T.Wellard

The BERA/SAGE Handbook of
Educational Research

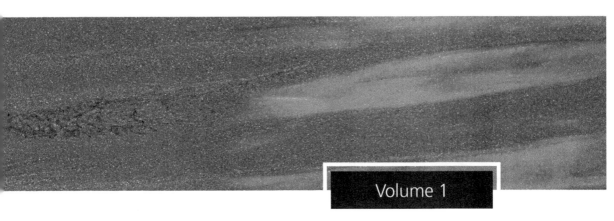

Volume 1

The BERA/SAGE Handbook of
Educational Research

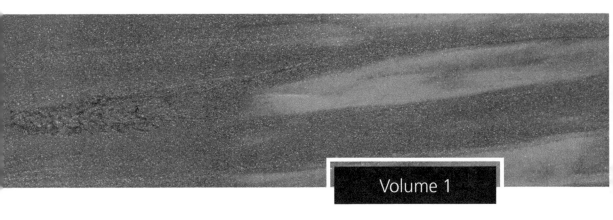

Volume 1

Edited by

Dominic Wyse, Neil Selwyn,
Emma Smith and Larry E. Suter

SAGE reference

Los Angeles | London | New Delhi | Singapore | Washington DC | Melbourne

BERA

BRITISH EDUCATIONAL RESEARCH ASSOCIATION

Los Angeles | London | New Delhi
Singapore | Washington DC | Melbourne

SAGE Publications Ltd
1 Oliver's Yard
55 City Road
London EC1Y 1SP

SAGE Publications Inc.
2455 Teller Road
Thousand Oaks, California 91320

SAGE Publications India Pvt Ltd
B 1/I 1 Mohan Cooperative Industrial Area
Mathura Road
New Delhi 110 044

SAGE Publications Asia-Pacific Pte Ltd
3 Church Street
#10-04 Samsung Hub
Singapore 049483

Editor: Marianne Lagrange
Assistant editor: Matthew Oldfield
Production editor: Sushant Nailwal
Copyeditor: Sunrise Setting Ltd.
Proofreader: Dick Davis
Indexer: Cathryn Pritchard
Marketing manager: Emma Turner
Cover design: Wendy Scott
Typeset by Cenveo Publisher Services
Printed by CPI Group (UK) Ltd,
Croydon, CR0 4YY

At SAGE we take sustainability seriously.
Most of our products are printed in the UK
using FSC papers and boards. When we
print overseas we ensure sustainable
papers are used as measured by the
PREPS grading system. We undertake an
annual audit to monitor our sustainability.

Library of Congress Control Number: 2016940833

British Library Cataloguing in Publication data

A catalogue record for this book is available from the British Library

ISBN 978-1-4739-1891-7

Contents

List of Figures

List of Tables

List of Boxes

Notes on the Editors
and Contributors

THE EDITORS

Dominic Wyse is Professor of Early Childhood and Primary Education at University College London (UCL), Institute of Education (IOE), and Academic Head of the Department of Learning and Leadership. Dominic is a Fellow of the Academy of Social Sciences (FAoSS), an elected member of the British Educational Research Association (BERA) Council, and a fellow of the Royal Society for the encouragement of Arts, Manufactures and Commerce (RSA). The main focus of Dominic's research is curriculum and pedagogy. Key areas of work are the teaching of writing, reading and creativity. Prior to his current role at the IOE as Head of the Academic Department Learning and Leadership Dominic was Faculty Director of Research. Before joining the IOE Dominic was a Senior Lecturer at the University of Cambridge. He was also appointed as the first Director of Music-Making at Churchill College Cambridge, where he was also a Fellow and Director of Studies for Education.

Neil Selwyn is a Professor in the Faculty of Education, Monash University. He worked previously at the Institute of Education – University College London, and before that at Cardiff University School of Social Sciences (UK). Neil's research and teaching focuses on the place of digital media in everyday life, and the sociology of technology (non)use in educational settings. Neil has written extensively on a number of issues, including digital exclusion, education technology policymaking and student experiences of technology-based learning.

Emma Smith is Professor of Education at the University of Leicester, UK. She researches issues of educational equity and the role that educational policy can play in reducing inequalities and closing achievement gaps in both the national and international context. Recent and on-going work has been in the following areas: shortages in the STEM workforce, special education and school account-ability, inequalities in participation in post-compulsory science programmes and school policy in England. She has a general interest in research methods and has taught on many research methods courses at both undergraduate and postgraduate level. Her particular area of interest is in the use of numeric secondary data and she is the author of 'Using Secondary Data in Educational and Social Research' published by the Open University Press.

Larry E. Suter is a consultant for educational research with experience in managing and analyzing large scale international surveys, informal education, measurement of student achievement, and measurement of 'soft skills' such as motivation, identity, and career interest. He received his undergraduate education in sociology at the College of Idaho and advanced degrees (MA and PhD) in sociology at Duke University in 1968 and 1975. He was employed for 21 years as a statistician at the US Census Bureau as chief of the Education statistics branch and at the National Center for Education Statistics where he expanded the program of international education to include large scale cross national surveys of science, mathematics, and reading. He worked for 21 years as a program director for research on science and mathematics education at the National Science Foundation. After retiring from the US government in 2011, he has continued conducting research on education as a visiting scholar at the University of Michigan and as a part-time lecturer at the Medical School of Harvard University. His published works include analysis of international comparative studies, studies of informal learning, and indicators of science education. He has been an adjunct professor at the University of Maryland, Georgetown University, and a visiting scholar at Stanford University where he taught courses in sociology, educational policy, and research design.

THE CONTRIBUTORS

Socorro Echevarria Aguja has been handling life science courses in both undergraduate and graduate levels for the past 15 years. She is currently a professor in the Graduate School of De La Salle Araneta University. She has also served as the Graduate Studies Coordinator (Coordenadora do Mestrado) at the Universidade Catolica de Mozambique (UCM) in Cuamba, Mozambique during her 3-year assignment as a VSO volunteer from AY2006–2009. During her stay at UCM, she developed the curriculum for Master of Science in Agriculture in collaboration with Universidad Publica de Navarra in Spain. Her current research activities are focused on science education, climate change studies, and environmental pollution. Dr Aguja also served as research and training consultant of research leaders and managers of State Universities and Colleges in the Philippines. Such involvement also extended to the Department of Education of the Philippine government, where Dr Aguja was a resource person and/or mentor for the Executive Program for School Superintendents in the country. Moreover, Dr Aguja facilitates the conduct of seminar workshops on Action Research in the different public schools in the country. Currently, she is actively involved in organizing and facilitating the Action Research Action Learning (ARAL) congress which started in 2015 at DLSU Manila.

Roser Beneito-Montagut is Lecturer in Digital Social Sciences at Cardiff University School of Social Sciences. Her research interests focus on the study of social interactions and emotions online, the exploration of the relationship between social isolation and social media use in later life online and the use of mix-methods in digital sociology. She is also interested in exploring methods to use the 'big data' produced by social media for social sciences. Her work has been supported by a range of funders including the Catalan Association of Public Universities 'La Caixa' Foundation.

Amanda Berry is Professor of Education at Royal Melbourne Institute of Technology, (RMIT) University, Melbourne, Australia. Amanda's work focuses on the development of teachers' knowledge and the ways in which that knowledge is shaped and articulated through teacher preparation, beginning teaching and in-service learning. In particular, Amanda's research concerns the ways in which teachers' learning can be studied from an insider perspective, as a means of enabling and empowering teachers and developing collectively understood knowledge of practice. Amanda has published extensively in the above areas, including books, Handbook chapters, international journals and academic texts. She is current editor of the journal *Studying Teacher Education*, an international journal of self-study, former Chair of the American Education Special Interest group in Self-study of Teacher education practices, and Associate Editor of *Research in Science Education*.

Stacey Bielick is Principal Researcher at the American Institutes for Research in Washington, DC where she oversees survey development for national education surveys in the United States. Ms Bielick has over 20 years of experience designing, managing, and analysing surveys and currently provides survey research expertise for parent and school administrator surveys sponsored by the US Department of Education. She has authored several publications on survey and education research and presented on and trained academic researchers in survey methods for education research in the United States and internationally. Ms Bielick holds an MS in Survey Methodology from the University of Maryland, Joint Program in Survey Methodology (JPSM).

Chris Brown (DPhil) is Senior Lecturer at UCL Institute of Education (UCL Centre for Knowledge Exchange and Impact in Education). With a long standing interest in how evidence can aid education policy and practice, Chris has written four books (including *Leading the Use of Research and Evidence in Schools*), several papers and has presented on the subject at a number of international conferences in Europe, and North America. Chris has extensive experience of leading a range of funded projects, many of which seek to help practitioners to identify and scale up best practice, and was recently awarded a significant grant by the Education Endowment Foundation to work with 100+ primary schools in England to increase their use of research. Other projects include an evaluation of England's progress towards an evidence informed school system (funded by England's Department for Education). In 2015 Chris was awarded the American Educational Research Association 'Emerging Scholar' award (Education Change SIG). The award is presented to an individual who, within the first eight years of the career of an educational scholar, has demonstrated a strong record of original and significant scholarship related to educational change.

Mary Brydon-Miller, PhD is Professor of Educational and Community-Based Action Research and Education and Social Change in the Educational Studies program at the University of Cincinnati where she also directs the University of Cincinnati's Action Research Center. She is Professor of Educational Leadership, Evaluation, and Organizational Development at the University of Louisville and the Director of the Action Research Consortium. She is a participatory action researcher who conducts work in both school and community settings. She is the co-editor, along with David Coghlan, of the *SAGE Encyclopedia of Action Research*. Her current research focuses on research ethics in educational and community settings and on the transformation of institutions of higher education through action research.

Lisa Calderwood is Director of Next Steps and Senior Survey Manager at UCL. Lisa's research is focussed on survey methodology, particularly in relation to longitudinal studies. She uses Next Steps and the British birth cohort studies of 1958, 1970 and 2000 in her research and has published on areas including: non-response, new methods of data collection, biomedical data collection and administrative data linkage.

Shannon Campe is a Research Associate and Project Coordinator at Education, Training, Research (ETR), a non-profit organization in California. Her work focuses on bridging research and practice in K-12 education. In recent years, her work has focused on youth and technology–specifically game programming as a way to engage all students and increase interest in and confidence of underrepresented youth in the field of computer science. Her understanding of both educational practice and computer programming has led to presentations and publications in the fields of education and computer science education. Ms. Campe's other contributions include writing grant proposals, designing projects, and coordinating large, multi-site research projects. She has been co-Principal Investigator on two projects funded by the National Science Foundation. Ms. Campe holds a Bachelors of Arts degree in Art History from the University of California and a California Multiple Subject Teaching Credential from California State University.

Kathleen M. T. Collins received her PhD in Education with an academic emphasis in Special Education and Research Methods-Qualitative Analysis from the Graduate School of Education at the University of California, Santa Barbara. She is a Professor in the Department of Curriculum and Instruction at the University of Arkansas at Fayetteville. Dr Collins has presented more than 100 papers at international, national, and regional conferences, and she has published more than 80 research articles, book chapters, and encyclopedia chapters. Dr Collins is lead editor of *Toward a Broader Understanding of Stress and Coping: Mixed Methods Approaches* (2010) (Information Age Publishing).

Susila Davis, BE and MSc, is currently studying for a Doctorate in Education at the University of Oxford. Her focus is on practitioner engagement with Oxford University Press Pathways to School Improvement. Her other research interests include youth programmes and alternative education provision. Susila was also a research and data analyst for several years at the Specialist Schools and Academies Trust. A recent related publication includes Sammons, P., Davis, S. and Gray, J. (2016) *Methodological Properties of School Effectiveness Research: Exploring the Underpinnings, Evolution and Future Directions of the Field.* In: C. Chapman et al (eds.) *Routledge International Handbook of Educational Effectiveness.*

Pamela Davis-Kean is Professor of Psychology at the University of Michigan where her research focuses on the various pathways that the socio-economic status (SES) of parents relates to the cognitive/achievement outcomes of their children. Her primary focus is on parental educational attainment and how it can influence the development of the home environment throughout childhood, adolescence, and the transition to adulthood. She has published extensively on the use of secondary datasets for use in psychological and educational research to enhance scientific integrity.

Sara Delamont was the first woman President of BERA in 1984. She was awarded the BERA John Nisbet Award for Lifetime Service in 2015. Her first degree was in Social Anthropology at Cambridge in 1968, and her PhD from Edinburgh was in Educational Sciences. She is the author of *Key themes in the Ethnography of Education* (Sage 2014) and *Fieldwork in Educational Settings* (Routledge, 2016, 3rd edition).

Jill Denner, PhD, is a senior research scientist at Education, Training, Research (ETR), a non-profit organization in California. She does applied research and evaluation and also has led the development of several after-school programs designed to increase children's opportunities to become producers, not just users, of technology. She is nationally recognized as an expert in strategies to engage girls/ women and Latino/a students in science, technology, engineering, and mathematics (STEM) fields in both K-12 and community college, and regularly does peer review of journal articles as well as grant proposals for the National Science Foundation. As part of a long-standing commitment to bridge research and practice, Dr Denner builds research-evaluation partnerships with universities, schools and after-school programs. She has been principal investigator on 20 federal grants, written numerous peer-reviewed articles, and co-edited two books. She earned her PhD in developmental psychology from Columbia University, Teachers College.

Rebecca Eynon is Associate Professor and Senior Research Fellow at the University of Oxford, where she holds a joint academic post between the Oxford Internet Institute (OII) and the Department of Education. Her research explores the connections between technology, learning and inequalities across the life course. Rebecca is co-editor of *Learning, Media and Technology* and is co-author of *Teenagers and Technology* (Routledge, 2013) and *Education and Technology: Major themes* (Routledge, 2015). Her work has been supported by a range of funders including the British Academy, the British Educational Communications and Technology Agency (BECTA), the Economic and Social Research Council (ESRC), the European Commission, Google and the NominetTrust.

Hannah Farrimond, PhD is Senior Lecturer in Medical Sociology at the University of Exeter, UK. Her research interests focus on the psycho-social dimensions of legal addictions (smoking, alcohol) as they intersect with new technologies (e-cigarettes, surveillance). She has a particular interest in research ethics, stemming from her experience of several years as a member of the Social Science and International Studies Ethics committee, including two as Chair. This knowledge has been synthesized into her book *Doing Ethical Research* (Palgrave Macmillan, 2012) which examines practical 'in the field' ethical issues from a firm theoretical basis, including in the field of education research.

Lyndsie N. Ferrara is an Instructor in the Forensic Science and Law program in the Bayer School of Natural and Environment Sciences at Duquesne University. She is also a doctoral student in the Health Care Ethics program and once communicated with a serial killer for a year. Prior to joining the faculty she was a former DNA analyst at the U.S. Army Criminal Investigation Laboratory and a forensics specialist/contractor for the Department of Justice's International Criminal Investigative Training Assistance Program. Her primary research interests include the improvement of ethics education in forensic science and DNA mixture interpretation.

Carrie Freie is Associate Professor of Education at Penn State Altoona. Her research uses qualitative methodology to study educational settings. Her areas of interest include social class, race, and gender as they intersect with student identities, student retention, and pedagogies. She is the author of *Class Construction: White working-class student identity in the new millennium* (Lexington, 2007) and co-editor with Amy Stich of *The Working Classes and Higher Education: Inequality of access, opportunity and outcome* (Routledge, 2016).

Harvey Goldstein was formerly Professor of Statistical Methods at the Institute of Education from 1997–2005. He is currently Professor of Social Statistics at the University of Bristol, and also professorial associate at University College London. He has been a member of the Council of the Royal Statistical Society, and chair of its Educational Strategy Group. He is joint editor of the Journal of the Royal Statistical Society, series A (2015–2018) He was awarded the RSS Guy medal in silver in 1998 and was elected a fellow of the British Academy in 1997. He has been the principal applicant on several major Economic and Social Research Council funded research projects since 1981. He has several major research interests. The first is the use of statistical modelling techniques in the construction and analysis of educational tests with a particular interest in institutional and international comparisons. He has written extensively on the use (and misuse) of item response modelling in educational testing. The second interest is in the methodology of multilevel modelling. His major recent book, *Multilevel Statistical Models* (Wiley, 2010, 4th edition) is the standard reference text in this important area of statistical data analysis. The third interest is developing efficient methods for handling missing data and measurement errors in multilevel models.

Roger Gomm, now retired, was Lecturer in Health and Social Welfare at the Open University. Trained as an anthropologist he has forty years of experience of social research, most of it evaluation research in education, health, social and community work and is the author of many papers on research methodology. He is author of *Social Research Methodology: a critical introduction* (2008) and *Key Concepts in Social Research Methods* (2009), both Palgrave Macmillan, and co-editor/co-author of *Evaluating Research in Health and Social Care* (2000) and *Case Study Method* (2000) (both Sage) and *Challenging the Qualitative-Quantitative Divide* (Continuum, 2012).

Stephen Gorard is Professor of Education and Public Policy, and Fellow of the Wolfson Research Institute, at Durham University. He is an advisor to the UK Cabinet Office, a member of the UK DfE Associate Pool, a Methods Expert for the US government Institute of Education Science, member of the British Academy grants panel, and of the ESRC commissioning panel for Strategic Networks, and Fellow of the Academy of Social Sciences. His work concerns the robust evaluation of education as a lifelong process, focused on issues of equity and effectiveness. He regularly gives advice to governments and other policy-makers, and is a widely read and cited methodologist, involved in international and regional capacity-building activities, and used regularly as an adviser on the design of evaluations by central and local governments, NGOs and charities. He is author of around 30 books and over 1,000 other publications.

Myrte Gosen is Assistant Professor at the Center for Language and Cognition Groningen at the University of Groningen, the Netherlands. She received her

PhD from the same university in 2012. Her thesis is titled *Tracing learning in interaction. An analysis of shared reading of picture books at kindergarten* and shows a research interest at the interface between education and communication. She has a particular interest in classroom interactions in relation to knowledge and she uses conversation analysis to identify the fundamental structures and practices in interaction that are related to knowledge construction. Currently, she is carrying out work to explore the interactional characteristics of (the development of) understanding of mathematics in primary education.

Christoph A. Hafner is Associate Professor in the Department of English, City University of Hong Kong. His main research interests include specialized discourse, digital literacies, and language learning and technology. In addition to his other publications, he is co-author of *Understanding Digital Literacies: A practical introduction* (Routledge, 2012), co-editor of *Transparency, Power and Control: Perspectives on legal communication* (Ashgate, 2012) and co-editor of *Discourse and Digital Practices: Doing discourse analysis in the digital age* (Routledge, 2015).

Frank Hardman is Professor of Education and International Development at the University of York, UK. He has published extensively in the areas of language and education, classroom learning, and teacher development in high and low income developing countries. Central to Professor Hardman's work has been the monitoring and evaluation of what takes place at the school and classroom level through baseline evaluations as a key indicator of the quality of education. He has secured large-scale funding from research councils and government and non-government agencies in the UK and overseas and his research has played an important role in policy formation and implementation in East Africa, South-east Asia and the Middle East.

Jan Hardman is Associate Professor in Language and Education in the Department of Education at the University of York, United Kingdom. She conducts research into classroom discourse and interaction, dialogic pedagogy and teacher education in high and low-income countries. She has been involved in a number of international research projects and has published widely on teacher professional development. She is currently carrying out a 2-year Randomised Controlled Trial of a teacher professional development intervention designed to improve the quality of classroom talk, learning and attainment in schools serving socially deprived areas of England. Informed by her research, Jan contributes to staff professional development courses on teaching and learning in schools and higher education.

David Hildebrand, 1997, PhD, Associate Professor and Chair of Philosophy at the University of Colorado Denver. Research Areas: John Dewey, pragmatism, neopragmatism, epistemology, aesthetics. Publications: *Dewey: A Beginner's*

Guide (Oxford: Oneworld Press, 2008), *Beyond Realism and Antirealism: John Dewey and the Neopragmatists* (Vanderbilt UP, 2003), numerous articles.

Justin Jager is Assistant Professor within the T. Denny Sanford School of Social and Family Dynamics at Arizona State University. His research focuses on how person-context interactions inform developmental trajectories across adolescence and the transition to adulthood. His more recent work also documents, through the latent modeling of dyadic and triadic data, unique and shared perspectives among family members regarding family functioning and family relationships.

R. Burke Johnson PhD, Professor of Professional Studies at University of South Alabama, Mobile, Alabama USA. His research areas include methods of social research; program evaluation; quantitative, qualitative and mixed methods; and philosophy of social science. Selected publications include *Research Methods, Design, and Analysis* (Pearson, 2014, with Larry Christensen and Lisa Turner); *Educational Research: Quantitative, Qualitative, and Mixed Approaches* (SAGE, 2017, with Larry Christensen); *The SAGE Dictionary of Statistics and Methodology* (SAGE, 2016, with Paul Vogt); and *The Oxford Handbook of Multimethod and Mixed Methods Research Inquiry* (Oxford University Press, 2015, with Sharlene Hesse-Biber).

Paul E. Jose is Professor of Psychology at Victoria University of Wellington and Director of the Roy McKenzie Centre for the Study of Families. He received his PhD in developmental psychology from Yale University in 1980, and since then has taught and conducted research on adolescent development, family dynamics, and developmental psychopathology, as well as research methods and statistics. He recently published a book on statistical mediation and moderation (2013), and is currently working on a book to describe curvilinear relationships among variables.

Barbara B. Kawulich is a Professor of Research at the University of West Georgia, Carrollton, GA, USA. Barbara's teaching has focused on qualitative research, particularly ethnographic methods, action research, and evaluation. Her research has centered on issues of interest to indigenous women, the Muscogee (Creek) women specifically, and issues related to the pedagogy of research methods. She is the past editor of the *Journal of Research in Education* and has published numerous articles and book chapters on various topics, such as ethics, participant observation, gatekeeping and students' conceptions of research. She co-edited two volumes with Claire Wagner and Mark Garner, *Teaching Research Methods in the Social Sciences* (2008), Ashgate, and *Doing Social Research: A global context* (2012), McGraw-Hill. Her evaluation work has included evaluating numerous grants funded, for example, by the National Science Foundation and The Centers for Disease Control.

Sean Kelly (PhD, Sociology; University of Wisconsin-Madison) is Associate Professor in the Department of Administrative and Policy Studies at the University of Pittsburgh. He studies the social organization of schools, student engagement, and teacher effectiveness. Dr Kelly's research has appeared in the *American Educational Research Journal, Educational Researcher, Teachers College Record, Sociology of Education, Social Science Research*, and elsewhere. He is the editor of *Assessing Teacher Quality: Understanding Teacher Effects on Instruction and Achievement* (Teachers College Press, 2011). In 2014 he received the Exemplary Research in Teaching and Teacher Education award from AERA's Division K. He teaches courses in educational reform, leadership, the sociology of education, and both introductory and advanced statistics for the social sciences.

Tom Koole is Professor of Language and Social Interaction at the University of Groningen. He has used conversation analysis to investigate classroom interaction, emergency calls and health communication. He is also a visiting professor in the Health Communication Research Unit of the University of the Witwatersrand, Johannesburg. His present research is concerned with the use in interaction of linguistic and embodied tokens of understanding. He has published in international journals such as *Research on Language and Social Interaction, Discourse Studies, Linguistics and Education* and *Journal of Pragmatics*.

Joshua J. Marland is a Doctoral Candidate in the Research in Educational Measurement and Psychometrics program at the University of Massachusetts Amherst. He is also Director of Data and Analytics for the Highlander Institute, where he is primarily responsible for researching the efficacy of educational software used in K-12 educational settings. His research interest is in growth and value-added models used for accountability purposes, and in the use of data for decision-making in organizations.

Erica Marsh is a Project Coordinator at Education, Training, Research (ETR), a non-profit organization in California. As a content coordinator, Ms. Marsh helps create and develop website taxonomies, and finds, assesses and adds, tags, and shares thousands of content items for multiple sites. Ms. Marsh also creates training and intervention products, coordinates projects that build mobile educational apps, and develops elearning courses and live webinars. She is currently coordinating a National Institutes of Health project for Dr Denner using serious games and baseball to teach math and science to middle schoolers. She holds a degree in psychology from San Francisco State University and has completed master's work in library and information science at San Jose State University.

Amir Marvasti is Associate Professor of Sociology at Penn State Altoona. His research (*Being Homeless*, Lexington Books, 2003 and *Middle Eastern Lives in America*, Rowman and Littlefield, 2004, with Karyn McKinney) explores how identities are socially constructed and managed in everyday encounters and in institutional settings. He also has an active publication record on the pedagogy of research. His books *Qualitative Research in Sociology* (Sage, 2004) and *Doing Qualitative Research: A Comprehensive Guide* (Sage, 2008, with David Silverman) provide overviews of qualitative research methods from data collection to analysis and writing.

Joseph A. Maxwell, PhD, is Professor in the College of Education and Human Development at George Mason University. His doctoral degree is in anthropology, but for the past 35 years his research has been mainly in education, with an increasing focus on methodology. He is the author of *Qualitative Research Design: An Interactive Approach* (3nd edition, Sage, 2013) and *A Realist Approach for Qualitative Research* (Sage, 2012), as well as articles on qualitative and mixed methods research, sociocultural theory, Native American societies, and medical education. His current research deals with using qualitative methods for causal explanation, validity in qualitative and quantitative research, the history and breadth of mixed methods research, the value of philosophic realism for research, and the importance of diversity and dialogue across research paradigms and methods.

D. Betsy McCoach, PhD is Professor and program coordinator of the Measurement, Evaluation and Assessment program at the University of Connecticut. Dr McCoach has co-authored over 100 peer-reviewed journal articles, book chapters, and books, including *Instrument Design in the Affective Domain and Multilevel Modeling of Educational Data.* Dr McCoach founded the *Modern Modeling Methods* conference, held annually at UCONN. She is also the Director of *DATIC*, which hosts workshops on a variety of modeling methods. Dr McCoach is co-Principal Investigator for the National Center for Research on Gifted Education Project and has served as Principal Investigator, co-Principal Investigator, and/or research methodologist for several other federally-funded research projects/grants.

Gary McCulloch is the Brian Simon Professor of the History of Education and Director of the International Centre for Historical Research in Education (ICHRE) at UCL Institute of Education, London. He is president-elect (president 2017–2019) of the British Educational Research Association and current Editor of the *British Journal of Educational Studies*. His recent publications include *The Struggle for the History of Education* (2011), *Secondary Education and the Raising of the School Leaving Age: Coming of Age?* (with Tom Woodin and Steven Cowan) (2013), and a special issue of *Paedagogica Historica* on Education, war and peace' (ed. With Georgina Brewis) (2016). He is currently completing a book on the social history of educational studies and research.

Ian Menter is a Fellow of the Academy of Social Sciences in the UK and was President of the British Educational Research Association, 2013–15. From 2012–2015 he was Professor of Teacher Education and Director of Professional

Programmes in the Department of Education at the University of Oxford. He previously worked at the Universities of Glasgow, the West of Scotland, London Metropolitan, the West of England and Gloucestershire. Before that he was a primary school teacher in Bristol, England. He is now a Visiting Professor at four UK universities and one in Australia. He was President of the Scottish Educational Research Association (SERA) from 2005–2007 and was a member of the steering group for the BERA/RSA Inquiry into Research and Teacher Education.

Inger Mewburn is an Associate Professor at the Australian National University specialising in the scholarship and teaching of in research education. She has been working in the field of research education for ten years and currently the holds the position of Director of Research Training responsible for *co-ordinating, communicating and measuring* research training activities at ANU. Inger is the founder and editor of The Thesis Whisperer blog, which at time of writing has 76,000 followers over Wordpress, Facebook and Twitter. Over its lifetime the blog has had over 5 million views with more than two and a half million unique visits. The blog is an active hub in the world wide community of PhD scholars which has had over 6 million visits at time of writing.

Mark Evan Nelson is Associate Professor of Media Education and Academic Director of the Language, Media and Learning Research Center at Kanda University of International Studies in Japan. He has also held academic posts in language and literacy teacher education at Deakin University in Australia and the National Institute of Education in Singapore. Mark received his PhD in Education in Language, Literacy and Culture from the University of California, Berkeley, and his research is principally focused on the semiotic, sociocultural, and pedagogical implications of multimodal communication, particularly across geographic and cultural boundaries and via digital media technologies.

Sarah D. Newton is an advanced doctoral student of Research Methods, Measurement, and Evaluation at the University of Connecticut. She also holds a BA in Criminology and an MS in Criminal Justice from Central Connecticut State University. At UConn, she has taught graduate-level courses, such as Principles and Methods in Educational Research, and was the Teaching Assistant for the Data Analysis Training Institute of Connecticut's Structural Equation Modeling course in 2016. Sarah's research interests include reliability, validity, factor analysis, and latent variable modeling, and her dissertation focuses on the performance of information criteria in multilevel modeling.

Sandy Oliver is Professor of Public Policy at UCL Institute of Education. For twenty five years her interests have focused on the interaction between researchers and people making decisions in their professional and personal lives. With this in mind she has been developing methods to collate knowledge from whole bodies of research – systematic reviews – not just single studies. Most recently this has been in the area of international development where she has conducted systematic reviews and built up a programme of support for research teams conducting reviews elsewhere. She works with Department for International Development and the Alliance for Health Policy and Systems Research at WHO to build capacity in systematic reviewing in developing countries.

Anthony J. Onwuegbuzie is Professor in the Department of Educational Leadership at Sam Houston State University. He teaches doctoral-level courses in qualitative research, quantitative research, and mixed research, including program evaluation, as well as teacher education courses and educational psychology courses. His research areas primarily involve social and behavioral science topics, including disadvantaged and under-served populations such as minorities, children living in war zones, students with special needs, and juvenile delinquents. Additionally, he writes extensively on qualitative, quantitative, and mixed methodological topics applicable to multiple disciplines within the field of the social and behavioral sciences. With a current h-index of 71, he has secured the publication of more than 400 works, including more than 300 journal articles, 50 book chapters, and 5 books. Most recently, he co-authored a book entitled *Seven Steps to a Comprehensive Literature Review* (Sage).

Chao-Ying Joanne Peng is Professor Emeritus of Inquiry Methodology and Adjunct Professor Emeritus of Statistics at Indiana University-Bloomington. She has conducted research in the areas of effect size measures, missing data methods, logistic regression, research design, and statistical computing using statistical software, such as, SAS, SPSS, SYSTAT, R, Minitab. She has published more than 120 refereed articles, book chapters, technical reports, and encyclopedia entries on methodology, psychometrics, and statistical computing. She is an author or co-author of four books on SAS® for statistical analyses and received one BEST PAPER Award at a SAS® users annual conference.

Terri Pigott is Dean and Professor of Research Methodology in the School of Education at Loyola University Chicago. She has served as Interim Dean and then Dean since November 2014. Prior to Loyola, she was Associate Program Officer at the Spencer Foundation in Chicago. Dr Pigott is the former co-Chair and current co-Editor of the Methods Group of the Campbell Collaboration, an international collaboration supporting the production of systematic reviews of social interventions. She has numerous publications on methods of meta-analysis, including work on handling missing data and computing power in meta-analysis. She is also interested in outcome reporting bias in education research, and its implications for systematic review. She serves on a number of editorial boards including Psychological Bulletin, Psychological Methods, and

Research Synthesis Methods. She is chair of the AERA SIG on Systematic Review and Meta-analysis, and a long-time member of the Society for Research Synthesis Methodology (SRSM).

Maricar S. Prudente is presently a Full Professor of the Science Education Department of De La Salle University-Manila, where she has been a faculty member for more than 20 years. She also serves as the Research Director of the Lasallian Institute for Development and Educational Research (LIDER). Dr Prudente has been actively involved as a resource person, facilitator and coordinator in various seminars, workshops and training programs dealing with action research, environmental issues and science education, specifically in the recent trainings of research directors of the State Universities and Colleges (SUCs) in the Philippines. She was also involved in the Leadership Training Program for the Schools Division Superintendents of the Department of Education. For the past 5 years, she is also actively conducting Action Research Seminar-Workshops for basic education teachers in the country. Dr Prudente is the lead organizer of *Action Research, Action Learning (ARAL)*, an Action Research Congress, which started in 2015 at DLSU-Manila. In the field of science education, her research work is focused on action research and on the integration of inquiry, technology and 21st century skills in the teaching of science. In view of her active involvement in research, Dr Prudente received the 2015 National Achievement Award from the National Research Council of the Philippines (NRCP) and the 2015 Lasallian Excellence Award on Research. Currently, Dr Prudente serves as the Chair of Division 1- Educational, Governmental and International Policies of the National Research Council of the Philippines.

Mary Lou Rasmussen is a Professor in the School of Sociology at the Australian National University. Her principal research areas are sexualities, gender, health, wellbeing and education. Currently, (with Peter Aggleton, Daniel Marshall and Rob Cover) she is part of the Queer Generations Research team, investigating the experiences of two generations of LGBT young people Australia. She is also leading another Australian Research Council funded project researching young Australian's perspectives of religions and non-religious worldviews. Recent books include *Progressive Sexuality Education: The Conceits of Secularism* (Routledge, 2016) and *The Cultural Politics of Queer Theory in Education Research* (Routledge, 2016).

Mark Rickinson is an Associate Professor and Associate Dean (Engagement) in the Faculty of Education at Monash University in Melbourne, Australia. Mark's work is focused on improving the use and usefulness of educational research in policy and practice. In Australia and before that in the UK, he has undertaken research, evaluation and consultancy projects relating to the use of evidence in educational policy and practice, and the role of learning in environmental and sustainability education. Book publications include: *Improving Research through User Engagement* (Routledge, 2011, with Judy Sebba and Anne Edwards), and *Environmental Learning: Insights from research into the student experience* (Springer, 2010, with Cecilia Lundholm and Nick Hopwood).

Pamela Sammons, BSocSci PhD HEA, is a Professor of Education at the Department of Education, University of Oxford and a Senior Research Fellow at Jesus College, Oxford. Previously she was a professor at the School of Education, University of Nottingham (2004–2009) and a professor at the Institute of Education University of London (1993–2004). Her research over more than 30 years has focused on school effectiveness and improvement, school leadership, teaching effectiveness and promoting equity and inclusion in education. She has a particular interest in longitudinal studies and the use of mixed methods research approaches. Pam is a governor of a secondary school in Oxford. Related publications include *Methodological Advances in Educational Effectiveness Research* (Routledge, 2010, with B. P. M. Creemers and L. Kyriakides), and *Methodological Properties of School Effectiveness Research: Exploring the underpinnings, evolution and future directions of the field* (2016, Routledge International Handbook of Educational Effectiveness, with Susila Davis and John Gray).

James B. Schreiber is Professor of Epidemiology and Statistics in the School of Nursing in at Duquesne University where he teaches research methods and statistics He has published over 60 articles, chapters, and reviews along with over 120 national and international presentations. He is the author of a research methods book with Wiley and Sons, and a book on motivation with Springer (due out in December 2016). He has been an Advisory Board member for the Lemelson Center for the Study of Innovation and Invention, Collaborative Pediatric Critical Care Research Network within the NICHD, and a panel reviewer with the IES and NSF. In addition, he held a research fellowship with the Smithsonian Institution from 2011–2012 and continues to consult for the education group at the United States Holocaust Memorial Museum. He is the former Editor-in-Chief of the *Journal of Educational Research, The Journal of Experimental Education, and Genetic, Social, and General Psychology Monographs*. He currently sits on 12 editorial boards. Recently he finished, as part of the team, that the initial framework for the PISA 2018 Global Competence Test for the Organization for Economic Co-operation and Developed. In his free time, he builds custom long boards.

David Scott is Professor of Curriculum, Pedagogy and Assessment at University College London, Institute of Education. Recent research projects include: *Teacher Cadre Management in Indian Schools*; *Teaching and Learning in Higher*

Education; Assessment for Learning in Hong Kong Schools; *National Curriculum Standards and Structures in Mexico*; *India Capacity Building to the Elementary Education Programme*; and *Professional Doctorates and Professional Development in Education*. He has been Editor of *The Curriculum Journal* 1995–2001. His most recent books are: *New Perspectives on Curriculum, Pedagogy and Assessment* (Springer, 2015); Scott, D. and Hargreaves, E., *Sage Handbook on Learning* (Sage, 2015); Scott, D., Evans, C., Watson, D., Hughes, G., Walter, C. and Burke, P.-J., *Transitions in Higher Education* (Palgrave Macmillan, 2013); Scott, D. and Usher, R., *Researching Education*, Continuum (Bloomsbury, 2011); *Education, Epistemology and Critical Realism* (Routledge, 2010); *Critical Essays on Major Curriculum Theorists* (Routledge, 2008); Scott, D. and Morrison, M., *Key Ideas in Educational Research* (Continuum, 2006); Scott, D., Lunt, I., Thorne, L. and Brown, A., *Professional Doctorates in Higher Education* (Open University Press, 2004); *Reading Educational Research and Policy* (RoutledgeFalmer, 2000); and *Realism and Educational Research: New Possibilities and Perspectives* (RoutledgeFalmer, 2000).

Stephen G. Sireci, PhD is Professor of Educational Policy, Research, and Administration, and Director of the Center for Educational Assessment at the University of Massachusetts Amherst. He specializes in educational test development and evaluation. His research focuses on improving educational testing through improved test development and administration practices, and empirical research targeted at how well tests fulfill their stated purposes. He has over 100 publications on topics such as content validation, cross-lingual assessment, standard setting, applied validity studies, test accommodations, computerized-adaptive testing, and educational assessment policy.

Guillermo Solano-Flores is Professor of Education at the Graduate School of Education, Stanford University. He specializes in the linguistic and cultural issues that are relevant to both international test comparisons and the testing of cultural and linguistic minorities. He is the author of the theory of test translation error. He has investigated the use of generalizability theory as an approach for examining validity in the testing of linguistically diverse populations. Current research projects examine academic language and testing, formative assessment practices for culturally diverse science classrooms, and the design and use of illustrations in international test comparisons.

Jeffrey T. Steedle, PhD, is a Senior Research Scientist at Pearson. He received his PhD in Educational Psychology and MS in Statistics from Stanford University. Currently, he provides psychometric support for state and national achievement testing program. His research interests include student motivation on assessments, forensic methods for detecting potential test security violations, and modeling the associations between test item features and their difficulty.

Tres Stefurak , 2004, PhD, Associate Professor & Department Chair, Department of Professional Studies, College of Education, University of South Alabama, Mobile, AL USA. *Research Areas:* child maltreatment & juvenile offending, vicarious trauma & trauma-informed care, program evaluation & mixed methods research, and psychology of religion & spirituality. *Publications:* Stefurak, T., Johnson, B., & Shatto, E. (2016). Mixed methods dialectical pluralism applied to an evaluation of a community-based interventions program for juvenile offenders. In L.A. Jason & D.S. Glenwick (Eds). *Handbook of Methodological Approaches to Community-Based Research: Qualitative, Quantitative and Mixed Methods.* New York: Oxford University. Johnson, B., & Stefurak, T. (2013). Considering the evidence-based debate in evaluation through the lens of Dialectical Pluralism. *New Directions for Evaluation, 138,* 37–48.

Alice Sullivan is Professor of Sociology at UCL and Director of the 1970 British Cohort Study (BCS70). Alice's research is focussed on social and educational inequalities in the life course. She has made extensive use of secondary data analysis of large-scale longitudinal data sets in her research, with a particular focus on the British birth cohort studies of 1958, 1970 and 2000. She has published on areas including: social class and gender differences in educational attainment, single-sex and co-educational schooling; private and grammar schools, cultural capital, reading for pleasure, and access to elite higher education.

Agnes Szabo is a Postdoctoral Researcher at Massey University and a Fellow of the Centre for Applied Cross-cultural Research at Victoria University of Wellington. She received her PhD in cross-cultural psychology from Victoria University of Wellington in 2015. Her research sits at the cross-roads of developmental and cross-cultural psychology with a particular focus on identity development, acculturative stress management, and cross-cultural research methods. As part of her postdoctoral fellowship, she is currently working on a longitudinal dataset drawn from a representative sample of older people in New Zealand, which was designed to gain a better understanding of the factors promoting healthy aging.

Monica Taylor is Associate Professor in the Secondary and Special Education department at Montclair State University, in Montclair, New Jersey, USA. For the past 15 years, she has worked collaboratively with Lesley Coia to develop co/autoethnography, a self-study research methodology. In 2014, they co-edited the volume, *Gender, Feminism, and Queer Theory in the Self-Study of Teacher Education Practices* (Sense Publisher, 2014). Some of Monica's other publications include: *A Year in the Life of a Third Space Urban Teacher Residency:*

Reinventing teacher education (Taylor & Klein, 2015) and *Whole Language Teaching, Whole Hearted Practice: Looking back, looking ahead* (Taylor, 2007).

Pat Thomson PhD, PSM, FAcSS, is Professor of Education at The University of Nottingham. A former school principal, she now researches in three areas: academic writing and doctoral education; the arts and creativity in school and community change; and critical approaches to educational leadership management and administration. She has ongoing research partnerships with Royal Shakespeare Company, Tate and Nottingham Contemporary. Her 2016 books are *Educational leadership and Pierre Bourdieu*, Routledge; *Place based methods for researching schools*, with Christine Hall, Bloomsbury and *Detox your writing: Strategies for doctoral researchers*, with Barbara Kamler, Routledge. She blogs as 'patter' about academic writing and doctoral education on patthomson.net and tweets as @ThomsonPat.

Robert Thornberg is Professor of Education in the Department of Behavioural Sciences and Learning at Linköping University in Sweden. He is also the Secretary and Board member of the Nordic Educational Research Association (NERA). His current research is on school bullying as moral and social processes. His second line of research is on school rules, student participation, and moral practices in everyday school life. His other research interests include teacher education, inter-professional collaboration in school, and classroom feedback. In his work, he uses a range of research methods such as qualitative interviewing, survey design, and ethnographic fieldwork, but has particular expertise in grounded theory.

Malcolm Tight is Professor of Higher Education at Lancaster University, UK. He previously worked at the University of Warwick, Birkbeck College London and the Open University. His current research interests are in research methodology, systematic review, and the development of higher education and higher education research.

Carole J. Torgerson is Professor of Education in the School of Education at Durham University. She is a methodologist with expertise in the design and conduct of randomised controlled trials. She has led over twenty five RCTs in diverse substantive topics, and also undertaken methodological research in trial design. Carole was Co-chair of the Campbell Collaboration Education Co-ordinating Group between 2006–9 and principal member of the United States Institutes of Education Sciences (IES) Reading and Writing and Science and Mathematics review panels, and a consultant methodologist to the IES on research design between 2006–13. She jointly established the annual international Randomised Controlled Trials in the Social Sciences Conference, now in its twelfth year.

David Torgerson is the Director of the York Trials Unit, which is the only UK trials unit that supports trials across the spectrum of health and the social sciences. He is a trial methodologist and has been involved in the design and conduct in a large number of randomized trials across the areas of health, education, crime and justice and the social sciences. He has published more than 240 peer reviewed papers many on trial design as well as empirical evaluations.

Janice Tripney is Lecturer in Social Policy and Programme Director for the MSc Social Policy and Social Research at UCL Institute of Education. Her research and teaching converge around an interest in the practice and politics of applying social research. She has many years' experience of conducting systematic reviews and supporting review teams, particularly in the areas of education and international development. Current work also includes the use of biographical methods to recount the history of a hidden network of women who shaped the practice and influence of British social science in the early twentieth century. She is an editorial board member of the *London Review of Education*.

Peter Tymms, PhD, is Director of iPIPS, an international study of children starting school. He was a school teacher for 20 years before taking up an academic career which has involved teaching, researching, the development of monitoring systems and leadership roles. His research has led to more than 100 academic papers and his leadership roles include being Head of Department in the School of Education at Durham University until 2013 and before that, Director of CEM at Durham University which runs monitoring systems for schools through which millions of pupils have been assessed across the UK and beyond each year. His main research interests are monitoring, assessment, interventions and research methodology generally. He set up the PIPS (Performance Indicators in Primary Schools) project which runs in thousands of schools around the world. Peter Tymms is an adviser to the German National Educational Panel Study and on the Education Advisory Group for the Sutton Trust.

Cornelis de Waal, 1997, PhD, Professor of Philosophy, Indiana University–Purdue University Indianapolis, USA. Editor-in-Chief *Transactions of the Charles S. Peirce Society. Research Areas:* Charles S. Peirce, Pragmatism, Metaphysics, Philosophy of Science, Philosophy of Mathematics. *Publications: The Illustrations of the Logic of Science by Charles S. Peirce.* Chicago: The Open Court, 2014. *Charles S. Peirce: A Guide for the Perplexed.* London: Continuum Press, 2013. *The Normative Thought of Charles S. Peirce.* New York: Fordham University Press, 2012 (with Krzysztof Skowroński). *Writings of Charles S. Peirce: A Chronological Edition*, Volume 8: 1890–1892. Bloomington: Indiana University Press, 2010 (Associate Editor). *On Pragmatism.* Belmont: Wadsworth, 2005.

Jerry West is a Research Affiliate with the Department of Human Development and Quantitative Methodology at the University of Maryland - College Park and a retired Senior Fellow with Mathematica Policy Research. He has more than 30 years of experience designing and conducting national studies of children, their families, and their early care and education experiences in the U.S. He has led the design and execution of large-scale studies of children from birth through middle childhood and played a key role in the development of many national studies of children and their families in the U.S., including the Head Start Family and Child Experiences Survey (FACES), the Early Childhood Longitudinal Study Birth (ECLS-B) and Kindergarten (ECLS-K) cohort studies, and the National Household Education Surveys Program (NHES). He has published extensively using data from these and other studies. He received a PhD degree in sociology from the University of North Carolina at Chapel Hill.

Patrick White is Associate Professor in the School of Media, Communication and Sociology at the University of Leicester. His empirical research has focused on education, training and the labour market. He has studied education and career choice at the end of compulsory schooling, participation in lifelong learning, and the supply and demand for both teachers and scientists. Patrick also worked on two projects aiming to research and improve the research capacity of the UK's educational research community. He has taught research methods for more than 15 years and has written about research questions, the use and teaching of statistics, and ethics. A second edition of his text, *Developing Research Questions*, is currently in preparation and a statistics textbook, provisionally titled *Sensible Statistics*, is also under contract.

Preface

BERA

 We believe that the development of a world-class education system depends upon high quality educational research. But this is a field where policy decisions are often driven by ideology rather than evidence.

BERA seeks to counterbalance the politicisation of education by carefully presenting the findings of the best in independent and critical research, through our projects, publications, responses to official consultations and other work on current issues.

In this way we help to strengthen the contribution educational research can make, not only to evaluating the effectiveness of current policies and practices, but also to generating fresh thinking and bringing a humanising influence to bear on proposals for reform.

As well as addressing practitioners and policymakers, we hope to raise wider public awareness and understanding of the value of educational research to our society and economy.

SAGE

 Founded in 1965, SAGE Publishing is a leading independent, academic and professional publisher of innovative, high-quality content.

Known for our commitment to quality and innovation, SAGE has helped inform and educate a global community of scholars, practitioners, researchers, and students across a broad range of subject areas.

With over 1,500 employees globally from principal offices in Los Angeles, London, New Delhi, Singapore, and Washington, D.C., we publish more than 950 journals and over 800 books, reference works and databases a year in business, humanities, social sciences, science, technology and medicine.

Believing passionately that engaged scholarship lies at the heart of any healthy society and that education is intrinsically valuable, SAGE aims to be the world's leading independent academic and professional publisher. This means playing a creative role in society by disseminating teaching and research on a global scale, the cornerstones of which are good, long-term relationships, a focus on our markets, and an ability to combine quality and innovation.

BERA and SAGE are delighted to collaborate on the BERA/SAGE Handbook of Educational Research. We believe it is a landmark reference work for everyone engaged in educational research, worldwide. We acknowledge the outstanding contribution of the editors, the editorial board and the contributors, drawn from the widest international community of researchers. As the editors state in their introduction,

Whatever the philosophical stance of the researcher about the origin of knowledge, the hope of nearly all educational researchers is that the results of their studies will somehow be translated into improvements of the process of learning and behaving in society. With these diverse goals in mind, how can the field of educational research accumulate knowledge for science and for practice? How can ideas and practices that one generation believes to be necessary for the education of the new generation of uneducated children be identified, implemented and modified as needed?

We hope that this Handbook will support researchers in achieving these ideals.

Editors' Introduction

Dominic Wyse, Emma Smith,
Neil Selwyn and Larry Suter

Education as a relatively young academic discipline has continued to grow in stature and significance. Part of the growth of education has been in understanding of the methodology and methods of educational research, an area which has matured over the last two decades. For these reasons The British Educational Research Association (BERA), SAGE publishers, and the editors of this Handbook felt it was timely that a significant new work on education research and methodology should be developed. The overarching concept of the book was conceived by council members of the BERA in collaboration with SAGE and the four editors. BERA was established in 1974 and since that time has developed as the leading learned society in the United Kingdom for research in the broad field of education. Over its lifetime, BERA has been associated with many important publications, including books, journals and pamphlets (see bera.ac.uk), but this is the first time such an ambitious work as the current Handbook has been compiled.

One of the main rationales of this book is to contribute to the development of education as a discipline by providing a cutting edge account of education research. In working on the proposal for the book the editors drew on a wide range of relevant texts that already existed. In this introduction it is only possible to cite a small minority. Examples of comparable books that we consulted include: *The SAGE Encyclopedia of Social Science Methods* (Lewis-Beck, Bryman, and Liao, 2004); *The SAGE Handbook of Qualitative Research* (Denzin and Lincoln, 2011); *The SAGE Handbook of Mixed Methods in Social and Behavioural Research* (Tashakkori and Teddlie, 2010); *A Companion to Research in Education* (Reid, Hart, and Peters, 2014); and the *Encyclopedia of Educational Theory and Philosophy* (Phillips, 2014).

In relation to methodology (and to sum up a very long-standing area of debate) the argument of this introduction is that education research has moved beyond crude opposing positions suggesting for example that either qualitative research or research in the *positivist* tradition is 'better' than the other. There is recognition that all research designs have strengths and weaknesses. However it is also true that some designs are better suited to answer some questions than others. For these reasons attention to the traditions of positivism and interpretivism, and quantitative and qualitative methods is balanced in the book as a whole. Another particularly important trend that arises, in part from greater understanding about the relative merits of different methodologies, is the growth in understanding of mixed methods approaches and the sophistication and systematicity with which these are now being used. The growth of mixed methods methodologies attracted epistemological questions from the start.

In addition to the prime attention to methodology and method the selection and use of examples of educational research as part of the chapters is an equally important element to the book. Authors were encouraged to select classic 'problems' in education that have attracted high quality research. For example the impact of teaching effectiveness on learning compared with the impact of socio-economic background of pupils. Criteria for selection of examples of research studies included: research that is generally regarded as noteworthy (by relatively objective measures); research that is of appropriate scale and significance; research that is peer-reviewed and professionally published in research journals or appropriate books. The examples of research include educational topics across the life course, so ensuring that particular age groups and phases of formal education were not excluded from the methodological explorations in the chapters.

Having collaboratively established a proposed rationale and set of contents for the book, authors with an international reputation for their work were invited to address one of the topics proposed in the contents. Early abstracts were peer-reviewed by the editors, and advice offered on content and scope. Subsequently first drafts of the chapters were peer-reviewed by at least one of the editors, and for about 10 percent of the chapters by two or three editors, as part of calibrating editors' expectations or if there were divided views about a particular chapter. Each chapter was also peer-reviewed by a member of the editorial board who were selected for their eminence in the world of educational research and to ensure that the editorial board's experiences and knowledge reflected a range of methodological expertise including in-depth knowledge of quantitative, qualitative and mixed-methods methodologies. Authors were required to systematically address peer-review comments. Following amendments to the chapters they were subject to final review by the lead editor for the chapter. The structure of the editors' introduction to the book was established collaboratively, with each editor proposing to write on an issue that is was agreed was significant to the field, taking into account the new knowledge noted in the chapters for the book. The contributions of the introduction were subject to review by all the editors and to further peer review.

One function of the chapters is to overview the methodological issues relevant to each particular topic. But the chapters also offer the reader practical guidance on how to use methods techniques. In view of the limitations on what can be covered in individual chapters, the use of further reading sections in each chapter provides readers with pointers to books and papers and other sources that will allow them to develop their knowledge further.

This introductory chapter begins with some reflections on the nature of academic disciplines. A selection of evidence and theory that has some bearing on the state of education research is also reviewed. The reflections on education as a discipline are followed by an account of some of the ways that knowledge is built through education research. The next sections of the introduction address two fundamental issues: the nature of paradigms and their place in educational thinking; and the changing nature of education research. The final section briefly introduces each of the six parts of the book.

EDUCATION AS A DISCIPLINE

Learning is an essential feature of human development, and education is a preeminent context for learning. Progress at different levels of society is inextricably linked with education. At the level of everyday life any activity that involves learning, individually or with others, can be described as educative, and indeed many of life's experiences are colloquially described as 'an education'. The characteristic of education to enhance progress, development, and change in people's lives is seen most notably in relation to human capital, and the associated opportunities to positively impact on well-being: for individuals, families, communities and nation states.

The way that education is conceptualized as an area of human thought is fundamental to how it can be approached as an area of scientific research. To many people education is seen as the vital work of early years' settings, schools, and universities. If we consider education not just in the realm of state provision but also its place in private enterprise then it includes facets such as apprenticeship, guilds, learned societies, think tanks, consultancy, philanthropic activity, and new technology to name but a few. However, the conception of education as an area of human thought is a contested space, for example in the depiction of education as a field versus a discipline. Even when recognized as a discipline it has been argued that education in universities has been 'dominated by its involvement with teacher education' (Furlong, 2013, p. 3) which, it is suggested, is a feature of the discipline's 'epistemological weakness' (Furlong, 2013, p. 3).

In examples of texts as early as the first half of the twelfth century the Anglo-Norman etymology of the word 'discipline' includes 'teaching, instruction' and 'rule or body of rules' (OED, 2016, online). From classical Latin the etymology included 'teaching, instruction' and 'branch of study'. A quotation from *The Lancet* in 1962 is an indication that not only has practical application been part of the etymology of the word discipline from its beginning but also that practical application is integral to disciplines other than education: 'Sir Leonard Parsons ... had been the first to draw into the paediatrics of his time other disciplines such as biochemistry and immunology' (OED, 2016, online).

The discipline of education can be seen as a 'young' discipline. Its major learned societies are only just one hundred years old. Examples include the American Educational Research Association (AERA) founded in 1916; the Australian Council for Educational Research (ACER), established in 1930; and the British Educational Research Association (BERA) in 1974. Compare these to the origins of the Royal Society which were 'in a 1660 'invisible college' of natural philosophers and physicians' (The Royal Society, 2016, online). However, serious scholarly attention to education as a topic can be traced back to the ancient Greeks. For example, the changes in ancient Greece from a mainly oral society to a literate society, as a result of the invention of the alphabet, challenged the status of the 'pedagogues', changes which were reflected in the philosophies of Plato, Socrates and Aristotle. This introduction is built on the premise that intellectually education is a discipline in every sense that other disciplines such as psychology, literary studies, medicine, linguistics, biology and so on are.

We have briefly traced Education as a subject of interest to society back to ancient Greece, and to the formation of major educational societies such as BERA. We now turn to a much more recent source of evidence about the state of different disciplines: systematic attempts, in different parts of the world, to 'measure' the quality of research. The Research Excellence Framework (REF), an exercise carried out every five years or so in the UK, provides some useful data. The REF uses panels of peer reviewers, selected from eminent researchers in a particular discipline, to grade research outputs, research impact, and research environment. The REF 2014 report's commentary included the following:

> in 23 education submissions [from universities], more than a quarter of the work submitted was judged to be 4* [world-leading research] – a rise from just five submissions of such quality in 2008. This is a similar figure to that reported by the Quacquarelli Symonds (QS) World University Rankings (2014), which lists 19 UK education departments in the top 100, including the first, fourth and seventh institutions. (REF, 2015a, p. 103)

In a different analysis, originating from government, the strength of UK education research in relation to research around the world was described as 'distinctively strong'. A risk was also noted, in a number of disciplines not just education, of not being able to recruit sufficient high quality postgraduate students (Department for Business, Innovation and Skills, 2011, p, 2).

The REF 2014 data suggested that education research was in many ways operating at a very high level, but also that there was considerable room for improvement when compared with some other disciplines. Although education performed well in relation to social-science there were other disciplines, such as natural sciences, performing better. This trend is evident not only in the UK data but can also be seen in the data from other regions, such as the Australian equivalent to the REF, Excellence in Research for Australia (ERA. Australian Government, 2015). However, the reasons for this underperformance are not necessarily 'epistemological weakness' as a result of links with professional practice. Other possibilities include the historical trajectory of disciplines, and more basically the amount of research funding available to different disciplines from governments and other sources commensurate with the funding needed to carry out world class research.

Our consideration of attempts to measure the nature of research in different disciplines also has to consider the ways in which such evidence is reported, summarized and communicated, because this also can reflect the state of a discipline. For example, it is interesting to compare the ways in which the place of professional practice in relation to research is summarized in life sciences research compared to education research. Contrary to some downbeat appraisals of the influence of professional practice on education research, the REF 2014 report from the life sciences fields was more positive about aspects of such links. In the UK, medical practitioners work mainly in the National Health Service (NHS). The REF sub-panel found:

> the beneficial effects of the increasingly close working relationship between UK academia and the NHS, almost certainly enhanced by the NIHR [National Institute for Health Research] funding awarded to the NHS partners. From identifying research problems and producing high quality research, to ensuring that this research is translated into bedside care, the unique partnership working between academia and the NHS in the UK clearly underpins a significant proportion of the excellence the sub-panel found in the submissions. (REF, 2015b, p. 26)

And perhaps of relevance when comparing the issue of large numbers of university staff in education departments not being eligible for submission to the REF, because of their work being largely dominated by teacher training, the panel for medicine found that:

> whilst outputs from basic science-led teams were well represented at the highest level, fewer were received from the scientifically trained investigator clinician. The sub-panel identified that fostering and maintaining a cadre of such individuals equipped to deliver experimental medicine studies in their clinical disciplines was important for the future UK biomedical vitality. (REF, 2015b, p. 26)

It may be that education research could learn from the beneficial effects of the close working relationships between academia and the professionals working for the NHS found in life sciences. In addition, the importance of fostering scientifically trained investigator clinicians in life science research may have a parallel with the need to engage teacher training staff in university departments with education research.

In addition to the researcher–professional dynamics addressed so far in this introduction, understanding the nature of a discipline requires attention to knowledge, an important topic that links the study of education with what is, or should be, at the heart of educational processes. Knowledge is not only central to the organization of universities and their disciplines and areas of study, but is also relevant to the organization of teaching in the other formal educational settings of early years, elementary/primary, and secondary education.

The debates about the place of knowledge have been, and continue to be, important in relation to education. To take a recent example of the debate, from a sociology of education perspective, it has been claimed that a lack of attention to knowledge is the defining feature of a crisis in educational thinking (more specifically in the study of curriculum – Young, 2013). Young saw the crisis as a manifestation of theoretical neglect of epistemological issues, in relation to forms of knowledge, that have philosophical and sociological dimensions. Others have in different ways articulated the roots of the crisis in the intersections between the *performativity* of educational policy and the intersections with research and practice (Hopman, 2010; Wyse, Hayward, and Pandya, 2016). In contradiction to Young's explanation of crisis, Lundgren (2015, p. 798) suggested that what is more important than specific forms of knowledge is continuing attention to 'the changing economic and cultural "conditions" for curriculum constructions as they govern and frame what content is possible for teachers to select and organize'. Critically reflecting on these theoretical positions we also have a new wave of empirical work that is challenging simple notions of linear routes from knowledge in the academy to knowledge taught through the curriculum in schools (see Wyse, Hayward, Livingston and Higgins, 2016).

These sociologically and philosophically informed positions encapsulate some historic foci for educational theory, and link with the best ways societies might organize learning and teaching through the control of educational content, including in national curricula. Understanding derived from philosophy has also identified the relativism–objectivism binary as a fundamental issue. For example, it has been argued that pragmatism, and particularly John Dewey's transactional framework, offers many possibilities for better understanding education, by moving away from the rather stale opposition of objectivism and relativism towards the idea of knowledge as transactional (Biesta, 2016). Biesta also reminds us of the important question that Herbert Spencer asked in 1854: 'what knowledge is of most worth?' – a question that was rephrased, from a critical theory perspective, by Michael Apple in the 1990s as '*whose* knowledge is of most worth?'. The epistemology of positions encapsulated by relativism, objectivism and pragmatism are central to the evolution of educational thinking, including its different paradigms and claims to warranted knowledge. The associated debates also reveal the capacity of education researchers to learn through multidisciplinary work, something that is another hallmark of education as a discipline.

BUILDING EDUCATIONAL KNOWLEDGE THROUGH RESEARCH

A key idea that links all the chapters in this book is the idea of building knowledge about education. Making a definitive, permanent statement of which methods are most likely to lead to greater knowledge is impossible because education itself is not a stable entity. Education is a practice of human to human exchange of cognitive and non-cognitive thought and behavior (parent to child, teacher to pupil, peer to peer, colleague to colleague). Conducting research about educational practices is a little like modeling a dance routine. The model must capture how both the forces of motion and the emotional experiences of the dancers are involved and integrated over space and time in a continuous changing interlude. Moreover, research on education is not only about the human psychology of learning, but also about the institutions that overlay the systems of exchange between the actors in the school or non-school setting. Therefore, building educational knowledge through research is a continuous process of concept construction, concept destruction, empirical observation, replication, and communication to multiple audiences. Conducting research is in fact as much a political process of convincing others about the significance of a method or intervention as it is a scientific process because knowledge must be shared and used in order to be 'known'.

Education contains both a discipline of scientific discovery and a field of practice. An emphasis on practice changes the focus of research discovery to the more immediate here and now rather than on broad long-range explanatory models of regularities. These kinds of distinctions are made clear in the widely adopted *Frascati Definition* of research:

> Research and experimental development (R&D) comprise creative and systematic work undertaken in order to increase the stock of knowledge – including knowledge of humankind, culture and society – and to devise new applications of available knowledge. (OECD, 2015, p. 44)

The *Frascati Manual* specifies that for an activity to be described as research or experimental development it must satisfy all five of the following criteria, so that it is: novel, creative, uncertain [re final outcomes], systematic, transferable and/or reproducible (OECD, 2015, p. 45). R&D is further distinguished from other activities as follows:

> The term R&D covers three types of activity: basic research, applied research and experimental development. Basic research is experimental or theoretical work undertaken primarily to acquire new knowledge of the underlying foundations of phenomena and observable facts,

without any particular application or use in view. Applied research is original investigation undertaken in order to acquire new knowledge. It is, however, directed primarily towards a specific, practical aim or objective. Experimental development is systematic work, drawing on knowledge gained from research and practical experience and producing additional knowledge, which is directed to producing new products or processes or to improving exist-ing products or processes. (OECD, 2015, p. 45)

For some education researchers, building knowledge in education research has included the need for reflection on philosophical beliefs about what education is. For example, a conception of education influenced by the ideas of social construc-tionism, which asserts that knowledge is continuously created, differs from the influence of behaviorist ideas, such as the learner as *tabula rasa* who receives fixed knowledge from the real world through one-way transmission from teacher to learner. Whatever the philosophical stance of the researcher about the origin of knowledge, the hope of nearly all educational researchers is that the results of their studies will somehow be translated into improvements of the process of learning and behaving in society. However, with these diverse goals in mind, how can edu-cational research accumulate knowledge for science and for practice? How can ideas and practices that one generation believes to be necessary for the education of the new generation of uneducated children be identified, implemented and modi-fied as needed?

The canons of the scientific method have provided guidance on how to orga-nize ideas and behaviors into logical forms of testing and replication. Knowledge may be best accumulated if researchers clearly identify how the concepts they are using in their research are related to concepts that have been used by others (so that not every observer is an 'island to themselves'). The scientific study of education requires that researchers explain how they objectively observe human behavior, how they describe and catalog it, and how they connect their concepts to existing models and theories. The goal of scientific research is to reach con-sensus about the meaning and validity of the constructed knowledge. The body of knowledge of education practices can grow only as long as researchers relate their studies to each other by testing, building on, and replicating previously known facts then by implementing new discoveries and testing/evaluating these.

The body of knowledge in education resides at many levels of generality, as is true in any field of science. At the first level, an *individual* experiences the natural world by bodily and brain processes, for example of language, quantities, and social relationships. The field of educational psychology provides frameworks for the study of human learning at this level. Educational research also deals with higher levels of aggregation that have power to control individuals such as the family, the school, the classroom, peers, local and national government, and even international events. Each of these systems may be an object of observation in a research study as they also have patterns of behavior that can be observed and studied scientifically. Because education resides in all aspects of human experiences the languages of many disciplines (psychology, economics, political science, sociology, physical sciences, and human ecology) may be required to adequately explain educational behavior. Consequently, a research problem in education may require a team of experts from several fields working together and addressing an educational problem from a variety of sciences.

An enduring philosophical question in relation to knowledge that is relevant to all disciplines is the nature of truth. While the scientific method has many forms of application, it is useful to draw upon an organizational framework provided by the philosopher Toulmin for guidance on how to know whether a proposition is true or not (Toulmin, 1958, and more recently Toulmin's arguments were examined by Zarębski, 2009). Agreeing on the rules of argument is a first step toward achieving consensus. According to Toulmin, science does not discover *new* facts or regularities in nature, but rather offers some new ways of seeing and understanding the physical world. Its basic, fundamental purpose is understanding through a relevant theory of phenomena with which we are already familiar. Understanding is established through a method of 'substantial argument' (taken from legal practice) which consists of six components: *claims*, *data*, *warrants*, *backing for warrants*, *rebuttals* and *modal qualifiers*. The *claim*, is an asserted thesis that someone tries to justify. The second element is the *data* (factual statements) that are proposed to support the claim advanced. The third element is the *warrant*, whose task is to show that the leap from data to 'conclusion' is legitimate. The fourth component is the *backing for warrant*, which gives some additional support for a warrant and indicates the ultimate basis that makes the warrant legitimate. The fifth element of the argument is called the *modal qualifier* which expresses the strength of the step from the data to the conclusion and has an adverbial form such as 'probably', 'almost certainly', and so on. Finally, the sixth component is the *rebuttal*, whose task is to point out the circumstances in which the leap from the grounds to the claim is not legitimate. Toulmin points out that each field of science develops its own methods and 'working logic' closely connected with the methods of representation accepted in that field. Therefore a new researcher must become initiated into the working logic of the field of educational studies through study and practice.

The best ways to build knowledge are also a concern for funding agencies which grapple with the problem of choosing the types of research projects most likely to contribute to the growth of a body of knowledge. In an effort to organize the field of research, a team of research managers for the National Science Foundation and the Institute of Educational Sciences in the USA proposed a set of guidelines for educational research that might be recognized and adopted as a systematic way of researching. These research activities form a hierarchy of development of ideas (Institute of Education Sciences, 2013) that form stages of study. The categories are:

1 *Foundational Research* provides the fundamental knowledge that may contribute to improved learning and other relevant education outcomes.
2 *Early-Stage or Exploratory Research* examines relationships among important constructs in education and learning.

3 *Design and Development Research* develops solutions to achieve a goal related to education or learning, such as improving student engagement or mastery of a set of skills.
4 *Efficacy Research* allows for testing of a strategy or intervention under 'ideal' circumstances, including with a higher level of support or developer involvement than would be the case under normal circumstances.
5 *Effectiveness Research* examines effectiveness of a strategy or intervention under circumstances that would typically prevail in the target context.
6 *Scale-up Research* examines effectiveness in a wide range of populations, contexts, and circumstances, without substantial developer involvement in implementation or evaluation. (Summarized from Institute of Education Sciences, 2013)

By defining stages of research the agencies sought to systematize the different approaches to education. Noteworthy in this list is the lack of emphasis on development of macro level theory or of limitations to research design. Rather, the organizational system for this recommendation appears to be an organized set of stages of explorations of educational practice. The stages reach from 'fundamental knowledge' that would presume to come from basic scientific disciplines, to 'scale-up' practices which would extend a system of interventions to a larger range of circumstances. The goal of this model of knowledge building is to base practices of education on scientifically based evidence and then following evidence of success in various conditions to expand the application to larger and larger populations. It is not the goal of this model to define knowledge of educational practices as a logical system tested with experimental design but to be tested with multiple forms of practice and observation.

Whether this model of defining educational research by a set list of stages of knowledge building is successful in its goal of organizing the field of educational research into a mechanism for recommending improvements in educational practices is yet to be determined. In a review of the model, Gutiérrez and Penuel (2014) concluded that the proposed model of research focuses too heavily on the uses of research for practice as the ultimate criterion for the field of research. They added:

> We also need to understand the limits of generalizability by answering questions of what works, under what conditions, and for whom. The challenge is that the effects of any instructional program as estimated in an efficacy trial are likely to vary widely, as is implementation, requiring identifying and mastering variation. In this connection, 'mastering variation' does not mean attempting to minimize variation in implementation but, rather, to learn from productive adaptations teachers make with learners from variety of backgrounds. It means developing and testing supports to broaden capacity of teachers to make such productive adaptations themselves, to increase the effectiveness of programs, and to promote equity. (Gutiérrez and Penuel, 2014, p. 22)

The goal of research is to make an original contribution, and in so doing to establish new knowledge. This goal is not straightforward for any research, nor is agreement from associations of researchers about what constitutes a contribution to knowledge. For a discipline like education the establishment of knowledge is complicated by its interdisciplinary influences and by its natural focus on the application of research for the benefit of society. These complications are what make education research and education as a discipline such a powerful, vital and fascinating area of human thought.

PARADIGMS AND RESEARCH

Despite significant progress in the accumulation of educational knowledge there remain many unanswered questions about fundamental areas of focus for education and its research. We do not know enough, for example, about the value of homework or of coursework; about whether it is more effective to teach students in large or small classes, of the lasting benefits, or otherwise, of single-sex teaching, or of how to effectively involve parents in their child's education, and even if and when it is desirable to do so. Some commentators attribute this lack of progress to methodological and philosophical divisions that have both defined and disrupted the discipline for the last 50 years. Indeed, over this period arguably the main methodological debate in education research and in social research more widely, has involved disputes over the competing *paradigms* that are considered, by some, to underlie the philosophies and principles upon which research in this field is grounded.

The origins of what are known as the 'paradigm wars' can be traced to the second half of the twentieth century when the growing field of qualitative enquiry, and its use of methods of data collection and analysis, began to challenge the perceived superiority of the established quantitative approaches (for example, Gage, 1989). The growth in qualitative enquiry coincided with a shift, among some social researchers, in the view that the social sciences had more in common with the humanities than they did with the natural sciences (Lather, 2004) and that the scientific method provided a poor basis for the study of people (Bryman, 1988). Indeed the 'paradigm wars' stemmed to a large extent from the rejection, by some social scientists, of a philosophical belief that 'positivist approaches' (too often lazily equated with numerical data per se) implied the existence of a single 'objective' reality that could be measured, analyzed and the conclusions generalized (for example, Guba and Lincoln, 1994).

While it is difficult to pin down which 'paradigms' were actually in dispute at this time – some commentators include positivism, post-positivism, constructivism, critical theory, interpretivism and/or Marxism, and post-modernism – the 'paradigm wars' were usually framed in terms of a 'battle' between positivist and constructivist philosophical positions (for example, Bryman, 2008; Hammersley, 1992). In this context, positivism and quantitative methods have been viewed as the dominant methodological approach; despite the claim that, in the UK at least, the majority of education researchers were using qualitative research techniques (Gorard, 2004).

Underlying these differing perspectives on the nature of the social world was Thomas Kuhn's notion of paradigms (Kuhn, 1970). Kuhn was a physicist and philosopher of science who challenged the claim that scientific discovery moved in a linear and cumulative manner. He argued that the early stages in the development of most sciences have been characterized by a number of distinct, competing and often incommensurable ways of viewing the world and practicing science within it.

According to Kuhn, 'normal science' (science that is based on past scientific advancements and which, at least for the time being, provides the foundation for further practice) proceeds through the accepted rules and norms within an established theoretical framework or paradigm. Any problems that cannot be solved by using these rules would lead to changes in the practice of science. This change, which Kuhn called a 'paradigm shift', occurs when new evidence suggests that there are anomalies within the data that need to be reconciled. Kuhn argued that science proceeds through successive scientific revolutions whereby one paradigm would be replaced by another until the anomalous eventually became the expected.

Kuhn's suggestion that it was not possible to understand one paradigm through the conceptual framework of another rival paradigm – that paradigms were incommensurable – contributed to a 'methodological revolution' in education (and other social science) research. It led to some members of the research community arguing that the emerging qualitative research procedures themselves represented a new, and incommensurable, paradigm. The importance of the 'paradigm wars' in influencing methodological development in the social sciences during the 1980s and 1990s cannot be underestimated: 'paradigm issues are crucial; no inquirer … ought to go about the business of inquiry without begin clear about just what paradigm informs and guides his or her approach' (Guba and Lincoln, 1994, p. 116). And central to the issue was the belief that different paradigms were incommensurable: 'constructivism and positivism/post-positivism cannot be logically accommodated any more than, say, the ideas of flat versus round earth can be logically accommodated' (Guba and Lincoln, 1994, p. 116; also Smith and Heshusuis, 1986).

However according to Hammersley (1995, p. 3), looking at social research methodology in terms of paradigms is unhelpful as it exaggerates empirical differences and leads to a narrow characterization of the difficult methodological issues that social researchers face: 'thinking about social research methodology in terms of paradigms obscures both potential and actual diversity in orientation, and it can lead us into making simplistic methodological decisions'.

While Kuhn's work was a major stimulus for the paradigm model of social research, a number of commentators (for example, Bryman, 1988; Gorard 2004) have suggested that Kuhn's argument has been misinterpreted and that the paradigm model is irrelevant to the social sciences because the social sciences are pre-paradigmatic as they are yet to reach an initial scientific consensus and so do not operate in the way that 'normal science' does: 'it remains an open question what parts of social science have yet acquired such paradigms at all' (Kuhn, 1970, p. 15). Nevertheless, Kuhn's notion of different, competing and incommensurable paradigms became fundamental to issues raised within the 'paradigm wars' in which their incommensurability became 'deeply ingrained' (Bryman, 2008) and, in the view of some, served to 'split the field into two non-communicating parts' (Gorard, 2004, p. 149).

Quantitative versus qualitative?

The focus of the 'paradigm wars' has largely rested on the merits and assumptions of quantitative versus qualitative research. However, even the terms 'quantitative research' and 'qualitative research' are problematic. All quantitative research involves qualitative judgments and all qualitative research involves quantitative judgments. In addition whereas the term qualitative research sums up a broad range of methodologies, the term quantitative research sums up a narrower range. The 'paradigm wars' were grounded in contrasting ontological beliefs and positions (theories of being or reality) and epistemological beliefs and positions (theories of knowledge) about the nature of the social world, and where quantitative and qualitative approaches were 'frequently depicted as mutually exclusive models of the research process' (Bryman, 1988, p. 105). For example in the idea that, 'you can't be a positivist and a constructivist'! Quite apart from the unhelpful dichotomy this represents, the idea that researchers can be labelled as one kind of '-ist' or another is somewhat ridiculous as these terms represent long-standing complex philosophical traditions of thinking.

Bryman (1988) has offered two perspectives on the paradigmatic differences between quantitative and qualitative research approaches – the epistemological and the technical – and argues that many writers 'shuttle uneasily' (p. 108) back and forth between the two. He argues that it is often unclear whether proponents of paradigmatic divisions are arguing that there *is* a link between epistemology and method or whether there *ought* to be. If there is a link, he argues that this might be exaggerated and that the two approaches might not be as far apart as is sometimes implied. For example, like qualitative research, quantitative research attempts to attribute meaning to the social world and quantitative methods can also gain access to people's interpretations and the ways in which they view the world: 'a preoccupation with meaning and subjects' perspectives is not exclusive to the qualitative tradition' (Bryman, 1988, p. 124). Indeed a seminal text on experimental design commented:

> The experiment is not a clear window that reveals nature directly to us. To the contrary, experiments yield hypothetical and fallible knowledge that is often dependent on context and imbued with many unstated theoretical assumptions … In this sense, all scientists are epistemological constructivists and relativists, the difference is whether they are strong or weak relativists. (Shadish, Cook and Campbell, 2002, p. 29)

Quantitative and qualitative approaches are each appropriate for different kinds of research design, implying that it is the research issue or research question that should determine which approach to research is used (for example, White, 2009), and the idea that research issues and questions should determine methodology is itself perhaps a form of philosophical pragmatism (and indeed pragmatic in the everyday meaning). Some research questions are better addressed by qualitative methods, others by quantitative methods. In other words, most research designs can accommodate most data collection techniques. For example, questionnaires can contain both open-ended questions and numerical scales; interview questions can have both numerical (for example, frequency of attending a particular class) and qualitative aspects (for example, how a respondent felt about attending that class). Similar arguments have been made about ethnographic, participant observation and diary methods of data collection (Maxwell, 2010; Allwood, 2012; Bryman, 1988).

From around the start of the 2000s a new perspective that offered an alternative to the methodological schism between quantitative and qualitative research that had dominated the field was emerging. Mixed methods research, considered by some to be a new paradigm, was defined as 'the class of research where the researcher mixes or combines quantitative and qualitative research techniques, methods, approaches, concepts or language into a single study' (Johnson and Onwuegbuzie, 2004, p. 17. Also see their chapter in this book.). Within mixed method research the research question was considered to be fundamental: research methods, including pluralist approaches to data collection, were to be derived from the most appropriate way to answer the research questions of the project in hand. The advent and establishment of mixed method research was an important development for the field and its quick popularity meant that according to some commentators 'to a very large extent, the "paradigm wars" can be considered to be over and peace can be regarded as having broken out' (Bryman, 2006, p. 112).

Beyond the 'paradigm wars'

If we accept that there is some consensus that the 'paradigm wars' in education have indeed ended, or at least abated, for example evident in the establishment of mixed method approaches to data collection, why is the rehearsal of the 'paradigm wars' in this introduction still necessary? Putting aside unhelpful polarized positions there are still important epistemological and practical distinctions to be understood in relation to the rationales for different methodologies and methods. In order to explore these distinctions we address two important overarching issues. The first is in relation to the call, by policymakers for example, for more 'scientifically valid' research in education. And the second issue is the persistence of paradigm debates in the teaching of education research methods especially at postgraduate level. Each will be considered in turn below.

In January 2002, President George W. Bush signed into law what was arguably the most important piece of US educational legislation for the past 35 years.

The *No Child Left Behind Act* linked government funding to strict improvement policies for America's public schools. It also emphasized the promotion of school wide reform strategies that 'use effective methods and instructional strategies that are based on scientifically based research' (US Department of Education, 2002, Sec1114) as well as defining what constituted 'scientifically based' research in education (US Department of Education, 2004).

This call for 'scientifically based' research proved to be contentious, with numerous commentators from within the education research community challenging this 'new scientific orthodoxy' (Howe, 2009, p. 428) in educational research (see also Lather, 2004). Of particular concern was the perceived privileging of quantitative research methods over qualitative approaches, with much of the consternation directed at the emphasis on experimental and quasi-experimental evaluative approaches, especially Randomized Controlled Trials (RCTs) (for example, Berliner, 2002). In an article in *Educational Researcher*, Robert Slavin (2002) put forward the case for adopting rigorous experimental approaches in education that would result in the same sort of advances seen in disciplines such as medicine and agriculture where replicable experimental approaches were well established. This 'optimism' (Olson, 2004, p. 24) for randomized experiments based on their success in evaluating medical treatments drew particular scrutiny from those who argued for the incommensurability of education and medicine, and where 'a school is not a hospital' (Furedi, 2013, online) or 'being a student is not an illness, just as teaching is not a cure' (Biesta, 2007, p. 8) are common refrains (but see also Slavin, 2004; Hanley et al., 2016).

Debates over the application of RCTs to the field of education as well as the value or otherwise of 'evidence-based' policies and 'scientifically valid' research have not been confined to the USA. In England in 2013 the Department of Education commissioned a report into 'the use of evidence in education policy and practice' (Goldacre, 2013). The report advocated the use of RCTs as the most reliable tool for finding out 'what works', but also cautioned that:

> we recognise that being a good doctor, or teacher, or manager, isn't about robotically following the numerical output of randomised trials; nor is it about ignoring the evidence, and following your hunches and personal experiences instead. We do best, by using the right combination of skills to get the best job done. (Goldacre, 2013, p. 19)

The resulting criticisms of the 'dogma of scientism' (Furedi, 2013) in Goldacre's report from some in the academic education community were perhaps unsurprising. In many ways the UK critics mirrored US commentators in their concern over both the 'medicalization' of education and the promotion, by government, of the primacy of quantitative methods:

> Answering these more nuanced questions often requires other forms of research, some of it qualitative rather than quantitative or experimental. We also need philosophical

> inquiry into whether the things that policy-makers or teachers want to do are worthwhile in the first place. (Whitty, 2013, online; also Furedi, 2013; James, 2013)

Arguably one of the main areas of contention over the 'considerable and ongoing dispute' (Hanley et al., 2016, p. 3) over the use of RCTs in education lie in their presentation as the 'gold standard' method for undertaking research in the field. As Hanley et al. (2016, p. 4) argue, this label has proven to be unhelpful: 'the term gold standard should be used judiciously if at all, implying as it does, that other alternatives are inferior'. However, it is important to note that many of the commentaries from within the research community that argue in favor of experimental approaches generally, do not advocate adopting these approaches in isolation and note the value of incorporating other approaches to data collection within what Gorard (2004) terms 'the cycle of research':

> Randomised trials are very good at showing that something works; they're not always so helpful for understanding why it worked ... 'Qualitative' research – such as asking people open questions about their experiences – can help give a better understanding of how and why things worked, or failed, on the ground. (Goldacre 2013, p. 13; see also Slavin, 2002; Capraro and Thompson, 2008)

Aligned with the types of research methods used by the education research community is, of course, the quality and nature of research methods training. One of the concerns being that if researchers are in some way dissuaded from adopting a particular approach during their training, they are unlikely to return to it in their professional lives. The next section considers these issues in relation to doctoral training in education.

> Investigators adopting an objectivist (or positivist) approach to the social world, and who treat it like the world of natural phenomena as being real and external to the individual will choose from a range of traditional options – surveys experiments and the like. Others favoring the more subjectivist (or anti-positivist) approach and who view the social word as being of a much more personal and humanly created kind will select from a comparable range of recent and emerging techniques – accounts, participant observation, personal constructs, for example. (Cohen, Manion, and Morrison, 2011, p. 6)

For those of us who might optimistically have thought that the 'paradigm wars' were indeed finally over, this extract from the introductory chapter of a bestselling education research methods textbook suggests otherwise. The book begins, as indicated above, with a discussion of the nature of reality, of different research paradigms and offers guidance on identifying one's epistemological position, which in turn, we are told, will inform the data collection methods that the researcher will adopt. This is the first encounter that many postgraduate students will have with research methods training, and the first thing this book, and many others like it, will do is to encourage them to pick sides and to decide whether they are an interpretivist or a positivist. This brings us to the second area where we risk a rerun of the 'paradigm wars' – the research methods training of novice researchers in particular at postgraduate level.

Education research has, at times, been described as having an 'awful' reputation (Kaestle, 1993) of being 'not very influential, useful or well-funded' (Burkhardt and Schoenfeld, 2003, p. 3), of following fads (Slavin, 1989) and of being of indifferent quality (Hargreaves, 1996). While these concerns may, or may not, have been justified, they prompted numerous calls to improve the research skills of the education research community. At the time of the criticisms, more than twenty years ago in some cases, the concerns were twofold: a lack of quantitative skills among education academics, and poor quality research methods training (for example, Henson et al., 2010).

In the UK, efforts to address these issues entailed ambitious, costly, long term programs by the Economic and Social Research Council, the Nuffield Foundation and the British Academy aimed at building capacity in the use of quantitative methods in the social sciences, including education. While the success of these initiatives in remedying the skills 'deficit' has been questioned (Platt, 2012), there has also been recognition that the UK lags behind other nations in terms of the quantitative research skills of the academic community:

> by far the most important barrier to change is the very low proportion of staff in university social science departments who themselves have quantitative skills, and the inertia in the system that makes raising this proportion difficult. (MacInnes et al., 2016, p. 15)

If there are issues with the capacity to undertake quantitative work within schools or departments of education then this will impact upon the quality of research methods training (for example, Capraro and Thompson, 2008). As Henson et al. (2010, p. 229) argue 'the nature and quality of research is inseparable from the nature and quality of the graduate education of future education researchers' and one of the main areas of concern is with the quality of quantitative research methods training, particularly at doctoral level. The foundations of these claims are perhaps obvious: if education academics/faculty are unfamiliar with the content and coverage of the quantitative methods curriculum then this is likely to lead to 'unproductive divides in graduate students' exposure to methodology concepts' (Henson et al., 2010, p. 238). These divisions will be particularly pronounced if quantitative methods training is provided by colleagues from a different discipline or department and where there may be a risk that technical statistical skills will be taught at the expense of applying those skills to the social (or educational) world. It is not sufficient simply to tell students what statistical test they need to use to analyze a particular piece of data; this risks producing 'button pushers', not social researchers. Instead students need to know why a particular technique may help them answer their research questions and how that technique can be accounted for in the design of their study and the collection of appropriate data and which will, of course, depend on what they want to find out. An overwhelmingly technical approach to teaching statistics, especially to students who have a limited mathematical background and may lack confidence in working with numbers, can lead to disengagement with quantitative methods and a reinforcement of the paradigmatic divisions that have been discussed here.

To summarize, despite the development of mixed methods research, and optimism that perhaps the 'paradigm wars' are finally over, methodological differences within the field of education remain and are apparent in the training that is provided to novice researchers. Over the last 15 years or so, the increased involvement of governments in the allocation of taxpayers' money to fund research in education has led to greater scrutiny over the types of research the community undertakes, the methods it uses and the warrant it attaches to its findings. Central to this have been disputes over the use of experimental methodologies that risk returning us back to the 'paradigm wars'. The purpose of education research, and subsequently its primary goal, is to improve education (Tymms, Chapter 7 this volume, Purposes for Educational Research). This may sound obvious, and is a goal that few within the education research community would dispute. However disagreement persists about the methods we use to inform the research we undertake into how we might seek this improvement. Looking back over the 'paradigm wars', it is remarkable to see the extent to which the debate has dominated methodological discourse in the field of education. And in doing this, it is difficult not to muse over what advances in knowledge might have been made had researchers not been encouraged to 'pick sides' and to fit the craft of research into divisive paradigms.

THE CHANGING NATURE OF EDUCATION RESEARCH

Most readers will want to use this Handbook as a means of improving their research knowledge and practice. Yet this book's chapters are also a useful prompt to thinking about some broader issues. In particular, the book, and this introduction, reflect the fast changing nature of what 'education research' is and what it means to be an 'education researcher' as we approach the 2020s. Thus, while highlighting many strengths of education research, reading this Handbook also raises a number of uncertainties and challenges. Some of these challenges relate as much to the politics of education research as to the practice of education research. The authors of the chapters do not merely set out to describe 'how' to conduct research in education settings, but also stimulate thought and reflection on what it is we are doing (and not doing) in the course of conducting education research.

One of the implicit assumptions throughout the book is the need for educational research to be conducted that is of the highest possible quality. The need to strive for the highest standards is driven by both professional and personal ambitions to do well, and increasingly driven by international, national and institutional audits of research quality. Yet it is worthwhile relating our individual ideals of what makes for high quality against criticisms that have been made about education research. While there is evidence that education has held up well in comparison to many other social science and humanities disciplines, anyone with even a passing involvement will be aware of the considerable criticism and pressure that education research has been subjected to over the past thirty years. These criticisms have come from a variety of sources, including some that have been self-inflicted, as we showed earlier in this introduction.

Education can find itself facing criticism from both academic communities and professional communities in spite of its serious engagement with both. For example, education research can be dismissed by other areas of the academy (that is, other disciplines that are part of universities) as an overly 'applied' area of research dominated by ex-teachers. At the same time, a professional and practical engagement with education inevitably results in careful thinking about 'what works' in relation to teaching and learning but this positive trait has been seen by some as an under-theorized focus on individual students, teachers and classroom (Biesta, 2007). Paradoxically though, a *lack* of attention to 'what works' in education research has been criticized by some policymakers, school leaders, parents, employers and teachers, who are themselves have a strong interest in practice (Berliner, 2002; Boekaerts and Cascaller, 2006; Beauchamp, Clarke, Hulme, and Murray, 2013). From these quarters, education research has been questioned in terms of its 'real-world relevance' and ideological biases. Some of these criticisms are not unique to education research because they are related to wider debates in social sciences. Savage and Burrows (2007) argued in 'The coming crisis of empirical sociology' that many of the social sciences that came to prominence in the 1950s, 1960s and 1970s were waning notably in prominence and purpose – facing growing challenges to their authority and jurisdiction, while stymied by their 'insular and self-regarding' (Savage and Burrows, 2007, p. 2) attitudes. Education scholarship certainly finds itself operating in very different conditions than were apparent even twenty years ago. A key question that therefore underlies all of the chapters in the book is simply: how can we ensure that education research can be considered to be 'fit for purpose' in these current times?

Awareness of, and reasoned arguments against, such criticisms can lead to higher quality education research. For example, some education researchers' work can benefit from a more comprehensive engagement with theory. Most researchers can benefit from being more open to engagement with different research approaches and traditions that we might not have favored previously. And we are in an era when dissemination of research in different forms in order to engage with different audiences is expected.

One of the important messages underpinning this book is the need to engage with broader shifts and innovations outside of the traditional methodologies used in education research: take, for instance, the recent 'Big Data' turn (see Chapter 45 this volume, Big Data and Educational Research). Indeed, the ongoing hyperbole surrounding big data is a good example of the changing (and challenging) landscape that education researchers now find themselves working within. In theory, recent development in networked digital technologies means that comprehensive data is being generated every day on/through the actions of educators and students in sufficient quality and scope to address many of the big questions that education faces in terms of education engagement and education outcomes. As Burrows and Savage (2014) note, big data offers the promise of being able to provide actual evidence of actions on a mass scale. Contrast, for example, the validity of using a traditional interview to understand the movements of an interviewee over a 48-hour period compared with the GPS data from their mobile telephone. Then consider this data for 10,000 (or 100,000 or 10 million) cases.

The huge datasets being generated by students, teachers and other education actors therefore offer 'to reveal the reality of human behavior at scale' (Carrigan 2015, online). Moreover, the implication is that these analyses can be conducted at a distance by distributed 'data scientists' rather than requiring efforts of education researchers 'in the field'. Policymakers, schools and parents have new sources from which to make decisions, inform practice and gain a general sense of trends and directions within education. What if big data might be able do a better job than researchers – providing insights that are far quicker and far cheaper? However, most readers of this book would probably feel that this is a reductive and distorted argument. So the challenge presented by methodological developments such as big data is what education researchers are going to do about it? On one hand, how can we develop convincing defenses against the wilder claims surrounding big data – re-asserting the value of nuanced, rigorous but comparatively small-scale research? How can education researchers produce explanations of education above and beyond what can apparently be achieved with big data? But also, how might the education research community best embrace aspects of big data – taking these methods and applying them carefully to education-specific contexts, for example through mixed methods approaches? Education researchers need to engage with *and* against new methodological and epistemological developments – striving to develop forms of research practice that are relevant to such changes. There is much in the book that might seem unfamiliar. The challenge, therefore, is to resist the temptation to skip past these chapters and topics. Instead we need to ask what does our own research genuinely do well that these familiar approaches cannot? What might our own research benefit from appropriating and incorporating?

This first part of the introduction to the Handbook has raised a series of issues, in relation to education as a discipline, how knowledge is built, epistemological debates such as the paradigm wars, and the challenges of new forms of data and research. These issues are both the explicit focus of some of the chapters but also the backdrop to the points raised in the different parts of the book. The following sections introduce the main content of each of the six parts.

PART I: UNDERSTANDING RESEARCH

One of the starting points for understanding education research comes from knowledge of the history of education. In relation to education as a discipline and a field we can trace roots back to classical Greek philosophy, as the opening chapters in this section do. In addition, as Ian Menter suggests in his chapter, more recent scholarship has sought to reflect epistemological and ontological considerations emerging from new understandings of cultural contexts other than Western ones. An important driver for education research continues to be its importance to society in a wide range of contexts.

Beyond considerations of the discipline of education and its history, perhaps one of the first issues that researchers encounter is the nature of theory and its place in research. Theory exists at many levels in relation to research, as the chapters in this section reveal. At a philosophical level theory can be seen in researcher's epistemological and ontological orientations. Yet some argue that such philosophical considerations have little merit in relation to empirical research. The debates about the place of theory include perceptions by some that binary opposites such as theory/practice or empirical/theoretical are in themselves unhelpful and have perhaps been a barrier to more sophisticated understandings of how researchers use and build theory.

Another highly significant topic for philosophers, and one that has increasingly important practical implications for all researchers, is ethics (as the BERA ethical guidelines illustrate www.bera.ac.uk/researchers-resources/resources-for-researchers). The growth of ethics scrutiny of research projects has been necessary but also comes with a range of challenges. One of these challenges is how to balance appropriate ethical scrutiny commensurate with the level of likely risk. As part of appropriate consideration of level of risk some low-risk projects are exempt from full Institutional Review Boards in the USA.

Another fundamental concept that affects all researchers is causality. It is sometimes argued that causality is the domain of natural science research only. But causality is of strong interest to social scientists as well. For example causal inferences need to be made about the effectiveness of different approaches to teaching. In this book it is argued that one of its contributions is to the recognition of sophisticated methodological knowledge in relation to qualitative, quantitative *and* mixed methods research designs. This is true of causality where it is recognized that causality is a concern in some qualitative research, just as it is in some quantitative and mixed methods studies. As Sean Kelly argues in his chapter, what links the concerns of a range of scientists (studying social and natural phenomena) are the basic principles of causality: (1) accounting for effects caused by chance; (2) ruling out competing explanations for effects; and (3) warranted explanations of causation, for example explanations for the effects of schools that can be attributed to teaching approaches, socio-economic factors, or to both.

The understanding of philosophy and theory, and their application in an ethically defensible way sometimes leading to causal explanations, are all implicated in the final chapter in this part of the book, by Joseph A. Maxwell, which addresses validity and reliability. Links with other chapters in this part are tangible because the author establishes a realist perspective on validity and reliability on the basis of ontological realism combined with constructivism.

PART II: PLANNING RESEARCH

This second section of the Handbook focuses on the crucial planning stage and considers the importance of developing robust research questions and research designs. Put simply, it emphasizes 'knowing what you want to find out' as the foundation for a high quality research study. However, when planning a study the researcher must first of all decide upon a topic. Ideas for topics can come from many sources – they may come simply from being recruited to work or study on an existing research project or may stem from somewhere more personal such as an experience or an observation, a chance conversation, a newspaper headline, a hunch or just simple curiosity. But, as Peter Tymms argues, one thing that these topics will, or should, share is a common purpose to improve education.

Having chosen a topic the next stage in planning research is to review the field and to understand what is already known about a particular area, where the gaps are and what the key issues and debates might be. A research or literature review is intended to provide this summary and, in turn, to help the researcher design a study that is both researchable and practicable for them, or their team, to undertake. This review might take the form of a traditional literature review or a systematic review or research synthesis. The growing number of outlets where research findings can be shared, in both print and electronic form, can make it daunting for the researcher, or the research consumer, to know what research is out there and how best to judge its quality. Examining the findings of high quality reviews from organizations like the US What Works Clearinghouse and the UK-based EPPI centre, or from peer-reviewed academic review journals such as the US *Review of Educational Research*, the Australian *Education Review* and UK *Review of Education* are good places to start.

From deciding upon the topic or area of study we move to developing research questions. Research questions are a crucial stage in the planning of research, they enable the study to have a clear focus and having well-developed research questions will help with the design of the study and in deciding upon the type of data that need to be collected. Research questions are an area that has achieved some recent prominence. Little was written about them before the turn of the century but they are now a feature of many research methods books and several text-books (for example, White, 2009). This is a welcome development but the extent to which education research is truly question-led remains a concern, as Patrick White indicates in his chapter.

Research questions and research design are linked: having clear and well-defined questions will help with the design of a project. Stephen Gorard refers to design as being the 'structure and organization of a research project' where a well-planned study will lead to more reliable methods of data collection, more credible findings and more warranted implications for policy and practice. Indeed while there are a number of different types of research design, as discussed in Part III of the Handbook, there is no such thing as one single good design or 'gold standard'. This is because the suitability of a design depends on the research questions and therefore 'any research design can, in principle, use any type of data collection and can use either qualitative or quantitative data' (de Vaus, 2001, p. 16). Indeed, only once the research design has been developed should the researcher make any final decisions about methods of data collection and analysis. Alongside issues of research design come the challenges of sampling. In particular an awareness of how to ensure that the sample is appropriate and representative of experiences or individuals, while also accounting for the ethical and practical challenges of maintaining an unbiased and relevant focus to data collection whatever sampling strategy is used.

If, as Gorard suggests, the design of a study acts as a type of conceptual framework, then its 'theoretical' framework is often informed by different (and sometimes contested) notions of the reality of the social world and the tools that can be used to study it. In this part of the Handbook we devote three chapters to considering the role of theory in educational research from three main orientations: positivist, interpretivist and pragmatic mixed method approaches.

PART III: APPROACHES TO RESEARCH

Progressing from initial research problems and philosophical assumptions the third section of the Handbook moves on to another important phase of the research process – the framing of more concrete research approaches. As will be clear from the chapters so far, education research is not a wholly mechanistic, value-free process. Any empirical inquiry has a guiding set of assumptions, agendas and viewpoints – what Guba (1990, p. 7) terms 'a basic set of beliefs that guide action'. It is important to be aware of what these beliefs are, and how they can be used to operationalize the initial stages of research outlined in the previous sections of this Handbook.

While important, consideration of research approaches can easily be neglected in the rush to 'get on with' the practicalities of conducting an empirical study.

Many researchers (particularly as they become more 'experienced' and/or set in their ways) will feel that they instinctively know how to go about approaching an empirical project, perhaps even before they have specified their research questions and research design. Indeed, the different approaches covered in the twelve chapters in this part of the book correspond closely with how many education researchers identify themselves – that is, 'I am a historian' or 'I am an ethnographer'. Yet people's certainty can sometimes belie a lack of consideration for the particularities of any new research project. On occasion what we presume to be a viable research approach for a new study might be driven by habit (that is, I have always conducted ethnographic research), presumed expertise (my strengths lie in ethnography), or lack of confidence (I don't know how to do anything but ethnography).

The chapters in this section, taken as a whole, suggest the case for striving to move regularly outside of one's methodological comfort zone and (re)consider each research approach on a case-by-case basis. Perhaps the issues that a research project is addressing actually merit a *different* approach than one might instinctively pursue. As such, it clearly makes sense to take the approach that is most congruent with the prevailing research ambitions and aims. For example, a project aiming to examine changes over time is likely to merit a longitudinal or perhaps historical approach. A project seeking to establish conditions of causality lends itself to a different approach. Regardless of personal convenience and/or comfort, there is no one research approach that is suitable for all circumstances.

Hopefully, the proceeding chapters will prompt reflection on how education researchers could (and should) set about approaching any empirical investigation. As all these chapters suggest, after having determined research questions and philosophy a lot more remains to the 'doing' of education research than simply enacting methods of data generation and analysis. Conducting research requires substantial amounts of planning, framing and preparing. The chapters offer a variety of ways that one might go about these tasks.

Some of these discussions are likely to appear familiar from readers' experiences of basic social research methods training. Here, approaches to research can be described in blunt terms of 'Quantitative', or 'Qualitative'. Clearly some of the chapters in this section are more 'quantitative' than others – for example, surveys, trend studies and experiments. Others are clearly more 'qualitative' – for example, ethnography, grounded theory and case studies. Yet there has been an understandable move away from these unhelpfully crude distinctions. How we go about research relates to a lot more than simply the nature of the data that is being generated. For example, Gorard (2013) offers the useful distinction in terms of research process between 'active' and 'passive' approaches – that is, whether or not a study involves some form of intervention, direct participation or treatment.

These various dichotomies highlight the range of important decisions that are taken when defining how any piece of research might be approached.

Are you setting out to build theory or test theory? Are you looking to explore or explain? Are you interested in mapping out the complexity of people's understandings and meaning-making, thereby acknowledging the inter-connected nature of social phenomenon over time and space? Are you looking to identify causal relationships between variables and generalize findings to larger groups and broader contexts? All of these intentions are very different in terms of the research approach that they point towards. The chapters in this part provide a thorough grounding in which approaches might best fit the guiding intentions of any piece of research.

One issue that is certainly worth reflecting on as these chapters progress is how the appropriation of each approach in *education* research differs from its origins. Most research approaches outlined in this section derive from disciplines other than education. For example, any educational ethnographer is clearly continuing an anthropological tradition dating back to the late nineteenth century. Grounded theory was born from sociological work over fifty years ago initially based on studies of expectations of death amongst hospital patients. Meta-analyses originated in psychology and medical research. These are not the sole preserve of education research.

A key dilemma that many of the chapters therefore touch on is the extent to which education research retains (or even extends) the strength of these approaches. Conversely, to what extent do education researchers compromise (or even perhaps lose sight altogether) of the essential qualities of these approaches? On one hand, as Sandy Oliver and Janice Tripney point out in their chapter, education researchers could be seen as having contributed greatly to advancing the use of meta-analyses in the social sciences. Yet, to what extent could the same be said of educational ethnography or experimental research? Indeed, Sara Delamont's chapter starts by chastising some education research for being 'misleadingly' touted as ethnography while it more honestly should be described as qualitative. Similarly, concepts such as grounded theory and action research sometimes feel stretched to the point of incredulity by some education researchers. All the chapters in this section therefore remind us of the benefit of looking back to the origins of the empirical traditions in which we are working, and not limiting our research imaginations solely to how things are done in the name of education research.

PART IV: ACQUIRING DATA

Moving beyond the planning and development stages of designing a research study, the fourth section of the Handbook covers what is perhaps the most exciting stage of all – acquiring the data. Assuming that the study has a clear focus, is researchable and has a well-thought out design, deciding which tools to use to actually gather the data ought to be straightforward.

However, one of the most important temptations that some, often novice, researchers have to resist is taking the decision about how they will acquire their data at the very start of their research project. As this Handbook demonstrates, good research proceeds incrementally – through developing an understanding about what research is, to considering a range of different research approaches, to finalizing the design of the study. Only then can the data be collected, analyzed and the findings shared. A well-designed research study would never begin with the researcher simply stating a wish to 'do interviews' or to 'do a survey'. So although the decision about how to acquire data can be the easiest stage in the entire process of research, this would only be the case if the previous steps in research development and design have been followed first.

So while deciding how data will be acquired ought to proceed logically from the earlier stages of research design, the actual process of data collection still requires a sound knowledge and understanding of the different techniques that might be used to effectively collect this data. This is the focus of the seven chapters in this section.

The first stage in acquiring data is, of course, gaining entry to the field. Accessing the field, particularly for primary data collection, can be challenging, especially if the researcher is external to the school or organization they wish to study, and gaining access can often require skillful and sensitive negotiation. Accessing secondary (or existing) data can sometimes be more straightforward especially with the increased accessibility of open data sources, although issues of privacy and data protection may still be present. Once in the field there are a number of strategies that the researcher might adopt in order to gather data and which will, of course, be apparent from the research questions and the design of the study. These data collection methods include observation techniques, interviews and questionnaires, as well as the gathering of textual data, from digital and non-digital sources; and techniques that focus on acquiring data from personal experiences, such as auto-ethnography and self-study.

Each of these techniques brings its own challenges and opportunities and the authors of these chapters offer advice and counsel on how best to acquire data using these different approaches. Based on their extensive experience of researching the field, the chapters balance practical advice and examples from the authors' own research projects, while at the same time locating the choice of data collection method within the wider process of designing a research study. For example, Amir Marvasti and Carrie Freie's chapter advises the researcher to select the type of interview (structured, in-depth, ethnographic, or focus group) that is best suited to the question being studied – a choice they suggest is made during the design phase of the study.

Being in the field gathering data can be one of the most exciting and challenging stages of the whole research process. The seven chapters in this section provide a useful guide to help us to do this and they encourage us to both reconnect with familiar methods and to explore new and exciting tools with which to acquire our data.

PART V: ANALYSING DATA

The word 'data' is derived from Latin meaning 'something given'. This section of the Handbook covers current practices in the application of analytical methods for managing data with techniques that allow the researcher to reduce massive amounts of information (data) into meaningful and useful knowledge. It includes chapters on the relationship between theory and data, methods of organizing data (cataloging and coding) which apply to any form of data reduction. Five chapters are devoted to quantitative analytical procedures such as descriptive statistics, inferential statistics, factor analysis, logistic regression, and multi-level analysis. And five chapters are devoted to qualitative methods such as coding qualitative data, content analysis, conversation analysis, discourse analysis and critical discourse analysis. One new area in educational research, known as 'big data', is defined for those who wish to consider how modern computational techniques are changing how information is created and potentially analyzed for new applications.

Data analysis in the twenty-first century invariably involves the use of computers to manipulate data which may be in the form of numbers, images, video, voice, or the printed page. The collection and classification of educational data include characteristics as diverse as psychological traits of individuals, classes of organizations, economic conditions, and geographic location. Such forms of data are an essential element of the scientific processes for both describing conditions and testing hypotheses about relationships between humans. The variety of educational data is so immense that the earliest definition of data as 'a given fact' has been replaced more often by the assumption that knowledge production is 'situated, partial and constitutive' (Phillips and Burbules, 2000). In other words, the meaning and use of data is a living event that depends as much on the point of view of the observer as on the object observed. Nevertheless, over the past hundred years or more, methods and procedures have been developed for assembling data in an orderly manner so that others might replicate the process. Education research is dependent on the ability of researchers to have shared understanding about the methods defined in the chapters of this section.

The chapters on data analysis were chosen to represent the expanse of data collection and reduction techniques used in the field of education today. Readers of this large variety of approaches to data analysis will notice that separating all of educational research into a dichotomy of quantitative and qualitative methods does not reflect reality. For example, in the chapter on discourse analysis Christoph A. Hafner makes the point that the methods of discourse analysis provide tools for observing and objectively recording student–teacher interactions. However, the researcher occasionally needs a means to establish whether some interactions are more common than others and thus a quantitative method is attached to the more qualitative observation method to provide counts of frequency of activities. Hafner rightly points out that the effort to turn a qualitative observation into a quantitative one invariably results in the loss of information. It may be essential for a full theoretical explanation of the essence of the interaction that affected the quality of educating a student that both qualitative and quantitative methods be applied equally in the same research study.

This identical dilemma occurs in reverse among researchers who conduct survey analysis because the survey researcher must develop a priori definitions of psychological functions or of social interactions to form an interview protocol or survey instrument. If the survey researcher collects too much information (such as hundreds of hours of video observation), the investigator is likely to be overwhelmed by detail and the analysis required is so time consuming that a full analysis is never completed nor insights discovered. Otherwise, if the researcher collects too little information about the behaviors of students or teachers then the analysis will provide only hackneyed conclusions that would have no important effect on knowledge building. Frequent compromises between a choice of rich observation and data reduction are a necessary element in ongoing research projects.

Likewise, the dilemma occurs in implementing statistical models, such as factor analysis. Betsy McCoach, in her chapter on confirmatory factor analysis, for example, explains that the researcher who confirms that an a priori defined set of latent structures is 'real', useful, reliable, and valid cannot be solely depend on the statistical functions of conducting a confirmatory analysis. The researcher must insert professional judgment about which data to include, how to include them, and when to end the process of analysis itself. The method does not provide the researcher with the mechanisms for making these judgments; the researchers must use professional experience to determine when to call an analysis scientifically meritorious. Of course, another judgment of merit occurs when a research paper is judged by peer reviewers.

Quantitative methods such as multi-level models, logistic regression, and inferential statistics have become easier to apply to large-scale databases in recent years as computational techniques have been developed to accommodate complex models. The value of these methods is that they solve some problems caused by the nature of data (such as whether a datum is nested within a larger unit which is also an important datum with variation that must be observed simultaneously). Such methods, however, have many hidden assumptions that users must acknowledge and understand as they describe their research results so that their study conclusions represent a reality that can be replicated and understood by others. The authors of these chapters have written to the general user so that the key errors that might be made in such analysis are defined.

One of the complaints about educational research is that rules of scientific observation and hypothesis testing are not universally followed or agreed upon (Shavelson and Towne, 2002). Consequently, recommendations for educational practices may be inconsistent simply because different forms of observation led to different conclusions. No single method or data collection procedure can eliminate the possibility of varying conclusions; therefore, multiple methods of study may be required before an observation is ready for application in the real world. For example, a carefully designed experiment conducted in the state of Tennessee reported convincing scientific evidence that small class sizes resulted in higher learning of students. The study was conducted in ways to remove any form of bias and thus was a 'pure' relationship. However, when one state implemented a plan to reduce class size throughout the state they found that student achievement did not increase. The assumptions of the Tennessee experiment were not matched. The implementation of smaller classes required the state to hire a large number of teachers, many of whom were not adequately prepared for their task. Thus, a simple observation made in a vacuum may not easily translate to implementation in the real world. Implementing a practice requires multiple forms of analysis and theory development involving multiple levels of aggregation and research methods.

Educational researchers operate within a history of research practices that have been acknowledged by scientific and professional associations and that provide guidance on how to assure that the communication of a research result can be explained adequately to be replicated by others. Individual researchers contribute to the growth and development of research methods by interpretation and implementation of these methods in their own research. Each of the chapters in the data analysis section describes the essential elements and rules of scientific rigor that are standard for that method. Since all stages of scientific research involve judgments by the researcher that may affect the outcome of the analysis, the techniques developed in each methodological domain contain rules and procedures to reduce (or openly specify) the researchers own personal biases. One goal of this Handbook is to provide a variety of examples of modern research analysis that successfully communicate the results of educational research results. Hopefully, these chapters have contributed to building a common language and knowledge of research analysis methods.

PART VI: REPORTING, DISSEMINATING & EVALUATING RESEARCH

The first five parts of this book identify and reflect on the conditions, contexts, processes and ways of thinking necessary for high quality educational research. Researchers implement their research to the best of their abilities in order to establish new findings. The extent to which the findings are an original contribution, established through rigorous methodology, and are significant, is ultimately determined through communication in writing (and other modes) and subject to review by expert peers. Reporting, disseminating & evaluating research are topics of the final section of the Handbook.

As part of dissemination and review the issue of generalizability is important. For some, generalizability is conceptualized through a particular theory, such as psychometric theories of measurement, as the first chapter in this part by Guillermo Solano-Flores does. A somewhat old-fashioned idea of research dissemination is the linear model from implementing the research design then publishing the outcomes in a research output aimed at an audience of researchers. While there is still a vital place for the peer-reviewed research journal article aimed at peers, over the last twenty years or so the complex and indirect nature of many ways of sharing research have grown in importance. Mark Rickinson's chapter argues for research utilization conceptualized as: instrumental research use; conceptual research use; and strategic or symbolic research use. Within these conceptualizations there are new ways in which the outcomes of research are being shared, for example social media as multiple hybrid modes of publishing.

A well as the growth in possibilities for disseminating research, and the new kinds of scrutiny this has brought, the evaluation of research and the accountability faced by researchers and their institutions has grown. National exercises that link research funding with evaluations of institutions' research quality are part of this. In addition, international league tables of institutions usually include scores for the research quality and intensity, which sometimes draw on national data. Of particular interest is the way that educational quality is assessed in the USA, for example, and how this compares with other regions of the world such as Australia, New Zealand and the UK, as Larry Suter's chapter discusses.

In spite of all the changes in educational research, including the growth of social media, bid data, multimodality, and so on the place of text and writing remains preeminent and integral to the research process as is clear from Pat Thomson's chapter (also see Wyse, forthcoming). The dominant 'three move structure' to an academic journal article is compared with approaches to writing based on problematization, and to alternative forms of written structure. Whichever ways education research is written, a key final question for researchers is to what extent their research will be used. This brings our discussion of education research back into the realm of politics and progress in society. Indeed the debates in relation to whether education researchers have done enough to engage with 'end users' of research, and whether practitioners and policymakers are sufficiently open-minded about research are addressed in the final chapter of this book, by Chris Brown.

We hope that you find the book's account of the discipline of education and its research compelling, thought-provoking, and practically useful. We also look forward to engaging with you about the theories, issues, and practices that are addressed, with the aim to continue the development of education as a discipline.

REFERENCES

Allwood, C. M. (2012) The distinction between qualitative and quantitative research methods is problematic. *Quality and Quantity*, 46, 1417–1429.

Australian Government: Australian Research Council (2015) *State of Australian University Research 2015–2016*. Australian Government.

Beauchamp, G., Clarke, L., Hulme, M., and Murray, J. (2013) Policy and practice within the United Kingdom. *Research and Teacher Education: The BERA-RSA Inquiry* (December). Retrieved on 27 September, 2016 from www.bera.ac.uk/system/files/ BERA Paper 1 UK Policy and Practice_0.pdf.

Berliner, D. C. (2002) Educational research: the hardest science of all. *Educational Researcher*, 31, 8, 18–20.

Biesta, G. (2007) Why 'what works' won't work: evidence-based practice and the democratic deficit in educational research. *Educational Theory*, 57 1, 1–22.

Biesta, G. (2016) Knowledge and the curriculum: a pragmatist approach. In D. Wyse, L. Hayward, and J. Pandya (Eds) *The SAGE Handbook of Curriculum, Pedagogy and Assessment*. London: Sage, 78–91

Boekaerts, M. and Cascallar, E. (2006) How far have we moved toward the integration of theory and practice in self-regulation? *Educational Psychology Review*, 18, 3, 199. doi: 10.1007/s10648-006-9013-4.

Bryman, A. (1988) *Quantity and Quality in Social Research*. London: Unwin Hyman.

Bryman, A. (2006) Paradigm peace and the implications for quality. *International Journal of Social Research Methodology*, 9, 2, 111–126.

Bryman, A. (2008) The end of the paradigm wars? In P. Alasuutari, L. Bickman, and J. Brannen (Eds) *The SAGE Handbook of Social Research Methods*. Los Angeles: Sage, 13–25.

Burkhardt, H. and Schoenfeld, A. H. (2003) Improving educational research: toward a more useful, more influential and better-funded enterprise. *Educational Researcher*, 32, 9, 3–14.

Burrows, R. and Savage, M. (2014) After the crisis? Big data and the methodological challenges of empirical sociology. *Big Data & Society*, April/June.

Capraro, R.M. and Thompson, B. (2008) The educational researcher defined: what will future researchers be trained to do? *The Journal of Educational Research*, 101, 4, 247–253.

Carrigan, M. (2015) *Towards a meta-critique of data science*. https://markcarrigan. net/2015/10/13/towards-a-meta-critique-of-data-science/ [last accessed 21th September 2016]

Cohen, L., Manion, L. and Morrison, K. (2011) *Research Methods in Education*, 7th Edition. London: Routledge.

Denzin, N. K. and Lincoln, Y. S. (Eds) (2011) *The SAGE Handbook of Qualitative Research*. London: Sage.

Department for Business, Innovation and Skills. (2011) *International Comparative Performance of the UK Research Base – 2011*. London: Department for Business, Innovation and Skills.

de Vaus, D. A. (2001) *Research Design in Social Research*. London: Sage.

Furedi, F. (2013) Teaching is not some kind of clinical cure. *Times Educational Supplement*, October 13.

Furlong, J. (2013) *Education – An Anatomy of the Discipline: Rescuing the University Project?* London: Routledge.

Gage, N.L. (1989) The paradigm wars and their aftermath: a 'historical' sketch of research on teaching. *Educational Researcher*, 18, 7, 4–10.

Goldacre, B. (2013) Building evidence into education. Retrieved on September 14, 2016 from http://media.education.gov.uk/assets/files/pdf/b/ben%20goldacre%20paper.pdf.

Gorard, S. (2004) *Combining Methods in Educational and Social Research*. Maidenhead: Open University Press.

Gorard, S. (2004) *Research Design*. Thousand Oaks, CA: Sage.

Guba, E. G. (1990) The alternative paradigm dialog. In E. Guba (Ed.) *The Paradigm Dialog*. Thousand Oaks, CA: Sage, 17–30.

Guba, E.G. and Lincoln, Y.S. (1994). Competing paradigms in qualitative research. In N. K. Denzin and Y. S. Lincoln (Eds.), *Handbook of Qualitative Research*. London: Sage, 105–117.

Gutiérrez, K.D. and Penuel, W.R. (2014) Relevance to Practice as a Criterion for Rigor. *Educational Researcher*, 43, 1, 19–23.

Hammersley, M. (1992) The paradigm wars: reports from the front. *British Journal of Sociology of Education*, 13, 1, 131–143.

Hammersley, M. (1995) The Politics of Social Research. London: Sage.

Hanley, P., Chambers, B., and Haslam, J. (2016) Reassessing RCTs as the 'gold standard': synergy not separation in evaluation designs. *International Journal of Research and Method in Education*, 39, 3, 287–298.

Hargreaves, D. (1996) Teaching as a research-based profession: possibilities and prospects, the Teacher Training Agency Annual Lecture April 1996. Retrieved in April 2016 from https://eppi.ioe.ac.uk/cms/Portals/0/ PDFreviewsandsummaries/ TTAHargreaveslecture.pdf.

Henson, R. K., Hull, D. M., and Williams, C. S. (2010) Methodology in our education research culture: toward a stronger collective quantitative proficiency. *Educational Researcher*, 39, 3, 229–240.

Hopman, S. (2010). When the battle's lost and won. Some observations concerning 'What ever happened to Curriculum Theory'. Stirling: University of Stirling.

Howe, K. R. (2009) Positivist dogmas, rhetoric, and the education science question. *Educational Researcher*, 38, 6, 428–440.

Institute of Education Sciences, US Department of Education and the National Science Foundation (2013) Common Guidelines for Education Research and Development. Washington DC: US Department of Education.

James, M. (2013) New (or not new) directions in evidence-based practice in education. Retrieved in April 2016 from www.bera.ac.uk/wpcontent/uploads/2014/02/Mary-james-New-or-not-new-directions-in-evidence-based-policy.-Response-to-Ben-Goldacre.pdf?noredirect=.

Johnson, R. B. and Onwuegbuzie, A. J. (2004) Mixed methods research: a research paradigm whose time has come. *Educational Researcher*, 33, 7, 14–26.

Kaestle, C. F. (1993) The awful reputation of education research. *Educational Researcher*, 22, 1, 23, 26–31.

Kuhn, T. S. (1970) *The Structure of Scientific Revolution*. Chicago, IL: University of Chicago Press.

Lather, P. (2004) This IS your father's paradigm: government intrusion and the case of qualitative research in education. *Qualitative Inquiry*, 10, 1, 15–34.

Lewis-Beck, M. S., Bryman, A., and Liao, T. F. (Eds) (2004) *The SAGE Encyclopedia of Social Science Methods*. London: SAGE Publications.

Lincoln, Y. S. (1994) Competing paradigms in qualitative research, in N. K. Denzin and Y. S. Lincoln (Eds) (2011) *The SAGE Handbook of Qualitative Research*. London: Sage, 105–117.

Locke, W., Whitchurch, C., Smith, H. and Mazenod, A. (2016) Shifting landscapes: meeting the staff development needs of the changing academic workforce. York, Higher Education Academy. Retrieved on September 14, 2016 from www.heacademy.ac.uk/sites/default/files/shifting_landscapes.pdf.

Lundgren, U. P. (2015) What's in a name? That which we call a crisis? A commentary on Michael Young's article 'Overcoming the crisis in curriculum theory'. *Journal of Curriculum Studies*, 47, 6, 787–801.

MacInnes, J., Breeze, M., de Haro, M., Kandlik, M., and Karels, M. (2016) *Measuring Up: International case studies on the teaching of quantitative methods in the social sciences*. London: The British Academy.

McKie, L. and Ryan, L. (2016) *An End to the Crisis of Empirical Sociology?* London: Routledge.

Maxwell, J. A. (2010) Using numbers in qualitative research. *Qualitative Inquiry*, 16, 6, 475–482.

OECD (2015) *Frascati Manual 2015: Guidelines for collecting and reporting data on research and experimental development, the measurement of scientific, technological and innovation activities*. Paris: OECD Publishing, doi: http://dx.doi.org/10.1787/9789264239012-en.

Oxford Dictionary Online (2016). Retrieved from www.oed.com (accessed 27 September, 2016).

Olson, D. (2004) The triumph of hope over experience in the search for 'what works': a response to Slavin. *Educational Researcher*, 33, 1, 24–26.

Phillips, D. (Ed.) (2014) *Encyclopedia of Educational Theory and Philosophy*. London: Sage.

Phillips D. C. and Burbules, N. C. (2000) *Postpositivism and Educational Research*. London: Rowman & Littlefield Publishers.

Platt, J. (2012) Making them count: how effective has official encouragement of quantitative methods been in British sociology? *Current Sociology*, 60, 5, 690–704.

Reid, Alan D., Hart, P., and Peters, M. A. (Eds) (2014) *A Companion to Research in Education*. The Netherlands: Springer.

Research Excellence Framework 2014. (2015a) *Overview report by Main Panel C and Sub-Panels 16 to 26*. Retrieved on September 14, 2016 from www.ref.ac.uk/panels/paneloverviewreports/.

Research Excellence Framework 2014. (2015b) *Overview report by Main Panel A and Sub-panels 1 to 6*. Retrieved on September 14, 2016 from www.ref.ac.uk/panels/paneloverviewreports/.

Savage, M. and Burrows, R. (2007) The coming crisis of empirical sociology. *Sociology*, 41, 5, 885–899.

Schrage, M. (2015) Why the future of social science is with private companies. *Harvard Business Review*, September 1. Retrieved on September 14, 2016 from https://hbr.org/2015/09/why-the-future-of-social-science-is-with-private-companies.

Shadish, W., Cook, T., & Campbell, D. (2002) *Experimental and Quasi-Experimental Designs for Generalized Causal Inference*. Belmont, CA.: Wadsworth.

Shavelson, R. J. and Towne, L. (Eds) (2002) *Scientific Research in Education*. Washington, DC: National Academy of Sciences.

Slavin, R. E. (1989) PET and the pendulum: faddism in education and how to stop it. *Phi Delta Kappan*, 70, 752–758.

Slavin, R. (2002) Evidence-based education policies: transforming educational practice and research. *Educational Researcher*, 31, 7, 15–21.

Slavin, R. (2004) Education research can and must address 'what works' questions. *Educational Researcher*, 33, 1, 27–28.

Smith, J. K. and Heshusuis, L. (1986) Closing down the conversation – the end of the quantitative–qualitative debate among educational inquirers. *Educational Researcher*, 15, 4–12.

Tashakkori, A. and Teddlie, C. (2010) *The SAGE Handbook of Mixed Methods in Social and Behavioural Research*. London: Sage.

The Royal Society (2016) History. Retrieved on September 14, 2016 from https://royalsociety.org/about-us/history/.

Toulmin, S. E. (1958), The Uses of Argument, Cambridge University Press, Cambridge.

US Department of Education (2002) Public Law 107–110, 107th Congress, Retrieved in April 2016 from www2.ed.gov/policy/elsec/leg/esea02/107-110.pdf.

US Department of Education (2004) Title IX – General provisions, Part A – definitions. Retrieved in April 2016 from www2.ed.gov/policy/elsec/leg/esea02/pg107.html.

White, P. (2009) *Developing Research Questions: A guide for social scientists*. Basingstoke: Palgrave Macmillan.

Whitty G. (2013) Evidence-informed policy and practice – we should welcome it, but also be realistic. Centre for Educational Research and Practice. Retrieved in April 2016 from https://cerp.aqa.org.uk/perspectives/evidence-informed-policy-practice.

Wyse, D. (forthcoming) *How Writing Works*. Cambridge: Cambridge University Press.

Wyse, D., Hayward, L. Livingston, K. and Higgins, S. (2016) Knowledge across the curriculum. The Curriculum Journal, 27, 3, online. Retrieved in September 2016 from http://www.tandfonline.com/doi/full/10.1080/09585176.2016.1207417

Wyse, D., Hayward, L. and Pandya, J. (Eds.) (2015). *The SAGE Handbook of Curriculum, Pedagogy and Assessment*. London: Sage.

Young, M. (2013) Overcoming the crisis in curriculum theory: a knowledge-based approach. *Journal of Curriculum Studies*, 45, 2, 101–118.

Zarębski, T. (2009). Toulmin's Model of Argument and the 'Logic' of Scientific Discovery. *Studies in Logic, Grammar and Rhetoric*, 16, 29, 267–283.

PART I
Understanding Research

1

Reasons for Education Research

Ian Menter

The word 'research' as here used does not describe any specific method or procedure. It designates a point of view – an attitude of enquiry and of willingness to test any theory against the evidence of the most carefully scrutinised and representative body of available facts. It implies a readiness to give up preconceived notions and to seek guidance not only from traditional interpretations but also from direct observation and experiment in any field of study. When successful, such research adds to the sum of human knowledge, and wise use of its findings leads to the husbanding of resources and the discovery of more satisfactory ways of living. (Fleming, 1952, p. v)

INTRODUCTION

The history of educational research is a very long one. In her work, *Research and the Basic Curriculum*, cited above, Dr C.M. Fleming is reviewing developments of the previous fifty years, that is, the first half of the twentieth century. Some would suggest that we can find the roots of our field, at least in the western world, in the works of Plato and Aristotle. Certainly it is not unusual for contemporary philosophers of education to cite the founders of classical philosophy in their deliberations. Philosophical debates on education also featured strongly during more recent considerations of human development and learning, such as Rousseau's *Emile* or in John Stuart Mill's *On Liberty*.

So, if philosophy provided the early foundations of our field, there was a major expansion in the late nineteenth and early twentieth centuries as the discipline of psychology was developed. For example, the influences of William James in the USA (James was also a philosopher) and Sigmund Freud in Europe can be detected in the discussions around child development and learning on both sides of the Atlantic that took place at that time. Within western thinking, many of the famous names in educational debate at this time – from John Dewey to Montessori, Pestalozzi and Froebel – were reacting to developments in our understanding of human learning and cognition and combining this with a set of clearly defined human values drawn from philosophy.

As the twentieth century progressed an increasingly scientific, even clinical and experimental perspective became significant. The work of the Swiss scientist Jean Piaget and of the Soviet psychologist Lev Vygotsky grew increasingly influential on how the processes of education – teaching and learning – were understood.

But also during the twentieth century there was an increasing influence from the discipline of sociology as educationists came to identify the influence of social factors on educational processes and outcomes. As well as the recognition of major connections between education and inequality, much deriving from the economic and political theories of Karl Marx, there was growing recognition of the fundamental social significance of national schooling systems through the work of Talcott Parsons in the USA.

So it was, that when educational studies emerged as a distinctive field around the middle of the twentieth century in the western world, it drew very heavily on philosophy, psychology and sociology, but also because of the way in which the trajectories of education systems were seen to be developing and evolving, history was seen as the fourth disciplinary partner (Tibble, 1966). It was during the twentieth century also that we saw the emergence of education departments in many universities around the world and the creation of a growing number of Professorships of Education, although earlier developments had taken place in Scotland (Hulme, 2013) and in continental Europe.

Of course, disciplines other than the four mentioned above also played a crucial part even if they were less visible. Anthropology, linguistics, economics and later cultural and media studies were also significant contributors, if less central (Furlong and Lawn, 2011). And, in referring to a western tradition it is also important to add two further caveats. First, there is not simply one single western tradition – to this day we can see enormous differences in the way that educational research is understood in different parts of Europe, with particular concepts that have developed within a Germanic tradition, such as 'bildung' (the idea of personal and cultural development being closely related), being very difficult for UK-based educationists to fully grasp. Or in the USA the dominance of sociological functionalism has long been apparent, with less support for more critical and historical paradigms (see Grace, 1984).

But second, in focusing on western developments it is necessary to recognise how important other traditions, elsewhere in the globe have been. Among those traditions that have a very different approach to an understanding of education would be those influenced by eastern philosophies and religions such as Confucianism and Buddhism or those that prevailed in pre-industrial civilisations in Africa (see Ukpokudu and Ukpokudu, 2012). In the west the development of state education was often connected to the promotion of a particular religious view – usually a Christian one – as well as to a belief in a form of rationalism inspired by the Enlightenment thinking that emerged so strongly in the eighteenth century. However the comparative study of education systems shows that the underlying premises of those systems may vary very significantly according to the cultural influences that have influenced the historical development of the system. In earlier comparative education studies there was a tendency to adopt a Eurocentric or Anglocentric approach, that is, to see 'the other' as strange in some ways. More recent developments in comparative education however are much more 'context sensitive' and culturally aware (Crossley and Watson, 2003; Phillips and Schweisfurth, 2007). So, if we can bring such sensitivity to study of education systems, we should also bring it to bear in our approaches to education research more generally.

In this chapter, as well as exploring some of the historical influences on the development of educational research, we consider what are the purposes of undertaking such work. Why is educational research important, what drives people to seek to understand and develop processes of education? Is education a field or a discipline? Is it a mainstream social science? Is it an applied or a pure science or what combination of the two? If educational research is important – and it will of course be argued that it is – then who should be responsible for ensuring its health, its development and its use in education policy and practice?

WHY UNDERTAKE EDUCATIONAL RESEARCH?

In the twenty-first century, throughout the 'advanced world', the provision of a system of education that is available to all young people with an ensuing phase of higher education for a section of the population is taken for granted as a necessary social good. There may be enormous disputes about how, when and where that provision is made, but the core idea of a system is not in dispute, in the way that it was in the nineteenth century, when at least in some capitalist societies the provision of universal education was seen as a major threat to the stability of society (Thompson, 1963; Simon, 1994).

State provision of education, with compulsory schooling at its core, is assumed to be one of the key responsibilities of governments and is a major element of government spending, through the allocation of part of the revenue raised through general taxation. Education therefore has become a matter for political decision-making. Most recently, as the world economies have become subject to the processes of 'globalisation' and increasingly politicians have talked of the importance of the 'knowledge economy', education provision has become not only political but has become increasingly 'politicised', that is a matter for notable dispute and contestation. One effect of the so-called Global Education Reform Movement (GERM) (Sahlberg, 2011) has been to create a very strong focus on education policies in countries throughout the world.

Therefore it has been strongly argued, especially in recent times, that one very strong driver for educational research should be to ensure that the large sums of public money that are spent on this social good are well spent. This is the *'accountability'* driver or 'value for money' driver for educational research. We will discuss later the real relationship between educational research, educational policy and educational practices. As we shall see, the relationship is not always a straightforward one, not least because education has become such an intensely ideological arena in the developed world, indeed in all parts of the world.

There are at least two other important reasons for undertaking educational research. One is the desire of those who are involved in the processes of education to ensure that what they are doing is going to be of the greatest possible benefit to the learners concerned and also to the wider society, indeed a desire to improve their practice. This motivation can be described as the *professional* driver for educational research. The third important reason for undertaking educational research is what one might call the quest for knowledge. In a complex, confusing and often contradictory world, many researchers are inspired by a simple passion for better understanding. This might be called the *intellectual* driver.

In the real world in which we live and research, these three motivations or drivers may very frequently overlap and interconnect, but there can be occasions when it is important to seek to identify the balance between them in particular undertakings.

WHAT IS EDUCATIONAL RESEARCH AND IS IT DIFFERENT FROM EDUCATION RESEARCH?

However, before proceeding any further with our discussion about purposes and the relationships between research, policy and practice, we would do well to define our terms. What actually is educational research? What makes research educational? Is educational research the same as education research? In the five-yearly national assessment of research quality in the UK, the 'unit' in which most university research is entered is called 'education', but yet the organisation which is producing this Handbook is the British Educational Research Association (BERA). A former President of BERA, Geoff Whitty, spent part of his inaugural address focusing on the question of whether there is a significant difference between these terms (Whitty, 2006, or Chapter 1 in Whitty, 2016). Simply stated, his conclusion was that the term 'educational research' implied a purpose of betterment or improvement of some kind in the intent of the research. Using the shorter prefix 'education' does not necessarily imply such an aspiration.

Education research can be research 'for its own sake' – what might be called 'blue skies' research – intellectually driven research to use the term adopted above – that does not necessarily have an intended impact on policy or practice. It is actually quite difficult to think of examples of education research that do not at least have the potential to influence policy or practice, but perhaps some highly theoretical analyses of educational processes or of cognitive functioning are so removed from the world or practice, that such a link may be difficult to establish.

So, if we cannot be clear-cut about the significance of the prefix (we will continue to use 'educational' in this chapter), can we at least be a bit more confident about the actual focus or foci of educational research? The British sociologist of education, Basil Bernstein, is often credited with pointing out the three 'message systems' of education – the three signifiers that define an approach to education in any particular context (Bernstein, 1971). These he called curriculum, pedagogy and evaluation – we would tend to use the word assessment nowadays in place of the last of these. So can we safely assert that all educational research will be concerned with one or more of these message systems? While it may be quite difficult to think of any educational research that does not fit within these three categories, it has been suggested that such has been the development of education in the 'knowledge economy' and such has been the scale of social and managerial change, that there is a need for a fourth category, to cover some of the more institutional aspects of education – the management and leadership arrangements. This is partly a response to the rapid development of 'policy sociology' in education during the later part of the twentieth century (Ball, 1994; Grace, 1984; Ozga, 2000; Whitty, 2002) and also a recognition perhaps that educational research should not be put into a (potential) silo or cocoon where it is disconnected from other aspects of social policy and social theory. So, whereas curriculum, pedagogy and assessment may all be seen as distinctively and inherently educational in their nature, management or leadership or policy are clearly categories with a much broader set of connotations and connections.

METHODOLOGIES FOR EDUCATIONAL RESEARCH

If we can confirm then, at least tentatively, that educational research is concerned with the study of curriculum, pedagogy, assessment and management, then are there limits on the kinds of methodology that can be deployed in pursuing our activity?

In the introduction to this chapter, reference was made to four foundation disciplines of education and of course each of these has its own range of methodologies that span a diverse set of ontological and epistemological bases. However, much of what takes place under the name of educational research is seen to be within the broad church of the social sciences. In his seminal work on these matters, and drawing on work by the founding President of BERA, John Nisbet, a more recent BERA President, John Furlong, argues that educational research:

> has gone through a number of stages of development, but, actually, the truth is more complex. Over the past 130 years, dominant discourses of educational research have certainly changed, but rather than one approach being succeeded by another, with old traditions withering away, the reality is that new ones have simply been added to previous traditions. As a result, today educational research is multivocal, embracing a range of different traditions each of which might claim different historical roots. (Furlong, 2013, pp. 21–2)

So, while educational research may now appear to have social science at its core, nevertheless there may still be a clear overlap with the humanities. For example much historical and philosophical research in education can be seen as falling under that umbrella (McCulloch and Richardson, 2000; Pring, 2000) and educational work within cultural and media studies may be seen also to be better described in this way.

If however, educational research now tends to be seen as predominantly a social science, what kind of methodological approaches may be taken? In the USA, in the latter part of the twentieth century, there were major tensions between quantitative and qualitative approaches, sometimes referred to as 'paradigm wars'. To some extent, these tensions reflected a struggle between positivism and interpretivism (St Clair, 2009). Major research funders – particularly government sources and large corporate organisations – have tended to favour the former, especially since the latter part of the twentieth century. There was also an influence from the media, with journalists strongly favouring stories in which numbers could be included. Something of the same 'warfare' has been experienced in the UK more recently, as again government sources have been seen to strongly favour a particular form of quantitative research in education, the randomised controlled trial, the RCT. In drawing comparisons with medical science, it has been argued that the comparison of the experiences of intervention and control groups, analogous to one group receiving a new drug and another group being given a placebo, will obviously lead to greater efficiency in education research (Goldacre, 2013; see also Torgerson and Torgerson, 2009).

In promoting these quantitative approaches, some scorn has been applied to small scale qualitative research (see Goldacre, 2013, for example). Yet, there is a very important tradition within education of what has variously been called educational action research (Elliot, 1991) or practitioner research (Campbell et al., 2004). Indeed the idea of 'teacher as researcher' was developed very significantly in the UK by another former BERA President, Lawrence Stenhouse (Stenhouse, 1975). In his groundbreaking work, drawing not least on ideas from John Dewey, he argued that the best researchers of education were teachers themselves. He saw teachers as curriculum researchers in particular, being in the best place to make decisions, based on evidence, about what should be taught – as well as how.

> The idea is that of an educational science in which each classroom is a laboratory, each teacher a member of the scientific community. (Stenhouse, 1975, p. 142)

It is curious that the current resurgence of interest in 'evidence-based teaching' in the UK (Thomas and Pring, 2004) seems often to ignore these important developments and to emphasise so exclusively one particular methodology. It is not that RCTs do not make an important contribution as one of a wide repertoire of approaches. However, largescale RCTs in education are very difficult to implement and small scale RCTs are only likely to have wider significance if they can be closely associated with each other – as some current moves within the Teaching Schools movement in England seek to do (Churches and Dommett, 2016). The importance of accumulating evidence in education research is one reason that systematic review and meta-analysis have become such important elements of the field in recent times (Gough et al., 2012; Hattie, 2008).

At (perhaps) the other extreme, there are arguments, often from a post-modern perspective, to the effect that conventional qualitative social science methods fail to capture the genuine complexity and messiness of the social world that we experience (see for example, Fenwick and Farrell, 2012). Indeed Law (2004) goes so far as to question the wisdom of an over-adherence to or over-reliance on 'method' per se:

> My hope is that we can learn to live in a way that is less dependent on the automatic. To live more in and through slow method. Multiple method. Modest method. Uncertain method. Diverse method. Such are the senses of method that I hope to see grow in and beyond social science. (Law, 2004, p. 11)

Such a call may seem almost metaphysical in its aspirations and calls into question the dominance of rationalism in social sciences. Educational research, in its efforts to make sense of complex human processes and phenomena, is certainly a suitable arena for imaginative methodological innovation, of the kind encouraged by Law.

THEORY AND EDUCATIONAL RESEARCH

The relationship between research and theory has been another interesting area of debate over many years. What is an educational theory? How may educational research draw upon wider social theory? Questions such as these have been considered by a number of scholars and we have an interesting array of answers.

During the late-twentieth century there was talk of 'grand theory' being discredited or at least being seen as not very useful, and the emergence of a greater range of theories (plural) that are fit for purpose in particular contexts. In education examples of grand theories might have been exemplified by 'correspondence theory', which broadly speaking suggested that schooling systems corresponded to wider society and so the inequalities within education were mirrors or reproductions of the inequalities in the wider society. Or in relation to teaching and learning, Piagetian theory suggested a number of stages of development through which a child would progress; Vygotskian theory espoused the view that thought and language are very closely related. Another example of a specifically educational theory might be Bernstein's 'classification and framing of educational knowledge' (Bernstein, 1971). In all of these examples we can see how these theories have influenced approaches taken to educational research. But many of these theories might be seen as being derived from wider psychological or sociological theories. For example correspondence theory as developed by Bowles and Gintis (1976), was at least partly derived from Althusserian 'structural Marxism'. And Bernstein drew on the work of sociologists such as Mannheim and Durkheim in developing his educational theories. So, perhaps rather than seeing these twentieth-century theories as discredited we should rather be acknowledging them as very significant influences on contemporary developments.

More recently, educational researchers who have pursued theory have tended to draw on 'post-structural' influences, notably, Bourdieu, Giddens, Foucault and Butler, not least as connections between education and, respectively, reproduction, agency, power and 'identity' have been identified. Ball has talked about the 'necessity for theory' in educational research (Ball, 2010) and contrasts an atheoretical technicist approach to research with a critical, intellectual approach which incorporates a theoretical dimension (Ball, 1995).

In similar vein, Anyon (2009) asserts the need for a combination of empirical work and theory:

> Neither data nor theory alone are adequate to the task of social explanation. Our view is that they imbricate and instantiate one another, forming and informing each other as the inquiry process unfolds. (p. 2)

She continues:

> We argue ... that, without theory, our data on school experience or social phenomena do not go very far, and do not tell us much that is not already obvious. Our data do not leave the ground on which they were found; our explanations do not soar, and they may fail to inspire. (p. 3)

And while these broadly sociological theories have become very visible in recent times, psychology has continued to play a significant part, not least in 'post-Vygotskyan' or neo-Vygotskyan approaches such as activity theory, sometimes narrowed to cultural-historical activity theory (Engestrom et al., 1999) or in the concept of 'communities of practice' (Wenger, 1998). Furthermore, the work of psychologists such as Dweck (2000), notably with her theory of 'mindsets', and the growing influence of neuroscientists in education (Howard-Jones, 2012) continue to demonstrate how psychology and related areas of study remain very important in educational research.

Theoretical innovation and development are seen to be very important elements in research of the highest quality and are certainly an expectation in the world-leading research that is worthy of the highest ratings in assessment exercises, such as the UK's Research Excellence Framework (REF) (see HEFCE, 2015). It is notable that in the UK – perhaps especially in England – this quest for theoretical development has not always had the widest support. In many education departments the teaching of educational theory has declined enormously (Furlong, 2013), in part in response to the increasing emphasis on skills development in teacher education (Murray and Mutton, 2016), although education studies as a discipline has helped to sustain the study of theory in some locations. But as long ago as 1981, the historian Brian Simon, in asking 'Why no pedagogy in England?' (reprinted in Simon, 1985), was calling for systematic study of teaching and learning of the sort that prevailed in the Soviet Union and also across much of continental Europe. He bemoaned the absence of serious scientific study of educational processes in the UK, especially in England. More recently, the similar cry 'Whatever happened to curriculum theory?' (Edwards, 2011) reflected a similar demise. Curriculum theory had been an important element of education courses in most education departments in the 1960s and 1970s and continued to be so in continental Europe but almost disappeared in the first part of this century, at least in the UK (Priestley and Biesta, 2013). In 2014 the inquiry that BERA established in cooperation with the Royal Society for the Arts called for all teachers to be equipped with 'research literacy' (BERA-RSA, 2014).

WHO RESOURCES EDUCATIONAL RESEARCH AND HOW?

It is now common practice for governments to allocate some part of their education budget to educational research. The ways in which they do this may vary significantly. In England, until 2010, the Department for Education had a significant research budget which it would deploy on areas of major priority and would fairly frequently put out open calls to tender to undertake projects. There had been considerable interest from university education departments in securing such contracts. However in the preceding twenty years or so, two factors tended to reduce the number of such research contracts going to universities. The first was growing competition from independent commercial organisations, often market research companies, which could often offer a more cost effective approach to the research than a higher education institution. The second tendency was a change in the nature of the projects that were being put out to tender. Increasingly these were short-term evaluations of new initiatives that the government was undertaking. The range and scope of research was thus narrowing and the opportunities to undertake work that would lead to major developments in understanding, let alone in educational theory were diminishing. Universities were also strongly influenced by the research assessment agenda (see below) which could mean that the kind of research that the government was sponsoring was less appealing to them. Furthermore, as was alluded to above, in recent times a major proportion of the money allocated for educational research by government had been handed over to an independent body, called the Educational Endowment Foundation – £125m over ten years – to support RCTs that are designed to address the educational needs of disadvantaged learners in particular (see: https://educationendowmentfoundation.org.uk/).

Governments in the other UK jurisdictions have at various times been important sponsors of research including some of them offering open calls for educational research. However, funding could also be found in the UK from charitable organisations such as The Nuffield Trust or The Leverhulme Foundation. These bodies have tended to be more amenable to imaginative proposals from researchers and to supporting longer-term research projects, than governments who are always working within an electoral cycle with a strong emphasis on policy effectiveness (the accountability driver).

Additionally the UK Research Councils and in particular the Economic and Social Research Council (ESRC) has been a funder of educational research. Indeed during the first years of this century the ESRC supported the most significant programme of independent research ever carried out in the UK, the Teaching and Learning Research Programme (TLRP) which managed to secure funds of over £40m over 14 years (Christie and Pollard, 2009). However, since the conclusion of the TLRP, educational researchers have found it extremely difficult to make successful applications, with significantly higher success rates being achieved in other disciplines including psychology and economics (see the BERA Observatory, Oancea and Mills, 2015). Where the recent support of the ESRC has been very important however has been in their doctoral training programme where significant numbers of students in education have been supported.

UK UNIVERSITIES AND EDUCATIONAL RESEARCH

Universities themselves have been key supporters of educational research. Education has been one of the main areas for research assessment in the five-yearly reviews carried out under the auspices of the Higher Education Funding

Councils of the UK. Although the Research Excellence Framework and its predecessors, Research Assessment Exercises, have had a number of unintended effects, nevertheless they have had the (intended) effect of making universities with education departments take the quality of educational research very seriously. The three criteria for assessing research outputs – originality, significance and rigour – have undoubtedly played a part in ensuring that UK education research is at the cutting edge of educational research internationally.

As the report from the 2014 REF sub-panel for education says:

> The REF outcome demonstrates the very high quality of much of the educational research which was submitted. Many universities submitting to the UOA for education produce work which is among the best from anywhere in the world. This work also compares well with the UK's best social science, to which it contributes. (HEFCE, 2015, para 4)

The recent addition of 'impact' as a key factor in the REF has also led to much discussion about the connections between research quality, and policy and practice in education. REF submissions from universities have had to include a general case about the impact of their research and to include some case studies of particular research and its impact on policy and/or practice (these can be viewed at: http://results.ref.ac.uk/Results/ByUoa/25).

Impact is not actually a new idea in educational research. As long ago as 1980 two former BERA Presidents, John Nisbet and Patricia Broadfoot, wrote about impact in a study commissioned by the forerunner of the ESRC, the Social Science Research Council. They adopted a rather more open view of impact than that prevalent today and bemoaned the weakness of theorising in educational research.

They said:

> If researchers argue that research impact is indirect, long-term and unpredictable, and that they need to do more 'thinking' before they launch into action, they may lose all sympathy and support.... Research in education must itself accept the same kind of questioning which it applies to the educational system. (Nisbet and Broadfoot, 1980, p. 66)

In other words they are calling for greater 'critical reflexivity' (as we might now call it) and accountability on the part of the educational research community and it would be reasonable to say that moves in both of these directions have ensued since that time.

The 'impact agenda' has been stimulated in particular by the accountability agenda – the economic driver of educational research. It has led to much debate and deliberation about the relationship between researchers and 'users' of research, about the relationships between the respective communities of research, policy and practice (Nutley et al., 2007; Levin, 2013; Whitty, 2016). Rickinson et al. (2011) talk of the importance of 'user engagement' with research, suggesting three different categories of user: the practitioner, the service user ('consumer') and the policymaker (see Chapter 51 in this volume). Terms such as knowledge transfer, knowledge exchange and knowledge mobilisation are among those that have been coined to describe these important processes (Fenwick and Farrell, 2012).

In the USA as well as in the UK, the impact agenda is part of what has led to an increasing emphasis on the purposes of educational research being restricted to the purpose of finding out 'what works' in education. In the US there has been a 'What Works' database that has offered a 'clearinghouse' for policymakers and others to ascertain the most effective interventions. In the UK the EEF has sponsored a 'teaching and learning toolkit' which includes a table listing the 'effects' of particular educational interventions in terms of how many weeks improvement they lead to in terms of outcomes (see: https://educationendowmentfoundation. org.uk/evidence/teaching-learning-toolkit). Such mechanistic measures have been strongly criticised as offering a simplistic view of educational processes and encouraging an uncritical approach to educational research, an approach that does not question underlying values or purposes but rather accepts existing status quo measures of educational success (Biesta, 2007).

The system of selective funding for higher education institutions in the UK means that there is a huge variation in the balance between funding for research and teaching in different university departments of education. Indeed there are many departments of education in UK universities that receive no funding for research from this source at all, often because senior managers judged it was not worth making a submission to the REF, given their low baseline in appropriate research.

This has led to significant questioning of whether it is appropriate for teacher education students to be on programmes led by universities where no such research is undertaken. The relationship between education and 'the academy' is a difficult one in many parts of the world. In the USA Labaree (2004) has talked of 'the trouble with ed schools'; in the UK, Furlong (2013) has examined this difficult relationship closely.

BUILDING CAPACITY IN EDUCATIONAL RESEARCH

Some reference was made above to the importance of training the next generation of educational researchers, in particular through doctoral programmes. However, there is a wider issue here, given the range of potential researchers who can make a contribution to the wider agenda. Certainly, the age profile of the existing research community is a factor that must be taken into account, as well as the institutional support – in all educational institutions – that is required to ensure the flourishing of our field.

Building capacity for the future is one of the major goals of associations such as BERA itself. In common with equivalent bodies elsewhere (the AERA; the

AARE; SERA; ESAI[1]) these associations are organisations for individual members who are committed to educational research. Their role in promoting and advancing educational research is a very important one. They tend to have a very broad and open understanding of what educational research is, one that is not limited to particular paradigms in the way that some other agencies are.

In the increasingly complex context in which educational research is taking place, the development of capacity has implications for policy and practice communities as well as the research community. For example, as the concept of 'close to practice' research becomes increasingly promoted, how can the wider community best ensure that research skills of the highest quality are deployed? There are enormous implications here for the education of professionals – teachers, lecturers and others, both in preparation to join their profession and in ongoing learning (BERA-RSA 2014).

In the UK the REF (referred to above) places a considerable emphasis on 'research environment' in making assessments about the quality of provision in universities. The education sub-panel emphasised the importance of providing support for the researchers themselves. In a paragraph headed 'People', they said:

> Submissions were highly rated when they demonstrated a strong policy and practical infrastructure for research capacity building and staff development. This frequently included evidence of recruitment and retention policies, including the advancement of equality and diversity.... The best submissions were able to demonstrate the intellectual vitality of the research environment for postgraduate research students, as well as having a high scale of enrolment, excellent supervision and sustained completions. (HEFCE, 2015, para 51)

The implications for the future of educational research are very clear. Investment is needed in the development of 'research capacity'. If educational research is to achieve its purposes, as set out at the beginning of this chapter, then it is essential that educational research is well funded, that future generations of educational researchers are trained and supported and that originality, significance and rigour are assiduously pursued by all concerned.

CONCLUSION

This chapter has explored the various motivations behind educational research. We have seen that among the important drivers are concerns about political accountability in education, about the need to make improvements in professional practice, as well as an intrinsic curiosity about processes, structures and outcomes. The sustenance of high quality educational research is an essential requirement in a modern democratic society.

In undertaking 'systematic enquiry made public' in education – to borrow Stenhouse's definition of research (Stenhouse, 1975) – it is crucial that researchers maintain their independence, their integrity and their criticality. There is no value in research setting out simply to affirm the value of what already exists. The purpose of high quality educational research is to provide a greater understanding, in order that changes can be brought about that are based on an explicit set of values. Indeed, it is always important that educational researchers are themselves explicit or 'reflexive' about their own values (Ozga, 2000).

There are times and places in this world where some of these commitments appear to be under threat or at least under serious pressure. In the ensuing chapters in this handbook, there are numerous examples of the kind of criticality, independence and integrity that is essential in the pursuit of these goals.

In 2010 BERA collaborated with the Universities Council for the Education of Teachers in reviewing the state of educational research across the UK and, following Furlong in his book on education as a discipline (Furlong, 2013, p. 86), this chapter closes with a reminder of the central importance of a strong educational research culture:

> No field of modern human endeavour, whether within or beyond the academy, can flourish without a strong research base. The enlargement of our understanding, the enhancement of the quality of public services, the nation's economic productivity, the well-being of the community, the wisdom and effectiveness of public policy all depend on the maintenance of a vibrant research culture. (BERA-UCET, 2012, para 98)

Note

1   American Educational Research Association; Australian Association for Educational Research; Scottish Educational Research Association; Educational Studies Association of Ireland.

REFERENCES

Anyon, J. (2009) *Theory and Educational Research: toward critical social explanation*. London: Routledge.

Ball, S. (1994) *Education Reform: a critical and post-structural approach*. Buckingham: Open University Press.

Ball, S. (1995) Intellectuals or technicians? The urgent role of theory in educational studies, *British Journal of Educational Studies*, 43, 3, 255–271.

Ball, S. (2010) The necessity and violence of theory. In P. Thomson and M. Walker (Eds) *The Routledge Doctoral Student's Companion*. London: Routledge, 68–75.

BERA-RSA (2014) *Research and the Teaching Profession: Building the capacity for a self-improving education system*. London: BERA. Available online: http://www.bera.ac.uk.

BERA-UCET (2012) *Prospects for Education Research in Education Departments in Higher Education Institutions in the UK*. London: BERA-UCET. Available online: http://www.bera.ac.uk/news/bera-ucet-report.

Bernstein, B. (1971) On the classification and framing of educational knowledge. In M. Young (Ed.) *Knowledge and Control: New directions in the sociology of education*. London: Collier-Macmillan, 47–69.

Biesta, G. (2007) Why 'what works' won't work: evidence-based practice and the democratic deficit of educational research. *Educational Theory*, 57, 1, 1–22.

Bowles, S. and Gintis, H. (1976) *Schooling in Capitalist America: education reform and the contradictions of economic life*. London: Routledge and Kegan Paul.

Campbell, A., McNamara, O. and Gilroy, P. (2004) *Practitioner Research and Professional Development in Education*. London: Paul Chapman.

Christie, D. and Pollard, A. (2009) Taking stock of educational research and the impact of the UK Teaching and Learning Research Program. In R. St Clair (Ed.) *Education Science: Critical perspectives*. Rotterdam: Sense, 25–40.

Churches, R. and Dommett, E. (2016) *Teacher-led Research: Designing and implementing randomised controlled trials and other forms of experimental research*. Carmarthen: Crown House.

Crossley, M. and Watson, K. (2003) *Comparative and International Research in Education: Globalisation, context and difference*. London: Routledge/Falmer.

Dweck, C. (2000) *Self-theories: their role in motivation, personality and development*. London: Routledge.

Edwards, R. (2011) Whatever happened to curriculum theory? *Pedagogy, Culture and Society*, 19, 173–174.

Elliot, J. (1991) *Action Research for Educational Change*. Buckingham: Open University.

Engestrom, Y., Miettinen, R. and Puanmakil, R.-L. (Eds) (1999) *Perspectives on Activity Theory*. Cambridge: University Press.

Fenwick, T. and Farrell, L. (Eds) (2012) *Knowledge Mobilization and Educational Research: Politics, languages and responsibilities*. London: Routledge.

Fleming, C. (1952) *Research and the Basic Curriculum* (2nd edition). London: University of London.

Furlong, J. (2013) *Education – the Anatomy of a Discipline*. London: Routledge.

Furlong, J. and Lawn, M. (Eds) (2011) *Disciplines of Education: Their role in the future of educational research*. London: Routledge.

Goldacre, B. (2013) *Building evidence into education*. Retrieved from www.education. gov.uk/inthenews/a00222740/building-evidence-into-education (accessedd on 7 August, 2016).

Gough, D., Oliver, S. and Thomas, J. (2012) *An Introduction to Systematic Reviews*. London: Sage Publications.

Grace, G. (1984) Urban education: policy science of critical policy scholarship? In G. Grace (Ed.) *Education and the City*. London: Routledge and Kegan Paul, 3–59.

Hattie, J. (2008) *Visible Learning: A synthesis of over 800 meta-analyses relating to achievement*. London: Routledge.

Higher Education Funding Council for England (HEFCE) (2015) Sub-panel 25: Education in *Research Excellence Framework 2014 Overview report by Main panel C and Sub-panels 16–26*. Retrieved on www.ref.ac.uk/media/ref/content/expanel/member/Main%20 Panel%20C%20overview%20report.pdf, pp 103–113 (accessed on 7 August, 2016).

Howard-Jones, P. (Ed.) (2012) *Education and Neuroscience: Evidence, theory and application*. London: Routledge.

Hulme, M. (2013) Research and practice. In T. Bryce, W. Humes, D. Gillies and A. Kennedy (Eds) *Scottish Education* (4th edition: Referendum). Edinburgh: University of Edinburgh, 938–948.

Labaree, D. (2004) *The Trouble with Ed Schools*. New Haven: Yale University.

Law, J. (2004) *After Method: Mess in social science research*. London: Routledge.

Levin, B. (2013) To know is not enough – research knowledge and its use. *Review of Education*, 1, 1, 2–3.

McCulloch, G. and Richardson, W. (2000) *Historical Research in Educational Settings*. Buckingham: Open University.

Murray, J. and Mutton, T. (2016) Teacher education in England: change in abundance, continuities in question. In Teacher Education Group, *Teacher Education in Times of Change*. Bristol: Policy Press, 57–74.

Nisbet, J. and Broadfoot, P. (1980) *The Impact of Research on Policy and Practice in Education*. Aberdeen: University Press.

Nutley, S., Walter, I. and Davies, H. (2007) *Using Evidence: How research can inform public services*. Bristol: Policy Press.

Oancea, A. and Mills, D. (2015) *The BERA Observatory*. London: BERA. Available online: www.bera.ac.uk/promoting-educational-research/projects/bera-observatory.

Ozga, J. (2000) *Policy Research in Educational Settings*. Buckingham: Open University.

Phillips, D. and Schweisfurth, M. (2007) *Comparative and International Education: An introduction to theory, method and practice*. London: Continuum

Priestley, M. and Biesta, G. (2013) Introduction: the new curriculum. In M. Priestley and G. Biesta (Eds) *Reinventing the Curriculum: New trends in curriculum policy and practice*. London: Bloomsbury, 1–12.

Pring, R. (2000) *Philosophy of Educational Research*. London: Continuum.

Rickinson, M., Sebba, J. and Edwards, A. (2011) *Improving Research through User Engagement*. London: Routledge.

Sahlberg, P. (2011) *Finnish Lessons: What can the world learn from educational change in Finland?* New York: Teachers' College Press.

Simon, B. (1985) *Does Education Matter?* London: Lawrence and Wishart.

Simon, B. (1994) *The State and Educational Change: Essays in the history of education and pedagogy*. London: Lawrence and Wishart.

St Clair, R. (Ed.) (2009) *Education Science: Critical perspectives*. Rotterdam: Sense.

Stenhouse, L. (1975) *An Introduction to Curriculum Research and Development*. London: Heinemann

Thomas, G. and Pring, R. (2004) *Evidence-based Practice in Education*. Maidenhead: McGraw-Hill.

Thompson E.P. (1963) *The Making of the English Working Class*. London: Victor Gollancz.

Tibble, J. (Ed.) (1966) *The Study of Education*. London: Routledge and Kegan Paul.

Torgerson, C. and Torgerson, D. (2009) Randomized controlled trials in education research. In R. St Clair (Ed.) (2009) *Education Science: Critical perspectives*. Rotterdam: Sense, 71–82.

Ukpokudu, O. and Ukpokudu, P. (Eds) (2012) *Contemporary Voices From The Margin: African educators on African and American education*. Charlotte, North Carolina: Information Age Publishing.

Wenger, E. (1998) *Communities of Practice: Learning, meaning and identity*. Cambridge: University Press.

Whitty, G. (2002) *Making Sense of Education Policy: Studies in the sociology and politics of education*. London: Paul Chapman.

Whitty, G. (2006) Education(al) research and education policy making: is conflict inevitable? *British Educational Research Journal*, 32, 2, 159–176.

Whitty, G. (2016) *Research and Policy in Education: Evidence, ideology and impact*. London: Institute of Education.

2

The Role of Theory in Research

Mary Lou Rasmussen

INTRODUCTION

Theory is a word that is evocative. It evokes confusion, frustration, trepidation, discomfort, shame, joy, disorientation, invention and derision. At times researchers will likely experience all of the above in regard to theory. Part of the joy of grappling with theory is this experience of confusion as one encounters new ideas, or attempts to create ideas that are new by bringing theory to a new problem, or different parts of existing theories together in order to look at a problem anew. Working with theory is invention, and this invention is not abstract. Theory is indispensible because it is intrinsic to the work of education.

Though the association of theory with education and educational research might not be automatic for some. Often when people think about theory it is often associated with science and its capacity to:

> make things visible or intelligible that are not immediately observable. In the natural sciences theory often performs this function by making plausible why certain laws – such as Ohm's law or Boyle's law – are as they are…. In the social sciences theory performs this function by trying to make plausible why people act as they act or do as they do. (Biesta et al., 2011, p. 227)

Theory helps us understand how others see and experience the world, how we develop our own understandings about the way we work and the way the world works. But theory in the social sciences is not set in stone – and this can be a source of anxiety for people new to theory in education. If theory is pliable, what does this mean for the rigour of arguments that are proposed? The measure of what constitutes good theory in people's minds might be a theory that can stand the test of time and that, like some theories in the natural sciences, is able to proffer a clear answer to a question that can be retested in different circumstances and proffer the same result.

Questions regarding a particular theory and its associated rigour are sometimes linked to more general anxieties about the quality of research in education. This association is reflected in Borko, Liston and Whitcomb's opening thoughts on empirical research in teacher education:

> Is empirical research on teacher education really so bad? Critics decry its inconsistent quality and inability to respond convincingly to some of the field's most vexing problems.... When we reviewed empirical research and reviews of research in teacher education ... we noted an excitement associated with working on the frontier of establishing a field of study, a willingness to critique the methodological rigor of our work, and a desire for our scholarship to have a constructive impact on teacher education policy and practice. (Borko et al., 2007, p. 3)

Anxiety about the rigour of theory and methodology in educational research is not confined to the discipline of education. Ien Ang, writing about the field of cultural studies, speaks to an 'ongoing sense of crisis, a general apprehensiveness over the question whether cultural studies is able to live up to its own self-declared aspirations, both intellectually and politically' (Ang, 2006, p. 184). She attributes this anxiety to the field's parameters being 'notoriously indefinite' (ibid.) and goes on to suggest that this lack of definition is one of the strengths of cultural studies, ensuring that the field does not stagnate intellectually or politically.

Similarly, in education, the parameters are indefinite, and the possibilities for reinvention might be

> derived precisely from its 'undisciplined' theoretical and methodological eclecticism, providing the space for researchers and students to flexibly 'mak[e] it up as they go along'. (Ang, 2006, p. 184)

Education as a field is pliable – answers to key questions in education, indeed the questions themselves, are not set in stone. Though in making this claim I don't mean to imply that anything goes with theory. Theory is an invaluable resource, with theory it is possible to apprehend and think about problems in education, formulate research questions that can interrogate these problems and proffer responses that enhance the field.

In the section below I consider the question 'what is theory' and its relationship to educational research. This is followed by a discussion of how theory relates to different research traditions, within and outside education. I also consider how theories are built and applied. Some suggestions for further readings are incorporated at the end of the chapter.

WHAT IS THEORY AND WHY IT IS IMPORTANT IN RELATION TO RESEARCH IN EDUCATION?

In an article entitled 'The theory question in research capacity building in education: towards an agenda for research and practice' Gert Biesta, Julie Allen and Richard Edwards identify 'unhelpful dichotomies such as theory versus practice, the theoretical versus the empirical, or theoretical versus useful. Such rhetorical moves have tended to give theory a bad name.' (Biesta et al., 2011, p. 226). These notions are unhelpful, they argue, because theory is not distinct from practice, theory informs practice and practice informs theory – affirming the two as distinct covers over this. Consequently, the connections between the two are often impossible to disentangle. Biesta et al. (2011) also resist the notion that theory is distinct from the empirical. The empirical that they evoke relates to types of data gathering (observation, interviews, surveys, discourse analysis, longitudinal studies, comparative studies, case studies), research methods which have come to be seen as indispensable to research in the field of education.

In *Theory for Education*, Greg Dimitriadis and George Kamberelis point to the problem of what C. Wright Mills called 'abstracted empiricism' – disconnected studies that take on individual empirical questions without regard to a larger 'research imaginary' (Dimitriadis and Kamberelis, 2006, p. vii). Binaries of theory versus practice and the theoretical versus the empirical also leave less space for inquiry that is predominantly historical and philosophical – educational research is increasingly produced as fundamentally about data collection – postgraduate students in education are asked to resolve the issue of whether they will utilize qualitative, quantitative or mixed methods – and they might deduce from set texts in methodology courses that the correct answer is the latter. Paul Standish argues new researchers in education will think that 'educational research is by default empirical' (Standish, 2007, p. 338) and the idea that research in education might be solely about an area of philosophical debate or historical inquiry is increasingly something of an oddity in educational research. To be clear, I continue to think that (along with many others) that there is an important place for historical and philosophical inquiry in educational research. Such scholarship plays a valuable role in helping researchers understand trends and contemporary problems in education, as well as assisting researchers to continually revisit the purposes of their inquiry.

Turning to the field of sexuality education, one of my own fields of research, it is possible to illustrate how the enactment of divisions between the empirical and the theoretical may lead researchers and consumers of research to assume that it is only possible to understand a phenomenon like sexting at school by doing fieldwork. Amy Dobson and Jessica Ringrose note sexting

combines the words 'sex' and 'texting' and has been connected to a range of practices where sexually explicit materials are digitally circulated, including the exchanging of nude, semi-nude, or sexually suggestive images and texts of and between peers via mobile phones or on social network sites. (Dobson and Ringrose, 2016, p. 8)

In research on sexting there might be an assumption that going out into the field and observing teachers and students talking about sexting in school contexts is fundamental to understanding the phenomenon of sexting. But we can't really apprehend what we have observed about sexting at school or in any other context, unless we utilize theory. This prompts the question not about 'what works best in regard to sexting prevention?' but rather 'what type of relationship to sexting are we trying to achieve?'. In order to answer this question it is important to have some idea of 'Why people sext?' And, to recognize that prevention might not only be impractical, it may also be undesirable if it assumes in advance that all sexting is malevolent. A combination of theory, practice and the empirical together make it possible to interrogate sexting and to develop an educative and legislative response. Sexting is an interesting case in point because practices associated with this phenomenon are in flux – different jurisdictions are coming up with different education and legal responses depending on school context, age of pupils, existing legislation and different understandings of young people and sexuality.

Good educational research about sexting will bring together diverse observations about sexting in education contexts, and a theoretical understanding of young people, sexuality and education. Ideally this research will also be informed by some grasp of the history of debates about young people, sexuality and education that continue to shape, in advance, what can and can't be said about sexting within school contexts. Too often, research in education focuses on what is observed, but fails to adequately contextualize these observations in relation to key philosophical and historical understandings. Such debates about the place of theory in research might seem esoteric, but they matter. These debates about the value of theory, and its relationship to different types of inquiry, can determine what types of educational research will be seen as legitimate, fundable, relevant for policy and useful for decision-making in schools, universities and government.

A recent example of educational research that illustrates the power of theory is Louisa Allen's exploration of the *Learning Sexualities* paper (course) she teaches at a university in New Zealand. In crafting her analysis of this paper Allen signals to the reader that

This is not a discussion about what queer pedagogy should look like at university, or whether it was 'successfully applied' in my course. These concerns are antithetical to queer theory itself, as a way of thinking that seeks to unsettle normative ideas around what, for example, constitutes a 'successful course'. Readers who are hoping for a template of how to do queer pedagogy at university should stop reading now, to avoid disappointment. (Allen, 2015, p. 764)

Rather than provide a recipe for queer pedagogy, Allen inquires into her own experiences of teaching this course in order to better understand 'the limits of queer pedagogy's thought, how can it see the boundaries of itself (in order to queer them)' (Allen, 2015, p. 765). In taking this route Allen's objective is to prompt a rethinking of existing practices associated with teaching and learning about sexuality in higher education.

This approach to utilizing theory in examining pedagogy articulates with Kalervo Gulson, Matthew Clarke and Eva Bendix Petersen's musings on the question 'what is theory'. Speaking to the question of what makes theory useful, they argue

> the task of scholarship is to begin to get a sense of one's own presuppositions, one's values and one's habituated ways of explaining things and of making sense, and, importantly, to get a sense of other possible presuppositions. (Gulson et al., 2015, pp. 3–4)

Following on from this reading theory isn't just about getting to know what others think, it is also, inevitably, about developing an understanding of how we have come to know, what we know, and to better understand our own prejudices, attachments and affiliations to particular ways of seeing and disciplinary approaches. Working out one's own theoretical affiliations ought not be confused with feeling a need to pick sides between approaches (quantitative or qualitative; critical or feminist). Often you will use a combination of approaches, methods, and methodologies, depending on the particularities of the research project you are undertaking.

Who and what we read matters for the type of theorizing one is able to do – and who or what we read is always a political, strategic and ethical decision. For example, it may be easy to apprehend that when you utilize critical race theory, disability studies or queer theory – your body, your politics and your ways of seeing (and being seen), feeling and being become enmeshed in the theorizing that you do. Though any type of theorizing we choose to do – or not to do – reveals our own prejudices and attachments regarding the work of theory. This is also part of the joy, shame, discomfort and disorientation of working with theory. Theory is not disembodied, but nor is it necessarily identity based (see Talburt and Rasmussen, 2010).

Whatever route we choose, debates about theory are embedded in the politics of knowledge. Raewyn Connell urges us to inquire into the colonizing politics that inform the theorists and theories we engage. Consequently, Connell urges researchers to take up the project of decolonizing theory – for more democratic theoretical conversations. Such conversations would surface knowledge from the global south (the periphery), at once refusing the dominance of northern theory – theoretical perspectives generated in the metropole (see Raewyn Connell's *Southern Theory*, 2007).

Another contemporary debate revolves around humanism and post-humanism in research. Helena Pedersen (2010), drawing on the writing of Donna Haraway (2008), asks researchers in education to think more about human-animal relations and post-humanism. She urges against thinking of post-humanism as a corrective to humanism that might 'reform education curricula in a more sustainable direction, without moving toward a deconstruction of the authoritative position of human subjectivity' (Haraway, 2008, p. 247). Rather she conceptualizes sites of education as post-human assemblages and advocates further exploration of 'how pedagogies are creatively tangled up with, and used by, regimes of biopower, biocapital, and other forms of embodied commodification of interspecies relationships' (ibid.) (see also Taylor and Blaise, forthcoming). From this theoretical perspective, the post-human isn't something that can be deferred, it is the assemblage in which we are currently embodied and entangled – the types of educational intra-actions it produces are messy, unpredictable and not subject to human authorship.

HOW DOES THEORY RELATE TO DIFFERENT RESEARCH TRADITIONS WITHIN AND OUTSIDE EDUCATION?

Above we have considered debates about what theory is, about rigour and theory, as well as looking at some contemporary debates regarding questions to consider when determining what theory to engage when conducting educational research. Now we take a step back and consider some different ways of seeing theory. In their introduction to *Theory for Education* Greg Dimitriadis and George Kamberelis make a distinction between the ways in which theorists inform research, and the 'ways in which different theoretical orientations inform approaches to research, particularly in education' (Dimitriadis and Kamberelis, 2006, p. ix). In making this distinction Dimitriadis and Kamberelis are referring to their analysis of 'historically and temporally situated ways of reading the world: *objectivism, interpretivism, scepticism, and defamiliarization*' (my emphasis) (see *On Qualitative Inquiry*, 2005). These ways of seeing are not confined to educational research; they are recognized as influential across the social sciences.

While Kamberelis and Dimitriadis break research down into ways of seeing, Biesta, Allan and Edwards find it more useful to classify theoretical approaches in terms of their purposes, highlighting three different roles of theory which perform quite distinct functions; namely 'research that aims to explain [objectivism], research that aims to understand [interpretivism], and research that aims to contribute to emancipation' (Biesta et al., 2011, p. 226). Below, some of the functions that are largely implicit in these different ways of seeing are elaborated.

Objectivism is a powerful approach within education research – it is important to recognize the continuing value and power of this tradition in educational research. Arguably, objectivism is the approach to educational research that continues to hold the most sway in terms of public policy; it is often characterized as robust, persuasive and the least politicized mode of research. Objectivism is rooted in scientific methods, founded on the notion that through observation and experimentation it is possible to gather reliable knowledge about the world around us, knowledge that is, as far as possible, unencumbered by human experience and subjectivity (Jonassen, 1991). Tony Vinson is an influential researcher in the objectivist tradition. His research focuses on systemic social disadvantage in the Australian context. Vinson examines and evaluates 'a series of 'hard' socioeconomic indicators (mortality, unemployment, low birth weight, childhood injuries, education, psychiatric admissions, crime, income, emergency relief) to identify factors indicative of localized poverty or socio-economic disadvantage by postcode and which could be aggregated into an index of socio-economic disadvantage' (Golding and Pattison, 2004, p. 110). This index of socio-economic disadvantage has been influential in education policy at federal and state levels, providing the basis for arguments about equity in numerous education sectors.

McClelland and Fine argue that 'without good science, we are not able to see or investigate a broad range of collateral consequences' (McClelland and Fine, 2008, p. 71) – this is certainly true of Vinson's research, without it would not be possible to draw robust conclusions about how different forms of advantage and disadvantage coagulate. At the same time, McClelland and Fine rail against what they term 'embedded science'; objectivist research that aligns with a specific political, social or economic agenda. Their use of the term embedded speaks to how 'the scientific endeavor – in this case, the federal funding of abstinence research [in the US] – is embedded in political frameworks that demand that data conform to already existing assumptions and how these ideologies "drip feed" into research method' (ibid., p. 72). The theoretical tools we utilize will already have a relationship to objectivism – it is important to critically assess such relationships, keeping in mind the value of science, as well as McClelland and Fine's cautions about embedded approaches to objectivism.

Interpretivism is another key way of seeing identified by Kamberelis and Dimitriadis. Biesta, Allan and Edwards also discuss the notion of interpretivism – describing this as an approach to research that sees a role for theory in

> deepening and broadening understanding of 'everyday' interpretations and experience. The task for theory here is not to describe *what* people are saying and doing, but to make intelligible *why* people are saying and doing what they are saying and doing. The primary interest of critical theory lies in exposing how hidden power structures influence and distort such interpretations and experiences. (Biesta et al., 2011, p. 226) (emphasis in original)

In coming to terms with theory, it is important to contextualize how the theory we use is situated, relative to other purposes of research. Apprehending these differences enables us to evaluate research with its purposes in mind. Graduate students who are new to research often make the mistake of assuming that all research has similar purposes, and thus they apply the same evaluative criteria to all the research they read, regardless of the theoretical approach it adopts. Coming to terms with theory requires a capacity to evaluate research according to the field in which it is situated. If we judge an interpretivist study as lacking because it has failed to expose hidden power structures – then we have quite likely misunderstood what the researchers set out to do.

Understanding distinctions underpinning different ways of seeing and different purposes of research helps us clarify how our ways of reading the world intersect with theory. This also helps us to understand how we, as researchers and as consumers of research, are necessarily affiliated particular ways of seeing. Jean Anyon, in *Theory and Educational Research: Toward critical social explanation*, suggests several motivations for choosing theories

> we think they will produce the most explanation parsimoniously, because their adoption may lead to new and interesting data and explanations, and-importantly-because they may provide some purchase on progressive strategies for social change. (Anyon, 2009, p. 8)

Anyon sees a role for theory in building new explanations, as well as gathering new data, but, most fundamentally, she sees theory, within the critical tradition, as about progressive social change. Such an approach to critical theory might be classified as emancipatory. Biesta, Allan and Edwards are useful in explaining how the critical-emancipatory approach to research might be distinguished from the interpretivist approach:

> those working within an interpretative approach would probably see their theoretical work as a way to contribute to the available interpretations of social actors...those working from a critical approach have a 'higher' ambition than just offering alternative interpretations. Their aim is to offer better interpretations than those generated by the social actors themselves, on the assumption that such first person interpretations may be distorted as a result of the workings of power.... The demarcation line between interpretative and critical forms of theorising thus separates those who aim to add interpretations to those of social actors themselves from those who aim to replace actor interpretations. While the ambition of both might be expressed in terms of 'adding plausibility', there is a fundamental difference in how 'plausibility' is understood. (Biesta et al., 2011, p. 231)

This association of critical theory with 'higher ambitions' has also led to variations of this approach having 'utopian tendencies' (Blake and Masschelein, 2002). Nigel Blake and Jan Masschelein in their entry on 'Critical theory and critical pedagogy' in the *Blackwell Guide to the Philosophy of Education* emphasize 'that there is no such as "the" critical theory'. This is also true of constructivism, feminism, interpretivism, objectivism and phenomenology – there are many scholars and schools of thought within and outside education that are loosely associated with these ways of seeing. As something of a feminist killjoy (Ahmed, 2010), in my own research I have found Wendy Brown (2005) and Lauren Berlant's (2011) theorizing of critical theory most productive precisely because they resist 'higher ambitions' for critical theory. Brown utilizes critical approaches inspired, in part, by Foucault to pry apart understandings of how we are governed. While Berlant's notion of 'cruel optimism' is useful because it demonstrates how 'higher ambitions' and desires for the 'good life', both of which are ubiquitous in education, can backfire (Rasmussen, 2015) and encourage fantasies that are unsupported by the structures of schooling. I also recognize that different ways of seeing, within and outside the tent of critical theory, have valuable roles to play in the production of educational research.

Given the difficulties in pinning down ways of understanding within objectivist, interpretivist and emancipatory approaches to inquiry, researchers often find it more helpful to associate themselves with particular theorists, theories or concepts. Gulson, Clarke and Petersen utilize this structure in their book on the role of theory in education policy research because they think it best 'reflects and constitutes how people tend to come to theory' (Gulson et al., 2015, p. 7). Counterpublics, queer theory, genealogy, affect and actor-network theory are just some of the concepts/theories selected by Gulson, Clarke and Petersen for further interrogation – and this list is by no means exhaustive. Gulson et al.'s collection also devotes chapters to theorists whose work has been influential in education (Bourdieu, Derrida, Foucault, de Certeau, Deleuze, Guattari and Lacan) – a similar approach is taken by Kamberelis and Dimitriadis in their *Theory for Education* (2006) – their selection incorporates most of the theorists mentioned above (sans de Certeau); but also incorporates others from diverse approaches to research (Piaget, Said, Vygotsky, Spivak, hooks and Freire). Neither book situates itself as the last word on theory in education; both are excellent introductory texts that provide valuable entrees providing concrete illustrations of how specific theories, theorists and concepts are applied in educational research.

Appreciating the distinctions between different approaches to research is fundamental to deciding what theories or theorists we might like to engage in relation to a particular project, question or problem. Grasping such distinctions is also useful in understanding how academic journals are organized, and therefore where one might look to find particular types of studies. For instance, journals will often signal the research tradition and theoretical approaches they favour based on the naming conventions they use. If one looks at the education and social science journals related to the topic of disability it is possible to understand some of the different ways in which knowledge on this topic is organized. There is the *Journal of Special Education, The International Journal of Inclusive Education, Disability and Society, Journal of Developmental and Physical Disabilities*. These different journal titles speak to different names researchers use to describe and imagine people with disabilities and the study of these people in diverse social and educational contexts. The *International Journal of Inclusive Education* is not specific to the study of disabilities, but sees disabilities as part of broader discourses of inclusion and exclusion. The journal welcomes contributions that are emancipatory, insofar as they might endeavour to identify and dismantle exclusions people experience in education across diverse constituencies and contexts, recognizing that different forms of inclusion and exclusion are not specific to disability or any other axis of difference.

The *Journal of Special Education* is more clearly aligned with the objectivist tradition. It has a specific focus on 'individuals with mild to severe disabilities' and studies in this journal will use the language of intervention, testing and evaluation, in accord with this purpose. *Disability and Society* is an interdisciplinary journal which tracks different ways in which the notion of disability is viewed and constructed across diverse contexts, explicitly rejecting segregated approaches to disability in policy and practice. This journal is also explicitly emancipatory – partially exemplified by its highlighting of the importance of incorporating 'the voice of disabled people' in the statement of its aims and purposes.

It is also important to consider our own relationship to theory – do certain traditions/theorists make us feel comfortable? It may be valuable to read theory precisely because it challenges our own preconceptions or habits of thought. In this regard it is useful to think about how we are drawn to theory, theorists and concepts, and to actively resist only reading theory that confirms what we think we already know about a particular question. For me, some of the most exciting theory makes the familiar appear strange, thereby calling me to question what I thought I already knew about a particular issue. It is also important to recognize that theory is dynamic, as is our relationship to it. Different theorists/traditions/concepts may appeal depending on the question under investigation – we don't need to be monogamous with theory.

Relationships to theory, theorists and theorizing also change over time in the field of education. At particular moments different theoretical ideas are predominant at conferences, in journals and in 'cutting edge' academic work. Given trends with theory it also worthwhile being wary of what Mark Dressman calls the 'siren song of a good theory' (Dressman, 2009, p. 95) – arguing that 'one likely outcome of a slavish devotion to a particular theoretical frame is the premature foreclosure of possible sources and types of data or analytical techniques, such as coding practices, that can significantly limit the range of possible interpretations of data in later stages of a study' (ibid., p. 97). In short, not all theories are applicable to all situations – it is important to ask whether or not the theory being utilized is appropriate for the context in which it is being put to work. Which isn't to say that new theoretical approaches cannot be adopted where previously they may have not been applied – it is to reckon with the siren song of theory and to recognize that at some point in our career we may all be susceptible to the seduction of the latest theoretical fashion – even when the fit may not be quite right.

THEORY BUILDING AND DATA ANALYSIS

Theory is not static. Educators utilize existing theories, but they also depend on research to build theory. Below I use some studies of young people and drug education in order to illustrate how people are building theory in order to look anew at existing approaches to health education and young people's consumption of drugs, in response to data they collected. I also consider some instances of theory building relating to the question of how data is understood and collected. This is recognition of the ways in which data and theory are always interconnected.

In an article entitled 'Assembling a health[y] subject: risky and shameful pedagogies in health education' Deana Leahy observes that a lot of researchers in health education have traced 'the myriad ways that neoliberalism and risk imbue both policy and curriculum hopes…' but she also notes few researchers have observed 'how neoliberal and risk-inspired governmental imperatives of health and health education are enacted' (Leahy, 2014, p. 172). By observing health education in action via an ethnographic study of health education classrooms Leahy argues it is possible to 'develop a more nuanced and sophisticated understanding of the politics of health education, its hopes and enactments' (ibid., p. 178). One of the insights Leahy developed through her observations was an appreciation of the ways risk discourses and neoliberal discourses of responsibilization in health education are interwoven with 'affective intensities of shame and disgust' in an effort to cultivate students as particular types of healthy subjects. Through Leahy's observations it apparent how, at least in the space of the classrooms in which she observed, young people were required to (and often did) acquiesce to the risk discourses that teachers' and governments mobilize, further affirming for educators their perceived value as a persuasive form of health education. This style of health education demands interrogation because of the ways in which it reinscribes particular people and practices as unhealthy and abject. It also fails/refuses to apprehend how young people engage/contest/ignore risk assemblages in their lives outside the classroom.

Leahy also utilizes contemporary theorizing regarding affect, specifically shame and embarrassment, to understand how risk discourses were further embedded via their entanglement in the production of 'melodramatic pedagogical moments' (Leahy, 2014, p. 177). Making this theoretical move helps Leahy understand a significant relationship between affect and risk discourse in health education. Those who had theorized the influence of risk in health education did not make this theoretical insight. Observing risk discourses in motion in a classroom setting enabled Leahy to make this theoretical leap. This move is important in shifting thinking about how health education engages risk, and how future health educators might resist the temptation to invoke the melodrama of risk.

In another study Adrian Farrugia argues that many existing theoretical approaches to drug consumption and education are problematic because they are tainted by the risk discourses identified by Leahy above. He observes that such approaches effectively close 'off any analysis of the kinds of positive practices and experiences' (Farrugia, 2015, p. 247) young men might associate with drug consumption. Farrugia underscores the importance of engaging theories

> that allowed for fluidity and change. In doing so, I have been able to map experiences, practices, and affects that are beyond the reach of peer pressure, hegemonic masculinity, and other approaches that assume social forces, working through the action of ontologically distinct bodies, impose themselves from above, or outside, local assemblages. (Farrugia, 2015, p. 252)

Farrugia argues that he is able to trouble common understandings of young people, risk and consumption of drugs via a combination of interviews with young men and the explicit crafting of a theoretical approach that resists framing their experience within the bounds of 'risk and harm'.

In the context of this chapter Farrugia's analysis is instructive because it demonstrates an explicit understanding of how different types of theorizing lead to specific types of data analysis. When one is crafting theory it is important to not only understand what a theory can do, but also to appreciate what theories might prevent us from doing. This is why it is important to read about different theoretical approaches and to try and become familiar with critiques of these approaches, especially approaches that might inform our own research. If we are not aware of the limits of the theoretical frameworks that we engage then researchers can too easily reproduce and affirm the received wisdom on a particular topic.

Building theory is also critical for apprehending how data infuses and produces contemporary ways of knowing, being and interrelating. In an article on the critical study of digital data in education Neil Selwyn suggests that digital sociological approaches

> start from the contention that data are political in nature – loaded with values, interests and assumptions that shape and limit what is done with it and by whom...acknowled[ing] data are profoundly shaping of, as well as shaped by, social interests. (Selwyn, 2015, p. 69)

In setting out a research agenda related to the critical study of data Selwyn proposes productive links that might be made with a number of social theorists (Foucault, Lyotard, Durkheim, Deleuze, Weber, Bourdieu and Bernstein) (Selwyn, 2015, p. 78). Drawing on social theorists such as those listed above, Selwyn argues digital data can never be conceptualized as a neutral object, but rather it is seen as part of an assemblage of discourses, practices and objects aligned with persistent struggles in education (ibid., p. 79).

A powerful example of the study of data related to my own field of research is Tom Waidzunas' (2012) article 'Young, gay and suicidal: dynamic nominalism and process of defining a social problem with statistics'. This research is published in a journal with a title that clearly welcomes interdisciplinary scholarship; *Science, Technology and Human Values*. Rather than starting from an understanding of 'gay youth suicide' as a point of departure for future research, Waidzunas set out to consider how 'gay youth suicide' had been brought into view as a powerful truth.

'Gay youth suicide' is in quotation marks here because Waidzunas' wants to complicate the emergence of this identity category 'as an at-risk identity' (Waidzunas, 2012, p. 218). He asks, how has it come to pass that researchers are able to mobilize 'gay youth' as a category for the basis of data collection and analysis? What do researchers mean when they talk about 'gay youth'? How is it possible to undertake credible statistical studies of people associated with an identity category that is incredibly heterogeneous and difficult to quantify with any statistical rigour?

Significantly, Waidzunas study resists the temptation to refine the processes of data collection pertaining to 'gay youth'. Rather, he theorizes the implications for social research of having an identity category 'gay youth'. One implication of the emergence of this category in this research is the co-production of statistics regarding 'gay youth suicide'. Research and practice continues to deploy specific truth claims utilizing statistical data to associate 'gay youth' and 'youth suicide'. These statistics, Waidzunas demonstrates, have incredible power and currency, partially through their constant repetition. Waidzunas' study is one example of building theory in order to help us question a range of data gathering techniques that have developed a compelling explanatory power.

Waidzunas turns to Ian Hacking's theory 'dynamic nominalism' to interrogate the categories of 'gay youth' and 'youth suicide'. Waidzunas is inspired by Hacking's ideas:

> To trace the historical ontology of a concept such as 'gay youth at risk for suicide' … not to discredit it, for it may indeed be a useful way of thinking about people. Rather, this kind of analysis offers the opportunity to denaturalize a concept, to realize its cultural and temporal specificity, and to raise questions about its universality. (Waidzunas, 2012, p. 203)

This is an example of theory building that has clear implications for research in education and other disciplines (public health, medicine, social work, and psychology) that may study 'gay youth' and mobilize the social problem 'gay teen suicide'. By studying the effects of a particular study by Paul Gibson that reported on levels of youth suicide among 'gay youth' Waidzunas' draws attention to the way in which this study became 'useful for framing scientific questions and acted as a powerful resource for justifying institutional change in schools' (Waidzunas, 2012, p. 212).

Waidzunas theorizes that the power attributed to these statistics is indicative of a political context in which hard data are needed to generate a policy response and argues:

> Given the credibility environment of the United States, such processes may be seen as a necessary means for setting in motion the definition of social problems and the generation of needed awareness, if other means fall on deaf ears because they are not sufficiently 'objective'. (Waidzunas, 2012, p. 219)

Waidzunas is not critical of objectivity here, rather he is utilizing theory in order to shine a light on the power of objectivity in framing truth claims regarding specific social problems. In thinking about the role of theory in this research, Waidzunas' theoretical framing does not seek to affirm or reject thinking within a particular tradition. Rather, he utilizes a theoretical approach that enables us to see how interpretivist and objectivist frameworks can become conflated when the need is great and the context demands the generation of a particular sort of data. Such research is building understanding of how data can morph in relation to a social problem. The *data* collected in Waidzunas' research comes in the form of a careful tracing of the ways in which statistics are generated, repeated, and authorized in order to make meanings that matter.

It is only by theorizing about data that is it is possible to appreciate the numerous ways in which it is politicized and always already embedded within broader debates within education and related fields. Waidzunas' research articulates well with Gayatri Spivak claim that without theory our society is doomed, because theory is epistemological and ethical healthcare for our society (Spivak, 2015).

For Spivak theory is fundamental to the health of society because without theory we will not be able to respond ethically to the challenges that confront us. While theory can be of great value, Becky Francis reflecting on the field of gender and education, argues against the enchantment of theory for theory's sake. She argues:

> finding the right theoretical tools is a necessary precursor to attaining impact for our work in educational policy and practice. Academic work in education is – at least in England – being notably marginalised in policy making, usurped by think tanks, voluntary organisations and charities, businesses, and individuals who have the ear of civil servants and ministers.... Within gender and education, we seem sometimes to have become more interested in analysing the phenomena than in using our findings to effect change. While we scoff at the naivety and lack of conceptual sophistication of some of the second-wave liberal feminist interventions in schools, our role in educational change has become muted. (Francis, 2013, p. 99)

Building theory is a part of academic work, but Francis worries that researchers might becomes so enchanted with theory that it becomes deracinated from practice. The idea that good theory can impact practice is meritorious. Time spent crafting theory requires justification – just as time spent on a particular practice in education requires justification. But I am also mindful of Standish's objections (see above) to the idea that all education research must by default be empirical. If the role of theory is to effect change – which appears to be Francis' measure – what is one to do if one's theory is out of favour with the government of the day? Or, if the purpose of our theorizing is not to effect change, but rather to change thinking?

Governments and school administrators will likely deploy theories that serve their political purposes – this is certainly often the case in education in Australia where commentators (academics, think tanks, charities) that have authority at a present moment are often likely to reflect the values of the administrators of the day. Given this state of affairs theory might produce valuable insights, but not immediately bring about change in policy and practice. What does this mean for the role of theory in research? This raises the question of how to craft theory that can address important questions but which isn't beholden to the politics of the day, nor removed from such politics.

In building theory in educational research researchers in education attend to many issues outside formal education institutions – including popular culture, equity, history, philosophy, ethics, digital data, marketization of education, creativity, inclusion, prisons, parenting, architecture, museums, identity, media and policy analysis (to name just a few topics). In short, theory building in education doesn't begin and end at the school gate.

FURTHER READING

All researchers need to be able to answer 'so what' questions (Boden et al., 2007) regarding the theory they are utilizing and the issue they are investigating. This is no doubt partially what Francis' is getting at above when she is underscoring the necessity of research having impact. How is the research drawing on theory to address questions of significance? How will the research contribute to knowledge? When writing research applications one is generally required to demonstrate the significance of the proposed research. Regardless of whether one is applying for funding, researchers need to be able to articulate what they are investigating and how they envisage this research contributing to existing literature and debates within this field of inquiry. It is not possible to answer these questions without engaging theory.

In *Getting Started on Research* Rebecca Boden, Jane Kenway and Debbie Epstein suggest new researchers need to be able to make a transition from articulating something as of personal interest

> to being able to frame it as a subject of academic research.... You must be able to frame your subject in such a way that you move from description to explaining what the data you have found means. In other words, you must be able to theorise your subject. (Boden et al., 2007, p. 14)

This *Getting Started on Research* kit is useful for thinking about how you can go about setting up a research agenda that will have the theoretical sophistication that enables it to persist beyond the level of doctoral research.

Acknowledging the need to engage with theory is important, but much easier than determining what theory one will engage. There are many different theorists, theories and concepts from which to choose. Different theorists and theories will be fashionable at different moments, while others are falling out of favour. Given these challenges, how does one decide what concepts, theories or theorists to engage? Collections like that of Anyon et al. (*Theory and Educational Research*), Dimitriadis and Kamberelis (*Theory for Education*) and Gulson, Clarke and Petersen (*Education Policy and Contemporary Theory*) are all useful introductory texts, but, as indicated above, it is important that they be construed as introductory. In my own experience, the only way to really get to know theoretical debates is to dedicate the time to reading key texts – others interpretations of these debates are no substitute.

Because educational research is interdisciplinary it is important to interrogate theories across disciplinary boundaries. For instance, Radhika Gorur (2015), in her discussion of Actor-network theory and policy analysis in Gulson et al.'s collection, provides references to specific texts of Bruno Latour. Latour is a key figure in this field of research. Following such leads is really helpful in navigating a way forward in engaging specific theories in research. There is so much one could read, it is imperative to be judicious about what we read. So while it is necessary to identify key thinkers within and outside education pertinent to the theory we are engaging, further reading can be contained by referring to the reading lists of scholars who are already well read in a particular field. While it is important to engage the work of researchers outside education in grasping theory, it is also important to be able to demonstrate familiarity with theoretical debates in education pertinent to your inquiry. It is also worthwhile remembering contemporary theorists in education will most likely be assessing, reviewing or examining contemporary scholarship, dissertations, and grant applications.

In locating theory in my own fields of research I find it helpful to go to the websites of publishing houses that are renowned for producing quality scholarship in the area. If the names of particular publishers and journals keep coming up in references, it is likely worthwhile examining other texts/issues produced by this publishing house, or searching extensively within a specific journal. I also find book reviews, blogs, and interviews with key figures really helpful points of departure in determining how much time I want to expend becoming familiar with a specific theorist or theory. Podcasts and vodcasts of lectures of key figures are also useful entrees, especially if the theory you are engaging is particularly dense.

When thinking about further reading it is also worthwhile spending time determining how many theorists one can be in conversation with in any one project.

Stuart Hall, a prominent cultural theorist, provides a salutary note on which to end this discussion of the role of theory in educational research. Hall reminds us of the challenges of doing interdisciplinary work well, and educational theorizing is invariably interdisciplinary:

> Interdisciplinarity is the most difficult intellectual practice of all. The slack thinking across disciplinary traditions – as if the traditions don't matter, as if they were funny things that were made up in the academy – is not serious thinking. It's not serious when we encourage students to do that kind of facile, theoretical, magpie approach. It doesn't get anywhere. The serious attempt to bring two constituted disciplinary fields genuinely together so that one is thinking at the point of articulation between them is serious business, hard business. (Hall, 1999)

In part, Hall is warning against the temptation to cast one's theoretical net too wide. While this may be tempting, it might also result in research that lacks depth in any one area, and therefore fails to contribute to knowledge in any meaningful way. Creating new ideas, building theory, especially when one is working across disciplines is hard work. But there is pleasure to be derived from immersing oneself in a field or across two fields, and being able to grasp at their limits in order to imagine potential new modes of inquiry, or to think anew about persistent questions within your field.

ACKNOWLEDGEMENTS

This chapter is dedicated to Greg Dimitriadis and Jean Anyon, two fine theorists of education. I would also like to thank the reviewers for the helpful comments.

REFERENCES

Ahmed, S (2010) *The Promise of Happiness*. Durham, NC: Duke University Press.

Allen, L. (2015) Queer pedagogy and the limits of thought: teaching sexualities at university. *Higher Education Research & Development*, 34, 4, 763–775.

Ang, I. (2006) From cultural studies to cultural research: engaged scholarship in the twenty-first century. *Cultural Studies Review*, 12, 2, 183–197.

Anyon, J. with Dumas, M.J., Linville, D., Nolan, K., Perez, M., Tuck, E. and Weiss, J. (2009). *Theory and Educational Research: Toward critical social explanation*. New York and London: Routledge.

Berlant, L. (2011) *Cruel Optimism*. Durham, NC: Duke University Press.

Biesta, G., Allan, J. and Edwards, R. (2011) The theory question in research capacity building in education: towards an agenda for research and practice. *British Journal of Educational Studies*, 59, 3, 225–239.

Blake, N. and Masschelein, J. (2002) Critical theory and critical pedagogy. In N. Blake, P. Smeyers, R. Smith and P. Standish (Eds) *The Blackwell Guide to the Philosophy of*

Education. Blackwell Reference Online. Retrieved from http://www.blackwellreference. com.virtual.anu.edu.au/subscriber/tocnode.html?id=g9780631221197_chunk_ g97806312211975 (accessed 3 August, 2016).

Boden, R., Kenway, J. and Epstein, D. (2007) *Getting Started on Research*. New York: Sage Publications.

Borko, H., Liston, D. and Whitcomb, J. A. (2007) Genres of empirical research in teacher education. *Journal of Teacher Education*, 58, 1, 3–11.

Brown, W. (2005) *Edgework: Critical Essays on Knowledge and Politics*. Princeton, NJ: Princeton University Press.

Connell, R. (2007) *Southern Theory: The global dynamics of knowledge in social science*. Cambridge: Polity.

Dimitriadis, G. and Kamberelis, G. (2006) *Theory for Education*. New York: Routledge.

Dobson, A. and Ringrose, J. (2016) Sext education: pedagogies of sex, gender and shame in the schoolyards of tagged and exposed. *Sex Education*, 16, 1, 8–21.

Dressman, M. (2009) *Using Social Theory in Educational Research: A practical guide*. New York: Routledge.

Farrugia, A. (2015) 'You can't just give your best mate a massive hug every day', young men, play and MDMA. *Contemporary Drug Problems*, 42, 3, 240–256.

Francis, B. (2013) Making an impact? In M.B. Weaver-Hightower and C. Skelton (Eds) *Leaders in Gender and Education: Intellectual self-portraits*. Rotterdam: Sense, 89–101.

Golding, B. and Pattison, S. (2004) Inequity in Australian vocational education and training by location, education and training. In K. Bowman (Ed.) *Equity in Vocational Education and Training. Research readings*. Adelaide, Australia: National Centre for Vocational Education Research, 108–119.

Gorur, R. (2015) Situated, relational and practice-oriented: The actor-network theory approach. In K. Gulson, M. Clarke and E. Petersen (Eds) *Education Policy and Contemporary Theory: Implications for research*. New York: Routledge, 87–98.

Gulson, K. N., Clarke, M. and Petersen, E. B. (Eds) (2015) *Education Policy and Contemporary Theory: Implications for research*. New York: Routledge.

Hall, S. (1999) A conversation with Stuart Hall. *The Journal of the International Institute*, 7, 1.

Haraway, D. J. (2008). *When Species Meet*. Minneapolis: University of Minnesota Press.

Jonassen, D. H. (1991) Objectivism versus constructivism: do we need a new philosophical paradigm?. *Educational Technology Research and Development*, 39, 3, 5–14.

Kamberelis, G. (2005) *On qualitative inquiry*. New York: Teachers College Press.

Leahy, D. (2014) Assembling a health[y] subject: risky and shameful pedagogies in health education. *Critical Public Health*, 24, 2, 171–181.

McClelland, S. I. and Fine, M. (2008) Embedded science: critical analysis of abstinence-only evaluation research. *Cultural Studies, Critical Methodologies*, 8, 1, 50–81.

Pedersen, H. (2010) Is 'the posthuman' educable? On the convergence of educational philosophy, animal studies, and posthumanist theory. *Discourse: Studies in the Cultural Politics of Education*, 31, 2, 237–250.

Rasmussen, M. L. (2015) 'Cruel optimism' and contemporary Australian critical theory in educational research. *Educational Philosophy and Theory*, 47, 2, 192–206.

Selwyn, N. (2015) Data entry: towards the critical study of digital data and education. *Learning, Media and Technology*, 40, 1, 64–82.

Spivak, G. C. (2015) A bit on theory! Retrieved from http://www.theeuropean-magazine. com/gayatri-c-spivak/10243-theory-and-education (accessed on 3 August, 2016).

Standish, P. (2007) Claims of philosophy, education and research. *Educational Review*, 59, 3, 331–341.

Talburt, S. and Rasmussen, M. L. (2010) 'After-queer' tendencies in queer research. *International Journal of Qualitative Studies in Education*, 23, 1, 1–14.

Taylor, A. and Blaise, M. (forthcoming). Queer departures into more-than-human-worlds. In L. Allen and M. Rasmussen (Eds) *Handbook of Sexualities Education*. New York: Palgrave.

Waidzunas, T. (2012). Young, gay, and suicidal: Dynamic nominalism and the process of defining a social problem with statistics. *Science, Technology & Human Values*, 37, 2, 199–255.

3

The Ethics of Research

Hannah Farrimond

Doing ethical research is a fundamentally important part of educational academic practice. Behaving 'well' in relation to your participants is not a new phenomenon. However, more recently, a more formal culture of ethics review through Institutional Review Boards (IRBs) and Research Ethics Committees (RECs) has emerged which has put the ethics of education research in the spotlight and, at times, questioned conventions of practice. It has been commonplace in education research, for example, for teachers/lecturers to give out surveys to their students to assess pedagogical issues. However this raises questions of whether consent of students is full and free if no real option to 'opt-out' is provided. Similarly, university/college education students often go into schools to undertake projects with school children and are assured by those in authority that 'everyone wants to take part'. Again, this raises questions about the power relationship between researchers, gatekeepers and the children involved – shouldn't children, like adults, also be allowed to say 'no' to being researched?

Although the spotlight of attention has fallen on the ethics of educational research, integrating ethics knowledge into research practices has lagged behind. Rees and colleagues have shown that out of 489 studies involving children or young people in school settings, only a third detailed their consent procedures in journal articles, and of this third, just under half (only one in ten) described seeking consent from children themselves rather than through proxy consent by teachers/parents (Rees et al., 2007). This suggests a laxity about reporting consent embedded in education research culture; it also suggests that the practice of asking children directly for consent or 'assent' has yet to find widespread acceptance. Felzmann suggests that there may be, erroneously, less focus on the ethics of schools-based research as it is perceived as 'practically risk free' (Felzmann 2009).

It is the case that some aspects of education research are relatively routinized, for example, education students doing observations or whole-class testing of education evaluation materials. This may mean only higher risk projects with vulnerable groups may end up featuring on the ethical radar. However, there are two good reasons for focusing on ethical issues across the span of educational research. The first is that given the requirements of formal ethical review are now embedded elsewhere in other research domains (for example, medicine, other social sciences), knowing about and deploying ethical practices is no longer an option. Schools of education often have their own ethics committees; journals are increasingly expecting ethical declarations to be made and Masters and PhD students have to include their ethics approval in their appendices. Second, there is considerable value in looking again at those taken-for-granted practices and reviewing whether they meet current ethical expectations. In particular, issues concerning consent and confidentiality have come back for re-examination, and new norms of ethics are emerging in relation to them.

This chapter has four main sections. The first outlines the parameters of ethical thinking in relation to research in education and childhood, focusing on the particular power relations and vulnerability of the subject group. The second identifies the relevant principles and codes which have developed to enshrine this ethical thinking. In the third, a closer look is taken at core issues in the ethics of education, focusing on two topics (1) consent/assent, including what to cover in consent, oral/written, hierarchies of consent, opt-in/out, researching with your own students and; (2) anonymity, confidentiality and disclosure, including how to deliver anonymity/confidentiality and if, when and how to disclose confidential information. Concrete suggestions on how to put together ethical protocols in relation to these are made here. Finally, the fourth section provides guidance on how to successfully meet institutional or organizational ethical requirements, such as formal ethical review. If you are new to, or need a refresher on, the parameters of ethical thinking in relation to education, the chapter can be read from start to finish. If you are facing an imminent deadline to submit an ethics application you may wish to start at the end and work backwards as time allows.

WHAT IS DISTINCT ABOUT THE RESEARCH ETHICS OF EDUCATION AND CHILDHOOD?

From the perspective of an ethics committee or IRB, children or 'minors' who are under 18 are identified as a 'vulnerable group' which requires special protection within research. This does not mean, however, that all projects involving children will necessarily be designated as 'high risk'. Some schools-based research which is minimally disruptive to students can be considered lower risk, such as reviewing existing teaching methods, unobtrusive observation or carrying out standard educational, psychological or cognitive assessment tests if they are anonymized. This may mean it is exempt from full IRB review in the states (Sieber, 2000, p. 121) or subject to a 'light touch' review in other countries. This does not mean it does not have ethical implications; rather that it is unlikely to pose significant harm to participants as part of their everyday educational experience.

Other types of educational research are considered 'higher risk' for a number of reasons. One is the age of the child, particularly if they are under 8, which would trigger a Level III IRB review or full ethics review in the UK. Another is the intrusiveness of the method or where the research requires pupils or students to engage in additional activities. This could involve individual level participation, for example, children or young people taking part in an experimental test or being interviewed about their experiences, or at a school-level, such as taking part in a country-wide evaluation of different types of reading schemes. This type of research is likely to require full review and careful consideration of the participants' perspectives (for example, whether the children assent to take part, what the experience of taking part will be like) as well as the permission of their parents/guardians and the school. Whether a particular piece of research might be considered part of normal educational practice and thus not subject to full review, or new research requiring full review, can be debatable; if in doubt, contact the ethics committee or representative and ask for advice.

Finally, some children are more vulnerable than others. Children may be 'multiply vulnerable' for a variety of reasons; such as the context they live in (for example, war zone, deprivation), their experiences (for example, having been sexually, physically or mentally abused, seriously ill) or having learning or developmental difficulties. There has been concern that multiply-vulnerable or 'problem' children may be more researched than other groups (Morrow and Richards, 1996). On the other hand, research with such groups can be viewed through a social justice lens as a form of inclusion and method of drawing attention to inequalities in educational experience and outcomes. This may be the case whether the research takes place in a school setting or outside.

Morrow and Richards identify three primary features of childhood which are problematic from the ethical perspective (Morrow and Richards 1996). The first of these is the 'vulnerability' of children. This encompasses both their physical/mental vulnerability with the corresponding need for 'care' by adults, and structural vulnerability in comparison with adults who have greater social, economic and political capital. Second, children are framed as 'incompetent', in the legal and moral sense, which can lead to others making decisions for them. The most notable example of this is that they are often not directly asked for consent, but proxies (such as their teacher, head teacher or parent) consent for them. Third, they are relatively powerless across a set of domains; school, home, in their leisure time which can lead not only to a loss of agency but also the loss of children's voices, both within research and wider sociopolitical contexts.

More recently, there has been an emphasis on children as 'social actors' in their own worlds, raising the possibility that there could be 'ethical symmetry' between researcher and subject (Christensen and Prout, 2002). Some researchers have advocated participatory approaches in childhood research in which participants themselves help set agendas, take part in data collection and frame results (Cocks, 2006). As such, they advocate creating research 'with' children rather than 'on' them (Flewitt, 2005). Recent thinking has emphasized that even very young children have rights to be heard and respected in research. For example, Einarsdóttir's study of 2–6-year-old children in a pre-school setting used a variety of child-friendly methods (for example, group and individual interviews, photos) at the right level of competency for the children, which revealed more than one 'voice' amongst the children and avoided treating them as a homogeneous group (Einarsdóttir, 2007). Using different methods with children, both traditional and innovative, can help dissipate some of the ethical issues inherent in childhood and education research (Punch, 2002).

However, even within a child-focused project, caution is needed. Research is rarely, if ever, the initiative of the child. It is always initiated by the researcher and on topics of their choosing (Einarsdóttir, 2007). Furthermore, such research has the potential to study (or intrude) into the private thoughts and everyday world of the child precisely because of the asymmetry of power. Children, particularly in school settings, may agree to participate as much because an authority figure has asked them, or they want to please them. For this reason, it has been argued that 'ethical symmetry' between children and adults is largely illusory given the ongoing disparity in the power relationship (Pole et al., 1999). Minimizing the distance between the adult researcher and the child through strategies such as being the 'least adult' and entering into the child's world through play have been suggested (Randall, 2012). However, this in turn carries another ethical risk, that children or young people may misunderstand the nature of the research relationship and perceive the researcher as a 'friend' now part of their lives (Thompson, 2002). Whatever strategy is chosen, the fact that the adults have more power than children in education research cannot really be escaped.

In conclusion, there is a need, when conducting research in education to 'think through' the ethical parameters of the specific piece of research being conducted and avoid generalization, for example, all school-based research is 'low risk'. Furthermore, educational research is shot through with issues concerning power (of adults over children) and agency (of children's decision-making capabilities), even at the 'lower risk' end of the research spectrum. The power differential is also formalized in school-based educational settings in which teachers are visibly and consistently 'in charge' which presents challenges to principles such as informed consent and confidentiality of data in particular.

ETHICAL PRINCIPLES AND CODES

Much ethical thinking about research is based on principles or values which are theorized to guide decision-making. Many of these principles have been derived from codes such as the Nuremberg Code and the Belmont Code which emerged after the mistreatment and torture of victims in medical research in World War II. The core set includes (taken from Kitchener and Kitchener, 2009; Shamoo and Resnick, 2009):

1 Respect for persons (autonomy, protection of the vulnerable)
2 Justice (treat people fairly)
3 Beneficence (do good)
4 Nonmaleficence (do no harm)
5 Fidelity (do not lie/fabricate, be trustworthy)
6 Academic freedom.

The first four of these are derived from the Belmont Code; fidelity has emerged as a key value in relation to preventing scientific misconduct (Shamoo and Resnick, 2009). I also add 'academic freedom' as increasingly the independence of research is compromised by competing interests (for example, vetoing research by a funder) or even by the research ethics system itself at times which can delay or prevent research (Hall, 1991). The competing interests of educators themselves are often overlooked or not declared in publications, for example, where the assessor of educational or schools-based programs are also the owners and commercial sellers of the copyright (Gorman and Conde, 2007). From a philosophical perspective, these principles are drawn from a variety of approaches, including Kantian 'first principles' or utilitarianism which weighs the benefit versus the risks of research at a social level. As such they represent abstract sets of desirable rules for the operation of morality in research.

The above core principles are the basis for most codes of practice. Relevant examples include the BERA guidelines 'Ethical Guidelines for Educational Research' (BERA, 2011) 'The Code of Ethics' of the American Educational Research Association (American Educational Research Association, 2011) and the EECERA Ethical Code for Early Childhood Researchers (European Early Childhood Education Research Association, 2014). These resources and others are usefully compiled together, for example, in the International Ethical Research Involving Children (ERIC) project (http://childethics.com/, accessed 4 April 2016).

Such codes are a good starting point for ethical discussion and decision-making. It also has to be remembered that they are essentially norms (that is, represent the agreement of the group) and may change over time as practice evolves. They are also abstract, to the extent that they describe general principles and practices. More recently, an 'ethics of care' approach has challenged these rule-based approaches, suggesting that the most important aspect of ethics is to respond responsively, sensitively and with compassion to the interpersonal situation which the ethics dilemma represents (Held, 2005). However, Goredema-Braid argues that it is not an 'either/or' situation, but pragmatic research with young people often ends up drawing on both abstract rules and situational decision-making (Goredema-Braid, 2010). For example, young people involved in crime should not be asked, and are very unlikely to agree, to sign a written consent form with identifying details. However the principle of autonomy to ask for their consent can still be upheld, for example, by using oral consent (Goredema-Braid, 2010, p. 48). In conclusion, rules-based approaches offer the key ethical principles for consideration, and the common practices derived from them. Situational-based ethics seeks to interrogate these practices and apply them to the contexts in which the research is taking place. Both are relevant in educational research.

CORE ISSUES IN EDUCATION RESEARCH

Consent and assent

The principle of 'informed consent' is a fundamental one in ethical research, stemming from the notion that individuals have personal autonomy and decision-making capacity to decide for themselves whether to participate in a given research project or not. How the principle of informed consent should be operationalized, however, has been the subject of considerable attention both in the clinical and educational research literature, with an increasing emphasis on seeking the consent or 'assent' of children themselves, and not just the consent of their 'proxies' such as teachers or parents (Alderson and Morrow, 2003; David et al., 2001; Lindeke et al., 2000). As Rees and colleagues' survey of schools-based research synthesis studies shows, however, the practice of asking children for consent/assent has yet to become the norm (Rees et al., 2007).

Gatekeeper (parental and school) consent

The best way to envisage consent in relation to schools-based research is in terms of 'hierarchies of consent'. Often numerous different levels of permission have to be sought to conduct research. Within the school setting itself, these may include the consent of the wider educational authority or local school district in which the school is located, permission from the individual school which may include the board or governors and the headteacher/principal, often in consultation with the staff, and permission from individual class teachers. In addition to this, parental consent is required from those with parental responsibility or a duty of care. This is usually parents, but may include other adults with responsibilities, such as foster carers and social workers. This is standard with under-16s, and sometimes older students, depending on the topic. As such, school-based research necessitates careful planning for gaining the consent from within these hierarchies, especially if it is time-dependent.

However, this does not mean that all education research requires consent from all levels of the hierarchy. Research which is unobtrusive and does not differ significantly from children's everyday practice (for example, being observed by students), research on different teaching methods and anonymous class-based tests/evaluations may be exempt from full ethics review/subject to an IRB waiver in the states (Sieber, 2000, p. 112). This does not mean informed consent is ignored; consent to run and analyze a standard set of evaluations might be sought from a head teacher or individual class teacher, but not necessarily from parents or the children themselves. In general, however, consent to participate is usually sought both from the school and from parents (or one parent, if the other is 'reasonably unavailable') as a necessity; children's consent/assent is then a final step before data collection starts.

Parental or school consent is usually formalized through sending written information forms and asking participants to sign consent sheets so that a record of involvement can be kept. It may also be worth considering additional methods of sharing information about the study, for example, doing a question and answer session at a staff meeting, running a parents' meeting in an appropriate location (for example, school hall or community centre) or setting up meetings with young people's project leaders. Not everyone will necessarily attend, but openness on the part of the researchers is likely to increase confidence and trust in participants. Within participatory research designs, where participants are involved in in designing research questions, being involved with data collection and producing analysis, such meetings are an integral part of the process of research (Khanlou and Peter, 2005; Ennew and Beasley, 2006). Such meetings give participants and gatekeepers the opportunity to assess the benefits and risks of participation for themselves and discuss their concerns in person rather than simply reading formulaic statements on an information sheet.

Another issue with hierarchies of consent is that they tend to replicate existing inequalities of power, with adults able to veto children's involvement or place restrictions on it. Skelton tells of a student project on older school children's attitudes towards P.E. which was eventually abandoned as the ethics committee insisted that chaperones in the form of teachers should be present even though the children reported they wouldn't be able to be honest in their presence (Skelton, 2008). Given the children involved were 14 plus, it seems contrary to the spirit of autonomy not to allow teenagers to speak freely. Skelton goes on to detail a successful project ESRC funded project 'Living on the edge' working with 16–25 year old gay young people which invoked 'Gillick competency' as a rationale for not involving parents in decisions of 16/17-year-olds to take part. 'Gillick competency', or the 'Fraser Guidelines', the legal guidance produced as a result of the Gillick case concerning contraceptive advice without parental consent, refers to the capacity of older children to understand information and make decisions about their medical treatment (Hunter and Pierscionek, 2007). A rationale for seeking child only consent might be where parental or school involvement is likely to prevent or inhibit research, such as in this example relating to sexuality, cheating in exams or illegal drug use. Many researchers have argued that it is important for older children (13 upwards/under the age of majority in the states) to be able to take part into such research into their lives without parents or teachers always knowing about it or being able to veto it (for a review see Williams, 2006). The use of 'Gillick competency' is somewhat controversial as it was originally established as a principle for medical treatment, although more recently it has been applied within research (Heath et al., 2009). It has also been pointed out that the researchers conducting the study should not assess it themselves as they have a vested interest in children participating (Hunter and Pierscionek, 2007). However, it can be a starting point for negotiation with ethics committees where educational researchers want to conduct research with older age children without necessarily seeking parental consent, if the research question justifies this.

Other instances of waiving parental consent might include where it is not possible to contact the parents (for example, in orphanages) or where children are at risk of abuse/in state or local authority care (where those in 'loco parentis' may give consent). This raises an important point which is that requiring parental consent assumes that all parents are stable, sensible and able to assess risks on behalf of their children which may not be the case (Goredema-Braid, 2010). Vargas and Montoya point out that parents may need additional time to 'think through' whether they want their children to participate in research, which is why parents require both information about participating, the time to consider it and the opportunity to ask questions (Vargas and Montoya, 2009). They also point out that cultures vary in terms of the autonomy afforded to children, so some parents will expect deference to authority, whilst others are more open to listening to the child's opinion. Finally, they argue that monetary incentives are particularly problematic with poorer families (Vargas and Montoya, 2009). For this reason, non-monetary incentives for the child and parent (for example, a tailored report, a picture of them engaging in the activity) are often used.

Opt-in/opt-out?

It seems intuitively obvious that individual consent should be given from the parents of each child involved in a research study. The default practice is to gain 'opt-in' individual consent, verified through parents sending back a signed consent form. However, in the real-world this can be difficult. Parents may not read information sheets or send them back signed within the short window in which research is to be conducted; children also lose these slips. If this happens, then the result can be a very incomplete dataset which is then unrepresentative of the age group the researchers had targeted. This is not just a design issue, but an ethical one, as it could be argued to be unethical to involve participants in a low-quality study that won't produce valid scientific information. In some instances, for example, in longitudinal studies where data is sought from a school cohort every year, a case for an 'opt-out' model can be made. The Department of Health, for example, uses an 'opt-out' model for the 'National Child Measurement Programme' which measures weight and height in primary age children to assess local and national trends. 'Opt-out' models should only be used sparingly, where there are real concerns about the analytic implications of incomplete datasets, but can be justified if these criteria are met.

Assent versus consent

In line with the developing capacity of the child over time, it has been suggested that children cannot fully consent to research, at least in a legal capacity, and that what should be sought is 'assent' which is an affirmative agreement to take part (Broome and Richards, 1998). Rather than an emphasis on written consent forms, assent is envisaged as an interpersonal act, such as agreeing to take part by saying 'yes' or by actively participating. Saying 'no' or not actively partici-pating would then become a refusal to give 'assent' and the participant should not be included in the study. Assent is a more appropriate mechanism to assess agreement with younger children. Specific age-appropriate materials have to be developed depending on the group, for example, using the appropriate language (for example, Makaton, sign language) and level of language (for example, visual methods such as pictures of sad face and word 'no' and happy face and word 'yes' can be used with the child pointing to their preference). These can be tried out on the group in question, in agreement with parents/teachers, to see whether assent is possible via these routes. Older children may respond better to more formal consent procedures, as they are in a position to assess the risks/ benefits of participation and level of confidentiality offered. This might include giving simple written information or both researcher and child signing an agreement.

There are several key steps to assessing 'assent': introducing yourself and who you are (for example, 'I'm X, a researcher looking at what children think about playtimes'), stating what the task will involve ('I would like to watch you playing at playtime and then ask you some questions about it, you could choose which friend comes with you for that part'), asking for participation ('is that ok?'), clarifying how the child can dissent (for example, 'you can stop at any time by telling me or the teacher you don't want to take part any more') and giving an opportunity to ask questions ('have you got any questions about taking part?').

Directly asking for the assent of children arguably gives children back some agency in the situation of research, making them feel more in control (Lindeke et al., 2000). However, is far from unproblematic. Given the power differential discussed earlier, children in a school context may not feel in a position to say 'no' to the adults in charge of them such as researcher or their teacher. Additionally, using language such as 'would you like to help me with this project?' can very much frame their participation towards agreement, feeding their desire to be perceived as 'good', so it is important to use more neutral language such as 'I would like to ask you about what you do at home-time' rather than loaded phrases about 'helping'. Furthermore, much participation in school-based projects is group or class-based, so there may be practical difficulties if a few children opt out of a study: arrangements may have to be made for them. It is also the case that asking the child if they are going to participate is usually the final step after the consent of gatekeepers such as parents and teachers has been sought. To this extent, their consent is conditional on that of those in authority, although this may not be the case with older teens as discussed in the last section.

Researching with your own students

Researching with your own students is a particular ethical challenge for educational researchers, particularly those at undergraduate or postgraduate level who are aiming to complete projects within a short time-frame. Using your own students or those known to you, or doing research within your own school appears to offer an ideal opportunity for research, as you already have rapport and trust both with gatekeepers and the potential population of children/young people, and access to them is easily facilitated. For all these reasons, such research is very commonly conducted; but often the ethical challenges this creates are overlooked. The most obvious problem is that researching your own students invariably compromises their ability to autonomously make a decision of whether to take part. This may be because you have built the activity into their schedule already, giving them no choice not to participate, but also because they feel a subtle social pressure to conform to your expectations about enthusiastic participation, or that they cannot envisage being the one person to say no and remove themselves from the classroom or lecture theatre. Being the class teacher or student researcher (and also the marker of their work or grades) doubles the power in the already asymmetric relationship. Students may also fear that the promised 'anonymity' may be compromised, as their handwriting/position in the class is recognizable.

So, what should ethically conscious teachers and researchers do? One solution is simply not to research your own groups or students. If you only require one class to participate, you could ask another teacher with a different set of students if they would mind allowing you 10 minutes at the end of their session to complete your questionnaire. This is easier where a culture of researching and testing already exists and where swapping classes to participate is an easy option. Another option is to make the anonymity of responses water-tight, for example, by using online submissions or simply by emphasizing that participants should not include their names/any identifying details in their answers. Another might be to create research opportunities out of the set-class time, for example, in lunch-breaks for those who are interested in participating. Ultimately, there is no easy answer, but increasingly ethics committees are putting the notion of 'informed consent' and the 'right to withdraw' under scrutiny within school-based research that, in some cases, appears not to offer these in the fullest sense.

Anonymity, confidentiality and disclosure

The purpose of offering participants anonymity (not using their real name) and confidentiality (not disclosing what they say to others) is to protect their privacy. Although conventions in research have grown up in relation to these, such as using anonymity as a default in studies, ultimately privacy is something that has to be negotiated with participants and gatekeepers, particularly if the research is at the higher end of intrusiveness.

Anonymity

Anonymity means to disguise or remove the identity of participants so that others outside the research setting do not know who they are. This is not just a matter of using a pseudonym or number instead of the real name, identifying data can include addresses and postcodes or distinctive features such as job titles or having a certain disorder or experience which others might recognize. There are several reasons for anonymizing research data: firstly it offers the participant privacy and confidentiality so that they can speak freely and honestly without others identifying them. As such, their data may be more authentic and insightful. Second, it ensures that participants are less likely to harm others, for example, by disclosing personal information or shared experiences about them, such as their opinions on a teacher or type of lesson. At a more serious level, it may protect participants if their disclosures are illegal (for example, if working on highly sensitive or criminal research). Finally, anonymization also helps researchers meet the data protection requirements in their countries. In the UK, for example, the Data Protection Act (1998) requires that identifying data is held for as short a time as possible and then destroyed, whereas anonymized data used for research purposes can be held indefinitely for future use.

There are several methods for ensuring anonymity. One way is not to collect identifying data in the first place. It may not be necessary, for example, if running an online school survey about students' understandings of a new educational IT system to collect their names at all. Avoiding identifiers is also sometimes used where the data collected is likely to be legally compromising for participants. In the US, waivers for data on criminality or drug use are available; in the UK, not collecting names/addresses may be the only way to engage with hard-to-reach youth on the margins of criminal activity/engaged with illegal drugs. The second way is to separate the identifying information, such as names and emails collected on consent forms, from the non-identifying at the collection stage. Here, each person, on entering the study, is assigned a number or pseudonym to their data. A separate list matching numbers to names is kept securely elsewhere. Often secondary datasets from large surveys or government sources come pre-anonymized with only numbers as identifiers. It can be harder to fully anonymize very personal qualitative interviews or ethnographic research; more than simply names may need to be changed to achieve anonymization. Furthermore, in schools-based research, the question is not only whether the individuals should be anonymized, but also the school itself; they need to be asked directly as part of the consent procedure.

In general, making data anonymous has become the default practice, and only a strong justification for departing from this is likely to be accepted from ethics committees. Examples might include where the person being interviewed is a public figure or someone speaking in their professional capacity that is happy for their words to be a matter of record. Schools may also be happy to be identified as having participated in an evaluation of a new educational intervention, even if individual children themselves are anonymized. Finally, some participants do not want to be anonymous, for example, Grinyer details the case of interviewing parents who had lost children to cancer who felt their anonymous pseudonyms originally given to them didn't relate to them at all; many were happy to be identified as a form of personal memorial (Grinyer, 2002). In summary, participants are protected by anonymity, so it makes sense to continue with it as a default practice in education research unless a strong reason to depart from it can be justified.

Confidentiality and disclosure

Confidentiality is a thorny issue in relation to studying children and educational practice. On the one hand, there is a need to reassure participants of the confidentiality of their data, in other words not sharing it beyond agreed limits. This is usually delivered through making data anonymous, but also through robust data protection and (usually) not discussing private details given by participants with other people outside the study. On the other hand, there may be legal and moral obligations to disclose information if the participant is themselves at risk or is experiencing harm, such as physical, emotional or sexual abuse or neglect. Sensitive information may also emerge during data collection regarding unsafe behavior, sexual practices, health status (for example, HIV status) or drug taking which may present a dilemma about whether others need to know. Researchers who cannot offer confidentiality at all are unlikely to gain full frank and scientifically valid data from children and young people about sensitive issues. So, what should the researcher do to balance the need for confidentiality against disclosure?

In the UK, many professional codes obligate the professional to disclose harm or neglect (for example, teacher, social worker). Whether there is a legal obligation for researchers is less clear; there may be a duty under the 1989 Children's Act to report instances where it is believed a young person is in danger from others or likely to cause danger (Heath et al., 2009). In the US, legal obligations do exist at state level to report sexual and elder abuse (Folkman, 2000). Legal or otherwise, the moral obligation to protect children remains.

There are several concrete steps that researchers can take to make their procedures as robust as possible before they arise:

1. Decide what is meant by 'confidentiality'. I suggest that confidentiality is agreed between the participant and the 'research team' rather than one individual (unless a good reason to do so) – which might include the researcher, supervisor if a student, other members of the team if a larger project. This means ethical discussion of tricky issues can be facilitated within the study as a whole (Farrimond, 2012). An example statement might include:

> Everything you say will be kept confidential, this means I won't share it with other people, except those in my research team, so that means me and my supervisor, is that ok?

2. Be upfront with participants that there are limits to confidentiality. It is important that children/young people know that what you are discussing is not completely secret between them and yourself, but that in exceptional circumstances, you may have to tell others what they have told you (Neill, 2005). If children are older, breaking confidentiality may be discussed with them first. Sample text includes:

> Everything you say will be kept confidential, except if you say something which makes us worry that you or someone else may be harmed, in which case we would talk to you first about what to do next.

3. Have a protocol in place for the disclosure of sensitive information or risk to the child. This is particularly important for studies with known high-risk or vulnerable populations. For example, if you were researching with children in care, this is a population known to have high rates of abuse and neglect, and so a protocol detailing what would happen at each stage after disclosure should be developed before any data collected. As a starting point, researchers should identify what I term 'the ethical chain of command' which is the hierarchy of those involved in ethical decision-making for this study (Farrimond, 2012). The first level is the researcher who is present in the situation along with the participant. If an ethical issue was identified that could not be solved by them, then it would go up the chain to the head of the study or principal investigator, and if not within the team itself, then they should involve outside ethical expertise. Good sources would include ethics representatives from the relevant department or the Chair of the ethics committee who can then seek additional advice or involve others as necessary (for example, legal advice, child protection services).

It is also worth noting that disclosure of sensitive or difficult material by children or young people is not just about the legal responsibility, but acting with compassion on the part of the researcher. From an 'ethics of care' perspective, this may involve strategies to help manage any upset or distress as well as practical information on accessing advice/assistance (for example, to a helpline, to appropriate services). Finally, safeguarding is a two-way street, in that children and young people must also be protected in research environments, which is why researchers working in UK education research usually need to undergo DBS checks (Disclosure and Barring Service (DBS) checks, formerly Criminal Records Bureau (CRB) checks).

MEETING THE REQUIREMENTS OF ETHICS REVIEW

The final aim of this chapter is to provide guidance on how to meet institutional ethical requirements. Making an ethics application is not the only time at which ethical issues are important in research. Ethical decision-making is present throughout the 'lifecycle' of a project from design through to dissemination (Farrimond, 2012). For example, sampling involves choices about who to include, exclude and whether to use proxies for consent. Analyzing results involves producing outputs that are scientifically meaningful and authentic. For example, if an educational evaluation suggests one program is more beneficial than another, then it may be widely adopted. A deliberate or accidental manipulation (for example, cherry picking) of data may lead to policy changes that change children's educations in non-beneficial ways (Mark and Gamble, 2009). Guillemin and Gilliam make a convincing distinction between research ethics at the organizational level, involving submitting ethics applications and committees, and 'ethics in practice' which concerns the myriad of sometimes unexpected ethical dilemmas which present themselves in real life (Guillemin and Gillam, 2004). Although ethical issues do indeed arise as projects are running, it is the case that for most students and researchers making an ethics application is the time-point at which ethical issues are brought into focus. Furthermore, it is also the point at which their 'ethical competence' has to be demonstrated to the satisfaction to the committee or IRB and, if they exist, where differences in ethical opinion or practice may occur. The following tips are aimed to help with writing a successful ethics proposal:

1. Find out what is required. This sounds incredibly obvious, but students and researchers get caught out by ethics procedures all the time. Not knowing the committee or IRB meeting dates, not having prepared the application thoroughly enough or a necessary institutional signatory such as supervisor being unavailable can mean a delay in approval. This can knock on into jeopardizing funding or completing a qualification. If you know you need ethics approval, read the relevant webpages and get in touch with the secretary or administrator early on to clarify what you have to do, download the forms and check you will meet the requirements. This has to be done locally (that is, at your institution) as procedures differ. One institution may require a one-page form to be submitted for undergraduate and Masters projects to an ethics representative, others may require full submission. Online forms

are increasingly common, as are committees specific to the discipline. If you are involving vulnerable subjects (otherwise vulnerable not just by virtue of being children, such as in care, living in poverty), sensitive topics (for example, sexuality, drug use in minors) or a particular issue (for example, whether to go for proxy consent with under-8s) then approach the Chair or ethics rep to ask for advice in advance, as review decisions are made on local precedents so it makes sense to write your application with them in mind (Stark and Hedgecoe, 2010).

2. Write the application in a concise but detailed way. Most ethics forms are pretty standard, which can mean that the temptation to cut and paste from a research funding application or other piece of work is high. This can work, as long as the basic principle is upheld – that it should be comprehensible to reasonably intelligent non-experts. There are usually sections on (a) the rationale and aims of the project, including some theory; (b) the methods; and (c) separate sections on various ethical aspects, which might include (but is not limited to) how you will manage consent, voluntariness, data protection, risks and benefits of the project and any international data collection issues. You may also be required to send documentation such as consent forms and information sheets, survey/instruments/experimental protocols/interview schedules and advertising materials; check in advance what your procedure requires. In particular, make sure the methods section is very clear and detailed; without this, the committee or IRB cannot make a judgement about whether what you are doing is ethically satisfactory. This should include who constitutes the sample, where the data will be collected, where it will be stored, how participants will be recruited and what will happen to participants throughout the study. Also, don't just identify ethical problems, explain what steps you are going to undertake to solve them. It is best to create a draft first, then perhaps send it to your ethics representative, supervisor or other members of the team for feedback for quality control purposes (if it goes to the ethics representative, they may be able to help you avoid common problems before it goes to the full committee).

3. Provide a realistic assessment of risks and benefits. Ethics forms usually ask for you to detail the possible harm/risks in your project, and solutions to those risks. It is also standard to include a brief section on the consent/information sheet detailing the risk and benefit to participants of taking part. Risks to participants can range from the physical, mental, social, economic, and reputational as well as to the researcher themselves (for example, safety, distress). In schools-based research, risks might focus on the voluntariness of participation (to what extent can the school, individual teachers and individual children say no to participation?) and disclosure (what strategies are in place if children disclose information about neglect/abuse/sensitive issues?) Researchers often veer between under-assessing (for example, 'there are no risks at all in this project') to over-assessment of risk (for example, suggesting counselling to deal with 'trauma' of interview). 'Minimal' or 'low' risk often has a specific meaning within research ethics: that the effects of participation are within the 'everyday experience' of the participants and won't be temporary or long-lasting. For example, talking about a time playing with friends that made you sad may be temporarily a bit distressing, but it is within the bounds of everyday experience for most children. A strategy for dealing with this may therefore be to offer existing support for children from within the school system if they wanted to talk about participating in a study which may bring up difficult feelings. Benefits of participation may be difficult to quantify and often relate to the perceived value of the study (for example, to change policy). Any individual benefits to children or parents should be specifically identified. For example, a study on weight and exercise might offer the opportunity to have individual feedback and advice. The key is to provide a realistic, not exaggerated, assessment of risks and harms, and more importantly, to show how risks will be managed.

Finally, the advice given here is addressed to individuals and research teams facing ethics review in the context of educational research. It is important to note however, that institutions have their own set of responsibilities to avoid creating a solely bureaucratic system of tick-boxes as is often the case (Hall, 1991; Hammersley, 2006) but to set up a research culture that engages genuinely and deeply with ethics and supports individuals to do so.

CONCLUSION

Education research, like research in general, has to tread a difficult path between ethical 'engagement' and ethical 'hypersensitivity'. The cause of producing good research is not served by overly bureaucratic systems or by researchers being afraid to engage with difficult or sensitive topics because of the perceived diffi-culties of ethics review. On the other hand, if many taken-for-granted practices in education research are now being questioned on the grounds of ethics without major detriment to the overall production of knowledge, the right balance will have been struck.

RECOMMENDED READINGS

Christensen, P and Prout, A. (2002) Working with ethical symmetry in social research with children, *Childhood*, 9, 4, 477–497.

Thomas, N. and O'Kane, C. (1998) The ethics of participatory research with children. *Children and Society*, 12, 336–348.

Flewitt, R. (2005) Conducting research with young children: some ethical considerations. *Early Child Development and Care*, 175, 6, 553–565.

REFERENCES

Alderson, P. and Morrow, V. (2003) *Ethics, Social Research and Consulting with Children and Young People*. Ilford: Barnados.

American Educational Research Association (2011) Code of ethics. Retrieved on 4 April 2016 from http://c.ymcdn.com/sites/www.weraonline.org/resource/resmgr/a_general/aera.pdf.

BERA (2011) Ethical guidelines for educational research. Retrieved on 4 April 2016 from www.bera.ac.uk/researchers-resources/publications/ethical-guidelines-for-educational-research-2011.

Broome, M. and Richards, D. (1998) Involving children in research. *Journal of Child and Family Nursing*, 1, 1, 3–7.

Christensen, P. and Prout, A. (2002) Working with ethical symmetry in social research with children. *Childhood*, 9, 4, 477–497.

Cocks, A. J. (2006) The ethical maze: finding an inclusive path towards gaining children's agreement to research participation. *Childhood*, 13, 2, 247–266.

David, M., Edwards, R. and Aldred, P. (2001) Children and school-based research: 'informed consent' or 'educated consent'? *British Educational Research Journal*, 27, 3, 347–365.

Einarsdóttir, J. (2007) Research with children: methodological and ethical challenges. *European Early Childhood Education Research*, 15, 2, 202–211.

Ennew, J. and Beasley, H. (2006) Participatory methods and approaches: the two tyrannies. In V. Desai and R. Potter (Eds) *Doing Development Studies*. London: Sage, 189–199.

European Early Childhood Education Research Association (2014) EECERA Ethical Code for Early Childhood Researchers. Retrieved on 4 April 2016 from www.eecera.org/documents/pdf/organisation/EECERA-Ethical-Code.pdf.

Farrimond, H. (2012) *Doing Ethical Research*. London: Palgrave Macmillan.

Felzmann, H. (2009) Ethical issues in school-based research. *Research Ethics Review*, 5, 3, 104–109.

Flewitt, R. (2005) Conducting research with young children: some ethical considerations. *Early Child Development and Care*, 175, 6, 553–566.

Folkman, S. (2000) Privacy and confidentiality. In B. D. Sales and S. Folkman (Eds) *Ethics in Research with Human Participants*. Washington, DC: American Psychological Association, 49–58

Goredema-Braid, B. (2010) Ethical research with young people. *Research Ethics Review*, 6, 2, 48–52.

Gorman, D. M. and Conde, E. (2007) Conflict of interest in the evaluation and dissemination of 'model' school-based drug and violence prevention programs. *Evaluation and Program Planning*, 30, 4, 422–429.

Grinyer, A. (2002) The anonymity of research participants: assumptions, ethics and practicalities. *Social Research Update*, 36.

Guillemin, M. and Gillam, L. (2004) Ethics, reflexivity, and 'ethically important moments' in research. *Qualitative Inquiry*, 10, 2, 261–280.

Hall, D. (1991) The research imperative and bureaucratic control: the case of clinical research. *Social Science and Medicine*, 32, 3, 333–342.

Hammersley, M. (2006) Are ethics committees ethical? *Qualitative Researcher*, 2, 4–8.

Heath, S. et al. (2009) *Researching Young People's Lives*. London, Thousand Oaks, CA, New Delhi and Singapore: SAGE Publications.

Held, V. (2005) *The Ethics of Care*. Oxford, UK: Oxford University Press.

Hunter, D. and Pierscionek, B. K. (2007) Children, Gillick competency and consent for involvement in research. *Journal of Medical Ethics*, 33, 11, 659–662.

Khanlou, N. and Peter, E. (2005) Participatory action research: considerations for ethical review. *Social Science and Medicine*, 60, 2333–2340.

Kitchener, K. S. and Kitchener, R. F. (2009) Social science research ethics: historical and philosophical issues. In D. M. Mertens and P. E. Ginsberg (Eds) *The Handbook of Social Research Ethics*. London, Thousand Oaks, CA, New Delhi and Singapore: Sage, 5–22.

Lindeke, L. L., Hauck, M. R. and Tanner, M. (2000) Practical issues in obtaining child assent for research. *Journal of Pediatric Nursing*, 15, 2, 99–104.

Mark, M. M. and Gamble, C. (2009) Experiments, quasi-experiments, and ethics. In D. M. Mertens and P. E. Ginsberg (Eds) *The Handbook of Social Research Ethics*. London, Thousand Oaks, CA, New Delhi and Singapore: Sage, 198–213.

Morrow, V. and Richards, M. (1996) The ethics of social research with children and young people: an overview. *Children and Society*, 10, 90–106.

Neill, S. J. (2005) Research with children: a critical review of the guidelines. *Journal of Child Health Care*, 9, 1, 46–58.

Pole, C., Mizen, P. and Bolton, A. (1999) Realising children's agency in research: partners or participants. *International Journal of Social Research Methodology*, 20, 39–54.

Punch, S. (2002) Research with children: the same or different from research with adults? *Childhood*, 9, 3, 321–341.

Randall, D. (2012) Revisiting Mandell's 'least adult' role and engaging with children's voices in research. *Nurse Researcher*, 19, 3, 39–43.

Rees, R. W., Garcia, J. and Oakley, A. (2007) Consent in school-based research involving children and young people: a survey of research from systematic reviews. *Research Ethics Review*, 3, 2, 35–39.

Shamoo, A. and Resnick, D. (2009) *Responsible Conduct of Research*, 2nd edition. New York: Oxford University Press.

Sieber, J.E. (1992) Planning Ethically Responsible Research: A Guide for Students and Internal Review Boards. London, California, Delhi: Sage.

Skelton, T. (2008) Research with children and young people: exploring the tensions between ethics, competence and participation. *Children's Geographies*, 6, 1, 21–36.

Stark, L. and Hedgecoe, A. (2010) A practical guide to research ethics. In I. Bourgeault, R. Dingwall and R. de Vries (Eds) *The SAGE Handbook of Qualitative Methods in Health Research*. London, Thousand Oaks, CA, New Delhi and Singapore: Sage, 589–607.

Thompson, S. (2002) My research friend? My friend the researcher? My friend, my researcher? Mis/informed consent and people with developmental disabilities. In W. C. van den Hoonaard (Ed.) *Walking the Tightrope: Ethical issue for qualitative researchers*. Toronto, Buffalo and London: University of Toronto Press, 95–106.

Vargas, L. A. and Montoya, M. E. (2009) Involving minors in research: ethics and law within multicultural settings. In D. M. Mertens and P. E. Ginsberg (Eds) *The Handbook of Social Research Ethics*. London, Thousand Oaks, CA, New Delhi and Singapore: Sage, 489–506.

Williams, B. (2006) Meaningful consent to participate in social research on the part of people under the age of eighteen. *Research Ethics Review*, 2, 1, 19–24.

4

Shared Principles of Causal Inference in Qualitative and Quantitative Research

Sean Kelly

In studying learning and socialization in the complex world of schools educational researchers must make inferences about educational problems and solutions from imperfect data and less than ideal research designs. Indeed, educational research-ers are often interested in studying educational problems as they naturally occur, or in curriculum or policy interventions that take place in an educational system all at once, without the benefit of proactively putting in place a study design. In quantitative research in education, a rich body of research has developed to under-stand and support causal inferences in quasi-experimental data, that is, data where the study design falls short of a true experimental design relying on random assignment to treatment and control conditions (Shadish and Luellen, 2006). While certainly not the only goal of qualitative research in education, this field of inquiry also strives to make inferences from limited data (Eisenhart, 2006; Riessman, 2002). In both methodological paradigms compelling research relies on three general principles of causal inference: accounting for chance, ruling out competing explanations, and explaining causation. The aim of this chapter is to provide a basic introduction to each of the principles, using examples from both qualitative and quantitative education research.[1]

DESCRIPTION VERSUS CAUSAL INFERENCE

Descriptive studies seek to demonstrate the prevalence, level, or pattern of edu-cational resources, contexts, and outcomes, while causal studies seek to document relationships or processes. Compared to the goal of description, it is much more difficult to develop understandings of causal relationships with a high level of confidence. Consider for example, the study of adolescent employment. Adolescent employment is a social phenomenon of interest to policymakers setting age of employment laws, educators who instruct both working and non-working students, and parents of working-age teens. What have educational researchers learned about adolescent employment?

Although there is some measurement error in self-reports of employment, with careful data collection, educational researchers are generally confident that they can establish the approximate prevalence rate of employment, and document changes in levels of adolescent employment over time (Marsh and Kleitman, 2005). In contrast, the causal effects of adolescent employment on student engagement and learning outcomes are inherently challenging to study. First, competing theories of employment argue that work reduces both time for academic pursuits and social-psychological commitment to schooling, or alternately, that work is a character-building activity leading to greater self-regulation and other developmental changes that facilitate school success. Second, the adolescents who seek employment may differ in unknown ways from those who do not, making inferences about the effect of working itself very difficult. What appears to be an effect of employment may instead stem from pre-existing attitudes towards school.

To see just how difficult it is to reach a causal inference about such effects, consider that we are really interested in knowing the effect of two potential outcomes for the same students; one set of outcomes where they were employed, one where they were not. This counterfactual 'what if' or 'alternate universe' comparison can only be approximated in an empirical study. Statistical methodologists, led by Rubin (1978, 1990), have demonstrated the many assumptions, often violated in practice, that separate real-world studies from pure counterfactual estimates of causality (see also Holland, 1986; Morgan and Winship, 2007). While analyses conducted by Marsh and Kleitman (2005), Warren and Lee (2003), and others have led to the conclusion that employment effects, on average, are probably modest for most schooling outcomes, it has taken much replication and further research to reach that conclusion.

Likewise, qualitative research in education, in addition to other aims, seeks both to describe educational phenomenon and understand causal relationships. Finley's (1984) seminal study of teacher tracking in a suburban high school provides an example of a qualitative study both describing a phenomenon and development of a causal model. At 'Suburban High' Finley found a system of teacher staffing in place where teachers were unevenly allocated to classrooms such that some teachers taught almost exclusively low-track students, while other teachers taught only high-track students. One focus of Finley's analysis was to describe teachers' perspective on tracked learning environments; at Suburban High, the high-track classes were almost unanimously perceived by teachers as the 'good classes'. Thus, the teacher-tracking system at Suburban was a system of status-differentiation for teachers. A second focus of Finley's analysis was more causal in nature, to understand what types of teachers were assigned to which tracks. Finley discovered that high-track teaching assignments were largely a function of tenure (length of service at Suburban), educational attainment, and motivation.

Yet, as with quantitative research, there is often uncertainty about both the internal and external validity of causal claims even in close ethnographic research. *Internal validity* refers to whether the observed findings were the result of a causal relationship. *External validity* concerns whether the observed relationship holds when applied to different persons, settings, treatments, or outcomes (Shadish et al., 2002). At Suburban, it is possible that one or more of the teacher characteristics that were found to lead to a high-track teaching assignment were really revealing the effect of an unmeasured characteristic. Finley did not, for example, have a measure of teachers' tested subject-matter proficiency, and it may be this factor, rather than educational attainment or tenure that is important. We might also wonder whether this staffing model was particular to the organizational context of Suburban. In this case, subsequent research by Kelly (2004) has supported Finley's model of teacher tracking, but this important phenomenon warrants further research.

Both quantitative and qualitative researchers are interested in beginning to make causal inferences from data. In this chapter I describe the shared challenges facing educational researchers, regardless of their overarching approach. However, as the examples above begin to show, some research designs may be better able to address a given principle of causal inference than others. The case study of Suburban High (Finley, 1984) introduces the common problem of accounting for chance in small scale studies of individual schools or classrooms.

ACCOUNTING FOR CHANCE

In her book, *Lower-track Classrooms*, Page (1991) contrasts instruction in regular- and low-track English and social studies classrooms in two high schools. Page's goal is both descriptive, to understand the nature of instruction in low-track compared to regular-track classrooms, and causal, to understand how tracking as an organizational practice affects classroom climate and teaching. She found that in general regular- and low-track classrooms spend their time doing similar activities like listening to lectures, participating in question and answer sessions, doing seatwork, small group work, and so forth. Yet, if regular- and low-track classrooms might look similar at first glance, a closer inspection reveals that low-track classrooms frequently have less academic content and a lack of engaging instruction. 'Ever notice how slooow this class is?' Page (1991, p. 87) overheard one low-track student remark to another. By the end of an intensive program of participant observations, interviews, and analysis of classroom transcripts, Page concluded that the highly-structured (and often boring) approach to teaching in low-track classrooms she observed was no accident, and was caused by the tracked system of curriculum organization itself, 'It is not the result of one teachers' ineptness. Nor is it necessitated by lower-track students rambunctiousness or indifference. Rather, it arises from and re-creates teachers' uncertainties regarding their role in lower-track classes' (Page, 1991, p. 104).

Might the results that Page so carefully detailed have been happenstance? Page studied only eight low-track classrooms in just two schools. If she had selected different schools or teachers, would the results have been different? In these cases, it seems likely the findings and patterns reflect underlying causal effects, both because the conclusions are supported by a larger body of research, and because the efforts to explain causation (see below) are so compelling. Nevertheless, accounting for chance is an inherent challenge in making causal inferences in educational research. When working with only a small set of students, classrooms, or schools, how do we know that any observed differences were systematic, and not due to chance? Indeed, while this problem of causal inference affects small datasets more so than large datasets, it nearly always poses a concern.

Accounting for chance is a cornerstone of quantitative research methods. Quantitative researchers use the science of statistics, which is based in principles of sampling, to conduct tests of statistical significance in order to estimate how likely a phenomenon, relationship, or difference might have been observed purely by chance. Importantly, there is a difference between merely measuring or quantifying an outcome, and generating a *statistic*. Just because you've counted something, doesn't make it a statistic.[2]

A *sample* is a part of a population selected for study, with the idea being that inferences will be made about the population itself. Populations may be finite (for example, all charter schools in a state), or infinite (for example, in a study of classroom discourse, all possible teacher utterances). Infinite populations are also called 'super-populations' and are common in educational research (Tipton, 2013). In discussing experimental research in particular, Shadish et al. (2002, p. 18) note that, 'Most experiments are highly local but have general aspirations'. The same might be said of discovery-oriented educational research using a variety of study designs.

In educational research, even when the populations we are interested in are technically finite, they tend to be very large indeed (for example, all students, teachers, or schools in an educational system). Even sub-populations (for example, all 4th grade English language learners) constitute a very large population. Thus, it is very seldom feasible to work with a population itself in educational research. Nor is it always desirable. Researchers are often able to obtain more robust results using a sample, because greater effort can be spent assuring high quality responses on a smaller set of respondents. Compared to using a population, sampling is often of lower cost, ensures greater timeliness of results, and

Table 4.1 Types of samples

Probability Samples		Non-probability Samples	
Simple Random Sample	Complex Random Samples: Cluster Samples, Stratified Samples, or some combination of both	Judgment Samples: Quota Samples	Convenience Samples: Volunteer Samples, Snowball Samples

allows for more detailed and accurate information to be collected about each case (Daniel, 2012; Fowler, 2002). Samples fall into two general types, *probability samples* and all other samples (see Table 4.1).

PROBABILITY SAMPLES

A probability sample is a sample in which the selection of elements has a known probability. The science of statistics is based on probability sampling. The most basic probability sample is the *simple random sample*, where each element of the population has an equal probability of being selected.[3] If you know nothing about the elements, and you select them from a list randomly, you have a simple random sample.

In educational research we are often fortunate to have an approximate *sampling frame*, a list of all possible elements in the population, from which to draw a probability sample. For example, in the United States, The National Center for Education Statistics keeps an updated list of all public schools, along with some basic descriptive information, in the Common Core of Data (CCD). Although there is no list of US students or teachers, it is still possible to produce a relatively robust estimate of at least the number of teachers and students, which are reported by school administrators in the CCD. With a list of elements, or even a solid estimate of the number of elements, it is possible to generate a probability sample. Educational samples are often generated by a complex, multi-stage process where students are *clustered* within schools, which are further *stratified* by school type (for example, public versus private). Stratification often improves the efficiency of sampling by increasing the variability in important variables. In contrast, clustering tends to reduce efficiency, since clustered cases tend to be more similar than a random selection from the population as a whole would be. On the other hand, clustering tends to make the data collection effort more cost effective, so any reduction in statistical power can generally be offset by collecting more data. In education research, because students are nested in classrooms in schools, clustering is a natural and unavoidable aspect of research, for better or worse. Most importantly, like their cousin, the simple random sample, such complex samples have the key ingredient of randomness. For a more detailed discussion of complex sampling elements see texts by Levy and Lemeshow (2008) or Daniel (2012).

Sample data are used to produce estimates, called *sample statistics*, of true population parameters. These parameters may be descriptive (prevalence rates, mean levels, and so on) or refer to causal relationships. Consider an example of descriptive statistics: the National Assessment of Educational Progress (NAEP) data, also known as the 'nation's report card' are used to produce nationally representative estimates of student achievement in the United States. The long-term trend version of NAEP is used to track changes in performance over time. In 2008, approximately 9,800 9-year-old students were selected to take the long-term trend NAEP reading test, and serve as a representative sample of the US as a whole. In the 2008 NAEP data collection the average 9-year-old had a scale score of 220 in reading. This value is an estimate of some unknown true average reading achievement level; a different group of 9,800 students would have produced a somewhat different conclusion about average reading performance.

The error that is due to taking a sample, the difference between the results from the sample, and the results that would obtain from having complete information about all respondents, is called *sampling error*. While we can never account for all possible sources of error (including errors of measurement such as who is sick the day of the test), the science of statistics allows us to quantify the amount of sampling error associated with a particular sample.[4] In 2004, the average reading scale score on the long-term trend NAEP data was 216, compared to 220 in 2008. In order to make an inference about some true possible change in reading achievement from 2004 to 2008, we need to take into account the amount of sampling error at each time point, the 'wiggle' between the sample statistic and what the true population value might be (picture an area of uncertainty around the average scale score in each year). Using the appropriate calculation given the sampling procedure, NCES concluded that there was indeed a 'statistically significant' increase in the 2008 NAEP reading scores from 2004. This phrase, 'statistically significant' simply means that the observed difference of four points of achievement is unlikely to be due to sampling error.

Returning to the basic principle of accounting for chance, my main point here is that the crucial component of this process, that which allows us to link a sample statistic to a true population value (or 'parameter'), is randomness. The amount of sampling error, the possible difference between an estimated sample statistic and the true population value can *only be validly established using a probability sample*. Without the assumption of a known probability of selection, we have no way, statistically, to link a sample statistic to its true underlying value in the population. Mathematically, it is possible to use the statistical formulas for assessing sampling error with the corresponding information from a non-probability sample (size of the sample, and so on), but the resulting inferences will be biased in unknown ways. Olsen et al. (2013) and Tipton (2014) provide discussion of generalizability in the context of purposeful sample selection.

NON-PROBABILITY SAMPLES

Early in his social science career, Kelly (2007) conducted a study of course taking policies in North Carolina High Schools. Not fully appreciating the importance of random sampling, Kelly took a non-probability sample, based on the average achievement level of all high schools in NC. Ordering all high schools by achievement, Kelly selected a balanced number of the 33 lowest, 33 middle, and 33 highest performing schools. Thus, the sample represented a stratified (by achievement level), but non-randomly selected sample, for instance, all of the top-performing schools were selected with certainty. At the time, Kelly reasoned that such an approach would provide good coverage of the range of possible course taking policies in North Carolina. However, this procedure did not produce a probability sample of high schools – some schools were guaranteed to be selected, while others had no chance of being selected. How might this have affected the results? Subsequent analyses have revealed that schools with greater variability in test scores have a more highly elaborated set of course taking policies (Kelly and Price, 2011). Thus, it seems likely that Kelly's (2007) initial study, where the within-school variation in achievement was relatively small, underestimated the robustness of high school tacking systems at that time, although the full extent of bias is unknown. In this case, Kelly's choice of data collection procedure was particularly unfortunate, because it would have been easy to incorporate random selection while still achieving coverage of a wide range of average achievement levels by using a stratified random sample, there was no reason not to sample schools with a known probability of selection.[5]

This example from the author's research is a case where the sampling frame, a list of the population of North Carolina high schools, was readily available. In much educational research however, it will not be possible to conduct a true probability sample. For example, even large-scale studies conducted at prominent educational research centers often use samples of schools that are in part selected for 'convenience', although 'feasibility' might be the more accurate term for this kind of sample. For example, in study designs that call for detailed observations of classrooms, researchers have to be able to physically get to the sampled classrooms several times a semester – it's often not feasible to select schools randomly from the CCD (Tipton, 2014). It is rarely desirable however, to employ a pure convenience sample. Rather, researchers develop a *judgment sample* that strives to be as representative as possible of their target population, despite not being a true random sample (Daniel, 2012). For example, selecting schools that cover a range of demographic contexts (for example, urban/rural/suburban, low/middle/high socio-economic status, and so on) does not guarantee, but does work towards, a representative sample. In a study of alternative teacher evaluation methods, Harris et al. (2014) studied 30 school principals and their teachers from a midsized school district in Florida. Although this was a non-probability, convenience sample, the participants were diverse, and similar in important respects to the national population of principals. Most importantly, this sampling strategy allowed them to assemble a variety of complex data, including a series of interviews that might otherwise have been impossible to conduct.

Sampling a diverse set of contexts has other implications for causal inference as well. If the researcher is interested in a particular 'X causes Y' (X→Y) relationship, then it will be easiest to detect a relationship when there is adequate variation in the independent (X) variable of interest. For example, non-experimental studies of the effect of class-size on instruction and learning often suffer from a lack of variation in class size, because for reasons of equity, school administrators work to keep class sizes as even as possible (Ehrenberg et al., 2001). On the other hand, it can be desirable to minimize variation in demographic contexts, such as school and neighborhood poverty concentrations, if this is not an explicit focus of the study. For example, Page (1991) purposefully selected a mostly white, middle-class district in order to study track effects free from the possibly confounding influence of demographic variables.

Indeed, the importance of careful sampling in making causal inferences holds in qualitative as well as quantitative research, in either case, it is crucial to make an effort to account for chance. Eckert's (1989) famous study of social categories and identity at Belten high, reported in the book *Jocks and Burnouts*, is an excellent example of a qualitative study that used a very careful sampling procedure. Eckert was interested in capturing an accurate portrait of social life at Belten. Early in her study, she created a procedure to increase the representativeness of her observations:

> I devised a schedule so that I spent blocks of time at all times of the day, and the week in each area of the school. This means that I spent hours sitting in back halls and odd corners, observing activities or its lack, and getting to know some people who rarely surfaced in other areas of the school. (Eckert, 1989, p. 32)

That being said, much of the cultural activity of the school took place in certain areas (for example, the courtyard), and these naturally received a great deal of her attention. Moreover, as her focus was on peer-group culture and interactions, Eckert's observations necessarily entailed a certain 'snowball' sampling; students often introduced her to their friends. To counteract the potential for non-representativeness, she regularly consulted grade-level lists of students, and randomly selected students for encounters and interactions. In *Jocks and Burnouts*, Eckert makes the causal argument that students' social identities as 'Jocks' and 'Burnouts' affects their academic success in school. Her conclusion is highly convincing, in part because of her efforts to sample the full range of adolescent social experience at Belten.

To summarize, accounting for the possibility that an observed relationship arose by chance is an important basic principle of causal inference. Quantitative research designs that employ a randomized sampling procedure allow the researcher to establish, with a formal test of statistical significance, how likely a group-difference or other statistic might have occurred merely from chance. Yet, even if no formal statistical analyses are planned, such as in a qualitative study, a careful sampling design will greatly improve the likelihood of producing representative findings.

RULING OUT COMPETING EXPLANATIONS

In addition to accounting for chance, researchers attempting to understand a causal relationship between a particular independent variable X and an educational outcome must make an effort to rule out competing explanations for an observed association (Shavelson and Towne, 2002; Campbell and Ross, 1968). Shadish et al. (2002) provide a discussion of common threats/process that may generate a misleading association between two variables. For example, in the study of time trend data, *history* (events occurring concurrently with the treatment or variable of interest) and *maturation* (naturally occurring changes over time in the persons/units being studied) could create an erroneous association. These threats and others were on display in Campbell and Ross's (1968) classic analysis of the 'Connecticut crack-down on speeding'.

In investigating the relationship between students' social identity as a Jock (with a pro-school alignment) or Burnout (with an 'anti-school' alignment) and student's success in school, Eckert had to address two highly compelling competing explanations for the association she observed. First, it could easily have been the case that success in school led to students adopting a given social identity, rather than the other way around. It seems only logical that a student who struggles in school would reorient his or her goals and aspirations away from school and towards other activities. Such a concern with *ambiguous temporal precedence* is especially common in non-experimental, observational data (Shadish et al., 2002). Second, Eckert also found a strong association between students' family background (that is, social class) and social identities in school. Perhaps the observed relationship between students' social identities and school success was really due to a common cause, students' family background. Through the course of her research, Eckert was able to rule out both of these competing explanations. While a lack of success in school certainly exacerbates students' anti-school alignment, students began to affiliate with Burnout peer groups in middle school, often well before they began to encounter difficulties in class, and while they were still active in school activities. Students' family background did seem to directly impac the likelihood of affiliating with the Jocks or Burnouts; Burnouts were much more likely to come from low-SES, working class families. Yet, Burnouts were also represented among the middle and upper-class students at Belten. Within social class categories, social identities had a profound effect on success in school. Successfully ruling out competing explanations is an important element in Eckert's ultimate conclusion, that it is the existence of social identity categories themselves, which is responsible for much of the educational inequality in high schools.

As in Eckert's ethnographic study, in addition to accounting for chance, quantitative researchers seek to improve causal inferences by ruling out the most likely alternative explanations for an observed relationship. While there are technically an infinite set of possible alternative explanations, this does not diminish the importance of ruling out competing explanations in improving causal inferences. Researchers need not concern themselves with explanations that constitute a series of improbable events (Schlesinger, 1991), such explanations amount to chance and are dealt with by careful sampling and replication of research studies. However, as in Eckert's study, there is often a finite set of specific, highly compelling alternative explanations for an observed event or association; it is essential to rule out these 'likely culprits'. For example, Foss et al. (2003) studied the effects of a social norms campaign to reduce high-risk drinking on the University of North Carolina-Chapel Hill campus over the period 1997–2002. In this study, it was important to consider changes in alcohol consumption that occurred during this time period on college campuses throughout the country, which might represent broad cultural trends influencing drinking behavior quite apart from the specific intervention taking place at UNC (a *history* effect).

Quantitative researchers use an array of experimental and quasi-experimental research designs to begin to rule out competing explanations (see Shadish et al., 2002 for an overview of alternative designs). Yet, it is particularly useful to consider the experimental approach, because it provides a 'gold-standard' frame of reference for understanding how quantitative researchers hope to rule out competing explanations, even when using quasi-experimental study designs (Shavelson and Towne, 2002).

EXPERIMENTS AND CAUSAL INFERENCE

In discovery-oriented, 'basic science' educational studies, *experiments* have yielded valuable insights into instruction and learning. In mathematics education, educational researchers have studied how the properties of manipulative objects affect counting and other mathematical skills. Many teaching supplies for use in elementary education are designed to be fun and attention-grabbing, such as small plastic giraffes or other animals. Teachers themselves report a strong preference for such 'perceptually-rich' manipulatives (Petersen and McNeil, 2013). But do such objects actually help children to perform mathematical operations, or might a more bland set of objects be preferable?

In a series of experiments, McNeil and colleagues have tested this question, randomly assigning some students to receive instruction using objects that are perceptually rich, familiar to the student, or both, while other students worked with simple solid-colored plastic discs or sticks (McNeil et al., 2009; Petersen and McNeil, 2013). Indeed it appears that the use of perceptually-rich objects, and especially familiar objects that are seen and used by children outside of school mathematics, reduce students' performance on counting tasks. One explanation for these results is that familiar, perceptually rich objects run the risk of attracting attention to the object itself and away from the mathematical concepts.

Experimental designs are also useful in studying larger scale questions of educational policy and reform. Researchers at the National Center on Performance Incentives have studied the relationship between incentive pay programs and teacher effectiveness. Yuan et al. (2013) report the results from three major studies involving the random assignment of teachers to incentive pay programs. Do incentive pay programs increase teachers' work effort and focus on instructional improvement? These studies, in Tennessee, Texas, and New York City, involved different grade levels and subject matters, and varying systems of teacher evaluation and bonus pay (as much as $15,000 for some teachers in the Tennessee study). The common feature was that teachers in the treatment group were *eligible* for performance-pay (if they met the standard for student achievement growth), while teachers in the control group were not eligible for the bonuses. Results showed that across the three programs, incentive pay had no effect in changing teachers' instructional practices. Teachers may not respond to incentive pay programs based on student-achievement growth criteria because of concerns about observed achievement growth reflecting the influence of family background and social context rather than their own instruction.

The power of an experiment to rule out competing explanations is due to the random assignment of participants to treatment and control groups. When the experimental treatment has been randomly assigned, we know that there are no other variables out there that are systematically related to the treatment, any relation is sheer chance, and unlikely to matter with a large enough sample size. For example, had Eckert been able to randomly assign students a social identity at Belten, she would not have had to worry about family background as a competing explanation, since the groups would contain a random mix of students of different family background.[6]

If experiments are generally effective at ruling out competing explanations and attaining internal validity, issues of external validity and generalizability often arise in experiments. In the case of research using constrained, laboratory-setting counting tasks, educators may wonder whether the results generalize to the classroom learning context more broadly. For example, in using manipulatives to teach basic mathematical operations, perceptually rich objects may be useful in keeping mathematical instruction fun and engaging over a series of lessons (Petersen and McNeil, 2013). In the case of experiments in educational policy, the results of small scale, local studies may not hold when 'going to scale'. For example, carefully designed experiments have shown benefits of class-size reduction, but such benefits may be much harder to achieve when enacted as a large scale policy in an entire state (Ehrenberg et al., 2001).[7] In addition, while experimental designs are a powerful tool for making causal inferences, they are often not feasible in the educational sciences. Thus, educational researchers often employ quasi-experimental research designs in an effort to rule out competing explanations.

CONTROLLING FOR CONFOUNDING VARIABLES IN OBSERVATIONAL STUDIES

Studies of curriculum and instruction in particular often involve naturalistic settings – real students in real classrooms and schools. For example, instead of studying differences in teacher expectations induced by a research team, researchers are interested in understanding the effects of teacher expectations that occur naturally, as teachers interact with students and develop cultural models of how students engage in schoolwork (see Jussim and Harber, 2005 for a review of the literature on teacher expectations). In this case, a *quasi-experimental* research design is preferred, where the effect of a key variable of interest (for example, teacher expectations) is identified using observational data, and analyzed with statistical models that account for relationships among observed variables. In quasi-experimental designs, quantitative researchers must carefully measure not only those variables directly related to their hypothesis (the independent, or predictor variable and the dependent, or outcome variable), but also potential *confounding variables*, which might be related to both the key independent variable and dependent variable in their study. Figure 4.1 shows an example of a potential confounding relationship schematically.[8]

If the researcher is able to identify and measure important potential confounding variables, these variables can be eliminated as competing explanations by

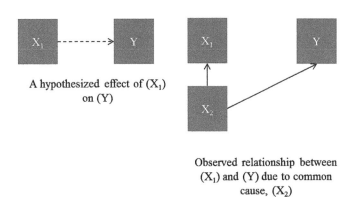

Figure 4.1   **Observed relationship attributed to a common cause**

using them as control variables in statistical models. *Regression models*, a family of statistical techniques well-suited to identifying the effect of a key independent variable while taking into account confounding variables, often form the basis of statistical analyses of quasi-experimental data (Harrison and Raudenbush, 2006). However, more basic techniques can also be used to control for confounding variables, although they are less flexible and efficient, statistically, than regression models. For example, by making comparisons only among respondents with the same attributes on the confounding variable (or *within categories* of the potentially confounding variable), we can rule out that variable as a competing explanation. This was the approach used by Eckert; among those students of similar family background, what effect does social identity seem to have on school success? Research on English and language arts achievement among students of Hispanic ethnicity provides a quantitative example of such an approach.

Hemphill et al. (2011) report data on reading achievement in the NAEP data that explores the achievement of Hispanic students. In 2009, the US national Hispanic-white reading gap was 25 points in Grade 4, and 24 points in Grade 8, a very large and statistically significant difference. While there are a host of factors which might explain this gap (Tienda and Mitchell, 2006), one of the most important is that many Hispanic students, and/or their families, are recent immigrants to the United States, and they begin school as English Language Learners (ELL students). Table 4.2 summarizes several of the findings from Hemphill et al's., report (8th graders only). In 2009, 35 percent of Hispanic 4th graders and 20 percent of Hispanic 8th graders were ELL students. An additional factor is that Hispanic students are more likely to be raised in families living at or near the poverty line; in 2009, 74 percent of Hispanic 8th grade students were eligible

Table 4.2   Selected results from the 2009 National Assessment of Educational Progress (NAEP) main assessments in reading, 8th grade (compiled from Hemphill et al., 2011).

	Non-Hispanic Whites		Hispanics		
	% of respondents	Mean Scale Score	% of respondents	Mean Scale Score	Achievement Gap
Total:	100	271	100	248	24
ELL	—	—	20	217	39[a]
Non-ELL	—	—	80	256	15[b]
Poor[b]	24	258	72	244	14
Non-Poor	76	276	28	259	17

Notes:

[a] Gap calculated between ELL Hispanic students and non-ELL Hispanic students.

[b] Gap calculated with overall non-Hispanic white mean.

[c] Eligible for the National School Lunch Program free- or reduced-price lunches.

— not reported due to small sample size (less < .5 % of sample).

for free or reduced price lunch due to poverty status, as opposed to only 24 percent of whites. Comparisons within categories of poverty and ELL status reveal that Hispanic ethnicity is less strongly associated with reduced reading achievement than an initial comparison might seem to imply. Considering only those non-Hispanic whites and Hispanics who are eligible for free or reduced lunch, the gap shrinks to 14 points. Similarly, there is only a 15-point gap between non-ELL Hispanic students and whites. Together, poverty status and English-Language Learner status account for much of the Hispanic-white achievement gap in reading.[9] In this example, the raw gap of 25 points is an accurate assessment of achievement differentials between Hispanics and non-Hispanic whites, but without taking into account a few basic explanatory variables, it might be easily misattributed to cultural differences (for example, hypotheses about parenting among Hispanics). While this example concerns a 'nonmanipulable' variable, it is nevertheless important to parse out the dimensions of such inequality because it can indicate the most fruitful ameliorative directions for intervention (Shadish et al., 2002, p. 8).

LONGITUDINAL ANALYSIS: PRE-TEST MEASURES OF ACHIEVEMENT IN EDUCATIONAL RESEARCH

Educational research is often focused on assessing achievement *growth*, how much students learn during a lesson, unit, or year. Unfortunately, what is often available as data from states and districts is *cross-sectional*: measures of achievement at a given point in time (Harris, 2011). It is tempting for researchers to make inferences about instructional effectiveness with cross-sectional data, but *longitudinal* data with repeated measures of achievement is much preferred for making causal inferences. Using longitudinal data helps address a simple competing explanation for group differences in performance in cross-sectional data, that the groups were different to begin with!

As an example consider, a study by Anderson et al. (1988) of reading development in elementary school, which used activity logs to track out-of-school time use over an extended period of weeks. Many studies have found that children vary a great deal in the amount of reading they do outside of school. In Anderson et al.'s study, children at the 90th percentile, the active readers at the top of the distribution, read for more than 40 minutes a day, which would amount to more than two million words per year, not counting words encountered at school. In contrast, the average child (50th percentile) reads very little, less than 15 minutes per day, only about 600,000 words per year outside of school. How does out-of-school reading affect reading comprehension, reading speed, or vocabulary as children learn new words by making context inferences? Anderson et al. found relatively strong correlations between reported reading time and these measures of literacy development in the fifth grade; the active readers scored much higher on reading comprehension, speed, and even vocabulary. However, closer analysis revealed that active readers were already higher achieving in second grade. Indeed, the observed association between reading out-of-school and vocabulary declined by 45 percent when considering growth as opposed to point-in-time vocabulary status. Out-of-school reading does appear to be an important component of literacy development, but the relationship is not quite as strong as it may appear at a given grade level.

SUMMARY

Quantitative researchers attempt to rule out competing explanations using experimental designs or by identifying and measuring important control variables in quasi-experimental observational studies. It is difficult to produce a causal inference using a quasi-experimental approach that is equivalent to results from an experiment, because the task of identifying potential confounding variables is open-ended, it's always possible to come up with new explanations that require additional data to investigate.[10] Moreover, we may have difficulty measuring certain variables in practice, and thus, not be able to fully control for a potential cause.[11] At the same time, using quasi-experimental methods we can rule out the likely culprits, which goes a long way towards improving causal inferences. Importantly, while quasi-experimental studies may lead to the use of complex statistical models, the underlying logic of controlling for confounding variables in a quantitative framework is similar to that used by qualitative researchers.

EXPLAINING CAUSATION

One reason for a healthy skepticism about findings from quasi-experimental studies is that it is possible to identify a statistically significant association between two variables, without having any real understanding of why that association might occur (Shadish et al., 2002). In educational research, a classic example of justifiable skepticism concerns school-to-school differences in observed achievement. It may seem only logical to conclude that schools with higher mean test scores are 'highly effective schools' where classroom instruction is exemplary, and schools with lower mean test scores are ineffective instructional environments. Indeed, the landmark No Child Left Behind Act in the US was premised on this assumption. Yet, hundreds of studies of school effects show otherwise; the vast majority of school-to-school differences in mean achievement have little to do with the effectiveness of a given school's instructional environments, but instead, can be traced to the non-school influences of families, neighborhoods, and society (Scheerens and Bosker, 1997; Coleman, 1990). Educational researchers are justifiably skeptical of those who would claim a causal relationship between two phenomena, merely because a statistically significant relationship has been observed. Instead, *causal inferences must be supported by one or more explanatory mechanisms.*

In Eckert's (1989) study of social categories in high school, it was vitally important to uncover the logic of students' affiliation with Burnout peer groups. It seems likely that an anti-school alignment would affect students' success in school (and Eckert presented a multitude of evidence showing how teachers and other school personnel responded to the Burnouts), but why would a student want to affiliate with a lower-status peer group in the first place? At Belten High, the Jocks competed fiercely for social status; it took a concerted effort to cultivate popularity and present an image of being 'flawless'. In contrast, the Burnouts cultivated a self-sufficient, egalitarian peer group with a high degree of social solidarity. Among the burnouts it was okay to have trouble at home or at school. Moreover, much of the Burnouts' social life occurred outside of school, while the Jocks immersed themselves in officially sponsored school activities. Rather than being seen primarily as low-status, the Burnouts saw themselves as independent young adults and each other as welcoming. Importantly, Eckert did not anticipate this understanding of the logic of peer group affiliation prior to her study. Rather, it developed over time from her in-depth observations and interviews of students. The flexibility to pursue new explanations as they arise during data collection is a defining feature of much ethnographic research that adopts a *Grounded* or *Emergent* perspective (Glaser, 1992; Glaser and Strauss, 1965; Jaccard and Jacoby, 2010).

Page's (1991) study of tracking is another example of emergent research that explains causation. In order to show how the tracking system itself affected classroom instruction, Page (1991) needed to show that teachers' instructional decisions were affected by deeply held cultural beliefs about low-track students, not simply to rational decisions about the appropriateness of materials and methods for any given lesson (see also Caughlan and Kelly, 2004).

As in these examples from qualitative research, *the best quantitative research tells a compelling story of how a causal relationship works.* In order to do so, quantitative researchers must identify and measure *mediating* (also called 'intervening') *variables.*

If we believe that the basic association between two variables, (X_1) and (Y) is causal, and that (X_1) causes (Y) and not the other way around, we might still posit that the effect of (X_1) on (Y) is indirect, that it operates through some other intervening variable (X_2). An intervening relationship is represented graphically in Figure 4.2.

In educational research, researchers have hypothesized, and demonstrated, a relationship between the quantity and quality of schooling an individual receives, and a wide variety of life outcomes, from political participation, physical health and well-being, psychological well-being, family outcomes, and so on. Pallas (2000) argues that many of these relationships might be accounted for by three

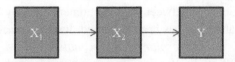

Figure 4.2   Effect of (X₁) mediated by (X₂)

broad categories of intervening variables; knowledge and cognitive development, socio-economic conditions, and other workplace conditions. For example, the relationship between education (X_1) and life expectancy (Y) might be accounted for by an intervening variable, income (X_2). Education has a positive effect on life expectancy *because* it increases income, making available better health care. Alternately, education might affect workplace conditions, such as the amount of stress, or environmental hazards encountered on the job, and thereby ultimately affect life expectancy. It is easy to see how the effect of education on life expectancy might be mediated by a host of processes that can be explicitly identified and measured.

Many social processes are complex, with multiple causes. An alternate schematic (Figure 4.3) represents an intervening relationship where the effect of (X_1) is only partially mediated or explained by (X_2). The simple relationship between (X_1) and (Y) is called the *total* or *reduced-form* effect. The direct effect of (X_1), represented by path (A*), that remains after controlling for (X_2), is called the *partial* effect. We call the effect of (X_1) on (Y) *via* (X_2), that part of the relationship that is accounted for by (X_2), the *indirect* effect.[12] Although more complicated, this is probably a more accurate representation of many causal effects in education.

Notice that mediating variables are in some sense quite similar, conceptually, to a confounding variable. In either case, we cannot adequately identify a direct causal effect (A*) of the key independent variable (X_1) on our dependent variable (Y), without measuring and accounting for (X_2). Yet, a mediating variable is very different from a confounding variable in that we posit that (X_1) causes

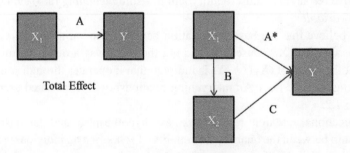

Figure 4.3   (X₁) has both a direct and indirect effect on (Y)

(X_2) and not the other way around. If (X_1) causes (X_2) then we think of the total or reduced-form effect as a true, meaningful effect, whereas if (X_2) is a common cause of (X_1) and (Y), the reduced-form relationship between (X_1) and (Y) is spurious. The difference between a confounding relationship and a mediating relationship becomes clear when we think about manipulating (X_1). In a situation where the association between (X_1) and (Y) is due to a confounding variable, increasing (X_1) would not have any effect on Y. In a situation where the association between (X_1) and (Y) was mediated by (X_2), increasing (X_1) would lead to a real increase in (Y), albeit by first affecting (X_2). Of course, documenting confounding relationships may be of important substantive interest to researchers interested in addressing common stereotypes or misconceptions.

Efforts to sort out various confounding, mediating, and other relationships between measured variables are an important part of quasi-experimental approaches to causal inference. Blau and Duncan's (1967) landmark study of the status attainment process in America, reported in *The American Occupational Structure*, was one of the first major empirical studies to parse out the direct and indirect effects of education on major life outcomes. Blau and Duncan were concerned with the so called 'intergenerational transmission of advantage', the tendency for individuals born into a high social status family to attain a high social status themselves. Generally speaking (Blau and Duncan broke the statistics down into various categories), if a respondent in the early 1960s had a father who had a white-collar occupation, they had about a 55 percent chance of their first job being in a white-collar occupation. In contrast, if the respondent's father had a blue-collar occupation, they had only about a 25 percent chance of having a white-collar occupation themselves. Was there a mediating variable that could explain the relationship between family background and the occupational status of the respondent? What accounts for the strong intergenerational transmission of advantage? Education of course! About 46 percent of the total association between fathers' and sons' occupational status (Path A in Figure 4.3) is explained by educational attainment (the indirect effect, Path B*C).[13]

Blau and Duncan estimated the importance of education in the status attainment process formally, performing calculations on regression coefficients to trace out effects and estimate the relative contribution of variables to an outcome in terms of specific percentages. The 'path models' they generated often involved many variables and multiple stages. However, basic relationships of the kind diagramed in Figure 4.3 can be estimated with correlation coefficients and simple regression models. Indeed, it is possible to capture the essence of explaining causation in a quasi-experimental study simply by performing a series of bivariate analyses sequentially; first showing the total relationship between the key independent (X_1) and dependent variable (Y), then showing how (X_1) is related to (X_2), then showing how (X_2) leads to (Y). Importantly though, the researcher must anticipate analyses of relevant intervening variables by identifying and measuring them as part of the data collection.

Crosnoe's (2011) research on the relationship between student perceptions of 'fitting-in' and academic outcomes is a good example of a simple, sequential approach to explaining causation. Crosnoe studied the relationship between feelings of not fitting in (for example, 'did not feel part of things at school', 'felt rejected or unwanted', and so on) and subsequent college enrollment in a longitudinal sample of more than 7,000 students. First, Crosnoe examined the link between the number of feelings of not fitting in and college attendance. The odds of attending college drop precipitously for students who don't fit in; compared to students who report no feelings of not fitting in, students reporting two such feelings were less than half as likely to go to college, while students reporting five feelings of not fitting in were five times less likely to go to college. Next, Crosnoe showed that feelings of not fitting in were associated with two important mechanisms linked with college attendance, academic preparation such as GPA and advanced academic course taking, and counterproductive coping mechanisms such as drug use and truancy. These mechanisms did indeed substantially explain the observed relationship between fitting in and college attendance. For example, among boys, students with one feeling of not fitting in had 48 percent lower odds of attending college than those who reported no such feelings. However, among boys who were similarly academically prepared, the difference in odds of college attendance dropped to just 22 percent.

As a final example of explaining causation, consider Lareau's (2000) qualitative study of social class and parental involvement reported in *Home Advantage*. As in other studies of parental involvement, Lareau found many important disparities in school involvement between working- and middle-class parents. In the views of many teachers, school administrators, and the public as a whole, the explanation for the reduced involvement of working-class parents is simple; they value education less than middle-class parents. As one principal put it:

> They don't value education because they don't have much of one themselves. [Since] they don't value education as much as they could, they don't put those values and expectations on their kids.

Another common explanation for lower levels of involvement among low-SES parents is institutional discrimination; schools are blamed for not reaching out to working-class parents. In the elementary schools Lareau studied, neither of these common explanations was sufficient to explain patterns of parental involvement. Contrary to the stereotype, working-class parents appeared to value education as much as any parent. Nor was there any lack of effort on the schools' part to solicit the involvement of working-class parents in their children's schooling.

Instead, Lareau identified several cultural factors, tightly linked with social class, which explained why working-class parents were often less involved, and when they were involved, less effective in securing additional resources or alternative schooling arrangements for their children. First, working-class parents often lack the educational skills to approach managing their children's career with confidence, to help them with school-work, and to interact with sophisti-cated teachers and school administrators. Parental involvement is literally harder and more anxiety-producing for working-class parents, something often over-looked when reduced involvement is attributed to values. Middle-class parents often think of teachers as contract-professionals, working in essence, for the bet-terment of their child, who should thus be highly responsive to parental requests. Meanwhile, working-class parents often regard teachers as expert-professionals, who they should *defer* to. Likewise, assisting a child with academic homework is not as easy for parents who rely less heavily on those skills in their own work lives. Second, working-class parents draw a sharp distinction between work and home, and consequently, school and home. After-school time is seen as an oppor-tunity to unwind and relax. Middle-class parents on the other hand, view a child's education as a 'twenty-four a day experience, which took place both at school *and* at home., just as the [middle-class] fathers labored both at work and at home' (Lareau, 2000, p. 115). Third, working-class parents lacked the social networks that provide them with important information that they can use to improve their kids' chances of success in school. Thus, working-class parents had less reason to be involved in the first place. Lareau concluded; 'Social class does make a dif-ference, but its effects are less direct and more complex than commonly believed' (ibid., p. 107).

The underlying logic employed by Blau and Duncan is similar to that of Lareau in *Home Advantage*. In both cases, the goal is to go beyond the total, or reduced-form relationship between two variables, in order to show how/why that relationship exists. Blau and Duncan's study was exemplary in using nation-ally representative data, and newly developed (at that time) statistical techniques, to show just how important education was in the status attainment process in America. Lareau used in-depth interviews and observations to identify the basic elements of culture that mediate the relationship between social class and parent-ing practices.

DATA MINING, AD HOC THEORIES, AND EXPLAINING CAUSATION

Students of empirical research are often taught the phrase, 'correlation does not imply causation'. This phrase is used by quantitative methodologists to convey reasoned skepticism; the observed relationship might not be causal at all, but due to some third, confounding variable, or even if truly causal, variable Y might be causing X rather than the other way around (Shadish et al., 2002). Unfortunately, I have sometimes seen this aphorism misunderstood to mean that observed cor-relations are essentially meaningless. Of course, any particular statistically sig-nificant correlation could indeed be merely chance, but that probability, by definition, is generally low. When an observed association between two variables is found repeatedly in many studies, we must admit that it has become an empirical regularity; *something* is clearly causing that association. For example, few would deny that girls now outperform boys in English and language arts at most grade levels (NCES, 2010), the question is why? The phrase, 'correlation does not imply causation' alerts us simply that it may not be the simplest or most commonly given explanation that accounts for the association. In particular, beyond a mere observed association, in order to believe that a particular variable (X) is causing another variable (Y), it is important to have further evidence that shows how that causation works.

In addition, some researchers take exception with the temporal-ordering of inductive quantitative research, believing that 'after-the-fact' explanations are inherently flawed. For example, taken to an extreme, the inductive approach to educational research might involve 'mining' an educational database for statistically significant associations; running thousands of correlations between pairs of variables until some interesting finding emerged. Then, taking an observed correlation as a starting point, the analyst might begin a more detailed investigation, ultimately formulating a theory to accommodate the data. Many researchers would object to this process as being 'ad hoc', and fundamentally a flawed approach to research. Indeed, quantitative researchers have shown that tests of statistical significance that result from data mining may be highly misleading, and have devised formal statistical tests to illustrate this concern (White, 2000; Sullivan et al., 2001). It's hardly surprising they argue; that when you consider thousands of possible statistical tests, a few should show up as statistically significant.

Yet, in other fields of research (public opinion research, marketing and consumer services, epidemiology, and so on), data mining, when carefully performed and when tests of statistical significance are appropriately based on new data, is considered perfectly legitimate (Obenshain, 2004; Murray et al., 2009). How can these two divergent viewpoints be reconciled? In some basic sense, I agree with Schlesinger (1991, p. 125) that, 'the time at which it is advanced makes absolutely no difference to the credibility of a hypothesis'. A good theory is one that explains the data, and a growing set of like phenomenon as new data is collected. The real problem that arises from extreme forms of inductive reasoning (that is, data mining) is not the timing of a hypothesis with respect to the data, but that a causal hypothesis might be put forth without also offering and testing a compelling mechanism or set of explanations.

In summary, educational researchers are justifiably skeptical of those who would claim a causal relationship between two phenomena merely because a statistically significant relationship has been observed. However, this skepticism is justified on the grounds that *causal inferences must be supported by one or more explanatory mechanisms*, not based on the time at which an explanation is advanced, or even how a researcher happened upon a hypothesis in the first place.

CONCLUSION

In this chapter, I have provided examples which illustrate that the best quantitative research has much in common with the best qualitative research. In both cases, causal inferences are supported by efforts to account for chance, rule out competing explanations, and explain causation. The quantitative approach differs from the qualitative principally in adopting a formalized, statistical approach to analyzing observed relationships – the fundamental issues in causal inference are the same.

In so far as quantitative studies often employ large probability samples, they are well-suited to account for chance. Ideally, quasi-experimental research begins with a careful probability sampling procedure, to generate a database that is representative of the population of interest. However, in educational research, true probability samples are often not feasible, in which case, a judgment sample can be obtained which is as representative as possible, and tests of statistical significance may be conducted with caution. Although accounting for chance is a less formal component of qualitative research, a careful approach to sampling will generate data that is as representative as possible of the phenomenon of interest.

Furthermore, in order to rule out competing explanations, educational researchers must identify and measure the most compelling alternative explanations, the likely culprits, for a hypothesized association. Then, the researcher must make an effort to explain causation, identifying one or more mediating variables. This places an important obligation on the researcher to pay close attention to theory building prior to study design and throughout the data collection.

Then again, in any single study, it may not be possible to anticipate all of the possible competing explanations and causal mechanisms, or to measure them fully. Quantitative researchers face the particular challenge of needing to have survey and other measures designed when data collection begins, and thus must anticipate competing explanations and the identification of causal mechanisms ahead of time. Qualitative researchers conducting long-term, in-depth analyses of the kind described in this chapter are perhaps better positioned to rule out competing explanations and explain causation because of the flexibility to pursue new explanations as they emerge during the data collection. Taken as a whole, the need to address all three principles of causal inference suggests that developing a deep understanding of educational problems and solutions is often a long-term endeavor involving a diverse set of research methods and replication in novel settings and with new measures.

Notes

1 In this chapter I make only passing reference to specific 'threats to validity' referenced in the causal inference literature (e.g. for internal validity: *history*, *maturation*, etc.). Shadish et al. (2002) provide a typology of validity including: statistical conclusion validity, internal validity, construct validity, and external validity. In this chapter, 'accounting for chance' concerns statistical conclusion validity,

while 'ruling out competing explanations' and 'explaining causation' concern internal validity. External validity is also discussed in this chapter to a lesser extent, but issues of construct validity are set aside.

2   Certain study designs in educational research lead to presentation of quantitative but not statistical findings, even if the researcher adopts an informal/liberal view on sampling and statistical inference. For example, Kelly and Caughlan (2011) studied instructional episodes depicted in well-known Hollywood teacher narratives. Using the same coding scheme employed in studies of real instruction (Gamoran et al., 1995; Gamoran and Kelly, 2003) Kelly and Caughlan compared Hollywood teachers' classroom discourse to real-world classrooms. They found that Hollywood teachers were far more likely to use engaging discourse practices (e.g. asking authentic, open-ended questions) than in real-world samples of instruction. However, it would not make sense to compare these carefully scripted instructional scenes statistically to real-world classrooms. The Hollywood film sample characteristics are 'statistics' only in the sense that we frequently refer to proportions, means, etc. as statistics, but they are not true sample statistics. In general, there may be many cases where instructional data is inherently non-representative of typical instruction (see also Caughlan et al., 2013).

3   Or more technically, 'A simple random sample is selected from a population such that each possible combination of the specified size has an equal probability of being chosen' (Neter et al., 1993). The distinction concerning combinations of sample elements as opposed to individual elements is important for understanding more complex sample designs.

4   A detailed discussion of the statistical logic of sampling, the assumptions and mathematical principles of sampling distributions, is beyond the scope of this chapter. We refer the reader to texts on sampling (Levy and Lemeshow, 2008) and statistics (Agresti and Finlay, 2009).

5   The data for this study were first collected in 1998 and results were later published (Kelly, 2007). While the statistical robustness of the data were compromised by the sampling procedure, the study was still useful in demonstrating a coding procedure for course taking policies and in generating preliminary results. Moreover, because the sample of 92 schools represents a large fraction of all high schools in North Carolina, the non-random sample was more informative than it otherwise might have been.

6   Randomization will tend to eliminate the risk of competing explanations *on average*. It is still possible, especially with smaller sample sizes for 'unhappy randomization' to occur, where the treatment and control group do differ on an important variable such as family background.

7   See Shadish et al.'s (2002) discussion of this as an issue of external validity (p. 88).

8   Terminology-wise, in Figure 4.1, both (X_1) and (X_2) are independent variables, but we might distinguish (X_1) as being the key variable of interest.

9   Keep in mind that binary categories like ELL and poor/non-poor are very rough simplifications of underlying continuous variables. If more robust measures of family background were available (e.g. income, parental education, home resources, etc.) the gap would shrink further.

10 In a quasi-experimental design those additional explanations, no matter how finite in number, must be foreseen *prior* to the study in order to be measured and included as statistical controls.

11 For example, in many cases, researchers rely on self-reported information from respondents (e.g. 'how often do you complete your homework each week?'). One source of error in self-reported data is social-desirability bias, where respondents give answers that make themselves look good or feel better. Observational data on homework completion for example, may produce a lower average level, and greater variability, than data from self-reports of homework completion. For a fuller discussion of potential errors in regression models see Berry (1993).

12 Mathematically, in a path model, the indirect effect would be calculated by multiplying path B and C together.

13 For the cross-national perspective on intergenerational mobility see Causa and Johansson (2009).

REFERENCES

Agresti, A., and Finlay, B. (2009) *Statistical Methods for the Social Sciences*, 4th Edition. Upper Saddle River, NJ: Pearson.

Anderson, R. C., Wilson, P. T., and Fielding, L. G. (1988) Growth in reading and how children spend their time outside of school. *Reading Research Quarterly*, 23, 285–303.

Berry, W. D. (1993) *Understanding Regression Assumptions*. Thousand Oaks, CA: Sage Publications.

Blau, P. M., and Duncan, O. D. (1967) *The American Occupational Structure*. New York: The Free Press.

Campbell, D. T., and Ross, H. L. (1968) The Connecticut crackdown on speeding: time-series data in quasi-experimental analysis. *Law & Society Review*, 3, 33–54.

Caughlan, S., and Kelly, S. (2004) Bridging methodological gaps: Instructional and institutional effects of tracking in two English classes. *Research in the Teaching of English*, 39, 20–62.

Caughlan, S, Juzwik, M., Borsheim-Black, C., Kelly, S., and Fine, J. (2013) English teacher candidates developing dialogically organized instructional practices. *Research in the Teaching of English*, 47, 212–246.

Causa, O., and Johansson, A. (2009) *Intergenerational social mobility*. OECD Economics Department Working Papers, No. 707, OECD Publishing.

Coleman, J. S. (1990) *Equality and Achievement in Education*. Boulder, CO: Westview Press.

Crosnoe, R. (2011) *Fitting In, Standing Out: Navigating the Social Challenges of High School to Get an Education*. Cambridge: Cambridge University Press.

Daniel, J. (2012) *Sampling Essentials: Practical guidelines for making sample choices*. Thousand Oaks, CA: Sage Publications.

Eckert, P. (1989) *Jocks and Burnouts: Social categories and identity in the high school*. New York: Teachers College Press.

Ehrenberg, R. G., Brewer, D., Gamoran, A., and Willms, J. D. (2001) Class size and student achievement. *Psychological Science in the Public Interest*, 2, 1–30.

Eisenhart, M. (2006) Representing qualitative data. In J. L. Green, G. Camilli, and P. B. Elmore (Eds), *Handbook of Complementary Methods in Education Research*). New York: American Educational Research Association and Routledge, 567–582.

Finley, M. K. (1984) Teachers and tracking in a comprehensive high school. *Sociology of Education*, 57, 233–243.

Foss, R., Diekman, S., Goodwin, A., and Bartley, C. (2003) *Enhancing a norms program to reduce high-risk drinking among first-year students*. Highway Safety Research Center: University of North Carolina-Chapel Hill.

Fowler, F. J. (2002) *Survey Research Methods*, 3rd edition. Thousand Oaks, CA: Sage Publications.

Gamoran, A. and Kelly, S. (2003) On what is learned in school to how schools work: learning and teaching in secondary school English classrooms. In M. T. Hallinan, A. Gamoran, W. Kubitschek, and T. Loveless (Eds) *Stability and Change in American Education: Structure, processes and outcomes*. Clinton Corners, NY: Eliot Werner Publications, 109–126.

Gamoran, A., Nystrand, M., Berends, M., and LePore, P. C. (1995) An organizational analysis of the effects of ability grouping. *American Educational Research Journal*, 32, 687–715.

Glaser, B. (1992) *Basics of Grounded Theory Analysis*. Mill Valley, CA: Sociology Press.

Glaser, B., and Strauss, A. (1965) *Awareness of Dying*. Chicago, IL: Aldine.

Harris, D. N. (2011) *Value-added Measures in Education: What every educator needs to know*. Cambridge, MA: Harvard Education Press.

Harris, D. N., Ingle, W. K., and Rutledge, S. A. (2014) How teacher evaluation methods matter for accountability: A comparative analysis of teacher effectiveness ratings by principals and teacher value-added measures. *American Educational Research Journal*, 51, 73–112.

Harrison, D. M., and Raudenbush, S. W. (2006) Linear regression and hierarchical linear models. In J. L. Greene, G. Camilli, and P. B. Elmore (Eds), *Handbook of Complementary Methods in Education Research*. New York: Routledge, 411–426.

Hemphill, F. C., Vanneman, A., and Rahman, T. (2011) *Achievement Gaps: How Hispanic and white students in public schools perform in mathematics and reading on the National Assessment of Educational Progress*. Statistical Analysis Report. US Department of Education, National Center for Education Statistics (NCES 2011–459).

Holland, P. W. (1986) Statistics and causal inference. *Journal of the American Statistical Association*, 81, 945–970.

Jaccard, J., and Jacoby, J. (2010) *Theory Construction and Model-building Skills: A practical guide for social scientists*. New York: The Guilford Press.

Jussim, L., and Harber, K. D. (2005) Teacher expectations and self-fullfilling prophecies: knowns and unknowns, resolved and unresolved controversies. *Personality and Social Psychology Review*, 9, 131–155.

Kelly, S. (2004) Do increased levels of parental involvement account for the social class difference in track placement? *Social Science Research*, 33, 626–659.

Kelly, S. (2007) The contours of tracking in North Carolina. *The High School Journal*, 90, 15–31.

Kelly, S., and Caughlan, S. (2011) The Hollywood teachers' perspective on authority. *Pedagogies*, 6, 46–65.

Kelly, S., and Price, H. (2011) The correlates of tracking policy: opportunity hoarding, status competition, or a technical-functional explanation? *American Educational Research Journal*, 48, 560–585.

Lareau, A. (2000) *Home Advantage*, 2nd edition. Lanham, MD: Rowman and Littlefield.

Levy, P. S., and Lemeshow, S. (2008) *Sampling of Populations: Methods and applications*, 4th edition. New York: Wiley & Sons.

Marsh, H. W., and Kleitman, S. (2005) Consequences of employment during high school: character building, subversion of academic goals, or a threshold? *American Educational Research Journal*, 42, 331–370.

McNeil, N. M., Uttal, D. H., Jarvin, L., and Sternberg, R. J. (2009) Should you show me the money? Concrete objects both hurt and help performance on mathematics problems. *Learning and Instruction*, 19, 171–184.

Morgan, S. L. and Winship, C. (2007) *Counterfactuals and Causal Inference: Methods and principals for social research*. New York: Cambridge University Press.

Murray, G. R., Riley, C., and Scime, A. (2009) Pre-election polling: Identifying likely voters using iterative expert data mining. *Public Opinion Quarterly*, 73, 159–171.

National Center for Education Statistics (NCES). (2010) *The condition of education, 2010*. US Department of Education (NCES 2010–028).

Neter, J., Wasserman, W., and Whitmore, G. A. (1993) *Applied Statistics*, 4th edition. Boston, MA: Allyn and Bacon.

Obenshain, M. K. (2004) Application of data mining techniques to healthcare data. *Infection Control and Hospital Epidemiology*, 25, 690–695.

Olsen, R. B., Orr, L. L., Bell, S. H., and Stuart, E. A. (2013) External validity in policy evaluations that choose sites purposefully. *Journal of Policy Analysis and Management*, 32, 107–121.

Page, R. N. (1991) *Lower-track Classrooms: A curricular and cultural perspective*. New York: Teachers College Press.

Pallas, A. M. (2000) The effects of schooling on individual lives. In M. Hallinan (Ed.) *Handbook of the Sociology of Education*. New York: Kluwer, 499–528.

Petersen, L. A., and McNeil, N. M. (2013) Effects of perceptually rich manipulatives on preschoolers' counting performance: established knowledge counts. *Child Development*, 84, 1020–1033.

Riessman, C. (2002) Narrative analysis. In A. M. Huberman and M. B. Miles (Eds) *The Qualitative Researchers' Companion*. Thousand Oaks, CA: SAGE Publications, 217–270.

Rubin, D. B. (1978) Bayesian inference for causal effects: the role of randomization. *Annals of Statistics*, 6, 34–58.

Rubin, D. B. (1990) Formal modes of statistical inference for causal effects. *Journal of Statistical Planning and Inference*, 25, 279–292.

Scheerens, J. and Bosker, R. (1997) *The Foundations of Educational Effectiveness*. Oxford: Pergamon.

Schlesinger, G. N. (1991) *The Sweep of Probability*. Notre Dame, IN: University of Notre Dame Press.

Shadish, W. R., and Luellen, J. K. (2006) Quasi-experimental design. In J. L. Green, G. Camilli, and P. B. Elmore (Eds) *Handbook of Complementary Methods In Education Research*. New York: American Educational Research Association and Routledge, 539–550.

Shadish, W. R., Cook, T. D., and Campbell, D. T. (2002) *Experimental and Quasi-experimental Designs for Generalized Causal Inference*. Belmont, CA: Wadsworth Cengage Learning.

Shavelson, R. J., and Towne, L. (Eds) (2002) *Scientific Research in Education*. Washington, DC: National Academy Press.

Sullivan, R., Timmermann, A., and White, H. (2001) Dangers of data mining: the case of calendar effects in stock returns. *Journal of Econometrics*, 105, 249–286.

Tienda, M., and Mitchell, F. (Eds) (2006) *Hispanics and the Future of America*. Washington, DC: The National Academies Press.

Tipton, E. (2013) Improving generalizations from experiments using propensity score subclassification: assumptions, properties, and contexts. *Journal of Educational and Behavioral Statistics*, 38, 239–266.

Tipton, E. (2014) Stratified sampling using cluster analysis: a sample selection strategy for improved generalizations from experiments. *Evaluation Review*, 1–31.

Warren, J. R., and Lee, J. C. (2003) The impact of adolescent employment on high school dropout: differences by individual and labor-market characteristics. *Social Science Research*, 32, 98–128.

White, H. (2000) A reality check for data snooping. *Econometrica*, 68, 1097–1126.

Yuan, K., Le, V-N., McCaffrey, D. F., Marsh, J. A., Hamilton, L., Stecher, B. M., and Springer, M. G. (2013) Incentive pay programs do not affect teacher motivation or reported practices: results from three randomized studies. *Educational Evaluation and Policy Analysis*, 35, 3–22.

5

The Validity and Reliability of Research: A Realist Perspective

Joseph A. Maxwell

Validity, in the broad sense of trustworthiness or credibility, is a fundamental concept for all research. It is hard to imagine anything that could be legitimately called 'research' if the validity of its inferences were substantially in question; as Shadish, Cook, and Campbell state, 'all science and all experiments rely on making such inferences validly' (2002, p. 33). However, the concept of validity has been seriously contested in the recent history of social research (for example, Guba and Lincoln, 1989; Lather, 1993; Lissitz, 2009; Miller, 2008; Teddlie and Tashakkori, 2003, pp. 12, 36–7), particularly between quantitative and qualitative researchers, and there is currently no consensus on what the term means, or even if it is appropriate for all forms of educational research.

In this chapter, I do not attempt to review all of the important work in this area. Instead, I present a specific perspective on validity issues that I believe is illuminating and useful for educational researchers. This perspective is based on philosophical realism, which has been an important, if not the dominant, approach in the philosophy of science, including the philosophy of the social sciences, for over 30 years (Baert, 1998, pp. 189–90), following the demise of logical positivism, which was explicitly operationalist and anti-realist (Norris, 1983; Phillips, 1987).

Philosophic realism in general was defined by Phillips (1987, p. 205) as 'the view that entities exist independently of being perceived, or independently of our theories about them'. In the philosophy of the social sciences, the most important manifestation of realism has been the 'critical realism' most closely associated with the work of Roy Bhaskar (1978, 1989) and others in this tradition (Archer et al., 1998). However, some prominent researchers (for example, Pawson, 2006, p. 20) have taken issue with Bhaskar's more recent development of what he

called 'dialectical critical realism' (Bhaskar, 1993), and have aligned themselves more with Donald Campbell's version of realism (Campbell, 1988),
which he termed 'evolutionary critical realism' (Cook and Campbell, 1979,
pp. 28–30).

The distinctive feature of the approach taken here, which is consistent with
both Bhaskar's and Campbell's positions, is that it combines ontological realism
(there is a real world that exists independently of our perceptions and constructions) with epistemological constructivism (our *knowledge* of this world is inherently our own construction, and not an 'objective' perception). Shadish et al.
(2002, p. 29) argued that 'all scientists are epistemological constructivists and
relativists' in the sense that they believe that *both* the ontological world and the
worlds of ideology, values, and so forth play a role in the construction of scientific knowledge. Conversely, Schwandt (1997), in his *Dictionary of Qualitative
Research*, stated that

> many (if not most, I suspect) qualitative researchers have a common-sense realist *ontology*,
> that is, they take seriously the existence of things, events, structures, people, meanings, and
> so forth in the environment as independent in some way from their experience with them.
> (Schwandt, 1997, p. 134)

I see these two positions as quite compatible, and as a productive stance for
approaching issues of validity in research. (For a much more detailed discussion
of this stance and its relevance for research, see Maxwell, 2013, and Maxwell
and Mittapalli, 2010.) Similar views have been adopted by both quantitative and
qualitative researchers (Hammersley, 1992; Henry et al., 1998; Mark et al., 2000;
Pawson, 2006; Pawson and Tilley, 1997; Seale, 1999). These views have gained
increasing attention even in qualitative research (Clark, 2008; Madill, 2008),
which has largely been dominated, at least in explicit philosophical statements,
by a radical constructivism that denied the existence of a 'real world' to which
our data, results, and theories refer (for example, Denzin and Lincoln, 2005;
Smith, 2008).

I also assume that validity is a more basic concept than reliability. It is generally recognized that the results of a study or measurement must be reliable in
order to be valid, but the reverse is not true–results can be highly reliable, but
invalid. Thus, the main focus of the chapter will be on validity; lack of reliability
is seen mainly as a possible *threat to* validity. Similarly, generalizability (for
example, 'external validity') is also taken to be a separate issue from validity
proper, although the line between these is often blurred.

There have been two main stances toward what makes a study, or its results,
'valid'. The first has treated the validity of a study primarily as a matter of the
design and methods used. In quantitative research, validity is often seen as
dependent on the use of specifically prescribed and well-established designs and
procedures (Brinberg and McGrath, 1985, p. 9). This has been labeled the 'instru-
mentalist' approach to validity (Norris, 1983); it was central to the philosophy of

science known as logical positivism, which had a profound influence on quantitative research. Logical positivists rejected the idea that there was anything other than our sense data that could be the object of scientific investigation; in this way, positivism was staunchly anti-realist in denying that there was a 'real world' beyond the reach of our senses, one to which our theories referred. They insisted that theoretical concepts must be defined in terms of the actual procedures used and the sense data these generated, and that theories were simply 'convenient fictions' that should be judged only by how well they predicted observations, not by their relationship to any external reality (Boyd, 2002; Niiniluoto, 2007; Norris, 1983).

This approach to validity has been prominent in the movement for 'science-based research' in education and other fields, which established a ranking of research designs in terms of their quality and rigor, with randomized experiments as the 'gold standard' for research. In the United States, this was particularly visible in the Education Sciences Reform Act of 2002, which transformed the Office of Educational Research and Improvement, the major source of government funding for educational research, into the Institute of Educational Sciences. This Act stated that 'The term "scientifically based research standards" means research standards that (i) apply rigorous, systematic, and objective methodology to obtain reliable and valid knowledge relevant to education activities and programs; and (ii) present findings and make claims that are appropriate to and supported by the methods that have been employed'. Even the National Research Council's report on *Scientific Research in Education* (2002), which attempted to present a broadly-based consensus that included both quantitative and qualitative research, contained unexamined positivist assumptions about causation that systematically prejudiced its treatment of qualitative research (Erickson and Gutierrez, 2002; Maxwell, 2004a).

In contrast, and partly in reaction to such views, many qualitative researchers repudiated the concept of 'validity' entirely, arguing that this assumed the possibility of 'objective' knowledge, a position that they saw as incompatible with constructivism. They developed alternative concepts such as 'trustworthiness' and 'authenticity', and proposed criteria for the quality of qualitative research that do not depend on the idea of objectivity (for example, Denzin and Lincoln, 2005, p. 24).

However, because these researchers denied the existence of a 'real world' to which their data and conclusions pertained, they typically defined trustworthiness and authenticity in terms of the methods and approaches used, similarly to positivists. For example, Lincoln's and Guba's influential formulation of criteria for trustworthiness in qualitative research, based on 'the assumption of multiple constructed realities' (Lincoln and Guba, 1985, p. 295), relied heavily on the use of specific procedures, such as member checks, self-reflection, prolonged engagement in the setting studied, peer review, rich description, and an 'audit trail' of the research.[1] This approach to validity continues to inform much qualitative research (Miller, 2008).

Despite the prevalence of these views in both qualitative and quantitative research, there is widespread agreement among philosophers that procedural criteria for validity or trustworthiness are seriously flawed. Phillips stated what seems to be a consensus: 'in general it must be recognized that there are *no* procedures that will regularly (or always) yield either sound data or true conclusions' (Phillips, 1987, p. 21). Brinberg and McGrath, dealing with social science generally, made the same point: 'validity is not a commodity that can be purchased with techniques... Rather, validity is like integrity, character, and quality, to be assessed relative to purposes and circumstances' (Brinberg and McGrath, 1985, p. 13; see also Briggs, 2008).

Validity, from this perspective, pertains to the accounts or conclusions reached by using a particular method in a particular context for a particular purpose, not to the method itself, and fundamentally refers to how well these accounts and conclusions help us to understand the actual phenomena studied. This is essentially a realist approach to validity (Hammersley, 1992, 1998; House, 1991; Maxwell, 1992; Norris, 1983; Porter, 2007; Seale, 1999, p. 157) that sees the validity of an account as inherent, not in the procedures used to produce and validate it, but in its relationship to those things that it is intended to be an account *of*.

This stance has gained substantial acceptance in measurement, stemming from Cronbach's statement that one validates interpretations of data, not tests themselves (Cronbach, 1971), and Messick's assertion that 'Validity is not a property of the test or assessment as such, but rather of the meaning of the test scores. These scores are a function not only of the items or stimulus conditions, but also of the persons responding as well as the context of the assessment' (Messick, 1995, p. 741; see also Borsboom et al., 2004, and Gehlbach and Brinkworth, 2011).

It has also been adopted by prominent scholars in both quantitative and qualitative research. Shadish et al., in what is widely recognized as the pre-eminent work on experimental and quasi-experimental designs, stated that 'Validity is a property of inferences. It is *not* a property of designs or methods, for the same designs may contribute to more or less valid inferences under different circumstances.... No method guarantees the validity of an inference' (Shadish et al., 2002, p. 34; italics in original). A classic work on survey research, after critiquing one study, asks 'May one, therefore, conclude that the Gluecks' measurements of these variables are invalid? In order to answer this question, it is necessary to ask what the Gluecks wish to learn from their data' (Hirschi and Selvin, 1973, p. 195). And for ethnographic research, Hammersley and Atkinson (1983, p. 191) state that 'Data in themselves cannot be valid or invalid; what is at issue are the inferences drawn from them'.

This approach does not dismiss the importance of design or methods; it only asserts that these must themselves be assessed in terms of the purposes for which they are used, the contexts of this use, the data, conclusions, and understandings that are drawn from them, and, most importantly, the ways that these understandings and conclusions could be *wrong* – the potential validity threats that must be addressed in order to give these conclusions credibility.

In characterizing this approach as 'realist', I mean that it assumes that there is a real world, one that our theories and research results are attempts to understand, and that validity depends fundamentally on how well these contribute to this understanding. This position sharply contrasts with the views of both logical positivists and radical constructivists, both of whom rejected the idea that there was anything beyond our sense data (for positivists) or constructions (for constructivists) to which our conclusions and theories referred.

This approach does not assume a 'correspondence theory' of truth or validity, since we have no way to independently access reality to determine if our conclusions or theories 'correspond' to this. It also does not assume that there is necessarily a single 'correct' understanding of some aspect of reality; reality is complex, and different theories may simply capture different aspects of that complexity (Greene, 2007, pp. 79–82; Keller, 1992, pp. 73–4). It does, however, assume that we can assess the *adequacy* of our conclusions and theories in enabling us to *deal with* reality – to take actions and anticipate their consequences.

The main challenge for a realist approach to validity is to explain how, if our understandings are inevitably our own fallible constructions rather than 'objective' perceptions or interpretations of actual phenomena, one can possibly have any basis for validity judgments that go beyond procedures and attempt to engage with these real phenomena. Thus, Smith (2008) argued that the absence of any theory-free knowledge 'mean[s] that there is no possibility that reality itself can be an independent referent point for judging the quality of research and for adjudicating among different knowledge claims' (pp. 752–3). For this reason, Smith stated that 'for relativists, the issue of criteria should be thought of as a list of characteristics that define what is considered good or bad inquiry' (p. 753), although he insisted that such lists are always subject to revision. This falls back on what is ultimately a procedural approach to validity.

Smith is certainly correct that realism provides no 'objective' or definitive measure of the validity or invalidity of the conclusions of a study. However, this does not entail that reality has *no* role in assessing the validity (trustworthiness, quality) of these conclusions. The reason for this is central to what is called the 'scientific method': the possibility of *testing* one's conclusions against both existing and potential evidence, with the goal of evaluating the plausibility of alternative interpretations or 'validity threats' to these conclusions (Platt, 1964). It involves identifying the plausible alternatives to the proposed explanation, interpretation, or conclusion, deciding what data exist or could be obtained that would count as evidence for or against this conclusion or the plausible alternatives, and then collecting or examining these data (and possibly other data that turn out to be relevant) to determine the plausibility of these conclusions.

There are numerous specific strategies that can be used for this purpose; for a detailed discussion of these strategies, see Shadish et al. (2002), for experimental research, and Miles and Huberman (1994) and Maxwell (2004b), for qualitative research. However, the important point for this argument is that any assessment of the 'validity' of a study's conclusions is not simply a matter of determining *whether* specific procedures have been used, or even of how carefully or rigorously they have been applied, but of considering the actual *results* of using these procedures, in this particular context, for these purposes, and of how potential validity threats to these results can be addressed. The evaluation of these results depend not simply on the appropriate use of the procedures, but on what the data generated by these procedures, in this specific situation, allow the researcher to legitimately conclude.

This strategy can be applied to both quantitative and qualitative research, although it is obviously incompatible with the radical constructivist position, taken by some qualitative researchers, that there are no phenomena independent of the constructions of the researcher – a stance that is both logically problematic and incompatible with our everyday practices. This approach to validity does, however, require that meanings, beliefs, and other mental and cultural phenomena be taken as real, and thus as things about which conclusions and interpretations can be assessed as more or less valid; this issue is discussed in more detail below.

One unfortunate implication of this stance toward validity is that there can be no generic criteria for definitively assessing validity, no checklist of characteristics or procedures that can be used, independently of the specific purposes, context, and conclusions of a study and the potential validity threats to these conclusions, to adequately evaluate a study in terms of the credibility or trustworthiness of its conclusions. The validity of the study's conclusions depends on the actual use of these procedures in the context of a particular study, and the evidence that this generates, to address the validity threats that are most salient for these conclusions.

Thus, a likely reason for the persistence of procedural criteria for validity, in both quantitative and qualitative research, is that procedures are much easier to identify and evaluate in publications or manuscripts than are the validity threats to the study's conclusions, and their plausibility in the specific context of the study. However, this resembles the joke about the person who had lost his car keys at night and was looking for them under the streetlight, rather than in the middle of the block where he dropped them, because the light was better there (Kaplan, 1964, p. 11).

Later in this chapter, I discuss the four traditional categories of validity in quantitative research (statistical conclusion validity, construct validity, internal validity, and external validity) and the qualitative analogues of these, and what counts as evidence for addressing validity issues. Before doing this, however, I want to address the kinds of *phenomena* that research aims at understanding, and the implications that these have for the types of validity with which researchers must deal. This is an area in which ontology is particularly relevant; the sorts of validity threats that are most salient, and the procedures that address these, depend on the nature of the phenomena investigated. I will briefly discuss three broad categories of phenomena to which validity can refer, and our understanding of these: description, meaning/interpretation, and explanation. These categories were described by Abraham Kaplan in his classic *The Conduct of Inquiry* (1964); for a slightly different treatment of these, see Maxwell (1992).

DESCRIPTION

The most basic phenomena that educational researchers deal with are the physical objects and events, and behavior (including speech) of participants, that occur in the settings we study. Although we have no 'objective' or neutral access to these, since our observations are inherently shaped by our own conceptual categories and assumptions (epistemological constructivism), these are the phenomena to which we have the *most* direct access, through our sense organs. Many potential validity threats to our descriptions of these (for example, researcher biases, selective perception, faulty memory) can be substantially addressed through video and audio recording, although these recordings still need to be interpreted by the researcher. It is possible that such recordings may not be adequate to resolve questions of descriptive validity; this is clear from the use of 'instant replay' in sports. However, what is also clear is that such data often *are* adequate to resolve these issues *beyond a reasonable doubt* – the everyday standard for such decisions (Scriven, 2008).

Descriptive validity can also pertain to numerically descriptive aspects of accounts (descriptive statistics). A claim that a certain phenomenon was frequent, typical, or rare in a specific situation at the time it was observed – for example, that few students raised their hands in response to the teacher's question – is also a descriptive claim, and numerical precision can support this claim.

The reliability of descriptive accounts, in my view, refers not to an aspect of validity, or to a separate issue from validity, but to a particular type of threat to validity. If different observers or methods produce descriptively different accounts of the same events or situations, this challenges the descriptive validity of the accounts. This problem could be resolved either by modification of the accounts, so that different researchers come to agree on their descriptive accuracy, or by realizing that the differences were due to differences in the perspectives, situations, and purposes of the researchers, and were both descriptively valid given these differences. Both of these outcomes are common results of efforts to assess reliability in qualitative research (Miller, 2008), and neither should be given priority over the other.

MEANING/INTERPRETATION

However, educational researchers are not concerned solely, or even primarily, with providing a valid description of the physical objects, events, and behaviors in the settings they study. They are also concerned with what these objects, events, and behaviors *mean* to the people engaged in and with them – 'meaning' being used in the broad sense of cognition, values, emotions, intentions, and other 'mental' phenomena. Ontologically, critical realists generally see meanings as just as 'real' as physical objects; they are simply not accessible to direct observation, and are understood by means of a different conceptual framework. (For a detailed justification for this understanding of meaning and mind, see Putnam, 1999, and Maxwell, 2013.) However, because the language and concepts used for these are inherently ideational or mental, rather than physical, the nature of the understanding, validity, and validity threats that pertain to them are substantially different from those involved in descriptive validity. In particular, the *misinterpretation* of participants' statements and responses is a serious threat to the validity of any conclusions about the meaning of these, or about their influence on other phenomena.

This category of phenomena is central to qualitative research, with its goal of understanding not simply behavior, but the 'participants' perspectives'. It is also fundamental to quantitative research that involves participants' responses to 'instruments' such as questionnaires, knowledge tests, and psychological assessments. This is an area for which qualitative methods can provide substantial validity support to quantitative research, both in the development of such instruments and in understanding the results (for detailed examples, see Weisner, 2002). Qualitative researchers have developed systematic methods for addressing such threats, both in interviewing techniques (for example, Weiss, 1994) and in follow-up strategies such as 'member checks' (Sandelowski, 2008).

EXPLANATION

Explanation, and the phenomena with which it deals, differ from both description and interpretation. An explanation is an answer to *why* something happened or exists; it incorporates description, interpretation, or both, but it involves integrating these into a *theory* of the phenomena studied. In quantitative research, explanation has usually meant *causal* explanation. However, there are two starkly contrasting views of causation in the quantitative research literature, and in philosophy.

The dominant view in quantitative research has been that causation is simply the regular, observable association of variables, a causal 'law' that may be probabilistic as well as deterministic; this view is derived from logical positivism, which rejected the idea of anything beyond observable relationships in our data. This view of causation is still prominent in quantitative research, and is implicit in some of the current, most respected quantitative approaches to causal research (for example, Mulaik, 2009, pp. 63–87; Murnane and Willett, 2010, pp. 26–38).

This theory led to the rejection of the entire concept of causation, and therefore causal explanation, by many qualitative researchers. (For a more detailed discussion of these issues, and strategies for dealing with potential validity threats, see Maxwell, 2004b, 2012a.)

However, a quite different understanding of causation has emerged in philosophy since the demise of positivism. Salmon (1984, 1989, 1998), one of the main proponents of this view, stated that this approach 'makes explanatory knowledge into knowledge of the ... mechanisms by which nature works.... It exhibits the ways in which the things we want to explain come about' (Salmon, 1989, pp. 182–3). This view is characteristic of realist approaches in the social sciences (for example, Huberman and Miles, 1985; Pawson and Tilley, 1997, pp. 67–8; Sayer, 1992, pp. 2–3). Pawson argued that

> The nature of causality in social programmes is such that any synthesis of evidence on whether they work will need to investigate how they work. This requires unearthing information on mechanisms, contexts, and outcomes. The central quest is to understand the conditions of programme efficacy and this will involve the synthesis in investigating for whom, in what circumstances, and in what respects a family of programmes work. (Pawson, 2006, p. 25)

These issues of mechanism (process) and context are ones for which qualitative research can make a substantial contribution to our understanding of causality in our research (Anderson and Scott, 2012; Donmoyer, 2012; Maxwell, 2012b). However, the theory of causation on which most quantitative research is based, and the bias toward quantitative and experimental methods that this produces, have largely excluded qualitative methods from 'causal' research, except in an exploratory and supporting capacity (for example, National Research Council, 2002; see Maxwell, 2004a).

These issues are obviously relevant to the validity of our research findings and how we can assess these. I therefore turn to the traditional categories of validity in research, and attempt to show the importance for these of the previous discussion. I will deal with these in a different order than is usual, because I think a realist perspective reveals some unexpected similarities and differences among these. (For a rather different view of the similarities and differences, see Shadish et al., 2002, pp. 93–5.)

CONSTRUCT VALIDITY AND INTERNAL VALIDITY

These two types of validity are the ones that directly pertain to the particular individuals and settings, and the actual phenomena (variables, relationships, events, or processes), on which data are collected – what Cronbach (1982, p. 78) called *utos*: the units, treatments, observations, and settings actually studied (Shadish et al., 2002, p. 19). Construct validity addresses the validity of the *constructs* in terms of which we understand these. Shadish et al. (2002, p. 38) state that this pertains specifically to inferences to 'higher order' constructs, based on particular observations, and thus treat construct validity as 'generalization' from procedures and data to these constructs. This is a quite different sense of 'generalization' from the way I am using it; also, from a constructivist epistemological perspective, *all* perception and understanding involves constructs whose validity is open to question. However, Shadish et al. provide a thoughtful discussion of inferences to constructs that is quite compatible with critical realism (2002, pp. 66–8), and they describe threats to construct validity, and ways of dealing with these (pp. 72–81), that are relevant to both quantitative and qualitative research (Maxwell, 2013, pp. 128-136).

In experimental research, internal validity is defined by Shadish et al. (2002, p. 38) as whether an observed difference or correlation is a *causal* relationship. This relates primarily to the category of phenomena I have termed 'explanation'. From a realist perspective, as discussed above, this should not be limited to *whether* a causal relationship exists, and its magnitude, but should include a theory of the mechanisms and processes that, in this context, produced the observed outcomes. As Shadish et al. stated,

> the unique strength of experimentation is in describing the consequences attributable to deliberately varying a treatment. We call this *causal description*. In contrast, experiments do less well in clarifying the mechanisms through which and the conditions under which that causal relationship holds—what we call *causal explanation*. (Shadish et al., 2002, p. 9; italics in original)

They list numerous threats to causal *description*, and these are also threats to causal explanations of this description, but causal explanation involves additional threats that relate specifically to the validity of theories, such as the possibility of alternative explanations for the results, and the existence of results that are incompatible with the proposed explanation.

Random assignment is often considered the 'gold standard' for internal validity. Shadish et al. state that 'random assignment eliminates selection bias definitionally, leaving a role only to chance differences' (p. 61). This is true, but it must be remembered that 'bias' refers only to systematic differences, and that chance difference can be a very serious validity threat; the possibility of such differences increases substantially with the number of possibly confounding variables. (See the later discussion of statistical conclusion validity.) In addition, random assignment provides no guarantee of the generalizability (external validity) of the results (Cartwright and Hardie, 2012).

For non-experimental research, internal validity is much less commonly invoked; such studies (often termed 'observational') don't usually attempt to establish causation, because they lack a key feature of experimental and quasi-experimental designs – the ability to manipulate a presumed causal factor and observe the result. Non-experimental studies that do address causation usually employ structural equation modeling or similar advanced statistical methods (for example, Mulaik, 2009; Murnane and Willett, 2010); the validity threats listed below, for statistical conclusion validity, are also relevant here.

STATISTICAL CONCLUSION VALIDITY AND EXTERNAL VALIDITY

The preceding discussion pertains fundamentally to the results, conclusions, or interpretations drawn about the actual people, treatments, attributes, outcomes, and situations on which data were collected. The extension of these results or conclusions to other individuals, interventions, measures, times, or settings than those actually studied is a different matter, which I will treat as generalizability, although in quantitative research these have usually been classified as forms of validity. I will discuss statistical conclusion validity, and the analogue of this for qualitative research, before dealing with external validity, and in substantially more detail, because of the widespread misunderstandings and misuses of statistical inference for addressing this. (For a more detailed discussion of generalization in qualitative research, see Maxwell and Chmiel, 2014.)

Statistical conclusion validity has played a major role in assessing the validity of quantitative conclusions, although this role is different in survey research and in experimental research. Unfortunately, many definitions of this concept (for example, Shadish et al., 2002, pp. 37–8) fail to state explicitly an important aspect of this concept – that it refers to inferences from the individuals actually included in the study, or from their specific assignment to experimental conditions, to the population from which these individuals were drawn or assigned; Yin (2003, p. 32) defined 'statistical generalization' as occurring when 'an inference is made about a population (or universe) on the basis of empirical data collected about a sample'. It has thus dealt primarily with threats that arise from the specific sampling or assignment procedures used. (For a detailed discussion of statistical conclusion validity and the threats that are relevant to this, see García-Pérez, 2012.)

Survey research is inherently focused on generalizing the results of a study to a larger population than those actually surveyed, usually through some type of systematic sampling. In survey research, inferential statistics (usually, null hypothesis significance testing, or NHST) are commonly used to assess the likelihood that the results found, for the sample actually studied, can be generalized to the population sampled. Researchers need to be aware, however, of two serious limitations on such uses.[2]

First, inferential statistics are only appropriately used when the units actually studied are a probability (simple random or stratified random) sample drawn from some defined population. (Specific tests may involve other assumptions as well, such as normality of distributions.) However, it is extremely difficult to draw a strictly random sample, in the mathematical sense, of some population of interest; such a sample requires that every member of that population have a known, non-zero probability of being selected. In addition, even a randomly selected sample can become effectively non-random through non-response or attrition, since willingness to participate in the study may be correlated with the variables studied. Finally, conscious or inadvertent sampling *bias* can be a serious threat to randomness.

Second, the results of a statistical test do *not* tell you what many researchers believe that they do – that is, the probability that your results are due to chance sampling variation, rather than to an actual relationship between variables in the sampled population. This point has been repeatedly emphasized by statisticians (Cohen, 1994; Gigerenzer, 2004; Nuzzo, 2014, Shadish et al., 2002, p. 43). What a p value actually tells you is the probability, *if* there were no correlation between these variables in the population randomly sampled, that you would find the relationship in your sample that you did (or one more extreme) by chance sampling variation alone. This is *not* the same as the probability that your result *is* due to chance sampling variation, and there is no way to derive the latter from the former unless you have information about the prior likelihood and magnitude of a correlation or difference in that population (Nuzzo, 2014) – information that is almost never available to researchers.[3]

A simple example can illustrate this point. Suppose you get a coin in change from a vending machine, it falls on the floor, and comes up heads. You wonder if this is a fair coin – one that comes up heads more often than tails in the long run. You flip it five times, and get five heads. This is a very unlikely occurrence (less than one chance in twenty, or p <.05) *if* it's a fair coin (one that has an equal likelihood of coming up heads or tails – the null hypothesis). However, it's still much more likely that this coin is fair, and that this particular result *is* due to chance, than it is that the coin is biased. In this case, the 'chance variation' explanation is unlikely, but all other plausible explanations are even more unlikely. If it came up heads *fifty* times, however, the latter possibilities become more plausible. The more improbable it is that your result could have happened by chance *if* you have a fair coin, the more likely it is that an alternative explanation for the result (that the coin is not fair, or that other factors are influencing the outcome), however implausible, is true.

As a result of these critiques, there has been a recent shift toward emphasizing effect sizes and confidence intervals, rather than p values (for example, American Psychological Association, 2010, p. 33; Cumming, 2012; Shadish et al., 2002, p. 43). However, confidence intervals are subject to the same error of interpretation as p values – of assuming that a confidence interval tells you the probability that the true population value falls within this interval. Instead, a 95 percent confidence interval tells you that 95 percent of the confidence intervals based on random samples of this size from this population will capture the true population value – whatever this is. As Cumming (2012) emphasizes, the true population value is not a variable, but a constant; it is the confidence intervals that vary with different samples. For this reason, one journal has now banned both p values and confidence intervals from its pages (Trafimow and Marks, 2015).

For experimental research, the primary purpose for using NHST is different from that for survey research. Randomized experiments rarely use random *sampling* of participants, since it is usually difficult to get randomly-sampled individuals to participate in an experiment. Instead, they typically rely on volunteers; this makes inferences to any larger population highly problematic, since volunteers systematically differ from non-volunteers in numerous, and often unpredictable, ways. However, NHST is used, not to make such inferences, but to determine whether the observed relationship between treatment and outcome variables is actually true of the population assigned to the different conditions, rather than being a result of chance *assignment* variation, which could create spurious differences in the outcomes.

Shadish et al. (2002, p. 38) defined statistical conclusion validity in experimental research as 'the validity of inferences about the correlation (covariation) between treatment and outcome'. They identify two aspects of this: whether the cause and effect covary, and if so, the magnitude of the covariation (ibid., p. 42), and inferential statistics are usually employed for this purpose. I treat this as also a form of generalization, because it involves generalizing from the results of a particular *assignment* of individuals to conditions, to the actual effect of the intervention in this sample.

However, the fundamental problem with this use of NHST is the same as for survey research – that a p value does *not* tell you the likelihood that your results are due to chance assignment variation, rather than to an actual relationship between the variables in the population sampled. Instead, it tells you the likelihood that you would get this result, or one more extreme, *if* there were no actual relationship in the group of participants in the experiment, and any difference or correlation was due only to chance assignment variation. As with survey research, there is no way to derive the former from the latter without additional information about the prior likelihood of a relationship.

This problem has plagued numerous areas of experimental research – in particular, fields such as parapsychology and the study of intercessory prayer (for example, Leibovici, 2001), in which highly significant experimental results are almost certainly artifacts of chance assignment variation, as well as of what has been termed 'p-hacking' – selecting hypotheses for testing, or deciding on sample size, after seeing the data (Nuzzo, 2014).

Chance sampling or assignment variation is always a potential validity threat to inferences from a sample to a population, or to the results of an experimental study, and the most effective ways of dealing with this, within a single study, are to use larger sample sizes than those in many published studies (Trafimow and Marks, 2015), and to stratify the sample or assignment on potentially important confounding variables. Replication is also an important, and underutilized, strategy; it has become a major scandal that many published studies in the social and behavioral sciences and medicine fail to replicate (Nuzzo, 2014; Saey, 2015).

In qualitative research, statistical inference is generally inappropriate, because qualitative researchers rarely use probability sampling. However, the task of generalization from the specific individuals, events, or settings on which data are collected, to the group, institution, or case studied, is still essential (cf. Brown-Saracino et al., 2008; Erickson, 1986; Maxwell and Chmiel, 2014), and such generalization obviously involves issues of sampling or selection. Miles and Huberman (1984, p. 36) asked, 'Knowing, then, that one cannot study everyone everywhere doing everything, even within a single case, how does one limit the parameters of a study?' They argued:

> Remember that you are not only sampling *people*, but also *settings, events, and processes*. It is important to line up these parameters with the research questions as well, and to consider whether your choices are doing a representative, time-efficient job of answering them. (ibid., p. 41)

For qualitative research, this type of generalization has been termed *petite generalization* (generalization *within* a case) by Erickson (1986), and *lower-order generalizability* (the generalizability of findings *within* the unit of analysis) by Brown-Saracino et al. (2008). Maxwell and Chmiel (2014) referred to these as *internal generalization*, as opposed to *external generalization* (the attempt to extend the findings or interpretations to other cases or populations than those actually studied, traditionally termed *external validity*).

Internal generalization is far more important for most qualitative studies than external generalization (generalization to *other* settings or cases), since qualitative researchers rarely make explicit claims about the external generalizability of their accounts. Indeed, the value of a qualitative study may depend on its *lack* of external generalizability in the sense of being representative of some larger population; it may provide an account of a setting or population that is illuminating as an extreme case or 'ideal type'. Freidson, discussing his qualitative study of a medical group practice, stated that

> There is more to truth or validity than statistical representativeness.... In this study I am less concerned with describing the range of variation than I am with describing in the detail what survey questionnaire methods do not permit to be described—the assumptions, behavior, and attitudes of a very special set of physicians. They are interesting *because* they were special. (Freidson, 1975, pp. 272–3)

He argued that his study makes an important contribution to theory and policy precisely because this was a group for whom social controls on practice should have been most likely to be effective. The failure of such controls in this case not only elucidates a social process that is likely to exist in other groups, but also provides a more persuasive argument for the unworkability of such controls than would a study of a 'representative' group.

Qualitative research almost always involves some degree of internal generalization, because it is impossible to observe everything even in one small setting. The sort of sampling done in qualitative research is usually what is called 'purposeful' (Patton, 2001) or 'theoretical' (Glaser and Strauss, 1967; Strauss, 1987) sampling, rather than random sampling or some other method of attaining statistical representativeness. The goal of the former types of sampling is twofold: to make sure one has adequately understood the *variation* in the phenomena of interest in the setting, and to test developing ideas about that setting by selecting individuals, settings, or events that are crucial to the validity of those ideas.

Interviewing poses some special problems for internal generalizability, because the researcher usually is in the presence of the person interviewed for only a brief period, and must necessarily draw inferences from what happened during that brief period to the rest of the informant's life, actions, and perspective. An account based on interviews may be descriptively, interpretively, and theoretically valid as an account of the person's actions and perspective *in that interview*, but may miss other aspects of the person's perspectives that were not expressed in the interview, and can easily lead to false inferences about her actions outside the interview situation. Thus, internal generalizability is a crucial issue in interpreting interviews, as is widely recognized (for example, Dexter, 1970), and has been (although not in these terms) a central focus of postmodernism. The interview is itself a social situation, and inherently involves a relationship between the interviewer and the informant. Understanding the nature of that situation and relationship, how it affects what goes on in the interview, and how the informant's actions and views could differ in other situations, is crucial to the validity of accounts based on interviews (Briggs, 1986; Mishler, 1986).

The distinction between internal and external generalizations is not clearcut or absolute in qualitative research. A researcher studying a school, for example, can rarely visit every classroom, or even gain information about these classrooms by other means, and the issue of whether to consider the generalizability of the account for those unstudied classrooms 'internal' or 'external' is moot. However, it is important to be aware of the extent to which the times and places actually observed may differ from those that were not observed.

External generalization (external validity), which involves the extension of findings from one (or more than one) population, setting, or case, to others that were *not* studied, involves a quite different logic than the previous types. Typically, we have no direct evidence on whether the results from a study, which may be well validated for that population or setting, would also apply more broadly. Cartwright and Hardie (2012) provide a detailed argument that generalization from randomized controlled trials (RCTs) to other settings or populations requires very different sorts of arguments and evidence from those involved in assessing the 'internal validity' of the RCT itself.

Consequently, there have been two types of arguments that have been used to support claims of generalizability: the *similarity* of other populations or settings to those involved in the original study, and the claimed generality of the *theory* employed to explain the results. These are often interrelated; the similarities that are relevant for generalization to other populations or settings are generally the ones that are most important for the theory that is held to explain the outcomes.

Yin (2003) has argued that what he termed 'analytical generalization' occurs when 'a previously developed theory is used as a template with which to compare the empirical results of the case study.' (Yin, 2003, pp. 32–3); Yin elsewhere described this strategy as 'generalizing to theory' (2003, p. 38. He claimed that this is the same process by which experimental results are generalized, and this would seem to be true for quantitative research generally.

However, other qualitative researchers have proposed a third approach to generalization, in which the emphasis is not on the *generality* of the findings or interpretations so much as on their case-to-case *transferability*; this has become the usual term for this approach (Guba and Lincoln, 1989, pp. 241–2; Jensen, 2008). This shifts the responsibility for making generalizations from the researcher to the reader or potential user of the findings, and Misco (2007, cited by Polit and Beck, 2010) has called this 'reader generalizability'. Lincoln and Guba (1985; Guba and Lincoln, 1989) and Schofield (1990) identified some of the properties that a qualitative study must possess in order for such transferability to be possible, and Donmoyer (1990, 2008) developed a model for how transferability operates. Schwandt stated that Lincoln and Guba 'urge the investigator to provide sufficient details … so that readers can engage in reasonable but modest speculation about whether the findings are applicable to other cases' (Schwandt, 1997, p. 58). This does not necessarily mean that the *outcomes* of the theory in the original case would transfer; Becker (1990, p. 240) provides a detailed example of how the same processes embodied in a theory, in different contexts, can lead to different, but understandable, outcomes.

Evidence

A realist approach, in contrast to most treatments of validity in research, gives a central role to the concept of evidence. This is as important for qualitative research as for quantitative (Freeman et al., 2007; Maxwell, 2009). Schwandt (2007, p. 98) defines evidence as 'information that bears on determining the validity (truth, falsity, accuracy, etc.) of a claim or what an inquirer provides, in part, to warrant a claim'. From a different perspective, Chandler, Davidson, and Harootunian, discussing Collingwood's view of evidence in history, likewise argue that 'question and evidence are therefore 'correlative' in the sense that facts can only become evidence in response to some particular question' (Chandler et al., 1994, p. 1).

Schwandt's definition, and Collingwood's argument, point to the inextricable connections between evidence, claim, and validity. A key property of evidence (as opposed to data) is that it does not exist in isolation, but only in relation to some claim (theory, hypothesis, interpretation, and so on). Evidence is thus in the same position as validity – it can't be assessed in context-independent ways, but only in relation to the particular question and purpose to which it is applied, and the specific context in which these are investigated.

In particular, evidence can't be evaluated solely in terms of the methods used to obtain it, as argued above for validity. Any attempt to establish a context-free hierarchy of kinds of evidence based entirely on the methods used to create that evidence, as proponents of 'evidence-based' approaches typically do, is inevitably flawed. While this emphasis on the context-dependence of evidence and conclusions is a key feature of critical realist approaches, it is shared by a much broader community of scholars.

The philosopher Peter Achinstein, who has probably done the most to systematically critique and reformulate the traditional philosophical view of evidence (2001, 2005), makes the related point that evidence isn't a single thing, but several; there is no essential property that all uses of 'evidence' possess (Achinstein, 2001, p. 15).

However, there is a key difference between the uses of evidence in quantitative and qualitative research, or between what Mohr (1982) called 'variance theory' and 'process theory'. Variance theory deals with variables and the relationship between them, and the main use of evidence is to show *that* a particular relationship exists, in the population studied, between different variables, by ruling out alternative explanations for the observed correlation, and to estimate its magnitude. Process theory, in contrast, is primarily concerned with events and processes, rather than variables, and the main use of evidence (and the main strength of qualitative research) is to support claims about these events and processes – to get inside the 'black box' of variance theory and to argue for what is actually happening in specific cases.

By 'what is happening', I (and critical realists in general) include participants' meanings, intentions, beliefs, and perspectives, which are essential parts of these events and processes. Claims about meanings and perspectives, which fall under the general category of 'interpretive' claims, require quite different sorts of evidence from claims about behavior, let alone claims about the relationships between variables. Thus, the kinds of claims, and the nature and evaluation of the evidence for these claims, is very different in qualitative research from that in quantitative research, and evidential standards appropriate for quantitative and experimental research can't uncritically be applied to qualitative research.

Achinstein draws a number of other conclusions from this claim-dependence and context-dependence of evidence. First, whether some fact is evidence for a particular claim depends on how the fact is obtained or generated (Achinstein, 2001, p. 8). This does not conflict with the previous point, that evidence can't be assessed strictly in terms of the methods used to obtain it. It simply asserts that how the evidence was obtained is often *relevant* to the support it lends to a particular claim, since the methods used may address (or create) certain validity threats that could threaten the support that the evidence provides for the claim.

Second, the degree of support that a particular piece of evidence provides for a particular claim depends on the plausibility of (and evidence for) *alternative* claims regarding the phenomena in question (Achinstein, 2001, pp. 7–10). Achinstein provides several examples from different sciences in which a finding that was once believed to be convincing evidence for a particular claim was no longer thought to be so when new evidence was produced or alternative explanations were proposed. Thus, part of the context that evidence for a particular claim depends on is the context of alternative possible theories and explanations for the phenomenon in question.

Third, the previous point entails that whether a fact or observation is evidence for some claim is an empirical question, not a logical one (Achinstein, 2001, p. 9). Evidence can only be assessed in the context of the particular claim that the evidence is asserted to support, the way the evidence was generated, and the epistemic situation in which these claims are made. This context is not given a priori, but needs to be empirically discovered. Achinstein argued that one of the main reasons that researchers have paid so little attention to philosophical work on evidence is that this work usually presumes that the link between claim and evidence is strictly logical, semantic, or mathematical, something that can be established by calculation rather than empirical investigation.

Finally, Achinstein argued that for a fact to be evidence for some claim, the fact's simply increasing the probability that the claim is true isn't enough; there must be some *explanatory connection* between the fact and the claim (Achinstein, 2001, p. 145 ff.). This is an essential component of realist approaches to explanation in general – that a valid explanation does not simply support the view *that* x causes y, but must address *how* it does so (Manicas, 2006; Salmon, 1998; Sayer, 1992, 2000).

The lack of attention to the processes by which a causal influence takes place is a major flaw in most 'evidence-based' approaches to research (Maxwell, 2004a; Pawson, 2006). Pawson argued that

> The nature of causality in social programmes is such that any synthesis of evidence on whether they work will need to investigate how they work. This requires unearthing information on mechanisms, contexts, and outcomes. The central quest is to understand the conditions of programme efficacy and this will involve the synthesis in investigating for whom, in what circumstances, and in what respects a family of programmes work. (Pawson, 2006, p. 25)

These are issues for which qualitative research can make a significant contribution. However, the theory of causation on which the 'evidence-based' movement relies, and the bias toward quantitative and experimental methods that this produces, have largely excluded qualitative evidence from the research syntheses that this movement has generated. In part because of this bias, qualitative researchers have long been either defensive about their use of evidence, or dismissive of the entire concept of evidence. I argue that there is no good reason for either of these reactions. A realist reformulation of the concept of evidence can provide a strong justification for the value of the evidence generated by qualitative research, and qualitative researchers have their own ways of obtaining and using such evidence that are just as legitimate for their purposes as quantitative researchers' are for theirs (Maxwell, 2004b).

A realist understanding of validity leads to a quite different approach to issues of quality, credibility, or trustworthiness than those normally employed in both qualitative and quantitative research. Rather than relying only on the designs or procedures used in a study to assess its quality, a realist perspective focuses attention on the credibility of the *interpretations* and *conclusions* drawn from the study, and the ways in which the researcher used the study's design, methods, and data to generate and test these interpretations and conclusions, and to address plausible alternatives to these. While the methods and approaches used are obviously an important issue in this assessment, they must themselves be assessed in terms of the actual context and purposes of their use. Rather than being employed as context-independent criteria for quality, their real value is as means of obtaining evidence that can deal with plausible threats to the validity of the study's interpretations and conclusions.

In summary, I have presented a realist perspective on the validity issues that I believe are involved in conducting and assessing research, and in extending the results of that research. I have argued that this approach, which bases validity on the kinds of understanding we can have of the phenomena we study, and the possible ways that we might be wrong, is more consistent and productive than prevailing positivist or constructivist typologies based on research procedures. A realist view of validity both avoids the philosophical and practical difficulties associated with the latter approaches, and seems to me to better represent what researchers actually do in assessing the validity of their accounts.

However, validity categories are of much less direct use in qualitative research than they are (or are assumed to be) in quantitative and experimental research. In the latter, many validity threats are addressed in an anonymous, generic fashion, by prior design features (such as random assignment and statistical controls); random assignment, for example, deals with both anticipated and unanticipated specific validity threats.

In qualitative research, such prior elimination of validity threats is less possible, both because qualitative research is more inductive, and because it focuses primarily on understanding particulars rather than generalizing to universals (Erickson, 1986). Qualitative researchers deal primarily with specific threats to the validity of particular features of their accounts, and they generally address such threats by seeking evidence that would allow them to rule out each of these threats.

This strategy of addressing particular validity threats, or 'alternative hypotheses', *after* a tentative conclusion or interpretation has been developed, rather than by attempting to eliminate such threats through prior features of the research design, is in fact more fundamental to scientific method than is the latter approach (Platt, 1964; Campbell, 1988). It is accepted by qualitative researchers from a wide range of philosophical positions (for example, Hammersley and Atkinson, 1983; Miles and Huberman, 1994; Eisner, 1998; Patton, 1990). Its application to causal inference has been labeled the 'generalized elimination model' by Scriven (2008, pp. 21–2), but the method has received little formal development in the qualitative research literature, although it is implicit in many substantive qualitative studies.

Thus, as argued above, researchers cannot use the framework presented here to directly and mechanically eliminate particular threats to the validity of their accounts. Researchers already have many methods for addressing validity threats, and although there are ways that the state of the art could be improved (cf. Miles and Huberman, 1994; Maxwell, 2004a; Seale, 1999; Shadish et al., 2002), reiterating these is not my main goal here. Instead, I am trying to clarify the validity concepts that researchers are using, explicitly or implicitly, in their work, to tie these concepts into a systematic model, and to reduce the discrepancy between researchers' 'logic-in-use' and their 'reconstructed logic' (Kaplan, 1964, pp. 3–11). I see my analysis as being useful in two ways. The first is as a framework for thinking about the nature of validity issues and possible threats to validity. The second is as a checklist of the *kinds* of understanding research can aim at, and of the kinds of validity issues that need to be considered. Gawande (2009) has argued that checklists are extremely useful in avoiding error in dealing with complex situations, and research certainly fits this description.

Notes

1 Guba and Lincoln later (1989) added a fifth criterion, authenticity, which relied more on the outcomes of the research, such as fairness in representing different realities, empowering members of the groups studied, and helping them to develop 'more sophisticated' understandings. However, the latter are firmly grounded in a 'relativist view that research accounts do no more than represent a sophisticated but temporary consensus of views about what is considered to be true' (Seale, 1999, p. 46), rejecting any reference to something beyond these views.

2 A third threat, one that has received much less attention but is nonetheless serious, is focusing on the average or typical value or category and ignoring the actual diversity in the population (Maxwell, 2012a, pp. 28–32, 49–51, 64–6; Rose, 2015).

3 One response to these issues has been to treat the p value for a particular hypothesis test as a sample from the entire population of hypothesis tests across all research studies, for example, 'the *p* value for the data from a given experiment relates to the uncountable times that such test has been applied to data from any experiment in any discipline' (García-Pérez, 2012). The problem with this is that we have no idea what the actual distribution of correlations or differences is in this population, which is critical to assessing the likelihood that the null hypothesis is true (Nuzzo, 2014).

REFERENCES

Achinstein, P. (2001) *The Book of Evidence*. Oxford: Oxford University Press.

Achinstein, P. (Ed.) (2005) *Scientific Evidence: Philosophical theories and applications*. Baltimore, MD: Johns Hopkins University Press.

American Psychological Association (2010) *Publication Manual of the American Psychological Association*, 6th edition. Washington, DC: American Psychological Association.

Anderson, G. L. and Scott, J. (2012) Toward an intersectional understanding of process causality and social context. *Qualitative Inquiry*, 18, 674–685.

Archer, M., Bhaskar, R., Collier, A., Lawson, T., and Norrie, A. (Eds) (1998) *Critical Realism: Essential readings*. London: Routledge.

Baert, P. (1998) *Social Theory in the Twentieth Century*. Washington Square, New York: New York University Press.

Becker, H. S. (1990) Generalizing from case studies. In E. W. Eisner and A. Peshkin (Eds) *Qualitative Inquiry in Education: The continuing debate*. New York, NY: Teachers College Press, 233–242.

Bhaskar, R. (1978) *A Realist Theory of Science*, 2nd edition. Brighton: Harvester.

Bhaskar, R. (1989) *Reclaiming Reality: A critical introduction to contemporary philosophy*. London Verso.

Bhaskar, R. (1993) *Dialectic: The pulse of freedom*. London: Verso.

Borsboom, D., Mellenbergh, G. J., and van Heerden, J. (2004) The concept of validity. *Psychological Review*, 111, 1061–1071. doi: 10.1037/0033–295X.111.4.1061.

Boyd, R. (2010). Scientific realism. In E. N. Zalta (Ed.), *The Stanford encyclopedia of philosophy (Summer 2010 Edition)*, <http://plato.stanford.edu/archives/sum2010/entries/scientific-realism/>.

Briggs, C. (1986) *Learning How to Ask*. Cambridge: Cambridge University Press.

Briggs, D. (2008). Comments on Slavin: Synthesizing causal inferences. *Educational Researcher*, *37*(1), 15-22.

Brinberg, D., and McGrath, J. E. (1985) *Validity and the Research Process*. Newbury Park, CA: Sage Publications.

Brown-Saracino, J., Thurk, J., and Fine, G. A. (2008) Beyond groups: seven pillars of peopled ethnography in organizations and communities. *Qualitative Research*, 8, 5, 547–567.

Campbell, D. T. (1988) *Methodology and Epistemology for Social Science: Selected papers* (S. Overman, Ed.). Chicago, IL: University of Chicago Press.

Cartwright, N. and Hardie, J. (2012). *Evidence-based Policy: A Practical Guide to Doing it Better*. Oxford: Oxford University Press.

Chandler, J., Davidson, A., and Harootunian, H. (1994) *Questions of Evidence: Proof, practice, and persuasion across the disciplines*. Chicago, IL: University of Chicago Press.

Clark, A. M. (2008) Critical realism. In L. Given (Ed.), *The SAGE Encyclopedia of Qualitative Research Methods*. Thousand Oaks, CA: SAGE Publications, 167–170.

Cohen, J. (1994) The Earth is round (p<.05). *American Psychologist*, 49, 12, 997–1003.

Cook, T. D., and Campbell, D. T. (1979) *Quasi-experimentation: Design and analysis issues for field settings*. Boston, MA: Houghton-Mifflin.

Cronbach, L. (1971) Test validation. In R. L. Thorndike (Ed.), *Educational Measurement*, 2nd edition. Washington, DC: American Council on Education, 443–507.

Cronbach, L. (1982) *Designing Evaluations of Educational and Social Programs*. San Francisco: Jossey-Bass.

Cumming, G. (2012) *Understanding the New Statistics: Effect sizes, confidence intervals, and meta-analysis*. London: Routledge.

Denzin, N. K., and Lincoln, Y. S. (2005) Introduction: the discipline and practice of qualitative research. In N. K. Denzin and Y. S. Lincoln (Eds) *The SAGE Handbook of Qualitative Research*, 3rd edition. Thousand Oaks, CA: SAGE Publications, 1–42.

Dexter, L. A. (1970) *Elite and Specialized Interviewing*. Evanston, IL: Northwestern University Press.

Donmoyer, R. (1990) Generalizability and the single-case study. In E. W. Eisner and A. Peshkin (Eds) *Qualitative Inquiry in Education: The continuing debate*. New York, NY: Teachers College Press, 175–200.

Donmoyer (2008) Generalizability. In L. Given (Ed.) *The SAGE Encyclopedia of Qualitative Research Methods*. Thousand Oaks, CA: SAGE Publications, 371–372.

Donmoyer (2012) Can qualitative researchers answer policymakers' what-works question? *Qualitative Inquiry*, 18, 8, 662–673.

Eisner, E. (1998) *The Enlightened Eye: Qualitative inquiry and the enhancement of educational practice*. Upper Saddle River, NJ: Prentice Hall.

Erickson, F. (1986) Qualitative methods. In M. Wittrock (Ed.) *Handbook of Research on Teaching*. New York: Macmillan. Reprinted separately in *Research in Teaching and Learning*, vol. 2. New York: Macmillan (1990), 77–194.

Erickson, F., and Gutierrez, K. (2002) Culture, rigor, and science in educational research. *Educational Researcher*, 31, 8, 21–24.

Freeman, M., deMarrais, K., Preissle, J., Roulston, K., and St. Pierre, E. A. (2007) Standards of evidence in qualitative research: an incitement to discourse. *Educational Researcher*, 36, 1, 25–32.

Freidson, E. (1975) *Doctoring Together: A study of professional social control*. Chicago, IL: University of Chicago Press.

García-Pérez, M. A. (2012) Statistical conclusion validity: some common threats and simple remedies. *Frontiers in Psychology*, 3, 325. Retrieved on 9/4/2016 from www.ncbi.nlm.nih.gov/pmc/articles/PMC3429930/.

Gawande, A. (2009) *The Checklist Manifesto: How to get things right*. New York, NY: Henry Holt.

Gehlbach, H. and Brinkworth, M. E. (2011) Measure twice, cut down error: a process for enhancing the validity of survey scales. *Review of General Psychology*, 15, 4, 380–387.

Gigerenzer, G. (2004) Mindless statistics. *The Journal of Socio-Economics*, 33, 587–606.

Glaser, B., and Strauss, A. (1967) *The Discovery of Grounded Theory: Strategies for Qualitative Research*. Chicago, IL: Aldine.

Greene, J. (2007) *Mixed Methods in Social Inquiry*. San Francisco: Wiley.

Guba, E.G., and Lincoln, Y.S. (1989) *Fourth Generation Evaluation*. Thousand Oaks, CA: Sage Publications.

Hammersley, M. (1992) Ethnography and realism. In M. Hammersley (Ed.) *What's Wrong with Ethnography? Methodological explorations*. London: Routledge, 43–56.

Hammersley, M. (1998) Get real! A defence of realism. In P. Hodkinson (Ed.) *The Nature of Educational Research: Realism, relativism, or postmodernism*. Crewe, UK: Crewe School of Education, Manchester Metropolitan University, 1998. Reprinted in H. Piper and I. Stronach (Eds) *Educational Research: Difference and diversity*. Aldershot: Ashgate (2004), 59–78.

Hammersley, M., and Atkinson, P. (1983) *Ethnography: Principles in practice*. London: Tavistock.

Henry, G., Julnes, J., and Mark, M. (1998) *Realist Evaluation: An emerging theory in support of practice*. New Directions for Evaluation 78. San Francisco, CA: Jossey-Bass.

Hirschi, T., and Selvin, H. C. (1973) *Principles of Survey Analysis*. New York: The Free Press.

House, E. (1991) Realism in research. *Educational Researcher*, 20, 6, 2–9, 25.

Huberman, A. M., and Miles, M. B. (1985) Assessing local causality in qualitative research. In D. N. Berg and K. K. Smith (Eds) *Exploring Clinical Methods for Social Research*. Beverly Hills, CA: SAGE Publications, 351–382.

Jensen, D. (2008) Transferability. In L. Given (Ed.) *The SAGE Encyclopedia of Qualitative Research Methods*. Thousand Oaks, CA: SAGE Publications, 886.

Kaplan, A. (1964) *The Conduct of Inquiry: Methodology for behavioral science*. San Francisco, CA: Chandler.

Keller, E. F. (1992) *Secrets of Life, Secrets of Death: Essays on language, gender, and science*. New York: Routledge.

Lather, P. (1993) Fertile obsession: validity after poststructuralism. *Sociological Quarterly*, 34, 4, 673–693.

Leibovici, L. (2001) Effects of remote, retroactive, intercessory prayer on outcomes in patients with bloodstream infection: randomised controlled trial. *British Medical Journal*, 323, 1450–1451.

Lincoln, Y. S., and Guba, E. G. (1985) *Naturalistic Inquiry*. Thousand Oaks, CA: Sage Publications.

Lissitz, R. W. (Ed.) (2009) *The Concept of Validity: Revisions, new directions, and applications*. Charlotte, NC: Information Age Publishing.

Little, D. (1995/1998) Causal explanation in the social sciences. *Southern Journal of Philosophy* (Supplement, 1995). Reprinted in D. Little, *Microfoundations, Method, and Causation.* New Brunswick, NJ: Transaction Publishers (1998), 197–214.

Manicas, P. T. (2006) *A Realist Philosophy of Social Science: Explanation and understanding*. Cambridge: Cambridge University Press.

Mark, M. M., Henry, G. T., and Julnes, G. (2000) *Evaluation: An integrated framework for understanding, guiding, and improving policies and programs*. San Francisco, CA: Jossey-Bass.

Maxwell, J. A. (1992) Understanding and validity in qualitative research. *Harvard Educational Review*, 62, 3, 279–300.

Maxwell, J. A. (2004a) Causal explanation, qualitative research, and scientific inquiry in education. *Educational Researcher*, 33, 2, 3–11.

Maxwell, J. A. (2004b) Using qualitative methods for causal explanation. *Field Methods*, 16, 3, 243–264.

Maxwell, J. A. (2009) Evidence: a critical realist perspective for qualitative research. In N. K. Denzin and M. D. Giardina (Eds) *Qualitative Inquiry and Social Justice*. Walnut Creek, CA: Left Coast Press, 108–122.

Maxwell, J. A. (2012a) *A Realist Approach for Qualitative Research*. Thousand Oaks, CA: Sage Publications.

Maxwell, J. A. (2012b) The importance of qualitative research for causal explanation in education. *Qualitative Inquiry*, 18, 8, 655–661.

Maxwell, J. A. (2013) *Qualitative Research Design: An interactive approach*, 3rd edition. Thousand Oaks, CA: Sage Publications.

Maxwell, J. A., and Chmiel, M. (2014) Generalization in and from qualitative analysis. In U. Flick (Ed.) *The SAGE Handbook of Qualitative Data Analysis*. Thousand Oaks, CA: SAGE Publications, 540–553.

Maxwell, J. A., and Mittapalli, K. (2010) Realism as a stance for mixed methods research. In A. Tashakkori and C. Teddlie (Eds) *Handbook of Mixed Methods in Social and Behavioral Research*, 2nd edition. Thousand Oaks, CA: SAGE Publications, 145–167.

Madill, A. (2008) Realism. In L. Given (Ed.) *The SAGE Encyclopedia of Qualitative Research Methods*. Thousand Oaks, CA: SAGE Publications, 731–735.

Messick, S. (1995) Validity of psychological assessment. *American Psychologist*, 5, 9, 741–749.

Miles, M. B. & Huberman, A. M., (1984). *Qualitative data analysis: A sourcebook of new methods*. Thousand Oaks, CA: Sage Publications

Miles, M. B., and Huberman, A. M. (1994) *Qualitative Data Analysis: An expanded sourcebook*. Thousand Oaks, CA: Sage Publications.

Miller, P. (2008) Validity. In L. Given (Ed.) *The SAGE Encyclopedia Of Qualitative Research Methods*. Thousand Oaks, CA: SAGE Publications, 909–910.

Misco, T. (2007) The frustrations of reader generalizability and grounded theory: alternative considerations for transferability. *Journal of Research Practice*, 3, 1, 1–11.

Mishler, E. (1986) *Research Interviewing: Context and narrative*. Cambridge, MA: Harvard University Press.

Mohr, L. B. (1982) *Explaining Organizational Behavior*. San Francisco, CA: Jossey-Bass.

Mulaik, S. (2009) *Linear Causal Modeling with Structural Equations.* Boca Raton, FL: Chapman & Hall/CRC Press.

Murnane, R. J., and Willett, J. B. (2010) *Methods Matter: Improving causal inference in educational and social science research*. Oxford, England: Oxford University Press.

National Research Council (2002). *Scientific Research in Education*. Washington. DC: National Academy Press.

Niiniluoto, I. (2007). Scientific progress. *Stanford Encyclopedia of Philosophy*, accessed at http://plato.stanford.edu/entries/scientific-progress/ Oct 18, 2010

Norris, S. P. (1983) The inconsistencies at the foundation of construct validation theory. In E. R. House (Ed.) *Philosophy of Evaluation*. New Directions for Program Evaluation, no. 19. San Francisco, CA: Jossey-Bass, 53–74.

Nuzzo, R. (2014) Statistical errors. *Nature 506* (13 February), 150– 152.

Patton, M. Q. (2001). *Qualitative evaluation and research methods* (3rd ed.). Thousand Oaks, CA: Sage Publications.

Pawson, R. (2006) *Evidence-based Policy: A realist perspective*. London: Sage Publications.

Pawson, R., and Tilley, N. (1997) *Realistic Evaluation*. London: Sage Publications.

Phillips, D. C. (1987) *Philosophy, Science, and Social Inquiry: Contemporary methodological controversies in social science and related applied fields of research*. Oxford: Pergamon Press.

Platt, J. (1964) Strong inference. *Science*, 146, 3642, 347–353.

Polit, D. F., and Beck, C. T. (2010) Generalization in quantitative and qualitative research: myths and strategies. *International Journal of Nursing Studies*, 47, 1451–1458.

Porter, S. (2007) Validity, trustworthiness, and rigour: reasserting realism in qualitative research. *Journal of Advanced Nursing*, 60, 1, 79–86.

Putnam, H. (1999) *The Threefold Cord: Mind, body, and world*. New York: Columbia University Press.

Rose, T. (2015) *The End of Average*. New York: HarperCollins.

Saey, T. H. (2015) Come again, research results? Scientists tackle the irreproducibility problem. *Science News*, 188, 13, 22.

Salmon, W. C. (1984) *Scientific Explanation and the Causal Structure of the World*. Princeton, NJ: Princeton University Press.

Salmon, W. C. (1989) Four decades of scientific explanation. In P. Kitcher and W. C. Salmon (Eds) *Scientific Explanation*. Minneapolis: University of Minnesota Press, 3–219.

Salmon, W. C. (1998) *Causality and Explanation*. New York: Oxford University Press.

Sandelowski, M. (2008). Theoretical saturation. In L. Given (ed.), *The SAGE Encyclopedia of Qualitative Research Methods*, Thousand Oaks, CA: SAGE Publications, 875-6.

Sayer, A. (1992) *Method in Social Science: A realist approach*, 2nd edition. London: Routledge.

Sayer, A. (2000) *Realism and Social Science*. London: SAGE Publications.

Schofield, J. W. (1990) Increasing the generalizability of qualitative research. In E. W Eisner and A. Peshkin (Eds) *Qualitative Inquiry in Education: The continuing debate*. New York: Teachers College Press, 13–103.

Schwandt, T. A. (1997) *The SAGE Dictionary of Qualitative Inquiry*. Thousand Oaks, CA: Sage Publications.

Schwandt, T. A. (2007) *The SAGE Dictionary of Qualitative Inquiry*, 3rd edition. Thousand Oaks, CA: SAGE Publications.

Scriven, M. (2008) A summative evaluation of RCT methodology: and an alternative approach to causal research. *Journal of Multidisciplinary Evaluation*, 5, 9, 11–24.

Seale, C. (1999) *The Quality of Qualitative Research*. London: Sage Publications.

Shadish, W. R., Cook, T. D., and Campbell, D. T. (2002) *Experimental and Quasi-experimental Designs for Generalized Causal Inference*. Boston, MA: Houghton Mifflin.

Smith, J. K. (2008) Relativism. In L. Given (Ed.) *The SAGE Encyclopedia of Qualitative Research Methods*. Thousand Oaks, CA: SAGE Publications, 749–753.

Strauss, A. (1987) *Qualitative Analysis for Social Scientists*. Cambridge: Cambridge University Press.

Teddlie, C, and Tashakkori, A. (2003) Major issues and controversies in the use of mixed methods in the social and behavioral sciences. In A. Tashakkori and C. Teddlie, *Handbook of Mixed Methods in Social and Behavioral Research*. Thousand Oaks, CA: SAGE Publications, 3–50.

Trafimow, D., and Marks, M. (2015) Editorial. *Basic and Applied Social Psychology*, 37, 1–2.

Weisner, T. S. (Ed.) (2002) *Discovering Successful Pathways in Children's Development: Mixed methods in the study of childhood and family life*. Chicago, IL: University of Chicago Press.

Weiss, R. S. (1994) *Learning from Strangers: The art and method of qualitative interviewing*. New York: The Free Press.

Yin, R. K. (2003) *Case Study Research: Design and methods*, 3rd edition. Thousand Oaks, CA: Sage Publications.

PART II

Planning Research

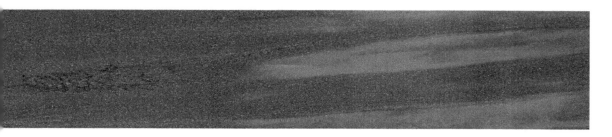

PART II

Planning Research

6

Approaches to Reviewing Research in Education

Jill Denner, Erica Marsh,
and Shannon Campe

The accumulation, organization and synthesis of research-based knowledge are critical components for building knowledge in the field of education and contributing to educational practice. However, to move the field of education forward, reviews require a systematic analytic methodology that is transparent and trustworthy for pulling together existing research. In this chapter, we provide a rationale for why research reviews are so important, and describe what we mean by systematic reviews. We then describe different approaches to conducting systematic reviews of research based on their study methods, including the strengths, limitations, and debates about each approach, as well as the contribution that each can make to educational research and practice. The next section gives an overview of the steps for conducting a systematic review, including how to define the scope of a review, how to identify a focus that will contribute to that field, strategies for locating relevant literature, how to decide what and how much to include in a review, steps for identifying, analyzing and synthesizing themes across studies, and examples of a final product. At each step, we discuss the debates and considerations, as well as key factors to consider. Next, a case study of a meta-synthesis is used to highlight an integrative and methodologically inclusive approach to systematically reviewing research studies; the focus is on the benefits to children of programming computer games. We conclude with a discussion of how systematic reviews of educational research can move the field forward, and the factors that must be considered to do this well.

INTRODUCTION TO STRATEGIES FOR REVIEWING EDUCATIONAL RESEARCH

Why review?

The goals of educational researchers are varied, and include both efforts to increase knowledge and to improve learning. To achieve these goals, individual studies must be informed by a thorough understanding of existing research – what is already known, where the gaps are, and what debates exist. Research reviews are designed to summarize the state of the field and typically result in a narrative that tells a trustworthy story. Reasons for reviewing research include: to advance theory and advance a field, provide efficient and trustworthy summaries of a research area, determine the effectiveness of practices or programs, inform policy, identify gaps in research, spark dialogue and debate, and create visibility and accessibility of a field (Cooper, 2010; Major and Savin-Baden, 2010; Suri, 2014). Reviews are important in many fields because a single study is unlikely to provide a generalizable and definitive answer to a research question (Suri, 2000) and more causal factors of a particular effect are likely to be detected by a research synthesis than by a single study (Cook et al., 1992).

Reviews play an increasingly critical role as the number of published studies has proliferated over the years. The number of journals that publish education research has grown and changed over time. For example, one review of over a decade of publications from leading academic journals in the field of higher education research found a growing number of research studies being published, increased internationalization of journals, and a growth in the representation of female authors (Tight, 2012). However, the growth may not reflect an increase in quality. For example, while the number of publications is growing, the number of studies that publish negative results is decreasing. Fanelli (2011) reports that the proportion of papers that found full or partial support for their hypothesis increased by more than 20 percent between 1990 and 2007; the trend was particularly strong in the social sciences and applied disciplines. When studies do not report insignificant results, or findings that run counter to popular belief, this limits what a research review can conclude. Similarly, the number of studies that aim to replicate findings remains very low – 13 percent of publications in the top 100 education journals (Makel and Plucker, 2014). The result of these trends is that the accumulation of knowledge that can inform educational practice stalls.

In educational research, knowledge accumulation tends to be slow and often haphazard, which limits its usefulness for educators, and increases redundancy. With the growing number of educational research journals and online publication outlets, it is difficult for researchers, policymakers, or educators to know what exists, and challenging to critically assess the findings within and across studies. The US Department of Education's What Works Clearinghouse addresses this issue by systematically reviewing research for evidence of effective programs and practices in education. However, their focus is on intervention studies that include a comparison group, not on broader questions about learning. In areas of study that use a range of methodologies and samples, it is particularly difficult to come to a consensus about what is known. In 2013, the US Department of Education and National Science Foundation published a framework that describes the progression from foundational research to the kind of scale-up studies that can be used to measure impact. Their definitions of the purpose and evidence produced by each of the six study types provide researchers with clear guidelines for how to move a field forward.

In addition to online clearinghouses, another response to these challenges is the creation of journals that exclusively publish reviews. The American Educational Research Association (AERA) began publishing Review of Educational Research in 1931, but the trend is more recent in other parts of the world. The Evidence for Policy and Practice Information and Co-ordinating Centre (EPPI-Centre) in the UK has been doing reviews, and supporting and developing methods for systematic reviews since 1993, but the Australian Council for Education first published the Australian Education Review in 2004, and the British Educational Research Association (BERA) created Review of Education as recently as 2013.

Systematic reviews

There is a long history of research summaries, but reviews have become increasingly more objective and systematic over time (Cooper, 2010). Many reviews simply affirm what we people already believe, or conclude that there is not enough trustworthy data so more research is needed (Davies and Powell, 2010). In contrast to a literature review, a systematic review has a clear question that is being addressed, often includes a systematic and comprehensive literature search, and involves some appraisal or assessment of quality of the primary studies. In the field of education, this shift is a result of discussion about how to conduct reviews that truly advance the field, which includes using synthesis methods that meet the same level of methodological rigor as the studies they are aiming to synthesize (Cooper, 2010). In this chapter, we focus on systematic reviews, or what others call research synthesis (Cooper, 2010). Gough, Oliver, and Thomas (2012, p. 2) define systematic reviews as 'a review of research literature using systematic and explicit accountable methods'. This includes a range of methodological approaches that involve systematic techniques to gather and analyze across studies, with the goal of contributing new knowledge to advance a field. Common features of influential research syntheses acknowledged by the AERA include using an inductive approach to identify common assumptions, theories, methods, and findings; performing a critical analysis of extant research; structuring the report along meaningful themes; and providing a unique conceptual framework to think about the topic, future research, practice, and policy (Suri and Clarke, 2009).

Systematic reviews provide the greatest likelihood of being used because they employ transparent approaches to synthesizing across research studies. They usually start with a focused question and have a clear protocol, including explicit methods for searching, appraising, and synthesizing studies. There are several online resources. The UK-based EPPI-Centre has identified methods of conducting systematic reviews that impact both policy and practice, which include working closely with decision-makers to inform the process as well as how the findings are written up, and addressing a range of research questions that go beyond just efficacy and certain types of evidence (Gough, Oliver, and Thomas, 2012). And a team from Switzerland and Canada write that 'important features of a systematic review are a comprehensive, reproducible search for primary studies, selection of studies using clear and transparent eligibility criteria, standardized critical appraisal of studies for quality, and investigation of heterogeneity among included studies' (Nordmann et al., 2012). What these approaches share is a commitment to rigor, which some view as striving toward objectivity and neutrality, while others focus on consistency, transparency, and reflexivity (Suri, 2014). As the US Department of Education and National Science Foundation report on common guidelines (2013) suggests, the definition of rigor, or evidence varies depending on the goal of the research.

Like the studies they use, systematic reviews are driven by a range of goals, including efforts to generate knowledge about: 'why', problems, what works, effective practice, and who to involve (Davies and Powell, 2010). The particular knowledge goal will determine the most appropriate methodological approach, including whether or not to do a comprehensive search, how or if quality and relevance will be appraised, and the actual synthesis process. In addition, the usefulness of the synthesis will be determined in part by the quality of the original studies, which includes the extent to which there is adequate description of participants and methods (Major and Savin-Baden, 2011). In the next section, we describe several factors to consider when choosing a systematic review method, and present the rationale and the limitations of conducting different types of systematic research reviews.

Choosing a methodological approach

The decision about what kind of review method to use will be driven by the *goals* of the review, the *epistemology* of the review team, the *maturity* of the field, and the *methodology* used in the existing literature. Gough et al., (2012) group the *goals* of systematic reviews into two categories: aggregative and configurative. They explain that reviews that aggregate data are deductive, and designed to test theories and answer questions such as 'How many?', 'How do phenomena compare?', and 'How are phenomena related?' Configurative approaches are designed to generate theories and ideas, and can be used to understand 'What is this phenomena?' and 'What is its meaning or value?' Many reviews employ elements of both approaches – for example, to describe not only IF a particular approach works, but also how and in what conditions.

The choice of a review method is determined in part by the synthesis team's *epistemological stance* – how the researchers think about evidence and rigor. Suri (2014) describes the range of epistemological positions in educational research, which include variations in what is worth knowing and what are legitimate ways of knowing. At one extreme are researchers who aim to take a neutral position, consider all perspectives, and let knowledge, regardless how complex or seemingly contradictory, emerge; at the other end are those who claim to take a position and use the synthesis to prove or disprove that point of view (Cooper et al., 2009). Most fall somewhere between these two approaches, since absolute neutrality is believed to be impossible. Regardless of the epistemology, it is important to be transparent about the position of the researchers (Major and Savin-Baden, 2011).

The methodological approach will also be influenced by the *maturity* of the field, which includes the number and quality of studies, as well as whether there are widely held beliefs and debates that warrant a need for a systematic synthesis. Within the field of educational research, there are many subfields – and sub-subfields – that have a range of membership and publications. For example, the AERA has 12 divisions and over 155 special interest groups, and BERA has 30 special interest groups. In the more established fields like studies of student achievement, Hattie et al. (2014) estimate that a new article is written every hour, which has resulted in a growing number of meta-analyses that aim to summarize what is known, as well as numerous syntheses of the meta-analyses. For younger fields (characterized by fewer numbers of studies, less diversity of study participants, and few theories) reviews of research may be more focused on understanding phenomena.

The synthesis approach will also be driven by the *methods* used in the original studies. Syntheses of purely quantitative studies are the most common, but there are a growing number of qualitative and mixed methods reviews (McMillan et al., 2013) and tools to synthesize studies across methods, disciplines, epistemologies, and theoretical frameworks. In recent decades, there has been an increase in scholarship about how to conduct reviews of qualitative and mixed methods studies. Though these methods are common in educational research, much of this work is in the health sciences (for example, Paterson and Canam, 2001), with social sciences a close second (Cooper, 2010; Major and Savin-Baden, 2010). Emerging frameworks aim to increase the rigor of methodologically inclusive synthesis in educational research (Suri and Clarke, 2009).

Below we review different approaches to conducting systematic reviews of research, and organize them based on the methodology of the studies being reviewed. We highlight the rationale for choosing each type of synthesis method, the limitations or biases inherent in each one, as well as the types of products that can result. We also discuss the disciplinary roots of each approach, and the extent to which each has been used in educational research.

QUANTITATIVE RESEARCH SYNTHESIS

A meta-analysis is a statistical approach to combining the data that results from a systematic review of quantitative studies. According to Bangert-Drowns and Rudner (1991), Gene Glass first used the term 'meta-analysis' in 1976 to refer to a philosophy, not a statistical technique. Glass argued that a literature review should be as systematic as primary research and should interpret the results of individual studies in the context of distributions of findings, partially determined by study characteristics and partially random. Since that time, meta-analysis has become a widely accepted research tool, encompassing a family of procedures used in a variety of disciplines. Starting in the early 1990s, the use of meta-analysis has grown exponentially in the field of education research (Hattie et al., 2014).

The meta-analysis is designed to translate statistical results from different studies to a common metric and statistically explore relations between study characteristics and findings. This includes a comprehensive and exhaustive literature search, and the aggregation of data to identify the frequency and relative weight of findings. Pooling the findings from many primary studies can increase statistical power to detect significant effects of interventions, as well as variation across demographic subgroups (Nordmann et al., 2012). The results are used to inform practice, as well as to resolve apparent contradictions in research findings.

There are several limitations or criticisms of meta-analysis. For example, some argue that by averaging simple numerical representations across studies, important contextual information is lost; other critics argue that meta-analyses lack the kind of reflection that can highlight debates and potentially conflicting results (Bangert-Drowns and Rudner, 1991). Other limitations of meta-analyses are that all primary studies must use the same measure or outcome in the same way at the same time intervals; they are inappropriate to use when the findings across studies are too heterogeneous to combine (Nordmann et al., 2012; Oliver and Tripney, this volume).

QUALITATIVE RESEARCH SYNTHESIS

The goal of a systematic synthesis of qualitative research is to integrate or compare the results across studies in order to increase understanding of a particular phenomenon, not to add studies together. Typically the aim is to identify broader themes or new theories – qualitative syntheses usually result in a narrative summary of cross-cutting or emerging themes or constructs, and/or conceptual models. For educational research, it can be particularly useful for exploring individual, relational, and contextual barriers and opportunities for promoting learning, and for providing educators and policymakers with cumulative knowledge that can be used to advance evidence-based policies and practices. However, qualitative research synthesis is not very common in the field of education. The challenges and limitations of doing a synthesis of qualitative research include coming up with a clear criteria for inclusion or exclusion.

There are several different but overlapping goals of qualitative research synthesis. Some reviews aim to *aggregate* data in order to identify the frequency and relative weight of themes, while others aim to *integrate* findings to 'create taxonomies of the range of conceptual findings and provide the foundation for the development of conceptual descriptions of phenomena across studies' (Saini and Shlonsky, 2012, p. 29). Reviews that have these goals typically start with a research question and/or concepts, which evolve over time. When the goal is *interpretive*, to uncover new insights or ways of interpreting data or relationships, questions and themes emerge and are revised during the synthesis process. Finally, some reviews aim to *deconstruct* existing narratives or assumptions in order to create dialogue rather than resolution (Suri, 2014). Many reviews have more than one goal. There are many existing guidebooks for carrying out qualitative research syntheses to meet a variety of goals, using a range of methods (for example, Barnett-Page and Thomas, 2009; Major and Savin-Baden, 2010; Saini and Shlonsky, 2012; Suri, 2014). In this section, we briefly highlight two approaches.

The first of these was a method of synthesizing qualitative research called the meta-ethnography (Noblit and Hare, 1988). The goal of this approach was to integrate and bring together narrative accounts, not for the purposes of reducing the results into a conclusion, but to develop explanatory theory or models. It follows a seven-phase systematic approach to combine data that involves identifying an interest or question, conducting an exhaustive search of relevant studies, identifying concepts within each study, translating the findings from each study into those from the other studies in the synthesis, and identifying similarity, dissimilarity, and a line of argument that builds across studies. This approach is particularly useful for synthesizing studies that offer a rich description of the research context, as it offers a way to synthesize the contexts in addition to the findings. Noblit and Hare (1988) include examples of how to synthesize ethnographic studies done in educational settings. Like all methods, there is variation in how well the steps are applied and the extent to which new insights result. The rigor depends on the level of saturation in the field, and the qualitative research skills of the synthesizer (Campbell et al., 2012). A recent review of health science meta-ethnographies found that only 38 percent resulted in new ideas, and only one-third clearly described their analytic and synthesis process (France et al., 2014).

The second approach was the best-fit framework, used to synthesize qualitative evidence and aggregate data. It has been used to produce context-specific conceptual models for describing or explaining decision-making and behaviors in health fields (Carroll et al., 2013). It begins by identifying a pre-existing conceptual model or framework, including all relevant qualitative studies that satisfy a specified criteria, mapping the data from included studies onto the framework, and using a grounded theory approach to generate new themes to supplement the framework's themes. The 'best fit' framework synthesis method can be used to test, reinforce, and build on an existing published model that was developed for a different population. The approach begins by identifying or creating a pre-existing conceptual model and coding data from the selected studies against that thematic or conceptual framework. It produces a relatively rapid, transparent, and pragmatic process when compared to more exclusively interpretative forms of synthesis because a substantial amount of the data to be included in the review is often coded against the a priori framework. Only data that cannot be accommodated within the framework requires considered, iterative interpretation using inductive, thematic analysis techniques.

MIXED METHODS RESEARCH SYNTHESIS

A review of primary studies that use either or both qualitative or quantitative methods requires a different approach because the object of the synthesis may vary – some findings are numbers, while others appear in written reports (Sandelowski et al., 2012). The purposes of a mixed methods synthesis vary and include the development of evidence summaries, the development of theory, and the identification of the active ingredients, effectiveness, and the factors that affect the effectiveness of interventions, programs, and policies (Pawson, 2006). The science of conducting rigorous synthesis of mixed methods research is still emerging, but there is now a substantial body of literature. Though much of this research comes from the field of health care (Pope et al., 2007; Sandelowski and Barroso, 2007), there are some more recent articles on the application to education and social science (Major and Savin-Baden, 2011; Suri, 2014). In this section, we describe two approaches to systematically reviewing studies that use a range of methods.

The first approach, the critical interpretive synthesis method, evolved from an attempt to use meta-ethnography to bring together findings from a large and methodologically diverse group of studies. The goal is theory generation, or the generation of a synthesizing argument (Dixon-Woods et al., 2006). The process begins with the formulation of an initial question or general focus, which is revised during the literature search and review, and throughout the process. The quality of research is appraised based on clear criteria, with emphasis on relevance and theoretical contribution. Key information is extracted and analyzed across studies, while maintaining a critical stance that includes contextualizing the information. The reviewers' perspective is expected to influence the interpretation and the results, and is made explicit.

The second approach, the meta-synthesis, is an interpretive integration of qualitative and quantitative research findings based on a systematic literature search and analysis process with an integrative approach that is methodologically inclusive.

The integrative review allows for a range of research methodologies to be included in syntheses and can inform evidence-based practice initiatives (Whittemore and Knafl, 2005). Meta-synthesis usually results in a narrative description, tables, or visual models. One challenge of doing meta-synthesis is to devise a set of criteria for appraising the quality of studies that use such different methodologies.

HOW TO DO A SYSTEMATIC REVIEW

In this section, we provide general guidelines for doing a systematic review of educational research, following Cooper's (2010) seven steps that can be applied to different review methods. While most of the review guidebooks follow similar steps, Suri (2014) has also advocated for ongoing and critical reflection in order to structure and inform decisions about methodology, and she lists a number of the key questions that should be considered at each stage. By reflecting on these questions, the team can increase the usefulness of the synthesis by being transparent at every stage – this means making each decision point clear, explaining why the decision was made, and making procedures (for example, searching, inclusion, appraisal, analyses) clear and consistent.

Define the scope

The success of a review depends in large part on how the field is defined. If the focus is too narrow, it will limit the extent to which there are new insights or understandings. On the other hand, if the focus is too broad, it will be difficult to draw conclusions, and the findings may not be relevant to any particular audience. The first step is to develop either a clear question, or identify a problem that the review can address. Doing this requires an understanding of the existing research, and an idea of how a review will contribute to the discipline or field in question. The contribution, including why the focus is important, as well as the audience, or who will benefit from the review, must be clearly articulated. The goal might be to fill a gap in the understanding of a phenomenon, address a debate, test assumptions about particular educational strategies, build theory, translate research into practical application, or address research gaps. When defining the scope, it must also be clear what is NOT being included initially and why.

A clear description of the scope will increase the likelihood that the review will make a contribution, but requires an initial scan of the literature. A scoping review is sometimes used as a first step to define the breadth of a systematic review; it can be used to determine the methodologies used and the maturity of the field. At this stage, there is usually not a specific question, and a scoping review is designed to pull together relevant literature in order to identify gaps, debates, and determine inclusion/exclusion criteria (Peters et al., 2015). This scan can help to identify pressing educational questions that have been studied in different ways by different research teams, using different theoretical frameworks and/or methods. The scan will also help to identify any widely held beliefs, lore, or shared understandings in the field that have come into question within certain populations or contexts. An effective review must also clarify who will benefit from the review – to who is the research review relevant, who is likely to use the findings, and who may be threatened by the results. To increase the likelihood the results will be used, some suggest it is important to involve the audience at all stages, to identify questions, interpret findings, and form conclusions (Suri, 2014).

Locate relevant literature

After the initial scan, a more systematic and thorough search of the literature is needed to ensure that the review is comprehensive. Relevant works can be identified from several sources: conference proceedings, online databases, cited references in existing papers, personal correspondence, published and unpublished works, and experts that are geographically dispersed (Conn et al., 2003). Once key papers are identified, Google Scholar can be used to search through the papers that have cited it. It is important to carefully document which databases or sites were searched, when, and what keywords were used. The literature search should be comprehensive enough to address the goal(s) of the review, and this process will be strengthened by including multiple researchers with different points of view, including both an emic and an etic approach (viewpoints from both inside and outside the field of study).

As part of the literature search, the review team needs to clearly document how papers were initially determined relevant (or not), and why. For example, initial decisions about relevance are often based on the title, but these decisions may be revised after reading the abstracts or the whole study to determine whether they are within the scope. The initial search may also be limited by specific parameters, such as a specified range of years; this may be particularly important if the topic area changes drastically over a short period of time (for example, technology education). Similarly, decisions about whether or not to include unpublished studies in the literature search must be clear and consistent. While some reviews include only peer reviewed papers, others include unpublished studies if they meet the team's quality criteria (Pierson, 2004). It is common to locate multiple papers describing the same study with the same participants, and these must be read as a cluster to determine whether to retain the most comprehensive paper, to group them together so they count as 'one' study but draw findings from across them, or to include them in different subsections of the synthesis if they contribute unique findings.

The process of reviewing the literature and creating a database of papers may lead to a restructuring of the question that drives the synthesis. This can happen if there are not enough papers to answer the question, or if there are too many papers to do a systematic synthesis. A revision of the review question may also result from reviewing abstracts and realizing that either a similar synthesis has been done already, or there is a more interesting or pressing question that a synthesis can address.

Extract key information

After initial decisions are made about what to include, and the focus is confirmed, the next step is to pull out the key pieces of information. The purpose is to make key information from each study easily accessible and searchable, to prepare for analysis. Decisions about what kind of information to include should be based on the primary and sub-questions that the review is designed to address. Categories (for example, sample size and ages) may be added or combined as each paper is read and key information extracted. Clear documentation of the paper is needed, including authors, date, and title, to avoid confusion that can result from multiple articles by the same authors in the same year and make article retrieval easier. In addition, the review team must make clear decisions about how to extract the results or evidence. For example, some teams copy and paste the authors' findings into a database, with no editing or interpretation, while others include interpretation based on a critical review of the methods. At this stage, it is important to include notes or questions about the methodology or authors' conclusions, ideas about how the findings will contribute to an overall conclusion, new categories to potentially analyze, and questions that arise from the study. This information will be used in the analysis stage.

This is the first time that most of the papers will be read in detail, and it provides an opportunity for the review team to revisit decisions about what to include from a paper, and whether a paper belongs in the synthesis. Although the quality and importance of each study will be assessed at the next stage, the extraction phase offers an opportunity to identify factors to consider, and to flag papers that might not meet those criteria. Papers that are ultimately not included in the review have their own value because they create opportunities for the team to revisit their criteria for 'evidence' and 'quality', and begin to identify questions that must be resolved in order to move to the analysis phase.

Evaluate the quality and importance of each study

The appraisal process involves first identifying the criteria for quality and importance. In some instances, quality will be associated with a certain type of research method, while in other cases it will be based on factors such as relevance to the review question or focus, or how generalizable the results are to other populations. For example, meta-analyses can only include studies with similar research designs and hypotheses, and with findings that can be converted into effect sizes (Cooper, 2010). On the other hand, Thomas and Harden (2008) assess the 'quality' of their studies in terms of their ability to answer their research question, rather than in terms of the research design. Major and Savin-Baden (2010) created the following rating system for evidence strength that can be adapted to assess different kinds of studies: Unequivocal (findings supported with clear and compelling evidence), Credible (findings that are plausible given the weight of evidence), Unsupported (findings are not supported by data). Ratings for generalizability can complement the evidence ratings because even if findings are unequivocal, it is possible that the participants, setting, or methodology are so unique that it is unlikely that the findings have relevance for any other situation. Clear documentation of the appraisal criteria is essential so that others can modify and build off of it, and know how to interpret the findings for their own use.

The appraisal process involves a careful reading of each paper, including the authors' conclusions, the evidence presented to support those conclusions, the rigor of the methods used to collect the evidence, and who participated (Harden and Gough, 2012). There is debate about whether or not to use checklists or criteria created by others to evaluate the quality and importance. Pawson et al. (2005) caution against the use of checklists, arguing that instead researchers need to indicate in the analysis phase which studies to be cautious about based on findings from other studies. But others, like Gawande (2009) stress that checklists can greatly increase efficiency and consistency. The Mixed Methods Appraisal tool is a checklist designed to be used in systematic reviews of literature that include a range of methodologies. It has been widely used, and preliminary tests of this tool have found it to have promising reliability (Pace et al., 2012). A detailed description and tutorial can be accessed online: http://mixedmethodsappraisaltoolpublic.pbworks.com/w/page/24607821/FrontPage.

Analyze and integrate the findings

In this phase, the review team will carefully analyze the evidence in each study, and begin to integrate the findings across studies in order to create new knowledge. The analysis process is a distinct stage, but it actually begins as soon as decisions are made about the scope of the review, and continues throughout. When the synthesis goal is aggregation, the analysis process includes running statistical analyses to combine and compare effect sizes across studies in order to give a measure of how big an intervention effect is (Cooper, 2010). A simpler version is to count the number of statistically significant findings, note the direction of the findings, as well as the number of non-significant findings, a procedure called vote counting (Cooper, 2010).

When the synthesis goal is configuration, analysis involves going beyond listing the findings from each study to identify cross-cutting themes, interconnected findings, and areas of debate (Thomas et al., 2012). One approach to the analysis and integration process is the constant comparison method, where concepts are generated and theories formed to integrate them (Dixon-Woods et al., 2006). Thomas and Harden (2008) suggest starting with a descriptive theme, which is a higher level statement than the findings from an individual study, and then looking across studies to develop an analytical theme, which involves going beyond the content of the original studies. Major and Savin-Baden (2010) describe a similar process, starting by developing first order themes and codes, then identifying first order themes across studies, combining themes across studies, and identifying second order themes across studies. The goal is not to identify similarities across studies or look for the lowest common denominator; it is to identify studies that disconfirm or challenge the collective understanding, and to generate a new way of understanding a phenomenon (Paterson et al., 2001; Suri, 2013).

Interpret the evidence

The analysis will lead to conclusions about what the data say in relation to the research questions, what the level of certainty is, and what the limitations are. The level of evidence (based on the criteria defined by the team) will influence the conclusions. For example, Harden and Gough (2012) describe how the Weight of Evidence Framework can be used to systematically assess a study's soundness, appropriateness of the study design for answering the review question, and the relevance to the review. The ratings can then be used to either exclude studies, or to determine their influence on the results. Harden and Gough (2012) also suggest that the weighting can simply be included in the review summary as information for the reader, and also be used in a sensitivity analysis, where the team assesses how the synthesis findings would change if the low evidence studies are excluded. At each decision point, the review team must be transparent about the extent to which a particular conclusion was based on the majority or a large set of studies, a single study with particularly strong evidence, or other criteria. The interpretation also leads to statements about how generalizable or specific the conclusions are over different populations, types of units, outcomes, and situations.

Communicate the results

The purpose of this stage is to summarize the findings and implications, and make recommendations about what research needs to be done, and which studies or methods they should build from. If members of the key audiences are involved throughout the process, what needs to be shared and the medium for sharing it can be discussed and presented in a variety of ways (Suri, 2014). This will increase the likelihood that the results will be useful and used. The findings need to be situated within the context of the field, so it is clear which gaps the review fills, which debates it contributes to or resolves, what new issues arose, as well as any implications for practice or future research.

EXAMPLE: A META-SYNTHESIS OF RESEARCH ON CHILDREN PROGRAMMING GAMES

In this section, we use a case study of a meta-synthesis to illustrate the steps, decisions, and challenges of conducting a systematic review of mixed methods educational research. To this end, we will describe the process followed by our team in a recent review of research on the benefits of children programming computer games (Denner et al., under review). Our team consisted of: a researcher trained in education and psychology, an educator who has both taught and done research on computer game programming (CGP), an education specialist with training in library and information science, and a computer science researcher/college professor. The overall goal was to pull together evidence of how and under what conditions children benefit from CGP, to identify the mechanisms through which students benefit (or do not), and generate new insights relating to the most effective approaches for teaching and studying CGP. We chose an integrative meta-synthesis approach for both practical and theoretical reasons. First, the studies came from a broad range of disciplines, and employ a range of theoretical perspectives, methods, epistemological foundations, and outcome foci. Second, we aimed to generate new ways of thinking about learning. We will describe the seven steps taken in this project, and emphasize the lessons learned in the meta-synthesis process, including the non-linear nature of the steps, key decision-making points, ongoing debates, unexpected challenges, and the range of expertise needed.

Define the scope: formulate the question

The focus of the review was driven by the recent and dramatic increase in the number of tools and classes for children to learn to program computer games. Despite this activity, there is no consensus on what children learn, the best pedagogical strategies, and which tools and learning environments promote different kinds of outcomes, and for whom. Our initial questions were about the benefits of CGP, including the kind of learning or motivation it is best suited to address, what kinds of students benefit the most, what is known about effective pedagogy and teacher training, what social and technical learning environments are most beneficial, and the research gaps. As the review progressed, additional questions emerged about the quality and range of research on CGP, the diversity of participants, and the range and advantages of different programming tools/environments. Because members of our review team had been studying CGP for over a decade, we were familiar with some of the popular assumptions about how it could benefit learning, but not sure the extent to which there was empirical evidence to support them.

Locate relevant literature

We conducted a comprehensive search using specific terms (for example, game programming, children game programming, game programming K-12, game programming schools, game design + novice, game design + novice + programmer) in the title and abstract and/or body, keywords, and metadata. The databases crossed academic and popular media sites, such as the ACM Digital Library and IEEE Xplore, as well as web search engines like Google Scholar and social media sites like Mendeley, ResearchGate and Academia.edu. We also searched conference proceedings and sent emails to key people who had published or worked in the area of children programming computer games. The search was limited to English language papers, because it is the primary language of the research team. Once our initial database search was exhausted, we searched the reference lists of the papers we had collected, to identify any published and unpublished papers we had missed in our online search and email communication.

A total of 408 articles were entered into an online database, but additional scrutiny was needed to determine their relevance. This required decisions about what is a 'game', and what is programming. We decided not to include studies of children modifying (rather than writing original) code, or studies of children programming as part of 'playing' a game. After reading the abstracts, we chose to only include papers that described studies of children programming what were described as games (versus digital storytelling or simulations), rather than studies of children designing games (on paper or verbally), reviews of research, or commentary. This left 236 papers, and gave our team ideas about determining the information that would be important to extract in the next phase.

Extract key information from each study

This process was designed to extract information by key categories that the team deemed necessary for understanding the sample, methods, evidence, and the context of the evidence. While this process can be reductionist, we aimed to include detail about study context and variations to avoid oversimplifying the findings. For each study, data were extracted on the following categories: demographic categories (for example, number of participants, grade level and age, race/ethnicity, country), program approach (for example, program setting, program hours, software), and measured outcomes (for example, academic content, CS learning, confidence). These data were entered into a searchable Excel database. Because so many papers lacked detail in one or more of these categories, we indicated when information was not found, or when it was unclear. One area in which our initial extraction categories broke down was the measured outcomes section, in part because our initial outcome categories were reductionist. We found that many papers did not fall into our big categories, such as academic content learning, so they were flagged as 'other' outcomes, but a key finding was that many studies were not designed to look at how children benefited. This insight was used later to help us think about what we mean by 'benefits'. Another challenge was how to clarify when the 'benefit' was clearly a result of CGP, and when it was part of a larger educational experience (so the extent to which CGP was the active ingredient could not be determined). Key decisions that had to be made at this stage included when to make inferences (for example, if the study authors were from Taiwan, should we assume the participants were too?) and what we mean by number of participants (for example, if a study has a comparison group of students who do NOT program games, do we count them as participants or not?). We decided not to make inferences, and wrote extensive notes to clarify the information for each category.

Extraction is a very time consuming process, and we learned to spend less time documenting details of studies that had obvious methodological flaws. Because this phase marked the first time that all papers were read in-depth, another round of decisions were made about which papers to include. Papers that were not included in the next phase were: duplicates (for example, reported the same findings from the same sample), studies that did not provide any evidence, or did not explain which evidence applied to K-12 students, and studies that did not clarify whether the evidence was based on students that actually programed games (or to a larger group). A reliability check was performed using two different reviewers working on approximately 30 articles; disagreements were resolved by discussion and the extraction process of the remaining 169 papers was done by individuals, who met regularly to discuss emerging issues and resolve questions. Additional categories were created in order to include notes about the strengths and limitations of the articles for addressing our review question.

Evaluate the quality and importance of each study

At this stage, our team relied on our expertise in research methods to critically evaluate the extent to which the conclusions made by the study authors were supported by evidence. To evaluate the quality of studies and determine which ones to include in the next (analysis) phase, we identified several criteria. For example, we used a modified version of Thomas and Harden's (2007) criteria to rate papers on their level of: Description (D), Validity (V), and Relevance (R). Each study was coded as yes/no on the following: (a) there was enough detail provided about the participants to assess generalizability (D), (b) there was enough detail provided about the research methods and data collected (D), (c) there were some findings and the conclusions were based on well-described evidence (V), (d) there was no obvious bias in the interpretation of findings (V), and (e) the findings were relevant to the key review questions (R). Based on these ratings, each paper was tagged as having evidence that was: Unsupported,

Credible, or Unequivocal, based on Major and Savin-Baden's (2010) criteria for evidence strength.

Unfortunately, the extraction matrix did not provide enough detail to make these decisions; therefore, the rating decisions required multiple readings of each paper and discussions amongst our interdisciplinary team about what counts as evidence. We ultimately defined evidence as 'a description of what students did and/or learned, where data are provided to support the authors' conclusions'. This process required ongoing critical reflection, because research shows that when a study challenges our expectations about outcomes, we are more likely to question the quality (Cooper, 2010). We retained papers in the first pass of the analysis if they had all five measures of description, validity, and relevance, which we termed unequivocal, or had 3–4 of these, which we termed credible. At the end of this process, there were 88 papers that met these criteria.

Analyze and integrate the findings

Our analysis approach followed Thomas and Harden's (2008) thematic synthesis approach. They distinguish between descriptive themes, which are higher level statements than the findings, and analytical themes, which involve going beyond the content of the original studies. Most prior mixed methods syntheses include ten or fewer studies, due to the complexity of analyzing and integrating across multiple papers. To create manageable groups, we took the 88 studies and grouped them into categories based on the specified outcome or benefit of CGP (for example, academic content, self-efficacy). This allowed us to compare and contrast the different ways that 'benefit' has been conceptualized and measured. However, this decision also had implications for the kinds of questions we could answer – for example, we could address questions about outcomes more easily than questions about pedagogical approach.

A key finding was that few studies were designed to address our question about how CGP benefited children. For example, during the analysis of papers in the academic content group, we identified two themes of how children benefited: evidence that students used academic content to make the games (for example, students made games about math), and evidence that students learned academic content as a result of making games. We labeled these two themes as 'integration', and 'learning'. The synthesis resulted in evidence for both kinds of benefits, but within specific parameters. For example, the evidence of learning benefits was stronger when students used academic content to make their games, than when they made games about academic content. In addition, there was evidence that programming computer games is a mechanism for engaging children in mathematical thinking, and for learning mathematics (followed by science), but only for certain types of math (for example, rates and proportions) and for younger children.

Interpret the evidence

A key result of our meta-synthesis review is that we have several recommendations for future research. Overall, the synthesis shows that there is a limited amount of credible evidence about the benefits of CGP. For example, most studies lack a clear theoretical perspective or research question, and few consider both outcomes and the context in which learning took place. Many are done with a small number of participants and rely on anecdotal, unsystematic observations of learning. More common is a focus on engagement, or the extent to which students enjoyed the process of designing and programming a game. But few include an analysis about what that might mean with regards to learning. In addition, many studies have an inadequate description of the participants or include only a highly experienced group of students, which prohibit generalization of findings. The incompleteness of the reports means that it is not always possible to highlight complementary or conflicting evidence.

Communicate the results

There are several final products that resulted from our synthesis. These include a narrative account of the findings – the descriptive and analytic themes that emerged, including a count of their frequency and the new ways of thinking about research on computer game programming. For example, one paper describes how studies using different research approaches attempt to justify the CGP approach, and the strengths and weaknesses of these methods in determining the educational benefits of CGP. Another paper will describe what evidence exists about assumptions that children learn computational thinking skills while programming computer games (Werner et al., under review). In addition to narrative, we have generated tables to provide a quick overview of the large number of studies in this field, in terms of their participants, programming language, data collection methods, and outcomes. These visual summaries can be used by readers to make their own judgments about the conclusions, and identify gaps in the research.

BENEFITS AND CHALLENGES OF A SYSTEMATIC REVIEW PROCESS FOR EDUCATIONAL RESEARCH FIELDS

It is well known that the accumulation, organization and synthesis of research-based knowledge are critical for advancing the field and contributing to educational practice (Shavelson and Towne, 2002). In particular, critical methods of research synthesis are needed to challenge the 'lore' and move a field forward (Suri, 2014). Fully understanding educational phenomena requires syntheses of studies that use a range of methodologies. However, traditional methods of research review are not designed to synthesize across different sample sizes, analytic methods, and criteria for evidence making. Rich, qualitative studies cannot be boiled down to the brief summaries that are needed to efficiently look across dozens of related studies.

In this chapter, we highlight several approaches to synthesizing research that use a range of methodological and epistemological approaches. The goal was to introduce the important and key issues to consider for students and researchers who are interested in pursuing a systematic research review, rather than to provide a set of detailed steps. There are a growing number of resources on how to conduct systematic reviews that include a range of methodologies, many of which were referenced in this chapter. However, less attention has been given to what happens to reviews. What makes a review effective? Who uses them? What happens if the findings contradict widely held beliefs? What kinds of presentations of results are needed for different audiences (for example, educators, policymakers, curriculum developers, researchers) to utilize them? How does the application of the results of a research review take place? How do people determine what parts of the synthesis to trust or apply, and what parts to not? To fully leverage the power of research syntheses, these questions must be addressed separately and collectively by subfields of educational research.

ACKNOWLEDGMENTS

The writing of this chapter was supported by a grant # 1252276 from the National Science Foundation. The authors are grateful to Linda Werner, for her important contributions to this work.

REFERENCES

Bangert-Drowns, R. L., and Rudner, L. M. (1991) *Meta-Analysis in Educational Research*. ERIC Digest.

Barnett-Page, E., and Thomas, J. (2009) Methods for the synthesis of qualitative research: a critical review. *BMC Medical Research Methodology*, 9, 1, 59. Retrieved on July 5, 2016 from http://eprints.ncrm.ac.uk/690/1/0109%2520Qualitative%2520 synthesis%2520methods%2520paper%2520NCRM.pdf.

Campbell, R., Pound, P., Morgan, M., Daker-White, G., Britten, N., Pill, R., ... and Donovan, J. (2012) Evaluating meta ethnography: systematic analysis and synthesis of qualitative research. *Health Technology Assessment*, 15, 43, 1–164.

Carroll, C., Booth, A., Leaviss, J., and Rick, J. (2013) 'Best fit' framework synthesis: refining the method. *BMC Medical Research Methodology*, 13, 1, 37.

Conn, V.S., Isaramalai, S., Rath, S., Jantarakupt, P., Wadhawan, R., and Dash, Y. (2003) Beyond MEDLINE for Literature Searches. *Journal of Nursing Scholarship*, 35, 2, 177–182.

Cook, T. D., Cooper, H., Cordray, D. S., Hartmann, H., Hedges, L. V., and Light, R. J. (Eds) (1992) *Meta-analysis for Explanation: A casebook*. London: Russell Sage Foundation.

Cooper, H. (2010) *Research Synthesis and Meta-analysis: A step-by-step approach*, 4th edition. Thousand Oaks, CA: Sage Publications.

Cooper, H., Hedges, L. V., and Valentine, J. C. (Eds) (2009) *The Handbook of Research Synthesis and Meta-analysis*. London: Russell Sage Foundation.

Davies, H., and Powell, A. (2010) *Helping social research make a difference: Exploration of a wider repertoire of approaches to communicating and influencing through research.* Research Unit for Research Utilisation, University of St Andrews. Retrieved on July 5, 2016 from www.ruru.ac.uk/pdf/Davies%20%20Powell%20-%20 Helping%20social%20research%20make%20a%20difference%20final.pdf.

Denner, J., Campe, S., Werner, L., and Marsh, E. (under review). Does computer game design and programming benefit children? A systematic review of research.

Dixon-Woods, M., Bonas, S., Booth, A., Jones, D. R., Miller, T., Sutton, A. J., ... and Young, B. (2006) How can systematic reviews incorporate qualitative research? A critical perspective. *Qualitative Research*, 6, 1, 27–44.

Fanelli, D. (2011) Negative results are disappearing from most disciplines and countries. *Scientometrics*, 903, 891–904.

France, E. F., Ring, N., Thomas, R., Noyes, J., Maxwell, M., and Jepson, R. (2014) A methodological systematic review of what's wrong with meta-ethnography reporting. *BMC Medical Research Methodology*, 14, 1, 119.

Gawande, A. (2009) *The Checklist Manifesto: How to get things right*. New York, NY: Metropolitan Books.

Glass, G. V. (1976) Primary, secondary, and meta-analysis of research. *Educational Researcher*, 3–8.

Gough, D., Oliver, S., and Thomas, J. (2012) *An Introduction To Systematic Reviews*. London: Sage Publications.

Gough, D., Thomas, J., and Oliver, S. (2012) Clarifying differences between review designs and methods. *Syst Rev*, 1, 1, 28. Retrieved on July 5, 2016 from http://www.systematicreviewsjournal.com/content/1/1/28.

Hattie, J., Rogers, H. J., and Swaminathan, H. (2014) The role of meta-analysis in educational research. In A. Reid, E. Hart, and M. Peters (Eds) *A Companion to Research in Education*. Netherlands: Springer, 197–207.

Harden, A. and Gough, D. (2012) Quality and relevance appraisal. In D. Gough, S. Oliver, and J. Thomas (2012) *An Introduction to Systematic Reviews*. London: SAGE Publications, 153–178.

Major, C. H., and Savin-Baden, M. (2010) *An Introduction to Qualitative Research Synthesis*. New York: Routledge.

Major, C. H., and Savin-Baden, M. (2011) Integration of qualitative evidence: towards construction of academic knowledge in social science and professional fields. *Qualitative Research*, 11, 6, 645–663.

Makel, M. C., and Plucker, J. A. (2014) Facts are more important than novelty replication in the education sciences. *Educational Researcher*, 43, 6, 304–316.

McMillan, J. H., Mohn, R. S., and Hammack, M. V. (2013) Quantitative research designs in educational research. DOI: 10.1093/obo/9780199756810-0113. Retrieved on July 5, 2016 from www.oxfordbibliographies.com/view/document/obo-9780199756810/ obo-9780199756810–0113.xml.

Noblit, G. W., and Hare, R. D. (1988) *Meta-ethnography: Synthesizing qualitative studies* (Vol. 11). London: Sage Publications.

Nordmann, A. J., Kasendaa, B., and Briel, M. (2012) Meta-analyses: what they can and cannot do. *Swiss Medical Weekly*, 142, w13518.

Pace, R., Pluye, P., Bartlett, G., Macaulay, A. C., Salsberg, J., Jagosh, J., and Seller, R. (2012) Testing the reliability and efficiency of the pilot Mixed Methods Appraisal Tool (MMAT) for systematic mixed studies review. *International Journal of Nursing Studies*, 49, 1, 47–53.

Paterson, B. L., and Canam, C. (2001) *Meta-study of Qualitative Health Research: A practical guide to meta-analysis and meta-synthesis* (Vol. 3). London: Sage Publications.

Pawson, R. (2006) *Evidence-based Policy: A realist perspective*. London: Sage Publications.

Pawson, R., Greenhalgh, T., Harvey, G., and Walshe, K. (2005) Realist review – a new method of systematic review designed for complex policy interventions. *Journal of Health Services Research & Policy*, 10 (suppl 1), 21–34.

Peters, M., Godfrey, C., McInerney, P., Soares, C., Khalil, H., and Parker, D. (2015) Methodology for JBI scoping reviews. Retrieved on July 5, 2016 from http://joannabriggs.org/assets/docs/sumari/Reviewers-Manual_Methodology-for-JBI-Scoping-Reviews_2015_v2.pdf.

Pierson, D. J. (2004) The top 10 reasons why manuscripts are not accepted for publication. *Respiratory Care*, 49, 10, 1246–1252.

Pope, C., Mays, N., and Popay, J. (2007) *Synthesising Qualitative and Quantitative Health Evidence: A guide to methods*. London: McGraw-Hill Education.

Saini, M., and Shlonsky, A. (2012) *Systematic Synthesis of Qualitative Research*. Oxford: Oxford University Press.

Sandelowski, M., and Barroso, J. (2007) *Handbook for Synthesizing Qualitative Research*. Berlin: Springer Publishing Company.

Sandelowski, M., Voils, C. I., Leeman, J., and Crandell, J. L. (2012) Mapping the mixed methods–mixed research synthesis terrain. *Journal of Mixed Methods Research*, 6, 4, 317–331.

Shavelson, R. J., and Towne, L. (2002) Scientific research in education. Committee on scientific principles for education research. *Center for Education. Division of Behavioral and Social Sciences and Education. National Research Council. Washington, DC: National Academy Press*.

Suri, H. (2000) A critique of contemporary methods of research synthesis. *Post-Script*, 1, 1, 49–55.

Suri, H. (2013) Epistemological pluralism in research synthesis methods. *International Journal of Qualitative Studies in Education*, 26, 7, 889–911.

Suri, H. (2014) *Towards Methodologically Inclusive Research Syntheses: Expanding possibilities*. London: Routledge.

Suri, H., and Clarke, D. (2009) Advancements in research synthesis methods: from a methodologically inclusive perspective. *Review of Educational Research*, 79, 1, 395–430.

Thomas, J. and Harden, A. (2007) Methods for the thematic synthesis of qualitative research in systematic reviews. ESRV National Centre for Research Methods, NCRM Working Paper Series, 10/07.

Thomas, J., and Harden, A. (2008) Methods for the thematic synthesis of qualitative research in systematic reviews. *BMC Medical Research Methodology*, 8, 1, 45.

Thomas, J., Harden, A., and Newman, M. (2012) Synthesis: combining results systematically and appropriately. In D. Gough, S. Oliver, and J. Thomas (2012) *An introduction to systemic reviews*. London: SAGE Publications, 179–227.

Tight, M. (2012) Higher education research 2000–2010: changing journal publication patterns. *Higher Education Research & Development*, 31, 5, 723–740.

US Department of Education and National Science Foundation report on common guidelines (2013) *Common guidelines for education research and development.* Retrieved on July 5, 2016 from http://ies.ed.gov/pdf/CommonGuidelines.pdf.

Werner, L., Denner, J., and Campe, S (under review). Children programming games: a synthesis of evidence of computational thinking.

Whittemore, R., and Knafl, K. (2005) The integrative review: updated methodology. *Journal of Advanced Nursing*, 52, 5, 546–553. Retrieved on July 5, 2016 from http://users.phhp.ufl.edu/rbauer/EBPP/whittemore_knafl_05.pdf.

7

Purposes for Educational Research

Peter Tymms

INTRODUCTION

Education is an artificial system (Simon, 1988) created by people and educational research should continually strive to improve that system. Research in the discipline of education is not about the fundamentals of philosophy, statistics, psychology, sociology or genetics, but rather about finding ways to improve how we learn and what we learn. It might seek, for example, to describe some aspect of education such as activity in the classroom, or problematise a politician's claim or establish the correlates of failure in examinations. These activities may or may not improve education, but if that is not their ultimate aim, then what is their purpose? To gain qualification or status for the researcher? To gain academic insight for its own end? To move up the university league tables? To justify a politician's policy? All these and others, are certainly purposes for educational research, but if we look behind the immediate aims and behind the rewards and ask about its ultimate purpose, it has to be to improve education.

That improvement might come about in many ways, for example, we might directly investigate whether approach A to teaching reading is more effective than approach B, or we might ask what the school experience of being labelled with a diagnosis of a disorder such as ADHD feels like, or we might ask if delaying the age of starting school helps children in the long run, and so on. In each case, we are exploring how education can be improved.

ADVANCE ORGANISER

This chapter builds the case for and elaborates the assertions in the last two paragraphs by first outlining the aspirations and perceptions of some selected researchers and then giving a position statement which sets out the author's ontological views. This is followed by an extended analogy which aims to show how a single topic can attract the interests of a very diverse set of researchers with varying mindsets and purposes. In trying to make sense of the diversity of disciplines attention is then directed at Herbert Simon's work, as providing an overarching structure and direction. The implications are then explored and, recognising that there are multiple purposes for educational research, a hierarchy of purposes is proposed. This is followed by a section which seeks to make more explicit the links between methods and purposes with two examples of chosen methods. Finally, the chapter is drawn to a conclusion with a call for more working together across disciplines.

DIFFERING PERCEPTION

A thoughtful overarching position was taken by Kerlinger (1973), in which he set out the case for the scientific approach. For him, the aim was to use the scientific method with the clear goal of creating theory '*the ultimate aim of science*'. Such a grand aspirational aim lies behind the development of the Tool Kit (Higgins et al., 2014), a synthesis of research on the impact of educational interventions and also a way to help schools spend their money wisely (http://educationendowmentfoundation.org.uk/). But the use of scientific procedures in educational research has been dismissed with the insult '*positivist!*', a term that refers back to a philosophy of the nineteenth century which has been rejected by mainstream natural scientists such as Heisenberg (1991), but the word continues to be used, often inappropriately, when describing quantitative educational research.

Unfortunately, for those who reject the scientific approach and for those who argue that more research will not allow us to establish universal education truths, we have evidence for both: we have examples of meaningful theory and have shown that educational truths are not always eternal. The former comes from the remarkably extensive work on reading (summarised by Delamont and Grigorenko, 2014). They synthesise work from psychologists, educationalists, geneticists and neuroscientists giving teachers a solid evidenced-based theoretical base from which help for those who struggle to learn to read can be constructed. Evidence for the latter has been building up over time, but two recent papers (Slavin et al., 2014 and Lemons et al., 2014), show that apparently well-established interventions do not consistently work across countries and over time. The paper by Slavin et al. recounts how a previously successful intervention involving cooperative learning in the USA simply did not work in the UK, despite two serious efforts using randomised control trials. They comment that 'Teaching methods proven to be effective in one culture and system cannot be assumed to be effective in another'. The work of Lemons et al. involved peer tutoring experiments repeated over several years which unexpectedly did not work after a series of successes. They ascribed the finding to 'the changed context' and wrote about the impact of 'the change agent – a no-nonsense Chief Instructional Officer'.

An additional purpose for educational research was set out by Simon (1988); creating systems that work. If, as educational researchers, our ultimate purpose is to improve education, then one way to do so is to create working systems. One significant example is provided by the A Level Information System project created by Fitz-Gibbon (1996), which led to a series of very successful monitoring systems for schools to evaluate the effectiveness of their own practice on students' progress and outcomes (Tymms and Coe, 2003). Interest has expanded in this way of working under the general heading of Design Research (Kelly, 2003 and Plomp, 2009).

In summary, the main purpose for educational research must be to improve education. That research may aim to analyse, describe or explain through various approaches but it may also be concerned with design. This might be the design of a teaching programme, an assessment system, a curriculum or an out of school activity. In each case, the aim is to improve the education of children.

POSITION STATEMENT

When writing about the purposes of educational research, it seems appropriate to set out what the author sees as the nature of the social world; in other words, to make an explicit statement about ontological belief. Educational researchers vary enormously in their stances and in what they write about the positions of others. This can vary from the caricatured extremes of positivism to an apparent belief that the world is entirely socially constructed. Between these, there are a range of views which are outlined below by analogy. But from the outset, I note that I believe in neither of these extreme positions which are of course incommensurate (Pring, 2000 and Coe, 2012) and which can distract us from a more pragmatic discourse; educational research is nothing, if not pragmatic.

TWO EXTREMES

The social world cannot be understood in the way that Isaac Newton was able to understand the movement of the earth around the sun. His was a staggering achievement, building on the data and the insights of others (Koestler and Butterfield, 1968). He was able to show that the same force which causes an apple to fall to the ground dictates the path of our planet around its star. He did this from a series of propositions and equations, generating a whole new branch of mathematics in the process (see for example Tymms, 2016). It is these advances, which allow us to predict eclipses to within a fraction of a second millennia ahead. But, Newton was aware that the solutions to his equations applied best to the problems involving two objects and that even with three, the solutions to the equations are not simple. In fact, as interactions occur, so do complications and the possibility that scientific chaos will ensue (see for example Gleick 1988) making prediction impossible even if the system obeys deterministic laws; a tantalising paradox. Of course, such unpredictability is not a problem for much of the movement of the massive bodies of our solar system where distances are large and near interactions are relatively rare but it is close at hand on a pool table. Even on a hypothetical perfect table with completely spherical balls the position after just a few impacts becomes unpredictable because tiny perturbations in the initial conditions take over the evolving system. In the social sciences, we need to take scientific chaos more seriously than we have to date, although there are strong movements to incorporate the insights which its study has generated (see for example Smith and Thelen, 2003). With these ideas in mind, I thought that I recalled the great Michael Scriven stating in a Keynote that 'The purpose, and the ultimate purpose, of educational research is to produce low level generalisation and explain them in an informal fashion'. But an Internet search failed to confirm my recollection and an email produced this response: 'That's an interesting quote, which sounds like something I'd say if it were a discussion: if it were for publication, I would have had to note that I believe there are some exceptions to this low-level generalization' (Scriven, 2014).

At the other extreme, is the view that the world is socially constructed. Note that this is not simply a claim that there are differing views, but that there is no reality per se (Fairhurst and Grant, 2010). A well-argued case is made for this proposition and it is clear we can doubt everything except our own existence: 'cogito ergo sum', as Descartes concluded in the charcoal burner's hut. Similarly, we can make a case that simply because the sun has risen every day for 4,000 million years, it does not follow that it will rise tomorrow (Ng, 2005). But I continue to live my life assuming that it will. I side *mutatis mutandis* with Samuel Johnson, who railed against Bishop Berkley's 'ingenuous sophistry' by kicking a stone and saying 'I refute it thus'. It is quite clear to me and I believe to most social scientists, that there is more substance to the world than that which is socially constructed. This is not to deny that there are different perceptions, even of a single incident and that those perceptions impact on the world, but it does not mean to say that, the world does not exist except in the mind.

I see the world as being based on a series of fundamental laws which are the province of physics and that these fundamental laws have dictated the nature of substances, from which our world is made. The study of these substances is the province of chemistry. From some of these substances, life evolved over the last

3.5 billion years on earth and much of this story is now becoming clear through the work of geneticists, biologists and others. We are merely one example of this life albeit with extraordinary brains. Our mental processes and states in all their complexity have been studied by psychologists whilst society, formed from groups of people, is the basis of sociological research.

Generally, and perhaps surprisingly, the various researchers and disciplines mentioned above have little to do with one another. It is even rare amongst proximate disciplines where it might be expected that sociologists would regularly refer to psychologists, or psychologists to biologists. By contrast, education departments in universities are quite likely to include an eclectic mix of psychologists, sociologists, historians, philosophers, economists and many other disciplines. They all study education often using their disciplinary perspectives and do, occasionally, collaborate.[1]

AN ANALOGY

If the world is not predictable, despite being the product of fundamental deterministic laws of nature, and if it is not simply in the eye of the beholder, how are we to perceive it and how might we study it? One way to start thinking this through is by using an inevitably imperfect analogy; studying education can be likened to studying rivers and streams. There will be some who might want to measure the water; its temperature, flow, depth and density. These measures might be related to known laws. For example, as the river flows down steep canyons the potential energy gets converted to heat and the changes can be satisfyingly modelled and predictions made. But others, might want to look at the flow of the water using a quite different qualitative lens, noting differences between fast running streams around cataracts and slow moving shallows and theorise about the a life of the river starting with the young stream with its fast bubbling brooks in high altitudes and then into the slow, moving middle age and finally, into slower moving old age as it comes to the sea. Such ideas might lead to aesthetically pleasing accounts involving the many shades of colour and the sounds generally by water flow. There will also be those who feel that their best way of studying the water is to become part of the river itself by jumping in and to study from within; to get an idea of how it feels to be water and, so far as it is possible, to become at one with the river. Yet others would claim that you cannot really understand the river without knowing its history. They might look at the paths formed by the water and build up layers of maps which allow us to see the different paths over the years. Or they might try to establish a history of the river through oral accounts and historic record. This could include comparing the river with other rivers. All these different ways of operating, or studying, are trying to make sense of what is going on.

Quite different groups will want to influence the way that the river behaves. Perhaps they want to avoid destructive flooding, improve the water quality, use the river's power to generate electricity or create a way in which the water can be released in a controlled fashion to irrigate crops efficiently. These groups would be advised to take cognisance of the research findings of the workers described in the previous paragraph – they need the knowledge – but their purpose is to change and improve, not to describe and understand. This improvement might also be to the river itself, to improve the quality of the water and the ecosystem that it supports.

There is, of course, a limit to the extent to which this analogy holds but it does illustrate various approaches. The researchers might come together and share their work, although it has to be acknowledged that different researchers might find that they were talking across each other even though they were all studying the same phenomenon! For many of the methodological approaches, there is no inherent purpose to studying the river other than to understand, but for those who would influence the river there are pre-stated purposes. These two positions (trying to understand and trying to change) are explored in the next two sections with a firm stance being taken for educational research.

SCIENCES OF THE ARTIFICIAL

In Herbert Simon's book, *The Sciences of the Artificial* (Simon, 1988) he outlines science in its traditional sense of physics, chemistry and biology which are natural sciences; the scientists working in these disciplines study and develop knowledge about objects and phenomena in the natural world. He distinguishes this natural science from sciences of the artificial. Although he notes that 'artificial' can have pejorative meanings, he argues that if artificial is taken to mean 'made by people' then there really is no problem. There is nothing pejorative in something which is created by people and which can, after creation, take on a life of its own as does a railway, a smartphone or a school. His focus is on things which can be designed. 'If we are talking about the artificial, we are thinking about things that are made, synthesised by people. They might imitate what happens in the natural world, not be of things of the actual world so that artificial things have function or goals or adaptation'. Artificial systems are likely to be so complex that, even though their basic structures may be fully understood by the sciences of the natural world they must be independently studied by scientific procedures. It follows that in order for an artificial system to be understood, it has to be created. For example, you must study the workings of computers to understand them rather than assuming that you will understand how they will work by looking at the well-understood hardware with logical algorithms. He hypothesises that there will be general laws that can be applied to these artificial systems.

Simon also sets out ways in which university curricula could be developed to study the sciences of the artificial and asserts that it is necessary to move in that direction with more formal and theoretical ways of thinking. Writing originally in 1969, he regretted the tendency for the natural sciences to occupy such a high status and thought that studies of the artificial had apparently suffered. This meant a general downplaying of studies such as journalism, library science and engineering whilst they themselves attempted, in a search for respectability, to mimic the natural sciences; 'the sciences of the artificial is always in danger of dissolving and vanishing and peculiar properties of the artefact, lie on the thin interface between natural laws within and natural laws without'. Whilst natural sciences are concerned with how things are, the artificial sciences should be concerned with how things ought to be, hence the emphasis on a science of design. There was already an extensive body of knowledge to help establish such disciplines but much has yet to be done. Great designs will not be perfect and he introduces the word 'satisficing' to underline the impossibility of perfect solutions. To satisfice is to do just what is necessary to solve a problem. What is needed, is something which is good enough, something which satisfices.

Of course, the university scene has evolved since the time of the first edition of Simon's work, but has it changed radically? Do we have education departments with a coherent focus on the science of education? To what extent do we seriously seek to design new and better systems? Do we still want, in our own ways, to emulate the disciplines from whence we came?

PASTEUR'S' QUADRANT

Stokes (1997), formulated what he termed 'Pasteur's quadrant' which (Figure 7.1) neatly categories research according to whether it was based on a quest for fundamental understanding and what the initial consideration of the use of the research was.

The top left hand quadrant corresponds to Simon's natural sciences and Stokes characterises this with the work of the physicist Neils Bohr. The top right hand quadrant is exemplified by the microbiologist Louis Pasteur, whose work was aimed at practical uses but involved developing fundamental understanding. The bottom right hand quadrant corresponds neatly with Simon's sciences of the artificial and is characterised by the work of the inventor and businessman Thomas Edison. Educational research also fits into that box with one proviso which is provided by Beckmann (2015). Beckmann uses the quadrants when thinking through the direction of psychological research. He argues that some of the work

Figure 7.1 Pasteur's quadrant

		Consideration of use?	
		No	Yes
Quest for fundamental understanding?	Yes	Pure basic research	User-inspired basic research
	No		Pure applied research

of psychologists, working in an applied discipline such as education, is aimed at use and inevitably, advances fundamental understanding. In this, he is surely right.

IMPLICATION

Both Simon's Sciences of the Artificial and Stoke's formulation have implications for educational research and its purpose. The first point is, that educational research can be considered to be a science of the artificial, which needs to focus on use and which can/should draw on the natural and other sciences and, in particular, on psychology and sociology whilst using tools derived from other disciplines such as medicine, ethnography, statistics and economics. Its purpose is not to search for fundamental understanding in the natural sciences sense, rather it should draw on fundamental understandings which have been established elsewhere. But it can be that the effort to improve education does advance fundamental understanding in a field such as psychology.

The second is that improvement might involve the designing of systems that work well enough, or, better than existing systems. This could be as grand as creating a national assessment system (Black, 1988), or as modest as designing a lesson plan. Each aims to satisfice, none is perfect and each can be improved.

Third, educational research can properly provide feedback to a system or part of the system. This may be as apparently small, but potentially vital, as giving observational feedback to a teacher, or as broad as systematically studying and reporting on standards (Tymms, 2004; Tymms and Merrell, 2007; Coe and Tymms 2008). It might also involve criticism (feedback) of existing systems; an aspect of feedback (Scriven, 1996).

A HIERARCHY OF PURPOSES

The purposes of educational research can be thought of as hierarchical (Figure 7.2). At the top level, the ultimate purpose for educational research is to improve education. The second level encompasses the implications noted above and fits well with Newby's (2014) three broad reasons for doing research in education and they are to explore the issues, to shape policy and to improve practice.

Below the second level come more differentiated purposes which start to blend into the methodologies hinted at earlier. That is to say as we move from general purposes we come to ways of doing research and these are usually linked to specific purposes; they include generalised themes such as literature searches, observations and interviews, testing ideas, thinking through the

purposes of education, thick descriptions, statistical analyses, creating local-
ised, national and cross-boundary systems. One of these, 'thinking through
the purposes of education', occupies an odd position in the hierarchy in that
one cannot logically decide how to improve education unless one knows what
its purposes are. Again a pragmatic view is taken. There is much agreement
about the overall purposes of education (to provide children with basic skills, to
enable fulfilling individual lives, to develop people who can contribute to society) but it is nonetheless not uncontroversial especially when the details behind
the broad headlines are examined, and thinking in this area should be seen as
evolving and potentially influencing our view of what it means to improve education in an iterative cycle.

As an aside, it is worth noting that it is common to see research design tackled
in books on educational research and this is often arranged within paradigms
(Cohen et al. 2000; Newby, 2014; Arthur et al., 2012; Green et al., 2012). The
paradigms might include broadly naturalistic or ethnographic research, correlational research, case studies, historical approaches and interventions; Cohen
et al. (2000) call these groupings 'Styles of Educational Research'. But within
the hierarchy research design does not appear *per se*, rather it can be conceived
as something which is necessary to the activity of educational research and which
should always have purpose(s) in mind. Research design is also the subject of
specific texts such as Middleton et al. (2008), Gerber and Green (2012) and
Creswell (2012).

At the fourth level come the tools of educational research and again many
texts, outline a plethora of different research techniques or approaches. Each of
those tools is able to answer particular kinds of questions, or rather, it is reasonable to seek answers to certain questions by using their tools. These include questionnaires, interviews, cognitive tests, randomised control trials, observational
checklists, meta-analysis and others too numerous to mention. For each of these
tools, we must be clear about their purposes, their potential and limitations for
educational research.

There is a danger that the purposes of educational research get lost in the
methods and the next section aims to make the link between methods and purposes clearer.

RESEARCH METHODS

Given the plethora of research methods available to the educational investigator,
two very different approaches are set out in more detail, by way of example, to
illustrate the kinds of questions (purposes) that can reasonably be asked using
the various methods. One involving questionnaires is usually associated with the
quantitative paradigms and the second, the ethnographic approach falls into the
naturalistic category.

Figure 7.2 Hierarchy of the purposes of educational research

1									
2	**To improve education**								
	Exploring the issues				**Shaping policy: examination of existing systems and practice; envisaging alternatives**			**Design: creating systems that work**	
3	Literature reviews including meta-analyses and systematic reviews	Observations, interviews	Identifying problems	Testing ideas through small-scale informal interventions through to large-scale clustered RCTs	Examining or purposes of education	Detailed thick descriptions of impact then on individuals and groups	Analyses of the workings through quantitative data including the validity of claims and unintended consequences	National – structures, curricula, assessment	Stand-alone: assessment systems, programmes of work, text books not restricted to one context	Specific, classroom organization, lesson planning
4									

QUESTIONNAIRES

Questionnaires (see for example Tymms, 2012), are responded to online, on paper or possibly on the telephone or face-to-face. They include a series of questions which can vary quite dramatically, from the very structured to the unstructured using yes/no types of responses to multiple choice, rank ordering, ratings and open ended questions. In doing this, the researcher can be expected to have a fairly advanced understanding of the issues of the topic being investigated. That is certainly the case if one is asking about questions involving rating scales; 'To what extent do you agree that …' which can be answered on a strongly disagree to strongly agree rating. Investigators would be ill-advised to ask such a question without preliminary investigation; this might be a series of interviews, or focus groups or reading the literature where other investigations have been carried out. A significant threat to the research is the possibility that respondents are prepared to give opinions of topics which they know little about or which are not relevant to them. Although, of course, it is accepted that questionnaires can begin in a very preliminary, open ended way and then focus in, with later instruments, as the key questions start to crystallise. Nevertheless, the kind of questions the researcher seeks to answer would be 'To what extent do participants feel that' and then some statement there or 'What is the general opinion about' or 'What is the estimated likely reaction to …'. Questionnaires can also be used as an instrument to measure such things as motivation or attitudes. They necessarily follow other theoretical or empirical work, which ascribes the kind of attitudes that we are interested in or the kind of structure behind motivation. It would not be possible or sensible to try to approach those later on.

Questionnaires seek to answer questions about people's feelings, attitudes and perceptions, having first decided what kind of attitudes and perceptions are relevant and valued. Of course, the open ended questionnaire is less constrained and can be used to develop a structure or theory through the analysis to the responses but even there, the questions that need to be asked need to be based on prior knowledge.

Sometimes, the technique is used to ask people why they did certain things but often they do not know or cannot remember accurately, even when they think they do. This lack of validity of introspection is evident for a number of investigations such as those into memory (McFarland et al., 1989) and social judgements (Nisbett and Bellows 1977). Both of these articles are discussed in more detail in Abelson et al. (2014).

But whatever the nature of a questionnaire and whatever the quality of the data it generates its purpose is embedded in the design of the research. Tools have multiple purposes and questionnaires could figure in several of the level 3 purposes in Figure 7.2. These are in turn linked to the levels above the point being that the specific approaches chosen for educational research should be subservient to the aims. Tools are there to be used for purposes not to define purposes.

THE ETHNOGRAPHIC APPROACH

The ethnographic approach of gathering information is quite different and is clearly outlined by for example, Anderson-Levitt (2006), Green and Bloome (2004), Rossman and Rallis (2011). The guiding principle is that, ethnography deals with culture and that the researcher takes the view of the insider and seeks to understand groups from within. It is about people and how they form meanings within groups. In other words, culture can be seen as the making of meaning. The researcher does not seek answers to the kind of questions that an evaluator might ask about impact; rather he or she 'seeks understandings of local situations' (Anderson-Levitt, 2006, p. 282). In other words, it describes the real world complexity of human behaviour. It asks: What is going on here? How does this happen? What does it mean? It does not measure variables nor does it test hypotheses. It is often used to tell stories, particularly of the less powerful (Bagley and Castro-Salazar, 2012), but it can also be used to study the powerful. The researcher might work in a field as a participant observer over a very long period of time.

It is instructive to note a passage from the Anderson-Levitt (2006), which gives a clear view of the purposes of the ethnographic approach:

> it is an ideal research strategy for seeking to understand real human behaviour in all its complexity and, therefore, *provides important background for any research that seeks real and lasting solutions to human problems*. (Anderson-Levitt, 2006, p. 282 emphasis added)

Note that the quote refers to a 'research strategy'. The author see the ethnographic approach not as an end in itself with its own purpose but as something which is subservient to a higher purpose.

CONCLUSION

Educational research is hard to categorise involving, as it does, many different academic disciplines. Indeed, one could be forgiven for not seeing educational research as a discipline in itself. But it can be unified under a single purpose which is to improve education. It can do this by exploring issues, shaping policy and crucially by design – creating systems that work. The methods it uses are extraordinarily diverse and very often they have restricted aims and operate only within well-defined boundaries. Nevertheless, educational research has built and is building an extraordinary body of knowledge and understanding which largely resides within the sub-compartments of educational research, the paradigms. Despite a widespread recognition that each approach has something to offer and despite important texts showing ways forward (Tashakkori and Teddlie, 2010;

Cooper et al., 2012), it remains the case that researchers often remain in their group running their own conferences, writing and reading their own journals. Moreover, there is probably more interdisciplinary interaction within education than is found between say sociology and psychology or between biology and chemistry. But we need more. Improving the education of our children can only be helped by bringing researchers from very different perspectives together. Curriculum design needs the insights of educational ethnographers just as it needs educational psychologists, psychometricians and practitioners. We have a common purpose and we should specifically aim to come together to fulfil that purpose.

Of course it is hard to get academics to agree with one another, not only are they naturally inclined to independent thought but career advancement can be forged by creating new theories and by pointing out the errors of others! But we do not have to agree with one another to work together. Given a common problem to solve – an educational design issue – researchers can and do come together remarkably well.

Note

1 One reviewer of this chapter commented: 'it is when these disciplines do not co-exist in a department that you get an insular view of small scale education research dominating'.

REFERENCES

Abelson, R. P., Frey, K. P. and Gregg, A. P. (2014) *Experiments with People: Revelations from social psychology*. London: Psychology Press.
Anderson-Levitt, K. M. (2006) Ethnography. In J. L. Green, G. Camilli and P. B. Elmore (Eds) *Handbook of Complementary Methods in Education Research*. London: Routledge, 279–296.
Arthur, J., Waring, M., Coe R. and Hedges L. (Eds) (2012) *Research Methods and Methodologies in Education*. London, California, New Delhi and Singapore: Sage Publications.
Bagley, C. and Castro-Salazar, R. (2012) Critical arts-based research in education: performing undocumented historias. *British Educational Research Journal*, 38, 2, 239–260.
Beckmann, J. F. (2015) Commentary – of quadrants and fish scales: reflections on new directions in research in child and adolescent development. *New directions for child and adolescent development*, 147, 127–133.
Black, P. J. (1988) *National Curriculum: Task group on assessment and testing, a report*. London: Department of Education and Science and Welsh Office.
Coe, R. (2012) The nature of educational research. In Arthur, J. et al. (Eds) *Research Methods and Methodologies in Education*. Los Angeles, London, New Delhi, Singapore and Washington: Sage Publications, 5–13.
Coe, R. and Tymms, P. (2008) Summary of research on changes in educational standards in the UK. In M. Harris (Ed.) *Education Briefing Book 2008: IoD Policy Paper*. London: Institute of Directors, 86–109.

Cohen, L., Manion, L. and Morrison, K. (2000) *Research Methods in Education*, 5th edition. London: Routledge Falmer.

Cooper, B., Glaesser, J., Gomm, R. and Hammersley, M. (2012) *Challenging the Qualitative–Quantitative Divide: Explorations in case-focused causal analysis*. London: Bloomsbury Publishing.

Creswell, J. W. (2012) *Qualitative Inquiry and Research Design: Choosing among five approaches*. London: Sage Publications.

Delamont, Elliott, J. G. and Grigorenko, E. L. (2014) *The Dyslexia Debate* (No. 14). Cambridge: Cambridge University Press.

Fairhurst, Gail T. and Grant, David (2010) The social construction of leadership: a sailing guide. *Management Communication Quarterly*, 24, 2, 171–210.

Fitz-Gibbon, C. T. (1996) *Monitoring Education: Indicators, quality and effectiveness*. London: Cassell.

Gerber, A. S. and Green, D. P. (2012) *Field Experiments: Design, analysis, and interpretation*. London: W. W. Norton.

Gleick, J. (1988) *Chaos: Making a new science*. London: Heinemann.

Green, J. L., Camilli, G. and Elmore, P. B. (2012) *Handbook of Complementary Methods in Education Research*. London: Routledge.

Green, J. and Bloome, D. (2004) Ethnography and ethnographers of and in education: a situated perspective. In J. Flood., S. B. Health and M. D. Lapp (Eds) *Handbook for Literacy Educators: Research in the Community and Visual Arts*. London: Routledge, 181–202.

Heisenberg, W. (1991) Positivism, metaphysics and religion. In T. Ferris (Ed.) *The World Treasury of Physics, Astronomy and Mathematics*. New York: Little, Brown & Co., 821–827.

Higgins, S., Katsipataki, M., Kokotsaki, D., Coleman, R., Major, L.E. and Coe, R. (2014) *The Sutton Trust-Education Endowment Foundation Teaching and Learning Toolkit*. London: Education Endowment Foundation.

Kelly, A. E. (2003) Research as design. *Educational Researcher: Theme Issue: The role of design in educational research*, 32, 1, 3–4.

Kerlinger, F. N. (1973) *The Foundations of Behavioral Research*, 2nd edition. London: Holt Rinehart and Winston.

Koestler, A., and Butterfield, H. (1968) *The Sleepwalkers*. London: Hutchinson.

Lemons, C. J., Fuchs, D., Gilbert, J. K. and Fuchs, L. S. (2014) Evidence-based practices in a changing world: reconsidering the counterfactual in educational research. *Educational Researcher*, 43, 5, 242–252.

McFarland, C., Ross, M. and DeCourville, N. (1989) Women's theories of menstruation and biases in recall of menstrual symptoms. *Journal of Personality and Social Psychology*, 57, 3, 522.

Middleton, J., Gorard, S., Taylor, C. and Bannan-Ritland, B. (2008) The 'compleat' design experiment: from soup to nuts. In A. E. Kelly, J. Y. Baek and R. A. Lesh (Eds) *Handbook of Design Research Methods in Education: Innovations in science, technology, engineering, and mathematics learning and teaching*. London: Routledge, 21–46.

Newby, P. (2014) *Research Methods for Education*, 2nd edition. Abingdon and New York: Routledge.

Ng, Y. K. (2005) *A critical analysis of the role of statistical significance testing in education research: With special attention to mathematics education* (Doctoral dissertation, Durham University).

Nisbett, R. E. and Bellows, N. (1977) Verbal reports about causal influences on social judgments: private access versus public theories. *Journal of Personality and Social Psychology*, 35, 9, 613.

Plomp, T. (2009) *Educational Design Research: An introduction.* Proceeding of the seminar conducted at the East China Normal University, Shanghai (PR China). SLO Netherlands Institute for curriculum development

Pring, R. (2000) The 'false dualism' of educational research. *Journal of Philosophy in Education*, 24, 2, 247–260.

Rossman, G. B. and Rallis, S. F. (2011) *Learning in the Field: An introduction to qualitative research.* London: Sage Publications.

Scriven, M. (1996) Types of evaluation and types of evaluator. *American Journal of Evaluation*, 17, 2, 151–161.

Scriven, M. (2014) Personal communication by email, 12 June.

Simon, H. A. (1988) *The Sciences of the Artificial*, 2nd edition. Cambridge, MA: The MIT Press.

Slavin, R. E., Sheard, M. and Hanley, P. (2014) Cooperative learning in mathematics: lessons from England. *Better: Evidence-based Education*, 6, 14–17.

Smith, L. B. and Thelen, E. (2003) Development as a dynamic system. *Trends in Cognitive Sciences*, 7, 8, 343–348.

Stokes, D. E. (1997) *Pasteur's Quadrant: Basic science and technological innovation.* Washington, DC: Brookings Institution Press.

Tashakkori, A. and Teddlie, C. (Eds) (2010) *Sage Handbook of Mixed Methods in Social and Behavioral Research.* London: Sage Publications.

Tymms, P. (2004) Are standards rising in English primary schools? *British Educational Research Journal*, 30, 477–494.

Tymms, P. (2012) Questionnaires. In J. Arthur, M. Waring, R. Coe and Larry V. Hedges (Eds) *Research Methods and Methodologies in Education.* London: SAGE Publications, 231–239.

Tymms, P. and Coe, R. (2003) Celebration of the success of distributed research with schools: the CEM Centre, Durham. *British Educational Research Journal*, 29, 5, 639–653.

Tymms, P. and Merrell, C. (2007) Standards and quality in English primary schools over time: The national evidence. Primary Review, University of Cambridge Faculty of Education. Retrieved from http://image.guardian.co.uk/sys-files/Education/documents/2007/11/01/overtime.pdf (accessed on 20 July, 2016).

Tymms, V. (2016) *Newtonian Mechanics for Undergraduates.* World Scientific Publishing Co. Pte. Ltd.

8

Research Questions in Education Research

Patrick White

Questions are everywhere; all you have to do is observe and be curious. (Graziano and Raulin, 2004, p. 57)

Until relatively recently, research questions were the 'elephant in the room' of social research. Very little was written about them, either in textbooks aimed at students or in the wider methods literature. Few methods texts discussed them in any great depth; many popular textbooks did not even have the term 'research question' listed in their indexes. Even in 2016 there are only three textbooks on research questions in print, all published since 2003. Apart from a pamphlet published in 1987 (Lewis and Munn, 2004) and a subject-specific academic study on the topic from 1984 (Campbell et al., 1982), no texts on the topic were available before the early 2000s.

This lack of guidance available to students and researchers in this area did not go unnoticed. In the mid-1970s Lundberg (1976, p. 6) complained that the literature on research questions was 'meagre and uneven' at that time and even two decades later, Flick (1998) noted that few textbooks provided detailed – or even any – discussion of this topic. There were notable exceptions, however, such as those written by Robson (1993), Creswell (1994) and Punch (1998), but by the end of the 1990s it was certainly not the case that research questions were routinely discussed in methods texts.

Considerable progress has been made since the turn of the century. Over the course of the last decade and a half the coverage of research questions in methods texts has increased, with many textbooks now covering the topic in some detail.

Popular texts such as those published by Bryman (2001, 2004, 2008, 2012) increased their coverage of research questions in each subsequent edition and other texts dedicated substantial space to the topic (for example, Denscombe, 2002; Booth et al., 2003; Maxwell, 2005).

While this is a welcome development, it is not one that has been reflected in either the discussion of research questions in the wider methods literature or the attention paid to research questions in substantive articles. Discussion of research questions in academic journals has been limited to a handful of papers in the past four decades, predominantly by researchers working in applied fields such as education (for example, Dillon, 1983, 1984; White, 2013), social work (for example, Milton, 2000; Mullen, 2002; Soydan, 2002) medicine (for example, Morrison, 2002; Stone, 2002) and management (for example, Alvesson and Sandberg, 2011; Sandberg and Alvesson, 2011).

Perhaps the most obvious neglect of research questions can be seen in published reports of substantive research. A brief survey of the latest editions of the *British Educational Research Journal* (*BERJ*), the *American Educational Research Journal* (*AERJ*), the *European Educational Research Journal* (*EERJ*) and *The Australian Educational Researcher* (*AER*) demonstrates the lack of visibility of research questions in research reports. These journals were chosen because of their high status, geographic coverage, connections with professional bodies and wide readership. Of those articles containing empirical research, more than half the papers (n=17/28) contained no references to either research questions or hypotheses. Even including explicit aims – as an alternative to questions or hypotheses – was far from universal.

It would be unwise to jump to any conclusions about the extent to which educational researchers report their research questions based only on a survey four issues of four different journals. However, a study of 79 empirical articles from *BERJ* and *AERJ* published between 2011 and 2012 found similar results (White, 2013) as did a larger scale survey of educational journals carried out in the early 1980s (Dillon 1983). Research by Bordage (2001) showed that 'insufficient problem formulation' was the second most common reason reviewers gave for rejecting articles submitted to medical education journals, suggesting that what is seen in published papers could be only the 'tip of the iceberg' in terms of the neglect of research questions; researchers may pay even less attention to research questions than surveys of publications suggest.

WHY HAVE RESEARCH QUESTIONS BEEN NEGLECTED?

This section of the chapter explores some possible explanations for the neglect of research questions. It starts by discussing the extent to which educational research is led by questions and the influence of particular philosophical standpoints. The related issue of methods-led research is explored next and the section ends by asking whether lack of attention to research questions is related to a wider neglect of research design.

How much of contemporary educational research is genuinely 'question-led'?

Some commentators have raised concerns about the extent to which some research is led by questions. These concerns have not focused solely on educational research but have also been directed at research in the social and natural sciences more widely. Views about the goals and purpose of research, prior assumptions about the way in which the world works and allegiances to particular political projects have all been seen as potential threats to research being question-led.

Lewins (1992, p. 8) suggests that the extent to which researchers are genuinely curious varies and argues that some investigators can be influenced 'by assumptions which prevent the right questions begin asked'. Researchers can become attached to certain explanations or theories and as a result are unwilling to pose questions that raise the possibility of these ideas being challenged. Others have acknowledged that the cultures of research communities do not always encourage genuine curiosity. Sellitz et al. (1965, p. 31) note that the 'habits of thought' cultivated within disciplines or research groups can also 'interfere with the discovery of the new and ... unexpected'. For research to be a meaningful activity, however, researchers have to acknowledge the possibility of unexpected (and even 'undesirable') findings. As Medawar (1979, p. 94), a biologist, argues, if research 'does not hold out the possibility of causing one to revise one's views, it is hard to see why it should be done at all'.

Emancipatory research

Discovery and the production of knowledge, however, are not always seen as the only or most important goal of 'research'. Commentators such as Griffiths (1998, p. 3) view 'taking sides', '*empowering* others; empowering oneself' and 'giving or getting a voice' as central to inquiry. Others have cited 'emancipation' (Brown and Jones, 2001) and 'fostering change' (Troyna and Carrington, 1989, p. 219) to be key research activities.

While few researchers would deny that they would like their research to have some kind of impact, some advocates of 'emancipatory' research argue that in order to achieve these goals research needs to be conducting in a different way. Rather than simply setting out with a set of questions to be answered, Griffiths (1998, p. 3) argues that researchers require a 'set of values' to guide both what is researched and how the research is conducted. Troyna (1995, p. 397) believes that political commitment must 'help to shape and direct all aspects of the research act' and Troyna and Carrington (1989, p. 201) add that political values should inform '*both* theory *and* practices' of research. Gitlin et al. (1993, p. 208) go further, asking researchers to 'reconceptualize method so it explicitly embodies the purpose of emancipatory change'. Such views are not uncommon and neither are they limited to a particular period of time or substantive area. Indeed, Hammersley (2002) noted that at the turn of the century such positions appeared to be growing in popularity.

The extent to which emancipatory research can be truly question-led is debatable. If the production of knowledge becomes subordinate to other goals, it is hard to see how research questions can remain central to a study. Hammersley (1995, p. 71) presents a rigorous and detailed case against such approaches, concluding that researchers' primary concern should always be 'the truth of claims, not their political implications or practical consequences'. He argues that those labelling themselves 'critical', 'anti-racist' or 'feminist' researchers do not offer a coherent alternative to more conventional approaches to research that prioritize the production of knowledge and concludes that 'fighting oppression is a good thing. However it is not the only good thing, and it is a different activity from doing research. The two should not be confused. Doing so serves neither well' (Hammersley, 1995, p. 44).

Post-modernist and post-structuralist approaches

An increase in 'emancipatory' research is not the only trend that may have led to some researchers neglecting research questions or even questioning their importance. Other developments have had the potential to marginalize research questions or at least render their answers futile. The influence of post-structuralism and post-modernism are two such developments.

Both post-modernism and post-structuralism have gained a degree of popularity among educational researchers over the past 25 years. Calls for these theories to inform research practice have come from within the educational research community (for example, Stronach and Maclure, 1997) and from the wider social sciences (for example, Alvesson, 2002). While more educational researchers appear to identify with post-structuralist rather than post-modernist ideas, Rosneau (1992) argues that the difference between the two approaches is one of emphasis rather than fundamentals. Paechter and Weiner (1996) noted the growing popularity of these ideas in the mid-1990s, particularly among feminist researchers. Twenty years later these schools of thought – post-structualism in particular – are still cited by many educational researchers as being influential on their practice.

These approaches have not escaped criticism. Although, as noted above, these ideas do not form a coherent whole, they share common features. By rejecting 'every standard that has governed enquiry since the Enlightenment' (Silverman, 2007, p. 139) they 'deny the possibility of there being any means for judging knowledge as being more or less true' (Gomm, 2004, p. 1), 'undermine the very basis for research' (Hammersley 1995, p. 43) and so 'make research a senseless activity' (Gomm 2004, p. 1). Benson and Stangroom (2006, p. 164) go further, arguing that those who do not believe in the 'existence or reality of truth' are fraudulent in defining themselves as researchers at all. They warn that those 'with a programmatic, or perhaps temperamental, disbelief in even the possibility of truth, have no business going into any branch of enquiry or pedagogy at all'.

It is important to emphasize that these critics are not setting up straw targets to attack. Paechter and Weiner (1996, p. 269), invited to edit a special issue on post-modernism and post-structuralism as acknowledged 'experts' in the area, cite belief in the existence of 'a multiplicity of truths' as a central tenet of these approaches. But if there really are no criteria for distinguishing between competing claims and no methods for evaluating how strong the evidence is for a particular phenomenon, the idea of evidence becomes meaningless. As a consequence, asking questions loses value as an activity, as if there is no correct answer to a question then striving to find one becomes either pointless or merely a charade.

Methods-led research versus question-led research

As has already been noted, even when researchers are genuinely curious, their training and the culture of research communities may mitigate against question-led research. Research can often be led by methods rather than questions or, at the very least, the range of questions some researchers address can be restricted by a preference for particular methods of data collection and analysis.

Campbell et al. (1982) conducted the first comprehensive study into the use of research questions, focusing on the practice of organizational researchers. Experienced researchers and stakeholders interviewed during the fieldwork frequently expressed concern that research was often led by researchers' preference for certain methods or techniques, rather than by particular questions. This was viewed as detrimental to the substantive area as a whole, as significant 'research milestones' were seen by the respondents as being led by the desire to address particular problems rather than use or develop specific research methods. Dillon's (1984) survey of published education research, also conducted in the early 1980s, produced similar findings, with the author concluding that education research was generally not question-led.

Two decades after Campbell et al.'s (1982) study, Taylor (2002) showed that similar concerns were still expressed in relation to education research. Key stakeholders in UK social science lamented the tendency of 'mono-method' researchers to use a single or narrow range of methods throughout their careers, with the then director of a large grant awarding body viewing question-led research as essential to the development of social science.

The development of identities based around methods is encouraged by the popular division of research methods into 'quantitative' and 'qualitative' categories. This can be found in the titles and contents of methods texts, in the titles of journals and Special Interest Groups, and the structure of research methods training. The fact that this distinction breaks down under even the most superficial scrutiny seems to have had little impact on its popularity. It is a division that has no logical basis, as no methods of data collection can be unproblematically categorized as either exclusively 'quantitative' or 'qualitative' (see: Gorard, 2002; Gorard and Taylor, 2004). As Punch (1998, p. 58) notes, data do 'not occur naturally in the form of numbers' and all data can be traced back to their non-numeric origins (Berka, 1983; Prandy, 2002). Even in the context of greater discussion of 'mixed methods' or 'combining methods' most commentaries use the 'qualitative/quantitative' division as their starting point (for example, Creswell, 2009; Teddlie and Tashakkori, 2009; but see Gorard and Taylor, 2004 for examples of alternative approaches).

This division also has consequences in terms of the presentation of research questions and hypotheses in methods texts and research reports, as some commentators see these as only necessary for 'quantitative' research. However, Sarantakos (1998), Flick (1998) and Agee (2009) warn that research questions are also crucial to 'qualitative' research. Mason (1996) notes that there can be resistance among some 'qualitative' researchers to using hypotheses, perhaps because of commentators such as Dobert (1982) warning that they are incompatible with ethnographic research and Creswell (2003) arguing that hypotheses and objectives are not stated in 'qualitative' research. Many experienced 'qualitative' researchers and ethnographers disagree, however, arguing not only that hypotheses can be useful in 'qualitative' studies (for example, Guba and Lincoln, 1994; Holliday, 2002) but also that they can be perfectly compatible with ethnographic research (for example, Barton and Lazarsfeld, 1969; Spradley, 1980; Reason, 1994) where 'hypothetical patterns' can be identified and tested (Hammersley and Atkinson, 1995, p. 19). In fact, there is also no logical reason why hypotheses cannot be used in any kind of research, as hypotheses and research questions are effectively two sides of the same coin (White, 2009).

Research methods versus research design

There are few areas of the methods literature that have not been the subject of extensive commentary and debate, as well as the focus of texts aimed at students. Research questions is one such area but research design has also received relatively little attention. There are far fewer texts on research design than there are on research methods, and some texts with 'research design' in the title predominantly cover methods of data collection and analysis, rather than design itself (for example, Creswell, 1994, 2003, 2009).

Although the terms 'research methods' and 'research design' are often used interchangeably, there are important differences between the two (White, 2009; Gorard, 2010, 2013). Developing a research design requires the investigator to make decisions about the kinds of evidence they require to answer their research questions (de Vaus, 2001). Research design is about the *logic* of inquiry – the links between research questions, data and conclusions – rather than the *logistics* of collecting and analyzing that data (Hakim, 2000). The latter receives a lot more attention than the former even although research design can be equally challenging.

Research questions and research design are linked, as having clear and well-defined questions helps with the design of a project (Denscombe, 2002; Stone, 2002); good research questions should point to the data required to answer them (Punch, 1998). Only once a research design has been constructed should the researcher make any final decisions about methods of data collection and analysis. Questions may change over the course of exploratory studies, and this may have implications for the most appropriate research design, but the two should be a good match at any particular point in this process.

As is the case with research questions, some researchers are resistant to the idea of research design being a central element of all studies. Research design has become associated with 'quantitative' studies, perhaps because some important elements of research design (change over time, comparison groups, selection of cases, randomization, and so on) are often more visible in larger scale studies where data have been quantified. This has led to some 'qualitative' researchers exempting themselves from the need to create research designs for their studies (Mason, 1996). However, as de Vaus (2001, p. 16) points out, 'any research design can, in principle, use any type of data collection and can use either qualitative or quantitative data'. He goes on to emphasize the primacy of research design over research methods and argues that decisions about data collection 'are all subsidiary to the matter of "What evidence do I need to collect?"' (de Vaus, 2001, p. 9). As Flick (1998) and Denscombe (2002) conclude, research designs are crucial to the conduct of any kind of research and 'qualitative' research is no different in this respect.

An effective research design can only be developed if a clear set of research questions have been formulated first (White, 2009; Gorard, 2013). Lack of attention to research design may go hand in hand with the neglect of research questions, as the two are so closely linked. As discussed earlier, philosophical, political and methodological identities, either individually or in combination, may also contribute to a lack of focus on research questions among researchers. Having attempted to highlight the problems that such neglect can raise, the remainder of this chapter examines issues relating to the development of research questions and provides some guidance on how to avoid common problems in question formulation.

WHAT MAKES A GOOD RESEARCH QUESTION?

Dillon (1990) notes that students find asking questions much harder than answering them and many commentators have reported that, in their experience, students and new researchers find it much easier to decide on a topic than to turn that topic into a research question. Before moving on to look at the form and content of questions, the relationships between topics, aims and research questions is discussed below.

Topics, aims and objectives, and research questions

Deciding on a topic is a necessary starting point for conducting research but a topic or area of interest does not provide sufficient direction for carrying out a well-designed study. Unlike research questions, topics or areas are too general to tell the researcher exactly what data they need or how these data can be analyzed most effectively. As Sellitz et al. (1965) note, not every topic can be translated into a feasible study and carrying out an investigation without developing research questions risks wasting time and resources and producing poor quality research.

It is usually necessary to narrow down topics considerably before trying to develop specific research questions (Labovitz and Hagedorn, 1971; Kane, 1984; Lewis and Munn, 1997). Developing research questions often involves moving from identifying a topic of interest, through thinking about aims and objectives, to developing and refining a set of coherent questions. Aims and objectives can be a useful bridge between topics and research questions, as they are more directive than topics but often easier to initially formulate than questions.

The following example shows how objectives and research questions can be developed from initial interest in a particular topic:

Objective

To find out why certain individuals and groups adopt new information and communication technologies before others.

Research Questions

1 What are the patterns of consumption of new information and communication technologies among adults in the city of Leicester?
2 What reasons do different individuals and groups provide for adopting or not adopting new information and communication technologies?

It is often necessary to break down a single objective into more than one question and this process starts to clarify exactly what data might be needed for a particular study. Aims and objectives can provide a useful springboard to formulating initial research questions but the first versions of questions are likely to need further development to make sure they are 'researchable' and to avoid some of the common problems associated with question design. Two issues that need to be considered in question design are the form and content of questions.

The form and content of research questions

Not all questions are social science research questions. Some questions do not relate to the social world and so are beyond the scope of social research. Other questions might be interesting to social scientists but cannot be answered using empirical evidence and so are not 'researchable'. Both the form and content of research questions are important. Problems with the form of a question stem from the way it is structured, whereas problems of subject relate to the topic that the question addresses. There are several issues relating to the form of questions that are useful to consider when formulating research questions.

Question form

Questions should be open-ended and interrogative. While this might sound obvious, Punch (1998) notes that even experienced researchers often reply with declarative statements, rather than interrogative ones, when asked about their research questions. In my experience, students and new researchers often start out wanting to 'prove', 'demonstrate' or 'find' something rather than *answer* a particular question.

A more subtle problem with the form of questions can arise when a particular question has different facets or contains underlying assumptions that may not be warranted. It is common for texts on questionnaire design to warn against asking more than one question at once, or making assumptions about respondents' knowledge, and similar issues can arise when formulating research questions. In order to be most effective in helping the researcher design their study, questions should only address one issue at a time.

The following statement actually contains two separate questions:

What were the aims of the 'comprehensivisation'[1] of secondary schools in England and Wales and to what extent were these aims achieved?

These questions require separate answers and different kinds of data are required to produce these answers. It would be more useful to separate this question into the following two questions:

1 What were the aims of the 'comprehensivisation' of secondary schools in England and Wales?
2 To what extent were these aims achieved?

The kind of data required to answer these two questions are very different and this has implications for research design, methods of data collection and methods of data analysis. The first question 'What were the aims of the comprehensivisation of secondary schools in England and Wales?' may require an analysis of policy documents and perhaps also interviews with policymakers and other actors involved with drafting and implementing the policy. The second question, 'To what extent were these aims achieved?', can only be answered after the first has been answered, and the aims of the policy established. It may require a longitudinal design, with any changes being tracked over time, in order to attempt to separate the effects of comprehensivisation from other potential influences. This could involve the analysis of secondary data on educational attainment and other aspects of student experience. It might also include interviews with teachers and students and the analysis of archived historical records.

A good research question should always indicate the type of data required to address it. This information can then help the researcher choose a suitable research design and methods of data collection and analysis. Breaking down compound questions into their constituent parts, as in the example above, can help clarify such decisions.

Another type of question that can be problematic are those that make what Fischer (1970) calls 'false presumptions'. An example of this might be:

At what age do boys stop underachieving at school?

The first presumption in this question is fairly obvious: that is, that boys underachieve at school. However, it also contains the presumption that their underachievement ends at some point. There is also the issue of what 'under-achievement' actually means, whether it can be measured and how this would be done (see Smith, 2005 for problems with this). Ignoring this issue of defining key terms for the moment – it is dealt with later in this chapter – this question can be usefully broken down into the following two questions:

1 Do boys 'underachieve' at any point in their compulsory schooling?
2 If so, during which periods of their schooling do they 'underachieve'?

These questions might be developed further to include differences between and with groups, as follows:

1 To what extent do boys 'underachieve' at any time during the compulsory schooling?
2 What is the timing and duration of any 'underachievement'?
3 What characteristics are associated with differences in the levels of 'underachievement' among boys?
4 Is the timing and duration of any 'underachievement' related to the characteristics of the 'underachievers'?

Originally problematic questions can be developed in this way in order to provide clearer direction on exactly what kinds of data are required to answer them. As can be seen in the example above, developing research questions is usually a multi-stage process. The questions were first broken down to ensure that they included no unwarranted assumptions and then developed further in order to ensure they captured more subtle variations and differences between and within groups.

They would doubtless benefit from further development before any decisions about research design are finalized.

The example above showed that some questions need to be addressed before others can even be asked. As is discussed later in this chapter, descriptive questions usually have to be addressed before explanatory ones can be tackled.

Another problem of question form relates to the use of dichotomies. Questions that include dichotomies are often used as essay questions, as they can be very useful for generating discussion and debate. However, as Fischer (1970) notes, they are rarely useful when constructing empirical research questions. An example of the kind of 'false dichotomy' that Fischer warns against can be seen in the following example:

> Comprehensive education: force for equality or lowest common denominator?

The problem with this question is that it proposes two possible answers with no room for a completely different alternative or any middle ground. It also precludes the possibility that the two situations could coexist. This would make a provocative title for a final report but is less helpful for the researcher when planning their research. While the example above could be seen as extreme or artificial, there is a much more subtle point to be made about the use of 'or' in research questions. As with terms such as 'why?' (see below), language that is common in everyday use is not always useful when formulating research questions because of the ambiguity that it can introduce into a question. As Fischer (1970, p. 11) notes, 'or' can mean:

a) either X or Y but not both
b) either X or Y or both
c) either X or Y or both, or neither.

This kind of ambiguity is perfectly fine in essay questions but works less well for research questions, when clarity is key. For this reason it is worth thinking very carefully about the use of 'or' in research questions and considering reformulating questions to avoid its use.

Problems of subject

As well as ensuring that a research question is structured as clearly as possible, it is also important that the focus of a question is appropriate for social research. Metaphysical, ethical and aesthetic questions cannot be answered through empirical study and so are not suitable topics for this kind of investigation (Cozby et al., 1989). But although it is unlikely that many researchers would attempt to answer obviously metaphysical questions, such as 'Do numbers exist independently of human thought?', there are subtle ways in which metaphysical, ethical or aesthetic elements can creep into research questions. Including norma-tive elements in research questions is one way that this can happen.

Normative questions relate to judgments concerning value or virtue. They are usually concerned with what is desirable or undesirable, right or wrong, or good or bad. Normative questions are concerned with ethical or aesthetic judgments and are sometimes known as 'deliberative' questions (Dillon, 1984). Philosophers contrast normative statements with descriptive statements. Descriptive statements can be tested through observation, at least in principle, but normative statements cannot. The following question is normative:

Should corporal punishment be re-introduced in secondary schools?

The key term that identifies this as a normative question is 'should'. This ques-tion cannot be answered using empirical evidence but, rather, is asking about an opinion on an ethical issue. There is no single correct answer to this question and, as with terms such as 'ought', it is best avoided in research questions in the social sciences (Nachmias and Nachmias, 1976; Kerlinger, 1986; Andrews, 2003). The question below relates to the same topic but is formulated in such a way that it avoids any normative element:

What proportion of parents think corporal punishment should be re-introduced in secondary schools in England and Wales?

In contrast to the first example, this question can be answered by empirical research. Rather than seeking a universal answer to a moral enquiry it aims to document and report the different views held on this issue by a particular group. At first sight difference between the two questions may appear to be subtle but it is very important in terms of both avoiding any normative element and providing guidance about the data required.

Questions including such terms as 'should' and 'ought' are easily identified as normative. But there are other commonly used terms that are also norma-tive in nature but are easier to overlook. Terms such as 'successful', 'effective', 'satisfaction', 'frequent' and 'elderly' are often value laden. Their meaning is not universal and so can vary according to context. As a general rule it is best to replace them with more specific terms but if their use is considered to be essential they need to be defined and operationalized clearly. Because it is easy to overlook these more subtle problems with language it is good practice to examine every word in a research question with an eye for this and similar issues.

In the next section, a distinction is made between descriptive and explanatory questions. 'Why?' questions are one of the most common types of explanatory question but, as Fischer (1970) argues, they are not always helpful to research-ers in the early stages of their research. All 'why?' questions do not necessar-ily require the same kind of answer, as they can seek causes, motives, reasons, descriptions, processes, purposes or justifications. Because of this, 'why?' can be a rather vague term and therefore problematic in terms of formulating research questions. Vague terms do not give clear direction about the kind of data needed to address them and so should be avoided in research questions where possible.

Fischer (1970) suggests using the other five 'W-questions' ('Who?', 'What?', 'When?', 'Where?' and 'How?') instead. Hamblin (1967) goes further, suggesting that that 'why?' questions and four of the other W-questions can all be usefully reformulated as 'what?' questions. Translating them into 'what?' questions can be a useful exercise in this respect. 'When?', for example, can be reformulated as 'at what time?', and 'where?' can be rephrased as 'at what place?' Similar results can be obtained with 'who', 'why' and even 'how'.

A distinction needs to be made here between how research questions might be presented at the end of a project – when it is quite clear what the term 'why?' might mean – and their role at the beginning of a study, when they need to be formulated in the way that is most effective in terms of providing direction for the research design. Some reviewers of my previous publications on research questions have reacted against this point strongly, arguing that 'why?' questions are important and must be asked. This is not under dispute. What is being argued here is that when research questions are being developed it can be a useful exercise to look at 'why?' questions more closely to determine exactly what kind of data is needed to answer them.

Question types

Having cautioned against the potential ambiguity of 'why?' questions, this section reintroduces the term in relation to the distinction between the two main types of questions used by social researchers: descriptive questions and explanatory questions. de Vaus (2001, p. 1) argues that this distinction usefully separates two different types of enquiry undertaken by researchers. These two types of questions and the associated types of research are as follows:

1 What is going on? (descriptive research)
2 Why is it going on? (explanatory research)

It is usually necessary to answer descriptive questions before answering explanatory ones, as it is important to know the 'what?' before trying to establish 'why?'. As was explained in the previous section, it may be necessary to examine 'why?' questions in greater detail, in order to clarify exactly what data are required to answer them, but an initial division into 'what?' and 'why?' questions can help identify questions as descriptive or explanatory.

Table 8.1 divides up the six 'W-Questions' (also known as the 'Journalistic Six') into those usually leading to descriptive research and those requiring

Table 8.1   Descriptive and explanatory questions

Descriptive Questions	Explanatory Questions
What?	Why?
Who?	How?
When?	
Where?	
How?	

explanatory research. This division is intended as an aid to thinking rather than a hard and fast categorization. As discussed earlier, most questions can be broken down into 'what?' questions even if this is not their initial form, and 'how?' questions could be either descriptive or explanatory depending on the context (and so are included in both sides of the table). Trying to work out which of your research questions are descriptive and which are explanatory can be helpful both in terms of thinking about the different stages of a project and also the order in which data must be collected and analyzed.

It is not uncommon for researchers to overlook the implications of this division for their research design. Neglect of the descriptive element of research has led to resources being wasted on ill-informed studies and policy initiatives that may have been unnecessary or even counterproductive. Describing what is actually happening accurately is a crucial prerequisite for seeking explanations.

Hypotheses

Hypotheses occupy a rather strange place in the methods literature. They are completely ignored in some texts but are discussed in detail in others. They were commonly discussed in methods texts from the 1950s to the 1970s, then appeared to fall out of favour, but have started to reappear as a topic in textbooks over the last 20 years. In some disciplines, such as psychology, greater attention is paid to hypotheses, perhaps reflecting differences in commonly used research designs. Hypotheses are usually covered in texts on statistical analysis but often only in the context of inferential statistical tests. As has already been discussed, the use of hypotheses is by no means restricted to so-called 'quantitative' research and hypotheses can be useful in a wide range of research designs. Nor do hypotheses have to be derived from existing theory, as some commentators suggest. They are simply 'hunches' about what you might find out (Verma and Beard, 1981).

Research questions and hypotheses are closely related. Because a hypothesis is a predicted answer to a research question, it is important to be clear about the question you are asking when formulating hypotheses, as well as the answer you expect. Thinking about hypotheses can sometimes help you develop your research questions and, as the following example shows, it is reasonably easy to move between research questions and hypotheses.

Hypothesis

On average, working mothers spend more time helping children with homework than employed fathers living in the same household.

Research question

Do working mothers spend more time helping children with homework, on average, than employed fathers living in the same household?

Whether hypotheses are useful in a research project will depend on many factors, including what is being researched and how much is already known about the topic. It is not the case that studies that use hypotheses are more scientific than those that do not (Sellitz et al., 1965). Whereas it is crucial that research questions are constructed for all studies, it is not necessarily the case that a lack of hypotheses will be detrimental to a project. In some cases hypotheses will simply not arise (Black, 1993) and researchers should not be concerned if their research is led by questions rather than predictions (Punch, 1998). Hypotheses can be used if they are useful but are not a prerequisite to high quality research. But whether hypotheses are used or not, the research questions that form the foundation of a study must be 'researchable'. In the following section the challenges to researchability are addressed.

Making questions researchable

> There are grand ideas, good ideas, and doable ideas.... In the case of executing a research project, being able to recognize these differences is essential. (Bradley, 2001, p. 569)

As was discussed earlier, some questions cannot be researched by social scientists. There are many questions, however, that are researchable in principle but may not be able to be answered for practical reasons. Throughout this chapter it has been stressed that first versions of research questions will usually require considerable work before they have been developed satisfactorily. One of the most important considerations in developing research questions is making sure they are 'researchable' (Lewis and Munn, 1997). Early versions of research questions are often too vague or too broad (Kane, 1984; Kerlinger, 1986) and researchers can also find it hard to contain their research within a reasonable number of questions (Mason, 1996). There are several strategies available to researchers to ensure that their questions remain researchable.

Prioritizing

Identifying an interesting topic is a crucial first stage in developing researchable questions but even reasonably specific topics can raise a large number of initial research questions. Listing these questions as they arise can be a useful stage on the way to choosing which particular ones to pursue, but the temptation to try to address too many questions should be resisted (Mason, 1996). Prioritizing questions can be a useful way of paring down an initial list (Jorgenson, 1989; Booth et al., 2003) but the scope of questions is as important as the number. Some questions will by their very nature be more ambitious than others and some combinations of questions will work better than others. Avoid adding questions to your list 'for interest's sake' (Andrews, 2003) as they will inevitably add to your workload but not necessarily add value to your research.

Main and subsidiary questions

Dividing questions hierarchically into 'main' and 'subsidiary' questions can be a useful exercise (Creswell, 1994, 2003; Denscombe, 2002). Subsidiary questions derive from the main questions and can be of two kinds: 'contributory' and 'ancillary' (Andrews, 2003). Contributory questions are smaller questions that must be answered in order to answer a main question. In contrast, auxiliary questions do not have to be answered in order to answer a main question but will provide additional information. Think carefully before including auxiliary questions, as there will always be interesting related issues but it is not always possible to address them. These are the types of questions that can easily extend your project beyond the available time and resources.

Spending time dividing your questions into main and subsidiary types, re-ordering them, combining them, reformulating them and discarding those that are unnecessary can help you think more clearly about your research. The following example, adapted from my own research (White, 2007), demonstrates the difference between main and subsidiary research questions.

Main research question

How do young people make career decisions at the end of compulsory schooling?

Subsidiary research questions

a) What factors do young people consider when making their choices?
b) What sources of information do they use to help their decision-making?

c) Which individuals are influential in shaping their choices?

d) To what extent do these factors, sources of information and influences vary between individuals and groups?

As can be seen, the sub-questions in this example are 'contributory' questions. In order to answer the main question comprehensively, these sub-questions all need to be addressed. This leads to the next issue: how many research questions are needed or appropriate? Most commentators recommend no more than two main questions, with a maximum of perhaps three or four subsidiary sub-questions per main question (Creswell, 2003; Stone, 2002; Punch, 1998). Miles and Huberman (1994) put the limit at a dozen in total, presumably including sub-questions.

Language

It is important to achieve a balance not only in the number of research questions but also in their length. For the purposes of thinking about research, questions may need to be reasonably long in order to be sufficiently specific. This does not mean, however, that they should not be as concise as possible. Stone (2002) and Kane (1984, p. 20) believe that all research questions should be able to be formulated as a single sentence, despite the belief of some that '*their* research is too complex' to be expressed in this way.

Clarity is also important both for the consumer of the research as well as for the researcher themselves (Nachmias and Nachmias, 1976). Being clear about the meaning of any terms included in a question is crucial for accurate interpretation of both the research aims and findings (Fischer, 1970) and Kane (1984) recommends examining every word used in each question. The aim should be to 'restrict the scope of each word as much as possible without interfering with what you hope to study' (Kane, 1984, p. 20). She warns against the use of words that are assumed to have common meanings but are problematic when examined in any detail (for example, 'frequent', 'effective', 'elderly', and so on). This avoids ambiguity in both the questions asked and the way the findings are interpreted by readers. Medawar (1972, p. 29) dismisses the view that some ideas, by virtue of their profundity, cannot be expressed clearly, concluding that 'no one who has something original or important to say will willingly run the risk of being misunderstood; people who write obscurely are either unskilled in writing or up to mischief'.

Research questions that are too vague or general are relatively common, even amongst professional researchers (see Campbell et al., 1982; Bordage, 2001). As is the case with lack of clarity, this can cause problems for both those conducting the research and those reading it. Research questions that lack precision often cannot provide enough direction for the research design and lead to poorly designed research (Morrison, 2002; Stone, 2002). As vague questions tend to produce vague answers, findings from such studies are often inconclusive and of limited use (Black, 1993; Denscombe, 2002).

A precisely stated research question needs to include certain information. In particular, it must be explicit about the 'what', the 'who', the 'where' and the 'when' of the research (Stone, 2002; Hudson-Barr, 2005). Unless the information is redundant, research questions should always include the answers to the following questions:

a) What is the focus of the project?
b) Who is to be studied?
c) Where is the research to be conducted?
d) When will the research be conducted?

These questions correspond to the following areas of information:

a) The substantive area of interest.
b) The population of interest and, if appropriate, study sample.
c) The study site or geographical coverage.
d) The historical period covered by the fieldwork or data.

The following example, adapted from Morrison (2002, p. 90) demonstrates how all of this information can be included in a single research question:

> Why do (*why*) second year (*when*) medical students (*who*) at Glasgow University (*where*) prefer learning about ethics (*what*) in small groups (*how*)?

This is a particular type of research question that depends upon a quite specific existing knowledge base (that is, that it has already been established, by descriptive research, that these students do prefer to learn in small groups). This example does show, however, how including all the relevant information immediately points to the data that would be required. The term 'prefer' suggests that data on preferences should be collected and as the question begins with 'why?' it seeks to look for reasons or rationales for these preferences. The preferences relate to a setting (small groups) for learning about a particular topic (ethics). It is clear from the question that the data must be collected from second year medical students at Glasgow University. As the research is not examining changes over time, a cross-sectional design is sufficient. Depending on the reason for conducting research and the detail required, the data could be collected using various methods. Questionnaires, interviews, focus groups or diaries may be most appropriate.

This example is not perfect, as some information is still missing. There is no information on what the alternative to small group learning might be. If, as is likely, different teaching methods are used with small and large groups, it may be the teaching method rather than the group that accounts for any differences. This distinction could become apparent in interview data or diaries but is less likely to do so in a questionnaire with only closed questions. Further development of this question would be useful in this respect. Research questions should only be finalized once it is clear that they all the necessary information to inform the research.

DISCUSSION

Research questions have historically been a neglected topic in the research methods literature. Things have certainly changed for the better over the course of the last two decades but while guidance for students is now commonly available in methods texts, wider methodological discussions are still relatively unusual. Research questions and hypotheses are certainly not included as a matter of course in published reports of empirical research.

The first section of this chapter offered some possible explanations for this neglect of research questions. Political and philosophical standpoints, mono-methods identities and the lack of attention given to research design are all possible contributors to this neglect. But have research questions been neglected simply because they are not very important? And does the neglect of research questions really matter? I have tried to argue that thinking about research questions is essential if a study is to be well-designed. I also believe that research questions need to be clearly stated in research reports, so that readers can effectively 'consume' research outputs and come to sound judgments on the quality of evidence they provide.

I have also attempted to convey what I consider to be the most important considerations when constructing, developing and refining research questions. Because of considerations of space, it has not been possible to provide a comprehensive guide to this process but this is something I have done, and continue to do, elsewhere (see White 2009, 2017). I hope that this chapter has provided new (or even more experienced) researchers with an insight into what, at first sight, may seem to be a simple and straightforward process. If those who read this chapter reflect on their research questions more than they did previously then I feel I will have succeeded in this respect.

Note

1 Comprehensivization was a policy pursued in England and Wales in the post-war period aimed at introducing non-selective secondary (high) schooling for 11–16-year-olds.

FURTHER READING

White (2009, 2017) offers a detailed discussion of where research questions come from and making questions 'researchable'.

Holliday (2002) provides a detailed review of the arguments for and against the use of hypotheses in 'qualitative' research.

White (2013) explores the neglect of research questions in greater detail and discusses the implication for teaching research methods.

Gorard's (2013) recent text on research design explores the relationship between research questions and research design in some detail.

Fischer (1970) discusses issues of question form and content in greater detail than was possible in this chapter.

REFERENCES

Agee, J. 2009. Developing qualitative research questions: a reflective process. *International Journal of Qualitative Studies in Education*, 22 (4): 431–447.

Alvesson, M. 2002. *Postmodernism and Social Research*. Buckingham: Open University Press.

Alvesson, M. and J. Sandberg. 2011. Generating research questions through problematization. *Academy of Management Review*, 36 (2): 247–271.

Andrews, R. 2003. *Research Questions*. London: Continuum.

Barton, A. H. and P. F. Lazarsfeld. 1969. Some functions of qualitative analysis in social research. In G. J. McCall and J. L. Simmons (Eds) *Issues in Participant Observation*. Reading, MA: Addison-Wesley, 216–228.

Benson, O. and J. Stangroom. 2006. *Why Truth Matters*. London: Continuum.

Berka, K. 1983. *Measurement: Its concepts, theories and problems*. London: D. Reidel.

Black, T. R. 1993. *Evaluating Social Science Research: An introduction*. London: SAGE Publications.

Booth, W. C., G. G. Columb and J. M. Williams. 2003. *The Craft of Research*, 2nd edition. Chicago, IL: University of Chicago Press.

Bordage, G. 2001. Reasons reviewers reject and accept manuscripts: the strengths and weaknesses in medical education reports. *Academic Medicine*, 76 (9): 889–896.

Bradley, D. B. 2001. Developing research questions through grant proposal development. *Educational Gerontology*, 27: 569–81.

Brown, T. and L. Jones. 2001. *Action Research and Postmodernism: Congruence and critique*. Buckingham: Open University Press.

Bryman, A. 2001. *Social Research Methods*, 1st edition. Oxford: Oxford University Press.

Bryman, A. 2004. *Social Research Methods*, 2nd edition. Oxford: Oxford University Press.

Bryman, A. 2008. *Social Research Methods*, 3rd edition. Oxford: Oxford University Press.

Bryman, A. 2012. *Social Research Methods*, 4th edition. Oxford: Oxford University Press.

Campbell, J. P., R. L. Daft, and C. L. Hulin. 1982. *What to Study: Generating and developing research questions*. Beverley Hills, CA: SAGE Publications.

Cozby, P. C., P. E. Worden and D. W. Kee. 1989. *Research Methods in Human Development*. Mountain View, CA: Mayfield.

Creswell, J. W. 1994. *Research Design: Qualitative, quantitative, and mixed methods approaches*, 1st edition. Thousand Oaks, CA: SAGE Publications.

Creswell, J. W. 2003. *Research Design: Qualitative, quantitative, and mixed methods approaches*, 2nd edition. Thousand Oaks, CA: SAGE Publications.

Creswell, J. W. 2009. *Research Design: Qualitative, quantitative, and mixed methods approaches*, 3rd edition. Thousand Oaks, CA: SAGE Publications.

de Vaus, D. A. 2001. *Research Design in Social Research*. London: SAGE Publications.

Denscombe, M. 2002. *Ground Rules for Good Research: A 10 point guide for social research*. Buckingham: Open University Press.

Dillon, J. T. 1983. Use of questions in educational research. *Educational Researcher*, 12 (9): 19–24.

Dillon, J. T. 1984. The classification of research questions. *Review of Educational Research*, 54 (3): 327–361.

Dillon, J. T. 1990. *The Practice of Questioning*. London: Routledge.

Dobert, M. L. 1982. *Ethnographic Research: Theory and application for modern schools and societies*. New York: Praeger.

Fischer, D. H. 1970. *'Historians' Fallacies: Toward a logic of historical thought*. New York: Harper and Row.

Flick, U. 1998. *An Introduction to Qualitative Research*. London: SAGE Publications.

Gitlin, A., M. Siegel and K. Boru. 1993. The politics of method: from leftist ethnography to educative research. In M. Hammersley (Ed.) *Educational Research: Current Issues*. London: Paul Chapman, 191–210.

Gomm, R. 2004. *Social Research Methodology: A critical introduction*. Basingstoke: Palgrave.

Gorard, S. 2002. Can we overcome the methodological schism? Four models for combining qualitative and quantitative evidence. *Research Papers in Education*, 17 (4): 345–361.

Gorard, S. 2010. Research design, as independent of methods. In C. Teddlie and A. Tashakkori (Eds) *Sage Handbook of Mixed Methods*. Thousand Oaks, CA: SAGE Publications, 237–252.

Gorard, S. 2013. *Research Design: Robust approaches for social science*. London: SAGE Publications.

Gorard, S. and C. Taylor. 2004. *Combining Methods in Educational and Social Research*. London: Open University Press.

Graziano, A. M. and M. L. Raulin. 2004. *Research Methods: A process of inquiry*, 5th edition. Boston, MA: Pearson.

Griffiths, M. 1998. *Educational Research for Social Justice: Getting off the fence*. Buckingham: Open University Press.

Guba, E. G. and Y. S. Lincoln. 1994. Competing Paradigms in Qualitative Research. In N. K. Denzin and Y. S. Lincoln (Eds) *Handbook of Qualitative Research*. Thousand Oaks, CA: SAGE Publications, 105–117.

Hakim, C. 2000. *Research Design: Successful designs for social and economic research*, 2nd edition. London: Routledge.

Hamblin, C. L. 1967. Questions. In P. Edwards (Ed.) *The Encyclopedia of Philosophy: Volume 7*. New York: Macmillan and the Free Press, 49–53.

Hammersley, M. 1995. *The Politics of Social Research*. London: SAGE Publications.

Hammersley, M. 2002. *Educational Research, Policymaking and Practice*. London: Paul Chapman.

Hammersley, M. and P. Atkinson. 1995. *Ethnography: Principles in practice*, 2nd edition. London: Routledge.

Holliday, A. 2002. *Doing and Writing Qualitative Research*. London: SAGE Publications.

Hudson-Barr, D. 2005. From research idea to research question: the who, what, where, when and why. *Journal for Specialists in Paediatric Nursing*, 10 (2): 90–92.

Jorgenson, D. L. 1989. *Participant Observation: A methodology for human studies*. Applied Social Research Methods Series Volume 15. Newbury Park, CA: SAGE Publications.

Kane, E. 1984. *Doing Your Own Research: Basic descriptive research in the social sciences and humanities*. London: Marion Boyars.

Kerlinger, F. N. 1986. *Foundations of Behavioural Research*, 3rd edition. New York: CBS Publishing.

Labovitz, S. and Hagedorn, R. (1971) *Introduction to Social Research*. New York: McGraw-Hill.

Lewins, F. 1992. *Social Science Methodology: A brief but critical introduction*. South Melbourne: MacMillan.

Lewis, I. and P. Munn. 2004. *So You Want to Do Research! A guide for beginners on how to formulate research questions*, 2nd edition, revised. Edinburgh: Scottish Council for Research in Education.

Lundberg, C. C. 1976. Hypothesis creation in organisational behaviour research. *Academy of Management Review*, 1 (2): 5–12.

Mason, J. 1996. *Qualitative Researching*. London: SAGE Publications.

Maxwell, J. 2005. *Qualitative Research Design: An interactive approach*, 2nd edition. Thousand Oaks, CA: SAGE Publications.

Medawar, P. B. 1972. *The Hope of Progress*. London: Methuen.

Medawar, P. B. 1979. *Advice to a Young Scientist*. New York: Harper and Row.

Miles, M. B. and Huberman, A. M. 1994. *Qualitative Data Analysis: An expanded sourcebook*. Thousand Oaks, CA: SAGE Publications.

Milton, P. 2000. Mind the gap! Translating practice problems into research questions in an evaluation of a welfare programme. *European Journal of Social Work*, 3 (1): 25–28.

Morrison, J. 2002. Developing research questions in medical education: the science and the art. *Medical Education*, 36: 596–597.

Mullen, E. J. 2002. Problem formulation in practitioner partnerships: a decade of experience at the center for the study of social work practice. *Social Work Education*, 21 (3): 323–336.

Nachmias, D. and Nachmias, C. 1976. *Research Methods in the Social Sciences*. London: Edward Arnold.

Paechter, C. and G. Weiner. 1996. Editorial. Special Issue on post-modernism and post-structuralism in educational research. *British Educational Research Journal*, 22 (3): 267–272.

Prandy, K. 2002. Measuring quantities: the qualitative foundation of quantity. *Building Research Capacity*, 2: 3–4.

Punch, K. F. 1998. *Introduction to Social Research: Quantitative and Qualitative Approaches*. London: SAGE Publications.

Reason, P. 1994. Three approaches to participative enquiry. In N. K. Denzin and Y. S. Lincoln (Eds) *Handbook of Qualitative Research*. Thousand Oaks, CA: SAGE Publications, 324–339.

Robson, C. 1993. *Real World Research: A resource for social scientists and practitioner–researchers*. Oxford: Blackwell.

Rosneau, P. M. 1992. *Post-modernism and the Social Sciences: Insights, inroads and intrusions*. Princeton, NJ: Princeton University Press.

Sandberg, J. and Alvesson, M. 2011. Ways of constructing research questions: gap-spotting or problematization?. *Organization*, 18: 23–44.

Sarantakos, S. 1998. *Social Research*, 2nd edition. Basingstoke: Palgrave.

Sellitz, C., M. Jahoda, M. Deutch, and S. W. Cook. 1965. *Research Methods in Social Relations*. London: Methuen.

Silverman, D. 2007. *A Very Short, Fairly Interesting and Reasonably Cheap Book about Qualitative Research*. London: SAGE Publications.

Smith, E. 2005. *Analysing Underachievement in Schools*. London: Continuum.

Soydan, H. 2002. Formulating research problems in practitioner–researcher partnerships. *Social Work Education*, 21 (3): 287–304.

Spradley, J. P. 1980. *Participant Observation*. New York: Holt, Rinehard and Winston.

Stone, P. 2002. Deciding upon and refining a research question. *Palliative Medicine*, 16: 265–267.

Stronach, I. and M. Maclure. 1997. *Educational Research Undone: The postmodern embrace*. Buckingham: Open University Press.

Taylor, C. 2002. *The RCBN Consultation Exercise: Stakeholder report*. Cardiff University School of Social Sciences Occasional Paper 50. Cardiff: Cardiff University.

Teddlie, C. and A. Tashakkori. 2009. *Foundations of Mixed Methods Research: Integrating quantitative and qualitative approaches in the social and behavioral sciences*. Thousand Oaks, CA: SAGE Publications.

Troyna, B. 1995. Beyond reasonable doubt? Researching 'race' in educational settings. *Oxford Review of Education*, 21 (4): 395–408.

Troyna, B. and B. Carrington. 1989. 'Whose side are we on?' Ethical dilemmas in research on 'race' and education. In R. G. Burgess (Ed.) *The Ethics of Educational Research*. London: Routledge, 189–202.

Verma, G. K. and Beard, R. M. 1981. *What Is Educational Research? Perspectives on techniques of research*. Aldershot: Ashgate.

White, P. 2007. *Education and Career Choice: A new model of decision making*. London: Palgrave.

White, P. 2009. *Developing Research Questions: A guide for social scientists*. London: Palgrave.

White, P. 2013. Who's afraid of research questions? The neglect of research questions in the methods literature and a call for question-led methods teaching. *International Journal of Research and Method in Education*, 36 (3): 213–227.

White, P. (2017) *Developing Research Questions*, 2nd edition. London: Palgrave.

9

An Introduction to the Importance of Research Design

Stephen Gorard

WHAT IS RESEARCH DESIGN?

Research design refers here to the structure and organisation of a research project. In particular it refers to the deployment of the cases (participants) involved in any study, the ways in which those cases can be allocated to subgroups for comparison, the timing and sequence of data collection episodes, and any interventions of interest to the researcher that could affect the research outcomes (de Vaus 2001; Shadish, Cook and Campbell, 2002; Gorard, 2013). The design must be appropriate for the research question(s) to be addressed, and will then make analysis easier, the results safer, and the conclusions drawn from the research more trustworthy. Given these major advantages it is surprising that so few methods resources and courses emphasise research design as much as they should, and so few researchers mention design in their reports and papers.

The elements of a design can be combined in a large variety of ways, only a few of which have clearly recognisable names. For example, where data is collected repeatedly from one group of cases the design is often called 'longitudinal' – which emphasises the time element (for example, Gorard, 2015). Where data is collected from two or more groups on one occasion the design can be called 'cross-sectional' or 'comparative' – emphasising that the cases are in subgroups (for example, See et al., 2016). Where there are two or more groups and some groups receive an intervention that other groups do not this forms the basis for a design that could be called 'experimental' or 'quasi-experimental' (for example, Siddiqui et al., 2015). As their use of different elements and their names suggest these designs have different roles. Experimental-type studies are good at answering causal questions (such as whether the intervention made a difference), the rest can only really address descriptive questions. Cross-sectional studies are good at answering comparative questions (such as whether one group of students has performed better than another). And so on.

Designs are usually expressed in a simple notation, which can be used by readers of research to summarise a design, and by writers to portray exactly what their design is (given that many people use similar terms for different designs, and most designs do not have an easily recognisable name). In design notation, time is represented by spacing across the page and different groups of cases (the subjects or participants) by spacing down the page. The letters R and N are used to portray how the cases have been selected and allocated to groups – with R representing randomised (picked by chance only) and N representing non-random or naturally occurring (all other methods). One of these letters would be placed to the left of the page on a separate line for each analytical pre-defined group in the study. The letter O is used to represent an episode of data collection, which could be observations, measurements, conversations, text or any other form of data. As explained further below any design is entirely independent of the methods of data collection used – so it is not necessary to be more specific at this stage.

(→Time→)

N   O   (Group 1)

N   O   (Group 2)

The illustration above shows a simple comparative design (the words in brackets are there to help and would not normally appear). It shows a study with two naturally occurring groups (such as male and female students, primary and secondary schools, or fact and fiction books), each of which has some data collected about it (such as their test results, staff:student ratio, or number of words).

Time is represented by the flow of events from left to right. The second illustration (below) would be a simple longitudinal study, with one naturally occurring group and repeated episodes of data collection. This is the design used by most birth cohort studies, for example. The kinds of data collected can vary at each stage. In a birth cohort study, data might include birth weight for the newborn baby, and their musical tastes once they are a teenager.

N   O   O   O   O....

Any intervention of interest (especially applying to only some of the groups) is denoted by the letter X. The next illustration is a little more complex than those above, and portrays a pre- and post-test experimental design or randomised controlled trial. Note that it includes both a comparative (more than one group) and a longitudinal (more than one episode of data collection) design. It is therefore more powerful in many ways than either of the above.

```
R  O  X  O

R  O     O
```

The cases are randomly allocated to one of two groups (R). This means that the two groups will be a fair comparison (unbiased). Pre-intervention data is collected from both (O), and then only one group receives an intervention (X). More data is collected from both groups. All other things being equal, any clear difference between the two groups at the end can be attributed to the effect of the intervention. This design could represent a trial where a large number of undergraduates had been randomly allocated to being taught traditionally in lectures (second row) or via a MOOC (first row). They could be tested for understanding of a topic before the trial, and again afterwards. The number of cases must be large, the randomisation fair, and no other systematic difference should occur between the groups (such as more teaching time for one group). If so, then the difference between groups in the progress of the students from pre- to post-test is a good estimate of the differential effectiveness of the two methods of teaching.

There are many more varieties of design than portrayed here. There can be any number of groups, episodes of data collection, interventions, methods of allocating cases to groups and so on. There is no one good design (no 'gold standard') because the suitability of a design depends solely on the research questions. A researcher using a case study to address a causal question is making a clear mistake (despite what other sources may state). A researcher using a randomised control trial to address a simple comparative question is making an equally clear mistake. Designs are not to be selected on the basis of purported research paradigms, nor do they have anything to do with the methods of data collection and analysis used in each O episode.

A SIMPLE CLASSIFICATION OF RESEARCH DESIGNS

One way of classifying designs is in terms of whether they are active or passive. An active design would include a controlled intervention, introduced as part of the study. Examples of active designs include randomised controlled trials (RCTs), and laboratory experiments, and may also include quasi-experiments (non-random allocation), action research, interrupted time series, regression discontinuity, and design studies. All of these are intrinsically more convincing in testing a causal claim than completely passive designs.

A passive design may consider changes over time but these changes do not occur as part of the research itself, because there is no specific or controlled intervention. Examples include standard cohort research, other longitudinal designs, trend designs, panel surveys, case studies, and comparative or cross-sectional approaches.

Another way of classifying designs could be in terms of whether they involve a pre-specified comparator group, or not. Obviously, comparative studies are intrinsically more convincing in testing a comparative claim than non-comparative ones. Examples include RCTs, natural experiments, and comparative research – all of which pre-specify subgroups for comparison. Non-comparative designs include standard longitudinal approaches and case studies.

Yet another way of classifying designs is in in terms of whether they involve repeated measures, or a planned gap in time from the outset to the final episode of data collection, or not. Such longitudinal designs are intrinsically more convincing in demonstrating a before-and-after claim than cross-sectional ones. Examples of designs with an automatic longitudinal element include standard cohort research, other longitudinal designs, RCTs, and natural experiments. Those usually without a longitudinal element include case studies, and comparative and cross-sectional approaches.

It is interesting that only RCTs and other experiments appear in the 'better' or positive half of each of these classifications. They are better than many designs for causal, comparative *and* time-dependent claims. In addition, RCTs have the advantage over quasi-experiments of having cases allocated to comparator groups at random. Given the right conditions and questions, an RCT or equivalent laboratory experiment is the best and most convincing design to use. Much of the rest of education research can be envisaged as working towards such a trial – whether it leads to an improvement in education policy, practice or simply understanding.

It is also notable that case studies are always in the worse half of each of these classifications. In themselves, they have no comparator, no intervention and no longitudinal element. They are simply an episode of data collection in the absence of any of the other elements of research design. By definition, they have no subgroups (else they would be comparative), and so no method of allocation to such groups, no repeated measures (else they would be longitudinal), no intervention and so on. Case studies can be valuable, especially towards the start of a research programme, largely because they are simple and quick to set up, but a case study, in isolation, should never be the preferred design for any research that aims to be convincing or definitive. Some commentators misunderstand this key point, and suggest that case studies are to be preferred because they allow a researcher to study a case in-depth. They forget that designs are independent of methods of data collection. It is as feasible that a case study was an examination of the financial accounts of one company as that a longitudinal study involved an in-depth observation of someone's adjustment to a new job over the first six months. No design has a monopoly on depth or breadth of data.

A similar point can be made to those who argue that we should select designs on the basis of research ethics – claiming, for example, that RCTs are intrinsically unethical because they deny treatment to some cases or because they involve interventions. This is not so. In fact, we ought to pick the most appropriate design, for only in this way can we hope to do research that will not waste the time of those involved in doing it, reading it or using the results, and will not waste the money of those funding it. This is the only ethical route. Students face interventions all of the time from policy-makers and practitioners. Using such interventions to plan research around cannot make them unethical. Denying an intervention to a student cannot be unethical unless we know that it works, in which case we should not be doing a trial, and so on. There are anyway many ways in which trials can be conducted so that no cases are denied the intervention (including wait-lists, as described in Gorard, 2013).

A fourth way of classifying designs would be in terms of the way cases are allocated to groups. With no comparator no comparison can be made. This may sound so obvious as to be not worth stating, yet comparisons without comparators are so prevalent in education research that they are almost the norm (and so perhaps hard to spot). Whenever a study picks a specific target to study and then works only with that target group (special needs, homeless learners, those living in poverty and so on) the study should make no comparative claims – including of course the claim that any research finding is specific to that target group. A recent newspaper report claimed that over 80 per cent of teachers had considered a different job, and the whole article and the quotations from commentators clearly envisaged that this was a much higher figure than for other jobs. This kind of unwarranted assumption is widespread in academic literature as well, as are claims about changes over time based on data from only one time point.

The need for warranted conclusions requires all researchers to identify the kind of claims to be made – such as descriptive, associative, or causal – and then ensure that the most appropriate possible design is used. A comparative claim *must* have an explicit and suitable comparator, for example. A research-based claim should be the simplest explanation for the available evidence. Good prior research design eliminates (or at least tests or allows for) a large number of alternate explanations before any claim to knowledge is made. In this way, the design makes analysis much easier, and strengthens research claims. Design makes research better.

THE ELEMENTS IN MORE DETAIL

Rather than picking a standard research design, it is better to work with the elements of design and create a framework that best suits the research question(s) you are addressing. This may lead to a clearly recognisable design such as longitudinal, but sometimes it will not. This is to be expected. Therefore, it will be helpful to consider the key elements of a design in more detail here, leaving the reader to use this knowledge to help them create suitable designs for their own work. Note that because so few methods resources consider design at all, and so many of those that consider it do not understand it, the points made in this chapter may conflict with the contents of other chapters in this book. For example, there is no need at all for researchers to go back to the basics of epistemology and ontology in real-life research, there are no paradigms such as 'quantitative' and 'qualitative' and case studies are a basically hopeless way of conducting research that matters. Research is much easier to conduct than is usually portrayed, as long as the design is right from the outset.

The cases in the study

The 'cases' are the individuals, organisations or objects selected to take part in the research. All possible cases that could take part form the 'population'. If possible, all possible cases should be used since this will minimise bias (as opposed to selecting only some cases from the population). If not possible, cases can be selected from the population. If these are selected randomly this produces the least bias (other than not selecting cases at all and using them all). If any other form of selection is used, such as convenience, the research is already considerably weakened in terms of its generality (whether the results would also be true for cases in the population but not in the study). In general, and all other things being equal, the more cases there are in any study the more trustworthy its findings are. Some reports discuss a 'power' analysis or using a minimal detectable effect size to compute the required sample size. Ignore these issues, as they depend on many assumptions almost none of which will be true for real-life research, and because they are predicated on the flawed technique of significance testing (Gorard, 2016).

More important is recording and reporting how many cases are missing (non-response, dropout, non-contactable) or have key missing data. All research reports should include a minimum set of information about the cases, such as the population, how many cases were selected, how many did not take part, and how many were later excluded for any other reason. In general, and all other things being equal, the fewer missing cases there are in any study the more trustworthy its findings are.

Creating comparator groups

If a researcher wants to make a comparison it is better (more convincing) that they specify this in advance, rather than dredging their data after collection. This specification would include how the comparator groups were created, and which variables or characteristics the groups will be compared on.

Where the comparator groups occur naturally (boys versus girls perhaps), they can be useful for making descriptive comparative claims using a cross-sectional design (such as girls get better exam results than boys). However, it is hard to make any other kind of research claim using such heterogeneous groups. Alternatively, researchers often want to create equivalent groups at the outset, such as the treatment and control groups in an experimental design. The surest way to do this is to randomly allocate each case to one of the subgroups in the study. This is the safest way because it caters for differences in terms of unknown variables that can never be matched as well as known variables that could be matched. If randomisation is not possible (a rare situation) then some kind of matching could be used. However, even when it is successful this procedure only matches the two groups in gross terms, and using only those variables that are available. For example, matching the average age of students in two groups does not mean that they are matched in terms of motivation (unlike with randomisation).

It is generally better for any subsequent research claim to have few groups and many cases per group. To a large extent, the safety of a research finding depends not on the total number of cases, but on the number of cases in the smallest group for the comparison (Gorard and Gorard, 2016), along with the number of cases missing (Gorard, 2014).

Matters of timing

When considering changes over time is important to beware of the difference between biographical and historical types of changes. Trend, or repeated cross-sectional, designs are useful for describing historical changes over time, but of limited use in explanatory research. The health of a nation may be improving (over successive generations), but the health of each individual in that nation may be declining (as they age). Longitudinal, or panel or cohort, designs are useful for tracking changes over the life-course of individuals (or cases), especially when looking for possible risk factors for subsequent events. The link between smoking and lung cancer was first discovered via this approach. However, neither design has been shown to be much good at predicting future events. Both are known to be misleading when assessing causal models – due to attrition as time goes on and changes arising that could not have been known at the outset.

Interventions and 'what works?'

Adding an intervention or treatment to a longitudinal or other study does not make it a useful test of causation. Before and after designs like this can be very misleading if treated as causal. It is well known that correlation is not causation, but nor is before-and-after. Giving school students an extra holiday and then discovering that their maths is improved a year later is not evidence that the holiday caused the improvement in maths. The design needs a counterfactual as well. What would have happened to these students if they had not had the holiday (most students improve over a year regardless of other factors)? Comparing these students with another group which did not receive the extra holiday is crucial, as is ensuring that both groups were as similar as possible to begin with – hence randomised trials. A post-test only experiment with two groups allocated at random is a simple powerful design. Adding a pre-test allows researchers to compare gain scores between groups. This can allow for slight variation in the initial scores between groups. Generally, experimental trials are powerful, relatively inexpensive, easy to conduct, and make subsequent analysis simpler. Despite some claims to the contrary they present few specific ethical or practical concerns

There is a range of alternatives that can be used when an experiment is genuinely not possible – including regression discontinuity, quasi-experiments, natural experiments, interrupted times series, difference in difference, instrumental variables, and Granger modelling (Gorard 2013). Apart from regression discontinuity none produces results as convincing as RCTs.

JUDGING THE TRUSTWORTHINESS OF RESEARCH CLAIMS

Research design is crucial to judging whether to believe or trust the findings from any research project (so that we should not believe comparative results from a study with no explicit comparator, for example). Gorard (2014) suggests a simple 'sieve' that can be used to help judge the quality of a piece of research. The first question to address is whether the research utilises a design that is appropriate for the research question. If the research is causal, has the study used a fair comparison group perhaps based on individual randomisation to treatment or control, and so on. The simplest design of two near-equivalents is usually the best. So, a post-test only experiment reduces the complications of initial errors, for example, in comparison to a pre- and post-test design. It is usually worth jotting down a summary of the design using the notation from this chapter whenever reading a new piece of research (even though for much reported 'research' there will be no design).

Note also the scale (is it large enough to be convincing?). The scale of the smallest group in any comparison drives (or should drive) our judgement about whether to trust the results. Note the missing data (both missing cases, and missing data from existing cases). Note whether the research actually reports missing data – if no data is reported missing then assume the worst. A sensitivity analysis can estimate how little of the missing data would have to differ to alter the substantive research findings (Gorard and Gorard 2016).

Perhaps the next most important aspect to consider is the quality of the data itself. Could there be errors in measurement, observation, or recording? Is the data quite precise (such as measurements of heights), less precise (such as records of student attainment), or rather vague (such as impressions, or psychological constructs like 'school self-concept')? Are there other threats to the validity of the study – such as a vested interest by the researcher?

All of these and other design issues need be judged and synthesised together. What the sieve (above) suggests is that research is rated in terms of its weakest link. If the scale is tiny (for example, a study with three cases) then none of the other factors really matter however strong they are. The research is probably not trustworthy. If the missing data is high (for example, 40 per cent) then again none of the other factors really matter, even if the study is very large. If the research draws a comparison over time with data from only one time point then it is not to be trusted whatever the strengths of its other attributes.

SUMMING UP

Research design is the friend of the researcher, where a bit of planning leads to a much more useful result. It is the friend of the funder, because it creates more believable research. And it is the friend of everyone else because it tends to produce more trustworthy results for education policy and practice. It is really quite simple. If the research question is causal in nature, then an experimental design or similar is necessary. If such a design is not used then the research is probably wasting everyone's time. If the research is to make comparative claims (even disguised comparative claims) then it must have explicit comparator groups from the outset. If such a design is not used then the research is probably misleading all readers. All of the designs and elements of design covered in this chapter are completely separate from issues about what data to collect. If a certain number of cases are needed to make a convincing research claim it does not matter at all how that data was collected. Design is a kind of conceptual framework for any research but it is far more important than what too many commentators call their 'theoretical framework' (which is usually not about a testable theory at all). Design is an ethical requirement for research, and it would be good if more ethics committees and similar bodies worried more than they currently do about the quality of research and its impact on the general public. Most of the harm done by research does not happen to individuals in the research process, but to the much greater number of individuals affected by bad interventions and untested policies.

REFERENCES

de Vaus, D. (2001) *Research Design In Social Research*. London: Sage Publications.

Gorard, S. (2013) *Research Design: Robust approaches for the social sciences*. London: Sage Publications.

Gorard, S. (2014) A proposal for judging the trustworthiness of research findings, *Radical Statistics*, 110, 47–60. Retrieved on July 5, 2016 from http://www.radstats.org.uk/no110/Gorard110.pdf.

Gorard, S. (2015) The uncertain future of comprehensive schooling in England, *European Educational Research Journal*, 14, 3–4, 257–268. Retrieved on July 5, 2016 from http://eer.sagepub.com/cgi/reprint/14/3–4/257.pdf?ijkey=6QSxgjXEXzExZC2&keytyp e=finite.

Gorard, S. (2016) Damaging real lives through obstinacy: re-emphasising why significance testing is wrong, *Sociological Research On-line*, 21, 1. Retrieved on July 5, 2016 from www.socresonline.org.uk/21/1/2.html.

Gorard, S. and Gorard, J. (2016) What to do instead of significance testing? Calculating the 'number of counterfactual cases needed to disturb a finding', *International Journal of Social Research Methodology*, 19, 4, 481–489. Retrieved on July 5, 2016 from http://tandfonline.com/doi/full/10.1080/13645579.2015.1091235.

See, B. H., Gorard, S. and Siddiqui, N. (2016) Can teachers use research evidence in practice?: a pilot study of the use of feedback to enhance learning, *Educational Research*, 58, 1, 56–72. Retrieved on July 5, 2016 from www.tandfonline.com/doi/full/10.1080/00131881.2015.1117798.

Shadish, W., Cook, T. and Campbell, D. (2002) *Experimental and Quasi-experimental Designs for Generalized Causal Inference*. Belmont: Wadsworth.

Siddiqui, N., Gorard, S. and See, BH (2015) Accelerated reader as a literacy catch-up intervention during the primary to secondary school transition phase, *Educational Review*, 68, 2, 139–154. Retrieved on July 5, 2016 from www.tandfonline.com/doi/full/10.1080/00131911.2015.1067883#.Vbs-W0_bKUk.

10

A Positivist Orientation: Hypothesis Testing and the 'Scientific Method'

Roger Gomm

INTRODUCTION

The term 'positivism' refers to the philosophical under-pinning of mainstream natural sciences. This assumes (ontologically) that there are entities and processes in the world that exist irrespective of what researchers might believe – 'mind-independent entities', and that scientists can approximate the truth about them: a position known as 'realism'. That world is conceptualized in terms of variables interacting with each other in cause and effect sequences which will always happen in similar ways in similar circumstances. For positivism, knowledge can only be justified as 'scientific' if it is:

- based on measured (quantitative) observations of empirical evidence – that is evidence of the senses – empiricism;
- produced in ways that are objective: that is open to audit by others: preferably in ways that can be checked by others repeating the study – reproducibility;
- and, as far as possible, with findings uninfluenced by the political, or religious desires or career aspirations of researchers – value neutrality.

'Unity of method' is a common associated prescription: that social and behavioural sciences such as educational research, should be modelled on the same approach as used in the natural sciences. Here the claim is that, while other ways of studying social, cultural and historical topics may be worthwhile, they are not 'scientific' (Popper, 1959, 1963 Verdugo, 2009).

Many social scientists reject this claim and use the term 'positivism' in a disparaging way either because they find it inappropriate or demeaning to describe social and psychological phenomena numerically, and/or because they think that sentient human activity cannot be captured in terms of interacting variables, and/or because they do not believe it is desirable, or possible, to insulate research from politics or religion. They propose alternative ways of doing research. These views are expressed elsewhere in this handbook. There has been a strongly anti-positivist tendency in sociology and to a lesser extent in psychology and hence in educational research. But from another direction there has been a growing concern at the increasing contrast between the remarkable achievements of the 'positivistic' natural sciences, and the poor showing of enterprises such as educational research. Expressions of this dissatisfaction have often claimed that educational research is not 'scientific' enough: not positivistic enough (Kaestle, 1993; Lagemann, 2000; Levin and O'Donnell, 1999; Tooley and Darley, 1998). This idea has become influential in decisions about state (and other) funding for educational research, tagged as SBR or 'science based research' in the USA (Feure et al., 2002; Shavelson and Towne, 2002a, 2002b; Towne et al., 2004) and associated with the promotion of evidence-based practice in the UK (Hargreaves, 1996; Hammersley, 2007; Thomas and Pring, 2004). In the UK this has resulted in the establishment by government of agencies to conduct such research in areas relevant to policy (Halpern 2015: pp. 266–298). For educational research these are the Education Endowment Foundation or Sutton Trust (https://educationen-dowmentfoundation.org.uk/) and the Early Intervention Foundation (http://www.eif.org.uk/). Both publish research-based 'toolkits' offering best practice advice to practitioners and or parents. These may give the impression that the research on which the advice is based is more certain and more generally applicable than is actually so, against the modern positivistic assumption that all knowledge is uncertain.

The characterization earlier of positivism as the philosophy of the natural sciences now has to be caveated, first by saying that natural scientists are far less likely to concern themselves with philosophical issues than those in social and behavioural fields. Few would call themselves 'positivists': most would just say they were 'scientists'. Second, the content of positivism has changed again and again since the term was coined by Compte in the 1830s. Positivism has always been riven with disputes, and what counts as best practice in 'scientific' research is constantly evolving. So there are many varieties of positivism and very little consensus about which approaches should be listed under that heading. For the last 60 years or so the approach called the 'hypothetico-deductive method' (H-DM) has been that most widely followed in the natural sciences and in much of psychology and educational research. Most of this chapter will deal with positivism of this kind.

So common, and successful for scientific output has this approach been that it is often simply called 'the scientific method' (Andersen and Hepburn 2016; 6.2) The main philosophical underpinning is usually taken to be Karl Popper's critical rationalism (Thornton, 2014) developed as a very different form of positivism from the logical positivism of the 1920s and 1930s (Creath, 2014) which was universally abandoned by 1970s. However, research practice has been much more influenced by the statistician Ronald Fisher (Fisher, 1935, 1937; Stanley, 1966) and for educational researchers the more important name is probably Donald Campbell (Campbell and Stanley, 1963).

What follow are:

- Section 1: a brief introduction to the hypothetico-deductive method, which will be dealt with in more detail through an example in Section 4.
- Section 2: an explanation of the philosophical rational for the H-DM and null hypothesis testing.
- Section 3: an introduction to the main example for this chapter with the reasons for choosing it.
- Section 4: a step-by-step exemplification of the hypothetico-deductive method featuring the example introduced in Section 3 and discussing important methodological points about the various components of the process.
- Section 5: a consideration of what it takes for research findings to be added the scientific knowledge-base.
- Section 6: some remarks on the limitations of the H-DM as an approach to research both in principle and as it is practised.

The chapter ends with some brief concluding remarks.

SECTION 1 THE HYPOTHETICO-DEDUCTIVE METHOD

This section gives a brief introduction to the hypothetic-deductive or 'scientific' method widely followed in the natural sciences and prescribed by some as the best approach to educational research.

An hypothesis is a conjecture or speculation. In this context it is a conjecture about what would be observable if a theoretical idea were false and what would be observable if it were true: respectively, a 'null hypothesis' – symbolized H_o and an' alternative' (or in an experiment, an 'experimental') hypothesis, symbolized H_a or H_e, or $H_{1(2, 3 etc.)}$. For the main research example for this chapter, the theoretical idea is that early childhood diet will influence later educational attainment. Here the alternative hypothesis might be that:

H_a IF early childhood diet DOES affect later educational attainment THEN there will be statistically significant associations between differences in diet and differences in educational attainment.

By the same IF–THEN logic, the null hypothesis would be something like:

H_o IF early childhood diet DOES NOT affect later educational attainment THEN there will be no statistically significant associations between differences in diet and differences in educational attainment.

Argument like this, from a general proposition to a specific instance is deductive argument: hence the 'deductive' in 'hypothetico-deductive'.

The null hypothesis is sometimes called the 'no-difference' hypothesis, and they are often phrased in this way, as if the null meant 'nil (difference)'. In fact the term was coined by R. A. Fisher saying that this was the hypothesis which should be tested: that the research should seek to 'nullify' it (Fisher, 1935, p. 8).

This kind of research then, is directed towards proving the null hypothesis true, hence falsifying the theory. Failure to prove the null leaves the alternative hypothesis standing. Those theoretical propositions which survive well-designed attempts to disprove them in this way, can be regarded as provisionally true: true for the time being: true until something better comes along which explains more. The term 'corroboration' is often used instead of 'proof', although 'proof' is quite appropriate in its original meaning which is 'subjected to test', rather than the modern 'put beyond doubt'. The approach may be variously called falsificationism, anti-verificationism, anti-justificationism, or anti-confirmationism.

The same deductive logic as above might apply in research evaluating (say) a drug education project, for example: *IF the project has been effective THEN the children who were involved will have more adverse attitudes towards illicit drugs than those who were not involved.* The null would be: [...] *there will be no difference in attitudes between the two groups of children [...].*

Any researcher who uses a statistical test of significance inevitably practises falsification. A statistically significant result is said to be one unlikely to have occurred by chance. The actual results are compared with what might have happened by chance. A model of the most likely chance outcomes is factored into the formula for the statistical test as the null situation. A much more detailed account of significance testing is given in Chapter 37 of this Handbook.

Before proceeding it is important to explain the rationale for falsification and null hypothesis testing (Section 2).

SECTION 2 THE PHILOSOPHICAL RATIONALE FOR THE HYPOTHETICO-DEDUCIVE METHOD: WHY TEST NULL HYPOTHESES?

This section explains the rationale for the null hypothesis testing which characterizes the hypothetico-deductive method.

In this branch of positivism, what demarcates science from other intellectual enterprises is that its propositions are capable of being proved false, if false they are, by reference to observable facts: empirically (Popper, 2002, pp. 17–20, 57–73; Dienes, 2008, Chapter 1).

There are at least three reasons for adopting a falsificationist position: a logical reason, a psychological reason (avoiding confirmation or verification bias) and an epistemological one (the problem of induction).

Avoiding a logical fallacy by testing the null

Suppose research showed an association between experiencing a particular diet, and (say) low achievement at school. This might actually be true, but without further evidence it would be a logical fallacy to assume that diet *caused* poor performance. It is a methodological cliché that, 'correlation doesn't necessarily indicate causation'. Instead an association between diet and educational attainment might be caused by a third factor, or a group of other factors. This fallacy – called 'affirming the consequent' (Hansen, 2015) is avoided by focusing on the null hypothesis.

Counteracting confirmation bias by trying to disprove theories rather than prove them true (Owad, 2006)

For researchers, confirmation bias is a bias in favour of reaching the conclusion they most hope for. Researchers are often very fond of their own theories especially those researchers in the politicized areas of educational research such Marxist, feminist, anti-racist or (dis)ability research (Chapter 1 in this Handbook) or in practitioner research (Chapter 29 in this Handbook) where the researcher-practitioner may have a lot invested in a particular pedagogic practice. Pressure from funding bodies can also lead to spurious findings, particularly where commercial interests are involved, as is well demonstrated by studies of research funded by the pharmaceutical and the food industries (Als-neilson et al., 2003; Lesser et al., 2007; Saini et al., 2014). These include some with educational relevance (for example the research backing the Brain Gym programme (Hyatt, 2007), or the Durham fish oil project (Goldacre, 2008, Chapter 8) or the DARE anti-drug programme (Hamilton, 1997)).The spurious research supporting the SCARE approach to discouraging juvenile delinquency is another example (Petrosino et al., 2013). It can be very easy to cherry-pick data, lose inconvenient findings, unilaterally exercise the benefit of the doubt where observations are ambiguous, and otherwise drum up evidence in support of a theory or practice, to say nothing of government censorship, or the issuing of libel suits or the employment of PR firms to mitigate criticism, especially if the aim is not so much truth as commercial gain or political impact (Mooney, 2005). Attention has been drawn to the suspiciously high rate of 'success' reported when evaluations are conducted with approaches other than described in this chapter (Logan, 1972; Oakley, 2000; Petrosino et al., 2013; Gomm, 2008, pp. 96–9). An approach which requires researchers to make serious attempts to *disprove* hypotheses they or their sponsors may favour, should reduce the influence of confirmation bias.

Outflanking the problem of induction by excluding error rather than confirming truths

A third reason for adopting a falsificationist approach via the hypothetico-deductive method is as an attempt to outflank the so-called 'problem of induction'. This is a centuries-old philosophical problem (Vickers, 2014). Induction means making inferences about what is true in general, based on observations about what is true in particular instances: the opposite of deduction (see Section 1). I might infer that, because the sun has risen in the morning every day of my life so far, that it will also rise tomorrow and the day after and so on. But since I have not yet observed, and cannot yet observe the sun rising tomorrow, I can have no proof that this is true: 'proof' in the sense of absolute certainty. Inductivist research usually consists of collecting more data in an attempt to confirm a theory: verificationism. But, however much data I collect about sunrises I will never have enough for certainty. However, a single contradictory observation can disprove my proposal. Einstein is quoted as saying, 'No amount of experimentation can ever prove me right; a single experiment can prove me wrong'. (Calaprice, 2005, p. 291)

Well, perhaps not a *single* contrary example, but certainly a small number of well-designed experiments, satisfactorily replicated (see Section 5).

The development of science through a process of eliminating erroneous theories is thus proposed as an alternative to inductivism: this is the H-DM.

Falsificationism is not an entirely satisfactory solution to confirmation bias or to the problem of induction. Nor does it provide a route to absolute certainty about what is true – far from it. Though the term 'positivism' once implied that it was possible to attain a 'foundation' of 'positive' or certain knowledge, it is uncertainty rather than certainty which characterizes modern positivism. The assumption is that what counts as scientific knowledge is not necessarily right, just less likely to be wrong than other knowledge (Popper, 2002, p. 94, Dennet, 1995, p. 380) In terms of the hypothetico-deductive method, while a piece of research, such as that to be described below (Section 3) might favour a particular explanation, it will always remain a possibility that the same evidence is better explained otherwise.

Now the rational for the H-DM has been explained, the next two sections illustrate the approach further through a major example: first an introduction to the example (Section 3) and then a step through some of the more common components with discussion about the methodological issues each raises (Section 4).

SECTION 3 THE MAIN EXAMPLE FOR THIS CHAPTER – ILLUSTRATING THE H-DM

The main example for this chapter concerns the influence of children's diet on their educational attainment (Feinstein et al., 2008; North and Emmett, 2000; Northstone et al., 2005; Wiles et al., 2007; Emmett, 2009,Emmett and Jones 2014,Emmett et al.,2015). It uses data from one of the British longitudinal surveys of child development (Chapter 20 in this Handbook): *ALSPAC*:

the *Avon Longitudinal Study of Parents and Children* or *Children of the Nineties* (Golding et al., 2001) and matched data from the *National Pupil Data Base* (Gov.UK, 2013). Most of what follows is based on 'Dietary patterns related to attainment in school: the importance of early eating patterns' (Feinstein et al., 2008). While the authors do not explicitly state null hypotheses, they do in effect test null hypotheses.

The ALSPAC survey recruited nearly all the children born in the then English Health Area of Avon between dates in 1991 and 1992. The relevant data collected are shown in Table 10.1. The research question is whether variations in diet (as they were measured) – the independent variable, predict variations in educational attainment (as measured) – the dependent variable. And if the one predicts the other, do dietary differences *explain* differences in educational performance? The researchers had dependent variable data from National Curriculum Tests or 'Key Stage Tests' (SATs), and independent variable data from food frequency questionnaires completed by parents enrolled in ALSPAC.

ALSPAC also provides data on 23 other demographic, socio-economic, health, and lifestyle factors and prior educational attainment which might contribute to differences in educational attainment (also treated as 'independent variables) which might confound (or confuse) any relationship shown between diet and attainment. These data allow the influence of such factors to be controlled out – discounted – in analysis.

This example was chosen for the following reasons:

- The research question is a fairly straightforward 'cause and effect' question. This is the kind of topic for which H-DM is most appropriate, rather than research designed to investigate the experiences and inner lives of other people for which qualitative or 'interpretative' research may be more appropriate.
- The mechanisms through which diet and educational attainment are linked, seem likely to be of the kinds dealt with successfully in natural sciences such as physiology, nutrition, and neurology and hence most amenable to investigation using a natural science approach.
- The example features survey data. H-DM is classically associated with experiments The design of controlled experiments is dealt with in Chapter 21 of this Handbook, however, in educational research, well designed experiments are often impractical, or ethically unjustifiable,or so unnaturalistic that it is doubtful whether findings can be extrapolated to real world circumstances. Or they may have samples so small and or unrepresentative that results are inconsequential. Good survey data often offers more opportunities for educational research.
- The example does indeed draw on 'good' survey data, on one of the major longitudinal studies of child development which are the jewels in the crown of data for educational researchers. The merits of large scale longitudinal surveys are described more fully in Chapter 20 of this handbook, and picked up again in Section 4 below.

The example is used to illustrate major steps, considerations and issues in an H-DM investigation. Of course, a different example would have highlighted a different set of issues.

Table 10.1 Data sources for study of the impact of diet on educational attainment (after Feinstein et al., 2008)

Who	What		How	When[3]
13,988 children born in Avon 1991–1992 and surviving.	Confounding (independent) variables	Data on 23 potentially confounding demographic, health, socio-economic and life-style variables	ALSPAC Questionnaires and interviews	At families' recruitment to survey and updated thereafter
5741 children for whom both dietary and attainment data were available [1]	Independent variable of interest	Dietary data	ALSPAC parent completed food frequency questionnaire	at 38 months (c 3yrs old) at 54 months (c 4yrs old) at 81 months (c 7yrs old)
	Dependent variable	Attainment data (from National Pupil Database (NPD)[2]	Teacher completed assessments of national curriculum tests (SATs)	
			maths, reading writing and language	at school entry (4–5 yrs)
			reading, writing and maths	at KS1 (6–7 yrs)
			English, maths and science	at KS2 (10–11 yrs)

Notes:

(1) 41 % of all children originally recruited and surviving. Since the characteristics of the missing 59% were known (see row 1) it was possible to estimate that the effect of attrition on the final results was probably small. Children from lower socio-economic groups and from ethnic minorities were most under-represented.

(2) Nearly all children in state funded education in England are assessed by their teachers in terms of a national testing framework. These data are recorded on the National Pupil Database (NPD).

(3) Food frequency data were collected at these points in time, but also referring to past periods of time.

SECTION 4 THE HYPOTHETICO-DEDUCTIVE METHOD EXEMPLIFIED IN DETAIL.

A deductive starting point (point 1 Figure 10.1)

The overall trajectory of Figure 10.1 extends (or restricts) an existing body of knowledge through logical deductions about the evidence which would enhance or detract from its credibility. Those theoretical propositions which survive a confrontation with evidence are candidates for inclusion in what counts as sound theory for the time being, at least by some sections of the research community. Thus theory is founded, confirmed, refined or overturned by many circuits like this.

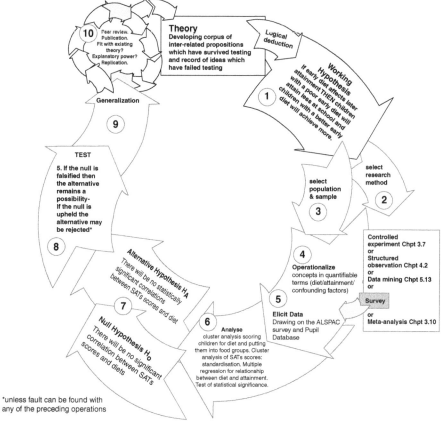

Note: steps 2–6 may occur in any order, or iteratively according to the method adopted

Figure 10.1   The hypothetico-deductive method illustrated with reference to Feinstein et al., 2008

Note: steps 2-6 may occur in any order, or iteratively according to the method adopted

Sometimes the starting point on such a circuit is not so much existing theory but a question arising from a hunch, an observation, a practical problem or a political interest, but carried forward with the same deductive logic. However, within a discipline too many new starts of this kind which don't extend or refine existing theory result in a corpus of fragmented, unrelated bits and pieces of knowledge. It has been claimed that this is so with educational research (Fidler and Gordon, 2013; Hargreaves, 1996, p. 7).

Whatever the initial inspiration for H-DM research, it usually includes an early scrutiny of existing knowledge – usually a 'literature review' (Chapter 7 in this Handbook) and then some deduction is made in the form of a statement of the logical consequences of (a) salient proposition(s) being either true or false. At point 1 Figure 10.1 the terms are insufficiently precise for testing. How are different diets to be distinguished, when are the critical periods, what is meant by 'educational attainment', how is 'corresponding' to be measured? Clarifying these points turns the working hypothesis into a set of operational hypotheses (see point 7 Figure 10.1): the null for statistical testing.

Choice of research method (point 2 Figure 10.1)

In our example, the choice of method was restricted to what was possible with survey data (Golding et al., 2001) since the study was based on a longitudinal cohort survey which was to form the basis for various studies of pregnancy, birth, health and child development. The advantages and some difficulties of using longitudinal surveys are dealt with in Chapter 20 in this handbook.

The iconic, textbook examples of the H-DM involve controlled (or manipulative) experiments where the researchers strongly modifies the environment in which the independent variable has its effects (Chapter 21 in this handbook). But there may be ethical and practical reasons why controlled experiments cannot be used in educational research especially when long time periods elapse between the independent variable and change in such dependent variable(s) it may or may not influence. It would be both impractical and unethical to attempt to control the independent variable here, because the independent variable is the eating behaviour of children continuously over seven to eight years or more. Hence the use here of a survey, but a survey used experimentally. Instead of subjects being subjected to different experiences under the control of the experimenter, survey data are used to discover what they do in the ordinary course of their lives. Then 'internal' or 'statistical' controls are created by analysing the survey data and then dividing people into categories – in this case into groups of children experiencing different diets – see Table 10.2. The general form of the implicit null hypotheses is that there will be no outcome differences between children experiencing different diets.

The dietary regimes are what happen 'naturally', outside the influence of the researchers, so this approach is often called a 'natural experiment' or an 'observational experiment'.

Table 10.2 The experimental logic of the 'natural experiment' on diet and educational attainment, after Feinstein et al., 2008 (KS= Key Stage)

Stage	*Exposure to independent variable*	*Measurement of dependent variable*	*Exposure to independent variable*	*Measurement of dependent variable*	*Exposure to independent variable*	*Measurement of dependent variable*
	Treatment -diet	Pre-test observation (Entry Level KS Score)	Treatment- diet	Post-test -previous treatment phase Pre-test for next treatment phase (KS1 score)	Treatment -diet	Post-test observation (KS2 score)
Timing	Continuous up to 4–5years (known up to 38 months)	Tested between 4–5years	Continuous 4–5 to 6–7 years	Tested between 6–7 years	Continuous up to 10–11years (known up to 81 months)	Tested between 10–11 years.
Diet Group j ('Junk')	T_{j1}	O_{j1}	T_{j2}	O_{j2}	T_{j3}	O_{j3}
Diet Group t ('Traditional')	T_{t1}	O_{t1}	T_{t2}	O_{t2}	T_{t3}	O_{t3}
Diet Group h ('Health-conscious')	T_{h1}	O_{h1}	T_{h2}	O_{h2}	T_{h3}	O_{h3}

Population, sampling, sample size and internal validity (point 3 Figure 10.1)

There are practical considerations in choosing a population and sample, about accessibility, about cooperativeness (Chapters 14 and 27 in this Handbook), and ethical concerns about not causing harm or distress (Chapter 4 of this Handbook). For our example, the population was pre-decided by the choice of a longitudinal survey in Avon. The extent to which Avon can stand for the rest of England was a consideration (Golding et al., 2001). The original pool of eligible subjects was 100 per cent of children born in the designated period 1991–1992, but the final sample here was the 41 per cent of children remaining: those for whom there were both dietary and educational records. Many relevant characteristics of those with incomplete records, or lost to the research were known, so it could be estimated how representative the sample continued to be of the whole population. Otherwise attrition of this sort can degrade a representative sample into a hopelessly unrepresentative one (Howe et al., 2013)

Representativeness is not an all or nothing matter, but depends on the diversity within the population which is relevant to the research question. A relatively small sample, properly recruited can be representative of the sex ratio in the population from which the sample was drawn, a larger sample would be needed for a sample to be representative of the diversity of human physiology, and an even larger one to be representative of the diversity of human psychology, or, as in this case, diet. Which are the relevant dimensions of diversity may not be known in advance of the research (or even afterwards). Controlled experiments (Chapter 21 in this Handbook) rarely achieve much in the way of representativeness, while properly conducted surveys usually do better.

Sample size and mode of recruitment can be very important for ensuring that the findings claimed are true for the data actually used: internal validity. And the smaller the sample the greater the error risked (Fox et al., 2007). Here the sample was large – just under 6,000 children, and provided adequate statistical 'elbow room' for controlling out the influence of potentially confounding variables, or at least those identified. The representativeness of samples is equally important for the credibility of *general* conclusions drawn from particular research findings – external validity, and will be dealt with later.

Creating testable hypotheses: operationalizing concepts (point 4 Figure 10.1)

To be testable the hypotheses need to be; stated in terms of unambiguous empirical indicators of the relevant variables conceptualized, phrased in quantitative terms amenable to appropriate statistical manipulation – see Chapters 36, 37, 44 and 45 in this handbook.

Indicators are rarely precisely and completely identical with the concepts they indicate. What is required is a good enough correspondence for the research task at hand: think of the relationships between a map and a landscape where the indicative symbols on the map are far from accurate in many respects, but accurate enough for the purposes for which a map is used.

Operationalization is done through creating data-collecting instruments and perhaps by transforming the data collected into forms more amenable to statistical manipulation. Instruments may be as simple as a yes/no/don't know question on a questionnaire, as complex as a population standardized aptitude test, as informal as the notes in a notebook, or as large scale and bureaucratized as the procedures for collecting key stage data for the National Curriculum tests.

Instruments generating indicative data need to be designed at least to:

- produce data that sufficiently represent the relevant aspects of whatever it is they are supposed to represent: *valid data*, with a good correspondence between the theoretical construct and its alleged indicator (Chapter 6 in this Handbook).
- be *reliable*: produce the same results if used by a different researcher – *inter-rater reliability*, or by the same researcher on a different occasions – *test-retest reliability* (assuming no change in the intervening period) and other kinds of consistent performance with regard to whatever is being measured (Chapter 6 in this Handbook).
- generate data which are suitable for the statistical manipulation required to answer the research question – see Chapters 4 and 5 – on levels of data and parametric and non-parametric statistics. Researchers who are not themselves statisticians are advised to consult one in designing their research. As Ronald Fisher said:

> To consult the statistician after an experiment is finished is often merely to ask him to conduct a post mortem examination. He can perhaps say what the experiment died of. (Fisher, 1938, p. 14)

Poor statistical practice is a major problem across all fields of science (Reinhart, 2014), including educational research (Schagen, 2008) but in quantitative research, unlike in qualitative research, these are errors which are detectable and sometimes correctable.

Feinstein et al. (2008) used the National Pupil Database as a source of data indicative of educational attainment (NFER 2009). These tests are precisely how a pupil's educational attainment is officially measured in real life. Thus there is a close match between concept and indicator (good *construct validity*), except that there are areas of educational attainment other than those measured in the tests featured in this research (less good *content validity*). For example, the tests do not measure the capacity to cooperate with others, emotional intelligence, physical prowess, musical or artistic ability and other matters which may be enhanced through education. And it would be impossible for the tests to be *unreliable* measures of educational attainment since the tests are what define educational attainment, whether or not assessing teachers are accurate judges of what children can do (Wiliam, 2001; Maughan et al., 2009). Insofar as teachers are poor judges, test results are less than valid measures of what children can actually do educationally speaking even if they are precisely accurate measures of the results of assessment.

The data on diet derive from parental questionnaires (North and Emmett, 2000; Northstone et al., 2005; Emmett, 2009, Emmett and Jones 2014, Emmett et al., 2015). Questionnaire data on diet are often inaccurate (Harper and Hallsworth, 2016, Unite for Sight, 2015; Brown, 2016). They often suffer from social desirability bias (Hebert et al 1995). Some of the data relied on parents' memory and ability to distinguish between different food types. People's estimates of past frequencies are similarly rather poor (Thompson et al., 2013). However, other researchers had followed up their own use of very similar questionnaires with interviews, to check them and found them reasonably accurate (Mouratidou et al., 2005).On validating research instruments see Chapter 4 and note the advantage of using an instrument similar to that used in other research, facilitating direct comparison of results between different pieces of research.

Data validity is not an all or nothing matter. You can improve or undermine the validity of data by redefining what data are being used as evidence for. For example if we replaced 'educational attainment' as the dependent variable, with 'cognitive development', then we might have a (construct) validity problem. Clever children sometimes perform badly at school, so key stage tests might not measure cognitive development accurately (validly) or reliably (consistently). For cognitive development, IQ scores, which were also recorded, would have been a better indicator for the dependent variable (Emmett and Jones 2014) though the IQ only records a narrow spectrum of cognitive competence. And issues of validity and reliability have to be judged in terms of the uses to which the data are put. A question here is whether any inaccuracies in the parental reporting of diet might obscure an association between diet and educational attainment – spuriously supporting the null hypothesis. Or there are two other possibilities: either the parents of children of low attainment might disproportionately and inaccurately report their diets as 'poor', *or* spurious characterizations of diet as 'good' might come disproportionately from the parents of the children showing higher educational attainment: in either case rejecting the null and wrongly saving the alternative hypothesis. Actually it seems unlikely that inaccuracies in the dietary data were structured in any of these of patterns of systematic error. A lot of small chance inaccuracies (random rather than systematic error) tend to cancel each other out in large samples (Niemi, 1993).

Data analysis (point 6 Figure 10.1)

The dietary data from parental questionnaires were analysed using Principal Components Analysis (PCA) – a type of factor analysis (Chapter 43 in this handbook) which creates groups of similarity No paragraph here. North and Emmett, 2000;

Northstone et al., 2005; Feinstein et al.,2008, Emmett, 2009, Smith et al., 2013, Emmett et al.,2015).The researchers distinguished three main diet types: one high in sugar and saturated fats – 'Junk food', one low in fats and sugars and high in fruit and vegetables – 'Health conscious', and the remainder labelled as 'Traditional'. Each child was given an individual diet score, these were standardized, and group means were calculated from this. Similarly factor analysis was used to create weightings employed in producing a single educational attainment score for each child (at each key stage) combining in one score the three or four component scores provided by the NPD for each child at each stage. The results were standardized so that the mean attainment score for all pupils was 0 and the standard deviation was 1. The purpose of standardization here is to bring both sorts of data onto a common measuring scale.

There were data on 23 other socio-economic, demographic and lifestyle variables (Feinstein et al., 2008, Table 1), many of which might both have an influence on educational attainment and a correlation with dietary patterns. For example, mothers with more advanced educational qualifications might both provide their children with an environment which facilitates educational achievement and with a 'healthy' diet. If this is not managed in the analysis, then what is caused by the mothers' education in the way of stimulating learning, might be mistaken by what is caused by the diet. All these potentially confounding factors had also to be operationalized in ways suitable for the intended statistical analysis: here multiple correlation analysis (Aiken, 2004) and t-tests of significance (Trochim, 2006).

Testing the hypotheses (point 8 Figure 10.1)

The result of the multiple correlation analysis (Aiken, 2004) showed a statistically significant correlation between a junk food diet at 38 months and lower educational attainment at Entry, KS1 and KS2, after discounting the effects of the confounding factors. Thus, the null or no difference hypothesis was falsified, and it remains probable that something like the alternative hypothesis is true and childhood diet does indeed have some causal effect on educational attainment. However, the effect of mothers' education, the socio-economic status of the family and of prior attainment on later educational attainment at KS1 and KS2 were many times greater.

The H-DM is almost co-terminus with the use of statistical testing with so-called 'Frequentist' or 'Fisherian' statistics, as in our example.

Gigerenzer et al. (2004) suggest in their title *The Null Ritual*, that such testing is often done ritualistically and without much understanding of what statistical significance means. The latter is hardly surprising since what 'significance' means is contested among professional statisticians and explained differently in different textbooks (ibid., pp. 394–408 and see also Dienes, 2008, Chapter 3; Nuzzo, 2014; Ioannidis, 2005).

Frequentist statistical testing is often criticized on two linked grounds: first, that it issues all or nothing verdicts: either an hypothesis is, or is not statistically significant at the given level: reject or don't reject. Second, that the 5 per cent, 1 per cent and 0.1 per cent levels are anyway arbitrary conventions without any rational justification. Such tests tend to treated as authoritative reasons to accept or reject an hypothesis, though Fisher intended them simply as one indication among several, of whether an hypothesis warranted a second look or not. There are alternatives in the frequentist toolkit which provide sliding scales of probability (Dienes, 2008, Chapter 3) but recently with increasing computing power there has been an increase in the use of Bayesian inference as a more radical alternative (Dienes, 2011).

Internal validity

Internal validity refers to whether a piece of research provides the most credible explanation for what the data show: credible in terms scientists might accept. Judging internal validity means evaluating all the procedures leading to the conclusion. Other chapters in this book deal with threats to internal validity and ways of managing them. However, the ultimate test of the internal validity of research is through independent replication by other researchers, although there is always a risk that while the results of the original were valid, they will not be replicated because of some unknown difference in sample, context or procedure. And the penultimate test is an audit of the research itself by peers who have access to all the data. Both of these require a high level of transparency – so-called procedural objectivity. This reproducibility of research will be discussed further in Section 5.

External validity, and generalization (point 9 Figure 10.1)

External validity depends on internal validity being achieved. Assuming that the exemplar study of diet and attainment has a high level of internal validity, and to all appearances it does, how far does it provide the basis for making inferences about the relationship between diet and educational attainment for other children in other places and at other times: how far does it contribute to general knowledge in this field: what is its external validity or generalizability?

A distinction can be drawn between two kinds of generalization (Gomm et al., 2000).

Empirical (statistical/enumerative/descriptive) generalizations

These are propositions about where, when and with what frequency the phenomenon will occur in the population *from which the research sample was drawn*. For example an empirical generalization might be that in the population of

Southern England those x per cent of children who, below the age of four in the 1990s, have experienced a diet with the same nutritional components as the junk food diet, will on average perform below the mean on Key Stage tests up to the age of 11.

Theoretical or analytical generalizations (or inference)

These are propositions about what will (probably) happen wherever specified circumstances occur: for example a theoretical proposition might be that below the age of four, experiencing a diet with the same nutritional components as the junk food diet in the Avon study, is among the factors which impair cognitive ability.

Empirical generalization is the stock in trade of survey research (Chapter 20 in this Handbook) where representative samples are used as the basis for making inferences about the actual populations from which the sample was drawn, perhaps extrapolated to similar populations.

In this regard, executing the H-DM using good representative survey data has the advantage of indicating the real-world distribution of the circumstances where the independent variable of interest has its effects, and hence potential sites for interventions, at least within a particular population. There are well-tried methods for determining adequate sample size in relation to the level of diversity of interest, tests for estimating the sensitivity of findings to missing data and imputation techniques to repair deviations from precise representativeness (Task Force on Imputation, 1997; Plewis et al., 2010). With such adjustments, the ALSPAC survey would provide data sufficient to identify the demographic profile of children who were most at risk of being disadvantaged in the way shown by the study and their prevalence. This could be done with most confidence for the Avon population at the time when the survey was made, with a little less for the South East of England at that time (Golding et al., 2001). Generalizing such prevalence estimates from one population to another is frequently done for disease conditions or specific learning difficulties such as dyslexia, adjusting for differences between populations using demographic and other benchmark data.

Extrapolating through time from a survey base (or any basis) is more prone to error when there are important cultural, social and political factors likely to change rapidly. For example, the nutritional compositions of the food brands featured in the example are changed frequently in response to marketing data, cost pressures and government legislation. Cultural factors now associated with both poor diet and poor attainment might change through time.

Controlled experiments, most of which employ the H-DM, rarely involve samples which are statistically representative of any finite population so they are a poor basis for any empirical generalization. Experiments typically create simplified situations better to disclose the cause–effect relationships of interest, which they often do well, especially randomized controlled trials (see Chapter 21 in this handbook). But as simplified situations they are often unlike what happens under non-experimental conditions, so that generalizing their results to a finite population (or indeed to any 'naturally occurring' population) may be problematic. A case in point is the generalization of effect sizes (Ellis 2010). Effect-sizes are measures of the strength of the effect of the independent variable on the dependent variable; for example of diet on Key Stage scores, or of some educational programme on scores on a student test (Biddix, n.d.; Wuensch, 2015).

Effect sizes cannot be read directly from the strength of statistical significance. They are quoted either as the difference in outcome attributable to the independent variable as between two groups of subjects treated differently/with different experiences, or as the amount of change in the dependent variable for each increase or decrease in the strength of the independent variable (Coe, 2002). Unless experiments are based on statistically representative samples, which is unusual, it is most unwise to assume that the effect size found in the experiment will be similar to that operating in some wider population (Staines, 2008). This means, for example, that a 'large effect' found in some evaluation study will not necessarily be reproduced when the intervention is rolled out to other sites. Some benchmarking of potential target sites for roll-out against likely relevant characteristics of the evaluation site, may help to select the most suitable targets, but it is rarely the case that all the relevant characteristics are known (Pawson and Tilly 1997, pp. 83–114; Gomm, 2000, pp. 171–91). The problem of generalizing effect sizes from unrepresentative experiments is not solved by the calculation of 'net' effect sizes through the meta-analysis of several studies (Chapter 23 in this Handbook), although attempts are often made to compensate for the non-representative nature of experimental samples. Effect sizes calculated from representative sample surveys are a rather better basis for generalizing effect sizes, but only to the population from which the sample was drawn at the time when it was drawn. In a similar way the 'research-based' 'took-kits' issued by agencies such as the Education Endowment Foundation will only be applicable successfully insofar as the circumstances of the research were representative of the circumstances in which the toolkit is put to use. Given the diversity among schools, classes, teachers, parents, households and pupils and changes through time, it is difficult to select samples which are widely representative (Gomm 2000).

Theoretical generalizations can be true in principle, irrespective of whether what they propose actually happens under naturally occurring conditions. In theory building, physicists after all, spend a great deal of time (and money) making fundamental particles do things that might rarely or never happen under naturally occurring circumstances. The main goal of most natural science has been to formulate law-like statements which will be widely applicable as explanations for what happens, whether such things happen naturally, or only when scientists alter characteristics of the world to make them happen, or even only in computer models of reality. The possibility of formulating law like statements relies on there being widespread cause-effect regularities, such that, for example, what can be said about some metal's electrical conductivity will be true for all examples of that metal under a range of specified circumstances. It is an open question as to how far the phenomena studied in educational research implicate robust cause–effect relationships. It seems credible that this is truer of some domains than of others, for example of neurological and physiological development, compared with classroom interaction. In our example a mechanism linking diet and educational attainment might be a physiological one.

Making theoretical generalizations is the point at which the H-DM itself comes up against the problem of induction (as discussed in Section 2). Theoretical generalization is an inductive move, asserting that what happened in a particular research project would also happen in every other situation with the same constellation of conditions. But somewhere out there, there may be negative instances yet to be discovered. Just as importantly, it is always possible that there is some explanation for the evidence other than the alternative hypothesis (including some flaw in the research). In terms of the H-DM then, the theoretical generalization of an unfalsified proposition remains provisional: perhaps as the best candidate yet for the truth, but not certainly so. The authors of our example are very circumspect about making such proposals. They draw attention to the possibility that home background factors (apart from diet) might not have been completely controlled out in the analysis, and might account for the association between diet and attainment. They rightly say 'results from this paper do not prove causality' (Feinstein et al., 2008, pp. 738).

In the last resort, judging whether research findings have external validity requires repeating the research with other subjects at other times. There are limits to how much this can be done, and there will always remain other unstudied populations which might negate the generalization or require it to be modified. For the practitioner wanting to base practice on extant research findings the question is about how closely the circumstances of practice match those of the research situation and on several dimensions (Gomm 2000,Pawson and Tilley 1997). In turn, for researchers wanting to present research relevant to practice it is important to supply large quantities of data characterizing the sample to help practitioners make this judgement. Note that the ALSPAC team provided data on 23 other demographic, socio-economic, health, and lifestyle factors and prior educational attainment as well as numerous physiological measurement such that it can be judged how like or unlike the ALSPAC sample is to some other population.

Section 5 Adding to the knowledge bank (point 10 Figure 10.1)

Theoretical propositions are not simply and naively accepted because they survive a testing procedure. In reality, the accumulation of knowledge is an untidy business, often ideologically or commercially driven, riven with conflicts, marred by biases and every now and then thrown into disarray by major paradigm shifts.

Nonetheless in the natural sciences at least, a great deal of knowledge does accumulate in the general way suggested by the diagram (Figure 10.1).

Peer review is an important part of this process. Over the last 20 years or so there has been move away from so called 'narrative' reviews without any agreed formal structure towards 'systematic' reviewing using standard sets of criteria about methodological quality (Chapters 7 and 23 in this Handbook). For educational research, the Campbell Collaboration (www.campbellcollaboration. org) sponsors and curates such reviews and meta-analyses as do the Education Endowment Foundation (https://educationendowmentfoundation.org.uk) and the Early Intervention Foundation (www.eif.org.uk/) although their combined content is dwarfed by the much larger Cochrane Collaboration for medical research. In the past, the constraints of hard-copy publishing limited the amount of information which could easily be provided for scrutiny, and it was rare for the raw data of research to be made available. But with electronic data storage and retrieval, these limits are lifted. Many funders now require that the raw data of research are archived and accessible. The ALSPAC data (Section 3), like that of all the major British longitudinal studies and data from many others studies worldwide, are archived and available to bona fide scholars. Preparing data for archiving, including anonymizing data on subjects who might otherwise be identified (U.K. Data Archive 2015), adds to the research burden. Curating data is itself now an important specialism among research occupations (Doorn and Tjalsma, 2007).

The term 'reproducibility' is used to refer to the extent to which the quality and availability of information provided, would facilitate the replication of the research. Confirmation of findings through replication by independent researchers is the most convincing reason for believing some proposition.

Scientific knowledge does not consist of propositions which are certainly true: rather it consists of those propositions which at the time seem more likely to be true than any competitors. Practical decisions about (say) implementing some educational programme do not and cannot wait for an absolute proof that they will be effective. A decision to act on evidence from research has to take into consideration not just the strength of the evidence of effectiveness in some context beyond the research situation, but the value of any effects which might be achieved, balanced against the material and non-material costs of the implementation. This involves unknown factors. Until recently a Bayesian approach was largely confined to management science and medical screening and its toolkit includes procedures for making decisions with cost–benefit considerations in the face of uncertainty (Christian, 2007).

According to Popper (2002, p. 9) for one theory to merit replacing another it should both explain what the earlier theory explains, and explain more. A great deal of hypothesis testing research consists not so much in generating new theories, but of more carefully specifying the conditional limits under which accepted theories are to be regarded as (provisionally) true. Further research following our example might take the form of identifying which of the 'junk' dietary components had most effect on school attainment, or whether intensive coaching could overcome the effects of diet. Or perhaps the research question might be tweaked to ask about cognitive development rather than educational attainment, by using an outcome measure such as IQ as an alternative to key stage tests. More ambitiously it might proceed to identify the mechanism which causes the demonstrable link between some diets and educational achievement. Is this a neuro-physiological matter: something about brain development, or a social-psychological mechanism – something about self-image or about the interaction of obese children and their peers and teachers? (Punder and Munsch, 2010). Other research from the ALSPAC team did not support a third possibility; that the link was via sugar-induced hyperactivity (Wiles et al., 2007).

SECTION 6 THE LIMITS OF THE H-DM IN THEORY AND AS PRACTISED

The H-DM is only suitable as an approach to cause and effect questions, and not questions about meanings and interpretations for which qualitative approaches are more suitable. It is subject to the critiques made of all quantitative methods by those who favour a qualitative approach, and of value-neutral research by those who favour value-led research, and these are dealt with elsewhere in this handbook. There are also other positivistic approaches, including a range of approaches with names including the term 'realism' (for example Pawson and Tilley, 1997; Chakravartty, 2015), and the increasingly popular Bayesian inference (Dienes, 2011). Reservations about tying research to the solution of practical problems (evidence-based practice), also bear critically on this approach (Hammersley, 2013).

Some other critiques are of more interest to philosophers than to practising researchers. They include the Duhem–Quine thesis (Harding, 1976) This notes that all theories are dependent on a wide range of assumptions – many unarticulated and most untested, and that any predictions are also dependent on these background assumptions – for example that the research methods are sound, that our eyes do not deceive us and so on. Therefore testing an hypothesis cannot refute the named theory, because the falsification might be due to flaws in any of the constituents of the package of beliefs of which the named theory is only a part. Moreover, any falsification of the focal theory can be evaded by modifying one of the background assumptions or inventing a new proposal which saves the theory from disconfirmation, or as in our example earlier (Section 4), changing the construct for which the evidence is supposed to stand. In this regard Popper drew attention to the many 'bolt-on' additions to Marxist and psychoanalytic theories which explained away the failure of their predictions (Popper 1963, pp. 35–8).

There is an ontological critique that the phenomena studied by educational researchers are in their nature not like the phenomena studied by the natural sciences, so that radically different approaches are required for educational research. This is probably true of some phenomena and not others.

There is a sociological critique, well supported by ethnographic accounts of scientists at work (for example Knorr-Cetina and Mulkay, 1983 for classic studies), which show that scientists do not rigidly follow the formulaic textbook versions of the scientific method (so why should educational researchers do so?). To which a Popperian would say, the H-DM was not supposed to be about how scientific ideas are discovered ('thought up') – which is every whichway, but how they are tested (Popper, 2002, pp. 7–8). The distinction is akin to that between the way a criminal investigation is conducted, and the way a prosecuting barrister lays out the case to be tested in court (Hoyningen-Huene, 1987). Others might say that natural science would be better if natural scientists more closely followed the model.

A case in point is the infrequency of replication outside a few areas of science, as against its crucial importance for accumulating quality controlled knowledge (Fidler and Gordon, 2013). Even more rarely is replication independent. Makel and Plucker (2013) found that in recent educational research only one in 500 articles were replications: 89 per cent of these confirmed original findings when done by the original researchers but only 54 per cent were confirmed when done independently: the latter figure being near to what would be expected by chance. Recently, 'reproducibility crises' have been declared widely across the sciences, from physics (Conrad, 2015) to psychology (Baker, 2015). The psychology 'Reproducibility Project' (Nosek et al., 2015) chose 100 well-thought of studies and had them replicated by a large international team of researchers. Of the 100 replications only 39 were successful. Ninety seven per cent of the original studies found a significant effect, only 36 per cent of replication studies found significant results. The average size of the effects found in replication was only half that reported in the original studies. Similar results have come from other sciences (*Economist*, 2013).

The fact that studies often do not reach the same results is unsurprising. Failures of replication should occur quite often if the enterprise of science is to be self-checking and self-correcting. What is worrying is, first, the rarity of independent replications and second the large number of studies which are so badly written up, or so coy about their data, that it would be impossible to replicate them anyway. This becomes even more alarming given the considerable extent of fraud in science (*Scientist*, 2015; Loewensein and Prelec, 2012; Fanelli, 2009). There is no evidence that educational research is any more prone to fraud than other research, but without replication how would anyone know. The H-DM may work against self-delusion in science (see Section 2), but reproducibility is the most effective antidote to fraud. Paradoxically this points to a strength of quantitative approaches over qualitative ones, most of which are largely unreproducible For example, sound and video recording apart, there is virtually no way of knowing whether an ethnographic study of a school, documents what other observers and readers would also have agreed to be true, or indeed if the ethnographic detail was pure or part invention.

There are reasons for bad practice. There is a perverse relationship between career incentives and good science. There are few rewards for confirming what someone else has already discovered. Journal editors are unwilling to publish confirmations of previous research, and have a bias for 'positive' findings, rather than for corroborations of null hypotheses: and the bigger the effect reported, the better! PhD students are often required to show that they have made 'an original contribution' to their field of study and steered away from the more mundane task of checking existing knowledge. Those who sponsor projects are not at all pleased to receive evaluation reports which tell them they wasted their money, and evaluators sometimes 'go native' and massage results to save the careers of those they might otherwise evaluate negatively. Systematic review and meta-analysis are poor substitutes for replication, and they frequently struggle with the incommensurability of pieces of research dealing with the same topic (Chapter 23 in this Handbook). While natural scientists usually use standard instruments and measurement scales, with well-known strengths and weaknesses, in educational research, apart from widely used psychometric tests, there is a tendency to create novel instruments, making different pieces of research difficult to compare with each other.

The problems noted above are not problems of positivism, or of H-DM in particular, but of a research culture awry. Doing positivism better seems the appropriate antidote, rather than abandoning it.

CONCLUSION

This chapter focused on one positivistic approach to research: the so-called hypothetico-deductive method (H-DM) which involves deductive reasoning to formulate conjectures (or hypotheses) about the evidence which would indicate whether some theoretical proposition should be believed or not. The emphasis is on attempting to prove the theory wrong rather than right. This may be counter-intuitive, but 'testing to destruction' is a common procedure in quality control systems, and the H-DM is, indeed, a quality control procedure for scientific knowledge. The approach is often called '*the* scientific method' and has been widely followed in the natural sciences, with considerable success in explaining the natural world. It has often been followed in educational research.

As a system of self-correcting knowledge production it relies heavily on repro-ducibility: that is on researchers providing all that is needed for their work to be audited and repeated (replicated) by others and on replications actually being carried out. Recently much concern has been expressed about the lack of effec-tive reproducibility in science generally, as well as in educational research. This, however, is not a case against the approach, but a case in favour of following it more closely. In this connection it is worth noting that most other approaches in educational research lack any rigorous quality control systems.

ACKNOWLEDGEMENT

My thanks to Martyn Hammersley and Emma Smith for their comments on an earlier version of this chapter.

FURTHER READING

The case for a 'scientific' approach to educational research is well-put in *Advancing Scientific Research in Education* (2004) edited by Towne, Winters and Wise: a report commissioned jointly by the (USA) Committee on Research in Education/Centre for Education/Division of Behavioural and Social Sciences and Education/National Research Council: Retrieved on 6 July 2016 from www.nap.edu/catalog/11112/advancing-scientific-research-in-education.

There are many text books on the statistical procedures of the H-DM, including those given in Chapters 36, 37, 44 and 45 of this Handbook. However, for a more critical approach which includes a good treatment of Bayesian alternatives to frequentist statistics try Dienes, *2008 Understanding Psychology as a Science: An introduction to scientific and statistical inference.* Palgrave Macmillan.

For a simple demonstration of Bayesian methods using an educational research example Eidswick's 2012 article 'A Bayesian alternative to null hypothesis significance testing' in the *Shiken Research Bulletin* 16(1) is available online at: https://www.academia.edu/2968429/A_Bayesian_alternative_to_null_hypothesis_significance_testing (retrieved 6 July 2016).

Given the widespread number of statistical mistakes in published research a reading of Schagen's, 'Simple guide to voodoo statistics' in the *Education Journal*, 2008 112: 33–36, would be worthwhile. Retrieved on 6 July 2016 from www.nfer.ac.uk/publications/55501/.

REFERENCES

Aiken, L. 2004. Multiple correlation. In M. Lewis-Beck, A. Bryman and T. Futin Lao (Eds) *SAGE Encyclopedia of Research Methods*. London: SAGE Publications.

Als-neilson, B., Chen, W., Gluud, C. and Kjaergard, L. 2003. Association of funding and conclusions in randomized drug trials: a reflection of treatment effect or adverse effects? *Journal of the American Medical Association*, 290: 921–928. Retrieved in September 2015 from http://jama.jamanetwork.com/article.aspx?articleid=197132.

Andersen, H., and Hepburn, B. 2016 Scientific Method, *The Stanford Encyclopedia of Philosophy* (Summer 2016 Edition), Edward N. Zalta (editor) Retrieved August 2016 from http://plato.stanford.edu/archives/sum2016/entries/scientific-method.

Baker, M. 2015. Over half of psychology studies fail reproducibility test. *Nature News* 27 August. Retrieved in September 2015 from www.nature.com/news/over-half-of-psychology-studies-fail-reproducibility-test-1.18248.

Biddix, J. n.d. Effect size. *Research Rundowns*. Retrieved in November 2015 from https://researchrundowns.wordpress.com/quantitative-methods/effect-size/.

Brown, P. 2016. Searching for a Fix to Unreliable Nutritional Research. *Med Page Today*. Retrieved in October 2016 from http://www.medpagetoday.com/primarycare/dietnutrition/55818.

Calaprice, A. 2005. *The New Quotable Einstein*. Hebrew University of Jerusalem and Princetown University Press.

Campbell, D. and Stanley, J. 1963. *Experimental and Quasi-experimental Designs for Research*, 1st edition. Chicago, IL: Rand McNally.

Chakravartty, A. 2015. Scientific realism. *The Stanford Encyclopedia of Philosophy* (Fall, 2015), Edward N. Zalta (Ed.). Retrieved in November 2015 from http://plato.stanford.edu/archives/fall2015/entries/scientific-realism/.

Christian, R. 2007. *The Bayesian Choice: From decision-theoretic foundations to computational implementation*, 2nd edition. Berlin: Springer.

Coe, R. 2002. It's the effect size stupid. Retrieved in September 2015 from www.cem.org/attachments/ebe/ESguide.pdf.

Conrad, J. 2015. Reproducibility: don't cry wolf. *Nature News*, 1 July. Retrieved in October 2015 from www.nature.com/news/reproducibility-don-t-cry-wolf-1.17859.

Creath, R. 2014. Logical empiricism. *The Stanford Encyclopedia of Philosophy* (Spring 2014), Edward N. Zalta (editor.). Retrieved in October 2015 from http://plato.stanford.edu/archives/spr2014/entries/logical-empiricism/.

Dennett, D. 1995 *Darwin's Dangerous Idea: Evolution and the meaning of life*. London: Allen Lane/Penguin.

Dienes, Z. 2008. *Understanding Psychology as a Science: An introduction to scientific and statistical inference*. London: Palgrave Macmillan.

Dienes, Z. 2011. Bayesian versus orthodox statistics: which side are you on? *Perspectives on Psychological Science*, 6(3), 274–290. Retrieved in September 2015 from www.lifesci.sussex.ac.uk/home/Zoltan_Dienes/Dienes%202011%20Bayes.pdf.

Doorn, P. and Tjalsma, H. 2007. Introduction: archiving research data. *Archival Science*, 7(1), 1–20.

Economist (The) 2013. Trouble at the lab: scientists like to think of science as self-correcting. To an alarming degree, it is not. *The Economist* 19 October. Retrieved in October 2015 from www.economist.com/news/briefing/21588057-scientists-think-science-self-correctingalarming-degree-it-not-trouble.

Eidswick, J. 2012. A Bayesian alternative to null hypothesis significance testing'. *Shiken Research Bulletin*, 16(1). Retrieved in July 2015 from www.academia.edu/2968429/A_Bayesian_alternative_to_null_hypothesis_significance_testing.

Ellis,P. 2010. *The Essential Guide to Effect Sizes*. Cambridge: Cambridge University Press.

Emmett, P. 2009. Dietary assessment in the Avon Longitudinal Study of Parents and Children. *European Journal of Clinical Nutrition Online*, 63. pp. S38–44. Retrieved in August 2015 from www.ncbi.nlm.nih.gov/pubmed/19190642.

Emmett, P., Newby, P., and Northstone, K. 2013. Dietary patterns obtained through principal components analysis: the effect of input variable quantification. *British Journal of Nutrition* 109(10):1881-91. RetSmith, A.rieved in August 2016 from www.ncbi.nlm.nih.gov/pubmed/22950853

Emmett, P., and Jones, L. 2014. Diet and Growth in infancy:relationship to socioeconomic background and to health and development in the Avon Longitudinal Study of Parents and Chidren. *Nutrition Review* 72(8):483-506. Retrieved August 2016 from www.ncbi.nlm.nih.gov/pubmed/?term=Diet+and+growth+in+infancy%3A+relationship+to+socioeconomic+background+and+to+health+and+development+in+the+Avon+Longitudinal+Study+of+Parents+and+Children.

Emmett, P., Jones, L., and Northstone,K. 2015. Dietary patterns in the Avon Longitudinal Study of Parents and Children. *Nutrition Review* 73:S3:207-230. Retrieved August 2016 from www.ncbi.nlm.nih.gov/pmc/articles/PMC4586449

Fanelli. D. 2009. How many scientists fabricate and falsify research? A systematic review and meta-analysis of survey data. PLOS ONE 4(5). doi: 10.1371/journal.pone.0005738. Retrieved in November 2015 from http://journals.plos.org/plosone/article?id=10.1371/journal.pone.0005738.

Feinstein, L., Sabates, R., Sorhaindo, A., Rogers, I., Herrick, D., Northstone, K. and Emmett, P. 2008. Dietary patterns related to attainment at school: the importance of early eating patterns. *Journal of Epidemiology & Community Health*, 62(8), 734–740. Retrieved in September 2015 from http://jech.bmj.com/content/62/8/734.full.

Feure, M., Towne, L. and Shavelson, R. 2002. Scientific culture and educational research. *Educational Researcher*, 31(8), 4–14. Retrieved in September 2015 from http://web.stanford.edu/dept/SUSE/SEAL/Reports_Papers/other_papers/Scientific%20Culture_ER.pdf.

Fidler, F. and Gordon, A. 2013. Science is in a reproducibility crisis: how do we resolve it? *The Conversation (online)*, 30 September. Retrieved in September 2015 from http://phys.org/news/2013–09-science-crisis.html#jCp.

Fisher, R. 1935 *Statistical Methods for Research Workers*. Edinburgh: Oliver & Boyd. [1st edition 1925]

Fisher, R. 1937. *The Design of Experiments*. Edinburgh: Oliver & Boyd.

Fisher, R. 1938. Presidential Address to the First Indian Statistical Congress, 1938. *Sankhya*, 4, 14–17.

Fox N., Hunn A. and Mathers N. 2007. *Sampling and sample size calculation*. The NIHR RDS for the East Midlands/Yorkshire and the Humber 2007.Retrieved in November 2015 from nihs-sampling_sample_size_calculation.pdf.

Gigerenzer, G., Krauss, S. and Vitouch, O. 2004. The null ritual: what you always wanted to know about significance testing but were afraid to ask. In D. Kaplan (Ed.) *The SAGE Handbook of Quantitative Methodology in the Social Sciences*. London: SAGE Publications, 391–408. Retrieved in November 2015 from http://library.mpib-berlin.mpg.de/ft/gg/GG_Null_2004.pdf.

Goldacre, B. 2008. *Bad Science*. London: 4th Estate.

Golding, J., Pembrey, M., Jones, R. and the ALSPAC Study Team. 2001. ALSPAC – the Avon Longitudinal Study of Parents and Children: study methodology. *Paediatric Perinatal Epidemiology*, 15, 74–87.

Gomm, R. 2000. But would it work here? In R. Gomm and C. Davies (Eds) *Using Evidence in Health and Social Care*. London: SAGE Publications, 171–191.

Gomm, R. 2008. *Social Research Methodology: A critical introduction*, 2nd edition. London: Palgrave Macmillan.

Gomm, R., Hammersley M. and Foster, P. 2000. Case study and generalization. In R. Gomm, M. Hammersley and P. Foster (Eds) *Case Study Method*. London: SAGE Publications, 98–115.

Gov.UK 2013. *National Pupil Database*. Retrieved in September 2015 from: https://www.gov.uk/government/collections/national-pupil-database.

Halpern, D. 2015. *Inside the Nudge Unit*. London:W.H.Allen.

Hamilton, D. 1997. The truth about DARE: the big bucks antidrug program for kids doesn't work. *Los Angeles New Times*, Issue 20 March.

Hammersley, M. 2007. *Educational Research and Evidence-Based Practice*. London: SAGE Publications.

Hammersley, M. 2013. *The Myth of Research-Based Policy and Practice*. London: SAGE Publications.

Hansen, H. 2015. Fallacies. *Stanford Encyclopedia of Philosophy*. Edited by N. Zalta. Retrieved in September 2015 from http://plato.stanford.edu/archives/sum2015/ entries/fallacies/.

Harding, S. 1976. *Can Theories be Refuted? Essays on the Dunhem-Quine thesis.* Berlin: D. Reidel/Springer Science Business and Media.

Hargreaves, D. 1996. *Teaching as a Research-Based Profession: Possibilities and prospects,* London: Teacher Training Agency. (Reprinted in Hammersley, 2007.)

Harper, H., and Hallsworth, M. 2016. Counting Calories: How under-reporting can explain the apparent fall in calorie intake. Behavioural Insights Team/Cabinet Office Retrieved in August 2016 from www.behaviouralinsights.co.uk/publications/counting-calories-how-under-reporting-can-explain-the-apparent-fall-in-calorie-intake/

Hebert, J., Clemow, L., Pbert, L, Ockene, I. and Ockene, J. 1995. Social desirability bias in dietary self-report may compromise the validity of dietary intake measures. *International Journal of Epidemiology*, 24(2), 389–398. Retrieved in November 2015 from www.ncbi.nlm.nih.gov/pubmed/7635601.

Tilling, K., Galobardes, B., and Lawlor, D. 2013. Loss to follow-up in cohort studies:bias in estimates of socioeconomic inequalities. *Journal of Epidemiology* 24(1):1-9 Retrieved August 2016 from www.ncbi.nlm.nih.gov/pubmed/23211345

Hoyningen-Huene, P. 1987. Context of discovery and context of justification. *Studies in the History and Philosophy of Science*, 18(54), 501–515. Retrieved in September 2015 from http://cfcul.fc.ul.pt/Seminarios/hoyningen-huene_Discovery%5B1%5D%5B1%5D.pdf.

Hyatt, K. 2007. Brain gym: building stronger brains or wishful thinking. *Remedial and Special Education*, 28(2), 117–124.

Ioannidis. J. 2005. Why most published research findings are false. *PLoS Med*, 2(8): e124. Retrieved in October 2015 from journals.plos.org/plosmedicine/article?id=10.1371/ journal.pmed.0020124.

Kaestle, C. 1993. The awful reputation of education research. *Educational Researcher*, pp. 26–31.

Knorr-Cetina, K. and Mulkay, M. 1983. *Science Observed: Perspectives on the social study of science.* London: SAGE Publications.

Lagemann, E. 2000. *An Elusive Science: The troubling history of education research.* Chicago, IL: University of Chicago Press.

Lesser, L., Ebbeling, C., Goozner, D., Wypij, D. and Ludwig, D. 2007. Relationship between funding source and conclusion among nutrition-related scientific articles. *Public Library of Science Medicine*, 4, 41–46. Retrieved in September 2015 from http://journals.plos.org/plosmedicine/article?id=10.1371/journal.pmed.0040005.

Levin, J. and O'Donnell, A. 1999. What to do about educational research's credibility gaps? *Issues in Education*, 5(2), 177–229.

Logan, C. 1972. Evaluation research in crime and delinquency: a reappraisal. *Journal of Criminal Law*, 63(3), 378–387.

Loewenstein, J. and Prelec, D. 2012. Measuring the prevalence of questionable research practices with incentives for truth telling. *Psychological Science*, 23(5), 524–532. Retrieved in November 2015 from www.cmu.edu/dietrich/sds/docs/loewenstein/ MeasPrevalQuestTruthTelling.pdf.

Makel, C. and Plucker, A. 2013. Facts are more important than novelty: replication in the education sciences. *Educational Researcher*, 43(6), 304–316. Retrieved in September 2015 from www.researchgate.net/publication/268522706_Facts_Are_More_ Important_Than_Novelty.

Maughan, S., Stylor, B., Yin, L. and Kircup, C. 2009. *Partial Estimates of Reliability: Parallel forms of reliability,* NFER/OfQual. Retrieved in September 2015 from www.

gov.uk/government/uploads/system/uploads/attachment_data/file/376735/2009-11-15-partial-estimates-of-reliability-report.pdf.

Mooney, C., 2005. *The Republican War on Science*. London: Basic Books.

Mouratidou, T., Ford, F. and Fraser, R. 2005. Validation of food-frequency questionnaire for use in pregnancy. *Public Health Nutrition*, 9(4), 515–522. Retrieved in August 2015 from http://journals.cambridge.org/download.php?file=%2FPHN%2FPHN9_04%2FS1368980006000863a.pdf&code=cb2e87a34e08b708be3d4e84592ebdd3.

NFER. 2009. *National Testing of Pupils in England, Wales and Northern Ireland*. National Foundation for Educational Research. Retrieved in September 2015 from www.nfer.ac.uk/shadomx/apps/fms/fmsdownload.cfm?file_uuid=67EAAF91-C29E-AD4D-07F1-A9373EA17105&siteName=nfer.

Niemi. L. 1993. Systematic error in behavioural measurement: comparing results from interview and time budget studies. *Social Indicators Research*, 30(2), 229–244.

North K and Emmett P. 2000 Multivariate analysis of diet among three-year-old children and associations with socio-demographic characteristics. The Avon Longitudinal Study of Pregnancy and Childhood (ALSPAC) Study Team.', *European Journal of Clinical Nutrition* 54 (1): 73-80. Retrieved in September 2015 from www.ncbi.nlm.nih.gov/pubmed/10696149

Northstone, K., Emmett, P. and the ALSPAC Study Team. 2005. Avon longitudinal study of pregnancy and childhood: multivariate analysis of diet among three-year-old children and associations with socio-demographic characteristics. *European Journal of Clinical Nutrition*, 59, 751–760. Retrieved in September 2015 from www.nature.com/ejcn/journal/v59/n6/full/1602136a.html.

Nosek, B., Cohoon, J. and Kidwell, M. 2015. Reproducibility project: psychology; summary report. *Open Science Framework*. Retrieved in November 2015 from https://osf.io/ezum7/.

Nuzzo, R. 2014. Scientific method: statistical errors. *Nature News*, 12 February. Retrieved in November 2015 from www.nature.com/news/scientific-method-statistical-errors-1.14700.

Oakley, A. 2000. *Experiments in Knowing: Gender and method in the social sciences*. London: Polity Press.

Owad, T. 2006. Confirmation bias: a ubiquitous phenomenon in many guises. *Review of General Psychology*, 2(2), 75–220.

Pawson, R. and Tilley, N. 1997. *Realistic Evaluation*. London: SAGE Publications.

Petrosino, A., Turpin-Petrosino C., Hollis-Peel M. and Lavenberg, J. 2013. 'Scared Straight' and other juvenile awareness programs for preventing juvenile delinquency. *Cochrane Database of Systematic Reviews* Issue 4. Art. No.: CD002796. Retrieved in November 2015 from http://onlinelibrary.wiley.com/doi/10.1002/14651858.CD002796.pub2/epdf/standard.

Plewis, I., Calderwood, L. and Ketende, S. 2010. *Sample Loss from Cohort Studies: Patterns, characteristics and adjustments*. Centre for Longitudinal Studies, Institute of Education University of London. Retrieved in August 2015 from http://eprints.ncrm.ac.uk/86/1/MethodsReviewPaperNCRM-002.pdf.

Popper, K. 1963. *Conjectures and Refutations: The growth of scientific knowledge*. London: Basic Books and many later editions. Retrieved in November 2015 from http://xxsy.library.nenu.edu.cn/pluginfile.php/1066/mod_resource/content/1/%5BKarl_Popper%5D_Conjectures_and_Refutations_The_Gro%28Bookos.org%29%20%281%29.pdf.

Popper, K. 2002. *The Logic of Scientific Discovery*. Routledge Classics/Taylor & Francis e-edition (electronic copy of the 1967 update of the first English edition (1959) which is a translation of the 1935 book. Retrieved in September 2015 from http://strangebeautiful.com/other-texts/popper-logic-scientific-discovery.pdf.

Punder, J. and Munsch, S. 2010. Psychological correlates of childhood obesity. *International Journal of Obesity*, 34(Supplement), S37–43.

Reinhart, A. 2014. *Statistics Done Wrong: The woefully complete guide*. Google Books.

Saini, P., Loke, Y., Gamble. C., Altman, D., Williamson, P. and Kirkman, J. 2014. Selective reporting bias of harm outcomes within studies: findings from a cohort of systematic reviews. *British Medical Journal*, 349, p. 6501. Retrieved in September 2015 from www.bmj.com/content/349/bmj.g6501.

Schagen, I. 2008. A simple guide to voodoo statistics. *Education Journal*, 112, 33–36. Retrieved in November 2015 from www.nfer.ac.uk/publications/55501/.

Scientist (The) 2015. Scientific fraud. *The Scientist*. Retrieved in November 2015 from www.the-scientist.com/?articles.list/tagNo/2642/tags/scientific-fraud/.

Shavelson, R. and Towne, L. 2002a *On Scientific Research in Education: Questions not methods should drive the enterprise*. Retrieved in August 2015 from web.stanford. edu/dept/SUSE/SEAL/Reports_Papers/On.

Shavelson, R. and Towne, L. 2002b. *Scientific Research in Education: Report for the Committee in Scientific Principles in Education Research*. Washington: National Academy Press. Retrieved in September 2015 from www.nap.edu/catalog/10236/ scientific-research-in-education.

Staines, G. 2008. The causal generalization paradox: the case of treatment outcome research. *Review of General Psychology*, 12(3), 236–252. Retrieved in September 2015 from http://citeseerx.ist.psu.edu/viewdoc/download?doi=10.1.1.406.2960&rep= rep1&type=pdf.

Stanley, J. 1966. The influence of Fisher's 'The Design of Experiments' on educational research thirty years later. *American Educational Research Journal*, 3(3), 223.

Task Force on Imputation 1997. *Report of the Task Force on Imputation; GSS Methodology Paper no 8*. Government Statistical Service. Retrieved in September 2015 from www.statistics.gov.uk. Then search on *GSS methodology*.

Thomas, G. and Pring, R. (Eds) 2004. *Evidence Based Practice in Education*. London: Open University Press.

Thompson, C., Skowronski, J., Steen, J. and Betz A. 2013. *Autobiographical Memory: Remembering what and remembering when*. London: Psychology Press.

Thornton, S. 2014. *Karl Popper*. Stanford Encyclopedia of Philosophy. Zalta, N. (Ed.). Retrieved in September 2015 from http://plato.stanford.edu/archives/sum2014/ entries/popper/.

Tooley, J. and Darley, D. 1998. *Educational Research: A critique*. OFSTED. Retrieved in September 2015 from http://webarchive.nationalarchives.gov.uk/20141124154759/ http://www.ofsted.gov.uk/resources/educational-research-critique-tooley-report.

Towne, L., Winters, T. and Wise, L. 2004. *Advancing Scientific Research in Education*. Committee on Research in Education/Centre for Education/Division of Behavioural and Social Sciences & Education/National Research Council. Retrieved in September 2015 from www.nap.edu/catalog/11112/advancing-scientific-research-in-education.

Trochim, W. 2006. The T-Test. *Research Knowledge Base*. Retrieved in November 2015 from http://dx.doi.org/10.4135/9781412950589.

UK Data Archive. 2015. *Anonymisation*. Retrieved in September 2015 from www.data-archive.ac.uk/create-manage/consent-ethics/anonymisation.

Unite for Sight. 2015. *The Challenges and Failures of Nutrition Studies*. Retrieved in October 2016 from. http://www.uniteforsight.org/global-health-university/nutrition-study.

Verdugo, C. 2009. Popper's theory of the unity of scientific method: method versus techniques. In Z. Parusnikva and R. Cohen (Eds) *Rethinking Popper: Boston studies in the philosophy of science*. Netherlands: Springer, 155–160.

Vickers, J. 2014. The problem of induction. In N. Zalta (Ed.) *The Stanford Encyclopedia of Philosophy*. Retrieved in September 2015 from http://plato.stanford.edu/archives/fall2014/entries/induction-problem/.

Wiles, N., Northstone, K., Emmett, P. and Lewis, G. 2007. 'Junk' food diet and childhood behavioural problems: results from the ALSPAC cohort. *European Journal of Clinical Nutrition Online*. Retrieved in September 2015 from www.nature.com/ejcn/journal/v63/n4/abs/1602967a.html.

Wiliam, D. 2001. Reliability, validity and all that jazz. *Education*, 29(3), 17–21. Retrieved in September 2015 from http://eprints.ioe.ac.uk/1156/1/Wiliam2001Reliability3_final.pdf.

Wuensch, K. 2015. Standard effect size estimates: why and how? *Karl Wuensch's Statistical Help Page*. University of East Carolina. Retrieved in November 2015 from http://core.ecu.edu/psyc/wuenschk/StatHelp/Effect%20Size%20Estimation.pdf.

11

Interpretivism as a Theory of Knowledge

David Scott

INTRODUCTION

There have recently been calls to adopt approaches to the study of the social world (in relation to educational research, see Moss (2015), and in relation to making judgements about educational research, see the Research Excellence Framework (2015)) which deny the need to address ontological and epistemological concerns – approaches which can be described as operating outside of and in opposition to philosophical framings about the nature of reality and how we can know it. Though the purpose of these approaches is to support and strengthen a particular ideological view of human behaviour, for example, that members of the educational research community working together can make reliable and valid judgements about its activities, in reality these approaches favour those forms of research and judgement that can be described as empiricist and technicist.

Ontological beliefs (theories of the nature of being or existence) and epistemological beliefs (theories of knowledge) underpin the development and use of strategies and methods by empirical researchers. In contrast, proponents of a pragmatic position, using this term in its ordinary language sense, argue that it is possible to separate out these beliefs from the adoption of methods and strategies. These methods and strategies then are determined by how useful they are, and even by whether they are fit for purpose.

If this is rejected, an alternative is required. The researcher is born into a world that is already resourced, and in the case of methodology, this consists of a series of opposing arguments for the use of certain types of approaches. A choice therefore has to be made, though of course the researcher may not be aware of all the possible options and indeed some options that have not yet been invented. As a result, they may only be able to make a limited choice, but a choice nonetheless. They use particular approaches, and draw conclusions from the data they collect, and in doing so implicitly claim that their version of reality is better than other possible versions. Making methodological choices per se means that the researcher is formulating a belief that the choice they make is a better choice than the one they did not make because it will lead to a more truthful representation of what they are trying to portray.

However, researchers may accept that they are working to a truth criterion, but then define their search for the truth in a way that is different from other researchers. Bridges (1999) suggests that there are five conceptions of truth (there may be more, but they have not yet been invented, or codified): truth as correspondence, truth as coherence, truth as what works, truth as consensus and truth as warranted belief. These different theories of truth are so framed that they imply a relationship between a statement and a referent, so a researcher can say, if they adopt a correspondence theory of truth, that a statement is true if it corresponds to a state of affairs in the world: 'P is true if and only if p – i.e. it corresponds with an actual state of affairs or condition' (Bridges, 1999, p. 601). Again, a researcher can say, if they adopt a conception of truth as coherence, that a proposition is true if it is consistent with a further set of propositions: 'P1... Pn are true if and only if they represent a coherent, consistent and comprehensive set of propositions' (Bridges, 1999, p. 603).

It is also possible to suggest that the referent in each particular case is of a different order, so, for example, a correspondence version of truth refers to an ontological state, whereas truth as warranted belief refers to whether it satisfies an epistemological test to determine its value. Furthermore, some of these conceptions of truth allow for the possibility of a relativistic element whereas others do not. So, truth as correspondence would suggest that a belief in epistemic relativism is unsound, whereas truth as consensus is predicated on a belief that a universal a-historical warrant cannot legitimately be developed. These different theories are so framed that belief in one precludes belief in another. Even if it is denied that a theory of truth is a logical requirement of proceeding in the world as a researcher, or at least that there is no universal warrant for truth, this does not contradict the assertion that is being argued for here: that in making a choice between alternatives that already have been formulated, the researcher is necessarily making a claim that the choice they make is better than one they did not make.

This position identifies a relation between a philosophical issue and empirical research; in the example above the issue is that of truth, but a similar exercise could have been conducted in relation to other philosophical concepts such as objectivity or ontology. It further suggests that any beliefs the researcher may have about the nature of the social world and even more importantly any beliefs they may have about how they can know it are so compelling that certain types of methods and strategies used by them are appropriate and others inappropriate. Thus, an experimental approach to the study of education can legitimately be adopted if the experimenter accepts a number of ontological and epistemological positions, which are justified and rationalized separately from their instantiation in the collection and analysis of data. These might consist of a belief that the social world is not mediated by consciousness so that it is possible to argue that controlled conditions replicate uncontrolled conditions in real-life situations. Or, they might consist of a belief that a controlled setting can eliminate the values, preconceptions and underpinning epistemic frames of the researcher.

The argument that I have made so far is that pragmatic approaches, again using this term in its ordinary language sense, to both educational research and making judgements about it are deficient because they do not take account of ontological and epistemological concerns. Four ontological and epistemological strategies have been identified: induction, deduction, retroduction/retrodiction and abduction. At appropriate points in this chapter explanations of these strategies are provided, arguments in favour and against each of them are made and a preferred approach is identified. In line with the approach set out above ontological and epistemological issues are foregrounded.

EPISTEMOLOGY

Epistemology has traditionally been concerned with what distinguishes different knowledge claims, specifically between legitimate knowledge *and* opinion and belief. When in the nineteenth century the social sciences were beginning to be developed, they did so under the shadow of the physical sciences. Therefore as immature sciences they sought to mirror the procedures and approaches adopted by the natural sciences (or at least by an etiolated version of scientific methodology which rarely equated with how scientists actually behaved).

Such positivist/empiricist approaches can be characterized in the following way. There is a real world out there and a correct way of describing it. This allows us to think that theorizing is simply a matter of following the right methods or procedures. What follows from this is that the knowledge produced from this algorithmic process is always considered to be superior to common sense understandings of the world, because it is systematic and rigorous. Science works by accumulating knowledge, that is, it builds incrementally on previous knowledge. However, it is hard to argue that the social sciences have developed a body of knowledge, which presents unequivocal truths about its subject matter. Furthermore, twentieth and twentieth-first century philosophy has generally accepted that any observations we make about the world, including those which are central to the research process and can be construed as 'facts', are always conditioned by prior understandings we have of the world. There are no theory-free facts (Quine (1951) – in this article Quine suggests that the distinction between synthetic and analytical truths is unsustainable), and this puts at risk the distinction made by positivists/empiricists between observation and theory.

The positivist/empiricist method equates legitimacy with an idealized view of scientific activity and is characterized as a set of general methodological rules. A clear distinction is made between knowers *and* people and objects in the world. Facts can be identified, free of the values and personal concerns of the observer. Thus, any assertions or statements made about this world are about observable measurable phenomena, and this implies that two theorists if they apply the correct method would come to the same conclusions. It is the correct application of the method that guarantees certainty and trust in the theories we produce. Although all these assumptions are significant in their own right, they give the impression that positivism and empiricism are simply highly idealized abstruse doctrines; however, such theories have important social consequences and speak as authorities in the world about social and physical matters.

This conception of theory-development has been disputed by interpretivists, critical theorists and postmodernists, who in their turn have been criticized for not providing a way of developing their theories which fulfils the Enlightenment desire for universal knowledge that is shorn of superstition, personal preference and special pleading. Interpretivists, critical theorists and postmodernists thus sought to provide an alternative to a view of theory-building which prioritized reduction to a set of variables, a separation between the knower and what they sought to know, a means for predicting and controlling the future, and a set of perfectly integrated descriptions of the world with a view of the social actor as mechanistic and determined. Interpretivist approaches provide one possible alternative. They focus on the meanings that social actors construct about their lives and in relation to the world, and argue that human beings negotiate these meanings in their social practices. Human action then cannot be separated from meaning-making, with our experiences organized through pre-formulated interpretive frames. We belong to traditions of thought, and the task of the theorist is to make sense of these interpretations, even though such interpretive activity is mediated by the theorist's own frame of reference. This is a practical matter for each individual, though of course they cannot make meanings on their own, since all meaning-making is located within cultural, linguistic and historical communities of practice. The field of study is therefore the meaningful actions of social actors and the social construction of reality; and one of the consequences is that the social sciences are now thought of as distinct from the natural sciences.

Being in the world is therefore understood as a practice, primed for investigation, but resistant to algorithmic and mechanistic methods for describing it used in the natural sciences. Critical theorists and critical realists take the interpretivist critique of positivism/empiricism one stage further. They look for a solution either in communicative competence (cf. Habermas (1981) or in the stratified nature of reality itself, cf. Bhaskar (2010)). The focus here is on the former and in particular Habermas' argument that any claim to theoretical credibility must be able to make the following assertions: this work is intelligible and hence meaningful in the light of the structuring principles of its discourse community; what is being asserted propositionally is true; what is being explained can be justified; and the person who is making these claims is sincere about what they are asserting. These four conditions if they are fulfilled allow a theorist to say something meaningful about knowing. The aim above all for a critical theorist is to develop knowledge that is potentially transformative or emancipatory. Its purposes are therefore the direct replacement of one set of values (unjust, muddled, and discriminatory) with another (rational, just and emancipatory).

The fourth framework is a postmodernist one and again it should be noted that it was developed in reaction to positivist and empiricist epistemic frameworks and in particular to all those epistemologies which posit a real world separate from the activities of the knower. As Lather (2007) suggests, any work or theory should give a voice to those social actors that have been traditionally marginalized (an explicit emancipatory purpose), and in the process undermine and subvert the agendas held by those with more power in the world than others; bring to the surface for public discussion those textual devices (both spoken and written) used in conventional theory-development, and suggest ways of countering these powerful knowledge constructions; question how theorists construct their texts and organize their sets of meaning in the world; and re-introduce the theorist into the research text by locating them within those frameworks which act to construct them as theorists and as human beings.

All these frameworks cannot be equally correct and this explains why theorists produce conflicting and contradictory results about important educational matters. However, the situation is more serious than this, since even though two theorists may subscribe to the same epistemology, they may still disagree with one another, even if they are focusing on the same set of social problems. The dispute might be about correct and incorrect uses of the method, different views and interpretations of the epistemological tradition to which they claim to belong, or the use of different interpretive frameworks. This has precipitated what has been called the crisis of representation, and it is hard to imagine how we can escape from it, since the alternative is to revert back to a pre-Enlightenment time of knowledge being privileged because of who could command the most attention.

However, theorizing is too important to simply ignore the problems of representation alluded to above. Indeed, we need to understand how our theories are constructed and how power is ever present in their construction. This is because theory-development is conducted with and through other people (some of them more powerful than others), and the theorist is always in the business of collecting, collating and synthesizing accounts by social actors of their lifeworlds and activities in the world.

In order to provide a full account of educational research, I therefore need to account for those epistemological and ontological frameworks which underpin processes, strategies and methods used by education researchers. In addition, I need to make explicit the way in which educational researchers move, sometimes in a seemingly effortless manner, from preconception, through data description to post-conception or summary of findings. Four approaches have been developed: induction, deduction, retroduction and abduction.

INDUCTION

A commonly used approach in educational research is that of grounded theory, developed by Glaser and Strauss (1967) in their seminal work, *The Discovery of Grounded Theory*, and, as we will see, modified by them and later collaborators in response to persistent criticisms. It is possible to plot the way in which grounded theory developed from its early emphasis on induction through to an acceptance that researchers bring with them to the data setting a variety of theoretical assumptions about the world, which they test against new data which is collected (see Chapter 18, Grounded Theory). However, it should not be assumed that grounded theorists have abandoned altogether their inductive orientation, and this approach is essentially one of discovery; theory develops from the data and not by the testing of deductively formulated hypotheses.

Grounded theorists argue that their method is both analytical and a specific way of understanding the social world. Glaser and Strauss originally recommended that the researcher should avoid presuppositions, other hypotheses and previous research studies, so that the data collected by the research team would be uncontaminated by theories developed by other people. They did, however, accept that at some stage the emergent theory should be tested against theory developed by other researchers, thus incorporating it into the cumulative development of theory about society. Strauss, but perhaps not Glaser, has since accepted that '… trained researchers are theoretically sensitised' (Corbin and Strauss, 2007, p. 227). The original tabula rasa approach was heavily criticized (cf. Bulmer, 1979) on the grounds that researchers bring with them to the setting a mass of partially formed theories and ways of understanding the social world, which inevitably impact upon initial decisions about data-collection, the boundaries of the field being studied and the methods used. However, though Strauss modified his position, his validity criterion was still whether the analysis is grounded in the data, that is, monosemically formed from it. This implies three tests: comprehensiveness (the theory takes account of all the data); logical coherence (the one correct way of organizing and representing the data is identified and applied); and phenomenological bracketing (the analyst is able to put to one side her preconceptions and prejudices during the analysis).

This leads onto the second point about the processes described above: the inductive nature of their project. Clearly, grounded theorists accept that theory always emerges from the data, though early theory is subsequently tested against later data; and, indeed, the emergent nature of theory-development means that both inductive and deductive processes are put to use. Furthermore, the emergent theory subsequently drives later data-collection methods; allowing grounded theorists to characterize the relationship between data and theory as dialectical. At different moments the one drives the other and vice versa. The inductive strategy that this represents has been described by Harré (2011) as consisting of three principles. The first of these is the principle of accumulation. Scientific knowledge consists of a series of facts about the world and it grows by the addition of new facts, which do not affect the integrity of the old facts. The second principle is the principle of induction, whereby 'there is a form of inference of laws from the accumulated simple facts, so that from true statements describing observations and the results of experiments, true laws may be inferred' (ibid., p. 42). The third principle is that of instance confirmation, whereby a greater number of instances of an observed event allows a greater degree of belief in the law.

DEDUCTION

A fairly typical deductive approach has a number of clearly defined steps. A research hypothesis is developed. This comprises the identification of a number of discrete variables, which the hypothesis suggests co-exist in a specified way. The hypothesis is operationalized, so that the relations between the variables and their applications can be construed as observational data and can be measured. Data are collected and a strategy, whether, for example, it is experimental, survey or case study, is chosen. In addition, a sample of cases is made, and the relationship between this sample and its parent population established. The empirical data are then used to confirm, disconfirm or partially confirm the original hypothesis or hypotheses. Finally, this process may be repeated, and, if this further process of testing is successful, the hypothesis becomes accepted as theory.

Critical rationalists such as Karl Popper (2002) argued that we cannot make observations without invoking a theoretical schema of one type or another; and that the inductive process, whereby theory-building always proceeds from the collection of observable facts, is flawed in both a logical and practical sense. His critique rests on the notion that because a number (however large) of similar events has occurred, we cannot conclude from this that a causal relationship has been identified. In other words, there are no logical grounds for extrapolating from past experiences to future occurrences. In addition, because Popper accepted that all observations are theory-dependent, then necessarily there is a deductive element in social theorizing.

Deductivists begin with implicit and explicit theories about the world, which they then proceed to test in and on the world. The precise origin of these theories is left deliberately obscure. However, this testing can never provide absolute proof of the truth of an hypothesis or theory; repeated testing only allows both the rejection of clearly false theories and the development and refinement of others. In addition, if a theory cannot be potentially falsified, it cannot be considered to be a theory at all.

For Popper (2002, pp. 89–90) the method of the social sciences comprises trying out tentative solutions to certain problems; problems emanating from the initial focus of the investigation and those foci formulated during it. Solutions are proposed and criticized. However, if a proposed solution is shown to be unable to be subject to criticism, then it is excluded as unscientific, although perhaps only temporarily. If the attempted solution is open to criticism, then an attempt is made to refute it, for all criticism consists of attempts at refutation. If it withstands criticism it is accepted temporarily; and accepted above all, as worthy of being discussed and criticized. The scientific method is one of tentative attempts to solve problems, by conjectures that are controlled by extensive criticism. It is a consciously critical development of the method of 'trial and error'.

Popper's solution depends on a distinction between knowing and being, or epistemology and ontology. Since the means of arriving at the truth are fallible and immersed in specific geo-historical traditions of knowledge (this is at the epistemological level), it is never possible to know reality directly (this is at the ontological level). Social scientists can in fact only make rational guesses about it and then test those guesses as best they can. However, since knowing is subject to changing conditions, to know absolutely is a fiction. Knowing, for Popper, does not have a teleological finesse about it; only by careful conjecture and refutation can theories be developed about both the natural and social worlds, which in turn and over time may be superseded by newer and better theories.

There are a number of problems with this approach. First, since all observations are theory-laden, the testing of theories against observations has a sense of circularity about it. Thus when Popper rejects the notion of psychoanalysis as unscientific, for example, because it cannot in theory be falsified, the test itself is unreliable because it assumes a particular configuration of observable data that is not shared by psychoanalysts. Second, the move from the critical deductive process to the rejection of theories if they cannot be potentially falsified does not follow logically. Popper is here making two separate points. Third, the rejection of the theory because it has been falsified rather than verified implies that reality can never be known as such. This is because his critical deductive approach never allows one to say that one theory is better than another because it accords with experience, but only that it might be a good theory because it has been modified as a result of being tested against a world of facts. In the end, this process of hypothesizing and re-hypothesizing is self-defeating.

Popper's celebrated critique of inductivism, and his advocacy of a deductive strategy, albeit one that has been considerably modified from traditional versions, points to the differences in the respective approaches adopted by inductivists and deductivists. However, as we observed with a typical quasi-inductive approach such as grounded theory, there are elements of both induction and deduction within it.

Popper's modified version of deduction nullifies one of the traditional criticisms made of this approach, which is that data can never be free of the preconceptions and frameworks of the data collector. However, more significantly, the method lacks predictive power because it is wholly based on events that occurred in the past. This is because it does not follow the inductive principle of inferring from past occurrences to future events. The deductive-nomological model (also known as Hempel's model or the Hempel–Oppenheim model or the Popper–Hempel model) is an extension of the original logical positivist model developed by Hempel, and it relies very much on probabilistic elements being introduced into the equation. It is also the dominant model in the field of education round the world. However, because neither inductive nor deductive research strategies have provided convincing explanations of how social scientists can develop knowledge of society, or educationalists of educational systems and activities, other strategies have been suggested: retroduction/retrodiction and abduction.

RETRODUCTION AND RETRODICTION

A way of solving the problems created by induction and deduction has been suggested by critical realists (cf. Bhaskar, 2010). Again, the first move that is made is to distinguish between the epistemological and the ontological realms (in fact, unless this is accomplished, Bhaskar (ibid.) argues, theorists are guilty of the ontic fallacy – the unjustified conflation of these two levels). Those constant conjunctions or patterns of events that are experienced are merely the appearance of reality; they reflect real mechanisms that are causal in nature and that exist at the transcendental level and therefore do not make themselves immediately known. In fact, he posits three levels or domains: the real, the actual and the empirical. In the domain of the real reside the mechanisms, powers of which drive actual events that produce actual experiences. These events are real, whether they are observed or not. If they are, they are located in the empirical domain. A theory is realist, therefore, if it acknowledges that something is objective, in that it exists whether it is known or not, and, furthermore, it may still be real without appearing so; all claims are fallible, in that they are always open to refutation and further exposure to the collection of new data; all claims to knowledge are transphenomenal, so that which is real goes beyond and underlies appearances, and these underlying mechanisms endure longer than their appearances and make them possible, indeed generate them; and finally, reality may actually be counter-phenomenal, in other words, knowledge of real structures certainly will go beyond appearances, but in addition may actually contradict those appearances. In order to understand these processes, careful experimentation has to take place in order to actualize mechanisms;

researchers set up a situation in which the three domains coincide. Bhaskar (2010, p. 4) suggests that

> we have in science a three-phase schema of development, in which in a continuing dialectic, science identifies a phenomenon (or range of phenomena), constructs explanations for it and empirically tests its explanations, leading to the identification of the generative mechanisms at work, which now becomes the phenomena to be explained, and so on. On this view of science, its essence lies in the move at any one level from manifest phenomena to the structures that generate them.

For Bhaskar, though this procedure more obviously applies in the natural sciences, a unity of method between the natural and social sciences is both possible and desirable.

This method or procedure can be understood at the levels of strategy and method as a series of steps or action-sets (cf. Bhaskar, 2010). The first entails a process of reasoning and analysing causal laws as expressions of the tendencies of natural and social objects. The second is resolving a concrete event occurring in a context into its components. The third is re-describing the components in theoretically significant ways. The fourth is a retroductive move or moving from describing the components of an event to proposing explanations about what produces the conditions or what are the conditions for the event. The fifth is eliminating alternative possible explanations. The sixth is identifying explanatorily crucial explanations. The seventh is correcting earlier proposed explanations in the light of the temporarily completed analysis. And finally there is a need to explain the parameters of these subsequent explanations and how they relate to the ontology and epistemology of the world.

Pratten (2007, p. 196) goes on to provide a second model of explanation, one more suited to the social world:

> referred to as applied (or practical or concrete) explanation, or the RRREI(C) model – a form that is essential when conditions are fundamentally open – proceeds in a manner that is somewhat different. First, a complex event or situation of interest is *Resolved* into its separate components, i.e. into the effects of its separate determinants; second, these components are then *Redescribed* in theoretically significant terms; third, a knowledge of independently validated tendency statements is utilized in the *Retrodiction* of possible antecedent conditions, which involves working out the way in which known causes may have been triggered and interacted with one another such as to give rise to the concrete phenomenon under investigation; whereupon, fourth, alternative accounts of possible causes are eliminated on evidential grounds. This may be followed by *Identification* and Correction as in the pure model (*i.e. the retroductive model described above*). (*My comments in italics.*)

Clearly, the viability of such a method depends on a belief in realism, albeit of a sophisticated kind. It also depends on a conceptualization of reality that includes unobservable entities. The existence of these mechanisms and structures is inferred from a complicated process of experimentation and testing.

ABDUCTION

The abductive strategy is the one generally used by hermeneutic or interpretive researchers and focuses on drawing out the meanings used by social actors as they live their daily lives. The principle is best expressed by Giddens (1986, p. 161), when he suggests that 'the production and reproduction of society thus has to be treated as a skilled performance on the part of its members, not as merely a mechanical series of processes'. What follows from this is that 'we cannot describe social activity at all without knowing what its constituent actors know, tacitly as well as discursively' (Giddens, 1986, p. 336). This perspective gives due weight to the descriptions that actors provide of their intentions, plans and projects. The alternative would be to fall into the trap of conceptualizing human actors as the agents of structural forces that are beyond their control and therefore do not allow them to act intentionally.

Three broad traditions have dominated sociological thought since its inception. The first focuses on the brute and imposing facticity of society and relegates the human actor to a subsidiary role. This may take the form of subservience to society as a functional whole (Parsons, 1970), to the overwhelming pressure exerted on the superstructure by economic arrangements (Marx, 2009) or to the constraining influence of discursive frames (Fairclough, 2001). These forms of downward conflation between the cultural and sociocultural spheres provide little real evidence that human actors can control their destinies and are reflexive beings who monitor and can thus by implication change their behaviours.

Pitted against this is a view that emphasizes the active and intentional flow of social life. Sociologists who work within this tradition recognize the central importance of the social actor in their descriptions of social life. More extreme versions ignore the pervasive and routinized character of much of that social life and seek to sustain a notion of Verstehen (Weber, 1964) without recourse to any constraining influences exerted by society. Such interpretive and interactive philosophies have found expression in movements such as symbolic interactionism, ethnomethodology and some forms of ethnography. More recently there have been various attempts to provide a synthesis and in doing so give full weight to both structure and agency in social life. This points to one of the major weaknesses of interactionist and interpretive methodologies. Prioritizing descriptions of the intentions and plans of social actors fails to position and locate these activities within the enabling and constraining contexts of life. The emphasis is on the agential thrust of activity, with a consequent neglect of structural influences.

The most compelling of the interpretive and meaning-based methodologies is symbolic interactionism, and much of the empirical literature in the field of the sociology of education over the past three decades and a half has been influenced by it in one form or another. Two important concepts are central to these analyses. The first is that of negotiated order: people negotiate the various roles they are expected to play. The second is that of interpretation. Roles, behaviours and understandings are dependent upon interpretive activity. The emphasis on the intentional aspect of human activity has been criticized because it involves a number of unwarranted assumptions about human behaviour and also fails to account for social constraints. Human beings are not equally able to control and influence events: society is stratified in various ways. This means that some human beings have greater degrees of freedom than others. Second, interaction-ism implies that society is simply the sum of a series of individual decisions, and cannot operate as a set of specific material constraints and enablements, a notion that is hard to sustain.

Symbolic interactionism leaves unanswered certain questions about episte-mology; in particular, about whether researchers should attempt to maintain the integrity of the phenomena they are studying. Most theorists working from an interpretivist perspective accept that social scientists need to build on the lay con-cepts of social actors. What is at issue is how far theorists and empirical research-ers should go; in other words, whether the concepts and ideas used by the social scientist should be anchored in lay discourses or whether it is methodologically acceptable to import other notions that these social actors may not recognize. This movement from first-order to second-order constructs involves abductive reasoning and may take a number of forms.

Schutz (1963), for instance, describes it as a process of developing models of typical social actors, which by virtue of how they have been constructed have typical motives and behave in typical ways. However, for him, these second-order constructs are always directly related to and anchored in lay descriptions of the social world. There is of course a sense in which the empirical researcher always goes beyond the self-constructed life-notions developed by participants. The process of collecting data is an intrusive act by the researcher; in the course of an interview, the researcher's biography imposes an order on how the social actor understands their life. When this is textually inscribed, a further process of intrusion takes place. The hermeneutic process always involves closure at some arbitrary point by the researcher. This closure takes the form of a 'going beyond' the way of understanding developed by the social actors under scrutiny. Abduction therefore comprises a movement from lay to technical accounts of social processes and lives, and is an alternative to inductive, deductive and retro-ductive/retrodictive strategies.

REASONS AND CAUSES

The key is answering the question as to whether reasons can be causes. This is of some importance because it impacts directly on the choice of methods for collecting data to understand human activity. Is it possible to determine ex post facto that the reasoning activity of an individual can provide an adequate explanation for a particular event in which this individual played a prominent part. Texts produced through interactive processes such as interviewing and involving interpretative activity can have a measure of truth about them. This argument hinges on the idea that the reasoning process undertaken by an individual can lead directly to actions; in other words, intentionality is a genuine idea. This doesn't mean that rationalizations of the reasons for their actions by individuals do not take place, and indeed, interviews as a methodological tool generally focus on these post-hoc rationalizations. However, the post-hoc rationalization is emergent from the actual reason for the activity and thus retains elements of it, though it is not reducible to it.

The difficulty then becomes that these reasons (which by necessity have a directive quality about them) are embedded in networks of reasons for doing things, which exist independently from the consciousness of the individual, though clearly the individual has the potentiality to access them. A person can have a reason for their action, is convinced that the reason that is given by them is the actual reason as to why the action took place, and believes that the action would not have taken place without the reason being developed prior to the action. And yet the reason that is given is not the real reason for that action. Furthermore the rationalization of the original reason does not necessarily comprise a distortion of that original reason, it may involve a redescription of that reason which now entails the placing of the action in wider social, political, economic and discursive contexts (some of which are developed during the research process by the researcher or trusted 'other'). The purpose is to grasp the reasoning action in its setting of rules, practices, conventions and fundamentally peoples' expectations.

What this implies is that there is always a cause–effect relationship in any particular action or event. And this in turn implies that in most circumstances the person is a skilled knower, especially with regards to their own reasons for their actions, even if the original and motivating reason is subsequently rationalized over time. And what this means is that the job of the researcher in the first place is to collect together accounts by key players in a particular event, with the proviso that, though reasons can be causes, there is always a difficulty with distinguishing between primary causes and subsequent rationalizations.

AN EXAMPLE OF ABDUCTIVE REASONING

In his 2003 book, *Class Strategies and the Education Market: The middle classes and social advantage*, Stephen Ball through a series of interviews with key respondents plots the still pervasive influence of class on the social structure. This is how he describes his work:

> I am interested in subtleties and nuances here rather than stark and distinct patterns and relationships, indeed this is not a field of analysis that lends itself to that sort of style of interpretation – if you are looking for some kind of clear-cut class story of stark oppressions and

determinisms then you are reading the wrong book. ... In good part, as I have indicated, the task of the book is the assembly of a toolbox of analytic possibilities rather than the display of findings. It is a cautious and stumbling text. It is a pragmatic or synthetic sociology rather than an ideological one. It is about exploring the way 'the social' works. It is about mapping rather than explaining. There is no pristine theoretical exposition to be displayed, nor any avant-garde posturing. I am attempting to gather together and elaborate a particular pack-age of concepts, or a 'moral vocabulary' (Parkin, 1979: 115) that may be useful for 'the exercise of making things intelligible' (114). In articulating this vocabulary I have sought, as far as possible, to escape from the seductive simplicities and the 'comforts of certainty' (Stronach and MacLure, 1997) offered by the binary. Both in class research and in qualitative analysis binaries have a certain obviousness to them. But binaries can obscure as much, if not more, than they reveal; they avoid complexity and divert our attention from what lies between, that which is neither one thing nor the other. This text is littered with the promises and pitfalls of the dual classification and not all of these are eschewed but neither are they indulged in without care.

Ball goes onto to argue that these voices always have to be contextualized:

This text is, then, a hybrid. It is part empirical; data are deployed in various ways – sometimes to illustrate, sometimes to demonstrate, sometimes to speculate and I shall endeavour to be clear about which is which. The aim is to achieve a degree of plausibility. The text is also, as already noted, in part conceptual. I am attempting to define, develop and relate together a set of concepts, which offers 'perspective' in understanding the complex relationships between social class and social justice in contemporary educational settings with a specific focus on the middle class. I shall focus on the rhythm and murmur of middle-class voices; their changing cadences and concerns, their expression of dilemmas and ambivalences. These are voices of confidence and uncertainty, which are sometimes also confused, voices which are articulate, persuasive and authoritative but also careful, measured and thoughtful. These voices are quoted at length in the text, in part because of what they tell us about class practices but also because they are a medium of practice. The middle class gets things done at home, work and in engagement with 'expert systems' through talk of a particular sort. They represent and perform themselves as moral subjects, as efficacious social actors and as classed agents, through talk. I shall be working across the surfaces of class and trying to eventualize class. (Ball, 2003, pp. 2–3)

This is an affirmation by Ball that the voices of key informants in a research study matter, and that even then they have to be positioned within already exist-ing material and discursive structures that constitute the conditions of existence within a society, and thus also determine the methodological approach that it is appropriate to adopt. This is the retroductive/abductive approach in action and, as I have argued throughout, both of these approaches in combination are framed by particular and specific ontological and epistemological positions. In a practical sense, this approach requires certain actions.

PRACTICAL METHODOLOGIES – RETRODUCTIVE AND ABDUCTIVE STRATEGIES

In pursuing causal explanation via a constant conjunction model, with its stress on that which can be observed and controlled, researchers have tended to overlook the liabilities, powers and potentialities of the programmes and people whose behaviours they seek to explain. A number of points need to be made here. First, if this is correct, then the data-collection methods and the research design are going to be different. The reason for this is that researchers are now committed to understanding mechanisms that may not actually operate in practice (that is, produce effects) because the external conditions for the release of the generative mechanism may not be present. Researchers therefore have to adopt a twofold strategy: identifying the appropriate generative mechanism and examining the actual conditions that have produced the effects that they have observed. Since the reality, which they wish to describe, is social in nature and comprises social actors interacting with each other, they cannot simply assume that those actors are compelled to behave in particular and specific ways by causal mechanisms which they cannot observe and which they do not understand. Causal relations need to be understood as configurations of social actors making decisions, whether appropriate or not, within certain determinate conditions, and further, the making of those decisions and the subsequent retroductions that are made changes both the contexts in which future decisions are made and the identity of those social actors.

In the first instance then, educational researchers need to examine a range of phenomena. The first of these – structural properties at each time point – may or may not have been activated in the particular circumstances, but provide access to understanding the essential contexts of action. In doing this, researchers need to try to understand a second phenomenon – interpretations of those relations by relevant social actors. Data needs to be collected about these interpretations because they provide access to those interpretations and their effects. Instead of assuming that a structural property always operates to facilitate human actions and interactions at every time point, it is important to understand when, where and how these different structures are influential; and furthermore, what the precise relationship is between them at specific moments and places during these interactions.

Researchers therefore need to gather data on those relations between different structures at each time point, and those perceived relations between different structures at each time point by the relevant social actors. This is a necessary part of the research process for two reasons. First, it provides access for the researcher to those real relations referred to above. Second, social actors' perceptions of those relations constitute a part of them. They may also be motivated by unconscious forces which compel them to behave in certain ways and which may conflict with the accounts they give of their reasons for action. By examining their intentions, it is possible to make a judgement about how much they know and how this impacts on decisions they make.

Educational and social researchers also need to consider the unintended consequences of actions. Some activities may be designed, and thus have a degree of intention behind them, which may change those structural properties; others less so. But more importantly, all actions have unintended consequences. After each interaction, however limited, its effects on those structures, which provide the contexts for future exchanges and interactions, need to be assessed. This last requirement for research therefore refers to the subsequent effects of those intended and unintended actions on structural properties. Finally, there is the focal point of any investigation: the degree of structural influence and the degree of agential freedom for each human interaction. This is the crux of the matter because it allows the researcher to understand the complex relationship between agency and structure at each time point.

REFERENCES

Ball, S. (2003) *Class Strategies and the Education Market: The middle classes and social advantage*. London: Routledge.

Bhaskar, R. (2010) *Reclaiming Reality*, 2nd edition. London and New York: Routledge.

Bridges, D. (1999) 'Educational Research: Pursuit of Truth or Flight of Fancy', *British Educational Research Journal*, 25 (5): 597–616.

Bulmer, M. (1979) 'Concepts in the Analysis of Qualitative Data', *Sociological Review*, 27 (4): 651–77.

Corbin, J. and Strauss, A. (2007) *Basics of Qualitative Research: Techniques and procedures for developing grounded theory*. London: Sage Publications.

Fairclough, N. (2001) *Language and Power*. London and New York: Pierson Educational Ltd.

Giddens, A. (1986) *The Constitution of Society*. Cambridge: Polity Press.

Glaser, B. and Strauss, A. (1967) *The Discovery of Grounded Theory: Strategies for qualitative research*. London: Weidenfeld and Nicolson.

Habermas, J. (1981) *The Theory of Communicative Action, Volume 1*, Thomas McCarthy (trans.). Boston, MA: Beacon Press.

Harré, R. (2011) *Theories and Things*. London: Sheed and Ward.

Lather, P. (2007) 'Validity, Qualitative', in George Ritzer (Ed.) *The Blackwell Encyclopaedia of Sociology*. Oxford: Blackwell Publishing, 5161–5165.

Marx, K. (2009) *Capital*, Vol. 1. Washington, DC: Regnery Publishing.

Moss, G. (2015) *Lecture at the British Educational Research Conference 2015*, Belfast: Queen's University, Belfast, Northern Ireland.

Parkin, F. (1979) *Marxism and Class Theory: A bourgeois critique*. London: Tavistock

Parsons, T. (1970) *Social Structure and Personality*. New York: Free Press.

Popper, K. (2002) *Conjectures and Refutations: The growth of scientific knowledge*. London: Routledge.

Pratten, S. (2007) 'Explanatory Critique', in Hartwig, M. (Ed.) *Dictionary of Critical Realism*, London and New York: Routledge.

Quine, W.V.O. (1951) 'Two Dogmas of Empiricism', *The Philosophical Review*, 60: 20–43.

Research Excellence Framework (REF) (2015) *The Research Effectiveness Framework*, Higher Education Funding Council for Wales, Higher Education Funding Council for England, Scottish Funding Council and Department for Employment and Learning.

Schutz, A. (1963) 'Common-sense and Scientific Interpretation of Human Action', in M. Natanson (Ed.) *Philosophy of Social Sciences*. New York: Random House, 302–54.

Stronach, I. M. and MacLure, M. (1997) *Educational Research Undone: The postmodern embrace*. Buckingham: Open University Press.

Weber, M. (1964) *The Theory of Social and Economic Organisation*. New York: Free Press.

12

Unpacking Pragmatism for Mixed Methods Research

R. Burke Johnson, Anthony J. Onwuegbuzie,
Cornelis de Waal, Tres Stefurak
and David Hildebrand

In 2004, Johnson and Onwuegbuzie summarized classical pragmatism (that is, Charles Sanders Peirce, William James, and John Dewey) in the context of mixed methods research (MMR). In that heavily cited article, the authors attempted to move understandings of pragmatism beyond one-line statements such as 'if it works it's true'. They attempted to make classical pragmatism more complex and more accurate, and in doing so they listed 22 general characteristics of classical pragmatism.

Today, some researchers still seem to view pragmatism as a simplistic philosophy. To continue our attempt to flesh-out pragmatism, we take a different approach in this chapter. In this chapter, we contrast the views of four well-known pragmatists: the three major classical pragmatists (Peirce, James, and Dewey) and one modern pragmatist (Richard Rorty). The goal remains to shift pragmatism beyond a one-line philosophy and to show its richness. The richness shown in this chapter will be seen in the different pragmatisms of the four philosophers. Another goal here is to provide much of our presentation of the pragmatists in their own words, thereby leaving less room for interpretation found in secondary sources.

In mixed methods research, pragmatism has been criticized by leading qualitative researchers. For example, Norman Denzin (2012, p. 81) stated: 'The MMR links to the pragmatism of Dewey, James, Mead, and Peirce are problematic.

Classic pragmatism is not a methodology per se. It is a doctrine of meaning, a theory of truth.... This concern goes beyond any given methodology or any problem-solving activity'. Denzin (2010, p. 420) also stated that pragmatism 'leaves little space for issues connected to empowerment, social justice, and a politics of hope'. Similarly, Yvonna Lincoln (2009) published the following statements: (a) 'Pragmatism is hiding many a positivist these days' (p. 7); 'Pragmatism is the new virtue, purism is the new doctrinal error, the paradigmatic sin' (p. 7); and 'The mixed methods pragmatists tell us nothing about their ontology or epistemology or axiological position' (p. 7). As the reader can see, these criticisms seem to be about both pragmatism and about the sort of pragmatism that they believe is popular in mixed methods research.

With these criticisms in mind, our goal in this chapter is to explain the ontologies, epistemologies, axiologies, and methodologies advocated by four prominent pragmatists, dispelling Lincoln's concern that this is not known among mixed methods researchers and dispelling Denzin's contention that mixed methods (MM) researchers (such as us) treat pragmatism just as a methodology and is disconnected from social justice. Ontology refers to our assumptions about the nature of reality and our beliefs about how it can be parsed. Epistemology is our theory of knowledge (for example, what is knowledge? how does one obtain knowledge? what standards must be met to conclude that one has knowledge?). Axiology, in educational research, refers to the ethical positions and values that we hold (this includes positions regarding social justice). Finally, methodology refers to specific approaches for the practice of empirical research (for example, experiments, correlational research, phenomenology, grounded theory). In explaining these positions, we provide nuance and sophistication to pragmatism for MMR.

Johnson, Onwuegbuzie, and Turner (2007) have shown that, rather than being a singular approach to mixed methods research, there are three major kinds of MMR: qualitatively driven (wherein qualitative component represents the dominant approach in a MMR study), quantitatively driven (wherein the quantitative component represents the dominant approach in a MMR study), and equal-status (wherein the qualitative component and quantitative component are [approximately] equally represented in a MMR study). And there are many smaller, but important, approaches to MMR. Below, we show that there is a specific pragmatism for each of the three major kinds of MMR. We specifically contend that quantitatively driven MMR can be partnered with Charles Sanders Peirce's realist pragmatism; qualitatively driven MMR can be partnered with the somewhat postmodern pragmatisms of Richard Rorty and William James; and, equal-status MMR can be partnered with John Dewey. One reason Dewey fits equal-status MMR well is because he famously attacked dualisms and dualistic argumentation, showing that, most often, one is not faced with an either/or logic but often with a both/and logic, and that oftentimes some truth content is found in the poles of dualisms and different perspectives, and the poles provide voices to be listened to and can be of use to research and practice in particular situations.

CHARLES SANDERS PEIRCE

Charles Sanders Peirce lived from 1839 to 1914. Our conceptual label for Peirce is 'The Natural Scientist and Classical Realist'.

Ontology

Peirce vehemently rejected nominalism, which is the view that reality is exhausted by particulars – all else is a mere mental construction or conceptual shorthand necessitated by the limitations of the human mind. This view, Peirce argued, dominated the modern era. It was favored by metaphysicians and uncritically assumed by the majority of scientists. To this view, Peirce opposed his realism. Starting from the 'fundamental hypothesis' that 'there are real things, whose characters are entirely independent of our opinions about them' (Peirce, 1877, p. 10), Peirce argued that existing as a particular thing is just one way in which something can be real. For example, Peirce allowed for real generals (or universals) and real possibilities. Consequently, variables, as they are used in quantitative research, can be real. Peirce's conception of real chance led him to a view he called tychism, which holds that the world is not fully predictable. Furthermore, rather than viewing reality as a set of separate entities in binary opposition, he viewed reality in terms of continua which he calls synechism – 'I have proposed to make synechism mean the tendency to regard everything as continuous' (Peirce, 1893/1998b, p. 1).

Epistemology

According to Peirce, research gets us closer to truth. 'Different minds may set out with the most antagonistic views, but the progress of investigation carries them by a force outside of themselves to one and the same [true] conclusion' (Peirce, 1878a). As he put it elsewhere,

> the truth of the proposition that Caesar crossed the Rubicon consists in the fact that the further we push our archaeological and other studies, the more strongly will that conclusion force itself on our minds forever – or would do so, if study were to go on forever. (Peirce, 1931–1958, 5.565)

Peirce next coined the term fallibilism, which means that although many of our beliefs may be true we cannot say for sure of any particular belief that it is true: '[we] cannot attain absolute certainty concerning questions of fact…our knowledge is never absolute' (Peirce, 1931–1958, 1.149).

Peirce also coined the term 'pragmatism', but, in 1905, replaced it with pragmaticism to disassociate his pragmatism with James's practicalism (as well as because of increasing use of the word pragmatism in 'literary journals, where it gets abused'; quoted in Haack, 1998, p. 55). Peirce philosophized that truth is immutable and is simultaneously independent from actual opinion (that is, fallibilism), and is discoverable (that is, anti-radical skepticism); this view of truth departs from the beliefs of other pragmatists such as James. Moreover, pragmaticism was meant to remind one that for Peirce, pragmatism was not about concrete practical consequences – a view he ascribed to James and which makes it always about particulars (see ontology above) – but, instead, was about the meaning of signs and scientific concepts and terms. Here is Peirce's pragmatic maxim: 'Consider what effects, which might conceivably have practical bearings, we conceive the object of our conception to have. Then, our conception of these effects is the whole of our conception of the object' (Peirce, 2014, p. 90). For example:

> When an experimentalist speaks of a phenomenon, such as "Hall's phenomenon" … he does not mean any particular event that did happen to somebody in the dead past, but what surely will happen to everybody in the living future who shall fulfill certain conditions.

In short, meaning is general, not particular (as in the case of James) (Peirce, 1998a, p. 340).

Axiology

Peirce, following Überweg, divided normative science (that is, inquiry that seeks to determine good ways to meet community-accepted goals, objectives, purposes, or the like) into aesthetics, ethics, and logic. He subsequently argued that logic – the theory of how we should reason – is grounded in the more general science of ethics, which he took, in turn, to be grounded in aesthetics. However, though the normative science of logic was Peirce's life-long project, he paid relatively little attention to ethics and aesthetics, and insofar as he did it, was only with an eye on how they grounded logic.

Methodology, science, and inquiry

Peirce had a much broader conception of science than is current today, including not only the so-called hard sciences, but also the social sciences and the humanities. What truly guides science, for Peirce, is not the adherence to a single 'scientific' method, but the genuine desire to have one's questions answered. Consequently, multiple methods are good for science. To illustrate his commitment to multiple methods, Peirce writes:

> One man may investigate the velocity of light by studying the transits of Venus and the aberration of the stars; another by the oppositions of Mars and the eclipses of Jupiter's satellites; a third by the method of Fizeau; a fourth by that of Foucault; a fifth by the motions of the curves of Lissajoux; a sixth, a seventh, an eighth, and a ninth, may follow the different methods of comparing the measures of statical and dynamical electricity. They may at first obtain different results, but, as each perfects his method and his processes, the results are found to move steadily together toward a destined centre. (Peirce 2014, p. 91)

Elsewhere Peirce provided a cable analogy, which sounds remarkably similar to triangulation.

> Philosophy ought to imitate the successful sciences in its methods.... Its reasoning should not form a chain which is no stronger than its weakest link, but a cable whose fibers may be ever so slender, provided they are sufficiently numerous and intimately connected. (Peirce, 1868, in Menand 1997, pp. 5–6).

Peirce's writings on science are relevant for mixed methods research. He has been popular among many scientists perhaps because he emphasized that the purpose of science is to answer questions, and that we should ask questions that we believe can be answered (that is, anti-radical skepticism). He believed we would obtain answers to carefully constructed questions that are specific and focused. Inquiry leads to true beliefs. 'It is unphilosophical to suppose', Peirce writes, 'that, with regard to any given question (which has any clear meaning), investigation would not bring forth a solution of it, if it were carried far enough' (Peirce, 2014, p. 99). 'The attainment of a stable belief – belief that will stand in the long run – is thus the goal of inquiry. Such belief we define as true, and its object is reality' (quoted in Scheffler, p. 60). 'The opinion which is fated to be ultimately agreed to by all who investigate, is what we mean by the truth, and the object represented in this opinion is the real' (Peirce, 1878a). Furthermore, methods are themselves products of scientific inquiry and will continually emerge in science. Finally, science is a social enterprise, which makes it stronger because ideas that survive criticisms and disputation are more likely to be true. As Peirce phrased it in an unpublished manuscript of 1894, 'In part what makes reasoning successful, even though it goes wrong so often, is the social aspect of inquiry' (Robin, 1967, p. 410). Peirce (1878b) stated that with respect to making inferences, 'logic is rooted in social principle' because inferences are dependent on a perspective which, essentially, is unrestricted.

WILLIAM JAMES

William James lived from 1842 to 1910. Our conceptual label James is 'The Psychologist and Radical Empiricist'.

Ontology

James was a radical empiricist. That is, the primary reality is in our ongoing experience in the local, immediate world. We all have an incomplete slice of experiential reality. According to radical empiricism, 'everything real must be experienceable somewhere, and every kind of thing experienced must somewhere be real' (James, 1912, p. 160). James also was an ontological pluralist. 'Pluralism involves indeterminism' (James, 1909, p. vi); 'Pluralism involves possible conflicts among things' (James, 1909, p. iv); and 'Things are "with" one another in many ways, but nothing includes everything, or dominates over everything' (James, 1909, p. 321).

James rejected strong determinism or what he called the block universe. 'The universe is not a block or an organism, but an all-navigable sea – a great neighborhood embracing lesser neighborhoods, in which accessibility is universal and intimacy proportional to propinquity' (quoted in Perry, 1935, p. 591). This entailed chance and freewill as important parts of the universe, as exemplified by the following quotations: 'My first act of free will shall be to believe in free will' (James, 1870, quoted in McDermott, 1977, p. 7); and 'Free-will pragmatically means novelties in the world ... the future may not identically repeat and imitate the past... [free-will] holds up improvement as at least possible.... Free-will is thus a general cosmological theory of promise' (James, 1907/1995, p. 46).

Epistemology

James rejected the 'copy view of truth' – which is similar to what came to be called the correspondence theory of truth, which represents the contention that the truth or falsity of a proposition is dependent entirely on its relationship to the world and the extent to which it accurately describes/corresponds with the world. He provided a combination of relativism and correspondence theory.

> To copy a reality is, indeed, one very important way of agreeing with it, but ... the essential thing is the process of being guided. Any idea that helps us deal, whether practically or intellectually ... that fits ... and adapts our life to the reality's whole setting, will agree sufficiently to meet the requirement. It will hold true of that reality. (James, 1907/1995, p. 82)

> 'Truth' in our ideas and beliefs means the same thing that it means in science. It means ... nothing but this, that ideas (which themselves are but parts of our experience) become true just in so far as they help us to get into satisfactory relation with other parts of our experience'. 'Any idea upon which we can ride, so to speak ... is true for just so much, true in so far forth, true instrumentally' (James, 1907/1995, p. 23).

A key question is not whether an idea 'matches' or 'copies' some reality but whether an idea is one that we 'can assimilate, validate, corroborate, and verify' (James, 1907/1995, p. 77).

James's goal was to radicalize the prevailing scientific thought of his time, which he deemed as representing 'agnostic positivism, radical materialism, mechanical rationalism, a vicious intellectualism' because it was devoid of any phenomena or explanation that was independent of the natural laws known at that time (Taylor, 1996, p. 112). He sought to bring science and the emerging field of psychology to the wellspring of rich and plural perspectives found in human experience. His radical empiricism insists on a foothold in human experience, rather than solely in abstractions of material observations: 'To be radical, an empiricism must neither admit into its constructions any element that is not directly experienced, nor exclude from them any element that is directly experienced' (James, 1912, p. 22). James believed that there were always multiple truths operating in the world. 'The world is indubitably one if you look at it in one way, but as indubitably is it many, if you look at it in another. It is both one and many – let us adopt a sort of pluralistic monism' (James, 1907, p. 5).

James was the first to use the word pragmatism in print. For him it meant the following: 'The whole function of philosophy ought to be to find out what definite difference it will make to you and me, at definite instants of our life, if this world-formula or that world-formula be the one which is true' (James, 1907/1995, p. 20). One of many uses was to solve previously indeterminate philosophical problems; for example, he used it to balance the dichotomy of rationalism and empiricism. He also used pragmatism to help us determine what was worth considering because a difference that makes no difference is no difference at all –

> The pragmatic method starts from the postulate that there is no difference of truth that doesn't make a difference of fact somewhere; and it seeks to determine the meaning of all differences of opinion by making the discussion hinge as soon as possible upon some practical or particular issue. (James, 1912, p. 81)

Axiology

James is a quintessential psychologist in morality. The route to social reform is through personal character and moral habits. According to James, we should Launch ourselves with as strong and decided an initiative as possible and.... Accumulate all the possible circumstances which shall reinforce the right motives; put yourself assiduously in conditions that encourage the new way ... take a public pledge.... This will give you a new beginning'; 'Never suffer an exception to occur till the new habit is securely rooted in your life' and 'Seize the very first possible opportunity to act on every resolution you make'. 'The course of history is nothing but the story of men's struggles from generation to generation to find the more and more inclusive order (James, 1891/1992, p. 610).

James was skeptical that abstract religion or philosophy could create a fixed ethical and moral system. Rather, he saw living an ethical life as a strenuous exercise requiring a constant commitment to a moral life. He viewed reliance on such fixed systems as a rejection of personal intuition, feeling and reasoning, which he saw as the real underlying mechanism creating good in the world.

> There is but one unconditional commandment, which is that we should seek incessantly, with fear and trembling, so to vote and to act as to bring about the very largest total universe of good which we can see. Abstract rules indeed can help; but they help the less in proportion as our intuitions are more piercing, and our vocation is the stronger for the moral life. (James, 1891/1992, p. 612)

Moral and ethical convictions don't need the sanction of external systems, merely the commitment and the felt conviction of each individual.

Methodology, science, and inquiry

As mentioned earlier, research determines what works which is a key criterion of truth. James took an instrumental and fallibilist approach to scientific theories:

> [N]o theory is absolutely a transcript of reality, but that any one of them may from some point of view be useful.... They are only man-made language, a conceptual shorthand, as someone calls them, in which we write our reports of nature. (James, 1907/1995, p. 22–23)

> You must bring out of each word its practical cash-value, set it at work within the stream of your experience.... Theories thus become instruments, not answers to enigmas, in which we can rest. Theories should be practical. We must find a theory that will work; and that means something extremely difficult ... It must derange common sense and previous belief as little as possible, and it must lead to some sensible terminus or other that can be verified exactly. To "work" means both these things. (James, 1907/1995, p. 21)

By modern standards James might qualify as a mixed methods researcher, or at least someone who valued pluralistic perspectives on research. In his own views on research methods he espoused quite clearly a phenomenological stance towards research methods, including an admonition that researchers remain interested in area of human consciousness that are often outside of the frame or objective empirical inquiry. He makes this point in *The Varieties of Religious Experience*, stating:

> Our normal waking consciousness, rational consciousness as we call it, is but one special type of consciousness, whilst all about it, parted from it by the filmiest of screens, there lie potential forms of consciousness entirely different. We may go through life without suspecting their existence; but apply the requisite stimulus, and at a touch they are there in all their completeness.... No account of the universe in its totality can be final which leaves these other forms of consciousness quite disregarded. How to regard them is the question.... At any rate, they forbid our premature closing of accounts with reality. (James, 1902/1994, p. 378)

Inquiry leads to new partial, provisional, working truths. Truth is fluid and each truth leads to a new formulation built upon the backs of existing truths. For James the march of discovery is an iterative process that can never be separated from the human endeavors before it to make sense of the same issue. The process by which an idea becomes a public truth is an ongoing, plodding, cumulative, and hard-won process:

> Our minds ... grow in spots; and like grease-spots, the spots spread. But we let them spread as little as possible; we keep unaltered as much of our old knowledge, as many of our old prejudices and beliefs, as we can. We patch and tinker more than we renew. The novelty

soaks in; it stains the ancient mass; but it is also tinged by what absorbs it. Our past apper-
ceives and co-operates; and in the new equilibrium in which each step forward in the process
of learning terminates, it happens relatively seldom that the new fact is added raw. More
usually it is embedded cooked, as one might say, or stewed down in the sauce of the old.
(James, 1907/1995, p. 64)

JOHN DEWEY

John Dewey lived from 1859 to 1952. Our conceptual label for Dewey is 'The Social
Psychologist, Educator, and Contextualist'.

Ontology

Although Dewey did not create a systematic view of reality (that is, a 'metaphysics'),
he discussed metaphysical ideas at length – he wrote on the nature of experience,
consciousness, nature, situations, necessity, and time, to name just a few familiar
foci of ontology. He also criticized, extensively, ontological dualisms basic to the
philosophical and scientific traditions; for example, mundane versus eternal,
substance versus accident, reality versus appearance, mind versus matter, and
experience versus nature. Dewey was troubled at how traditional ontology
attempted to describe 'what there is' or 'what exists' from a purely neutral and
abstract standpoint – a 'God's Eye Point of View', as Hilary Putnam labeled it
(Putnam, 1981, p. xx). Such a standpoint was incoherent, Dewey argued, and cut
inquirers off from the world in which they could make a difference. Still, the fact
that we all inhabit a particular standpoint (or perspective) does not isolate us,
solipsistically. There is nothing to prevent inquiries into what Dewey called the
'generic traits' of reality; we can describe, fallibilistically, what we find – our
experience in and of nature – through observation and experiment. This enterprise (of describing what is experienced persistently and commonly) can, in fact,
create very useful resources and is a process, Dewey thought, not so different
than science. Dewey wrote:

This is the extent and method of my 'metaphysics': – the large and constant features of
human sufferings, enjoyments, trials, failures and successes together with the institutions of
art, science, technology, politics, and religion which mark them, communicate genuine
features of the world within which man lives. The method differs no whit from that of any
investigator who, by making certain observations and experiments, and by utilizing the
existing body of ideas available for calculation and interpretation, concludes that he really
succeeds in finding out something about some limited aspect of nature. (Dewey, *Later Works*,
3, pp. 75–6)

Dewey likened metaphysical investigation to the creation of a map; by noting
what recurs in experience, we increase our understanding of ourselves and our
environment and gain power and control regarding where and what to do next.

But such understanding is never 'apart' from the practical world; the needs and purposes of that world always drive inquiry, including ontological or metaphysical inquiry. 'Things are what they can do and what can be done with them – things that can be found by deliberate trying' (Dewey, *Middle Works*, 12, p. 146). 'The true "stuff" of experience is recognized to be the adaptive courses of action, habits, active functions, connections of doing and undergoing' (Dewey, *Middle Works*, 12, p. 132). In short, reality is not something apart from experiencing organisms interacting in environments; rather, reality is both nature and experience in transaction.

Epistemology

Dewey's account of knowing is best described as a 'theory of inquiry', one which shifts the traditional focus from argument types and rules to the wider process in which people manage situations using inquiry. In Dewey's view, once inquiry becomes the dominant focus, justification (the reason supporting one's conclusion and, possibly, actions) then becomes much more important than 'truth'. Why? Because any revision of the overall reasoning chain – necessitated, for example, by the fact that things did not work out – requires revisiting the specific parts of that chain to see how to do better the next time. So, one might say, for Dewey, justification (not absolute or universal or eternal truth) is the salient factor in the process of truth and knowledge.

> Knowledge or warranted assertion depends upon inquiry ... it also provides for probability, and for determination of degrees of probability in rejecting all intrinsically dogmatic statements, where "dogmatic"' applies to any statement asserted to possess inherent self-evident truth'. Dewey's theory rejects the idea that propositions can ever have be true in ways that are 'self-sufficient, self-possessed, and self-evident but must instead find 'the test and mark of truth in consequences of sort' (Dewey, *Later Works*, 14, p. 172).

Again, this is to see knowledge as 'knowing', which is a process. Here is Dewey's instrumental or experimental approach to knowing:

> When the practice of knowledge ... became experimental, knowing became preoccupied with changes and the test of knowledge became the ability to bring about certain changes. Knowing, for the experimental sciences, means a certain kind of intelligently conducted doing; it ceases to be contemplative and becomes in a true sense practical.... The [real] ceases to be something ready-made and final ... [and the ideal and rational] represent intelligent thought-out possibilities of the existent world which may be used as methods for making over and improving it. (Dewey, *Middle Works*, 12, pp. 149–50)

According to Dewey, knowledge is a temporal and transactional process: 'Knowing begins with specific observations that define the problem and ends with specific observations that test a hypothesis for its solution ... but that ... requires careful scrutiny and prolonged development' (Dewey, *Middle Works*, 12, p. 165). 'There is a genuine objective standard.... One will further ... in reaching his end while another will hamper him' (Dewey, *Middle Works*, 12, p. 129) replaced the historically popular epistemic distinction between subject and external object with the process-oriented organism–environment transaction:

> The organism acts in accordance with its own structure, simple or complex, upon its sur-roundings. As a consequence the changes produced in the environment react upon the organism and its activities. The living creature undergoes, suffers, the consequences of its own behavior. This close connection between doing and suffering or undergoing forms what we call experience. [Furthermore] ... disturbance of the organism-environment integration is also a disequilibration of the energy-relations within the organism; recovery of equilibration of organism-environment is a re-integration of organism. (Dewey, *Middle Works*, 15, p. 250)

When forced to address directly the term truth by his critics, Dewey pointed out that

> [T]he 'truth' [of any present proposition] is, by the definition, subject to the outcome of continued inquiries; its 'truth', if the word must be used, is provisional; as near the truth as inquiry has as yet come, a matter determined not by a guess at some future belief but by the care and pains with which inquiry has conducted up to the present time. (Dewey, *Later Works*, 14, pp. 56–7)

Further, '[t]he hypothesis that works is the true one; and truth is an abstract noun applied to the collection of cases, actual, foreseen and desired, that receive confirmation in their works and consequences' (Dewey, *Middle Works*, 12, p. 170).

In discussing pragmatism, Dewey stated that it is nothing 'but the systematic elaboration of the logic and ethics of scientific inquiry' (Dewey, *Later Works*, 15, p. 24). 'Pragmatism regards both knowledge and truth as bridges which enable us to approach our purposes' (Dewey, *Middle Works*, 12, p. 213). Pragmatism should be applied broadly. 'It lies in the nature of pragmatism that it should be applied as widely as possible; and to things as diverse as controversies, beliefs, truths, ideas, and objects' (Dewey, *Middle Works*, 4, p. 101). Dewey's pragmatism was a philosophy that 'takes its stand with daily life' (Dewey, *Middle Works*, 10, p. 39) and remains committed to the 'actual crises of life' (Dewey, *Middle Works*, 10, p. 43).

Experimental science enables human beings 'to effect a deliberate control of his environment' (Dewey, *Middle Works*, 12, p. 134) and when 'experience ceased to be empirical and became experimental, something of radical importance occurred.... Now, old experience is used to suggest aims and methods for developing a new and improved experience.... Consequently experience becomes is so far constructively self-regulative' (Dewey, *Middle Works*, 12, pp. 133–4). To make a positive difference in the world means that we are required continually to learn and to grow and to act intelligently: 'Intelligence ... is not something possessed once and for all. It is in constant process of forming, and its retention requires constant alertness in observing consequences, an open-minded will to learn and courage in re-adjustment' (Dewey, *Middle Works*, 12, p. 135).

Axiology

Values and ethics were paramount for Dewey: 'It is incompatibility of ends which necessitates consideration of the true worth of a given end; and such consideration it is which brings the experience into the moral sphere' (Dewey, *Middle Works*, 5, p. 194).

> [A moral law] is a formula of the way to respond when specified conditions present themselves.... Its soundness and pertinence are tested by what happens when it is acted upon. Its claim or authority rests finally upon the imperativeness of the situation that has to be dealt with, not upon its own intrinsic nature. (Dewey, *Later Works*, 4, p. 222)

Dewey rejected all monocausal theories of morality – for example, those seeking to explain 'right' and 'wrong' by way of consequences or motives or even character – and instead emphasized a complex, contextual morality. 'Whatever may be the difference which separate moral theories, all postulate one single principle as an explanation of moral life' (Dewey, *Later Works*, 5, p. 280).

> [A] moral situation is one in which judgment and choice are required ... the action needed to satisfy it – is not self-evident. It has to be searched for. There are conflicting desires and alternative apparent goods. What is needed is to find the right course of action, the right good...that provides a balance of interests. (Dewey, *Middle Works*, 12, p. 174)

> 'Moral progress and the sharpening of character depend on the ability to make delicate distinctions, to perceive aspects of good and of evil not previously noticed, and to take into account that fact that doubt and the need for choice impinge at every turn'. (Dewey, *Later Works*, 5, p. 280)

> A truly moral (or right) act is one which is intelligent in an emphatic and peculiar sense; it is a reasonable act. It is ... one which will continue to be thought of as "good" in the most alert and persistent reflection (Dewey, *Middle Works*, 5, p. 279).

Ultimately, 'growth itself is the only moral 'end' (Dewey, *Middle Works*, 12, p. 181).

Many called Dewey an 'optimist' because of his philosophy was constantly focusing on some new problem or conflict. In response, Dewey explained that he was neither an optimist nor a pessimist, because both of those positions imply some 'view from above' about the ultimate state of things. Instead, he advocated that 'meliorism [which] is the belief that the specific conditions which exist at one moment, be they comparatively bad or comparatively good, in any event may be bettered. It encourages intelligence to study the positive means of good and the obstructions to their realization' (Dewey, *Middle Works*, 12, p. 102). Part and parcel of those 'positive means', was free and collective inquiry in the form of deliberative democracy: '[W]e now have to re-create by deliberate and determined endeavor the kind of democracy which in its origin one hundred and fifty years ago was largely the product of a fortunate combination of men and circumstances' (Dewey, *Later Works*, 14, p. 225). 'At the present time, the frontier is moral, not physical. The period of free lands that seemed boundless in extent has vanished. Unused resources are now human rather than material' (Dewey, *Later Works*, 14, p. 225).

Methodology, science, and inquiry

Dewey defined inquiry (in *Logic: The Theory of Inquiry*) as 'the directed or controlled transformation of an indeterminate situation into a determinately unified one' (Dewey, *Later Works*, 12, p. 109). 'The attainment of settle beliefs is a progressive matter; there is no belief so settled as not to be exposed to further inquiry' (Dewey, *Later Works*, 12, p. 16). Paraphrasing Dewey, Hildebrand (2008, pp. 53–6) shows the four steps of inquiry for Dewey: (a) 'An indeterminate situation in which a difficulty is felt – Something is wrong...' (b) 'The institution of a problem; its location and definition – The problem seems to be...' (c) 'Hypothesis of a possibly solution – Maybe what I should do is...' and (d) 'Reasoning out the bearings of the suggestion – Doing that would mean...'.

For Dewey, '[t]he scientific attitude that has actually proved itself in scientific progress is ... a practical attitude.... Its interest in change is in what it leads to, that can be done with it, to what use it can be put' (Dewey, *Middle Works*, 12, p. 152). 'Inquiry is emancipated. It is encouraged to attend to every fact that is relevant to defining the problem or need, and to follow up every suggestion that promises a clue' (Dewey, *Middle Works*, 12, p. 164). 'The purpose is so to clarify the disturbed and confused situation that reasonable ways of dealing with it may be suggested' (Dewey, *Middle Works*, 12, p. 161).

We hear MMR intimated in Dewey's thought 'We must be able to move promptly and definitely from one tool of attack to another' (Dewey, *Middle Works*, 12, p. 169).

> Conceptions, theories and systems of thought are always open to development through use.... They are tools. As in the case of all tools, their value resides not in themselves but in their capacity to work shown in the consequences of their use. (Dewey, *Middle Works*, 12, p. 163)

RICHARD RORTY

Richard Rorty lived from 1931 to 2007. Our conceptual label for Rorty is 'The Conversationalist Philosopher following the Linguistic Turn'.

Ontology

Rorty, the most postmodern of the pragmatists, declared that 'There is no authority called Reality before whom we need bow down' (Rorty in Brandom, 2001,
p. 376). 'There is no such thing as [singular] Reality to be gotten right, only
snow, fog, Olympian deities, relative aesthetic worth, the elementary particles,
human rights, the divine right of kings, the Trinity, and the like' (Rorty in
Brandom, 2001, p. 375). 'To say that we get snow mostly right is not to say that
we represent snow with reasonable accuracy' (Rorty in Brandom, 2001, p. 376)
However, Rorty does not deny that there is a reality: 'even if there is no Way the
World Is, even if there is no such thing as "the intrinsic nature of reality", there
are still causal pressures' (Rorty, 1999, p. 33).

Epistemology

Rorty rejected representationalism or the 'picture theory' of reality (similar to
the correspondence theory of truth), which is the idea that our knowledge can
directly and accurately represent a singular reality. A mirror also implies an
objective standpoint for viewing reality. In his words:

> The picture which holds traditional philosophy captive is that of the mind as a great mirror,
> containing various representations – some accurate, some not....Without the notion of the
> mind as mirror, the notion of knowledge as accuracy of representation would not have sug-
> gested itself. (Rorty, 2009. p. 12)

'The notion of 'accurate representation' is simply an automatic and empty com-
pliment which we pay to those beliefs which are successful in helping us to do
what we want to do' (Rorty, 2009, p. 10). 'No area of culture, and no period of
history, gets Reality more right than any other. The differences between areas
and epochs is their relative efficiency at accomplishing various purposes' (Rorty
in Brandom, 2001, p. 375).

Rorty replaced representationalism with conversationalism; that is, the best
we can do in science is to have useful conversations about topics of interest. 'The
true and the right are matters of social practice' (Rorty, 1979, p. 178). 'Reweaving
a web of beliefs ... is ... all anybody can do' (Rorty, 1991, p. 101) 'A necessary
truth is just a statement such that nobody has given us any interesting alternatives
which would lead us to question it' (Rorty, 1980, p. 175). Truth is 'what our peers
will, ceteris paribus, let us get away with saying' (Rorty, 1980, p. 176). Rorty
integrates truth 'with the consensus of a community rather than a relation to a
nonhuman reality' (Rorty, 1991, p. 23). 'Truth is not the sort of thing one should
expect to have a philosophically interesting opinion about' (Rorty, 1982, p. xiii).

Rorty viewed himself as a pragmatist, which is 'the doctrine that there are no
constraints on inquiry save conversational ones – no wholesale constraints derived
from the nature of the objects, or of the mind, or of language, but only those retail

constraints provided by the remarks of our fellow inquirers' (Rorty, 1982, p. 165). 'For pragmatists, the desire for objectivity is not the desire to escape the limitations of one's community, but simply the desire for as much intersubjective agreement as possible' (Rorty, 1991, p. 23). Rorty's form of pragmatism also has been labeled as neopragmatism (also called linguistic pragmatism), wherein scientific and philosophical methods represent solely a set of contingent terminologies that people use or ignore over time in accordance with social conventions.

Axiology

Social values were embedded in Rorty's philosophy. 'There is no epistemological difference between truth about what ought to be and truth about what is, nor any metaphysical difference between facts and values, nor any methodological difference between morality and science' (Rorty, 1982, p. 163). Rorty believed that democratic socialism was the best current form of government (for example, Norway). 'In the end … what matters is our loyalty to other human beings clinging together against the dark, not our hope of getting things right' (Rorty, 1982, p. 166).

Methodology, science, and inquiry

For Rorty, the pattern of all inquiry – scientific as well as moral – is deliberation concerning the relative attractions of various concrete alternatives. 'The idea that in science or philosophy we can substitute 'method' for deliberation between alternative results of speculation is just wishful thinking' (Rorty, 1982, pp. 163–4). '[T]here is no such thing as the search for truth, as distinct from the search for happiness.… "Happiness", in the relevant sense, means getting more of the things we keep developing new descriptive vocabularies in order to get' (Rorty in Brandom, 2001, p. 376). Rorty rejected the scientific method as a way to 'avoid the need for conversations and deliberation and simply tick off the way things are' (Rorty, 1982, p. 164). For a Rortian pragmatist scientist, 'there would be less talk about rigor and more about originality. The image of the great scientist would not be of somebody who got it right but of somebody who made it new' (Rorty, 1991, p. 44). Science is just another form of ethnocentrism, like any other paradigm. Rortian inquiry leads to conversational agreement within ethnocentric communities such as science.

PARADIGMS

Rorty's work also is relevant for discussions on paradigms. He thought that we lived in language communities which are similar to paradigms. They are 'ethnocentric'. This is fine because it leads to support and within-group solidarity.

> When we say that our ancestors believed, falsely, that the sun went around the earth, and we believe, truly, that the earth goes around the sun, we are saying that we have a better

tool than our ancestors did. Our ancestors might rejoin that their tool enabled them to believe in the literal truth of the Christian Scriptures, whereas ours does not. Our reply has to be, I think, that the benefits of modern astronomy and of space travel outweigh the advantages of Christian fundamentalism. The argument between us and our medieval ancestors should not be about which of us has the universe right. It should be about the point of holding views about the motion of heavenly bodies, the ends to be achieved by the use of certain tools. Confirming the truth of scripture is one such aim, space travel is another. (Rorty, 1999, p. xxv)

If you want to influence someone representing a different paradigm, you should expose those 'others' to alternative languages or vocabularies. If you want to reflect and to critique your own paradigm then use the method of irony by violating some norms within your paradigm. Ironists are 'never quite able to take themselves seriously because [they are] always aware that the terms in which they describe themselves are subject to change, always aware of the contingency and fragility of their final vocabularies, and thus of themselves'. (Rorty, 1989, p. 73f).

SIMILARITIES AMONG THE FOUR PRAGMATISTS

We have examined, in some detail, the characteristics and nuances of the four pragmatists. The reader may wonder 'Do the pragmatists have anything in common?' and 'What makes all four philosophers "pragmatists"?' Certainly there are commonalities, as seen in the following bulleted points.

- Their positions always fell between the extremes of dogmatism and skepticism. They preferred action to philosophizing, where pragmatism is, in a sense, an anti-philosophy.
- They rejected reductionisms and indeterminate dualisms, and they viewed many longstanding metaphysical disputes as being suspect and too far removed from day-to-day reality to worry about.
- They all developed views on what is real (for example, trees and mountains, but also possibilities) and what is constructed, enabling them to overcome entrenched dualisms, such as idealism versus materialism.
- All, except Rorty, endorsed empiricism to determine what works as a criterion of tentative truth.
- They endorsed practical theory and viewed theories instrumentally that are true to different degrees based on how well they currently work; workability is judged especially on the criteria of predictability and applicability.
- They viewed humans as constantly adapting to new situations and environments. Our thinking follows a dynamic-homeostatic process of belief, doubt, inquiry, modified belief, new doubt, new inquiry, ..., in an infinite loop, where the person or researcher (and research community) constantly attempts to improve upon past understandings in a way that fits and works in the world in which he or she operates. The present is always a new starting point.
- They emphasized that the starting point of philosophy is lived experience, where experience is not merely sense experience or an intuitive, subjective awareness of mental content but includes a world of people, objects, and events that are encountered and mediated through the cultural, historical, and personal backgrounds which, together, comprise perspective.

- Scientific and individual experimentation (to see what works) are key to inquiry.
- They endorsed some version of eclecticism and pluralism (for example, different theories and perspectives can be useful; observation, experience, and experiments are all useful ways to gain an understanding of people and the world).
- They endorsed fallibilism (current beliefs and research conclusions are rarely, if ever, viewed as perfect, certain, or absolute).

DIFFERENCES AMONG THE FOUR PRAGMATISTS

We examined above, in some detail, the characteristics and nuances of the four pragmatists. The reader therefore understands the many differences among these pragmatists. In the following bulleted points, we provide what we view as some major differences separating the pragmatists:

- Peirce was more comfortable referring to 'objective reality' than the other pragmatists.
- Only Peirce viewed each research question as converging on one single truth (the 'final' opinion) if inquiry were to continue long enough. James and Rorty believed in multiple, provisional truths about phenomena as what we obtain and live by.
- Dewey and James viewed current truth, meaning, and knowledge as tentative and as changing over time. Accordingly, what we obtain on a daily basis in research should be viewed as partial, temporary, working, or provisional truths. Truth is not 'stagnant', and, therefore, James (1907/1995, p. 86) stated that we must 'be ready tomorrow to call it falsehood'.

Peirce would disagree, with the others, that to call something true is just to list it as a present resource for inquiry.

- Peirce was a conceptual realist, but James was a conceptual nominalist. For example, some concepts and variables were real for Peirce, whereas these were abstract constructions for James who was focused on particulars.
- According only to Rorty, warrant or justification comes by conversation that leads to seemingly better linguistic devices, rather than from experience or satisfaction of the conditions that initiated the initial research problem.
- In contrast to the other pragmatists who would argue that language is a tool, Rorty would contend that there is nothing beyond language that can be appealed to in philosophical argument. This is Rorty's linguistic turn. Actually, Peirce also was a forerunner of the linguistic turn with his semiotic turn. He would, however, object to Rorty, pointing out that Rorty's notion of language is far too limited and primitive.
- Regarding inquiry, Rorty contended that no specific methods or patterns of inquiry are discoverable.
- The other pragmatists disagreed with Rorty's contention that the best we can do in science is to have useful conversations.
- Versions of the pragmatic maxim were keys to the thought of Peirce and James, but not the other pragmatists; also, for Peirce the maxim was a theory of meaning; however, for James, it was a theory of (determining) truth.
- Dewey and Rorty emphasized social justice in many of their writings; they explicitly endorsed shared values such as democracy, freedom, equality, and progress.

APPLICATIONS TO MIXED METHODS RESEARCH

Mixed methods research must navigate (and thrive on) many intellectual tensions and dualisms (Johnson, 2016). The pragmatists (especially Dewey) were anti-dualists, and provided alternative logics. Here are some of the many dualisms that pragmatism can help navigate by using a 'both-and' logic rather than an either-or logic: (a) micro versus macro level of reality; (b) subjective/intersubjective versus objective reality; (c) emic versus etic viewpoints; (d) categories versus variables; (e) facts versus values; (f) value embedded versus value neutral research; (g) agency versus structure as causal factors; (h) change versus order; (i) constructivism versus realism; (j) perspective versus truth; (k) human science versus natural science; (l) idealism versus physicalism/materialism; (m) knowledge versus wisdom; (n) particulars versus universals; (o) rationalism versus empiricism; (p) relativism versus absolutism; (q) humanism versus scientific naturalism; (r) freedom versus equality; (s) reason versus creative 'imagination'; (t) local needs versus national needs; (u) means versus ends; (v) similarity versus difference; and (w) single versus multiple logics such as induction, deduction, abduction, dialectic, dialogic, and critical. By interacting with the poles on these dualisms and finding a third approach or synthesis or balance, mixed methods research relying on pragmatism offers a larger and more complex type of research (Johnson, 2016).

Following are some added values that pragmatism brings to MMR: (a) pragmatism justifies the compatibility thesis and mixing and matching of qualitative and quantitative methods, methodologies, and paradigms. It asks the key empirical question 'Does it work?' It also justifies the use of multiple purposes even if they appear to conflict or to suggest different epistemologies; (b) pragmatism emphasizes practical theory (that is, emphasizes the construction of theory that understands context and is likely to work locally); (c) pragmatism is a philosophy of freedom to do what works, rather than being controlled by dogmatic a priori claims of what can and cannot be done in research; (d) pragmatism supports the fundamental principle articulated by Johnson and Christensen (and Onwuegbuzie) 2017 (p. 51), which 'advises researchers to thoughtfully and strategically mix or combine qualitative and quantitative research methods, approaches, procedures, concepts, and other paradigm characteristics in a way that produces an overall design with multiple (divergent and convergent) and complementary (broadly viewed) strengths and nonoverlapping weaknesses'; (e) pragmatism focuses on problem solving via research and practice; (f) pragmatism provides a flexible philosophy, supporting emergence in design and conduct of research; (g) pragmatism is open to creative combinations with additional paradigms (for example, transformative-pragmatism, critical realist-pragmatism, constructivist-pragmatism).

There are some similarities among combinations of the four pragmatists with regard to axiomatic/assumptive components (that is, ontology, epistemology, axiology, and methodology) that we have highlighted in this chapter. The fact that several differences prevail among these brands of pragmatism supports the contention of methodologists (for example, Johnson and Onwuegbuzie, 2004; Johnson et al., 2007) that there are multiple types of pragmatism, which, in turn, means that as an overarching research philosophy, pragmatism is highly inclusive. This inclusiveness may afford researchers more flexibility when conducting MMR, compared to other prevailing research philosophies used in MMR, such as the critical realist orientation (Houston, 2001; Maxwell, 2004; McEvoy and Richards, 2003, 2006), anti-conflationist philosophy (Bryman, 1992; Hammersley, 1992; Layder, 1993; Roberts, 2002), complementary strengths stance (Brewer and Hunter, 1989; Morse, 2003), transformative-emancipatory stance (Mertens, 2003), a-paradigmatic stance (Patton, 2002; Reichardt and Cook, 1979), substantive theory stance (Chen, 2006), and communities of practice stance (Denscombe, 2008) – although it should be acknowledged that each of these other research philosophies plays a very important role in MMR. The only philosophical approach in MMR that is more inclusive than pragmatism is dialectical pluralism (see Johnson, 2016).

As evidenced in this chapter, pragmatism promotes a multiple approach to MMR, allowing MM researchers to utilize a both/and logic that is non-dogmatic, non-skeptic, anti-dualistic, eclectic, and pluralistic by conducting qualitatively driven, quantitatively driven, and equal-status MMR. It should be noted here that within each of these three major kinds of MMR there is a multiplicity of MMR designs, such that these three MMR types lie on an interactive continuum, with qualitatively driven MMR and quantitatively driven MMR being situated at the opposite ends of the continuum, and equal-status MMR lying between these two poles. Thus, via a pragmatist lens, as noted by Johnson and Onwuegbuzie (2004, p. 20), 'Ultimately, the possible number of ways that studies can involve mixing is very large … [and] truly opens up an exciting and almost unlimited potential for future research'. Thus, it should not be surprising that pragmatism, in some form, remains the dominant research philosophy used by MM researchers.

REFERENCES

Brandom, R. B. (Ed.) (2001). *Rorty and his Critics*. Malden, MA: Blackwell.
Brewer, J., and Hunter, A. (1989). *Multimethod Research*. Thousand Oaks, CA: Sage.
Bryman, A. (1992). Quantitative and qualitative research: further reflections on their integration. In J. Brannen (Ed.) *Mixing Methods: Qualitative and quantitative research* (pp. 89–111). Aldershot: Avebury Press.
Chen, H. T. (2006). A theory-driven evaluation perspective on mixed methods research. *Research in the Schools*, 13(1), 75–83.
Denscombe, M. (2008). Communities of practice: a research paradigm for the mixed methods approach. *Journal of Mixed Methods Research*, 2, 270–283.

Denzin, N. K. (2010). Moments, mixed methods, and paradigm dialogs. *Qualitative Inquiry*, 16, 419–427.

Denzin, N. (2012). Triangulation 2.0. *Journal of Mixed Methods Research*, 6, 80–88.

Dewey, J. (1920). Reconstruction in philosophy. In Jo Ann Boydston (Ed.) *The Middle Works (1899–1924)* (pp. 77–201). Carbondale, IL: Southern Illinois University Press.

Dewey, J. (1969–1972). *John Dewey: The early works* (5 vols.). Carbondale, IL: Southern Illinois University Press.

Dewey, J. (1976–1988). John Dewey: *The Middle Works* (15 vols). Carbondale, IL: Southern Illinois University Press.

Dewey, J. (1981–1991). *John Dewey: The Later Works* (17 vols). Carbondale, IL: Southern Illinois University Press.

Haack, S. (1998). *Manifesto of a Passionate Moderate: Unfashionable essay*. Chicago, IL: University of Chicago Press.

Hammersley, M. (1992). Deconstructing the qualitative–quantitative divide. In J. Brannen (Ed.) *Mixing Methods: Qualitative and quantitative research* (pp. 39–55). Aldershot: Avebury Press.

Hildebrand, D. (2008). *Dewey*. Oxford, England: Oneworld Publications.

Houston, S. (2001). Beyond social constructionism: critical realism and social work. *British Journal of Social Work*, 31, 845–861.

James, W. (1992 [1891]). *The Moral Philosopher and the Moral Life*. New York, NY: Library of America.

James, W. (1902/1994). *The Varieties of Religious Experience*. New York. Modern Library.

James, W. (1907/1995). *Pragmatism*. Toronto, Canada: Dover Books.

James, W. (1909) *A Pluralistic Universe*. Reprinted 1996, Lincoln Nebraska: University of Nebraska Press.

James, W. (1912). *Essays in Radical Empiricism*. New York, NY: Longmans, Green, and Co.

Johnson, R. B. (2016). (OnlineFirst, waiting for volume and issue). Dialectical pluralism: A metaparadigm whose time has come. *Journal of Mixed Methods Research*, 1–18, doi:10.1177/1558689815607692

Johnson, R. B., and Christensen, L. B. (2017). *Educational research: Quantitative, qualitative, and mixed approaches* (6th ed.). Los Angeles, CA: Sage.

Johnson, R. B., and Onwuegbuzie, A. J. (2004). Mixed methods research: a research paradigm whose time has come. *Educational Researcher*, 33(7), 14–26.

Johnson, R. B., Onwuegbuzie, A. J., and Turner, L. A. (2007). Toward a definition of mixed methods research. *Journal of Mixed Methods Research*, 1, 112–133.

Layder, D. (1993) *New Strategies in Social Research: An introduction and guide*. Cambridge: Polity Press.

Lincoln, Y. S. (2009). 'What a long, strange trip it's been...': Twenty-five years of qualitative and new paradigm research. *Qualitative Inquiry*, 16, 3–9.

Maxwell, J. A. (2004). *Realism as a stance for mixed methods research*. Paper presented at the annual meeting of the American Educational Research Association, San Diego, CA.

McDermott, J. J. (1977). *The Writings of William James: A comprehensive edition*. Chicago: IL: University of Chicago Press.

McEvoy, P., and Richards, D. (2003). Critical realism: a way forward for evaluation research in nursing? *Journal of Advanced Nursing*, 43, 411–420.

McEvoy, P., and Richards, D. (2006). A critical realist rationale for using a combination of quantitative and qualitative methods. *Journal of Research in Nursing*, 11, 66–78.

Menand, L. (1997). *Pragmatism: a reader*. New York, NY: Vintage Books.

Mertens, D. (2003). Mixed methods and the politics of human research: the transformative-emancipatory perspective. In A. Tashakkori and C. Teddlie (Eds)

Handbook of Mixed Methods in Social and Behavioral Research (pp. 135–164). Thousand Oaks, CA: Sage.

Morse, J. M. (2003). Principles of mixed methods and multimethod research design. In A. Tashakkori and C. Teddlie (Eds) *Handbook of Mixed Methods in Social and Behavioral Research* (pp. 189–208). Thousand Oaks, CA: Sage.

Patton, M. Q. (2002). *Qualitative Research and Evaluation Methods*. Thousand Oaks, CA: Sage.

Peirce, C. S. (1868). Some consequences of four incapacities. *Journal of Speculative Philosophy*, 2, 140–157.

Peirce, C. S. (1877). The fixation of belief. *Popular Science Monthly*, 12, 1–15.

Peirce, C. S. (1878a). How to make our ideas clear. *Popular Science Monthly*, 12, 286–302.

Peirce, C. S. (1878b), The doctrine of chances. *Popular Science Monthly*, 12, 604–615.

Peirce, C. S. (1931–1958). *Collected Papers of Charles Sanders Peirce*. C. Hartshorne, P. Weiss, and A, Burks (Eds). Cambridge, MA: Harvard University Press. Referred to by volume and section number.

Peirce, C. S. (1998a). *The Essential Peirce: Selected philosophical writings*, vol. 2. Bloomington, IN: Indiana University Press.

Peirce, C. S. (1998b). Immortality in the light of synechism. In *The Essential Peirce* (vol. 2) (pp. 1–10). Bloomington, IN: Indiana University Press (original work published 1893).

Peirce, C. S. (2014) *Illustrations of the Logic of Science*. Cornelis de Waal (Ed.) Chicago, IL: Open Court.

Perry, R. B. (1935). *The Thought and Character of William James*, vol. 1. Boston, MA: Little, Brown.

Putnam, H. (1981). *Reason, Truth and History*. Cambridge: Cambridge University Press.

Reichardt, C. S., and Cook, T. D. (1979). Beyond qualitative versus quantitative methods. In T. D. Cook and C. S. Reichardt (Eds) *Qualitative and Quantitative Methods in Evaluation Research* (pp. 7–32). Thousand Oaks, CA: Sage.

Roberts, A. (2002). A principled complementarity of method: in defence of methodological eclecticism and the qualitative–qualitative debate. *The Qualitative Report*, 7(3). Retrieved on July 7, 2016 from www.nova.edu/ssss/QR/QR7–3/roberts.html.

Robin, R. (1967). *Annotated Catalogue of the Papers of Charles S. Peirce*. Amherst: University of Massachusetts Press.

Rorty, R. (1979). *Philosophy and the Mirror of Nature*. Princeton, NJ: Princeton University Press.

Rorty, R. (1980). *Philosophy and the Mirror of Nature*. Oxford: Oxford University Press.

Rorty, R. (1982). *Consequences of Pragmatism*. Minneapolis, MN: University of Minnesota Press.

Rorty, R. (1989). *Contingency, Irony, and Solidarity*. Cambridge: Cambridge University Press.

Rorty, R. (1991). *Objectivity, Relativism, and Truth*. Cambridge: Cambridge University Press.

Rorty, R. (1999). *Philosophy and Social Hope*. London, England: Penguin.

Rorty, R. (2009). *Philosophy and the Mirror of Nature*. Princeton, NJ: Princeton University Press.

Scheffler, I. (1974). *Four Pragmatists: A Critical Introduction to Peirce, James, Mead, and Dewey*. London: Routledge & Kegan Paul.

Taylor, E. (1996). *William James on Consciousness Beyond the Margin*. Princeton, NJ: Princeton University Press.

13

Sampling Decisions in Educational Research

Kathleen M. T. Collins

The researcher's underlying intention when conceptualizing educational research is to conduct high-quality research, in which the design is defensible, the research process transparent, the outcomes justified, and the conclusions are viewed as relevant by the research consumer (Collins, 2015). Also contributing to the conduct of high-quality research is the transparency of the logic underpinning researchers' sampling decisions, and the degree that the resulting sampling design (that is, sampling scheme and sample size) will provide an adequate sample to address the research question.

However, the reality of conducting educational research in practical contexts can be compromised by multifaceted situational contexts and the inquiry's evolving positioning as it progresses through the research process (Berliner, 2002; Greene, 2012). There are several critical decisions involved in traversing successfully these stages; one example is the intertwined decision of deciding the sample design and responding to sampling challenges when implementing the design in practice. It is this intertwined decision that is the topic of this chapter.

Typically, sampling decisions are viewed as decisions made to implement procedures to attain efficiently estimates of a population and to select cases based on specific criteria. However, the reality of educational research in practice requires the researcher to make a series of sampling decisions at different stages of the research process. My perspective and the premise guiding this chapter is that these decisions are influenced by the researcher's ontological and epistemological assumptions about what constitutes credible data, and that data are created by the researcher – not simply collected. Rather, data construction is filtered by the researcher's experiences, qualifications, beliefs, and motivations for exploring the research topic, all of which are influenced by the context surrounding the inquiry (Malterud, 2001; Maxwell, 2010; Sandelowski et al., 2009).

ORGANIZATION OF THE CHAPTER

To structure this discussion, examples of sampling decisions accompanied by sampling criteria are outlined at the following stages of the research process: conceptualization, design, implementation, and outcome. Also presented are selective examples of sampling challenges and recommended responses to these challenges are discussed. To support points made in the chapter and as illustrative applications of sampling designs in practice, selective examples of decisions about sampling designs are embedded throughout the chapter.

Sampling decisions and sampling criteria

Conceptualization stage

Goal. At this point, the researcher identifies the aim of the study, the stakeholders and the sample characteristics of interest (Collins, 2015). In quantitative research, samples, (for example, individuals, contexts, groups, observations, events) are selected to be representative of the characteristics of interest in the target population within the known boundaries of sampling error (Shadish et al., 2002). The selection process is designed to minimize the likelihood of obtaining faulty relationships (type 1 error) or missing relationships (type 2 error).

The goal is to select a representative sample. The process begins by defining the target population, and identifying the accessible population, which the researcher has reasonable access. The sampling frame is then delineated to list all elements in the selected population. Typically, probability sampling schemes are used to ensure that every member of the selected population has an equal chance of selection. Sample size is determined by a power analysis using a software package such as G Power or consulting published tables (cf. Krejcie and Morgan, 1970).

The goal of qualitative sampling is based on the concept of 'sampling for meaning', and its logic is evident in four distinct ways (Luborsky and Rubinstein, 1995, p. 6). First, the individual's perspective is context-specific and contains referential interpretations based on similar and dissimilar events in the individual person's life. Second, the individual's interpretations are based experientially, and these experiences are not fixed entities; rather they evolve as the individual is immersed in the lifecycle. Third, the relationship between researcher and participant also is context specific, and can provide stimuli toward prompting a discussion of the topic that might not have occurred independent of the relationship. Last, participant's level of interpretation is affected by sociocultural standards comprising culture and community standards.

Sample selection begins by developing a sampling boundary to delimit the number of cases and to select a sample that is information-rich thereby increasing the likelihood of reaching saturation (Lincoln and Guba, 1985). However, to achieve saturation with less number of cases, it is advisable to narrow extraneous characteristics, not pertinent to the study's focus (Guest et al., 2006). Sample selection is made, typically, using purposive sampling schemes defined by specific criteria. However, random selection of the sample can be used to select a criterion sample to minimize selection bias (Miles et al., 2014).

Combining results from the cycles of data collection and analyses occurring within the quantitative and qualitative phases is characteristic of mixed research[1] and multiple methods designs. The rationale is that multiple approaches accompanied by multiple data sources will provide a broader interpretation of a topic in contrast to using one approach and one method. The goal in mixed research is to integrate conclusions derived from the quantitative and qualitative phases at the outcome stage, and, depending on the design, at other stages of the research process. The degree that this goal is achieved is predicated on addressing the goals of quantitative and qualitative sampling when designing the mixed and multiple methods research studies.

Objective. The objective is the researcher's decision about generalizing the results, and this decision is shaped by the goals underpinning quantitative and qualitative research. Researcher's choice of generalization lies at a point on a particularistic-universalistic continuum (Onwuegbuzie et al., 2009). This continuum is anchored at one end by particularistic generalizations that are formed based on investigated phenomena that can be applied to a specific context, such as single classroom or only to the participants involved in that particular study. The other end of the continuum represents universalistic generalizations that are formed based on phenomena that can be applied more broadly, to contexts other than the context of the study and to individuals other than the study's participants. Midpoint on the continuum represents phenomena that can be generalized to a specific context such as a primary or elementary level classroom in a specific school, and, depending on the sampling design, results also can be generalized to multiple primary or elementary level classrooms in multiple schools. Table 13.1 specifies seven types of generalizations.

Rationale and Purpose. The rationale for developing the sample design is filtered by the researcher's preference for one data approach involving the use of variables and correlations (that is, variance theory [Mohr, 1982]) or the preference for the alternative data approach involving events and processes surrounding these events (that is, process theory [Mohr, 1982]). The sampling purpose reflects the degree that the sample design is aligned to the assumptions underpinning probability sampling and purposive sampling.

Probability Sampling. One assumption underlining probability sampling is that the selected sampling unit has a known probability of being selected and this probability provides the basis for the inference to generalize (that is, external

Table 13.1 Types of generalizations and definitions

Types	Definition
External Statistical Generalization	Assuming the number of sampling units is representative of the characteristics of interest in the population, units are selected randomly, and data are analyzed using statistical techniques, will allow the researcher to apply external statistical generalizations to the target population. (i.e., universalistic generalization).
Internal Statistical Generalization (Onwuegbuzie and Leech, 2007)	Data generated from a subset of respondents who are representative of the sample, are key informants, data are analyzed statistically, and the conclusions are generalized only to that particular sample (i.e., particularistic generalization).
Moderatum Generalization (Payne and Williams, 2005)	Occurrences in everyday existence are generalized pragmatically to similar contexts based on the individual's personal experiences, thereby 'bringing a semblance of order and consistency to social interaction, [and] make everyday life possible (Payne and Williams, 2005, p. 296).
Internal Generalization Maxwell (1992)	Findings are generalized to the sample that participated in the study.
Analytic Generalization (Yin, 2014)	Findings generated from a case study design are generalized to other contexts based on theory or logical argument.
Case-to-Case Transfer Generalization (Firestone, 1993)	Case findings are generalized to other cases based on the degree of similarity between the cases.
Naturalistic Generalization (Stake, 2005)	Stakeholders interpret the findings based on their own personal or vicarious experiences, and use these experiences to determine the degree that the findings are generalized or applicable to other contexts.

statistical generalization to the target population) (Lohr, 2010). Another assumption is that the sample is selected randomly using a probabilistic sample scheme to minimize systemic error (Lohr, 2010). A third assumption is that the sample units are similar to each other, and that the population characteristics can be represented by the selected sample (Lohr, 2010).

Purposive Sampling. One assumption underlying purposive sampling is that the sampling scheme will prompt discovery of the informant's insider perspective on specific dimensions of interest. Sample selection can result in a sample that is homogeneous or heterogeneous with respect to these dimensions (Sofaer, 2002). Sample selection criteria are based on whether the researcher is examining informants' shared experiences or their unique experiences (Sofaer, 2002). Another assumption is that the selected sample will generate quality data. Too large a sample introduces logistical problems in managing a large dataset, and too small a sample can compromise saturation and theory development (for example, grounded theory) (Lincoln and Guba, 1985; Miles et al., 2014). To guide decisions about sample selection, researchers can conduct prebriefing interviews of potential participants, as part of the selection process, to screen if the sample is relevant toward addressing the research question (Collins et al., 2006b).

Design stage

In quantitative research, probability sampling is used to select randomly a sample representative of the target population. Purposive sampling schemes are used in quantitative research when a probability scheme is not viable as in the case of a population considered difficult to access. One strategy is using snow-balling sampling to obtain a sample recruited from referrals. Rosenberg et al. (2015) designed a study to tested components of goal disruption theory to inves-tigate mental health of military personnel. The potential stigma surrounding any discussion of mental health prompted these investigators to use a snowballing sampling scheme to recruit their sample. Representative sample size in quantita-tive research is determined prior to collecting data, as noted earlier in the chapter, by conducting a power analysis using a software package such as G Power or consulting published tables (cf. Krejcie and Morgan, 1970).

In qualitative research, purposive sampling schemes are used to select a sam-ple based on specific criteria. The sample size evolves as the researcher strives to attain saturation using sequential cycles of data collection, analysis, and interpre-tation. These cycles continue to the point that sampling further will not generate additional information (Glaser and Strauss, 1967; Lincoln and Guba, 1985).

In multisite research, the process of selecting the sites, typically, is discussed minimally in the reporting of the study, a point made by Sharp et al. (2012). These researchers addressed this point in their multisite longitudinal study. Sharp et al. (2012) used a four-stage sequential (that is, each preceding stage impacted a subsequent stage) mixed research approach to select their high school sample. Sharp et al. (2012) developed their sampling design using a MaxMinCon strategy proposed by Tashakkori and Teddlie (1998). This strategy was used to maximize and minimize specific site characteristics and to minimize sampling error by controlling extraneous variables. At each stage, schools were selected based on site characteristics, and collection and analysis of quantitative and qualitative data obtained at the schools across the stages led to the selection of a sample of eight schools. The site selection process was transparent and ensured that the collection and analysis processes were 'practical, contextual, responsive and consequential' leading to defensible outcomes (Datta, 1997, as cited in Sharp et al., 2012, p. 49).

In mixed research, the sample design per phase can facilitate or can limit the degree that inferences can be made approximately equally from results generated in the quantitative and qualitative phases. For example, in a hypothetical study that has two phases of data collection, a randomly selected sample (n = 100) partici-pated in the quantitative phase (phase one) by completing a detailed questionnaire assessing anxiety levels when enrolled in research courses. In phase two, the researcher selected a criterion sample comprised of 20 percent of the sample of 100 to participate in interviews. The disparity in the two sample sizes (100, 20), and the type of scheme[s] used for selection (probability, purposive) can compromise successful integration at the conclusion stage and affect the generalizability of the findings. To address these issues, researchers can implement a 'representativeness/saturation tradeoff' by placing more emphasis or weight on the results generated from one phrase in contrast to the other phase when drawing inferences (Teddlie and Tashakkori, 2009, p. 184). A second recommendation is to identify the relationship between the samples participating in each phase of the study. Onwuegbuzie and Collins (2007) provide four examples of possible relationships between the samples. Identical relationship indicates that the same sampling units participated in each phase of the study. A parallel relationship indicates that samples in each phase are different but are chosen from the same population. Nested sample relationship indicates that sample in one phase serves as the source for selecting a subset of sampling units to participate in another phase. Multilevel sampling relationship specifies that each sample per phase comprises different sampling units, and each sample has a hierarchical level of engagement with the variable of interest, such as superintendents, principals, and teachers. Specifying the relationship can add to the transparency of the sampling design and credibility to the conclusions and generalizations. In studies using transformed data, the sample size is a critical part of the decision to implement the transformation. Transformation refers to the process of converting quantitative data into qualitative data that can be analyzed using qualitative techniques and/or converting qualitative codes or themes into numerical data and analyzed using statistical techniques (Tashakkori and Teddlie, 1998). Sample size affects the type of analyses possible in terms of having a sufficient sample size to permit the use of advanced data analytical techniques associated with quantitative research, and or allowing a more detailed qualitative analysis, as in the cases of Q methodology, Q factor analysis (cf. Newman and Ramlo, 2010) and correspondence analysis (cf. Maltseva, 2016).

Implementation stage

At the implementation stage, sampling schemes accompanied by sample sizes guide the data collection process. Researchers make decisions about data in terms of collection, analysis, validation, and interpretation. The sampling design directs the data collection activities and the quality of data collected is related to the type(s) of sampling schemes used to select the sampling units, and the number of sampling units to meet the requirements of power, saturation, and transformation. At this stage, the researcher might adapt the sampling design to accommodate the practical aspects of conducting educational research in practice.

Outcome stage

At the outcome stage, the study is documented and decisions made throughout the research process are detailed for the research consumer. At this point, any changes to the initial sampling design, such as attrition, that occurred as the study progressed are discussed, and included in that discussion are details specifying how these changes impact or limit the conclusion(s) and generalization(s).

Examples of sampling challenges

In this section, discussed are the challenges of selecting a representative sample, selecting samples that lead to successful integration of results and inferences, and meeting ethical responsibilities when engaging with participants and the members of the research team.

Challenge of representation

In quantitative research, the concept of representation is related to the concept of statistical inference, and the goal of selecting a representative sample is to generalize conclusions to the target population (Kruskal and Mosteller, 1979a). In qualitative research, the concept of representation is related to the concept of transferability, and goal of selecting a representative sample is to generalize or apply the conclusions to other individuals or contexts (Lincoln and Guba, 1985).

Kruskal and Mosteller (1979a, 1979b) point out that without providing details about the sampling design, and, stating only the term representative sample in the narrative, could imply a 'seal of approval' that the sample is representative of the target population (Kruskal and Mosteller, 1979a, p. 14). Kruskal and Mosteller (1979a, 1979b) also note variation of interpretations of representative sample. For example, a representative sample can be interpreted as 'miniature or small replica of the population', or 'typical of the population' and, typical could be further explained 'in terms of the average, the mode, the ideal', or 'coverage of a population'. Interpretation of coverage could be further delineated as 'heterogeneity' or 'inclusion of extreme cases' or coverage could be interpreted as 'partitioning a population into disjoint classes [that are] regarded as homogeneous' but not necessarily represented proportionately (Kruskal and Mosteller, 1979a, 1979b, p. 14). They recommend researchers define their interpretations of representative, use probability sample schemes to narrow unwanted variability, and identify the specific sampling schemes.

Selection Bias. Selection bias can occur due to the researcher's own unintended biases (Lohr, 2010). For example, Luborsky and Rubinstein (1995) note that cultural values define researchers' perceptions of representation, and these perceptions impact the degree that proportional representation of minority persons is addressed in sample selection. Selection bias also occurs using judgment samples (that is, researcher uses his or her judgment to select the sample) and convenience samples (that is, sampling unit is handily available). Selection decisions in both cases lack a theoretical rationalization and compromise the quality of data by not positioning it within a theoretical framework (Walford, 2001). Also, these selection decisions compromise representation because the sample members might be dissimilar to the target population (Lohr, 2010).

Generalizing from events and activities that are observed by researchers when they are present, assuming their presence is not continuous, could lead to flawed conclusions because the selective viewing of events and activities might not be representative of the pattern of events or activities characterizing the topic of interest (Miles et al., 2014). Sampling bias also can occur when researchers select participants who are willing to participate, or who are perceived as 'articulate, insightful, attractive, and intellectually responsive' or who are selected because they are key informants. Bias can occur if the participants' perspectives are not representative of the actual variability occurring within the population of interest (Sankoff, 1971 as cited in Maxwell, 2010; Miles et al., 2014, p. 295).

To address these issues, Miles et al. (2014) recommend increasing the number of cases and including cases that represent alternative perspectives, such as negative cases, for contrasting purposes. Other strategies are to select randomly individuals, events, and activities to observe and organize data based on these selections into a matrix. This matrix can be used to review the observed cases to detect a potential pattern of missing information (Miles et al., 2014).

Attrition. Although, all designs can be affected by attrition, longitudinal studies, in particular, are affected due to the study's length of time and number of contacts for data collection. Number of data points and length of collection can be perceived as 'burdensome or invasive', a point addressed by Boyden and James (2014, p. 21) in their longitudinal study; specifically, they minimized the number and length of visits, and the number of data collection instruments. Gay et al. (2012) point out that dropouts typically occur in the treatment group because participation in the treatment requires effort and control group participation requires little or no effort. Hypothetically, dropouts might be less motivated individuals, and, this is problematic because the treatment group now represents a group higher in motivation in contrast to the control group (Gay et al., 2012). Subsequently, information about attrition should be reported in the write-up of the study and discussed as a potential limitation.

Challenge of integration

The degree that the researcher integrates results of each approach into inferences that are supported by the research design is a characteristic of high-quality research (Collins, 2015). Typically, integration is interpreted as triangulation. Triangulation is an iterative process of comparing and contrasting theories, data generated by different methods, and different perspectives introduced by using investigators who might have differing ontological and epistemological assumptions about research (Denzin, 2009). One or more of these definitions of triangulation shape the research process and the outcomes leading to the integration of knowledge. However, triangulation as the purpose for mixing approaches can be conceptualized in different ways.

Bazeley and Kemp (2012) point out that triangulation can serve the purpose of validation, which occurs when the results converge, or complementarity, which occurs when integration of results leads to broader insights and more complex interpretations of the topic of interest. Another purpose is divergence, which occurs when the researcher is looking for findings that contradict leading potentially to different types of research questions or topics to explore (Greene, 2007). Torrance (2012) recommends interpreting respondent validation or member check as a form of triangulation. Asking participants to review initial data collected, such as interview transcripts and/or video of events can validate that the data are representative of their perspectives. Member validation can be extended to asking participants to review preliminary analysis and the emerging draft of the findings (Creswell, 2013; Torrance, 2012). In the event that there is a discrepancy, the dissention can be addressed, and, if not resolved, can be noted as a point of dissention in the report of findings (Lincoln and Guba, 1985; Torrance, 2012).

Interpretive Consistency. In designs involving cycles of data collection and analysis, the degree that the sample design per cycle supports the integration of inferences is defined as interpretive consistency, and it is another defining characteristic of high-quality research (Collins, 2015; Collins et al., 2006a). Interpretive consistency is the consistency between the sampling design and the credibility of the researcher's inferences and chosen generalizations.

To address interpretive consistency, a researcher can use an identical sample in all phases or implement a 'representativeness/saturation tradeoff' (Teddlie and Tashakkori, 2009, p. 184), as discussed earlier in the chapter. The generalization chosen by the researcher guides this decision. Expanding on the hypothetical example used earlier in the chapter, phase one a randomly selected sample (n = 100) participated in the quantitative component, and phase two, 20 individuals selected from the 100 participated in the qualitative component. If the researcher wanted to draw external statistical generalizations, she or he would place emphasis on the quantitative results due to the use of a random sampling scheme and a sample size of 100. However, the researcher also could have more than one generalization. Continuing with this hypothetical example, the researcher also is interested in specific demographics, and the degree that these demographics affect participants' perspectives. Subsequently, to select the subgroup of 20, the researcher used a stratified purposeful sample to obtain homogeneous subgroups representing the specific demographics. The researcher integrated the findings into a synthesis, and avoided interpretive inconsistency by choosing case-to-case transfer generalization of the qualitative findings and external statistical generalization of the quantitative results.

Challenge of ethics

The challenge of ethics evolves around the relationships between researchers and multilevel stakeholders, including participants, practitioners, and policy-makers. This challenge also extends to the relationships between researchers collaborating on a study who are members of different intellectual communities, and who view the study's design and conclusions through the lens of their selected community and area of expertise. Examples of intellectual communities are traditional scientific research, social construction/constructivist interpretivist research, artistic/evocative research, critical change research, and program evaluation research (Patton, 2015). Other examples of intellectual communities are emergent communities comprised of mixed researchers, interdisciplinary researchers, interparadigmatic researchers, and action researchers (Collins et al., 2012).

A diverse array of expertise can be an asset – assuming team members have discussed their philosophical standpoints, and the team has reached a consensus about moving forward in designing the study. In the case of mixed research and multiple methods research, this consensus also supports integration of results and inferences. Tensions can occur when the integration of findings from qualitative and quantitative phases present contradictions or inconsistences. On one hand, these contradictions and inconsistences can lead to what Thomas Cook (1985) called an 'empirical puzzle – a puzzle that warrants further investigative analysis' (as cited in Greene, 2007, p. 103). On the other hand, these contradictions and inconsistencies can occur when there is an imbalance between the presentation of emic (that is, members of a group participating in the study) and etic (that is, individual researcher or team of researchers) perspectives in the final report. Implementing member checking and debriefing interviews of the researcher or research team to ask questions identifying areas of potential bias can address this challenge (cf. Onwuegbuzie, et al., 2010 for examples of questions).

Sample selection can present an ethical challenge as the researcher balances the responsibility of ensuring the participants' rights (for example, voluntary participation, informed consent, anonymity, confidentiality, risk minimization), and developing a sample design to achieve credible outcomes and generalizations (Dattalo, 2010). Preferential selection of specific sampling methods over other methods by the researcher could present 'methodological privileging' and limit potentially the 'possibilities of the inquiry' (Preissle et al., 2015, p. 150). Participants respond to stimuli based on the 'meaning that these things have for them not on the basis of the meaning that these things have for the outside scholar' (Blumer, 1969, p. 51, as quoted in Torrance, 2012). An ethical dilemma can occur when participants are included because they present a specific perspective of interest to the researcher, and, other potential participants are excluded because they do not share this perspective, leading to compromised results and inferences.

CONCLUSION

This chapter began with a discussion of the inter-related points of high-quality research, complexity of doing educational research in practice, and, the intertwined decision of deciding the sample design and responding to sampling challenges. In this chapter, sampling was discussed as a series of decisions made by the researcher across the research process, and these decisions are influenced by ontological and epistemological assumptions about what constitutes credible data.

The reader was presented with examples of sampling designs accompanied by sampling criteria applicable for quantitative, qualitative, mixed and multiple methods designs. Sampling issues related to representation, integration, and ethics were presented to illustrate the complexity of creating sampling designs in educational research contexts.

The specificity of the researcher's language when describing a representative sample and defining triangulation as a purpose for integration was noted as important toward explicating the logic underpinning sampling decisions, and enhancing credibility of results. Interpretive consistency was discussed illustrate how sampling design contributes to successful integration.

Ethics was presented in the context of relationships and researchers' responsibilities toward protecting participants' rights. An important part of this conversation was how researchers' philosophical standpoints impact team collaboration when designing the research and interpreting data leading to the balanced reporting of results. I hope that this chapter's content will contribute to the conversation surrounding sampling decisions in educational research.

Note

1   Although, the term mixed methods research is used most frequently to define the process of mixing approaches, the term mixed research is used in this chapter because mixed research designs are not just about methods. Mixed research is also about philosophy and values. Therefore, the term mixed research encapsulates the breadth and depth of the process of mixing approaches.

REFERENCES

Bazeley, P., and Kemp, L. (2012). Mosaics, triangles, and DNA: metaphors for integrated analysis in mixed methods research. *Journal of Mixed Methods Research*, 6, 55–72.

Berliner, D. C. (2002). Comment: Educational research: the hardest science of all. *Educational Researcher*, 31(8), 18–20.

Boyden, J., and James, Z. (2014). Schooling, childhood poverty and international development: choices and challenges in a longitudinal study. *Oxford Review of Education*, 40(1), 10–29.

Collins, K. M. T. (2015). Validity in multimethod and mixed research. In S. Hesse-Biber and R. B. Johnson (Eds) *The Oxford Handbook of Multimethod and Mixed Methods Research Inquiry* (pp. 240–256). New York: Oxford University Press.

Collins, K. M. T., Onwuegbuzie, A. J., and Jiao, Q. G. (2006a). Prevalence of mixed methods sampling designs in social science research. *Evaluation and Research in Education*, 19(2), 83–101.

Collins, K. M. T., Onwuegbuzie, A. J., and Johnson, R. B. (2012). Securing a place at the table: introducing legitimation criteria for the conduct of mixed research. Special Issue, *American Behavioral Scientist*, 56, 849–865.

Collins, K. M. T., Onwuegbuzie, A. J., and Sutton, I. L. (2006b). A model incorporating the rationale and purpose for conducting mixed methods research in special education and beyond. *Learning Disabilities: A Contemporary Journal*, 4(1), 67–100.

Creswell, J. W. (2013). *Qualitative Inquiry and Research Design: Choosing among five approaches*, 3rd edition. Thousand Oaks, CA: Sage.

Dattalo, P. (2010). Ethical dilemmas in sampling. *Journal of Social Work Values and Ethics*, 7(1). Retrieved on July 7, 2016 from www.socialworker.com/jswve/spring2010/2dattalo.pdf.

Denzin N. K. (2009). *The Research Act: A theoretical introduction to sociological methods*, 4th edition. Piscataway, NJ: Aldine Transaction.

Firestone, W. A. (1993). Alternative arguments for generalizing data as to qualitative research. *Educational Researcher*, 2(4), 16–23.

Gay, L. R., Mills, G. E., and Airasian, P. (2012). *Educational Research: Competencies for analysis and applications*, 10th edition. Upper Saddle River,NJ: Pearson Education.

Glaser, B. G., and Strauss, A. L. (1967). *The Discovery of Grounded Theory: Strategies for qualitative research*. Chicago, IL: Aldine.

Greene, J. C. (2007). *Mixed Methods in Social Inquiry*. San Francisco, CA: Jossey–Bass.

Greene, J. C. (2012). Engaging critical issues in social inquiry by mixing methods. Special Issue, *American Behavioral Scientist*, 56, 755–773.

Guest, G., Bunce, A., and Johnson, L. (2006). How many interviews are enough? An experiment with data saturation and variability. *Field Methods*, 18, 59–82.

Krejcie, R. V., and Morgan, D. W. (1970). Determining the sample size for research activities. *Educational and Psychological Measurement*, 30, 608.

Kruskal, W., and Mosteller, F. (1979a). Representative sampling, I: Nonscientific literature. *International Statistical Review*, 47, 13–24.

Kruskal, W., and Mosteller F. (1979b). Representative sampling II: Scientific literature, excluding statistics. *International Statistical Review*, 47, 111–127.

Lincoln, Y. S., and Guba, E. G. (1985). *Naturalistic Inquiry*. Newbury Park: CA: Sage.

Lohr, S. L. (2010). *Sampling: Design and analysis*, 2nd edition. Boston, MA: Brooks/Cole.

Luborsky, M. R., and Rubinstein, R. L. (1995). Sampling in qualitative research. *Research on Aging*, 17, 89–111.

Malterud, K. (2001). Qualitative research: standards, challenges, and guidelines. *The Lancet*, 358, 483–488.

Maltseva, K. (2016). Using correspondence analysis of scales as part of mixed methods design to access cultural models in ethnographic fieldwork: prosocial cooperation in Sweden. *Journal of Mixed Methods Research*, 10, 82–111.

Maxwell, J. A. (1992). Understanding and validity in qualitative research. *Harvard Educational Review*, 62, 279–300.

Maxwell, J. A. (2010). Using numbers in qualitative research. *Qualitative Inquiry*, 16, 475–482.

Miles, M. B., Huberman, A. M., and Saldaña, L. (2014). Qualitative Data Analysis: A methods sourcebook, 3rd edition. Thousand Oaks, CA: Sage.

Mohr, L. B. (1982). *Explaining Organizational Behavior*. San Francisco, CA: Jossey-Bass.

Newman, I., and Ramlo, S. (2010). Using Q methodology and Q factor analysis in mixed methods research. In A. Tashakkori and C. Teddlie (Eds), *SAGE Handbook of Mixed Methods in Social and Behavioral Research*, 2nd edition (pp. 505–530). Thousand Oaks, CA: Sage.

Onwuegbuzie, A. J., and Collins, K. M. T. (2007). A typology of mixed methods sampling designs in social science research. *The Qualitative Report*, 12, 281–316.

Onwuegbuzie, A. J., and Leech, N. L. (2007). A call for qualitative power analysis. *Quality and Quantity: International Journal of Methodology*, 41(1),105–121.

Onwuegbuzie, A. J., Leech, N. L., and Collins, K. M. T. (2010). Innovative data collection strategies in qualitative research. *The Qualitative Report*, 15, 696–726.

Onwuegbuzie, A. J., Slate, J. R., Leech, N. L., and Collins, K. M. T. (2009). Mixed data analysis: advanced integration techniques. *International Journal of Multiple Research Approaches*, 3, 13–33.

Patton, M. Q. (2015). *Qualitative Evaluation and Research Methods*, 4th edition. Thousand Oaks, CA: Sage.

Payne, G., and Williams, M. (2005). Generalizations in qualitative research. *Sociology*, 39, 295–314.

Preissle, J., Glover-Kudon, R. M., Rohan, E. A., Boehm, J. E., and DeGroff, A. (2015). Putting ethics on the mixed methods map. In S. Hesse-Biber and R. B. Johnson (Eds) *The Oxford Handbook of Multimethod and Mixed Methods Research Inquiry* (pp. 144–163). New York: Oxford University Press.

Rosenberg, B. D., Lewandowski, J. A., and Siegel, J. T. (2015). Goal disruption theory, military personnel, and the creation of merged profiles: a mixed methods investigation. *Journal of Mixed Methods Research*, 9, 51–69.

Sandelowski, M., Voils, C. I., and Knafl, G. (2009). On quantitizing. *Journal of Mixed Methods Research*, 3, 208–222.

Shadish, W. R., Cook, T. D., and Campbell, D. T. (2002). *Experimental and Quasi-Experimental Designs for Generalized Causal Inferences*. Boston, MA: Houghton Mifflin.

Sharp, J. L., Mobley, C., Hammond, C., Withington, C., Drew, S., Stringfield, S., and Stipanovic, N. (2012). A mixed methods sampling methodology for a multisite case study. *Journal of Mixed Methods Research*, 6, 34–54.

Sofaer, S. (2002). Qualitative research methods. *International Journal for Quality in Health Care*, 14, 329–336.

Stake, R. E. (2005). Qualitative case studies. In N. K. Denzin and Y. S. Lincoln (Eds) *The Sage Handbook Of Qualitative Research*, 3rd edition (pp. 443–466). Thousand Oaks, CA: Sage.

Tashakkori, A., and Teddlie, C. (1998). *Mixed Methodology: Combining qualitative and quantitative approaches* (Applied Social Research Methods Series, No. 46). Thousand Oaks, CA: Sage.

Teddlie, C., and Tashakkori, A. (2009). *Foundations of Mixed Methods Research: Integrating quantitative and qualitative approaches in the social and behavioral sciences*. Thousand Oaks, CA: Sage.

Torrance, H. (2012). Triangulation, respondent validation, and democratic participation in mixed methods research. *Journal of Mixed Methods Research*, 6, 111–123.

Walford, G. (2001). Site selection within a comparative case study and ethnographic research. *Compare: A Journal of Comparative and International Education*, 31, 151–164.

Yin, R. K. (2014). *Case Study Research: Design and methods*, 5th edition. Thousand Oaks, CA: Sage.

PART III

Approaches to Research

14

Historical Research

Gary McCulloch

INTRODUCTION

This chapter explores the kinds of engagement with historical sources of evidence that constitutes historical research in the field of education. In doing so, it assesses the kinds of historical sources that can be deployed as evidence to support a fuller understanding of education, and the methodological issues that arise from these (see also McCulloch and Richardson, 2000 for an earlier and more detailed discussion of related issues).

There is first of all a range of published and readily accessible sources that may be used for this purpose. These include published policy reports, records of parliamentary debates, contemporary books and treatises, textbooks, autobiographies, newspapers, periodicals, novels, short stories, children's books, comics, drama, poetry, and art.

Other kinds of evidence may be more difficult to reach, especially unpublished material of different kinds. Archival documentary evidence is well established as a key source of historical data, and the chapter will investigate the uses and limitations of the archive, explaining the impact of recent technological advances in helping archival research. Archives can support the study of educational policy and administration, national and local organisations, and specific educational institutions such as schools and universities. Personal papers and records are also invaluable in biographical studies or life histories. Such unpublished evidence can have considerable advantages over published sources in that they enable the researcher to look behind the scenes to determine motivations and trace the development of arguments and conflicts that may not always become fully public in nature.

The chapter will also review the use of oral sources, visual evidence and physical artefacts in historical research. Oral history, based on interviews with surviving witnesses of historical events, has become an increasingly popular type of historical research, and can have some advantages over a reliance on documentary sources alone (Thompson, 1988). In particular, it can provide a means of exploring the educational experiences of different groups, such as girls and women, ethnic minorities, and disabled people, as well as of former pupils and teachers (Gardner, 2003). Visual history makes use of evidence from paintings, murals, drawings, photography, films, cartoons, television documentaries, and plans. The material conditions or materiality of education also provides significant evidence for historical researchers; for example, buildings, school desks, slates, and many kinds of physical artefacts (Lawn and Grosvenor, 2001).

This chapter will also introduce quantitative sources in historical study. Quantitative methods deploying datasets such as large-scale surveys, census returns, marriage registers and questionnaires supply an important resource for historical research in education, providing an alternative approach to the qualitative studies that are often favoured. Statistical analysis supported by computerised data is the main basis for such research (Carpentier 2008).

In addition, the chapter will provide some examples of combining different kinds of historical sources in investigating a research problem related to education. For instance, it is possible to combine different kinds of documentary sources, or oral and documentary sources, or to use qualitative and quantitative methods as complementary devices. The use of more than one method can address particularly complex and difficult issues, and also a wide range of historical, educational and social scientific problems. A critical awareness and understanding of these aspects of historical evidence is a prerequisite for a historical analysis and interpretation of events and issues in education, and is the main focus of this chapter. The sources that are available for historians define what is possible for them to research. They are severely limited in the amount and type of evidence that they can produce themselves, and must perforce rely on what has survived from the past into the present for them to seek to understand.

There is a range of further issues around historical research in education, outside the scope of the current chapter. It should be borne in mind that this field of research has changed substantially in a number of ways in recent years, and these long-term historiographical developments are discussed elsewhere (see for example McCulloch, 2011b, 2016a). Different ways of interpreting evidence to develop historical arguments are examined for instance in McCulloch (2015). Specific areas of historical research in education are analysed in detail for example in Raftery and Crook (2012), McCulloch (2016b) and McCulloch (2016c). There are some collections of articles that showcase the strongest articles and best practice across a wide range of literature from the past forty years (for example

Lowe, 2000; McCulloch, 2005). Further contributions highlight current trends in the international field especially in the United States (for instance Reese and Rury, 2008; Popkewitz, 2013) and Europe (Depaepe 2012).

DOCUMENTARY SOURCES

Documentary sources are the staple type of evidence used in historical research. A document may be defined briefly as a record of an event or process. Such records may be produced by individuals or groups, and take many different forms. They have been created at another time and by others, rather than in the process of the research or by the researcher. Historians place particular weight on this kind of evidence, especially when it is produced as a direct account at the time and place that they are interested in, and seek to evaluate their worth as historical sources (see also McCulloch, 2004 and 2011a, for more detailed treatments of historical and documentary research).

There is an established difference between primary documents and secondary documents, although this difference is more complex than it may at first appear. Primary documents are produced as a direct record of an event or process by a witness or subject involved in it, and it is this kind of source that historians generally depend on. Secondary documents are formed through an analysis of primary documents to provide an account of the event or process in question, often in relation to others. However, many documents do not fit easily into this basic dichotomy. For example, autobiographies are primary documents by virtue of the author being a witness or participant in the relevant events, but are often produced years or even decades later, and so may be affected by memory or selective recall. They might also be regarded as secondary documents to the extent that they seek to analyse the changing times through which the autobiographer has lived (for instance Hobsbawm, 2002; Morgan, 2015).

Moreover, some documents are edited and collected versions of diaries, letters and autobiographies. These might be described as hybrid documents. These are more widely accessible than the original primary document, but have gone through an editing process that may alter some of their characteristics, whether subtly or substantially. In producing a published work of this kind, editors may tend to emphasise particular types of material to make it more interesting or more or less flattering to the authors of the document, or else to reflect specific interests (Fothergill, 1974). In such cases, one might say that some features of the primary document have been compromised by the process of being edited and presented in this way.

Broad distinctions may be drawn between types of primary documentary sources, and it is important to observe these, although they are not always rigid typologies. One distinction that can be made, for example, is between the documents created by private individuals and family groups in their everyday lives, and the records produced by local, national and international authorities and small or large organisations (Hodder, 1998). The former class of personal or private documents might include diaries, letters, photographs, blogs, autobiographies and suicide notes (Plummer, 2001). The latter group of public and official records would include committee minutes, reports and memoranda, but also formal items such as birth, marriage and death certificates, driving licences and bank statements (Scott, 1990).

There are preliminary issues around ascertaining the authenticity of the document; that is, verifying the author, place and date of its production. In some cases the document may have been forged, or the authorship is in doubt. Historical research also takes into account the reliability of the document, for example, the credibility of the account of an event in terms of the bias of the author, the access to the event, and the interpretation of the observer. The differential survival rate of documents creates a further issue of reliability, and raises questions about how representative, typical and generalisable the surviving documents may be (Scott, 1990, p. 7).

A distinction may also be drawn between documents that are based on written text and other forms produced through other means. Until very recently, most written documents were produced on paper or similar materials, either by hand or mechanically. The past two decades have witnessed the exponential growth of electronic documents such as electronic mail and data communicated and stored through the Internet. This constitutes a contemporary revolution in the nature of documents, albeit that electronic documents may well retain and incorporate elements of the print culture developed over the past five centuries (McCulloch, 2004, p. 2).

Virtual documents, that is, primary documents stored electronically for access through the Internet, are available through 'the click of a mouse' (Travis, 2003). These are often most valuable for researchers, although government and other organisational websites which store documents in this way may seek to cast the government or organisation in a favourable light. On the other hand such digital documents lose the immediacy of the original paper document that they represent (McCulloch, 2004, pp. 34–42).

Diaries, letters and autobiographies are generally regarded as personal documents, although they can often reveal a great deal about public issues and debates. In some cases, they may provide commentary on contemporary social developments, and they often record meetings or other events in which the author has been involved. Diaries are generally produced soon after the event, although this varies, and may give detailed and intimate evidence of individuals and daily life for women no less than for men (Blodgett, 1988). In many cases, as with the published diaries of the composer Benjamin Britten, they document the tensions of adolescence and early adulthood (Britten, 2009). Political diaries, such as those of the British politician Tony Benn, can be highly revealing about policy changes, as in the case of the self-styled 'Great Debate' on education in Britain in 1976 (Benn, 1990). They also reveal much, often unintentionally, about the diarists themselves (Pimlott, 2002). School log books have an official function in that they are generally required to include specific information about the pupils, teachers and management of the school, but in some cases they may reveal the everyday life and interactions of the headteacher concerned (see for example McCulloch, 1989, Chapter 8).

Letter writing as a means of communication has generated a further type of documentary source, one that has been rivalled in recent times by devices such as the telephone and transformed through electronic media. They are interactive in character, forming explicitly part of a dialogue, and may again be both personal and formal in their style and substance (Earle, 1999; Dobson, 2009). Many letters relating to education, such as those from parents to a school or to a newspaper or to a Minister of Education, reflect the interaction between the personal or family domain and the concerns of an established institution (see for instance Heward, 1988). By contrast, autobiographies and memoirs are essentially introspective, and provide an inside account of lives and relationships. They often give particular emphasis to the early life and schooling. For example, David Vincent's major study of working-class autobiographies in nineteenth-century England, based on 142 accounts of this kind, demonstrates the nature of their involvement in a social network of family, friends, colleagues and acquaintances (Vincent, 1981).

Fictional works might also be classed as personal documents. Although not intended to convey the literal truth about particular events, these may represent deeper realities about social experiences. In relation to education, they can provide insights into everyday life from the imagined viewpoints of pupils and teachers, notwithstanding the dramatisation and stereotyped forms that it generally depends upon for plots and characterisation. Novels and plays have been especially useful for their depiction of teachers and teaching. James Hilton's *Goodbye, Mr Chips*, for example, is a classic account of the life story of a male veteran teacher in an elite English boarding school (Hilton, 1934), while the plays of Alan Bennett such as *Forty Years On* (1969) and *The History Boys* (2004) have evoked resilient cultural images (McCulloch, 2009). Susan Ellsmore has also explored representations of the teaching profession in films, including the film of *Goodbye, Mr Chips* produced in 1939 (Ellsmore, 2005).

The printed press embodies a further important source of primary documentary evidence. This provides a day-to-day public record very soon after the event being studied (Vella, 2009, p. 194), albeit one that caters for particular kinds of public taste and interest and by no means comprehensive in its coverage. Peter Cunningham has made interesting use of newspapers as a documentary source by examining the development of the image of the teacher in the British press from 1950 to 1990 (Cunningham, 1992). Cunningham's work compares newspaper coverage of teachers in 1950, 1970 and 1990, using *The Times* in its unofficial capacity as a newspaper of record as well as major mass-circulation newspapers of the political left and right. This has been taken further in other work that examines political cartoons involving teachers in the British press since the 1970s (Warburton and Saunders, 1996). Other particular features of newspapers also offer interesting and useful material for researchers, including leading articles, letters columns and advertisements.

School magazines have a limited circulation in and around their own institution, but constitute a significant record on behalf of the institution itself, with detailed information on everyday life and interests as well as transmitting the received values of the school. J.A. Mangan's research on English public schools in the late-nineteenth century demonstrated the role of school magazines as the official record of school life, reflecting in many cases an emphasis on games and sports as opposed to examinations (Mangan, 1986). Nevertheless, unofficial magazines may also provide important clues to debates and differences within the school (see for example McCulloch, 2007, Chapter 6).

Over the past five hundred years, books in their modern printed format have been repositories of knowledge and scholarship, besides also being a key means of challenging established orthodoxies. Tracts and treatises are important sources of documentary evidence that often embody the principal themes of debate in politics and society, although they do not always fully convey wider attitudes in a particular context, and their representative nature and influence are often exaggerated. A specific type of book that is often useful for researchers in education is the textbook, produced for schools and other educational institutions since the 1830s when the term itself appeared (Stray, 1994, p. 2). They are generally used to support teachers, lecturers, pupils and students to follow a syllabus, and are significant partly for the way in which they present information but also for how they project approved values and ideologies. Stuart Foster, for example, has investigated the treatment of ethnic groups in history textbooks in the United States in terms of a struggle for American identity, arguing that such works have represented the views and interests of a white, male, Protestant middle or upper class, and have tended to support the capitalist system, traditional lifestyles, and Western traditions (Foster, 1999).

Published reports are a further significant source of research evidence in this area of study. Governments as well as organisations and pressure groups produce reports in order to examine particular defined problems and to propose solutions. The information that they provide is often very helpful, although it cannot be assumed that this is always accurate, and it should be checked against other sources. Policy reports are also important for revealing the kinds of assumptions that underlie policy reforms. They represent an outlook or ideology (Scott, 2000, p. 27), and also embody the contradictions and tensions that are inherent in state policy (Codd, 1988). Some reports are voluminous, taking up several volumes including appendices of oral and written evidence provided by witnesses, whereas in recent decades reports have tended to become shorter in length, more limited in focus and more reader-friendly in format to promote their public appeal.

Again, care needs to be taken to resist assuming that such reports reflect educational practices in a straightforward manner.

The Crowther Report of 1959, *15 to 18*, is an example of a published primary source which can itself be the focus of historical research. It was produced by the Central Advisory Council for Education (England), which was set up under the Education Act of 1944 (Ministry of Education 1959). The chair of the CAC during this inquiry was Geoffrey Crowther, the deputy chair of the *Economist Newspaper* Ltd, and the report took its name from him. The Committee itself comprised 27 members, of whom seven were from the universities, two from the local education authorities, two from technical colleges, seven from schools (maintained and independent), one from teacher education, two from trade unions, two from employers and three from elsewhere. The Report took over three and a half years to be produced and was eventually published at the end of 1959. Two of its key recommendations concerned the raising of the school leaving age from fifteen to sixteen, and the establishment of an 'alternative road', more practical in nature in relation to the academic route that led to universities. The first of these was eventually supported by the Conservative government despite opposition from the Treasury, and although further economic problems delayed its introduction it was eventually introduced in 1972–1973 (McCulloch et al., 2012; Woodin et al., 2013). The second was not followed up by the government, but a number of schools and interest groups attempted to put it into practice over the following decade (McCulloch 1989, Chapter 7). Tracing and analysing the origins of the report, the processes that went into its production, its initial reception and longer-term impact entails consideration of a range of source material including national and local archives, newspapers and personal documents.

The proceedings of parliamentary debates and committees provide another kind of official publication. In Britain, these are known as Hansard, after Thomas Hansard, who began publishing the debates of the House of Commons and House of Lords in 1812, and are now available online (www.parliament.the-stationery-office.co.uk; see also www.parliament.uk). An online record of the history of education in England including the full text of the key published official reports of the past two centuries, compiled by Derek Gillard, is at www.educationengland.org.uk/history. In the USA, the Congressional Record provides a similar service, also available on the Internet (www.gpoaccess.gov/crecord/index.html). This was first published in 1873, and provides up-to-date and complete proceedings of debates in the House of Representatives and the Senate. Many datasets produced by governments, organisations and research project teams are also readily accessible, and these lend themselves to secondary analysis. Hakim has defined this in terms of the further analysis of existing datasets which develops the original interpretations and findings of the inquiry in a different way (Hakim, 1982). These include population census reports and datasets specially related to education such as many of those in the data resources of the Economic and Social Research Council (www.esrc.ac.uk/research/our-research/uk-data-service/).

Much research employs one or two of these kinds of document as the principal source of data, but different combinations of personal and public documents may be applied depending on the problem being studied. For example, an education policy report may be examined through the study of the report itself, of the files of the committee that produced it, and of newspapers relating to its reception after publication. The changes in the curriculum at a university might be appraised through institutional records, lecture notes and student diaries where these exist (see for example Slee, 1986). The different perspectives of parents, children and teachers may also be revealed through a combination of such methods, as in the case of the Simon family and their experiences with Gresham's School in the 1930s (McCulloch and Woodin, 2010).

As we have seen, many documentary records are available quite readily through research libraries or the Internet. In other cases, they are stored in an organised format, usually in numbered files for identification, in archives and record offices. Archives are repositories of accumulated knowledge, in many ways the institutional memory of modern societies, and these also exist in a number of forms.

National archives preserve the official records of government departments, and local record offices those of the particular location where appropriate, and in many countries around the world these are preserved carefully and methodically to store the collective memory. In some cases they date from the nineteenth century or even earlier, and they often reflect the specific national and social characteristics (Joyce, 1999). The French Archives Nationales, set up in 1790, developed with a strong focus on the centralised State (Sheppard, 1980). Much documentary evidence has been lost for a number of reasons, whether due to being discarded by the original owners, or failing to survive changes of location, or for lack of space or resources. Thus the researcher is left with only the documents, whether recent or from earlier periods of time, that remain to be examined today. There are many silences in the documents that do survive (Andrew, 1985, p. 156). The experience of working in an archive can also be a challenge. Beyond the costs and the time that may be involved in reaching an archive, it is often difficult to anticipate the amount and quality of documentary material that is available on a particular topic (Steedman, 2001, p. 29).

At the same time, the establishment and spread of online archives over the past ten years have transformed the nature of archival research. In many cases the archive catalogue or inventory of holdings is available in searchable form on the Internet so that the researcher is able to check in advance before traveling to the archive. Increasingly also the documents themselves may be researched digitally (for the UK National Archives see www.nationalarchives.gov.uk). In Britain, the results of the census up to and including 1911 are online (www.ukcensusonline. com/census/1911.php). Full newspaper records (www.britishnewspaperarchive. co.uk) including for example more than 150 years of the newspaper *The Guardian* (http://www.archive.guardian.co.uk; see also *The Guardian*, 2007) have been made available online. Cabinet minutes and discussions are also accessible by this means (www.nationalarchives.gov.uk/cabinetpapers/). For example Cabinet discussion of the Conservative government on education policy in the early 1970s (Cabinet file CAB.128/50/55) may be consulted in this way. The online archive of the former British Prime Minister Margaret Thatcher, which has many references to education, can also be consulted at www.margaretthatcher.org/archive. However, there are some restrictions in terms of coverage and a subscription or other cost may often be applied.

ORAL, VISUAL AND QUANTITATIVE EVIDENCE

Such written, printed and electronic texts might be contrasted with oral, visual and quantitative evidence. Oral evidence is most commonly accrued through interviews with surviving witnesses of or participants in historical events, although other oral sources may include sound recordings of speeches. Visual documents take graphic or pictorial form, such as photographs, paintings and films (Prosser, 1998; Grosvenor, 2007; Tinkler, 2013), although it should be noted that texts in contemporary society have become increasingly multi-semiotic in combining and juxtaposing language and visual forms (Fairclough, 1995). One may also distinguish textual records from material artefacts like fossils, slates, desks and buildings. Quantitative methods making use of datasets such as large-scale surveys and questionnaires have also attracted many historical researchers with an interest in education.

Oral history based on interviews has become an increasingly popular strategy for research on the history of the twentieth century. In relation to education, for example, interviews may be conducted with former teachers or students, designed for them to recall their own experiences and those of their peers. For historical research such as this, oral history has a number of advantages over conventional documentary sources. In the first place, documentary records maintained by the State or by major institutions tend to be a record of the views and interactions of policymakers and administrators, who are also in the main successful in their own experience of the education system. For this reason, oral history can support alternative accounts of groups that have historically been less successful or visible in western-style schooling, in particular working-class youth, girls and women, and many ethnic minorities and indigenous groups.

For example, Stephen Humphries (Humphries, 1981) seeks to explore the world of working-class childhood and youth in England from 1889 to 1939. He argues that working-class children and youth tried to resist the values imposed upon them by a hegemonic dominant culture. He therefore portrays them not as 'hooligans', as they were often viewed in official documents, but as 'rebels'. In order to understand the nature of their 'resistance', which he claims is 'under-recorded and under-researched', he prefers oral rather than documentary sources. Thus, according to Humphries,

> Clearly, any account of an underprivileged and largely anonymous group like working-class youth requires a methodological approach different from that ordinarily employed by historians. Since the control of manuscript and printed evidence by adults (normally middle-class adults) is absolute, most documentary sources present a biased and distorted view of the resistance of working-class youth. This book will attempt to redress this balance by rewriting the history of working-class childhood and youth largely in the words of working-class people who themselves experienced it between 1889 and 1939; official accounts of disruptive and delinquent behaviour will be assessed in the light of their reminiscences. (Humphries, 1981, p. 3)

Humphries insists that oral history 'offers a viable method of placing this class resistance back at the centre of analysis' (Humphries, 1981, p. 27). In particular, he contends, interviews illuminate 'the precise circumstances and consequences of opposition to school authority because official records often distort the motives and underestimate the frequency of children's resistance' (Humphries, 1981, p. 29). In order to redress the balance, he concludes, 'we must listen to the testimony of those old working-class people who stand accused in the official records of acts of resistance against rational state instruction' (Humphries, 1981, p. 29). On the other hand, it is important to note that Humphries' emphasis on the idea of 'resistance' has itself been challenged by other historians, who have found a high level of support for such schools from many working-class children and youth of the period (Rose, 2001).

A second and related way in which oral history can often go beyond documentary data is in its capacity to shed light on the interface between teaching and learning, in the classroom. Thus, Cunningham and Gardner conducted over 300 oral history interviews with former teachers to develop detailed accounts of, for example, the historical experience of student teachers, and of teaching in the Second World War (Gardner, 1996; Gardner and Cunningham, 1997; Cunningham and Gardner, 2004). Gardner's oral history research on the use of corporal punishment by teachers in English working-class elementary schools in the 1920s (Gardner, 1996) highlights a distinction between teacher accounts and pupil or student narratives. Gardner points out several practical difficulties involved in interviewing former teachers, for example, the relatively smaller number of teachers compared with their pupils, their relatively greater age and the sensitivity of the topic, as well as the generally distorting effects of memory. On the other hand, he reports, 'The memories of such individuals promise a source of intimate and detailed information capable both of refining the bland messages inscribed in the official documents and tempering the pained, passionate classroom recollections of former pupils' (Gardner, 1996, p. 144). The conclusions from his research based on these teacher accounts suggest that corporal punishment was 'a more prominent part of classroom life than the documentary record can ever admit' (Gardner, 1996, p. 163), but also that it was not as universal, intensive or uncontrolled as might be implied in pupil recollections such as those studied by Humphries (Humphries, 1981).

Life history research may also be used to reflect on the educational experiences of individuals during their childhood and youth and also over their lives as a whole (Goodson and Sikes, 2001). For example, O'Donoghue and Harford present a number of accounts as topical life stories in which the focus is on the participants' memories of their secondary schooling (O'Donoghue and Harford, 2016, p. 6). In this case, the authors first introduce some general aspects of different types of secondary schools in Ireland in the twentieth century, and then provide edited narratives of former pupils at these schools.

The records of oral media such as the radio are also of great potential value for historical research. For instance, Cox (1996) examines school music broadcasts and the British Broadcasting Corporation (BBC), 1924–1947, based on records held at the BBC Written Archives Centre in Caversham and at the National Sound Archive in London, while Stephen Parker has investigated religious broadcasting at the BBC based on similar sources (Parker, 2010, 2015).

Visual sources have attracted increasing attention as a basis for historical research. They have long been used as a means of illustrating historical accounts, but they also have potential as a form of historical evidence that can be analysed in depth (Burke, 2001). Ines Dussel and others have pointed to a 'visual turn' in historical research that has been particularly noticeable in relation to education (Dussel, 2013; see also for example Rousmaniere, 2001; Mietzner et al., 2005; Prosser, 2007). Paintings, for example, were used by the French historian Philippe Aries to help support his argument that childhood was a modern invention that became established only from the seventeenth century onwards. Thus, he claimed, in early medieval art children tended to be portrayed as if they were small versions of adults, in adult clothing and in the same proportions as adult bodies (Aries, 1962). Jeroen Dekker has examined seventeenth-century Dutch genre paintings for the 'educational messages' that they transmitted, 'presenting the image of the desired adult personality and explaining the purpose of upbringing' (Dekker, 1996, p. 160). Dekker has also shown that seventeenth-century family and children's portraits, and the portraits of dead children that were also common, were vivid representations of Dutch culture, providing insights into 'how and why people in the past continued to remember their already dead children as members of their family' (Dekker, 2015, p. 715).

Photographs are similarly powerful as visual images in historical research (see for example Tinkler, 2013). Even when they are artificially posed, as school photographs of class groups or sports teams, they can tell us a great deal about hierarchies and institutionally approved images (Mangan, 1986; see also for example O'Donoghue, 2010). Moving pictures, or films, can also be highly significant as historical data, for instance, propaganda films in the Second World

War (Cunningham, 2000), and documentary films (Warmington et al., 2011). Archives of these kinds of sources are accessible through online databases, for example that of the BBC, and media libraries.

Physical artefacts of education, such as school desks and buildings, have also been given due recognition as historical sources. Remnants or remains of earlier periods have in many cases survived into the twenty-first century, often protected under the aegis of museums of education and of childhood. Herman et al. (2011) have traced the historical development of school desks (see also Betts, 1981; Moreno Martinez, 2005). School buildings such as those produced by the architect E. R. Robson for the London School Board in the late-nineteenth century have been examined by Burke and Grosvenor (Burke and Grosvenor, 2013).

Quantitative approaches to historical research have been widely advocated in the area of education, and have yielded substantial results. Peter Laslett and his Cambridge Group for the History of Population and Social Structure pioneered the systematic study of archival sources over several centuries to compute literacy rates and other data in 'the world we have lost' (Laslett 1965/1983). Lawrence Stone, another prominent social historian, strongly advocated the use of quantitative methods for historical research in the area of education. In the 1960s, Stone produced two key articles on the 'educational revolution' of early modern England (Stone, 1964), and on literacy and education in England between 1640 and 1990 (Stone, 1969). He emphasised that historical research into the relationship between schooling and society should deploy statistical evidence wherever possible (Stone, 1976). In the 1980s, Carl Kaestle, a leading American historian of education, noted that quantitative historical research has been further stimulated by the wider availability of computer programmes and the broader sociological implications of the outcomes of schooling. On the other hand, the techniques involved have been unfamiliar and difficult for many historical researchers, as well as time consuming and expensive compared with library-based or archival research of a qualitative nature (Kaestle, 1988). A.J. Christopher discusses the problems involved in examining census data material over the long term in the context of South Africa (Christopher, 2015). Over the past few decades, these issues have begun to be addressed in the context of digital sources and databases, often through greater use of research teams in funded projects, as opposed to separate researchers working in isolation from each other (see for example O'Neill, 2014, Lassig, 2015).

At the same time, a number of historical researchers recommend a partnership between qualitative and quantitative approaches in developing a full treatment of a historical topic relating to education. For example, William E. Marsden drew extensively on the returns of census enumerators from the nineteenth century to support his study of local school provision, but also made the point that quantitatively processed aggregate assessments of social situations can effectively divorce researchers from the lived experience of urban localities and education in the nineteenth century. He therefore sought to complement such source material with personal sources such as school log books, newspaper accounts and diaries (Marsden, 1979). Another case of this kind of partnership is Kerckhoff et al. (1996), which examines the spread of comprehensive schools in England and Wales from the 1940s to the 1970s. This work examines ten case studies of the process of comprehensive reorganisation in ten different local authority areas, using detailed qualitative methods based on documentary sources. The study then goes on to complement these case studies with the use of longitudinal data drawn from the National Child Development Study, and then applies a series of multinomial logistic regression analyses to this to help explain the nature of local variations within the general process of reorganisation.

Such mixed methods can often be used in historical research to good effect. Documentary research may frequently be allied to good effect with other research methods in education (see for example McCulloch, 2004 on combining archive and interview research). Interviews with teachers about their curriculum and pedagogic practices may be compared with documentary evidence of changing policy in these areas over the past thirty years, as in the case of research by McCulloch et al. (2000).

CONCLUDING REFLECTIONS

Historical research in education stands on the frontiers of a number of fertile fields and disciplines of research: education and history most obviously, but also a wide range of the humanities and social sciences. It has gained much from its close articulation with these bodies of knowledge, and continues to engage freely with them (see McCulloch, 2011b, 2012). Nevertheless, historical research in education has a strong tradition in its own right, with well-established standards of rigour and claims to originality. It has a recognised research base in primary documents, but has also found new means of revising and reorienting its work, partly through different approaches being taken to established sources but also through increased awareness and theorisation of a wider range of historical evidence.

The late Richard Aldrich also argued that historical research in education has developed a powerful and distinctive ethical base, with a particular set of values insomuch as its practitioners are bound by a characteristic approach to three familiar duties of the historian: the duty to the people of the past, the duty to our own generation, and the duty to search after the truth (Aldrich, 2003). Historical research in education addresses many profound social and political issues (Aldrich, 2014), and it must pay careful attention to ethical considerations in its archival research no less than in any other method, whatever may be the particular theme (see for example Tesar, 2015).

REFERENCES

Aldrich, R. (2003) 'The three duties of the historian of education', *History of Education*, 32/2, 133–143.

Aldrich, R. (2014) 'In search of an ethical history of education', *International Journal for the Historiography of Education*, 4/2, 277–284.

Andrew, A. (1985) 'In pursuit of the past: some problems in the collection, analysis and use of historical documentary evidence', in R. G. Burgess (Ed.) *Strategies of Educational Research*. London: Falmer Press, 153–178.

Aries, P. (1962) *Centuries of Childhood: A social history of family life*. London: Vintage Books.

Benn, T. (1990) *Against the Tide: Diaries 1973–76*. London: Arrow.

Bennett, A. (1969) *Forty Years On*. London: Faber and Faber.

Bennett, A. (2004) *The History Boys*. London: Faber and Faber.

Betts, R. (1981) 'The school desk in the nineteenth century', *History of Education Society Bulletin*, 27, 24–35.

Blodgett, H. (1988) *Centuries of Female Days: Englishwomen's private diaries*. Brunswick, NJ: Rutgers University Press.

Britten, B. (2009) *Journeying Boy: The diaries of the young Benjamin Britten, 1928–1938*, J. Evans (Ed.). London: Faber.

Burgess, R. (Ed.) (1985) *Strategies of Educational Research: Qualitative methods*. London: Falmer.

Burke, C. and Grosvenor, I. (2013) 'An exploration of the writing and reading of a life: the "body parts" of the Victorian school architect E.R. Robson', in T. Popkewitz (Ed.) *Rethinking the History of Education*. New York: Palgrave Macmillan, 201–20.

Burke, P. (2001) *Eyewitnessing: The uses of images as historical evidence*. London, Reaktion Books.

Carpentier, V. (2008) 'Quantitative sources for the history of education', *History of Education*, 37/5, 701–720.

Christopher, A.J. (2015) 'Educational attainment in South Africa: a view from the census, 1865–2011', *History of Education*, 44/4, 503–522.

Codd, J. (1988) 'The construction and deconstruction of educational policy documents', *Journal of Education Policy*, 3/3, 235–247.

Cox, G. (1996) 'School music broadcasts and the BBC, 1924–47', *History of Education*, 25/4, 363–371.

Cunningham, P. (1992) 'Teachers' professional image and the press, 1950–1990', *History of Education*, 21/1, 37–56.

Cunningham, P. (2000) 'Moving images: propaganda film and British education', *Paedagogica Historica*, 36/1, 389–406.

Cunningham, P. and Gardner, P. (2004) *Becoming Teachers: Texts and testimonies 1904–1950*. London: Woburn Press

Dekker, J. (1996) 'A republic of educators: educational messages in seventeenth-century Dutch genre painting', *History of Education*, 36/2, 155–182.

Dekker, J. (2015) 'Images as representations: visual sources on education and childhood in the past', *Paedagogica Historica*, 51/6, 702–715.

Depaepe, M. (2012) *Between Educationalization and Appropriation: Selected writings on the history of modern educational systems*. Leuven: Leuven University Press

Dobson, M. (2009) 'Letters', in M. Dobson and B. Ziemann (Eds) *Reading Primary Sources: The interpretation of texts from nineteenth and twentieth-century history*. Oxon: Routledge, 57–73.

Dobson, M. and Ziemann, B. (Eds) (2009) *Reading Primary Sources: The Interpretation of texts from nineteenth- and twentieth-century history*. Oxon: Routledge.

Dussel, I. (2013) 'The visual turn in the history of education: four comments for a historiographical discussion', in T. Popkewitz (Ed.) *Rethinking the History of Education*. New York: Palgrave Macmillan, 29–49.

Earle, R. (Ed.) (1999) *Epistolary Selves: Letters and Letter-Writers, 1600–1945*. Aldershot: Ashgate.

Ellsmore, S. (2005) *Carry On, Teachers! Representations of the teaching profession in screen culture*. Stoke on Trent: Trentham.

Fairclough, N. (1995) *Critical Discourse Analysis: The critical study of language*. London: Longman.

Foster, S. (1999) 'The struggle for American identity: treatment of ethnic groups in United States history textbooks', *History of Education*, 28/3, 251–278.

Fothergill, R. (1974) *Private Chronicles: A study of English diaries*. London: Oxford University Press.

Gardner, P. (1996) 'The giant at the front: young teachers and corporal punishment in inter-war elementary schools', *History of Education*, 23/2, 141–163.

Gardner, P. (2003) 'Oral history in education: teacher's memory and teachers' history', *History of Education*, 32/2, 175–188.

Gardner, P. and Cunningham, P. (1997) 'Oral history and teachers' professional practice: a wartime turning point?', *Cambridge Journal of Education*, 27/3, 231–242.

Goodson, I. and Sikes, P. (2001) *Life History Research in Educational Settings*. Buckingham: Open University Press.

Grosvenor, I. (2007) 'From the "eye of history" to a "second gaze": the visual archive and the marginalized in the history of education', *History of Education*, 36/4–5, 607–622.

Hakim, C. (1982) *Secondary Analysis in Social Research: A guide to data sources and methods with examples*. London, George Allen and Unwin.

Herman, F., Van Gorp, A., Simon, F. and Depaepe, M. (2011) 'The school desk: from concept to object', *History of Education*, 40/1, pp. 97–117.

Heward, C. (1988) *Making a Man of Him: Parents and their sons' education at an English public school, 1929–50*. London: Routledge.

Hilton, J. (1934) *Goodbye, Mr Chips*. London: Hodder and Stoughton.

Hobsbawm, E. (2002) *Interesting Times: A twentieth-century life*. London: Allen Lane.

Hodder, I. (1998) 'The interpretation of documents and material culture', in N. K. Denzin and Y. S. Lincoln (Eds) *Collecting and Interpreting Qualitative Materials*. London: Sage, 110–129.

Humphries, S. (1981) *Hooligans or Rebels?: An oral history of working class childhood and youth*. Oxford: Blackwell.

Joyce, P. (1999) 'The politics of the liberal archive', *History of the Human Sciences*, 12/2, 35–49.

Kaestle, C. (1988) 'Recent methodological developments in the history of American education', in R. M. Jaeger (Ed.) *Complementary Methods for Research in Education*. Washington, DC: American Educational Research Association, 61–71, 79–80.

Kerckhoff, A., Fogelman, K., Crook, D. and Reeder, D. (1996) *Going Comprehensive in England and Wales: A study of uneven change*. London, Woburn Press.

Laslett, P. (1965/1983) *The World we Have Lost*, 3rd edition. London: Methuen.

Lassig, S. (2015) 'Digital humanities: we need to talk', *International Journal for the Historiography of Education*, 5/1, 72–79.

Lawn, M. and Grosvenor, I. (2001) '"When in doubt, preserve": exploring the traces of teaching and material culture in English schools', *History of Education*, 30/2, 117–127.

Lowe, R. (Ed.) (2000) *History of Education: Major themes* (4 vols.). London: Routledge.

McCulloch, G. (1989) *The Secondary Technical School: A Usable Past?*. London: Falmer.

McCulloch, G. (2004) *Documentary Research in Education, History and the Social Sciences*. London: Routledge.

McCulloch, G. (Ed.) (2005) *The RoutledgeFalmer Reader in the History of Education*. London: RoutledgeFalmer.

McCulloch, G. (2007) *Cyril Norwood and the Ideal of Secondary Education*. New York: Palgrave Macmillan.

McCulloch, G. (2009) 'The moral universe of Mr Chips: veteran teachers in British literature and drama', *Teachers and Teaching*, 15/4, 409–420.

McCulloch, G. (2011a) 'Historical and documentary methods', in L. Cohen, L. Manion and K. Morrison (Eds) *Research Methods in Education*, 7th edition. London: Routledge, 248–255.

McCulloch, G. (2011b) *The Struggle for the History of Education*. London: Routledge.

McCulloch, G. (2012) 'The changing rationales of the history of education: history, education, and social science', in J. E. Larsen (Ed.) *Knowledge, Politics and the History of Education*. Berlin: Lit Verlag, 25–38.

McCulloch, G. (2015) 'A footnote to Plato: interpreting the history of secondary education in mid-twentieth-century England', in P. Smeyers, D. Bridges, B. C. Burbules and M. Griffiths (Eds) *International Handbook of Interpretation in Educational Research, Part 2*. Dordrecht: Springer, 873–891.

McCulloch, G. (2016a) 'New directions in the history of education', *Journal of International and Comparative Education*, 5/1, 47–56.

McCulloch, G. (2016b) 'History of the curriculum', in D. Wyse, L. Hayward and J. Hayward (Eds), *The SAGE Handbook of Curriculum, Pedagogy and Assessment*, vol. 1. London: Sage, 47–62.

McCulloch, G. (2016c) 'Histories of urban education in the United Kingdom', in W. T. Pink and G. W. Noblit (Eds) *Second International Handbook of Urban Education*. Dordrecht: Springer, in press.

McCulloch, G., Cowan, S. and Woodin, T. (2012) 'The British Conservative government and the raising of the school leaving age, 1959–1964', *Journal of Education Policy*, 27/4, 509–527.

McCulloch, G., Helsby, G. and Knight, P. (2000) *The Politics of Professionalism: Teachers and the curriculum*. London: Continuum.

McCulloch, G. and Richardson, W. (2000) *Historical Research in Educational Settings*. Buckingham: Open University Press.

McCulloch, G. and Woodin, T. (2010) 'Learning and liberal education: the case of the Simon family, 1912–1939', *Oxford Review of Education*, 36/2, 187–201.

Mangan, J. A. (1986) *Athleticism in the Victorian and Edwardian Public School: The emergence and consolidation of an educational ideology*. London: Falmer.

Marsden, W. E. (1979) 'Census enumerators' returns, schooling and social areas in the late Victorian town: the case of Bootle', in R. Lowe (Ed.) *New Approaches to the Study of Popular Education, 1851–1902*. Leicester: Leicester University Press, 16–35.

Moreno Martinez, P.M. (2005) 'History of school desk development in terms of hygiene and pedagogy in Spain (1838–1936)', in M. Lawn and I. Grosvenor (Eds) *Materialities of Schooling*. Oxford: Symposium Books, 71–95.

Mietzner, U., Myers, K. and Peim, N. (Eds) (2005) *Visual History: Images of education*. Oxford: Peter Lang.

Ministry of Education (1959) *15 To 18 (Crowther Report)*, 2 vols. London: HMSO.

Morgan, K. (2015) *My Histories*. Cardiff: University of Wales Press.

O'Donoghue, D. (2010) 'Classrooms as installations: a conceptual framework for analysing classroom photographs from the past', *History of Education*, 39/3, 401–415.

O'Donoghue, T. and Harford, J. (2016) *Secondary School Education in Ireland: History, Memories and Life Stories, 1922–1967*. New York: Palgrave Macmillan.

O'Neill, C. (2014) *Catholics of Consequence: Transnational Education, Social Mobility, and the Irish Catholic Elite, 1850–1900*. Oxford: Oxford University Press.

Parker, S. (2010) '"Teach them to pray Auntie": Children's Hour prayers at the BBC, 1940–1961', *History of Education*, 39/5, 659–676.

Parker, S. (2015) 'Mediatizing childhood religion: the BBC, John G. Williams and collective worship for schools in England, 1940–1975', *Paedagogica Historica*, 51/5, 614–630.

Pimlott, B. (2002) 'Dear diary...', *The Guardian G2*, 18 October, 2–3.

Plummer, K. (2001) *Documents of Life 2: An invitation to a critical humanism*. London: Sage.

Popkewitz, T. (Ed.) (2013) *Rethinking the History of Education: Transnational perspectives on its questions, methods, and knowledge*. New York: Palgrave Macmillan.

Prosser, J. (Ed.) (1998) *Image-Based Research: A Sourcebook for Qualitative Researchers*. London: Falmer.

Prosser, J. (2007) 'Visual methods and the visual culture of schools', *Visual Studies*, 22/1, 13–30.

Raftery, D. and Crook, D. (2012) 'Forty years of History of Education, 1972–2011', *History of Education*, special issue, 41/1.

Reese, W. J. and Rury, J. (Eds) (2008) *Rethinking the History of American Education*. New York: Palgrave Macmillan.

Rose, J. (2001) *The Intellectual Life of the British Working Classes*. London: Yale University Press.

Rousmaniere, K. (2001) 'Questioning the visual in the history of education', *History of Education*, 30/2, 109–116.

Scott, D. (2000) *Reading Educational Research and Policy*. London: RoutledgeFalmer.

Scott, J. (1990) *A Matter of Record: Documentary Sources in Social Research*. Cambridge: Polity Press.

Sheppard, J. (1980) 'Vive la difference?: An outsider's view of French archives', *Archives*, 14, 151–162.

Slee, P. (1986) *Learning and a Liberal Education: The study of modern history in the universities of Oxford, Cambridge and Manchester, 1800–1914*. Manchester: Manchester University Press.

Steedman, C. (2001) *Dust*. Manchester: Manchester University Press.

Stone, L. (1964) 'The educational revolution in England, 1560–1640', *Past and Present*, 28, 41–80.

Stone, L. (1969) 'Literacy and education in England, 1640–1900', *Past and Present*, 42, 69–139.

Stone, L. (Ed.) (1976) *Schooling and Society: Studies in the history of education*. Baltimore, Johns Hopkins University Press.

Stray, C. (1994) 'Paradigms regained: towards a historical sociology of the textbook', *Journal of Curriculum Studies*, 26/1, 1–29.

Tesar, M. (2015) 'Ethics and truth in archival research', *History of Education*, 44/4, 101–114.

Thompson, P. (1988) *The Voice of the Past: Oral history*. Oxford: Oxford University Press.

Tinkler, P. (2013) *Using Photographs in Social and Historical Research*. London, Sage.

Travis, A. (2003) 'Online archive brings Britain's migration story to life', *The Guardian*, 30 July, p. 7.

The Guardian (2007) 'The Archive', 3 November.

Vella, S. (2009) 'Newspapers', in M. Dobson and B. Ziemann (Eds) *Reading Primary Sources: The interpretation of texts from nineteenth- and twentieth-century history*. Oxon: Routledge, 192–208.

Vincent, D. (1981) *Bread, Knowledge and Freedom: A Study of Nineteenth-Century Working Class Autobiography*. London: Europa.

Warburton, T. and Saunders, M. (1996) 'Representing teachers' professional culture through cartoons', *British Journal of Educational Studies*, 44/3, 307–325.

Warmington, P., van Gorp, A., Grosvenor, I. (2011), 'Education in motion: uses of documentary film in educational research', *Paedagogica Historica*, 47/4, 457–472.

Woodin, T., McCulloch, G. and Cowan, S. (2013) *Secondary Education and the Raising of the School-Leaving Age: Coming of Age?*. New York: Palgrave Macmillan.

WEBSITES

British Cabinet papers online. www.nationalarchives.gov.uk/cabinetpapers/

British Census (1911). www.ukcensusonline.com/census/1911.php

British Newspaper Archive. www.britishnewspaperarchive.co.uk

British Parliamentary Committee proceedings, evidence and reports. www.parliament.uk

British Parliamentary Debates. www.parliament.the-stationery-office.co.uk

Economic and Social Research Council (ESRC) data service. www.esrc.ac.uk/research/our-research/uk-data-service

History of education in England, compiled by Derek Gillard. www.educationengland.org.uk/history

National Archives UK online catalogue. www.nationalarchives.gov.uk

The Guardian Archive. http://archive.guardian.co.uk

US Congressional Record. www.gpoaccess.gov/crecord/index.html

15

Using International Comparative Studies in Achievement

Larry E. Suter

INTRODUCTION OF INTERNATIONAL COMPARISONS TO EDUCATIONAL RESEARCHERS

Making comparisons between human activities either individually, across organizations, or between large national systems is an essential tool of scientific research (Cummings, 1999). Comparisons provide context for observed human behaviors. Are they absent or present, frequent or infrequent, or large or small when compared with other settings? Thus, making comparisons to other countries can improve the chances for drawing a correct inference by expanding the number of possibilities. Yet, if measurements of individuals are aggregated to an entire country level, the significant amount of variation between individuals within the country is masked thus simple comparisons of countries as units may lead to erroneous inferences regarding the nature of individual behavior – an ecological fallacy. Yet, the field of educational research has continued to produce massive studies and create entire journals and professional associations for International Comparative Education. What can be learned about educational practices by making comparisons of students, teachers, and educational content across countries? What problems do they solve and what errors should be avoided by educational researchers? How can the discipline of educational research benefit from making international comparisons of educational behaviors and student performance?

Some answers to these questions are provided by two educational researchers who have been engaged in conducting comparative studies. Their review of research illustrates the range of uses made from results of international comparative studies. Dossey and Wu explain that:

> The purpose [of international comparative studies] appears to be the creation of a platform for illustrating and relating students' achievement to salient policy variables such as distribution of achievement across racial and cultural groups, the relative performance of different genders in mathematical situations, the distribution of resources and teachers across geographical units, the relationships between the flow of students through the academic mathematics pipeline, and the relationship of various levels of output to national needs and labor projections. Within education, the output of such studies is of direct interest to curriculum experts, teacher educators, and those involved in professional development programmes, and textbook writers and publishers of mathematical learning materials, as in Kilpatrick, Mesa, and Sloane (2007). (Dossey and Wu, 2012, p 1014)

In a second review, Martin Carnoy describes how changes in national policies are affected by the global competition for information and knowledge and he discusses how that information is needed for educational planning by country leaders (Carnoy, 1999). Carnoy wrote,

> The quality of national educational systems is increasingly being compared internationally. This has placed increased emphasis on mathematics and science curricula, English as a foreign language and communication skills. Testing and standards are part of a broader effort to increase accountability by measuring knowledge production and using such measures to assess education workers (teachers) and managers. Yet, the way testing is used to 'improve quality' is heavily influenced by the political context and purposes of the evaluation system. Again, to develop effective policies for education improvement, the ideological-political content of a testing programme has to be clearly separated from its educational management content. (Carnoy, 1999, p. 16)

Key themes that emerge from these statements, and from textbooks on comparative education such as Bray, Adamson, and Mason (2007) and Philips and Schweisfurth (2014) are that comparative studies substitute objective measurement of behaviors and performances of students and teachers for ideological discussions of ways for improving educational practices; comparative studies provide useful descriptions of the variety of individual behaviors possible in educational practices; and international comparison surveys have increased the focus of attention about educational practices on measures of student achievement and its antecedents.

The field of educational research has a long history of the use of comparisons between countries to advise policymakers about what forms of educational practices are most successful (Peaker, 1975, Husén, 1987; Medrich and Griffith, 1992; Carnoy, 2006; Heyneman, 2003). Textbooks on Comparative International Education assert that the field of comparative international education is old (from the early 1800s says Phillips and Schweisfurth, 2014), that it is growing because the world is increasingly connected, and that it can save the field of education by advancing systematic inquiry (Bray et al., 2007; Philips and Schweisfurth, 2014). For educational researchers, comparisons among country educational systems and practices can be used to test hypotheses or generate new hypotheses (Porter and Gamoran, 2002). For educational practitioners, the examples of systems of educational organization, teaching practices, curriculum design, and daily school policies observed in one country may form a model for advancing changes in another country (Lewis and Takahashi, 2011). Experiments in redesigning educational practices in some countries, such as Sweden in the 1960s, have provided a laboratory for other researchers to consider as a source of scientific evidence of education (Husén and Boalt, 1967; Dahllöf, 1973, 1966). While the use of international comparative studies for research and policymaking has led to an extensive debate about whether the results have been used appropriately for establishing new educational policies (Berliner and Biddle, 1995; Glass, 2008; Bracey, 2006), many researchers and policymakers agree that their effect on education research as well as policy has been substantial (Husén, 1987; Brown, 1998; Floden, 2002; Porter and Gamoran, 2002).

Future educational researchers will contribute to the creation of an objective knowledge base for educational theory by replicating and reanalyzing enduring educational issues such as the causes of student achievement, the influence of teaching practices, the role of different forms of curriculum, the changing nature of parental influence on students, the measurement of student non-cognitive factors, and many other topics (see Chapter 37 on Theory in this volume). As shown by reports of cross-national studies, nearly all associations with student achievement vary in strength over time and space (OECD, 2007; Willms, 2006). Fortunately, at this point in the twenty-first century, a large enough body of well-constructed cross-national surveys is available to every researcher. The content of these surveys include measurement of student knowledge of mathematics, science, reading, civics, and computer technology. They also include measures of student attitudes toward subjects, the student family background, relationships to peers and to teachers, and after-school activities. Some surveys include reports directly from school administrators and parents.

SOURCES OF INTERNATIONAL COMPARATIVE STUDIES

Examples from two large systems of international comparative educational data collection and analyses will be discussed to demonstrate the type of issues addressed by these international comparative studies in the twenty first century. Researchers concerned about variations in student achievement should consult the reports from these studies early in the planning for new projects.

The two international organizations that conduct regular surveys of students, schools, and teachers are The International Association for the Evaluation of Educational Achievement (IEA) and the Organisation for Economic Co-operation and Development (OECD). These organizations conduct the Trends in International Mathematics and Science Study (TIMSS), the Programme for International Student Assessment (PISA) and Progress in International Reading Literacy Study (PIRLS). Each survey organization has conducted other related studies that will not be described here in detail. The two studies have been repeated six times between 1995 and 2016. TIMSS was conducted every four years between 1995 and 2016 and PISA every three years from 2000 to 2015. Each study has produced an extensive number of analytical reports and each release the survey files to anyone for secondary analysis (IEA, 2016; OECD, 2016). By 2012 altogether 79 countries, about half of all world countries, participated in international assessments of either TIMSS or in PISA (14 countries participated exclusively in TIMSS, 37 exclusively PISA, and 28 participated in both studies). The participating countries range from the least developed to the most highly developed. Thus they are not only a massive resource for examining changes in student performance and school practices for participating countries (OECD, 2010) the frameworks and cross-national evidence from these studies could potentially form a common basis for accumulating knowledge of educational systems across the field of educational research (see OECD, 2007, 2009b, 2010, 2013b, and 2014; IEA 2011, 2016).

The IEA surveys have followed a model of studying how school content (curriculum) is intended by the nation, implemented by teachers, and learned by students (Travers and Westbury, 1989; Schmidt et al., 1998). These surveys are a resource in particular for analyzing issues regarding the content of a curriculum and student achievement (Suter, 2017, forthcoming). Whereas the PISA surveys have emphasized student preparation for the workforce and are a resource for analyzing how individual and family factors associated with higher levels of knowledge of science, mathematics, and reading differ in different cultures.

ISSUES AND RESPONSES OF LARGE SCALE INTERNATIONAL COMPARATIVE STUDIES

The first educational researchers to conduct empirical measurement of student differences across countries felt that they were undertaking an impossible task (Foshay et al., 1962; Husén, 1967a) and in fact many of the original concerns for these studies continues to be debated (Freudenthal, 1975; Berliner and Biddle, 1995; Glass, 2008; Bracey 2006; Brown, 1998; Carnoy and Rothstein, 2013; Heyneman, 2003), The earliest surveys of achievement began with a pilot study of 13-year-olds in 10 countries in 1959–1961 (Walker, 1962; International Association for the Evaluation of Educational Achievement, 2011). The members of the research team were an international group of recognized scholars from the University of Chicago, Columbia University, University of Stockholm, and the National Foundation for Educational Research in England and Wales. These researchers believed that cross-national studies provided a natural laboratory with which to investigate the factors that impacted student learning (Foshay et al., 1962; IEA, 2011; Grisay and Griffin, 2006; Husén, 1979; Ross and Genevois, 2006) and that practices within a single country were limited by the laws and customs of that each nation. The discovery of best practices would require expanding education observations throughout the world (Ross and Genevois, 2006; Foshay et al., 1962). The first researchers were not centrally organized as they are today but represented individual country research centers that had demonstrated that they had had prior experience in conducting empirical studies of education. Consequently, the quality of execution of the first studies was questioned (Bracey, 2006; Papanastasiou et al., 2011).

Mathematics was chosen as the subject of the first major study because mathematics was believed to be the subject most commonly taught among different countries. However, that assumption was strongly challenged by mathematics educators such as Freudenthal (1975) who argued that mathematics was variable and not a perfect reflection of the entire educational domain. The First International Mathematics Study was conducted by the IEA in 12 countries in 1965 (Australia, Belgium, England, Finland, France, Germany, Israel, Japan, the Netherlands, Scotland, Sweden and the United States; Husén, 1967b). The study included students who were in the grade normally attended by 13-year-olds and students who were in the final year of school (Husén, 1967a, 1967b). Studies in other fields followed in the 1960s and 1980s in science, foreign language, reading literature, writing and civics education (Purves, 1973). However, the results of these studies had little impact on educational research or on policy. The researchers were careful to not draw invidious comparisons between countries and instead focused attention of differences of relationships within the countries (Husén, 1967a). The results were ambiguous. But others did wish to make comparisons and it was the secondary analysis by Barbara Lerner in 1982 that created direct comparisons, drew relationships with expenditures, and thus formed the basis for a public debate about the value of public education in the United States (Lerner, 1982; National Commission on Excellence, 1993).

One issue that plagued the interpretation of cross-national studies was whether or not the test questions accurately represented the body of knowledge as taught in schools for each participating country. Did countries teach the same types of mathematics in a similar sequence? And if they didn't, could the effect on student achievement be detected? That question formed the basis for an expansive survey of opportunity to learn in the Second IEA Mathematics Study (SIMS) that was conducted during 1981–1982 in 14 countries (McKnight et al., 1987; Travers and Westbury, 1989). The second study attempted to tackle the issue of causality between curriculum coverage and student achievement by measuring achievement at the beginning and end of the school year in eight countries (Burstein, 1993); the only time pre and post student measures were attempted.

The outcome of the analysis is expressed in the US national report title, 'The Underachieving Curriculum' (McKnight et al., 1987) which brought more focus on the educational practices after the attention given to the significance of family and home rather than the school following the earlier publication of the 'Coleman report' in 1966 (Coleman et al., 1966). The IEA continued conducting surveys of mathematics and science in the 4th, 8th, and occasionally 12th grades between 1995 and 2015 (IEA International Study Center, 2016) that further explored the relationship between the intended, the implemented, and the achieved curriculum (Travers and Westbury, 1989). Questions about the significance of establishing national standards in curriculum are still worthy of investigation by new researchers who could replicate the analyses with existing survey data made available by the two research organizations (Dossey and Wu, 2012).

In the year 2000 the OECD created PISA to make comparisons across countries of an entire age group (age 15), rather than a school class as the IEA had done (for 4th, 8th, and sometimes 12th grade), and it sought to make a test that represented what students needed to know for successful employment in a modern economy. The analytical reports that come out of the PISA surveys are about student performance in each field (reading, mathematics and science) with detailed analyses of student family background, student attitudes toward learning school subjects, number of hours of study, language spoken at home, immigration and experiences outside of the formal school system (see reference list for partial set of publication by OECD). The contributions of PISA to the discussion of student achievement have been widely heralded by researchers and journalists (Ripley, 2013) as having raised attention to country level achievements even further. Thus, since the year 2000, two models of educational measurement compete. They differ in definitions of student knowledge, in selecting the characteristics of the school system that are measured, in how to present differences within and between countries, and in emphasis of the role of family background compared with educational practices (an issue that was made salient by both the Coleman and Plowden Reports of 1967). Each survey model offers researchers ample resource opportunities for advancing a systematic analysis of educational practices.

WHAT CAN BE LEARNED FROM CONDUCTING RESEARCH BY COMPARING COUNTRIES:

While the results of the international comparisons conducted over the past 50 years have provided some durable findings (such as the role of a demanding curriculum; Floden, 2002; Schmidt et al., 2013) their role in inferring causal links between school factors and outcomes of individual students or schools is limited because of the complex nature of comparing entire systems and limitations on measuring complex human interactions (Carnoy and Rothstein, 2013;

Willms, 2006). Yet, the surveys have addressed practical issues in education that can be enacted as educational policies that had not been addressed in other studies such as measuring whether all members of a population have equal opportunity to learn all topics in mathematics (Schmidt and McKnight, 1995; Schmidt et al., 1997a; Schmidt et al., 1998; Schmidt et al., 2001). Government policymakers have paid considerable attention to the findings of these studies and have used the reports to inform policy decisions about weaknesses and strengths in their school systems (Dossey and Wu, 2012; National Commission on Excellence in Education, 1983; Ertl, 2006; Grek, 2009).

The information collected in current ongoing international comparative studies is well suited for investigating enduring issues in educational practices such as equality and equity, opportunity to learn, quality of instruction, material resources for students and schools, types of teaching practices, home environment, time on learning tasks, and student proclivities toward learning. The cross sectional nature of most of the surveys permits only correlational analysis between factors at one point in time, thus reducing the ability to create causal models of effectives of school interventions on achievement. The strength of the studies is that they provide a comprehensive measurement of levels of performance and background factors that are associated with higher levels of school performance and they have been repeated over a sufficient length of time to measure changes in levels of performance of entire systems.

Some of the innovations in educational policies and practices that have resulted from the conduct and analysis of large-scale international comparisons in education are selected here to illustrate the breadth of educational research topics that can be undertaken with the existing databases provided by these studies. Examples of major contributions that emerged from the international comparative studies will be discussed in the following sections including the topics:

1   The emphasis on academic achievement (what knowledge of achievement in different subjects can contribute to policy);
2   Establishment of policy frameworks (standards);
3   Expansion of non-cognitive inputs and outcomes;
4   Expansion of analysis from between individuals to between schools and between countries.

ACHIEVEMENT AS OUTCOME

The main function of the ongoing international comparisons is to assess student achievement of elementary and secondary school students in subjects such as mathematics, science, reading, civics, and technology (see IEA and PISA websites) and of literacy, numeracy, and problem solving among adults (OECD, 2001, 2009, 2013). Other subjects, such as writing and literature, have been attempted but the judgment of psychometricians was that the variability between countries on what constituted high quality writing was too great to be tested among countries (Bloom, 1971; Purves, 1973). When the results of international comparisons are released by the survey organizations, the results invariably are reported widely by news organizations in each country thereby leading to specula-tion and debate about the meaning of the results (Ripley, 2013). The consequence of the discussions of these studies when they were released in the 1980s was to bring greater attention by policymakers, educators, and parents to academic achievement itself as a product of schooling (National Commission on Excellence, 1993). Thus, we can say that the public discussions of educational differences between countries have been a factor in altering discussions of the role of increas-ing student achievement in formal education (Ertl, 2006; Husén, 1987).

Testing an entire subject area of student knowledge with short 40-minute tests challenges the capacity of educational researchers to validly and reliably measure student learning. Assessing student knowledge fairly across countries is compli-cated by differences in language, curriculum, and many unknown factors that may affect how a student perceives a question. The two international compara-tive studies discussed in this chapter use different approaches for designing their assessment framework. The TIMSS, for example, is designed to assess whether the intended curriculum of a country was learned by the students (Travers and Westbury, 1989; Robitaille et al., 1993). Thus, the test items in TIMSS are designed to align with a representation of the curriculum of the tested countries. Consequently, for the TIMSS international comparisons to be fair, science top-ics that are experienced equally across the globe must be selected. Similarly, for all subjects, the content of the test must be perceived as a fair representation of the intended curriculum of each country (Travers and Westbury, 1989). The experience of designing test items for curriculum-based tests in science for many countries can be visualized by imagining how to create a test item on the origin of seasons. Such an attempt failed because the question was considered inappropri-ate by Indonesians who do not experience dramatic seasonal changes.

The model for assessment used by OECD for the PISA science, mathematics, and reading achievement is not tied to the curriculum instead they are designed to portray the 'yield' of a country's education system to prepare youth to function in a knowledge economy. The PISA questions involve examples of problem solving given a situation that a student would find in everyday living or at work condi-tions. Furthermore, the PISA test is not grade-based as in TIMSS but is given to an age group of 15-year-olds. That age was chosen to represent the accumulation of knowledge by students at the end of formal school.

The experience of international researchers over the past 50 years with devel-oping tests that are appropriate across countries has led to improvements in understanding testing itself and in reporting the results of these tests (Hencke et al., 2012). Technical reports produced by each study describe how the content of tests are defined and how items are created (Mullis and Martin, 2011; OECD, 2009a, 2009b, 2012, 2014, 2013b). These reports not only inform researchers about the test development for these particular studies but they also provide examples to educational researchers of best testing practices because they were developed with highly skilled researchers working together across many countries. Once test items are developed to measure the variety of study knowledge of each area the final selected items are then reduced to measurement scales of content areas and presented in statistical tables as scores along a continuum (Martin et al., 2004; OECD, 2009a, 2012, 2014).

Since the earliest international comparative studies educators have been wary that a single test given to multiple countries could adequately measure an entire field of mathematics, science, or reading (Freudenthal, 1978; Grisay and Griffen, 2006). Therefore, analysists of the international studies have developed techniques to measure the applicability of a test item to the local school system. For example, in 1995 the teachers participating in TIMSS were asked to which extent their classes covered 21 mathematics topics. Second a smaller set of topics represented by mathematics problem sets were posed to teachers who reported on whether these topics were used in classrooms. Then, the entire set of test items was reviewed by a country level mathematics curriculum specialist who determined whether each test item was 'matched' with the country's 'intended' curriculum. The 'matched item' exercise has been carried out in each TIMSS survey and reported in a table of the official reports (Beaton, 1998; Martin, et al., 2004). For example, the 2011 international report on TIMSS described the following procedures for establishing whether the test item was 'matched' to the country curriculum: National Research Coordinators were asked to indicate whether each of the TIMSS 2011 mathematics topics was included in their countries' intended curriculum through the fourth or eighth grade, and if so, whether the topics were intended to be taught to 'all or almost all students' or 'only the more able students.' (Mullis et al., 2012). The percentage of TIMSS test items that were signified as covered by the curriculum expert ranged from about 80 to 95 percent of items (Suter, 2017).

Beaton and Mullis have reported that the country rankings would be the same no matter whether the item selection represented only those rated as being matched or not (Beaton, 1998; Mullis and Martin, 2011; Mullis et al., 2012). A more recent analysis of how test items that are matched or not to each country was conducted with the items of the 2003 TIMSS by Hencke et al., (2012) using modern scaling methods of Item Response Theory (IRT, see Muthen, 1991). IRT creates scales that are equivalent and thus can be more reliably compared with each other than simple averages of percent correct. Hencke et al. computed IRT scores for all combinations of items by whether they were matched or not to each country (Hencke et al., 2012). Their findings support the IEA International center claim that virtually any combination of test items produced scores that were highly correlated with the items considered appropriate for each country. No matter which combination of test items was used, the rankings of countries on that subject were identical (with an r of .999 or 1 for the 46 tested countries in 2003). This finding is surprising because the percentage of mathematics items reported in some countries as 'not covered' ranged from 8 percent in arithmetic to 19 percent in geometry. In other words, the ranking of student performance differences between countries does not appear to be affected by whether or not the test items were said to be covered in the classrooms. However, in more recent years the number of countries participating in testing has increased and as a greater variety of countries is tested in the IEA and OECD studies the greater the differences are likely to be (Suter, 2017).

POLICY FRAMEWORKS AND EDUCATIONAL STANDARDS

Another consequence of the wide public discussion of international comparative studies has been increased attention to the content of the school curriculum. One way to consider the relationship between policy and student learning is through how the curriculum is implemented in the classroom. Travers and Westbury (1989; Dossey and Wu, 2012) outlined the IEA model of intended curriculum (as defined by the state), the implemented curriculum (as the content was presented in the classroom) and the achieved curriculum (as learned by the students). The intended curriculum is established by policies of the governments and textbook publishers in most countries (Westbury, 2008). The basis for making fair international comparison of student achievement begins with the development of a common framework of the content of curriculum in each subject field, such as mathematics and reading. The framework must include topics intended to be covered in each participating country while omitting those topics that are unique to a few countries (Robitaille et al., 1993; Mullis et al., 2003a; OECD, 2013b). The frameworks must also be sensitive to the implemented curriculum that may differ from the intended. Thus, the assessment frameworks used by the international comparative studies have served two functions. First, they provide a common basis for organizing a test with items that form the basis for making fair comparisons between countries. Second, the very existence of a professionally developed classification of a content area contributes a significant organizational system for defining standards for school instruction and student achievement of particular areas such as science and mathematics (Dossey and Wu, 2012; Ertl, 2006; National Council of Teachers of Mathematics, 1989, 2000).

Dossey and Wu (2012) describe in detail how the progression of development from the first, second and third IEA international mathematics studies led toward the mathematics professional organizations instituting a published set of standards in education in the United States during the 1980s and 1990s (Dossey and Wu, 2012; National Council of Teachers of Mathematics, 1989, 2000). They also discussed how the results of PISA supported the development of national goals in Belgium, New Zealand, Sweden (Owen et al., 2004) and even high achieving Finland (Välijärvi et al., 2002). Following the release of the 2000 PISA results in reading, German officials urged for reform measures in education (Ertl, 2006).

Also, Grek (2009) outlined in some detail how Finland and Germany modified their educational systems following the publication of PISA results between 2000 and 2006. Thus, the comparative studies have affected educational policy not only by publication of comparative 'league' tables that showed countries ranked by achievement levels but also by developing an organizational system for defining educational content and practices. As Grek points out, the testing frameworks are often widely accepted by policy leaders because the survey organizations are considered to be 'highly competent' (Grek, 2009).

Assessment frameworks usually have multiple dimensions made of subject matter content in one dimension and categories of knowledge in another. For many years, Bloom's taxonomy of learning has been used as a dimension of test development. Those categories of Bloom's taxonomy (Bloom, 1956) are:

A. Factual Knowledge – The basic elements that students must know to be acquainted with a discipline or solve problems in it. Terminology, details and elements.
B. Conceptual Knowledge – The interrelationships among the basic elements within a larger structure that enable them to function together. Classifications, categories, principles, generalizations, theories, models, and structures.
C. Procedural Knowledge – How to do something; methods of inquiry, and criteria for using skills, algorithms, techniques, and methods.
D. Metacognitive Knowledge – Knowledge of cognition in general as well as awareness and knowledge of one's own cognition: Strategic, contextual, and conditional knowledge and self-knowledge.

But these categories have been modified in recent years. Three examples of a framework for science illustrate how different conceptualizations of school-based science can be created for test development. The first example shown here is a framework published by the US National Academy of Sciences (National Research Council, 2012). It illustrates how test items are developed to fit into cells of a multi-dimensional matrix of level of cognitive demand by school content areas (Figure 15.1).

Figure 15.1

Science Content performance	Cognitive Demand	Cross-Cutting and Interdisciplinary Content				
		Knowing	Applying	Reasoning	Inquiry Skills	
					Basic	Advanced
Biology						
Chemistry						
Physics						
Earth/Space Science						

Source: National Research Council (2012).

Second, the two international frameworks used for science student assessment in the TIMSS and PISA assessments illustrate how definitions of content areas may differ greatly even though the resulting ranking of countries is similar. The TIMSS framework is school-based with a theoretical structure based on the elements of the content of instruction in the intended curriculum and relates the impact of that curriculum to the implemented curriculum and attained curriculum (Travers and Westbury, 1989). The framework developed for the 1995 TIMSS included the following dimensions for each topic mathematics and science (Robitaille et al., 1993):

- Content areas (80 specific scientific disciplines; 44 mathematics topics)
- Performance expectations (understanding, theorizing, using tools, investigating, communicating)
- Perspectives (attitudes, career expectations, participation, interest, safety, and habits of mind).

The TIMSS frameworks were developed from topics found in textbooks and national definitions of content areas, not from general theory of learning (Dossey and Wu, 2012) following criticism of how mathematics topics were selected for the 1965 IEA mathematics study by mathematics educators (Freudenthal, 1978). Extensive empirical analysis of how the topics of mathematics and science were covered in elementary and secondary schools of many countries was conducted prior to the creation of the TIMSS achievement tests (Schmidt and McKnight, 1995). The results of the empirical analysis of content coverage across countries found that while not every topic of mathematics or science is taught at the same grade in every country, that eventually all topics in mathematics and science were covered in all countries (Schmidt et al., 1997a). The model of defining specific content areas a priori led to an extensive research program questions about the effect of differences in patterns of curriculum coverage on student achievement (Schmidt et al., 2001; Suter and Cai, 2014). However, the frameworks do not remain stable over time. This framework was modified in later versions of TIMSS as data analysis and changes in the countries participating led the framers of the study to change the emphasis to fit new demands of analysis (Mullis, et al. 2003a, 2009, 2011).

The PISA framework, on the other hand, began through a cooperative systematic effort by country members of OECD to establish a new basis for an international educational statistical system that was relevant for working conditions. The PISA framework explicitly includes 'inquiry' as an aspect of science learning by an international committee of education and science experts. The test items tend to be items of general problems faced by engineers, for example, but that could be solved with logic and experience (rather than by rote memory as in TIMSS). The OECD Framework for Science published in 2006 used four areas of student performance (OECD, 2009b, p. 34, 2013b):

- Context: recognizing life situations involving science and technology.
- Knowledge: understanding the natural world on the basis of scientific knowledge that includes both knowledge of the natural world, and knowledge.

- Competencies: demonstrating scientific competencies that include identifying scientific issues, explaining phenomena scientifically, and drawing.
- Attitudes: indicating an interest in science, support for scientific enquiry, and motivation to act responsibly towards, for example, natural resources and environments.

The content frameworks provide a structure for item selection and scale development for a student assessment. For example, the content framework for TIMSS science lists 80 topics in science areas that are likely to be found in elementary–secondary school classrooms. PISA created a framework that defined general properties of education without specific content areas. Hundreds of specific test items are written by item writers for the key topics of the framework (Mullis et al. 2005, 2009). Scales are created from the final chosen items with statistical procures such as the IRT model that force items to be ranked from high to low ability. The results of these scales are then evaluated by content experts to judge whether they actually appear to reflect the content that was intended in the framework.

The question of whether countries differ in achievement because of differences in how the curriculum is organized has been a matter of continual research and discussion (Travers and Westbury, 1989). For example, the comparative rankings of countries have shown that Asian countries such as Japan, China and Korea have the highest levels of achievement in mathematics and that concepts of algebra and advanced geometry are introduced earlier in those curricula but that the school systems do not repeat the topics in later years (Suter and Cai, 2014; Schmidt et al., 1998; McKnight et al., 1987). These findings have led mathematics educators some countries, such as the United States, to systematically alter the textbooks and policies to introduce the teaching of algebra topics at earlier grades (Kilpatrick et al., 2007).

NON-COGNITIVE ASSESSMENT

The international frameworks for test development categorize only cognitive behaviors (such as knowing, applying, and reasoning). Existing frameworks for achievement rarely include attitudes or engagement practices, qualities that are also affected by schooling. The 1995 TIMSS framework contained a dimension called 'Perspectives' that was made up of attitudes, career expectations, and habits of mind that are characteristics of persons who are most likely to continue with a career in the science and mathematics (Robitaille et al., 1993). But that dimension was never fully populated with test items because none of the researchers involved with subject matter item development had experience with combining content (science or mathematics) with non-cognitive behaviors. The framework was dropped from TIMSS frameworks after 2000 (Mullis, et al. 2009). While the IEA and OECD surveys both include items that ask students about their attitudes toward a subject (especially science or mathematics), they are conceived mainly as explanatory concepts rather than outcomes of learning experiences. The attitude items chosen for the surveys do not appear to emanate from an existing theory of learning or goal setting. The PISA surveys especially in 2006 include an extensive battery of attitude scales that are related to country level performances in publications of science achievement and are somewhat related to theories of student motivation such as the expectancy-value theory model (Wigfield and Eccles, 2000; Eccles et al., 1989) Nine scales made from 50 items in the 2006 PISA survey most clearly demonstrate the content of non-cognitive measurement methods in the international comparative studies. The attitude measures for science, as an example, included:

1 General value of science
2 Personal value of science
3 Self-efficacy in science
4 Self-concept in science
5 General interest in science
6 Enjoyment of science
7 Instrumental motivation to learn science
8 Future-oriented motivation to learn science
9 Science-related activities.

The association between attitude scales of motivation is mostly positively related to the cognitive test scores, but the average level of association is weak at only around .20 (PISA, 2007, Chapter 3). Thus, it is possible to conclude that the two dimensions of student learning – cognitive and attitudinal – are more independent from each other than are dependent and as such are worthy of continuing research and analysis. The non-cognitive measures included in each of the surveys have changed over the years as researchers have examined their power to explain student achievement differences.

EXPANSION OF ANALYSIS FROM BETWEEN INDIVIDUALS TO BETWEEN SCHOOLS AND BETWEEN COUNTRIES

How the large scale international comparative studies may be used to examine the differences between individuals, between schools and between countries is illustrated by an example of research conducted by Willms (2006). Willms conducted an analysis of reading achievement in two international studies collected during years 2000 to 2002. One aim of this example is to illustrate how large databases may be used to examine country to country differences in how factors known to affect student achievement, such as socio-economic status. The example uses methods to compute gradients in relationships between socio-economic status and reading literacy. The report of the full study includes an expansive explanation of how the statistical models are computed and presented.

The two studies are the Progress in International Reading Literacy Study (PIRLS) which was conducted in 2001 under the auspices of the International Association for the Evaluation of Educational Achievement (IEA). It involved 35 countries to assess the literacy skills of pupils in their fourth grade of elementary school using a comprehensive measure of early literacy skills. The study included surveys of students, parents, teachers and school administrators. Findings are presented in PIRLS 2001 International Report (Mullis et al., 2003b). The second survey included in this example is the Programme for International Student Assessment (PISA) which is a collaborative initiative of member countries of the Organisation for Economic Co-operation and Development (OECD) to assess the knowledge and life skills of 15-year-old youth as they approach the end of their compulsory period of schooling. The PISA reading literacy tests are primarily concerned with whether measuring whether students can apply the knowledge they have learned at school, rather than the measuring the content of secondary school curricula. The PISA assessment was conducted included 46 countries. The assessment also collected extensive information on students' family background, including family structure, the education level and occupation of parents, and several aspects of social and cultural capital available to students (OECD, 2001).

The social outcome in this study example is students' reading performance and a socio-economic gradient is defined as the relationship between reading achievement and socio-economic status for individuals in a specific jurisdiction, such as a school, a province or state, or a country (Willms, 2003). The PISA measure of socio-economic status (SES) was derived from survey reports of parental education, occupation and possessions in the home. The PIRLS measure was based on parents' level of education, occupational status and family income. The level of the gradient is defined as the expected score on the outcome measure for a person with average SES. The level of a gradient for a country (or for a province, state or school) is an indicator of its average performance, after taking account of students' socio-economic status. The slope of the gradient indicates the extent of inequality attributable to SES. Steeper gradients indicate a greater impact of SES on student performance – that is, more inequality – while more gradual gradients indicate a lower impact of SES – that is, less inequality. The strength of the gradient refers to the proportion of variance in the social outcome that is explained by SES. If the strength of the relationship is strong, then a considerable amount of the variation in the outcome measure is associated with SES, whereas a weak relationship indicates that relatively little of the variation is associated with SES.

The most basic hypothesis about the slopes of SES gradients is that there is a significant bivariate relationship between reading literacy and SES. In the simplest case, this hypothesis can be tested for a continuous outcome measure, such as reading performance using ordinary least squares regression analysis and displaying the socio-economic gradients graphically (Willms, 2006, p. 32). The results show clearly that the levels of achievement and the slopes between socio-economic status and achievement vary considerably among countries for grade 4 students assessed in PIRLS and for 15-year-old students assessed in PISA.

Thus, the answer to the question, 'Do schools vary in their educational performance?' is unequivocal: there are large and statistically significant differences among schools in their performance within and among countries. At grade 4, countries with the highest mean scores tend to be more homogeneous in their achievement and have fewer students with very low scores. At age 15, the differences among schools and among countries are larger in absolute terms, and as at grade 4, the most successful countries are those with fewer students with very low scores. In other words, the countries with the highest scores tend to achieve their high performance not simply by raising all students' scores uniformly but also by reducing the number of children with very low scores.

The policy question of whether placing students in schools with an equal distribution of socio-economic status rather than placing them in schools selective of high or low status affects the learning outcomes of students was explored by Willms. He examined between-school and between-classroom segregation of students with differing ability and SES. In countries with large differences in characteristics of students from school to school (compositional effects), there are two basic strategies for raising and levelling the socio-economic gradient. One is through reforms aimed at bolstering the achievement levels of low SES schools. The other strategy is through inclusive reforms aimed at decreasing the segregation between schools as was performed in Sweden during the 1960s (Dahllöf, 1966). The schooling systems that have the best results, meaning high and equitable student performance, with very few exceptions have low levels of between-school segregation. When students are segregated into different kinds of programs, the gap tends to increase and overall levels of performance become worse as they progress through school. This is evident if the PIRLS and PISA results for Bulgaria, Germany, Hungary, Latvia and the Russian Federation, which have highly selective school systems after age 10, are compared with the results for Canada, New Zealand and Sweden which have more inclusive systems through the end of secondary school. At the grade 4 level, the former group of countries had relatively high average levels of achievement on the PIRLS reading test, with scores ranging from 528 to 550. However, the PISA results for 15-year-olds for the more selective systems were all below the OECD mean (a notable exception is Hong Kong its scores in PIRLS and PISA were comparable to those of New Zealand, even though its system is quite selective). Thus, this analysis of reading supports the claim that school composition affects students differently at different ages (Willms 2003, 2006).

RESOURCES FOR COMPARATIVE EDUCATION DATA

All surveys conducted by the IEA are available to researchers for secondary analysis. They may be found at the IEA data repository (http://www.iea.nl/data.html).

Databases for the IEA has conducted 11 surveys in mathematics and science (TIMSS and the first and second mathematics and science studies separately), five surveys in use of computer technology, four studies of reading, two of civics education and one of teaching. Most of the survey data for these surveys are available from the IEA website.

Also, all surveys conducted by OECD are available on the PISA website for use by researchers (http://www.oecd.org/pisa/pisaproducts/). For each of the survey years from 2000 to 2012, the OECD website includes reports of analysis of the students, schools and countries; research papers, test questions, background questionnaires, by students, school principals and parents. It includes the assessment frameworks and technical reports that describe how the surveys were implemented. And the website contains the actual survey data with manuals and data analysis techniques. As well as translation manuals and guidelines.

The extensive catalogues of reports and data files prepared by these two organizations are a resource for all researchers. The databases may be used as a basis for comparison to local studies as well as for exploration of particular hypotheses. For example, the PISA survey in its attempt to measure how students use time after school have created some of the few survey measurements of time use for formal and informal settings. The analyses of these data have created a new set of hypotheses for informal learning (Suter, 2017).

CONCLUSION

The theme of this chapter is that the development of large scale international comparative studies conducted by the IEA and OECD have developed over the past 50 years to become a basic resource for all researchers in education for theory, measurement, and practice. The studies provide a basis for objective analysis of student achievement, the surveys are developed by highly skilled researchers and thus are authoritative. If the results and procedures found in the published reports and available databases were more widely exploited by researchers, the result could be an increase in the accumulation of knowledge of educational practices.

It was a political event, the launching of Sputnik in 1958, that led to high levels of national interest in the quality of education of Western countries and thus to increased level of funding for objective studies of student achievement. The release of ranks of comparisons of achievement between countries has been used by some countries as a lever to gain support for educational practices. But, politics were not the intent of the originators of the studies. Leading educational researchers used the opportunity of conducting cross national studies to create objective analysis rather than draw invidious comparisons (Husén, 1967a). They intended the comparative studies to be used to increase knowledge of education by using differences in educational practices throughout the world as a 'natural laboratory' for a scientific description and analysis. This chapter provides an introduction to two international comparative surveys and provides an example of how the data were used to address policy questions of great importance to educational equity.

Research using cross-national comparisons of educational outcomes and practices has expanded greatly over the past 50 years in both quantity of surveys and quality of methods used (Papanastasiou et al., 2011). The surveys collect detailed information for samples of students in many topics and several ages and over periods of time. The significance of international comparative surveys is that they are useful to generate, and test, new hypotheses about relationships between student achievement and student and teacher characteristics. The publicly available databases themselves provide a source of reliable methodologies for conducting investigations that help to place local studies within a larger context.

Beginning and experienced researchers cannot ignore the body of evidence produced by these studies. The analytical reports and survey data bases have been made easily available on public websites. Moreover, the published technical reports, questionnaires, analytical reports, and basic tabulations of the IEA and PISA cross-national studies provide a good foundation of useful methods and baseline comparisons for many new research projects. These reports and methodologies are broad based enough and well enough tested that they could form the basis for a broader accumulation of knowledge of educational processes if researchers included some of the PISA or IEA survey items and methods as a piggy back to their own studies of local educational systems (Porter and Gamoran, 2002).

This chapter does not provide a formula for conducting analyses of cross-national studies nor did it attempt to introduce all of the measurement concepts that are available in them. It introduced the issues that stimulated the development of large international comparative surveys with the expectation that new researchers could use the information provided by the studies a resource for new studies and provides an example of one such analysis. Researchers with access to the reports, analyses, and data bases should be able to develop and test hypotheses about such issues as student performance, family background, curriculum coverage, family influences on students, study habits, and work attitudes. For example, the relationships between attending after school programs and student achievement may be studied with PISA surveys unlike in any other study (Bray, 1999; Suter, 2017).

REFERENCES

Beaton, A. E. (1998). Comparing cross-national student performance on TIMSS using different test items. *International Journal of Educational Research*, 29(6), 529–542.

Bloom, B. S. (1956). *Taxonomy of Educational Objectives*. Handbook I: Cognitive domain. New York: David McKay Company.

Bloom, B. S. (1971). Mastery learning, in J. H. Block (Ed.) *Mastery Learning. Theory and Practice* (pp. 47–63). New York: Holt, Rinehart & Winston.

Bracey, G. W. (2006). *Reading Educational Research: How to avoid getting statistically snookered.* Portsmouth, NH: Heinemann.

Bray, M. (1999). The shadow education system: private tutoring and its implication for planners. *Fundamentals of Education Planning*, 61. Paris: UNESCO.

Bray, M., Adamson, R., and Mason, M. (2007). *Comparative Education Research: Approaches and Methods.* CERC Studies in Comparative Education, University of Hong Kong. Springer.

Brown, M. (1998). *The Tyranny of the International Horse Race.* books.google.com.

Burstein, L. (Ed.) (1993). *The IEA Study of Mathematics III: Student growth and classroom processes.* Oxford: Pergamon.

Carnoy, M. (1999). *Globalization and Educational Reform: What planners need to know.* Paris: United Nations Education, Scientific, and Cultural Organisation.

Carnoy, M. (2006). Rethinking the comparative and the international. *Comparative Education Review*, 50(4), 551–570.

Carnoy, M. and Rothstein, R. (2013). *What do International Tests Really Show about US Student Performance?* Washington, DC: Economic Policy Institute.

Coleman, J. S., Campbell, E. Q., Hobson, C. J., McPartland, J., Mood, A. M., Weinfeld, F. D., and York, R. L. (1966). Equality of educational opportunity. Washington, DC: U.S. Government Printing Office

Cummings, W. (1999). The Institutions of Education, Compare, Compare, Compare!, *Comparative Education Review*, 43 (November), 413–437.

Dahllöf, U. (1966). Recent reforms of secondary education in Sweden. *Comparative Education*, 2, 71–92.

Dahllöf U. (1973). The curriculum development system in Sweden: some comments on present trends and problems. *International Review of Education*, 19(2), 218.

Dossey, J. A. and Wu, M. L. (2012). Implications of international studies for national and local policy in mathematics education, in Alan J. Bishop, Christine Keitel, Jeremy Kilpatrick, and Frederick K. S. Leun (Eds) *Third International Handbook of Mathematics Education* (pp. 1009–1042). Dordrecht: Springer.

Eccles, J. S., Wigfield, A., Flanagan, C., Miller, C., Reuman, D., and Yee, D. (1989). Self-concept, domain values, and self-esteem: relations and changes at early adolescence. *Journal of Personality*, 57, 283–310.

Ertl, H. (2006). Educational standards and the changing discourse on education: the reception and consequences of the PISA study in Germany. *Oxford Review of Education*, 32(5), 619–634.

Floden, R. E. (2002). The measurement of opportunity to learn. In A. C. Porter and A. Gamoran (Eds) *Methodological Advances in Cross-National Surveys of Educational Achievement* (pp. 231–266). Washington, DC: National Academy Press.

Foshay, A. W., Thorndike, R. L. Hotyat, F., Pidgeon, D. A., and Walker, D. A (1962). *Educational Achievements of Thirteen-Year-Olds in Twelve Countries. Results of an international research project, 1959–1961.* Hamburg: UNESCO Institute for Education.

Freudenthal, H. (1975). Pupils' achievement internationally compared – the IEA. *Educational Studies in Mathematics*, 6, 127–186.

Freudenthal, H. (1978). *Weeding and Sowing: Preface to a science of mathematical education.* Amsterdam: Reidel.

Glass, G. V. (2008). *Fertilizers, Pills, and Magnetic Strips: The fate of public education in America.* Charlotte, NC: Information Age Publishing.

Grek, S. (2009). Governing by numbers: The PISA 'effect' in Europe. *Journal of Educational Policy*, 24(1), 23–37.

Grisay, A. and Griffin, P. (2006). What are the main cross-national surveys. In K. N. Ross and J. Genevois (2006). *Cross-National Studies of the Quality of Education: Planning their design and managing their impact*. UNESCO, International Institute for Educational Planning, 67–96.

Hencke, J., Rutkowski, L., Neuschmidt, O., and Gonzalez, E. (2012). Curriculum coverage and scale correlation on TIMSS 2003. IERI Monograph Series: Issues and Methodologies In Large-Scale Assessments.

Heyneman, S. P. (2003). International education: a retrospective. *Peabody Journal of Education*, 78(1), 33.

Husén, T. (1967b). *International Study of Achievement in Mathematics: A comparison of twelve countries*, Vol. 2. New York: Wiley.

Husén, T. (1967a). *International Study of Achievement in Mathematics: A comparison of twelve countries*, Vol. 1. New York: Wiley.

Husén, T. (1979). An international research venture in retrospect: the IEA surveys. *Comparative Education Review*, 23.

Husén, T. (1987). Policy impact of IEA research. *Comparative Education Review*, 31.

Husén, T. and Boalt, G. (1967). *Educational Research and Educational Change: The case of Sweden*. Stockholm: Almqvist & Wiksell; New York: John Wiley.

International Association for the Evaluation of Educational Achievement (IEA). (2011). Brief history of the IEA. Retrieved on 8/20/2015 from www.iea.nl/brief_history_of_iea. html

Kilpatrick, J., Mesa, V., and Sloane, F. (2007). US algebra performance in an international context. In Tom Loveless (Ed.) *Lessons Learned: What international assessments tell us about math achievement* (pp. 85–126). Washington, DC: Brookings Institution Press.

Lerner, B. (1982). American Education: How are we Doing?, The Public Interest. 0, 69, 59–82 (Retrieved on August 15, 2016 from ProQuest Information and Learning Company, 2001).

Lewis, C. and Takahashi A. (2011). Facilitating curriculum reforms through lesson study. *International Journal for Learning and Lesson Studies*, 2, 3, 207–217.

Martin, M., Mullis, I., and Chrostowksi, S. (2004). TIMSS 2003 technical report. Chestnut Hill, MA: TIMSS & PIRLS International Study Center, Lynch School of Education, Boston College.

McKnight, C. C., Crosswhite, F. J., Dossey, J. A., Kifer, E., Swafford, J. O., Travers, K. J., and Cooney, T. J. (1987). *The underachieving curriculum: Assessing US school mathematics from an international perspective*. Champaign, IL: Stipes Publishing.

Medrich, E. A. and Griffith, J. E. (1992). International mathematics and science assessments: What have we learned? Retrieved on 4/13/2012 from nces.ed.gov.opac. acc.msmc.edu.

Mullis, I., Martin, M., Smith, T., Garden, R., Gregory, K., Gonzalez, E., Chrostowksi, S., and O'Connor, K. (2003a). *TIMSS Assessment Frameworks and Specification 2003*, 2nd edition. Chestnut Hill, MA: TIMSS & PIRLS International Study Center, Lynch School of Education, Boston College.

Mullis, I. V. S., Martin, M. O., Gonzalez, E. J., and Kennedy, A. M. (2003b). *PIRLS 2001 International Report: IEA's Study of reading literacy achievement in primary schools*. Chesnut Hill, MA: Boston College.

Mullis, I.V.S., Martin, M. O., Ruddock, G. J., O'Sullivan, C.Y., Arora, A., and Eberber, E. (2005). TIMSS 2007 Assessment Frameworks

Mullis, I. V. S., Martin, M. O., Ruddock, G. J., O'Sullivan, C. Y., and Preuschoff, C. (2009). *TIMSS 2011 Assessment Frameworks*. Chestnut Hill, MA: TIMSS & PIRLS International Study Center, Boston College.

Mullis, I. V. S., and Martin, M. O. (2011). *TIMSS 2011 Item Writing Process and Guidelines*. TIMSS and PIRLS International Study Center, Boston College.

Mullis, I. V. S., Martin, M. O., Foy, P. and Arora, A. (2012). *TIMSS 2011 International Results in Mathematics*. Amsterdam, the Netherlands: TIMSS & PIRLS International Study Center, Lynch School of Education, Boston College Chestnut Hill, MA, USA.

Muthén, B. O., Kao, Chih-Fen and Burstein, L (1991): Instructional Sensitivity in Mathematics Achievement Test Items: Application of a New IRT-Based Detection Technique Journal of Educational Measurement, Vol. 28, No. 1 (Spring, 1991), pp. 1–22.

National Commission on Excellence in Education. (1983). A nation at risk: The imperatives of education reform. Washington, DC. Retrieved on 9/13/16 from www2.ed.gov/pubs/NatAtRisk/index.html

National Council of Teachers of Mathematics. (1989). *Curriculum and Evaluation Standards for School Mathematics*. Reston, VA: NCTM.

National Council of Teachers of Mathematics. (2000). *Principles and Standards for School Mathematics*. Reston, VA: NCTM.

National Research Council. (2012). A Framework for K-12 Science Education: Practices, Crosscutting Concepts, and Core Ideas. Committee on a Conceptual Framework for New K-12 Science Education Standards. Board on Science Education, Division of Behavioral and Social Sciences and Education. Washington, DC: The National Academies Press.

Organisation for Economic Co-operation and Development. (2001). Knowledge and skills for life: first results from the OECD programme for international student assessment (PISA) 2000. Paris: OECD.

Organisation for Economic Cooperation and Development. (2007). PISA 2006: science competencies for tomorrow's world. Paris: OECD.

Organisation for Economic Co-operation and Development. (2009a). PISA 2006 technical report. Paris: OECD.

Organisation for Economic Co-operation and Development. (2009b). PISA 2009 assessment framework key competencies in reading, mathematics and science. Paris: OECD.

Organisation for Economic Co-operation and Development. (2010). PISA 2009 results volume v. 'learning trends: changes in student performance since 2000, looks at the progress countries have made in raising student performance and improving equity in the distribution of learning opportunities'. Paris: OECD.

Organisation for Economic Co-operation and Development. (2012), PISA 2009 technical report, PISA. Paris: OECD Publishing. Retrieved on 8/1/2015 from http://dx.doi.org/10.1787/9789264167872-en.

Organisation for Economic Co-operation and Development. (2013a). Programme for the international assessment of adult competencies. Paris: OECD. Retrieved on 8/15/2015 from oecd.org/site/piaac/mainelementsofthesurveyofadultskills.htm.

Organisation for Economic Co-operation and Development. (2013b). PISA 2012 assessment and analytical framework – mathematics, reading, science, problem solving and financial literacy. Paris: OECD.

Organisation for Economic Co-operation and Development. (2014). PISA 2012 technical report. OECD Publishing. Retrieved on 6/13/2013 from www.oecd.org/pisa/pisaproducts/PISA-2012-technical-report-final.pdf.

Organisation for Economic Co-operation and Development. (2016). PISA products. Retrieved on 3/12/2016 from www.oecd.org/pisa/pisaproducts/.

Owen, E., Stephens, M., Moskowitz, J., and Gil, G. (2004). Toward education improvement: the future of international assessment. In J. H. Moskowitz and

M. Stephens (Eds) *Comparing Learning Outcomes: International assessments and educational policy* (pp. 3–23). London: RoutledgeFalmer.

Papanastasiou, C. Plomp, T., and Papanastasiou, E.C. (Eds.). (2011). *IEA 1958–2008. 50 years of experiences and memories*. Nicosia, Cyprus: Cultural Center of the Kykkos Monastery.

Peaker, Gilbert. (1975). *An Empirical Study of Education in Twenty-one Countries: A technical report*. New York: Wiley.

Philips, D. and Schweisfurth, M. (2014). *Comparative and International Education: An introduction to theory, method, and practice*, 2nd edition. London, Bloomsbury.

Plowden, B. Central Advisory Council for Education (England). (1967). Children and their Primary Schools. London: Her Majesty's Stationery Office. Retrieved on 13/9/16 from www.educationengland.org.uk/documents/plowden/.

Porter, A. C. and Gamoran, A. (Eds) (2002). *Methodological Advances in Cross-National Surveys of Educational Achievement*. Washington, DC: National Academy Press.

Purves, A. C. (1973). *Literature Education in Ten Countries*. Stockholm: Almquist & Wiksell; New York: John Wiley & Sons.

Ripley, A. (2013). *The Smartist Kids in the World and How they Got that Way*. New York: Simon and Schuster.

Robitaille, David. F., Schmidt, William. H., Raizen, Senta., McKnight, Curtis., Britton, Edward., and Nocol, C. (1993). *Curriculum Frameworks for Mathematics And Science*. Vancouver: Pacific Educational Press.

Ross, K. N. and Genevois, J. (2006). *Cross-National Studies of the Quality of Education: Planning their design and managing their impact*. UNESCO, International Institute for Educational Planning.

Schmidt, W. H. and McKnight, C. C. (1995). Surveying educational opportunity in mathematics and science: an international perspective. *Educational Evaluation and Policy Analysis*, 17(3), 337–353.

Schmidt, W. H., Jakwerth, P. M., and McKnight, C. C. (1998). Curriculum sensitive assessment: content does make a difference. *International Journal of Educational Research*, 29(6), 503–527.

Schmidt, W. H., McKnight, C. C., and Raizen, S. A. (1997a). *A Splintered Vision: An investigation of US science and mathematics education*. Dordrecht, the Netherlands: Kluwer.

Schmidt, W., Zoido, P., and Cogan, L. (2013). Schooling matters: opportunity to learn in PISA 2012, OECD Education Working Papers, No. 95. Paris: OECD. Retrieved on 6/10/14 from http://dx.doi.org/10.1787/5k3v0hldmchl-en.

Schmidt, W. H., McKnight, C. C., Valverde, G. A., Houang, R. T., and Wiley, D. E. (Eds) (1997b). *Many Visions, Many Aims (TIMSS Volume I): A cross-national investigation of curricular intention in school mathematics*. Dordrecht, the Netherlands: Kluwer.

Schmidt, W. H., McKnight, C. C., Houang, R. T., Wang, H. C., Wiley, D. E., Cogan, L. S., and Wolfe, R. G. (2001).*Why Schools Matter: A cross-national comparison of curriculum and schooling*. San Francisco, CA: Jossey-Bass.

Suter. L.E. (2017 forthcoming). How international studies contributed to educational theory and methods through measurement of opportunity to learn mathematics. Accepted by Comparative and International Education.

Suter, L. E. and Cai, J. (2014). Characterizing Chinese mathematics curriculum a cross-national comparative perspective. In B. Sriraman, J. Cai, L. Kyeong-Hwa et al. (Eds). *The First Sourcebook on Asian Research in Mathematics Education: China, Korea, Singapore, Japan, Malaysia, and India* (pp. 365–392). Charlotte, NC: Information Age Publishing.

Travers, K. J. and Westbury, I. (Eds) (1989).*The IEA Study of Mathematics II: The analysis of mathematics curricula*. Oxford: Pergamon.

Välijärvi, J., Linnakylä, P., Kupari, P., Reinikainen, P., and Arffman, I. (2002). *The Finnish Success in PISA – and Some Reasons Behind It*. Jyväskylä, Finland: Finnish Institute for Educational Research, University of Jyväskylä.

Walker, D. A. (1962). An analysis of the reactions of Scottish teachers and pupils to items in the geography, mathematics and science tests. In A. W. Foshay, R. L. Thorndike, F. Hotyat, D. A. Pidgeon, and D. A. Walker (Eds) *Educational Achievement of Thirteen-Year-Olds in Twelve Countries*. Retrieved on 2/2/2012 from http://unesdoc.unesco.org/images/0013/001314/131437eo.pdf.

Westbury, I. (2008). Making curricula: Why do states make curricula, and how? In F. M. Connelly, M. F. He and J. Phillion (Eds) *The SAGE Handbook of Curriculum and Instruction* (pp. 45–69 London: Sage Publications.

Wigfield, A. and Eccles, J. S. (2000). Expectancy-value theory of achievement motivation. *Contemporary Educational Psychology*, 25, 68–81.

Willms, J. D. (2006). *Learning Divides: Ten policy questions about the performance and equity of schools and schooling systems*. UNESCO Institute for Statistics. Montreal, Quebec Canada.

Willms, J.D. (2003). Ten hypotheses about socioeconomic gradients and community differences in children's developmental outcomes. Report prepared for Human Resources Development Canada.

16

Ethnography

Sara Delamont

INTRODUCTION

The chapter defines ethnography, a variety of qualitative research, and briefly outlines the history of ethnographic research in education, contrasting the anthropological and sociological traditions. Centrally it explains the stages of an ethnographic project, with advice on key aspects of conducting it successfully, including analysis and writing up. Examples come from the whole age-range and from formal and informal educational settings. Longer and more elaborated versions of the argument can be found elsewhere (Delamont, 2012a, 2012b, 2012c, 2014, 2016a).

This chapter focuses on 'pure' ethnography (defined here as research based on long term immersion in a field site) and briefly on the use of ethnographic approaches in mixed method designs. Ethnography is sometimes used misleadingly to include interview-based projects, for which 'qualitative' is a more accurate term. It is unhelpful to label work as ethnographic if it is not primarily based on long-term fieldwork. My position is a somewhat traditional or conservative one (like Atkinson et al., 2003; Hammersley and Atkinson, 2007), and more controversial approaches can be found in Somerville (2008) and Bagley (2009). The most important determinant of which methods are chosen must be the research questions, the confidence the researcher has in them and the data they produce. Ethnography is one type of qualitative research, and the terms 'participant observation' and 'fieldwork' are often used as synonyms for it. While the centrepiece of an ethnographic project is the observer(s) being physically present in the online or offline setting (Second Life or a university chemistry lab) watching and listening to the interaction, good researchers gather other types of data too. They talk to people in the setting, formally and informally, individually or in groups or both. Documents are collected, pictures taken, maps drawn, and censuses and surveys done. The usual actors in the setting may be asked to write for the project, or draw, or take pictures. Sounds, smells, tastes and textures in the setting are also part of the data. No competent ethnographer just watches passively, but being present is vital and fundamental. Boellstorff (2008) is the seminal ethnography in a virtual world, just as Proweller (1998) is a classic in the offline world. This chapter focuses primarily on offline settings because educational ethnography in online settings has so far been relatively uncommon (but see Girvan et al., 2013; Girvan and Savage, 2010, 2012; Webster and da Silva, 2013). Boellstorff et al. (2012) is a useful text on how to do ethnography in virtual worlds.

ETHNOGRAPHY AND EDUCATION

There have been regular overviews of ethnographic research on educational settings and processes for over sixty years, such as those by Spindler (1955), Burnett (1974), Hammersley (1980), Wilcox (1982), Jacob (1987), Gordon, Holland and Lahelma (2001), Yon (2003) and Delamont (2012c, 2014).Projects can be done with ethnography as the main method (for example, Pascoe, 2012; Moffat, 1989) or incorporating some ethnographic data gathering into a more mixed method design such as the ORACLE projects (for example, Galton and Willcocks, 1983, Hargreaves and Galton, 2002) – see below. Anthropologists regard ethnography, especially long-term, sustained fieldwork in a setting (such as a Mexican village), as their discipline's fundamental method. In educational research there is a long history of anthropological work (Spindler, 1955), mostly conducted by scholars based in north America, with a focus on ethnic minorities (Ogbu, 1981), Native Americans and Canadians (King, 1967; Wolcott, 1967) and areas of the world where US influence is strong such as Mexico and the Philippines. Anderson-Levitt (2012) and Levinson and Pollock (2011) have edited compilations of the best of the anthropology of education. Despite its long history the anthropological approach is the minority one. The majority of the educational projects done using ethnographic methods have had either an explicitly sociological focus (for example, Swidler 1979) – an approach that dates back to Hollingshead (1947) in the USA and Hargreaves (1967) in the UK – or show no specific disciplinary or theoretical stance.

Sociological ethnography in education is bedevilled by typologies, qualifiers and confusing links to epistemology or grand theory. It is easy to read six ethnographic monographs about urban secondary schools in English-speaking countries that report very similar interactions, perspectives and strategies among the pupils and the staff, but are characterised very differently. Such studies can be described by intimidating labels such as 'critical' or 'neo-materialist' or 'neo-realist' or 'poststructuralist' or 'feminist', and locate their authors as 'critical race theorists', or 'constructivists' or 'phenomenologists' or 'Foucauldians'. None of that, or any other categorisation or branding, helps the novice do their own research, or trace and make sense of any of the previous studies done over the past sixty years (see Delamont, 2012c, 2014). Given the continuities of schooling, such as the hierarchical cliques in the American High School (Ortner, 2003; Crosnoe, 2011), or the fears British children have about their transfer to secondary schools (Mellor and Delamont, 2011), that is a serious problem for the new scholar.

Scholars in educational research can always benefit from exploring publications on methods from outside educational research. Issues of research design, research ethics, or writing and analysis are not specific to educational research. On the contrary, issues of method are generic across any and every research setting. Ethnographers of educational settings need not only to read beyond their national boundaries; they also need to read beyond the confines of education. We can always, in principle, learn about educational institutions by examining institutions of other kinds – workplaces, total institutions, therapeutic settings, and so on. There are multiple social processes that transcend taken-for-granted distinctions. Equally, ethnographers of educational settings need to define 'education' as broadly as possible, paying attention to processes of learning and enculturation wherever and whenever they occur. Ethnographic understanding is not fostered by too narrow an analytic focus, while a thoroughly comparative perspective can often encourage the generation of ideas that are generic and not tied to any one local setting or institutional type. By the same token, such comparative thought is not fruitful if analysts waste time focusing on small local differences rather than the development of broad, generic analytic concepts and frameworks. In general, ethnographers need to avoid parochial styles of thought, whether based on ethnocentrism, ignorance, or narrow disciplinary emphasis. There is always value in working comparatively across time, across disciplines, and across countries in order to fight familiarity (see Delamont, 2005, 2014, 2016a). An elite boarding school in Australia (Yeo, 2010) has similarities with similar schools in the USA (Proweller, 1998; Yon, 2000; Kahn, 2011, Kahn and Jerolmack, 2012), or the UK that researchers benefit from recognising.

In order to promote a pragmatic approach to the nature and conduct of ethnographic research, in this chapter I draw on material across time, and across the Anglophone world. I do not dwell on confusing labels and qualifiers preferring to focus on practicalities. There are many textbooks that provide advice on how to conduct an ethnography (Walford, 2008; Mills and Morton, 2013; Delamont, 2016a), but beginners may well learn more from what is sometimes called the 'confessional' literature. That label implies that the authors have done terrible things, but actually it refers to autobiographical accounts by researchers of what actually happened when they set out to conduct an ethnography. Reading how a big name, such as Lois Weis or Diane Reay, actually did their project can be more helpful than textbook advice. Walford (2002) edited a collection of reflections on doctoral projects, which is particularly useful for doctoral students to consult. Among the collections of autobiographical papers relevant to educational research are Burgess (1984, 1985a, 1985b, 1985c), de Marrais (1998), Spindler (1982, 2000), Spindler and Spindler (1987) and Walford (1987, 1991, 1994).

Ethnography has been used in all areas of formal education, from pre-schools and kindergartens to postdoctoral programmes, in formal settings outside conventional 'education', such as martial arts classes, dance studios, army training and driving schools, and in informal contexts where enculturation takes place such as hunting, fishing, basket weaving and becoming a medium. The range of settings where educational ethnography has taken place is displayed in Delamont (2012a), and in Singleton (1998). Some ethnographers undertake to learn things themselves, such as the researchers in the Tobias (1990) project who enrolled for science and maths classes at university alongside 'genuine' American undergraduates or Brown and Jennings (2013) learning Kung Fu. What makes an ethnography 'educational' is not its location within a school or a college, but its analytic emphasis on formal or informal arrangements and processes that contribute to the socialisation or enculturation of members, of modes of knowledge-transmission, and practices of pedagogy.

Sometimes claims are made that 'traditional' ethnographic projects are vanishing and that it is 'impossible' to get book length ethnographies published: see, for example, St Pierre and Roulston (2006). Yet researchers continue to do ethnographic projects and publishers still produce books (monographs) such as Ward (2015), Pascoe (2012), Fitzpatrick (2013), Kahn (2011), Crosnoe (2011) Weis et al. (2014), Casanova (2010), and Griffin (2015). It is also arguable that because of the growth of formal and informal education in virtual worlds, there will be a golden age of educational ethnography centred on studies of online teaching and learning.

Stages of educational ethnography

The stages are essentially similar to all research projects. However, one of the chief characteristics of ethnographic research is that it does not follow a linear research design. Access, for example is continuously and continually negotiated, (re)negotiated, extended, restricted, terminated and begun again. Writing up is done from the genesis of the research questions until long after the actual fieldwork ends. Some stages overlap more than others, and some are more clearly demarcated, especially entering and leaving the field. In the eleven subsections there is reference to two types of record that an ethnographer must keep: fieldnotes taken in situ and an 'out-of-the-field' diary, which is a resource for the analytic, methodological and personal reflection that characterises the fieldwork process (see subsection 5).

RESEARCH QUESTIONS OR FORESHADOWED PROBLEMS

Ethnographers rarely talk about hypotheses, but do have research questions, and generally formulate them as foreshadowed problems. They do not enter the field with empty minds. Fieldwork started without foreshadowed problems is much harder: entering the field with some ideas, usually from the literature, prevents the first days in the field (Geer, 1964) being vacuous. However one of the core principles of ethnography is to be prepared to abandon any preconceptions if the data collected offer other avenues for the investigator. Imagine an ethnographer with access to study doctoral students in education in the UK starting with fore-shadowed problems based on the findings of the 1983 BERA enquiry (Eggleston and Delamont, 1983) into the experiences of postgraduate students. The ethnographer might expect that the key issues for students would be problems with methods of data collection and analysis, and two kinds of isolation (a destructive social isolation and an essential, but scary intellectual isolation): the key problems reported in 1983. However in 2016 the researcher might find that the students were excited about and empowered by the methods training they had had (a plausible change since 1983) and used social media so successfully they did not feel socially isolated: so two of the three foreshadowed problems no longer existed. The students now had two preoccupations entirely absent from the 1983 study: what their supervisors meant by two mysterious (to the students) phenomena. That is, the Impact Factors of journals and the UK Research Excellence Framework requirement for Impact Case Studies. These could be confusing because the word 'Impact' means two distinct things that staff need to be concerned about. The ethnographer would rapidly change the focus to exploring those preoccupations. Such a shift of focus is normal, even essential in the development of an ethnographic project.

Research strategy

It is rare for ethnographers to talk of a research design, but they do have strategies to ensure good data collection. The plan has to be flexible and the investigator has to be self-consciously and self critically reflexive. Many pitfalls can be avoided if the ethnographer proceeds systematically. Among many other issues, the field researcher repeatedly has to think about the range and variety of people and/or situations that are to be observed. In a school, it can be too comfortable to find a clique of students or teachers and spend all the time with them. Cusick (1973) for example found one group of young men, and his portrait of the high school is actually only their view of it. No teacher perspectives, no female viewpoints, and no other students' behaviour or experiences are covered. Of course a study of one male clique is fine as a project, but is not a study of high school. US high schools have diverse cultures (Palonsky 1975), and different sexes, races and classes use the time, space, curricula and opportunities very differently (Crosnoe 2011).

The strategies must ensure that before the end of the fieldwork researchers have observed the learners and the teachers in all the possible spaces, at all the possible times, have seen the whole curriculum and discovered what the school offers. Sometimes it is not possible to get access to everything, but that is itself a finding and should be carefully, and reflexively, documented in the fieldnotes and the 'diary'. If the ethnographer is female, and a clique of male teachers meet in private space at lunchtime and play poker, it may not be possible to follow them there, but that inaccessibility is itself a discovery about the gender regime of the staff groups. This reflects what fieldworkers need to understand in terms of sampling. Ethnographers do not sample according to pre-set criteria, or statistically-based notions of representation. Rather, as the fieldwork progresses, a process of purposive sampling develops, to ensure an adequate exposure to different settings, to different times of the year/semester/week/day, to different categories of learners and teachers (successful/unsuccessful, experienced/novice, and so on). These categories will reflect the emergent analytic categories of the research itself, and are not predetermined. In other words, the 'design' of the research is a series of strategic decisions and responses, and is itself a process.

ETHICS

There are three aspects to the ethical issues that all ethnographers have to face: duty to the people in the fieldsite(s) whose confidentiality and safety have to be paramount, the mental comfort of the researcher who should not do anything that they would not want done to them, and the organisational regulations that projects have to satisfy. These three aspects apply to research in the offline and online worlds, and of course many possible research sites involve informants who move seamlessly between offline and online 'worlds'.

Webster and da Silva have a useful discussion of ethics for the researcher who wants to gather data 'only online or through a blended approach (online and offline)'. The central issue is that notions of 'public' and 'private' are constantly changing in online worlds and 'new' facilities (such as Periscope at the time of writing) develop fast. I went to a martial arts class in 2015 and found that the teacher had set his phone up with Periscope 'switched on' to transmit the proceedings to all his 'followers'. That possibility was not in the application made to my university for ethical approval because I had not foreseen that any instructor would do such a thing. So Webster and da Silva (2013, p. 125) are correct to state that: 'the ethnographic researcher must think about her own ontological assumptions about space and privacy'.

Ethnographers must remember that they may have a better understanding of how public exposure can damage informants than the informants themselves.

If, for example, a newspaper decides to 'expose' some subculture, and is able to discover the 'real' identities of a teenage gang, or a group of traveller gypsies or a coven of neopagan witches, via the ethnographer's writing or lectures or media participation, the researcher has failed in his or her duty of care. Ball's (1984) careful protection of the 'real' Beachside Comprehensive School is a good model to follow.

Apart from the ethnographer's own moral sense, it is important to think about how the ethics issues have been addressed by the 'experts'. The learned societies for anthropology (AAA in the USA, ASA in the UK) publish ethical guidelines for ethnographic research, and it is helpful to consult them alongside those of the educational research organisations such as AERA and BERA. There are some notorious cases of ethnographic research in the past that are today judged to have been unethical such as Humphries's (1970). UK universities have ethics committees, and American ones have Institutional Review Boards (IRBs) which give formal approval to projects. Because it can take time to get a project 'past' an ethics committee it is wise to start the process in good time, and to acquire copies of successful ethnographic applications which did get ethical approval to use as models. Rossman and Rallis (2010) is a special issue of *International Journal of Qualitative Studies in Education* on Everyday Ethics that raises key topics. Where the educational setting involves children, researchers in the UK will need to have an official statement that they do not have a criminal record, and many types of data collection, especially visual methods, will need informed parental consent for each child involved as well as the consent of the teachers, and the students themselves.

Current ethical regulation in many institutional contexts is unhelpfully and inappropriately individualistic. As Liberman (1999) suggests, it reflects a distinctively Western preoccupation with individual rights and obligations. It pays insufficient attention to the ethnographer's necessary collective engagement with groups, cultures, organisations or networks. It is also inappropriate to universalise or globalise individualistic, neo-liberal views of social values and commitments. Consequently, ethnographers can find it troublesome to be faithful simultaneously to their preferred research strategy and to externally imposed ethical, or even legal, requirements.

ACCESS: INITIAL AND NEGOTIATED

Access negotiations with formal organisations such as hospitals, prisons or schools nearly always take much longer than the novice expects. Therefore it is sensible to start the negotiations early, expect delays, and have other tasks to get on with while the institutional processes go on. On the plus side a formal organisation is more likely to have a fixed address and a hierarchical structure so it is clearer who can give official approval. Formal requests, often in writing, are often the best way to approach formal organisations. Delamont's (2016a) chapter on access has examples of request letters, and strategies for approaching potential fieldwork sites. Researchers who hope to do an ethnography in a school near their university often find that those schools complain they are over-researched. Schools further away from any university may be more receptive. Other sorts of places where non-formal education takes place, such as skateboarding venues (Petrone, 2010), or Umbanda centres where novices learn how to become possessed by spirits (Leacock and Leacock 1972), or neopagan covens (Greenwood, 2001) where beginners learn how to practice witchcraft, may be harder to find, and lack visible hierarchies or authority structures, but can be easier to access by personal interaction. Even when formal approval has been given, the ethnographer has to work hard every day to establish and maintain it with the actors in the setting. Most informants will not have understood what the research 'meant', because good researchers do not handicap themselves by giving enormous amounts of detail, but seek general access by saying things like: 'I hope to understand more about how the new intake make sense of physical education' or 'I'm interested in how school science is actually taught and learnt'. Actors in the fieldsite have not usually had an experience of observational research, and find the reality is not what they expected. So they ask questions such as 'Why do you want to watch my lacrosse lesson?' 'Why are you writing things down?'. Also, informants may deliberately test the researcher. Teachers leave the ethnographer 'in charge' of a class, or require her to join the pupils on the cross country run, or announce that they are going to let the boys play cards while they mark exam scripts but 'don't tell the Head'. Similarly pupils may deliberately disrupt their class, go shoplifting, or boast about their sexual conquests (Pascoe, 2012 Appendix, 175–194) to see if the ethnographer's promise of confidentiality is 'real'.

It is particularly complicated if some people withdraw their consent while the research is going on. And that is why treating research ethics on an individualistic basis can be difficult, as standard ethical procedures normally expect individual consent, when the individual may withdraw from the research at any stage. A field project (say in a youth orchestra) cannot come to a halt if just one participant 'withdraws'. In practice, researchers often have to deal with reluctant or recalcitrant members by explicitly agreeing not to approach them for interview, or avoiding small-group occasions when they participate. Sometimes more formal face-to-face explanations and clarifications may also be needed. Like all aspects of the ethnography, it requires strategic decision-making and action on the part of the fieldworker, which must be documented.

VARIETIES OF DATA

It is hard to make final decisions about what varieties of data to collect (that is, what are desirable and what are possible) before the researcher is installed in the setting.

The central data of any ethnography are fieldnotes (Emerson et al., 2011). Traditionally these were written by hand by the observer in the field, and amplified and expanded. That second stage involved researchers dictating the notes for a secretary to type or typing them herself. More recently researchers have used voice recognition software, or taken a keyboard into the field and typed the notes ab initio. As audio equipment has got more portable and cheaper, its use has increased, with speech, and ambient sounds being captured in situ. Cameras and video recorders have also become cheaper and more portable, increasing their use to make visual records of events and locations. Other sources of data are interviews (formal and informal), documents (both those that already exist, and those solicited from informants such as diaries or student essays). Where the fieldsite is an online one, such as Second Life or Mumsnet, the 'data' are likely to be the blogs, tweets, and posts of actors, and can be the interaction an avatar has with other avatars (see Boellestorff et al., 2012).

Ethnographers also get informants to draw, make collages, create maps, and are generally creative about encouraging them to give 'voice' to their perceptions, understandings and ways of seeing their social worlds. Seyer-Ochs (2006) used maps, drawn by the high school students she studied in San Francisco. It is important, whatever the types of data being collected, that the rationale for their collection, reflections on how it worked and on how the researcher's race, class, gender, and self-presentation may have influenced the collection are all recorded in the diary. So, for example, if the ethnographer's avatar is a glamorous blonde woman the data will be different from those gathered by an avatar who is an elderly Rastafarian with waist-length dreadlocks. Good ethnography depends on thoughtful inclusion of such things in the reflections.

READING AND WRITING EN ROUTE

Good ethnography involves a great deal of reading and writing. The reading is vital to force the ethnographer to keep comparing and contrasting their fieldsite with other social settings (Delamont, 2014, 2016a). The writing becomes the data, the reflexivity and the eventual outputs. If the fieldnotes are scrappy and inadequate, it is hard to produce a useful thesis or article. If the out of the field reflexive diary is not comprehensive and richly detailed it is hard to reconstruct the research process. Regular reading, reflected upon, enriches the data and the diary. Few ethnographies or textbooks are explicit enough about what to write and how to write either fieldnotes or the diary. Walford (2009) interviewed four experienced education ethnographers, exploring and comparing in detail the creation of fieldnotes. Emerson et al. (2011) is more explicit than most textbooks, and Delamont (2016a) has a chapter in which the 'raw' scribbles, the written up narrative, the diary and the eventual publication, of a savate (French kick boxing) class are set out. To illustrate what can and should go into the fieldnotes I have used an example of what I write when doing observation of a capoeira (the Brazilian martial art) class for adults. I developed these focuses and strategies doing research in schools, and adapted them for the capoeira fieldwork.

What to Write: When I get into the space (classroom, gym, chemistry lab or swimming pool) I find somewhere safe and unobtrusive where I will not impede on the action. Then I draw the hall, noting the floor (wooden, stone, matting?), any equipment (a ballet bar, wall mirrors, exercise mats, hula hoops) and record some of the physical context of the space. For example whether there are changing rooms and showers for use after class, a kitchen, lavatories. Moving on to the teacher(s) and the students I focus on their clothing. In a school I would record how the teachers are dressed (gowns? smart suits? lab coats?) and what proportion of the pupils are in uniform. In the capoeira research I check whether teachers and students come with their capoeira kit on under their street clothes, or do they just change in public view? If the latter, is it men only, or both sexes? Is there a clock? Is it right? What temperature is it? What notices are posted? Do they say 'no drugs, no guns, no knives' or 'Can you help with the bingo on Wednesdays?' or both? Do they stress keeping everything locked up, and are the windows covered with wire netting or bars? On my diagram I mark where I stood or sat, and if I move to see something, hear something or even join in, I note that too.

I count the students, by sex and race. I record how many were prompt, and add any latecomers. Capoeira in Britain is done in uniform, and I count how many people are in full kit, in partial uniform, and in ordinary clothes. Beginners' classes usually have lots of people in ordinary clothing, advanced students generally own uniforms, so a clothing census indicates how many are new to capoeira. Capoeira groups mostly have a grading system with belts of different colours. If I know the colour hierarchy of the group, a count of the belts of each colour will tell me how many of those present are beginners versus more advanced learners. If I do not know the hierarchy, I record the colours anyway and ask later, or look on the website.

A typical class opens with a warm up, of running, stretching and bending. Most teachers train with a CD of capoeira music on. I will find out what the CD is and record that, and describe the warm up – how many press-ups? Squat thrusts? Lunges? Does the teacher do all the warm-up exercises himself, or mostly yell instructions, or get an advanced student to lead it for him? Once the teaching begins, I record each move taught (by its Portuguese name), in as much technical detail as I can. I note what the teacher says, verbatim if I can: so my notes will include things like 'T yells "Look ahead, look ahead"', or 'T stresses the angle of the kicking leg'. If the students are strangers to me, so I do not yet know their names, I'll give them brief descriptions (large man in red kit – 'LMRK') or mnemonics (girl looks like Kelly Holmes – KH). If I later get introduced, or watch the class again I'll add their real and capoeira nicknames into the notes retrospectively.

As the class proceeds I might record a variety of other things. Some are factual such as how sweaty people are, how the money is collected, whether there is live music. Others are more judgemental, such as how hard the lesson is and how fiercely the people play. However I am careful to record the signs I use to make these judgements. I have watched over 800 lessons, so I can tell a simple class from a hard one, as it would be rated by students who have been learning for three years or so, but I will note both my judgement and the way the students in that class are responding to it. So I might write 'All but two of the men are struggling to do this sequence, and it seems hard to me'.

Reflecting afterwards: Ethnographers in educational settings have observed contexts in which they were expert, and those of which they knew nothing, and all types of learning milieu in between. Each produces problems. If the researcher is an expert it is very hard not to be judgemental, rather than dispassionate. If the researcher knows nothing – for example German lessons when they have no knowledge of that language – it is hard to study the content of the course. The most important thing is to be reflexive, and focus on how the knowledge or lack of it, is affecting the data collection. My early days in capoeira classes are recorded in notes that reflected my bafflement, but phrased as questions I needed to explore (for example, 'I must ask Achilles why he is so insistent on how the hands are placed on the floor'). When I decided I was becoming too 'expert' in capoeira I started observing a different martial art (savate) to force myself back into a novice 'outsider' role.

In the field I write very brief notes, mostly in abbreviations. As soon as I get to a quiet place away from the field I copy up a much longer version, spelling out all the abbreviations, such as 'KH', to remind me what I meant (a woman of about 25 who looks like the athlete Kelly Holmes), and filling in a lot more detail while it is fresh. So to amplify the note 'all but two of the men are struggling'. I would add: 'nearly everyone can do the initial kick and escape it but almost all the pairs are unable to move from the escape (an angola laterale) over into the bridge (ponte) and/or go on up into the corkscrew – like one handed spin (s-dobrado). So the sequence begins ok, but collapses into failure at the third or fourth step'. Notes such as these still have real names and identifying features in them, so have to be anonymised before publication, but I can analyse them for my own use.

Separately I write an entry in my out of the field diary reflecting on that bit of fieldwork. So I have three different notebooks. These days most people I know word-process their written up notes so they are online, either by typing them or via word-recognition software. The most important thing is that the sooner the rough notes are written up, and the reflexive writing is done, the better.

ENTERING AND LEAVING THE FIELD

There is a bigger literature on 'First days in the field' or 'Initial Encounters' than on leaving it. All the textbooks and the confessional accounts explore initial encounters. Geer (1964) remains the classic, but many confessional texts focus on early weeks (for example, Deyhle, 1998) and especially on mistakes the researcher made. The importance of initial encounters is that the ethnographer will see things and hear things and smell things and feel things that are novel and these sensations need to be documented before they become familiar. Detailed notes and a good deal of reflexive writing are both particularly important at the initial encounter stage.

Very few scholars have explored leaving the field. Iverson (2009) explores exits, based on research experience and some literature. There is a dedicated chapter in Delamont (2016a) and a 'confessional' paper (Delamont, 2016b). A section in the collection edited by Shaffir et al. (1980) draws on a survey of some leading American male sociologists of the 1960s about exit. Altheide (1980) has an insightful piece on how, once a fixed exit date was made public, he could collect different types of data, and interact with informants in a different way. It is important to ensure that informants know that the research is ending and that all the exit processes are documented.

Relationships in the field

In the ideal ethnographic project, the actors in the setting come to like and trust the researcher, to be a friend, and vice versa. The investigator is adopted into the social networks being studied, and informants explain everything openly and honestly. In reality such idyllic relationships have to be worked at. There is ample advice on how to establish good rapport with informants in the textbooks and most of the autobiographical accounts focus on how the ethnographer managed life in the staffrooms, the classes, and the playground or the non-school setting. Being careful to follow the ethical guidelines, guarding the confidentiality of people, and remaining slightly neutral (that is, not stating strong positions) help. It can be good to do 'chores' and be practically helpful, but not at the expense of data collection or enough to change the norms of the setting. Again reflexivity is important. If a teacher or group of teachers are suspicious or hostile, hard thinking about why and whether it will damage the research is needed. Rallis (2010) is a very useful account of the breakdown of all relationships in a school, which is helpful to read.

ANALYSIS

The classic text on analysis is Coffey and Atkinson (1996), coupled with Becker (1986, 1998). While software packages have been developed that can make some of the retrieval of coded data more systematic (usually called CAQDAS – computer aided qualitative data analysis software) they do not replace human creativity. They can retrieve material tagged, classified or coded by a human being with social science imagination. If the ethnographer is interested in heteronormativity, or aesthetic judgements, or sibling labelling, that ethnographer has to be brave enough to categorise some features of the data (fieldnotes, transcripts, documents or whatever) as 'about' those things. Informants are unlikely to use the social science label 'heteronormativity'; but might use phrases like 'I hate those Julian Clary boys', or 'I cannot be doing with sissies and mummy's boys who don't try at rugby' or 'I don't like the girls coming to school in slacks all the time' or 'Did you see the little Patel girl in the playground draped round Fatima Mohani? I can't bear to see it'. The researcher has to classify those as statements of heterosexual norms held by teachers and/or as gender stereotyping of the sort reported by Peterson (1964) and Datnow (1997, 1998). In those, very 'dated', comments I have also tried to suggest things that might be said by teachers at the end of their career, rather than newly qualified staff, because the mode of expression of prejudices, stereotypes and labels may differ by the age and generation of the teachers.

The most important thing is never to let the data pile up untranscribed and unanalysed: even if that means coming out of the field for a day or so to catch up. Provisional analysis is essential, because the provisional conclusions lead to changing the working hypotheses, and collecting different data to 'test' them. Writing analytic memos as you go is vital so the ongoing analysis is also reflected upon. Generally it makes sense to work with middle-order concepts in the first instance. These can help the researcher to develop a detailed analysis of the local setting, and facilitate comparison with other settings. Moving quickly to all-encompassing issues ('power', 'postcolonialism') can short-circuit such analysis, resulting in reductionist accounts that merely illustrate some grand theoretical scheme, and losing sight of the concrete detail revealed by the fieldwork.

WRITING AGAIN

How ethnographic work is written for others to read has been much discussed since Atkinson (1982, 1990, 1992) and Clifford and Marcus (1986). The four-volume set edited by Atkinson and Delamont (2008) contains papers on how ethnography is represented. Briefly, there have been three changes: first, writing and reading are done in reflexive ways, second, there is more emphasis on presenting different 'voices' in the publications, and third, many literary forms (such as poems, plays, dialogues and so on) are used instead of one impersonal dispassionate authoritative authorial 'voice'. The *International Journal of Qualitative Studies in Education* has specialised in the 'new' literary forms, and on de-centering the author. At the more practical level, there are several excellent advice books on how to write up qualitative research (for example, Wolcott, 2001; Delamont 2016a, Chapter 12). The more regularly people write the better they get at it, and so the best advice is (a) 'Write early and write often' and then (b) 'Don't get it right, get it written' which does not mean getting it wrong, but does mean that drafting and redrafting text improves it. A blank page cannot be redrafted, a scrappy paragraph can be.

ETHNOGRAPHY IN MIXED METHODS DESIGNS

The most important thing about incorporating ethnographic data collection into a mixed method project is that different methods derive their strengths from contrasting philosophical positions. A quasi-experiment is based on a positivist philosophy, which aims to be scientific, so relies on ideas of the reliability and validity of objective data, while an ethnographic project is based on the idea that social worlds are socially constructed, and 'objectivity' is not an achievable or desirable goal for social science. Mixed method research designs are generally fixed, to answer set research questions or text hypotheses, whereas ethnographers work in a series of loops, following the initial findings by adapting the ideas and changing the focus of the data collection. So there are some fundamental incompatibility in working procedures. If one researcher is able to collect different types of data and use them that is not a big problem, because the individual researcher can build a portrait of the setting from different social science angles, keeping an open mind about the philosophy, and being pragmatic. It is harder when an interdisciplinary team work with a mixed method project, and there is not equal intellectual confidence in all the methods across the team. It is utterly miserable to be the ethnographer in a team if some other people disparage the data being collected: see Rallis (2010).

My main experience of working as the lone ethnographer in a mixed method, but largely process-product qualitative study, was the first ORACLE (Observational Research and Classroom Learning environment) study from 1976 to 1981. There was a team of researchers but none had done ethnographic work before. I was responsible for the ethnographic study of pupils' first month in the six 'secondary' schools, observing in four of the six myself, and publishing from everyone's fieldnotes (Delamont, 1983, Delamont and Galton, 1986). The qualitative data were valued, but it was very clear, in retrospect, that I should have insisted on all the research assistants having intensive training in ethnographic methods (see Galton and Delamont, 1985). I only realised that they needed it after the data collection was over.

Very often in mixed methods designs qualitative data of all kinds are intended, as and used as, illustrations of findings provided by the tests and surveys: for example if the girls' physics test scores are poor, observational and interview data about girls' in physics classes are used to make their dislike of the subject 'come alive' for readers. Any ethnographer employed to gather and write up such data has a duty to do that.

The legacy and achievements of educational ethnography

Ethnographers of teaching and learning can celebrate the depth, breadth and strength of the research done with their chosen method across the globe. Delamont (2014) is an overview of the achievements of educational ethnography, broadly defined, and examples of excellence across a time period of seventy years are reprinted in compilations of papers from throughout the Anglophone world edited by Torrance (2010) and Delamont (2012b). The approach has made a substantial contribution to educational knowledge. Ethnographic research in educational settings has proved to be both memorable, and enduring. The well written ethnographic monograph is surprisingly long-lasting. The most insightful study of medical students, still readable and informative in 2016, is Becker et al.'s (1961) *Boys in White* reporting research done in 1958 in Kansas. Many of the experiences of and reactions to medical education found in that cohort of men – all now long retired from the profession – are repeatedly found in today's medical schools all over the world. The ethnographies of the American high school and its hierarchical cliques, conducted from Hollingshead (1947) onwards, reveal an institution which is enduring in its positive and its negative outcomes for students, and is profoundly 'American' in ways that American researchers have repeatedly failed to notice (see Ortner, 2003). The cumulative returns of ethnographic research often make uncomfortable reading, but that is itself a strength of the research tradition. Many of the results of qualitative work, such as the finding that ability grouping and grade retention both polarise pupils and produce anti-school feelings in those stigmatised by being in 'low' streams or held back to repeat a year, are best understood when the insightful ethnographies, such as Lacey (1970) or Jones (1991) are read.

CONCLUSION

Ethnographic research is not an easy option. It is hard to do, because it is very tiring, mentally and physically, particularly because reflexivity is itself exhausting. However when done carefully and conscientiously, the data can be powerful, enduring and make great social science. Ethnographic research is not intended simply to generate one-off 'case-studies'. As suggested here, it should be thought of as both cumulative and comparative. Further, such comparisons should not be confined to narrowly-defined studies of education, restricted to the most obvious of educational institutions. Teaching and learning take place in a wide variety of settings, and the ethnographer's analytic stance should be equally wide-ranging. Illustrations in this chapter from martial-arts classes illustrate the point. Comparative fieldwork helps us to overcome any sense of over-familiarity with, say, schools and classrooms. And even if such first-hand fieldwork itself is not conducted, then comparative reading will help develop a suitable analytic framework.

The ethnographic purpose is always to move between the local – the specifics of the chosen field site – to the generic, and reciprocally to bring generic ideas to an understanding of the particular.

REFERENCES

Altheide, D. L. (1980) Leaving the newsroom, in W. B. Shaffir, R. A. Stebbins and A. Turowetz (Eds) *Fieldwork Experience*. New York: St Martin's Press, 301–310.

Anderson-Levitt, K. M. (Ed.) (2012) *Anthropologies of Education*. New York: Berghahn.

Atkinson, P. A. (1982) Writing ethnography, in H. J. Helle (Ed.) *Kultur und Institution*. Berlin: Dunker and Humblot, 77–105.

Atkinson, P. A. (1990) *The Ethnographic Imagination*. London: Routledge.

Atkinson, P. A. (1992) *Understanding Ethnographic Texts*. Newbury Park, CA: Sage.

Atkinson, P., Coffey, A. and Delamont, S. (2003) *Key Themes in Qualitative Research*. Walnut Creek, CA: Alta Mira Press.

Atkinson, P. A. and Delamont, S. (Eds) (2008) *Representing Ethnography*, 4 volumes. London: Sage.

Bagley, C. (Ed.) (2009) Shifting boundaries in ethnographic methodology. Special Issue of *Ethnography and Education*, 4, 3, 251–414.

Ball, S. (1984) Beachside reconsidered, in R. G. Burgess (Ed.) *The Research Process in Educational Settings*. London: Falmer, 69–96.

Becker, H. S. (1986) *Writing for Social Scientists*. Chicago, IL: The University of Chicago Press.

Becker, H. S. (1998) *Tricks of the Trade*. Chicago, IL: The University of Chicago Press.

Becker, H. S., Geer, B., Strauss, A. L. and Hughes, E. (1961) *Boys in White*. Chicago, IL: The University of Chicago Press.

Boellstorff, T. (2008) *Coming of Age in Second Life*. Princeton, NJ: Princeton University Press.

Boellstorff, T., Nardi, B., Pearce, C. and Taylor, T. L. (2012) *Ethnography and Virtual Worlds*. Princeton, NJ: Princeton University Press.

Brown, D. and Jennings, G. (2013). In search of a martial habitus, in R. S. Garcia and D.C. Spencer (Eds) *Fighting Scholars*. London: Anthem, 33–48.

Burgess, R.G. (Ed.) (1984) *The Research Process in Educational Settings*. London: Falmer.

Burgess, R. G. (Ed.) (1985a) *Field Methods in the Study of Education*. London: Falmer.

Burgess, R. G. (Ed.) (1985b) *Strategies of Educational Research*. London: Falmer.

Burgess, R. G. (Ed.) (1985c) *Issues in Educational Research*. London: Falmer.

Burnett, J. H. (1974) *Anthropology and Education*. The Hague: Mouton.

Casanova, U. (2010) *Si Se Puede!* New York: Teachers College Press.

Clifford, J. and Marcus, G. (Eds) (1986) *Writing Culture*. Berkeley, CA: California University Press.

Coffey, A. and Atkinson, P. A. (1996) *Making Sense of Qualitative Data*. Thousand Oaks, CA: Sage.

Crosnoe, R. (2011) *Fitting In, Standing Out*. Cambridge: Cambridge University Press.

Cusick, P. (1973) *Inside High School*. New York: Holt, Rinehart and Winson.

Datnow, A. (1997) Using gender to preserve tracking's status hierarchy. *Anthropology and Education Quarterly*, 28, 2, 204–228. Reprinted in S. Delamont (Ed) (2012b) *Ethnographic Methods in Education*, 4 volumes. London: Sage volume IV, 317–339.

Datnow, A. (1998) *The Gender Politics of Educational Change*. London: Falmer.

de Marrais, K.B. (Ed.) (1998) *Inside Stories*. Mahwah, NJ: Erlbaum.

Delamont, S. (1983) The ethnography of transfer, in Part 4 of M. Galton and J. Willcocks (Eds) *Moving from the Primary Classroom*. London: Routledge, 97–153.

Delamont, S. (2005) Four great gates. *Research Papers in Education*, 20, 1, 85–100.

Delamont, S. (Ed.) (2012a) *Handbook of Qualitative Research in Education*. Cheltenham: Edward Elgar.

Delamont, S. (Ed.) (2012b) *Ethnographic Methods in Education*, 4 volumes. London: Sage.

Delamont, S. (2012c) The parochial paradox, in K. Anderson-Levitt (Ed.) *Anthropologies of Education*. New York: Berghahn, 49–70.

Delamont, S. (2014) *Key Themes in the Ethnography of Education*. London: Sage.

Delamont, S. (2016a) *Fieldwork in Educational Settings*, 3rd edition. London: Routledge.

Delamont, S. (2016b) Time to kill the witch? In M. Ward (Ed.) *Gender Identity and Research Relationships*. Bingley: Emerald, 3–22.

Delamont, S. and Galton, M. (1986) *Inside the Secondary Classroom*. London: Routledge.

Deyhle, D. (1998) The role of the applied anthropologist: between schools and the Navaho Nation, in K. Bennett de Marrais (Ed.) *Inside Stories*. Mahwah, NJ: L. Erlbaum, 35–48.

Eggleston, J. F. and Delamont, S. (1983) *Supervision of Students for Research Degrees*. Kendall: Dixons for BERA.

Emerson, R. M., Fretz, R. and Shaw, L. (2011) *Writing Ethnographic Fieldnotes*, 2nd edition. Chicago, IL: The University of Chicago Press.

Fitzpatrick, K. (2013) *Critical Pedagogy, Physical Education and Urban Schooling*. Berlin: Peter Lang.

Galton, M. and Delamont, S. (1985) Speaking with forked tongue, in R. G. Burgess (Ed.) *Field Methods in the Study of Education*. London: Falmer Press, 163–190.

Galton, M. and Willcocks, J. (1983) *Moving from the Primary Classroom*. London: Routledge.

Geer, B. (1964) First days in the field, in P. Hammond (Ed.) *Sociologists at Work*. New York: Basic Books, 372–398.

Girvan, C. and Savage, T. (2010) Identifying an appropriate pedagogy for virtual worlds. *Computers and Education*, 55, 342–349.

Girvan, C. and Savage, T. (2012) Ethical consideration for educational research in a virtual world. *Interactive Learning Environments*, 20, 3, 239–251.

Girvan, C., Tangey, B. and Savage, T. (2013) SLurtles: supporting constructionist learning in Second Life. *Computers and Education*, 61, 115–130.

Gordon, T., Holland, J. and Lahelma, E. (2001) Ethnographic Research in Educational Settings. In P. Atkinson et al. (eds) *Handbook of Ethnography*. London: Sage 188–203.

Greenwood, S. (2001) *Magic, Witchcraft and the Otherworld*. Oxford: Berg.

Griffin, S.R. (2015) *Those Kids, Our Schools*. Cambridge, MA: Harvard University Press.

Hammersley, M. (1980) Classroom ethnography. *Educational Analysis*, 2, 1, 47–74.

Hammersley, M. and Atkinson, P. (2007) *Ethnography: Principles in practice*, 3rd edition. London: Routledge.

Hargreaves, D.H. (1967) *Social Relations in a Secondary School*. London: Routledge.

Hargreaves, L. and Galton, M. (1999) *Transfer from the Primary Classroom: Twenty years on*. London: Routledge.

Hollingshead, A.B. (1947) *Elmtown's Youth*. New York: John Wiley and Sons.

Humphries, L. (1970) *Tearoom Trade*. London: Duckworth.

Iverson, R. R. (2009) 'Getting out' in ethnography. *Qualitative Social Work*, 8, 1, 9–26.

Jacob, E. (1987) Qualitative research traditions. *Review of Educational Research*, 57, 1, 1–50.

Jones, A. (1991) *At School I've Got a Chance*. Palmerstone North: Dunmore Press.

Kahn, S. (2011) *Privilege*. Princeton, NJ: Princeton University Press.

Kahn, S. and Jerolmack, C. (2012) Saying meritocracy and doing privilege. *The Sociological Quarterly*, 54: 9–19.

King, A.R. (1967) *The School at Mopass*. New York: Holt, Rinehart and Winston.

Lacey, C. (1970) *Hightown Grammar*. Manchester: Manchester University Press.

Leacock, S. and Leacock, R. (1972) *Spirits of the Deep*. New York: Doubleday.

Levinson, B. and Pollock, M. (Eds) (2011) *A Companion to the Anthropology of Education*. Oxford: Wiley-Blackwell.

Liberman, K. (1999) From walkabout to meditation: craft and ethics in field inquiry. *Qualitative Inquiry*, 5, 1, 47–63.

Mellor, D. and Delamont, S. (2011) Old anticipations, new anxieties? *Cambridge Journal of Education*, 41, 3, 333–344.

Mills, D. and Morton, M. (2013) *Ethnography in Education*. London: Sage.

Moffat, M. (1989) *Coming of Age in New Jersey*. New Brunswick, NJ: Rutgers University Press.

Ogbu, J. U. (1981) School ethnography. *Anthropology and Education Quarterly*, 12, 1, 3–29.

Ortner, S. (2003) *New Jersey Dreaming*. Durham, NC: Duke University Press.

Palonsky, S. B. (1975) Hempies and squeaks, truckers and cruises: A participant observer study in a city high school. *Educational Administration Quarterly*, 11, 2, 86–103. Reprinted in S. Delamont (Ed.) (2012b) *Ethnographic Methods in Education*, 4 volumes. London: Sage.

Pascoe, C. J. (2012) *Dude, You're a Fag. Masculinity and sexuality in high school*. Berkeley, CA: California University Press

Peterson, W. A. (1964) Age, teacher's role and the institutional setting, in B. J. Biddle and W. Ellena (Eds) *Contemporary Research on Teacher Effectiveness*. New York: Holt, Rinehart and Winston, 264–315.

Petrone, R. (2010) You have to get hit a couple of times. *Teaching and Teacher Education*, 26, 1, 119–127. Reprinted in S. Delamont (Ed.) (2012b) *Ethnographic Methods in Education*, 4 volumes. London: Sage.

Proweller, A. (1998) *Constructing Female Identities*. Albany, NY: SUNY Press.

Rallis, S.F. (2010) 'That is NOT what's happening at Horizon!' *International Journal of Qualitative Studies in Education*, 23, 4, 435–448.

Rossman, G. B. and Rallis, S. F. (Eds) (2010) Everyday ethics. Special Issue of *International Journal of Qualitative Studies in Education*, 23, 4, 379–500.

St Pierre, E. A. and Roulston, K. (Eds) (2006) The state of qualitative inquiry. Special Issue of *International Journal of Qualitative Studies in Education*, 19, 6, 673–811.

Seyer-Ochs, L. (2006) Lived landscapes of the Fillmore, in G. Spindler and L. Hammond (Eds) *Innovations in Educational Ethnography*. Mahwah, NJ: Erlbaum, 169–232.

Shaffir, W. et al. (Eds) (1980) *Fieldwork Experience*. New York: St Martin's Press.

Singleton, J. (Ed.) (1998) *Learning in Likely Places*. Cambridge: Cambridge University Press.

Somerville, M. (Ed.) (2008) Emergent Methodologies. Special Issue of *International Journal of Qualitative Studies in Education*, 21, 3, 209–311.

Spindler, G. (1955) *Education and Anthropology*. Stanford, CA: Stanford University Press.

Spindler, G. (Ed.) (1982) *Doing the Ethnography of Education*. New York: Holt, Rinehart and Winston.

Spindler, G. (Ed.) (2000) *Fifty Years of Anthropology and Education*. Mahwah, NJ: Erlbaum.

Spindler, G. and Spindler, L. (Eds) (1987) *Interpretive Ethnography of Education*. Hillside, NJ: Erlbaum.

Swidler, A. (1979) *Organisation without Authority*. Cambridge, MA: Harvard University Press.

Tobias, S. (1990) *They're not Dumb, They're Different*. Tucson, AZ: Research Corporation.

Torrance, H. (Ed.) (2010) *Qualitative Research Methods in Education*, 4 volumes. London: Sage.

Walford, G. (Ed.) (1987) *Doing Sociology of Education*. London: Falmer.

Walford, G. (Ed.) (1991) *Doing Educational Research*. London: Falmer.

Walford, G. (Ed.) (1994) *Researching the Powerful in Education*. London: UCL Press.

Walford, G. (Ed.) (2002) *Doing a Doctorate in Educational Ethnography*. New York: JAI Press.

Walford, G. (Ed.) (2008) *How to do Educational Ethnography*. London: Tufnell Press.

Walford, G. (2009) The practice of writing ethnographic fieldnotes. *Ethnography and Education*, 4, 2, 117–130.

Ward, M. (2015) *From Labouring to Learning*. London: Palgrave Macmillan.

Webster, J. P. and da Silva, S. M. (Eds) (2013) Doing educational ethnography in an online world. Special Issue of *Ethnography and Education*, 8, 2, 123–272.

Weis, L., Cipollone, K. and Jenkins, H. (2014) *Class Warfare*. Chicago, IL: The University of Chicago Press.

Wilcox, K. (1982) Ethnography as a methodology and its applications to the study of schooling, in G. Spindler (Ed.) *Doing the Ethnography of Schooling*. New York: Holt, Rinehart and Winston, 456–485.

Wolcott, H. F. (1967) *A Kwakiutl Village and School*. New York: Holt, Rinehart and Winston.

Wolcott, H. F. (2001) *How to Write Up Qualitative Research*. London: Sage.

Yeo, W. L. (2010) Belonging to 'Chinatown'. *International Studies in Sociology of Education*, 20, 1, 53–64.

Yon, D. A. (2000) *Elusive Culture*. Albany, NY: SUNY Press.

Yon, D. A. (2003) Highlights and overview of the history of educational ethnography. *Annual Review of Anthropology*, 32, 411–429.

17

Grounded Theory

Robert Thornberg

BACKGROUND

Grounded theory (GT) is a qualitative, iterative, and inductive research approach designed to explore and analyze data to generate a theory on the studied phenomenon (Glaser and Strauss, 1967). It is particularly helpful for investigating individual, social psychological and wider social processes, interaction patterns, and participants' actions and meanings (Charmaz, 2014). Research can for instance include teaching and learning processes, classroom management, group work, peer conflicts, classroom activities, and school bullying. The *iterative* dimension of GT means that the researchers move back and forth between data collection and analysis. The *inductive* logic of GT refers to the idea of beginning by studying individual cases or instances from which more abstract concepts and finally theories are developed.

Although GT is often described as an inductive method, many grounded theorists have understood that GT is actually being based on interplay between induction and abduction (for example, Bryant, 2009; Kelle, 2005; Reichertz, 2010; Richardson and Kramer, 2006; Thornberg and Charmaz, 2014). *Abduction* refers to a selective and creative process in which the researchers carefully examine which hypothesis explains a particular case or segment of data better than any other candidate hypotheses for further investigation (Douven, 2011; Peirce, 1960, 1979). Hence, adopting GT is like doing detective work in which the grounded theorist constantly moves back and forth between data and pre-existing or emerging conceptions, and makes comparisons and interpretations in the search for patterns and best possible explanations.

GT was originally developed by sociologists Barney Glaser and Anselm Strauss while they conducted a field study on dying in hospitals (Glaser and Strauss, 1965, 1968). They defined GT as 'the discovery of theory from data' (Glaser and Strauss, 1967, p. 1). Although they acknowledged the hypothetic-deductive use and verification of 'grand theories' by quantitative methods that dominated the field of social research of the 1960s, they criticized its dominance and overconfidence in 'grand theories' which might not always be adequate to understand and explain people's everyday lives, as well as the lack of aims and methods to discover and generate new theories. In contrast, they offered a set of qualitative methods for constructing theories from data.

Since 1967, GT has been further developed in different versions, and the three most widespread versions today are *Glaserian* GT, *Straussian* GT, and *constructivist* GT.[1] Glaser has published a number of books and articles, but to best understand Glaserian GT (sometimes called 'classic GT' by his advocates, for example, Holton, 2007), the three most important books are *Theoretical Sensitivity* (1978), *Doing Grounded Theory* (1998), and *The Grounded Theory Perspective III: Theoretical coding* (2005). Strauss first presented his further development of GT in his book *Qualitative Analysis for Social Scientists* (1987), and then developed it further, together with Juliet Corbin, in two editions of *Basics of Qualitative Research* (Strauss and Corbin, 1990, 1998). Corbin later released two further editions of this book (Corbin and Strauss, 2008, 2015). Thus, although the label 'Straussian GT' is common, Corbin's contribution to this version has to be recognized. The most prominent scholar in the development of constructivist GT is sociologist Kathy Charmaz, who has written a number of book chapters in various research method books as well as two editions of her book *Constructing Grounded Theory* (2006, 2014). The aim of this chapter is to introduce the main methods and concepts of GT and to describe the main similarities and differences between these three types of GT.

EPISTEMOLOGY

The original GT (Glaser and Strauss, 1967) and Glaser's developed version of GT has often been considered as positivistic or rooted in both positivism and pragmatism. Glaser (2003, 2005, 2009, 2013) however dismisses this and claims that his GT has no epistemology at all. 'The quest for an ontology and epistemology for justifying GT is not necessary' (Glaser, 2005, p. 145). A certain epistemological framework would simply work as a problematic influence or preconception that will hinder the researcher to be open and unbiased. Thus, he takes an anti-philosophical or anti-foundational stance. The researcher needs to only trust in and properly engage with GT. Holton (2007) in turn argued that GT should not be confined to a certain perspective but 'can adopt any epistemological perspective appropriate to the data and the ontological stance of the researcher' (Holton, 2007, p. 269).

Although Strauss and Corbin (1990, 1998) did not make explicit their episte-mological stance in the two first editions of their book, Straussian GT has often been considered a post-positivist approach. However, in the third and fourth edi-tion of their book (Corbin and Strauss, 2008, 2015), Corbin claims that their version of GT is rooted in the Chicago School tradition of symbolic interaction-ism and the philosophy of pragmatism (which actually makes sense considering Strauss' background in the Chicago School and some of his other writings, for example, Strauss, 1991). Knowledge assumes to be created through action and interaction, and inquiry often starts from a problematic situation. Knowledge is viewed as cultural embedded, accumulative and provisional. Corbin (in Corbin and Strauss, 2015) agrees with the position of the constructivist GT that 'concepts and theories are *constructed* by researchers out of stories that are constructed by research participants who are trying to explain and make sense out of their expe-riences and lives' (Corbin and Strauss, 2015, p. 26).

Constructivist GT in turn is explicitly rooted in pragmatism, symbolic inter-actionism, and relativist epistemology (Charmaz, 2006, 2014; Charmaz et al., forthcoming). Data and theories are not simply discovered but constructed by the researchers as a result of their interactions with the field and its participants (Charmaz, 2006, 2014; Thornberg and Charmaz, 2014). Data are assumed to be co-constructed by the researcher and participants. Both the research process and product are situated in a social-cultural context and influenced by researchers' perspectives, values, privileges, positions, interactions, and geographic locations (Charmaz, 2006, 2014). Constructivist GT takes a middle ground between the realist and postmodernist positions (Charmaz, 1995) by assuming an 'obdurate reality' (cf. Blumer, 1969) while at the same time assuming multiple realities and multiple perspectives on these realities (Charmaz, 2008, 2009, 2014). Charmaz (2014) stated that both Straussian GT (as further discussed by Corbin) and con-structivist GT fit a theory-methods package of symbolic interactionism and GT, although at the same time she emphasizes that symbolic interactionism is not the only possible theoretical perspective, but grounded theorists can integrate several theoretical perspectives (also see Thornberg, 2012).

THE PLACE OF LITERATURE REVIEW

In line with the ideal of an unbiased *tabula rasa* researcher who without preconception discovers a theory from the data, Glaserian GT advises researchers to delay the literature review until the analysis is nearly completed. The main reasons for this are to keep the researchers as free and open to discovery as possible, and to avoid contamination, in other words forcing data into pre-existing concepts that distort the analysis (Glaser, 1978, 1998, 2001, 2005, 2013). This is Glaser's (2013) dictum of no preconception. In contrast, Strauss and Corbin (1990, 1998; Corbin and Strauss, 2015) argue that literature can be used more actively in GT research as long as the researcher does not allow it to block creativity and get in the way of discovery. According to them, familiarity with relevant literature can enhance sensitivity to subtle nuances in data, provide a source of useful concepts for comparing data, stimulate questions during the analysis process such as when there is a discrepancy between a researcher's data and the findings reported in the literature, and suggest areas for theoretical sampling. Using the literature enriches the analysis, while simultaneously encouraging the researcher to take a critical stance and challenge 'emergent' concepts and ideas.

This is also the approach to literature in constructivist GT, in which the researchers neither dismiss the literature nor apply it mechanically to data but rather use it as a possible source of ideas, creative associations, critical reflections, and multiple lenses (Charmaz, 2014; Charmaz et al., forthcoming; Thornberg, 2012; Thornberg and Charmaz, 2014; Thornberg et al., 2015). As Dey (1999, p. 251) has stated, 'there is a difference between an open mind and an empty head'. Instead of running the risk of reinventing the wheel, missing well-known issues and coming up with trivial products or repeating others' mistakes, grounded theorists should consult the literature at the outset and during the research process. Thornberg (2012) has reviewed and suggested strategies on how to use literature in a data-sensitive way. And of course, the final literature reviews that researchers will write in their research reports are not the same as the initial and on-going literature reviews but have been put together to fit the specific purpose and constructed grounded theory of their research report (Charmaz, 2014).

RESEARCH PROBLEM

The three versions of GT differ when considering the research problem as the starting point of a study. Glaser (1992, 1998, 2001, 2013) states that grounded theorists begin by simply choosing a particular area to investigate (which in the field of educational research might be elementary classroom, mathematic lessons, teachers' work, and students' lives at school), and then enter the area of interest with no particular research problem in mind. There are at least two reasons for that: (a) a research problem is usually derived from literature and will contaminate the study with preconceptions which in turn are at risk of distorting data and reducing openness and sensitivity, and (b) the relevant research problem cannot be known beforehand. Instead of starting with a research problem, the grounded theorist moves into the area of interest with wondering and open questions such as 'What is going on here?' and, 'What is this a study of?' Glaser (1992, p. 21) argues that 'the research problem and its delimitation are discovered or emergent as the open coding begins on the first interviews and observations. They soon become quite clear and structured as coding, collection and analyzing begin'. The problem that the researcher has to discover is always in the data. It is about the participants' main concern and how they continually resolve their main concern.

In contrast to Glaserian GT, Strauss and Corbin (1990, 1998) claim that grounded theorists normally choose a research problem, and they identify various possible sources such as the literature, which might point to unexplored areas or a need for further development, contradictions, and needing a new approach. Other sources could be personal and professional experiences. They also acknowledge the possibility of entering the field with a general notion about what the researcher might want to study but with no specific research problem. Initial data collection and analysis could then lead to discovering the research problem, which is 'the issues that are important or problematic in the respondents' lives' (Strauss and Corbin, 1998, p. 38). This last option is thus very similar to Glaser's standpoint. Furthermore, and in contrast with Glaserian GT, Strauss and Corbin (1998) argue that the researcher has to state a research question based on the initial research problem. The initial research question starts out broadly and then becomes more focused during the research process. 'So, the research question begins as an open and broad one, but not so open, of course, as to allow for the entire universe of possibilities' (Strauss and Corbin, 1998, p. 41). Additionally, formulating an initial research problem and a delineation of the research question(s) is necessary when writing research proposals and applications (Corbin and Strauss, 2015).

Like Straussian GT, constructivist grounded theorists begin their studies with an open research problem and one or a couple of open research questions (Charmaz, 2014; Charmaz et al., forthcoming; Thornberg et al., 2015). Furthermore, Charmaz (2014) suggests that grounded theorists can use so-called *sensitizing concepts* (Blumer, 1969) as a starting point. A sensitizing concept lacks specific, definitive characteristics, and is a more flexible, open, and loose concept that 'gives the user a general sense of reference and guidance in approaching empirical instances' (Blumer, 1969, p. 148). Examples of sensitizing concepts include culture, institutions, resistance, socialization, power, management, social structures, learning, meaning-making, motivation, identity, negotiation, interaction, and group processes. According to Charmaz (2014), grounded theorists can treat sensitizing concepts as points of departure for studying the area of interest, in which they form a loose frame for looking at the initial research interests. At the same time, researchers have to be open and ready to dispense sensitizing concepts if they prove to be irrelevant. It is crucial to understand that the initial problem formulation and research questions are always treated as tentative in GT and thus can be modified during the research process as a result of the ongoing analysis of data. Examples of possible initial research questions in educational research might be: How do teachers manage students who show poor academic motivation? What happens in school when a student complains of being bullied? What goes on while students are doing group work? How do teachers manage disorder in the classroom? What happens in everyday classroom life?

DATA COLLECTION

Grounded theorists are not fixed to a particular data collection method but use those which best fit the actual research problem and the ongoing analysis of the data. Possible sources of data might be interviews, field observations, informal conversations, focus groups, videos, documents, drawings, diaries, or questionnaires. Although GT is open to a range of methods of data gathering, common methods in GT research literature are qualitative interviews, field observations, and different forms of written reports from participants. In the beginning of a GT study, the research problem might point to one method or a mix of methods for data collection. For example, if the grounded theorists would like to examine how teachers manage disorder in the classroom, doing classroom observations might be a reasonable start.

During the research process, the ongoing data analysis might then lead the grounded theorist to change or add a new data gathering method. For instance, after collecting and analyzing a certain amount of classroom observation data, the researchers might realize that they have to focus on particular situations, incidents, or participants, shift from fieldnotes to video recording, conduct observations in another classroom with certain characteristics, or begin to interview the participants in order to pursue the analysis further. If the researchers work with qualitative interviews, the iterative process between data collection and analysis might lead them to add or revise their interview guide, and return to all or certain participants, or turn to new participants with the same or a new set of interview questions. Thus, as Charmaz (2014, p. 25) stated, we can 'add new pieces to the research puzzle or conjure entire new puzzles *while we gather data*, and that can even occur late in the analysis'.

There are some differences concerning how to document or record data. When doing Glaserian GT, Glaser (1998, 2001) strongly advices researchers not to tape or audio record interviews, but instead take notes. He argues that audio recording produces overwhelming and unnecessary data, slows the researchers down in the iterative process between data collection and analysis, and thus delays theoretical sampling (see below). In contrast, both in the Straussian and constructivist versions of GT, audio recording interviews is the norm when documenting interviews (Charmaz, 2014; Corbin and Strauss, 2015), even though Corbin and Strauss (2015) recommend that researchers bring paper and pencils in addition to a recorder in case the participants begin to report new or more elaborated and interesting data when the recorder is turned off. Charmaz (2014) argues that if researchers use a recorder when interviewing, it would allow them to give full attention to their participants during the conversation and to gather much more detailed data overall.

CONSTANT COMPARISON

Constant comparison is a core method in GT for all three versions (Charmaz, 2014; Corbin and Strauss, 2015; Glaser, 1992, 2011). By this method, the grounded theorists compare data with data, data with codes, codes with codes, data with categories, codes with categories, and categories with categories to find similarities and differences (Glaser and Strauss, 1967). According to Glaser (2011), the aim is to discover patterns in data to code. Constant comparison is thus essential when coding. 'Data that appear to be conceptually similar are grouped together under a conceptual label' (Corbin and Strauss, 2015, p. 94). According to Corbin and Strauss (2015), this constant comparative method helps the researcher to reduce data to concepts. Charmaz (2014) states that the constant comparative method is used to establish analytic distinctions and to make comparisons at each level of the analysis. I will therefore come back to this method in the different sections below.

CODING

Coding begins directly as the first data are gathered, and then goes hand in hand with data collection throughout the research process. Coding is about creating codes and categories grounded in the data by scrutinizing and interacting with the data – by constant comparisons and asking analytical questions. A *code* is a label that the researcher constructs to depict what is happening in a piece of data (Charmaz, 2014). Codes capture patterns or themes, and can vary in levels of abstraction. A *category* in turn is a higher-level code that is more abstract (Corbin and Strauss, 2015), and has been given a conceptual definition (Charmaz, 2014). According to Glaser (1978), coding refers to fracturing the data and then conceptually grouping it into codes to later become the theory. Glaser (1998, p. 137) also states 'coding is the generating of categories and their properties by constant comparison of incidents and categories'. Corbin and Strauss (2015, p. 57) define coding as 'denoting concepts to stand for meaning'. Charmaz (2014, p. 111) in turn defines coding as 'naming segments of data with a label that simultaneously categorizes, summarizes, and account for each piece of data'. Learning about coding in GT literature can confuse the novice because the three main GT versions differ and use various labels when writing about coding. Figure 17.1 offers an overview on the coding phases in the three GT versions.

In Glaserian GT, there is a basic distinction between substantive coding and theoretical coding (Glaser, 1978, 1998, 2005). In *substantive coding*, the researchers generate codes that conceptualize the empirical substance. The researchers construct these codes from the data. Substantive coding in turn consists of two phases: open coding and selective coding. Substantive coding is contrasted with theoretical coding. In Straussian GT, coding moves through three phases: open coding, axial coding, and selective coding (Strauss, 1987; Strauss and Corbin, 1990, 1998). According to constructivist GT, coding consists of two phases: initial coding and focused coding (Charmaz, 2006, 2014). However, coding in GT is not a linear process. Rather, researchers have to move back and forth between the coding phases and be sensitive to data and their analysis.

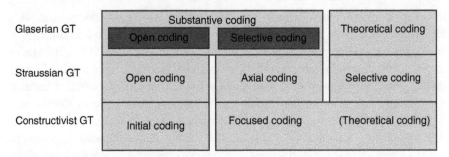

Figure 17.1   Coding in Glaserian, Straussian and constructivist versions of GT

Open coding/initial coding

In all three versions of GT the first step of coding is similar. It is called *open coding* in Glaserian GT and Straussian GT, and *initial coding* in constructivist GT. In all three versions, the researchers stay close to the data and remain open to exploring what they define is going on in these data. They ask a set of analytical questions such as 'What is this data a study of?' 'What category does this incident indicate?' 'What is actually happening in the data?' (Glaser, 1978, p. 57); 'What is the participant's main concern?' (Glaser, 1998, p. 140). Constructivist GT problematizes the last question and may highlight multiple concerns (Charmaz, 2014).

Additional analytical questions suggested in the constructivist GT are: 'What do the data suggest? Pronounce? Leave unsaid?' 'From whose point of view?' (Charmaz, 2014, p. 116); 'What process(es) is at issue here? How can I define it?' 'How does this process develop?' 'How does the research participant(s) act while involved in this process?' 'What does the research participant(s) profess to think and feel while involved in this process? What might his or her observed behavior indicate?' 'When, why, and how does the process change?' 'What are the consequences of the process?' (Charmaz, 2014, p. 127).

During this first step of coding, 'data are broken down into discrete parts, closely examined, and compared for similarities and differences' (Strauss and Corbin, 1998, p. 102). The researchers read and analyze the data word by word and line by line. Through this careful reading they construct codes that represent what they see (interpret) in the segments of data. Charmaz (2014) recommends that researchers remain open, stay close to the data, keep the codes simple and precise, construct short codes, and preserve actions, while comparing data with data. Table 17.1 illustrates an example of line-by-line coding. The excerpt is from a group interview with some students in a GT field study on rules in everyday school life (Thornberg, 2007, 2008, 2009). Note that the codes are kept close to the data and are focused on action and process.

All constructed codes are always considered as provisional and constantly open for modification and refinement during the analysis to improve their fit

Table 17.1   Open/initial coding

Open/Initial Coding	Group Interview Data
Puzzling over teacher response; Angry responding; Confirming responding; Inconsistent teacher;	*John:* It's strange! Sometimes she [the teacher] gets angry and yells at the students if someone starts to talk without raising his hand, but sometimes she will not act like that. She just says, 'Oh, that's right!' *Interviewer:* Why is that strange?
Not knowing how to act; Unsure if 'hand-up-before-talk' rule has to be followed	*John:* Well, but then you don't know what to do. *Robin:* No, you don't know if you need to put your hand up or not

Source: The excerpt and the codes are examples from open/initial coding that preceded the result in Thornberg (2007).

with the data. While coding, the researchers use the constant comparative method (data are compared to data; codes are compared to new or other data; and codes are compared with each other), which gradually leads to sorting and clustering codes based on similarities and differences. Eventually, the researchers will group certain codes under a more abstract higher order code, and thus the amount of codes decrease as they are grouped into fewer but more comprehensive codes. Although there are a lot of similarities in the first phase of coding, the three versions of GT become more differentiated in the steps that follow.

Selective coding (Glaserian)

According to Glaserian GT (Glaser, 1978), the aim of open coding is to finally discover the *core category*. This refers to the most significant and frequent code and related to as many other codes as possible and more than other candidates for the core category. Furthermore, the core category is based on the participants' continual resolving of their main concern, and thus 'the prime mover of most of the behavior seen and talked about in the substantive area' (Glaser, 1998, p. 115). Glaser uses the terms core category, core concept and core variable interchangeably.

When the core category has been identified, the researcher shifts from open to *selective coding*. The subsequent gathering and coding of data are now delimited to the core category and those codes that relate to the core category (Glaser, 1978, 1998; Holton, 2007). The study becomes more focused, and the core category is the guide to further data collection, theoretical sampling (see below), and analysis. Learning more about the core category and its relation to other categories is now the focus, because the aim is to generate a theory on the core category, in other words a theory of the continually resolving of the main concern. Selective coding continues until the grounded theorist has sufficiently integrated the core category, its properties and relations with other relevant codes or categories.

Theoretical coding

Pretty much in parallel with selective coding, the researchers have to conduct *theoretical coding*, in which they analyze how categories and codes constructed from data (substantive codes) might relate to each other as hypotheses to be integrated into a theory (Glaser, 1978, 1998, 2005). To achieve this, researchers have to inspect, choose and adopt *theoretical codes* as analytical tools. Theoretical codes 'consist of ideas and perspectives that researchers import to the research process as analytic tools and lenses from outside, from a range of theories' (Thornberg and Charmaz, 2014, p. 159). They refer to underlying logics on how to relate, organize and integrate concepts that could be found in various theories across different disciplines. Therefore, theoretical codes 'conceptualize how the substantive codes may relate to each other as hypotheses to be integrated into the theory' (Glaser, 1978, p. 55). Theoretical coding means, as Charmaz (2006) noted, that Glaserian GT is ambiguous – it is neither entirely inductive nor free from influence from extant theories and concepts.

Glaser argues that by studying many theories across different disciplines, the researchers may identify numerous theoretical codes embedded in these theories and thus develop and enhance their own knowledge base on theoretical codes (Glaser, 1998, 2005). As a guide for researchers, Glaser (1978, pp. 72–82; 1998, pp. 170–5; 2005, pp. 21–30) compiled a list of theoretical codes which are organized in a typology of *coding families*, but he emphasizes that his list is not exhaustive, and there are considerable overlaps between them. Examples of coding families presented by Glaser are:

- *The 'six Cs':* causes, contexts, contingencies, consequences, co-variations and conditions.
- *Process family:* phases, stages, progressions, passages, transitions, careers, trajectories, cycling, and so on.
- *Basic family:* basic social process, basic social psychological process, basic social structural condition, and so on.
- *Cultural family:* social norms, social values, social beliefs, and so on.
- *Degree family:* limit, range, grade, continuum, level, and so on.
- *Type family:* type, kind, styles, classes, genre, and so on.
- *Strategy family:* strategies, tactics, manipulation, dealing with, positioning, dominating, and so on.
- *Identity-self family:* self-image, self-concept, self-worth, self-evaluation, identity, transformations of self, self-realization, and so on.
- *Consensus family:* agreements, contracts, conformity, homogeneity–heterogeneity, conflict, dissensus, and so on.
- *Cutting point family:* boundary, cutting point, turning point, breaking point, deviance, and so on.
- *Paired opposite family:* ingroup–outgroup, in–out, manifest–latent, explicit–implicit, overt–covert, formal–informal, and so on.

Glaser (1978) highlights how theoretical codes must not be forced into the analysis but should earn their way by constant and careful comparisons between theoretical codes, data, substantive codes, and memos (see below). Theoretical codes must work, have relevance and fit with data and substantive codes (that is, the core category and related codes or categories). A combination of many theoretical codes most often captures the relationships between substantive codes, and thus used when linking, organizing, and integrating them into a grounded theory.

Focused coding

Instead of selective coding, Charmaz (2000, 2006, 2014) suggests *focused coding* as the next phase after initial coding. The researchers use the most significant or frequent codes that have been constructed during the initial coding and treat them as *focused codes*. These codes are used to sift, sort, synthesize, and analyze large amount of data. This is reminiscent of Glaser's selective coding, however instead of choosing one significant code (the core category), a set of significant codes (focused codes) is chosen as a guide to further the data collection, theoretical sampling, and analysis. 'Focused coding requires decisions about which initial codes make the most analytic sense to categorize your data incisively and completely' (Charmaz, 2014, p. 138).

Charmaz' position could be considered more flexible than Glaser's by being open for more than one significant/frequent code, and the researchers continue to determine the adequacy of those codes throughout the focused coding phase. They remain sensitive and open to modifying their focused codes and to being surprised by the data (Thornberg and Charmaz, 2012, 2014). Focused codes are usually more conceptual and comprehensive than initial codes, and the researchers have to concentrate on what their focused codes say and the comparison they make with and between them. During the focused coding, the grounded theorists explore and decide which codes best capture what they see happening in the data, and raise these codes up to tentative conceptual categories, which means that they give them conceptual definitions and begin to examine the relationships between them (Charmaz, 2006, 2014). Thus, it is important to construct working definitions of the relevant codes. In order to construct and refine categories, grounded theorists have to make various constant comparisons (Thornberg and Charmaz, 2012):

- Comparing and grouping codes and comparing codes with emerging categories.
- Comparing various incidents.
- Comparing data from the same or similar phenomenon, action or process in different situations and contexts.
- Comparing different people (their beliefs, situations, actions, accounts or experiences).
- Comparing data from the same individuals at different points in time.
- Comparing specific data with the criteria for category.
- Comparing categories in the analysis with other categories.

For example, during the focused coding, Thornberg (2007) established a limited set of focused codes such as 'inconsistencies in teacher's rule-making', 'difficulties in predicting teacher responses' and, 'not knowing if rule is in force', which later on were developed into the categories 'rule diffusion', 'prediction loss', and 'negotiation loss'. Constructivist GT as proposed by Charmaz (2000, 2006, 2014) only emphasizes two necessary phases of coding: initial coding and focused coding. However, what about theoretical coding? In general Charmaz (2014) claims that the researchers do not need to make explicit attempts to integrate their focused codes through theoretical coding. Instead, the direction of the analysis will emerge from the data and focused coding. She points to the risk of mere application when doing theoretical coding.

On the other hand, Charmaz (2014, p. 151) recognizes that if 'you use them skilfully, theoretical codes may hone your work with a sharp analytic edge. These codes can add precision and clarity – as long as they fit your data and substantive analysis'. Within the constructivist version, GT is viewed as providing rigorous yet flexible guidelines (Charmaz, 2006, 2014), and it is up to the researchers to decide if they would like to do theoretical coding in an explicit fashion or let it be embedded more implicitly in focused coding (Charmaz, 2014; Thornberg and Charmaz, 2014). If the former, the researchers have to conduct theoretical coding in parallel with focused coding as an iterative process.

Axial coding

The next step after open coding is *axial coding* in Straussian GT (Strauss, 1987; Strauss and Corbin, 1990, 1998). During the open coding, the researchers in Straussian GT begin to construct categories, which are higher-order concepts, and these are developed through defining their properties and describing how these properties vary along their dimensional range. Whereas open coding is about fracturing data into separate pieces, axial coding is about bringing the data back into a coherent picture of the data. The researchers 'look for answers to questions such as why or how come, where, when, how, and with what results' (Strauss and Corbin, 1998, p. 127) by uncovering relationships among categories.

There is a focus on both *structure* that sets the stage and *process* that denotes the action/interaction over time. Straussian GT offers a *coding paradigm* as a conceptual analytic device for sorting out and organizing the relationships between the categories (Strauss, 1987; Strauss and Corbin, 1990, 1998). The basic components in the coding paradigm are: (a) *conditions*: the circumstances or sets of events/ happenings that create the situations, issues and problems; (b) *action/interaction*: participants' strategies or routine responses to issues, problems, or events; and (c) *consequences*: outcomes of actions/interactions. However, the paradigm should not be used in rigid ways but as a possible perspective to discover the ways the categories are related to each other (Corbin and Strauss, 2015; Strauss and Corbin, 1998).

Selective coding (Straussian)

According to Strauss and Corbin (1998, p. 143), selective coding is 'the process of integrating and refining the theory'. The first step in selective coding is to choose a *central category* among or based on the constructed categories from earlier coding. A central category has to be related to all other major categories, appear frequently in the data, and be able to account for considerable variation with categories (Strauss and Corbin, 1998). Thus, it is reminiscent of what Glaser (1978) defines as the core category. In fact, at first Strauss (1987), and later Strauss and Corbin in their first edition (1990), actually used the term 'core category' – a term that Corbin then returns to in 2008 and 2015 editions of their book. The core/central category is simply defined as 'what researchers determine is the main theme of the research' (Corbin and Strauss, 2015, p. 188). They do not refer to how participants constantly resolve their main concern, as Glaser does.

Strauss and Corbin (1998) offer a range of techniques to facilitate identification of the core/central category and the integration of categories, such as identifying and writing the storyline, making use of diagrams, and reviewing and sorting memos (see below). When the researchers have outlined the main theoretical scheme, the next step is to refine the theory by reviewing the constructed theoretical scheme or storyline for internal consistency and (for gaps in) logic, filling in poorly developed categories (enhancing precision of properties and variation of the category by reviewing memos or data and looking for data that might have been overlooked), trimming the theory (deleting categories that do not fit the theory), and validating the theory scheme (go back and compare the scheme against the data or report the story to the participants and let them evaluate how well it seems to fit their cases).

MEMO WRITING

While researchers are collecting, coding and analyzing data, they will also raise new questions and come up with ideas and thoughts about their codes and relationships between their codes. To aid memory they write them down in so called *memos*, which are analytical, conceptual or theoretical notes. According to Glaser (1978, p. 83), memos are 'the theorizing write-up of ideas about codes and their relationships as they strike the analyst while coding'. By *memo writing*, the grounded theorists step back and ask, 'What is going on here?' and, 'How can I make sense of this?' Writing memos helps the researcher to build up and maintain 'a storehouse of analytical ideas that can be sorted, ordered, and reordered' (Corbin and Strauss, 2008, p. 120). The researchers put things down on paper (or document on a computer), and this makes codes, categories, ideas and reflections manageable and stimulates further theorizing. Codes, categories, and the emergent theory are explored and scrutinized.

According to Pidgeon and Henwood (1996), among other things memos can consist of working definitions of codes/categories; comparisons between data and between codes/categories; identified gaps or vagueness in categories; hunches or questions to be checked out and further investigated; fresh ideas and newly created concepts; comparisons between categories and a range of theoretical codes, investigations of possible relationships between categories by using theoretical codes; and comparisons with and links to relevant literature. Grounded theorists in all three main GT versions engage in simultaneous data gathering and analysis, and hence write memos at the outset of the research process. Their early memos are usually shorter, less conceptualized, and cover analytical questions and hunches. Later, the memos become longer, more conceptualized, and more like written findings. Researchers also compare memos with memos and sort memos, which is the key to constructing the theory and writing drafts of papers.

In addition, the issue of *reflexivity* is addressed differently in the three versions of GT. In Glaserian GT, reflexivity has no place at all. Glaser (2001) talks about *reflexivity paralysis* when researchers try to locate and critique themselves, their data and their findings. For him, reflexivity is 'paralyzing, self-destructive and stifling of productivity' (Glaser, 2001, p. 47), and is completely irrelevant when generating categories and the emerging theory. In contrast, both the Straussian and constructivist versions of GT acknowledge the importance of reflexivity when doing research. In Straussian GT, reflexivity is a strategy for controlling researcher perspectives, biases and assumptions during the research process (Corbin and Strauss, 2015). In constructivist GT, researchers take a reflexive stance toward the research process and product and on how the researchers' own positions, perspectives, and assumptions influence the work. This is done in order to be sensitive to data and to avoid thoughtlessly reproducing current ideologies, discourses, and power relationships (Charmaz, 2014). Both Corbin and Strauss (2015) and Charmaz (2014) recommend that the researcher keep a journal to engage in reflexivity.

THEORETICAL SAMPLING AND SATURATION

Coding and constant comparisons will produce categories and ideas about relationships between categories, which are written down in memos. In order to explore categories and relationships further, to fill out their properties, and, at the final stage, to examine and complete the emerging theory, the grounded theorist engages in *theoretical sampling* (Charmaz, 2014; Corbin and Strauss, 2015; Glaser, 1978, 1998; Glaser and Strauss, 1967; Strauss, 1987). Glaser and Strauss (1967, p. 45) define theoretical sampling as 'the process of data collection for generating theory whereby the analyst jointly collects, codes, and analyzes his data and decides what data to collect next and where to find them'. It is 'the process by which data collection is continually guided' (Glaser, 1992, p. 102).

Coding, constant comparison and memo writing guide the researchers to decide which data will illuminate their theoretical ideas and where these data might be found. The iterative process between data collection and analysis thus became more conceptual-driven and make data collection more focused. According to

Charmaz (2014), theoretical sampling is primarily seeking and gathering data to elaborate the properties of the researchers' theoretical categories as well as defining the variation within a category and specifying relations between categories. At the same time, it prevents researchers from becoming unfocused and overwhelmed by unnecessary data. The researcher is like a detective, according to Corbin and Strauss (2015, p. 134), who 'follows the leads of the concepts, never quite certain where they will lead but always open to what might be discovered'.

Theoretical sampling continues until the study reaches *theoretical saturation*, which is the point when all relevant categories are saturated, elaborated and integrated into the emerging theory (Glaser, 1992), when 'theoretical completeness' has been reached (Glaser, 1998), 'all concepts are well defined and explained' (Corbin and Strauss, 2008, p. 145), and when 'gathering fresh data no longer sparks new theoretical insights, nor reveals new properties of your core theoretical categories' (Charmaz, 2006, p. 113).

According to the Glaserian GT, when theoretical saturation has been reached, the researcher has completed a final *grounded theory* as a theory on the core category that will only include those categories which are associated with the core category (Glaser, 1978). Thus, the outcome is a 'conceptual substantive theory that explains how a main concern is continually resolved' (Glaser, 2013, p. 65).

In the Straussian GT, constructed grounded theory is also around a central or core category (Strauss and Corbin, 1998; Corbin and Strauss, 2015), and 'its categories and concepts are integrated around a core category to form a structure that offers a theoretical explanation about the why and how something happens' (Corbin and Strauss, 2015, p. 15). Context and process – or more specified, conditions, actions/interactions and consequences – are expected components in the theory. The theory should have 'explanatory power', which means the ability to explain what might happen in a given situation. Variation should also be built into the theory (Strauss and Corbin, 1998).

In the constructivist GT, the constructed grounded theory gives *abstract understanding* greater priority than abstract explanation. It aims to 'understand meanings and actions and how people construct them' (Charmaz, 2014, p. 231). Such theory interprets the assumptions on which participants construct their actions and meanings. Furthermore, theorizing in constructivist GT is not confined to analyzing how participants resolve their main concern, but is open to pursue varied emerged analytical goals and foci. Finally, constructivist grounded theories are situated in their social, historical, local, and interactional contexts (Charmaz, 2014).

EXAMPLES OF GT STUDIES IN EDUCATIONAL RESEARCH

The contemporary field of educational research illustrates the wide-ranging contribution that GT studies offer educational research and practice. Focus is generally on teachers' and/or students' actions, processes, and meanings in a particular educational context. Some studies rely on the Glaserian GT tradition. For example, Yalof (2014) examined online students in higher education and generated a GT of marshalling resources, which explains how peer support sustains motivation towards successful programme completion. In Hakel's (2015) study of university students, *optimizing personal resources* emerged from the analysis of data as the participants' main concern. Depending on their evaluation of the actual situation, they resolve this problem by oscillating between various strategies.

Other studies are located within or close to the Straussian GT tradition. For example, Smart and Igo (2010) conducted and analyzed teacher interviews. They developed a theoretical model describing novice teachers' tendencies to select and implement different behaviour management strategies related to the severity of student behaviour. Webster and Son (2015) examined technology use both in and out of the classroom by English teachers at a Korean University. Data was collected through semi-structured interviews, questionnaires, and classroom observations. They developed a GT entitled 'what works' and that helped explain the myriad of decisions that teachers make while trying to manage their goals.

Finally, there is a growing body of GT studies guided by a constructivist GT tradition. For example, Keane (2011) examined the social class-differentiated behaviours of undergraduate students. She identified and developed concepts to describe and explain engagement in various forms of distancing behaviours motivated by a desire to self-protect and based on perceived relative social positioning. She illustrates some ways in which both disadvantage and privilege are performed. Perhamus (2010) used a sociology of childhood framework and conducted in-depth interviews. She constructed a GT on how children and adults kinaesthetically recontextualize standardized, official health messages into personally meaningful, context-specific health knowledge.

CRITICISMS OF GT

As any other methodological tradition in social and educational research, GT has attracted criticisms. A recurring criticism is the reliance on induction and the idea of a researcher who collects and analyses theory-free data without being influenced by any prior theoretical knowledge or preconceptions (Alvesson and Kärreman, 2011; Layder, 1982; Thomas and James, 2006). However, in a strict sense this criticism affects only the Glaserian version, since both Straussian GT and constructivist GT reject the ideal of the tabula rasa position (no preconception) and acknowledge literature and prior theories as valuable resources when conducting a GT study. A constructivist grounded theorist would in fact agree with Alvesson and Kärreman (2011, p. 37) that openness is 'not a matter of avoiding theory or postponing the use of it, but instead demands that we include a broadening of the repertoire of vocabularies and theories that can be mobilized', which Thornberg (2012) discusses in terms of *theoretical agnosticism* and *theoretical pluralism* in GT. In addition, several grounded theorists argue that induction is not enough and that abduction is an essential component in GT methodology, including imagination and creativity (see Thornberg, 2012). Furthermore, the accusation that GT shares a belief in a clear separation of theory and data, in which data can speak for itself, might be a problem for Glaserian GT and earlier publications of Straussian GT, whereas both constructivist GT and Corbin in her later writings on Straussian GT recognize data as 'theory-laden' and constructed by researchers and co-constructed by researchers and participants (Charmaz, 2014; Corbin and Strauss, 2008, 2015; Thornberg, 2012).

Another criticism is to accuse GT of taking a positivistic view on theory – that the outcome of inquiry is a middle range theory with the power of *explaining* and *predicting* things, rather than being a theory in a loose sense that help us understand things (Thomas and James, 2006). Although Glaserian GT and Straussian GT are most vulnerable to this criticism, Glaser for instance emphasizes that a grounded theory is always hypothetical and tentative, and is therefore open to modification in further studies. In addition, Charmaz (2014) rejects a binary categorization of defining theory as either explanation or understanding, and states that it would be more useful to view 'positivist' and 'interpretivist' theories as located in a continuum. Constructivist GT is then closer to a definition of theory that 'emphasizes interpretation and gives *abstract understanding* greater priority than explanation' (Charmaz, 2014, p. 230). Still, there are plural definitions and understandings of theory in educational research, which might be considered as a challenge when talking about theory in GT.

GT has also been criticized for limiting its level of analysis to a micro-level (for example, people's interpretations and main concerns, social interactions in everyday life, and social psychological processes), while ignoring or downplaying the macro-level (for example, social structures, power and hegemonies in society) (Layder, 1982). Nevertheless, Charmaz (2014) argues that GT strategies can be adopted in social justice research to 'locate subjective and collective experience in larger social structures and increase understanding of how these structures work' (Charmaz, 2014, p. 326). The constructivist GT attends to context, positions, discourses, meanings and actions in a way that could advance understandings of how power, norms, oppression, inequities and social structure influence individuals, groups and categories of people in various ways (Charmaz, 2005). While consulting and interacting with diverse theories prior to and during the research process (Thornberg, 2012), GT can take a critical stance in examining the interplay between agency and structure, and between agency and discourse (Charmaz et al., forthcoming).

CONCLUSION

In this chapter, I have described three main versions of GT in the literature and it is crucial that researchers who adopt GT are aware of them and other versions, their own positioning in this field, and what consequences their positioning has in terms of epistemological and methodological assumptions. At the same time, GT will continue to evolve in different directions such as more critical directions (for example, Denzin, 2010; Gibson, 2007) and postmodern versions like situational analysis (Clarke, 2005) and discursive GT (McCreaddie and Payne, 2010). Thus, entering the field of GT requires a curious, unorthodox and open mind, a willingness to develop methodological awareness to understand similarities and differences across the various versions, as well as reflexivity and a critical stance, including a self-critical stance.

Note

1 Other noteworthy versions of GT are Clarke's (2005) postmodern version called *situational analysis*; *multi-GT* (Goldkuhl and Cronholm, 2010); *discursive GT* (McCreaddie and Payne, 2010); a and Dey's (1999) version with an elaborated view on categorization, process, causality, and structure/agency.

REFERENCES

Alvesson, M. and Kärreman, D. (2011). *Qualitative Research and Theory Development*. London: Sage.

Blumer, H. (1969). *Symbolic Interactionism*. Englewood Cliffs, NJ: Prentice Hall.

Bryant, A. (2009). Grounded theory and pragmatism: the curious case of Anselm Strauss. *Forum: Qualitative Social Research*, 10(3), Art. 2. Retrieved 4 July 2011 from www.qualitative-research.net/index.php/fqs/article/viewArticle/1358/2850.

Charmaz, K. (1995). Between positivism and postmodernism: implications for methods. *Studies in Symbolic Interaction*, 17, 43–72.

Charmaz, K. (2000). Constructivist and objectivist grounded theory. In N. K. Denzin and Y. S. Lincoln (Eds) *The SAGE Handbook of Qualitative Research*, 2nd edition (pp. 509–535). Thousand Oaks CA: Sage.

Charmaz, K. (2005). Grounded theory in the 21st century: applications for advancing social justice studies. In N. K. Denzin and Y. S. Lincoln (Eds) *The SAGE Handbook of Qualitative Research*, 3rd edition (pp. 507–535). Thousand Oaks, CA: Sage.

Charmaz, K. (2006). *Constructing Grounded Theory: A practical guide through qualitative analysis*. London: Sage.

Charmaz, K. (2008). Constructionism and the grounded theory method. In J. A. Holstein and J. F. Gubrium (Eds) *Handbook of Constructionist Research* (pp. 397–412). New York: The Guilford Press.

Charmaz, K. (2009). Shifting the grounds: Constructivist grounded theory methods for the twenty-first century. In J. M. Morse, P. N. Stern, J. Corbin, B. Bowers, K. Charmaz, and A. E. Clarke (Eds) *Developing Grounded Theory: The second generation* (pp. 127–154). Walnut Creek, CA: Left Coast Press.

Charmaz, K. (2014) *Constructing Grounded Theory*, 2nd edition. Thousand Oaks, CA: Sage.

Charmaz, K., Thornberg, R. and Keane, E. (forthcoming). Evolving grounded theory and social justice inquiry. In N. K. Denzin and Y. S. Lincoln (Eds.), *The SAGE Handbook of Qualitative Research*, 5th edition. Thousand Oaks, CA: Sage.

Clarke, A. E. (2005). *Situational Analysis: Grounded theory after the postmodern turn*. Thousand Oaks, CA: Sage.

Corbin, J. and Strauss, A. (2008). *Basics of Qualitative Research*, 3rd edition. Thousand Oaks, CA: Sage.

Corbin, J. and Strauss, A. (2015). *Basics of Qualitative Research*, 4th edition. Thousand Oaks, CA: Sage.

Denzin, N. K. (2010). Grounded and indigenous theories and the politics of pragmatism. *Sociological Inquiry*, 80, 296–312.

Dey, I. (1999). *Grounding Grounded Theory*. San Diego: Academic Press.

Douven, I. (2011). Peirce on abduction. In E. N. Zalta (Principal Ed.), *Stanford Encyclopedia of Philosophy*. Retrieved 16 January 2014 from http://plato.stanford.edu/entries/abduction/.

Gibson, B. (2007). Accommodating critical theory. In A. Bryant and K. Charmaz (Eds) *The SAGE Handbook of Grounded Theory* (pp. 436–453). Los Angeles: Sage.

Glaser, B. G. (1978). *Theoretical Sensitivity*. Mill Valley, CA: Sociology Press.

Glaser, B. G. (1992). *Basics of Grounded Theory Analysis*. Mill Valley, CA: Sociology Press.

Glaser, B. G. (1998). *Doing Grounded Theory: Issues and discussions*. Mill Valley, CA: Sociology Press.

Glaser, B. G. (2001). *The Grounded Theory Perspective I: Conceptualization contrasted with description*. Mill Valley, CA: Sociology Press.

Glaser, B. G. (2003). *The Grounded Theory Perspective II: Description's remodeling of grounded theory methodology*. Mill Valley, CA: Sociology Press.

Glaser, B. G. (2005). *The Grounded Theory Perspective III: Theoretical coding*. Mill Valley, CA: Sociology Press.

Glaser, B. G. (2009). *Jargonizing: Using the grounded theory vocabulary*. Mill Valley, CA: Sociology Press.

Glaser, B. G. (2011). *Getting Out of the Data: Grounded theory conceptualization*. Mill Valley, CA: Sociology Press.

Glaser, B. G. (2013). *No Preconceptions: The grounded theory dictum*. Mill Valley, CA: Sociology Press.

Glaser, B. G. and Strauss, A. L. (1965). *Awareness of Dying*. Chicago, IL: Aldine.

Glaser, B. G. and Strauss, A. L. (1967). *The Discovery of Grounded Theory: Strategies for Qualitative Research*. Chicago, IL: Aldine.

Glaser, B. G. and Strauss, A. L. (1968). *Time for Dying*. Chicago, IL: Aldine.

Goldkuhl, G. and Cronholm, S. (2010). Adding theoretical grounding to grounded theory: toward multi-grounded theory. *International Journal of Qualitative Methods*, 9, 187–205.

Hakel, K. (2015). Oscillating between conservation and investment: A grounded theory of students' strategies for optimizing personal resources. *The Grounded Theory Review*, 14, 11–25.

Holton, J. A. (2007). The coding process and its challenges. In A. Bryant and K. Charmaz (Eds) *The SAGE Handbook of Grounded Theory* (pp. 265–289). Los Angeles: Sage.

Keane, E. (2011). Distancing to self-protect: The perpetuation of inequality in higher education through socio-relational dis/engagement. *British Journal of Sociology of Education*, 32, 449–466.

Kelle, U. (2005). 'Emergence' vs. 'forcing' of empirical data? A crucial problem of 'grounded theory' reconsidered. *Forum: Qualitative Social Research*, 6(2), Art. 27. Retrieved 4 July 2011, from www.qualitative-research.net/index.php/fqs/article/viewArticle/467/1000.

Layder, D. (1982). Grounded theory: a constructive critique. *Journal for the Theory of Social Behavior*, 12, 103–122.

McCreaddie, M. and Payne, S. (2010). Evolving grounded theory methodology: towards a discursive approach. *International Journal of Nursing Studies*, 47, 781–793.

Peirce, C. S. (1960). *Collected Papers of Charles Sanders Peirce. Vol. I: Principles of philosophy; Vol. II: Elements of logic* (Ed. A. W. Burks). Cambridge, MA: Harvard University Press.

Peirce, C. S. (1979). *Collected Papers of Charles Sanders Peirce. Vol. III: Science and philosophy* (Ed. A. W. Burks). Cambridge, MA: Harvard University Press.

Perhamus, L. M. (2010). 'But your body would rather have this ...': conceptualizing health through kinesthetic experience. *International Journal of Qualitative Studies in Education*, 23, 845–868.

Pidgeon, N. and Henwood, K. (1996). Grounded theory: practical implementation. In J. T. E. Richardson (Ed.) *Handbook of Qualitative Research Methods for Psychology and the Social Sciences* (pp. 86–101). Leicester: The British Psychological Society.

Reichertz, J. (2010). Abduction: the logic of discovery of grounded theory. *Forum: Qualitative Social Research*, 11 (1), Art. 13. Retrieved 6 december 2013 from http://nbn-resolving.de/urn:nbn:de:0114-fqs1001135.

Richardson, R. and Kramer, E. H. (2006). Abduction as the type of inference that characterizes the development of a grounded theory. *Qualitative Research*, 6, 245–249.

Smart, J. B. and Igo, L. B. (2010). A grounded theory of behavior management strategy selection, implementation, and perceived effectiveness reported by first-year elementary teachers. *The Elementary School Journal*, 110, 567–584.

Strauss, A. L. (1987). *Qualitative Analysis for Social Scientists*. New York: Cambridge University Press.

Strauss, A. (1991). The Chicago tradition's ongoing theory of action/interaction. In A. Strauss (Ed.) *Creating Sociological Awareness* (pp. 3–32). New Brunswick, NJ: Transaction.

Strauss, A. and Corbin, J. (1990). *Basics of Qualitative Research: Grounded theory procedures and techniques*. Newbury Park, CA: Sage.

Strauss, A. and Corbin, J. (1998). *Basics of Qualitative Research: Grounded theory procedures and techniques*, 2nd edition. Thousand Oaks, CA: Sage.

Thomas, G. and James, D. (2006). Reinventing grounded theory: some questions about theory, ground and discovery. *British Educational Research Journal*, 32, 767–795.

Thornberg, R. (2007). Inconsistencies in everyday patterns of school rules. *Ethnography and Education*, 2, 401–416.

Thornberg, R. (2008). School children's reasoning about school rules. *Research Papers in Education*, 23, 37–52.

Thornberg, R. (2009). The moral construction of the good pupil embedded in school rules. *Education, Citizenship and Social Justice*, 4, 245–261.

Thornberg, R. (2012). Informed grounded theory. *Scandinavian Journal of Educational Research*, 56, 243–259.

Thornberg, R. and Charmaz, K. (2012). Grounded theory. In S. D. Lapan, M. T. Quartaroli and F. J. Reimer (Eds) *Qualitative Research: An introduction to methods and designs* (pp. 41–67). San Francisco, CA: John Wiley/Jossey-Bass.

Thornberg, R. and Charmaz, K. (2014). Grounded theory and theoretical coding. In U. Flick (Ed.) *The SAGE Handbook of Qualitative Data Analysis* (pp. 153–169). London: Sage.

Thornberg, R., Perhamus, L. M. and Charmaz, K. (2015). Grounded theory. In O. Saracho (Ed.) *Handbook of Research Methods in Early Childhood Education* (pp. 405–439). Charlotte, NC: Information Age Publishing.

Webster, T. E. and Son, J-B. (2015). Doing what works: a grounded theory case study of technology use by teachers of English at a Korean university. *Computers and Education*, 80, 84–94.

Yalof, B. (2014). Marshaling resources: a classic grounded theory study of online learners. *The Grounded Theory Review*, 13, 16–28.

18

Case Study Research

Malcolm Tight

INTRODUCTION

This chapter argues that case study is a research design rather than a method, approach, style or strategy, and that case studies are small-scale research projects with meaning. Like other research designs, case study has strengths and weaknesses, with the latter focusing in particular on the question of generalization. As well as reviewing the literature on case study, and arguing for a revised conceptualization, the chapter offers practical advice on doing a case study, and some suggestions for further reading.

OVERVIEW

In this section, we look briefly at the history of case study, consider what case studies are and the different approaches that may be taken, and discuss the relationship between case study and theory.

Origins and history

Burgess (1927, p. 114) notes that 'The case-study method was first introduced into social science as a handmaiden to statistics', with the latter regarded as the most desirable way of undertaking research. Case study was seen as a means for fleshing out and providing detailed exemplification to complement statistical analyses, rather than as an alternative to them. Symonds (1945, p. 357) argued that:

> much remains to be done to improve its methodology so that case materials may be amassed and treated in a manner that includes, on the one hand, objective appraisal and statistical integrity and that, on the other hand, never loses sight of the integrated, dynamic, holistic picture of human personality which the case study approach to research uniquely may give.

From its beginnings, a great deal of attention has always been given to trying to devise common standards or approaches to case study (for example, Foreman, 1948).

In the 1950s, case study was in less favour in the social sciences. Platt (1992) associates this decline with its imprecise usage, the issues of generalization and prediction, problems with the articulation of case study analysis, and increased competition from the development of more sophisticated quantitative techniques. Case study began to make a comeback in the 1980s, as qualitative techniques assumed a greater importance and popularity, particularly outside of North America:

> In the last 25 years the shift away from quantification and large scale survey methods in the social sciences, alongside the increasing attention being given to language and meaning in constructing identity and social relations, has seen a significant revival in case study methods. This has led to a range of reappraisals of the method, and an increased emphasis upon lived experience, the life-story and the biographical/autobiographical in social research. (David 2006, p. xxxix)

What is a case study?

As with any important idea, the meaning of case study is the subject of debate, and many definitions can be found in the literature. Four are given as examples in Box 18.1. These definitions usefully draw attention to some common elements of our understanding of case study.

Thus, Stake points out that the case being studied is both particular and complex, while Thomas emphasizes that its study should be holistic; if neither of these points applies, the case would scarcely be worth studying. Merriam (1998) and Bassey both note that the case needs to be bounded or delimited; if it isn't, it isn't a case, and you are not then engaged in case study but in some other kind of research.

Other elements of the definitions stress aspects of case study which most of its proponents would agree with. Bassey stresses that the case is to be studied in its 'natural' context. Cases are not artificial entities, they are not experiments, but are part of our reality, from which – even though, as cases, they are bounded – they cannot be separated. Bassey (1999) also writes of case studies focusing on 'interesting aspects' and 'significant features', leading to the construction of a 'worthwhile argument'; while Thomas sees the case as illuminating and explicating a particular phenomenon of interest.

Box 18.1   Definitions of Case Study

Case study is the study of the particularity and complexity of a single case, coming to understand its activity within important circumstances. (Stake, 1995, p. xi)

The single most defining characteristic of case study research lies in delimiting the object of study, the case.... If the phenomenon you are interested in studying is not intrinsically bounded, it is not a case. (Merriam, 1998, p. 27)

An educational case study is an empirical enquiry which is: conducted within a localized boundary of space and time ... into *interesting* aspects of an educational activity, or programme, or institution, or system; mainly in its natural context and within an ethic of respect for persons; in order to inform the judgements and decisions of practitioners or policy-makers; or of theoreticians who are working to these ends; in such a way that sufficient data are collected for the researcher to be able ... to explore *significant* features of the case ... create *plausible* interpretations ... test for the[ir] trustworthiness ... construct a *worthwhile* argument ...[and] convey *convincingly* to an audience this argument. (Bassey, 1999, p. 58)

Case studies are analyses of persons, events, decisions, periods, projects, policies, institutions or other systems which are studied holistically by one or more methods. The case that is the subject of the inquiry will be an instance of a class of phenomena that provides an analytical frame – an object – within which the study is conducted and which the case illuminates and explicates. (Thomas, 2011a, p. 23)

It is not surprising that we can also readily identify differences between these definitions, but the commonalities between them are stronger. As well as clarifying what case study is, they help to make it clear what case study is not. We can be reasonably confident, then, in stating that case study involves the study of a particular case, or a number of cases, that the case will be complex and bounded, that it will be studied in its context, and that the analysis undertaken will seek to be holistic. Case study is, in other words, small-scale research with meaning.

It has been argued that 'almost anything can serve as a case' (Punch 2005, p. 144), but this does not mean that all research can or should be designated as case study (whether single or multiple). Of course, 'case' is a generic term, and all research could be said to involve the study of cases. It is critically important, therefore, that we exercise care and discretion in using the label 'case study', restricting it to research which explicitly employs a case study design: that is, the focus of the research is on one or more cases.

The attention given to case study in the social research methods literature varies. May (2001) devotes only a page and a half to case study research, at the end of a chapter on participant observation, with which he links and compares it. Punch (2005) discusses case study as an approach to qualitative research design, alongside ethnography, grounded theory and action research. Bryman (2004) also treats case study as a research design, but contrasts it with experimental, cross-sectional, longitudinal and comparative designs. Cohen et al. (2007) take a third approach, seeing case study as a style of (educational) research, together with ethnographic, historical, action, experimental, internet-based and survey styles.

There are many other social research methods texts which we might examine, but this small sample already illustrates the range of alternative perspectives that are taken towards case study. Judging by these texts, we could view case study as a method, approach, style, strategy or design. Whichever of these it might be, it can be conceived of in relation to a wide, but differing, range of other social research methods, approaches, styles, strategies or designs; including action research, comparative studies, cross-sectional studies, ethnography, experiments, grounded theory, historical studies, internet-based studies, longitudinal studies and surveys.

While recognizing that the terms method, approach, style, strategy and design share overlapping meanings, the perspective taken here is that it is most sensible to be clear and consistent, and to view case study as a research design. Within this research design, particular methods, approaches, styles or strategies may then be adopted in order to progress the research.

Status and role

Case study is widely used as a research design, not just in education but throughout the social sciences and beyond. Swanborn (2010) identifies several disciplinary sources of importance in the development of case study, including the health sciences, clinical psychotherapy, law, cultural anthropology, sociology, political science, psychology and many policy fields.

Currently, the use of case study is particularly evident in the business/management area, and in other professional disciplines such as health, law, psychoanalysis and social work, as well as in education. In some, case study is used as a teaching method as well as, or instead of, a research design. This is common in the health/medicine field, in law and social work, and in business/management studies. Case studies are used to explore and illustrate particular medical conditions, legal precedents or business problems. Teaching and research case studies may also overlap.

Case study research has, unsurprisingly, been caught up in the debate over the relative merits of qualitative and quantitative forms of research. Sometimes it has been defined and approached as if it was qualitative research, probably because of its small-scale and in-depth focus. This is, however, both erroneous and unnecessary. While most case study research in education is primarily qualitative, case studies may make use of quantitative techniques as well as, or instead of, qualitative methods. Indeed, they are well suited to the pragmatic, mixed methods, approach that has been advocated by some (Dunning et al., 2008; Tashakkori and Teddlie, 1998), though this approach is also less common.

Types and examples

Proponents of case study have long recognized that there are different sorts of, or approaches to, case study. Box 18.2 summarizes four categorizations. Each seems fairly simple, identifying just three categories, and there are similarities between them.

Thus, Cunningham (1997) distinguishes comparative case studies, while Stake (2005) and Yin (2009) use the alternative terms multiple or collective.

Box 18.2   Types of Case Study

1 The intensive case study (including interpretative and explanatory)
2 Comparative case studies (case surveys, case comparisons, creative interpretations)
3 Action research ('a term for describing a spectrum of cases that focus on research and learning through intervening and observing the process of change'). (Cunningham, 1997, pp. 402, 405)

1 Descriptive (exploratory-descriptive, focused-descriptive)
2 Theoretical-heuristic (grounded theory building, hermeneutic work)
3 Theory-testing (testing propositions within grounded theory, metatheoretical construction). (Edwards, 1998)

1 Intrinsic ('if the study is undertaken because, first and last, one wants better understanding of this particular case')
2 Instrumental ('if a particular case is examined mainly to provide insight into an issue or to redraw a generalization')
3 Multiple or collective ('a number of cases may be studied jointly in order to investigate a phenomenon, population or general condition'). (Stake, 2005, p. 445)

1 Explanatory or causal
2 Descriptive
3 Exploratory.

All of which may be single or multiple. (Yin, 2009, pp. 19–21)

Whether or not the focus of the case study is on theory is a key concern, conveyed by Edwards (1998) in the 'theoretical-heuristic' and 'theory-testing' distinctions, and by Yin in his 'explanatory/causal' category. The opposite focus is classified by both Edwards and Yin as 'descriptive'.

While no typology seems entirely satisfactory, and the usage of alternative terms to mean much the same thing can be confusing, the analysis so far suggests that there are three major factors to bear in mind when considering examples of, or undertaking, case studies:

- Whether they focus on a single case or involve a comparative study or two or more cases;
- Whether they confine themselves to description or engage with theory; and
- Whether they are intended primarily to support teaching or research.

Box 18.3 briefly describes and discusses three varied examples of published case study research to indicate some of the possibilities.

Multiple case studies

For those committed to the case study approach, one of the key decisions concerns moving from single case studies to carrying out and/or analysing multiple case studies. This decision is bound up with a whole range of issues, including generalization and theory development and testing, as well as with building up the credibility of case study as a research design.

Box 18.3   Examples of Case Study Research

Snyder (2012) offers a 'case study of a case study' developed from 'a study which tracked the transformative journeys of four career-changing women from STEM fields into secondary education', using 'archived writing, journaling, participant-generated photography, interviews, member-checking, and reflexive analytical memos' (p. 1). This, then, would qualify as a multiple case study (that is, four women were studied). It was a qualitative and longitudinal study, making use of varied sources of data. The author sets out very clearly how she collected and analysed the data. While there was a theoretical framework to the study, to do with women's career development, this is not the focus of, and is not exemplified in, the article.

Canen (1999) reflects on the challenges of conducting ethnographic case study research in a UK teacher education institution. She encountered an ethical dilemma when further access was refused part way through her study, resulting in its early termination. This was a single case study (that is, one institution), informed theoretically by a transformative approach to competence. A qualitative and ethnographic approach was taken to data collection, making use of observation (shadowing) of trainee teachers, analysis of institutional documents and selected in-depth interviews.

Corcoran, Walker and Wals (2004) consider the use of case study methodology to research sustainability in higher education, arguing that this design is 'the ideal research tool to investigate sustainability in higher education' (p. 10). They review 54 journal articles published in selected environmental journals over the 1996-2001 period, raising concerns about the lack of theorising and/or understanding of methodology displayed. They then set out a series of conditions for critical case study development. This is clearly a meta-analysis of multiple case study reports.

Over 40 years ago Lijphart (1975) defined what he referred to as the comparative method, which he presented as an alternative to the statistical method. By selecting similar sorts of cases for study, the researcher would be able to assess whether the same sorts of relationships between variables could be observed within them, and thus provide support, or otherwise, for their hypotheses about how these relationships worked. More recently, Odell (2001) has argued that single case studies, multiple case studies and statistical analyses lie on a spectrum of research designs.

If you are carrying out a multiple case study, there are additional factors to bear in mind in sampling and selection (Small, 2009). McClintock (1985, p. 220) recommends the use of the case cluster method, which 'offers a way to structure case study research so that data collection, analysis and reporting can be accommodated in a more focused manner'. George and Bennett (2005) emphasize the importance of structured and focused comparison:

> The method is 'structured' in that the researcher writes general questions that reflect the research objective and that these questions are asked of each case under study to guide and standardize data collection, thereby making systematic comparison and cumulation of the findings of the cases possible. The method is 'focused' in that it deals only with certain aspects of the ... cases examined. (George and Bennett, 2005, p. 67)

They also make the point that such studies are made easier when the work is all undertaken by a single researcher. If this is not feasible, and the research planned necessitates the involvement of a number of researchers, then the importance of training, piloting and calibrating the work done becomes critical, especially if it is international in scope.

Gerring and McDermott (2007) seek to provide what they term an experimental template for comparative case study research, proposing four alternative designs: dynamic comparison (involving the use of both temporal and spatial variation), longitudinal (that is, temporal) comparison, spatial comparison and counterfactual (imagined) comparison. Larsson (1993) takes the discussion in a different direction, towards what is commonly termed meta-analysis or synthesis, which he terms the case survey method:

> The basic procedure of the case survey is (1) select a group of existing case studies relevant to the chosen research questions, (2) design a coding scheme for systematic conversion of the qualitative case descriptions into quantified variables, (3) use multiple raters to code the cases and measure their interrater reliability, and (4) statistically analyze the coded data. (Larsson, 1993, pp. 1516–17)

The quantification of qualitative data proposed transforms the case study design into something that many small-scale researchers might be uncomfortable with, but illustrates the potential if numbers of similar existing case studies are available.

Case study and theory

As with any research design, the relationship between case study and theory is important. While critics of case study argue that, because it is small-scale, it is not suitable for theory development or testing, its advocates contend that, precisely because it is so in-depth, it is well suited to theory development; and that, when suitably replicated, case studies may also test theories. Of course, much depends, as Hammersley (2012) points out, on what type of theory you are talking about and/or what you mean by theory.

Eisenhardt (1989), in a much cited article (see Ravenswood, 2011), offers a roadmap for building theories from case study research. She argues that, while theory building may begin from the analysis of a single case, to progress further additional case studies need to be undertaken or examined. Dooley (2002) offers a similar formulation:

> The researcher who embarks on case study research is usually interested in a specific phenomenon and wishes to understand it completely.... From this single observation, the start of a theory may be formed, and this may provoke the researcher to study the same phenomenon within the boundaries of another case, and then another, and another (single cases studied independently), or between individual cases (cross-case analysis) as the theory begins to take shape. (Dooley, 2002, p. 336)

Hoon (2013; cf. Larsson's proposal in the previous section) goes further in arguing for the use of meta-synthesis – analyzing multiple case studies – for building theory from qualitative case studies:

> a meta-synthesis of qualitative case studies is proposed to have major potential in synthesizing qualitative evidence on a particular topic to build theory ... building theory out of published case studies holds great potential especially if a reliable synthesis process is augmented through the application of ... rigorous procedures ... the greatest challenge that a qualitative synthesis faces is viewed in the heterogeneity inherent in the primary studies' underlying paradigmatic perspectives, methods, and quality. (Hoon, 2013, p. 543)

The third point rather undermines the first two, however, in pointing out the difficulty in identifying multiple case studies, by multiple researchers, which can be compared.

Welch et al. (2011) identify four methods of theorizing from case studies:

- Inductive theory building (inducing new theory from empirical data);
- Natural experiment (using deductive logic to test propositions);
- Interpretive sense-making (seeking to understand the particular rather than the general); and
- Contextualized explanation (understanding how an outcome was brought about in a particular case).

These methods vary in terms of their emphasis on contextualization and causal explanation.

As well as using case studies to build or develop theory, they may also be employed to test theory. Yin (2009) links this with the issue of generalization, arguing that case studies may be used to perform what he terms analytic generalization:

> in which a previously developed theory is used as a template with which to compare the empirical results of the case study. If two or more cases are shown to support the same theory, replication may be claimed. The empirical results may be considered yet more potent if two or more cases support the same theory but do not support an equally plausible, *rival* theory. (Yin, 2009, pp. 38–9)

By building up more and more case studies, theory may, in this way, be tested and verified, or rejected and then modified.

Clearly, then, there is a divergence of opinion on the use of case study in theory development and testing, but a general recognition that this is made easier when multiple case studies are carried out or available.

STRENGTHS AND WEAKNESSES

Criticisms of case study are of long standing (Atkinson and Delamont, 1985; Platt, 1992). Hence, those in favour of case study as a research design often feel obliged to defend their choice:

> case studies of whatever form are a reliable and respectable procedure of social analysis and ... much criticism of their reliability and validity has been based on a misconception of the basis upon which the analyst may justifiably extrapolate from an individual case study to the social process in general.... The validity of the extrapolation depends not on the typicality or representativeness of the case but upon the cogency of the theoretical reasoning. (Mitchell, 1983, p. 207)

Proponents of case study sometimes try and anticipate their critics by identifying the criticisms that have been made, and then articulating responses to these. Flyvbjerg, for example identifies what he terms 'five misunderstandings or oversimplifications':

1 General, theoretical (context-independent) knowledge is more valuable than concrete, practical (context-dependent) knowledge.
2 One cannot generalize on the basis of an individual case...
3 The case study is most useful for generating hypotheses ... while other methods are more suitable for hypothesis testing and theory-building.
4 The case study contains a bias towards verification, that is, a tendency to confirm the researcher's preconceived notions.
5 It is often difficult to summarize and develop general propositions and theories on the basis of specific case studies. (Flyvbjerg, 2004, p. 391)

On the first point, Flyvbjerg argues that in social research 'we have only specific cases and context-dependent knowledge' (p. 392). On the second and third points, he contends that it depends upon the case and how it is chosen. On the fourth point, Flyvbjerg argues that this criticism is true for all methods of social research, and on the fifth that:

> The problems … are due more often to the properties of the reality studied than to the case study as a research method. Often it is not desirable to summarize and generalize case studies. Good studies should be read as narratives in their entirety. (Flyvbjerg, 2004, p. 402)

Many others have wrestled with these issues over the years. Feagin et al. (1991) outline how issues of reliability and validity can be handled by conducting team research and triangulating data sources, and assert the strengths of case study in providing a close reading set within its context. Ragin and Becker (1992) argue that the response to criticisms of case study is implicit in its practice:

> Social scientists who conduct case studies argue that their cases are typical or exemplary or extreme or theoretically decisive in some other way. Thus, even in case-study research the principle of repetition is often implicated in statements concerning the relation between the chosen case and other cases. (Ragin and Becker, 1992, p. 2)

Gomm et al. argue that 'while *some* case study research may be able to avoid "the problem of generalization" because the case(s) studied have sufficient intrinsic relevance, this is not true of most of it' (Gomm et al., 2000, p. 102, emphasis in original). They then articulate effective strategies for drawing general conclusions, involving theoretical inference and empirical generalization, either to a larger population or within cases.

Strengths

These debates enable us to construct a shortlist of the strengths and weaknesses of case study as a research design. Let us start by emphasizing the strengths. Thus, case studies are in-depth, detailed and particular; they allow a close focus on the case, which the researcher thoroughly studies. Second, and relatedly, the research is holistic, aimed at understanding everything – or, at least, as much as possible – about the particularity of the case in question (hence the importance of using a range of methods in studying it). These characteristics are in contrast to much other social research, which tends to focus on a limited range of variables or factors, and inevitably over-simplifies what is going on.

Third, the case being studied may be typical or exemplary, and, if this can be demonstrated, then the likelihood of the findings from it being of broader relevance increase. Or, alternatively, if the case being studied is critical or extreme, it is the very particularity of the case, rather than its broader significance, that is important.

Finally, a very important advantage of case study research from the point of view of the small-scale researcher is that it is bounded and, therefore, more feasible. When there are limits – of time and other resources – on what the researcher can afford to spend on a particular piece of research, it is highly pragmatic to be able to tightly and precisely define what is going to be researched. Of course, at the same time, the researcher will still wish to complete a piece of research that is useful and meaningful.

We may add to these strengths three desirable qualities for case study (and other forms of) research. First, the case study needs to be approached and carried out rigorously. Second, it should have a theoretical framework, enabling the development of a fuller understanding of how it works. And, third, it is highly desirable that the findings are triangulated in some way, for example by comparison with other similar case studies or other kinds of evidence.

Weaknesses

Turning now to weaknesses, the major criticism of case study as a research design, which has already been touched upon a number of times, undoubtedly has to do with generalizability. We might seek to argue that this is to overlook the strength of case study, its focus on the particular, and assert that what really matters is the quality of the case study, but – as we have seen – there are many who would reject this position.

The main response to this criticism has been to argue for the accumulation of single case studies on the same topic to allow for the identification of similarities and differences. This is how case studies have long been used in certain disciplines. Jensen and Rodgers (2001) argue that such meta-analysis may be used to cumulate what they refer to as 'the intellectual gold' of case study research. In this light, Ruzzene (2012, p. 99) demands that 'the emphasis should be placed on the comparability of the study rather than on the typicality of the case'.

Evers and Wu (2006) take a different tack, arguing that it is possible to generalize from single cases:

> cases possess considerably more structure than is commonly supposed ... researchers bring to a case much more knowledge than is often supposed ... an ongoing trajectory of inquiry through time and changing circumstances makes it less likely that a stable match between patterns of researcher expectations and what is observed is sheer coincidence. (Evers and Wu, 2006, p. 524)

Clearly, the researcher's experience will be a key factor here, suggesting that generalization is much more difficult or risky, though often difficult to resist, for the novice researcher.

Thomas (2011b, p. 33) reminds us that generalization is an issue throughout the social sciences: 'to seek *generalizable knowledge*, in whatever form – everyday or special – is to miss the point about what may be offered by certain kinds of inquiry, which is *exemplary knowledge*'. We study particular cases for their interest and what we can learn from them.

Other perceived weaknesses of case study are those of validity and reliability. Riege (2003) considers which validity and reliability tests can most appropriately be used at each stage of case study research. He argues that:

> The four design tests of construct validity, internal validity, external validity and reliability are commonly applied to the theoretical paradigm of positivism. Similarly, however, they can be used for the realism paradigm, which includes case study research.... In addition to using the four 'traditional' design tests, the application of four 'corresponding' design tests is recommended to enhance validity and reliability, that is credibility, trustworthiness (transferability), confirmability and dependability. (Riege, 2003, p. 84)

Riege here introduces different measures of validity: construct (whether the constructs which are being used to measure concepts of interest are appropriate), internal (the quality of the explanation of the phenomena examined) and external (whether the findings can be extrapolated beyond the case studied). He also introduces four alternative ways of judging the quality of a piece of case study research, which have the benefit of being both more immediately intelligible and more suitable to qualitative forms of research.

Most researchers, though, have sought to remain true to the 'traditional' ideas of validity and reliability when assessing the results of case study research. Thus, Diefenbach (2009, p. 892) concludes that: 'many qualitative case studies either do not go far beyond a mere description of particular aspects or the generalizations provided are not based on a very sound methodological basis'.

One of the strongest contemporary advocates of case study, Yin (2013), offers rather more hope, discussing a range of different approaches that have been taken towards addressing validity and generalization in case study evaluations, including alternative explanations, triangulation, logic models, and analytic generalization and theory.

Clearly, as practitioners of case study research, we need to be aware of its limitations, and do what we can to overcome them, but we should also emphasize the strengths of this research design. In the end, perhaps it does come down to how well the case study has been carried out, and how useful, interesting or meaningful the story it tells is.

DOING A CASE STUDY

Most of the issues and processes involved in carrying out a case study – choosing what to study, how to study it and how to analyse and write up your findings – are common to those faced when applying other research designs. The key difference is that, in case study research, we choose to focus in detail on a particular example or a small number of examples.

Those who offer guidance on doing case studies tend to organize this – as I am doing here – into a series of stages or tasks. For example, Stuart et al. identify five 'steps' (2002), Stake gives six 'responsibilities' (2005), George and Bennett suggest five 'tasks' (2005) and Pan and Tan list eight 'steps' (2011). The number of points identified and the labels given to them differ, but all of these authors present a sequential listing of tasks to be undertaken, from defining the research question, through developing a data collection strategy, data gathering, seeking patterns in the data, aligning theory and data, to writing up and disseminating the results.

While presenting the practice of doing a case study as a sequence of steps can be helpful, it should also be recognized that it is artificial and over-simplified. Actually doing a case study, as with any other form of research, can be a messy and confusing business, with, for example, data collection and analysis taking place more or less simultaneously, and research questions being altered to better fit emerging findings.

Macpherson et al. (2000) take a rather different approach, offering a set of six principles to guide case study practice: contextuality, sensitivity, authenticity, applicability, growth and communicability.

Research questions

Many researchers would argue that your research questions are key, and should drive all your other research decisions:

> A question is the starting point for your research. Begin with a question, not a presupposition that you are going to do a case study. A case study should follow logically from your question or else you should not do one. (Thomas, 2011a, p. 30)

It would be unusual to conduct research without any idea of what you were researching and why. However, having only a general idea gives you quite a lot of scope for wasted time and effort; hence the importance of being as specific as possible about what you want to research. Research questions should be short, specific, clearly answerable and limited in number.

Sampling and selection

Sampling and selection are fundamental processes in almost any research project, unless you plan to study every example of the particular population of interest to you. This is so even if you have already identified the case you intend to study. Many small-scale researchers select their own case – for example, where they work – or have it selected for them by their funder or employer. But you should carefully consider other options, if possible, and be aware of the consequences of engaging in 'insider' research, as well as the comparative characteristics of your case.

Thomas identified three main reasons for choosing a particular case to study:

> You may choose it because you know a great deal about the case in question and you want to understand some feature of that subject.... Alternatively, you may choose it because it provides a particularly good example of something. The other option is that the case may reveal something interesting because it is different from the norm. (Thomas, 2011a, pp. 95–6)

The first of these reasons applies when you study your own institution, hoping to better understand its operation and be able to make practical recommendations for improvement. For Thomas's other two options, your choice is determined more by whether your findings might be of wider interest, either because the case studied is more typical or because it is unusual. Seawright and Gerring (2008) identify more case study designs – typical case, diverse cases, extreme case, deviant case, influential case, most similar/most different cases – all of which seem worthy of consideration.

A key issue in sampling and selection is having access to the people, institutions, documents or whatever it is that you need to study to understand the case. Clearly, gaining only limited access, or being refused access at the beginning – or part way through – your study, will not help you answer your research question(s). This also helps to explain why so many small-scale researchers opt to research within their own institution, because access seems to be assured. Yet, this is not the only factor of importance: 'you should choose the case(s) that will most likely illuminate your research questions' (Yin, 2009, p. 26).

Selecting cases for study solely on the basis of convenience and ease of access may limit the usefulness of the research you carry out. The greater effort, and possible delays, involved in going beyond the familiar may yield significant benefits in the longer run:

> insufficient concern is often given to the choice of research sites. Far too often it seems that researchers settle for research sites to which they can easily gain convenient and ready access rather than thinking through the implications of particular choices... however difficult access may be, it is crucial that obtaining access is not seen as the primary consideration in selecting an appropriate site. (Walford, 2001, p. 151)

Selecting the right case or cases for study may involve quite a bit of work, but it should be worth it when you finish. While the ideal selection strategy may be unrealizable, the researcher should always be aware of, and be prepared to justify, the factors they took into account in making their selection.

Boundary and environment

Given the importance that case study researchers accord to bounding the case, and understanding its place within the surrounding environment, it is surprising how little explicit attention is given to these issues. This may be because, as with so much about case study, the notion of bounding the case is simply specialist terminology for what is a much more generic process. All researchers have to place limits on their research projects. This is particularly so in small-scale research, where focusing the research is of key importance if it is to be manageable and deliverable within time and resource constraints. The same considerations are involved in bounding the case.

This is readily apparent in the advice given by Baxter and Jack (2008, p. 547): 'Suggestions on how to bind a case include: (a) by time and place; (b) time and activity; and (c) by definition and context'. To take the first two of these suggestions, you might bound your case in terms of when and where it occurred, and when and what was of interest. The third suggestion, by definition and context, sounds very like case and environment. It is important to always bear in mind that, if you had defined your case somewhat differently, your findings might be significantly different.

Collecting and analysing data

Approaches to the collection and analysis of data vary within case study: in terms of methodological strategy adopted and the level of sophistication sought. In principle, any of the wide range of qualitative and quantitative approaches might be used, singly or in combination.

Amongst case study researchers, Swanborn (2010) distinguishes five traditions:

1 Analysis of data collected in the field of changing organizations [by which he means simply organizational change research], according to Yin.
2 Analysis of data collected in one of the qualitative traditions, especially the grounded theory approach of Strauss and Corbin.
3 Data analysis and presentation according to the work of Miles and Huberman.
4 Time-series analysis.
5 Data analysis according to Ragin's method, using Boolean logic and fuzzy-set theory. (Swanborn, 2010, pp. 114–15)

Yin (2009, pp. 136–60) himself identifies five analytic techniques: pattern matching (that is, comparing the pattern found with that expected), building an explanation about the case, time-series analysis (examining what happens in the case over time), logic models (which predict and then test complex chains of events), cross-case synthesis (for example, using multiple cases or meta-analysis).

Assessing your work

A number of authors provide checklists for judging the worth of a completed case study. These may, of course, be used to assess published case studies as well as your own. Yin (2009, pp. 185–90) identifies five 'general characteristics of an exemplary case study': it must 'be significant ... be "complete" ... consider alternative perspectives ... display sufficient evidence ... be composed in an engaging manner'. All of these characteristics are, of course, couched in rather subjective language: what, for example, is significant or engaging, and who is to be the judge of this? These characteristics are also, however, generic in nature, and could be applied to any piece of research.

Thomas (2011a, pp. 67–8) provides another checklist. He stresses quality, which he suggests can be assessed through three questions:

1 How well has the case been chosen?
2 How well has the context for the study been explained and justified?
3 How well have the arguments been made? Have rival explanations for the same kinds of observations been explored?

The first of these questions is similar to Yin's point about significance, while the last encompasses aspects of Yin's strictures regarding the consideration of alternative explanations and writing in an engaging manner. Thomas's second question, however, opens up another aspect for evaluation, the context for the case study, and takes us back to considerations of bounding.

Writing up

Another way of assessing the quality of a case study, particularly one you have recently completed, is to write it up for publication, and find out what others (editors, reviewers, readers) think of it. Academic publishing is a competitive practice, and almost always involves the author(s) undertaking some significant revision of what they originally drafted, in the light of comments made by reviewers, if they are to proceed to publication. Successful publication in a reputable academic journal is a significant achievement and a strong (but by no means foolproof) indication of quality.

One obvious way to get a grip on what is involved in writing up your case study is to examine previous examples (Darke et al., 1998). Whatever genre of publication you are attempting – for example, an academic journal article, a book chapter, a report, a conference paper or a dissertation – there will be existing examples you can access and study. Get advice, if you can, on particularly good examples; or focus on those which are highly cited by other researchers. Look at the way in which the writing has been organized, and the balance of space devoted to the different sections. Note the kind of language used, the way references to other publications are brought in, and how the author(s) put forward their argument.

Alternatively, there are also guides available to writing up. For example, Pan and Tan (2011) recommend that a case study paper should contain six sections: introduction, literature review, research method, results, discussion and conclusion. That is a perfectly reasonable structure to adopt for writing up a case study, but it is generic, and would do just as well for many other kinds of research. Don't be afraid to move away from such formulaic approaches.

CONCLUSION

Hopefully, reading this chapter will have given you a clear idea of the range of options available in case study research, and how you might go about doing yours. Make sure that you enjoy it and that it has meaning.

FURTHER READING

Swanborn, P. (2010) *Case Study Research: What, why and how?* London: Sage.
Thomas, G. (2011) *How to do your Case Study: A guide for students and researchers*. London: Sage.
Yin, R. (2014) *Case Study Research: Design and methods*, 5th edition. Los Angeles, CA: Sage.

REFERENCES

Atkinson, P. and Delamont, S. (1985) Bread and dreams or bread and circuses? A critique of 'case study' research in education, in M Shipman (Ed.) *Educational Research: Principles, policies and practices* (pp. 26–45). London: Falmer.
Bassey, M. (1999) *Case Study Research in Educational Settings*. Buckingham, Open University Press.
Baxter, P. and Jack, S. (2008) Qualitative case study methodology: study design and implementation for novice researchers. *The Qualitative Report*, 13, 4, 544–559.
Bryman, A. (2004) *Social Research Methods*, 2nd edition. Oxford, Oxford University Press.
Burgess, E. (1927) Statistics and case studies as methods of sociological research. *Sociology and Social Research*, 11, 103–120.
Canen, A. (1999) The challenges of conducting an ethnographic case study of a United Kingdom teacher education institution. *Journal of Teacher Education*, 50, 1, 50–56.
Cohen, L., Manion, L. and Morrison, K. (2007) *Research Methods in Education*, 6th edition. London: Routledge.
Cunningham, J (1997) Case study principles for different types of case. *Quality and Quantity*, 31, 401–423.
Darke, P., Shanks, G. and Broadbent, M. (1998) Successfully completing case study research: combining rigour, relevance and pragmatism. *Information Systems Journal*, 8, 273–289.

David, M. (2006) Editor's introduction, in M. David (Ed.) *Case Study Research*, 4 volumes (pp. xxiii–xlii). London: Sage.

Diefenbach, T. (2009) Are case studies more than sophisticated storytelling? Methodological problems of qualitative empirical research mainly based on semi-structured interviews. *Quality and Quantity*, 43, 875–894.

Dooley, L. (2002) Case study research and theory building. *Advances in Developing Human Resources*, 4, 3, 335–354.

Dunning, H., Williams, A., Abonyi, S. and Crooks, V. (2008) A mixed method approach to quality of life research: a case study approach. *Social Indicators Research*, 85, 1, 145–158.

Edwards, D. (1998) Types of case study work: a conceptual framework for case-based research. *Journal of Humanistic Psychology*, 38, 3, 36–70.

Eisenhardt, K. (1989) Building theories from case study research. *Academy of Management Review*, 14, 4, 532–550.

Evers, C. and Wu, E. (2006) On generalising from single case studies: epistemological reflections. *Journal of Philosophy of Education*, 40, 4, 511–526.

Feagin, J., Orum, A. and Sjoberg, G. (Eds) (1991) *A Case for the Case Study*. Chapel Hill, NC: University of North Carolina Press.

Flyvbjerg, B (2004) Five Misunderstandings about Case Study Research. pp. 390–404 in C. Seale, G. Gobo, J. Gubrium and D. Silverman (Eds) *Qualitative Research Practice*. London: Sage.

Foreman, P. (1948), The theory of case studies. *Social Forces*, 26, 4, 408–419.

George, A. and Bennett, A. (2005) *Case Studies and Theory Development in the Social Sciences*. Cambridge, MA: MIT Press.

Gerring, J. and McDermott, R. (2007) An experimental template for case study research. *American Journal of Political Science*, 51, 3, 688–701.

Gomm, R., Hammersley, M. and Foster, P. (2000) Case study and generalization, in R. Gomm, M. Hammersley and P. Foster (Eds) *Case Study Method: Key issues, key texts* (pp. 98–115). London: Sage.

Hammersley, M. (2012) Troubling theory in case study research. *Higher Education Research and Development*, 31, 3, 393–405.

Hoon, C. (2013) Meta-synthesis of qualitative case studies: an approach to theory building. *Organizational Research Methods*, 16, 4, 522–556.

Jensen, J. and Rodgers, R. (2001) Cumulating the intellectual gold of case study research. *Public Administration Review*, 61, 2, 235–246.

Larsson, R (1993) Case survey methodology: quantitative analysis of patterns across case studies. *Academy of Management Journal*, 36, 6, 1515–1546.

Lijphart, A. (1975) The comparable-cases strategy in comparative research. *Comparative Political Studies*, 8, 2, 158–177.

Macpherson, I., Brooker, R. and Ainsworth, P. (2000) Case study in the contemporary world of research: using notions of purpose, place, process and product to develop some principles for practice. *International Journal of Social Research Methodology*, 3, 1, 49–61.

May, T (2001) *Social Research: Issues, methods and process*, 3rd edition. Buckingham: Open University Press.

McClintock, C. (1985) Process sampling: a method for case study research on administrative behaviour. *Educational Administration Quarterly*, 21, 3, 205–222.

Merriam, S. (1998) *Qualitative Research and Case Study Applications in Education*. San Francisco, CA: Jossey-Bass.

Mitchell, C. (1983) Case and situation analysis. *Sociological Review*, 31, 2, 187–211.

Odell, J. (2001) Case study methods in international political economy. *International Studies Perspectives*, 2, 161–176.

Pan, S. and Tan, B. (2011) Demystifying case research: a structured-pragmatic-situational (SPS) approach to conducting case studies. *Information and Organization*, 21, 161–176.

Platt, J. (1992) 'Case study' in American methodological thought. *Current Sociology*, 40, 1, 17–48.

Punch, K. (2005) *Introduction to Social Research: Quantitative and qualitative approaches*, 2nd edition. London: Sage.

Ragin, C. and Becker, H. (Eds) (1992) *What is a Case? Exploring the foundations of social inquiry*. Cambridge: Cambridge University Press.

Ravenswood, K. (2011) Eisenhardt's impact on theory in case study research. *Journal of Business Research*, 64, 680–686.

Riege, A. (2003) Validity and reliability tests in case study research: a literature review with 'hands-on' applications for each research phase. *Qualitative Market Research*, 6, 2, 75–86.

Ruzzene, A. (2012) Drawing lessons from case studies by enhancing comparability. *Philosophy of the Social Sciences*, 42, 1, 99–120.

Seawright, J. and Gerring, J. (2008) Case selection techniques in case study research: a menu of qualitative and quantitative options. *Political Research Quarterly*, 61, 2, 294–308.

Small, M. (2009) 'How many cases do I need?': on science and the logic of case selection in field-based research. *Ethnography*, 10, 1, 5–38.

Snyder, C. (2012) A case study of a case study: analysis of a robust qualitative research methodology. *The Qualitative Report*, 17, Article 21, 1–21.

Stake, R. (1995) *The Art of Case Study Research*. Thousand Oaks, CA: Sage.

Stake, R. (2005) Qualitative case studies, in N. Denzin and Y. Lincoln (Eds) *The Sage Handbook of Qualitative Research*, 3rd edition (pp. 443–466). Thousand Oaks, CA: Sage.

Stuart, I., McCutcheon, D., Handfield, R., McLachlin, R. and Samson, D. (2002) Effective case research in operations management: a process perspective. *Journal of Operations Management*, 20, 419–433.

Swanborn, P. (2010) *Case Study Research: What, why and how?* London, Sage.

Symonds, P. (1945), The case study as a research method. *Review of Educational Research*, 15, 5, 352–359.

Tashakkori, A. and Teddlie, C. (1998) *Mixed Methodology: Combining qualitative and quantitative approaches*. Thousand Oaks, CA: Sage.

Thomas, G. (2011a) *How to Do Your Case Study: A guide for students and researchers*. London, Sage.

Thomas, G. (2011b) The case: generalization, theory and phronesis in case study. *Oxford Review of Education*, 37, 1, 21–35.

Walford, G. (2001) Site selection within comparative case study and ethnographic research. *Compare*, 31, 2, 151–164.

Welch, C., Piekkari, R., Plakoyiannaki, E. and Paavilainen-Mantymaki, E. (2011) Theorising from case studies: towards a pluralist future for international business research. *Journal of International Business Studies*, 42, 740–762.

Yin, R. (2009) *Case Study Research: Design and methods*, 4th edition. Thousand Oaks, Sage.

Yin, R. (2013) Validity and generalization in future case study evaluations. *Evaluation*, 19, 3, 321–332.

19

Surveys: Longitudinal, Cross-sectional and Trend Studies

Alice Sullivan and Lisa Calderwood

INTRODUCTION

Survey research has made vital contributions to our understanding of social and educational questions. Seminal early contributions include Jean Floud's work with A. H. Halsey and F. M. Martin (Floud et al., 1956), which showed the way in which the selection of children for grammar school places was biased against working class children, and Douglas's (1964) study of children at primary school during the 1950s, which also emphasised the wastage of working class talent.

Quantitative research fell out of favour for a time, at least among British sociologists, during the 1970s. Cathie Marsh pointed out that criticism of surveys seemed to grow in popularity as the funds for surveys declined (Marsh, 1982). Nevertheless, the tradition of quantitative work on the influence of social origins on educational outcomes continued, notably including Halsey Heath and Ridge's work on 'origins and destinations' (Halsey et al., 1980). This school of research, known as the 'political arithmetic' tradition (Heath 2000), has a strong focus on social and policy problems, notably those concerning educational inequalities.

Large surveys have been vital in addressing questions of social reproduction and social mobility, and the link between social origins, educational experiences and attainment, and adult occupational status for men and (somewhat belatedly) for women (Blanden et al., 2004; Blanden et al., 2007; Bowles and Gintis, 1976; Glass, 1954; Goldthorpe and Mills, 2008; Goldthorpe et al., 1980; Jencks, 1972; Joshi et al., 2007).

Survey research has made substantial contributions to the evidence base on schools, and how they may improve outcomes for their pupils. The Coleman Report (Coleman et al., 1966) was a landmark study, showing that student socio-economic background and race were far more important predictors of children's attainment than the characteristics of the school they attended. While not contradicting these findings, subsequent work (Rutter et al., 1979) showed that schools do matter to children's outcomes. Further research in this tradition has interrogated the reasons for differential school effectiveness (Nuttall et al., 1989).

The wealth of survey data now available and the ease of data analysis with current software would have been the envy of previous generations of researchers. The potential of survey research to help us to answer vital educational questions, and the need for education researchers to develop the skills to exploit quantitative data, are now generally acknowledged. Contributions to education research come from across the disciplines, and are increasingly multidisciplinary. The range of educational questions that have been tackled using survey data is huge, including education and skills from the earliest years to adulthood, and the precursors and consequences of educational experiences and attainment throughout life for diverse groups.

This chapter provides an overview of different types of survey and shows how survey research can be used to address a range of educational research questions. We also provide practical guidance on how to get access to survey data.

We explain the pros and cons of primary data collection and secondary data analysis, before going on to address the strengths and weaknesses of different types of survey data for addressing particular types of questions. A large range of data resources relevant to education research is available, and we can only scratch the surface here, but we provide some key examples of existing data. We also provide some illustrative examples of education research using these resources. For a wider selection of examples, a good starting point is (Gorard, 2008).

We go on to address data collection, including sampling, questionnaires and fieldwork methods.

Finally, we give a brief summary of statistical tools for the analysis of survey data. A more thorough treatment is available in the relevant chapter of this volume.

PRIMARY AND SECONDARY DATA AND ANALYSIS

Secondary data analysis

Secondary data analysis simply means analysing data that is already available, rather than gathering your own data. Illustrative examples of this kind of research are provided under the sections on specific types of survey data.

Advantages

Secondary data analysis has some important advantages.

1 You have access to large-scale surveys, which contain far more cases than you would be able to survey if you were collecting your own data. This provides greater *statistical power* – that is, the ability of a test to detect an effect, if the effect actually exists. It also allows you to carry out relatively complex statistical analyses, using a range of variables.
2 Many of the datasets that are available for data analysis are representative of a given population. A sample is representative to the extent that it is similar to the population from which it is drawn. The population that is sampled will depend on the nature of the study. A representative sample can be used to draw inferences regarding the population the sample is drawn from. If your analysis is based on a non-representative sample, then you cannot generalise those findings to the wider population. So, for example, if you use data collected from children in only one school, the findings would not necessarily be generalisable to pupils in other schools.
3 By using available data, rather than collecting your own, you save a huge amount of time and effort. This leaves much more time for data analysis. A PhD student who uses secondary data is more likely to have time to submit journal articles for publication during their course of study, compared to a student who carries our primary data collection.

Disadvantages

There are also constraints and disadvantages inherent in using secondary data analysis.

1 You have no control over the measures in the dataset. If you have a particular hypothesis that you want to test, you may find that the measures you would ideally want to use are not available. Care is needed to avoid using weak proxies for the measures that you would ideally have liked to use.
2 The population that you are interested in may not be covered by existing datasets. For example, existing data may be out of date.
3 Other researchers may have similar ideas for analysis to you, and access to the same data. They may publish similar findings before you complete your work.

Getting hold of data

We are fortunate in the UK in having a wealth of data resources readily available at the UK Data Archive.[1] The archive contains over 6,000 data collections, including both UK and international datasets. This includes both quantitative and qualitative datasets, spanning many disciplines and themes. The datasets can be searched by data type, theme or geography. The data types are: cross-national surveys; longitudinal surveys; international macrodata; census data; business microdata; and qualitative/mixed methods data. The themes are: ageing; crime; education; environment and energy; ethnicity; health and health behaviour; housing and the local environment; information and communication; and the labour market. This gives some idea of the breadth of data resources available, and the potential range of topics and projects that could be addressed using these datasets.

The UK Data Archive website provides guidance on the process for registration and for downloading data. It also provides guidance on a range of other international data providers. A list of sources of more information on the datasets mentioned in this chapter is provided at the end of the chapter.

Primary data collection

Small-scale primary data collection is an alternative to secondary data analysis. Often, data collection is carried out within educational settings such as schools or universities.

Advantages

The advantages and disadvantages of using primary data collection are essentially the mirror image of those for secondary data analysis.

1 The key advantage of collecting your own data is control. You are able to develop your own survey instruments, and really attempt to get to the heart of what you are trying to measure. If you are interested in a particular theoretical concept, you can *operationalise* that concept – that is, develop a set of measures that tap into the concept. This is particularly important if existing surveys do not have adequate measures of the thing that you are interested in, or if developing new measurement tools is the focus of your study.
2 You are able to focus on a sample that interests you. For example, some researchers may be interested in the current experiences of a particular tightly-defined group, such as pupils at a particular school or set of schools.
3 Primary data collection facilitates mixed-methods designs, using both qualitative and quantitative data (Gorard and Taylor, 2004). For example, you could do an in-depth study of a school, using observation, qualitative interviews, and questionnaires. Alternatively, you may consider combining quantitative secondary data analysis using existing data with qualitative data collection.

Disadvantages

1 Data collection is time-consuming and difficult. The work involved in gaining access to research subjects, designing survey instruments, administering the data collection, and creating a usable dataset, should not be underestimated. A pilot study must be carried out before the main stage of fieldwork in order to assess whether the instruments and protocols are working as hoped, and to allow adjustments to address any problems.
2 You may encounter problems with data quality, including low response rates.

Example

An example of small-scale data collection in the context of a PhD project is provided by the doctoral research of one of the authors of the current chapter (Sullivan, 2001, 2002). The research sets out to assess the claims of Bourdieu's theory of cultural reproduction (Bourdieu and Passeron, [1977] 1990). According to this theory, children from middle-class families are advantaged in gaining educational credentials due to their possession of 'cultural capital', which can be defined as familiarity with the culture of the dominant social class. Sullivan was frustrated by the lack of adequate measures of cultural capital in existing data-sets, and set out to develop a broad operationalisation of the concept of cultural capital. She surveyed 465 year 11 pupils in four comprehensive schools. The questionnaire covered both the pupils' own and their parents' cultural capital. The assessments of pupils' cultural capital included a cultural knowledge score and vocabulary test. The study concluded that, in line with Bourdieu's theory, cultural capital is transmitted within the home, and has an effect on the level of school qualifications achieved at age 16. However, a large, direct, effect of social class on school attainment remained when cultural capital had been controlled for. Therefore, the conclusion was that 'cultural reproduction' can only provide a partial explanation of social class differences in educational attainment.

TYPES OF SURVEY

This section explains some of the different kinds of surveys: cross-sectional surveys; trend studies; and longitudinal surveys.

There is an extensive literature on surveys. For an introduction to the survey method see Marsh (1982). For an extended discussion of the strengths, weak-nesses and different type of longitudinal surveys see Lynn (2009). For a general overview of quantitative methods in education research, see Gorard (2001).

Cross-sectional surveys

Cross-sectional surveys provide information about a specific population at a single point in time. This can be very useful for providing one-off information about the attributes of that population. These attributes could be attitudes, behaviours, knowledge, or socio-demographic status measures such as occupational and mari-tal status. So, for example, a cross-sectional survey could tell researchers what proportion of the population hold certain political or social attitudes, engage in particular health behaviours such as smoking and drinking, are married or single, are in paid employment and so on. They can also be used to look at the association between different population attributes at a particular point in time. For example, how ethnic groups vary in their level of educational qualifications and income. They can be used by government to develop policies and to plan the delivery of services, by academic researchers to answer a range of research questions and by the third-sector and businesses to provide information on their client groups.

Advantages

1 Because cross-sectional surveys only involve the collection of data at a single time point, results are available relatively quickly and they can be relatively inexpensive to carry out.

2 Cross-sectional surveys are often developed to answer specific policy or research questions, which means that they can benefit from clarity and specificity of purpose and being highly relevant and timely.
3 The fact that cross-sectional surveys are designed as a one-off survey means that researchers can be less concerned about future proofing and longevity of the data.

Disadvantages

However, cross-sectional surveys also have some disadvantages and limitations arising from their one-off nature.

1 The fact that cross-sectional surveys are limited to a particular point in time means that they cannot be used to study change over time, either at the level of the individual or household or at the level of the population. For example, a cross-sectional survey may provide information on what proportion of the population hold particular attitudes or engage in particular behaviours at a particular time, but researchers may be interested in how these things have changed over time. For this reason, often cross-sectional surveys are repeated on more than one occasion.

In practice, most major cross-sectional studies are repeated cross-sections, which are addressed in the following section.

Repeated cross-sectional or trend surveys

Repeated cross-sectional surveys involve collecting the same or similar information about the same population on more than one occasion. Independent samples are used for each survey, so the information is not collected from the same individuals on more than one occasion. The intervals between repeated surveys can vary. Many repeated cross-sectional surveys take place annually, and some collect data on a continuous basis. These surveys are very useful for monitoring trends in population attributes over time.

In order to be able to compare trends over time reliably, it is important that key design aspects such as the questionnaire used in the survey, the sampling frame and method used and the data collection mode and period are kept the same over time. This is because these design features can influence survey measurement. If the design of the survey changes between one wave and the next, and the surveys give different estimates of the prevalence of particular attributes in the population, it may be that this is not a genuine change, rather it is an artefact of the change in survey design. This is a major concern for repeated cross-sectional surveys, particularly those responsible for monitoring key national statistics such as the unemployment, crime and poverty rates. In order to mitigate this risk, where changes in survey design are needed, they are often introduced in the form of a split or parallel run, which allows the impact on the design change on key survey estimates to be measured and trend data calibrated for this change.

Many government departments have their own repeated cross-sectional survey. For example, the Health Survey for England run by the Department of Health, the

Crime Survey for England and Wales run by the Home Office, and the Family Resources Survey run by the Department of Work and Pensions. As well as allowing government to monitor trends in key population attributes, they can also be used to evaluate at a population level whether policies designed to change behaviour have been effective. For example, have government guidelines or targets such as recommended amounts of exercise per week or consumption of fruit and vegetables been met? Although it is not possible to causally attribute changes in the attributes of the population to specific policies, such surveys help government to prioritise areas of concern for policy intervention and to change priorities over time.

Repeated cross-sectional studies in educational research include international comparative studies such as PISA (Programme for International Student Assessment), TIMMS (Trends in International Mathematics and Science Study) and PIRLS (Progress in International Reading Literacy Study). These studies aim to evaluate education systems worldwide, and assess changes in how countries fare over time by testing students. The Survey of Adult Basic Skills (PIAAC Programme for the International Assessment of Adult Competencies) is a similar study of the adult population. However, data issues, such as differentially unrepresentative samples across countries or across time, need to be taken into account when interpreting the results from this kind of study (Jerrim, 2013).

Repeated cross-sectional surveys can also be used to look at the relationship between population attributes and whether this relationship changes over time. For example, using a repeated cross-sectional survey it would be possible to establish the relationship between parents' social class and children's educational attainment, and whether this relationship has changed over time.

Advantages

1 Repeated cross-sections combine the general advantages of cross-sectional surveys with the ability to track population change over time.
2 Some of the particular disadvantages of longitudinal data collection do not apply. For example, the problem of *attrition*, which occurs in longitudinal surveys when the sample diminishes over time is not an issue for cross-sectional surveys.

Disadvantages

1 The repeated nature of trend surveys means that they are usually more expensive than one-off cross-sectional surveys, and the need for repeated standardised measurement over time means that they have limited flexibility to adapt their content to emerging policy, research or societal issues.
2 A major disadvantage and limitation of repeated cross-sectional surveys is that they are only able to observe change over time at a population level rather than an individual level. This is due to the fact that they don't follow the same sample of individuals over time. This also limits their ability to explain the reasons for change over time. For example, it is possible to observe what types of individuals engage in different behaviours at different points in time, but they can only observe change over time at a population level not an individual level. They cannot tell us which

types of individuals changed their behaviour, and what factors were associated with individual behaviour change. For many policy interventions, understanding the factors associated with individual behaviour change is crucial for designing interventions. For this, we need longitudinal surveys, which follow the same sample of individuals over time.

Example

The British Social Attitudes (BSA) survey has been carried out annually since 1983 by the National Centre for Social Research (NatCen). The survey tracks people's changing social, political and moral attitudes and informs the development of public policy. The survey has over 3,000 respondents annually, and questions are repeated periodically. The people selected to participate in the survey are chosen using random probability sampling, which means that the results are representative of the British population.

One of the issues that the British Social Attitudes survey has tracked over time is people's attitudes towards education. Zimdars et al. (2012) report on attitudes to higher education in particular. Issues such as the question of how many young people should go to university, and how their education should be paid for, are controversial, so it is interesting to track how these have changed over time.

The following question has repeatedly been included in the survey

Do you feel that opportunities for young people in Britain to go on to higher education – to a university or college – should be increased or reduced, or are they at about the right level now?

Figure 19.1 describes the trends recorded since this question was first asked. It shows that, in 2010, as in 1983, there are more people in England who think the level of higher education opportunities is 'about right' than believe they should be increased or reduced. But the similarity ends there because in 2010 the proportion favouring further expansion has reached a low point (35 per cent), while the percentage recommending reduced rates of university participation has reached its highest level to date (16 per cent). Thus, as the proportion of young people in higher education has continued to increase in recent years, so support for further increasing participation has gone into decline.

Since 2004, respondents have also been asked about their attitudes towards tuition fees (Table 19.1).

Table 19.1 shows that the proportion of people wholly opposed to students and families paying towards tuition costs fell from 25 per cent in 2007 to 16 per cent in 2010. The increased proportion of people stating that students or their families should pay fees may reflect increasing acceptance of tuition fees (introduced in the UK in 1998) as the status quo.

Longitudinal surveys

Longitudinal surveys follow the same individuals over time in order to measure change over time.

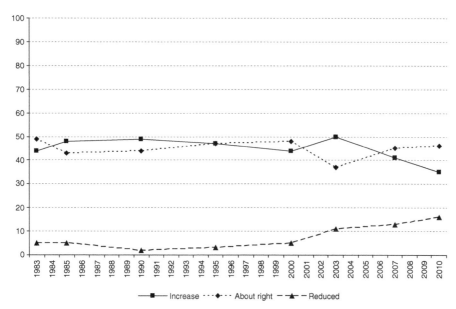

Figure 19.1   Trends in views on the level of higher education participation, 1983–2010

In terms of measuring change, longitudinal surveys have several advantages compared with repeated cross-sectional surveys.

Advantages

1 Longitudinal data allows us to assess change over time at the individual level. For example, we can track children's learning over time, and assess which factors are linked to particular learning trajectories.
2 Another important advantage of longitudinal surveys is that they are able to measure persistence of particular states, for example poverty or lone parenthood, and also the factors associated with moving in and out of particular states over time. This could for example allow researchers to assess the impact of persistent versus temporary family poverty on children's learning.
3 The temporal ordering of events can also help researchers to go beyond looking at the association between factors to addressing issues of causality. For example, cross sectional data may

Table 19.1   Attitudes towards tuition fees over time, 2004–2010

	2004	*2005*	*2007*	*2010*
Who should pay towards tuition costs?	*%*	*%*	*%*	*%*
All students/families should pay	11	9	8	13
Some students/families should pay	66	67	66	70
No students/families should pay	22	22	25	16
Bases	*2684*	*1796*	*2617*	*913*

tell us that people with health problems are more likely to be unemployed compared to healthy people. But does ill-health cause unemployment, or does unemployment cause ill-health? Both processes may occur. Longitudinal data allows us to assess individual trajectories and understand 'which came first' in people's lives – ill health or unemployment.

4   Longitudinal data allows us to control for unobserved individual characteristics over time. This can get us closer to being able to make causal inferences. For example, researchers are interested in whether the type of school that young people have attended affects their educational and occupational attainment. But it can be difficult to assess whether the apparent advantages of a particular type of school are really due to differential selectivity into the school. For example, do pupils at private schools get good results because of the school itself, or because the pupils are well-off and already doing well in ability tests before they start secondary school? Variables that affect both the outcome (for example, exam results) and the treatment (for example, the type of school a child attends) are known as confounders. To the extent that these confounders are accurately observed in the data, we can control for them. While it is difficult to rule out the possibility of measurement error or unobserved confounders, rich, longitudinal data gives the analyst a greater chance of using an adequate set of controls.

5   Longitudinal data can be used to measure the long-term impacts of circumstances early on in life, for example during childhood and adolescence, on outcomes later in life, for example in middle or old age. For example, does having been breastfed as an infant mean that you are more likely to be upwardly mobile as an adult? Does maternal depression during childhood affect the child's mental health in mid-life?

Disadvantages

1   One of the major disadvantages of longitudinal surveys is that they can be more expensive than cross-sectional surveys, due to the need to follow people and keep in touch with them over time.

2   *Attrition* is an important problem in longitudinal surveys. Attrition refers to people dropping out of the longitudinal sample over time. This may be due to factors such as death or emigration, but is also often due to difficulties in keeping in touch with cohort members (for example when they change address), or simply because people no longer wish to participate. Attrition reduces sample size, and can also lead to the sample becoming unrepresentative over time if particular types of people are more likely to drop out, for example, if men drop out more often than women.

3   *Panel conditioning* is a possible consequence of longitudinal data collection. This happens if the subjects of the research are influenced by the fact that they are in the study. For example, members of a longitudinal panel on dietary habits and health may be more aware of what they are eating, due to completing regular dietary diaries. This may lead to them changing their eating habits.

4   Data collected are bound by the interests and questions of the time, and these may not reflect the issues that future researchers would have liked to be covered.

Longitudinal Datasets

There are a large number of longitudinal datasets that can be used by education researchers, but here we highlight some of the most widely used British examples. There are also many international cohort studies suitable for education research, including Growing up in Ireland (GUI), Growing up in Scotland (GUS), the French Longitudinal Study of Children (ELFE), the German National

Educational Panel Study (NEPS), Growing up in Australia, and the US National Education Longitudinal Studies (NELS), to name a few. Catalogues of resources are available from national data archives www.data-archive.ac.uk/find/international-archives

The British Birth Cohort Studies

Britain is unique in having a series of national birth cohort studies which track individuals from birth (Pearson, 2016). The first of these studies started in 1946. Subsequent cohorts began in 1958, 1970 and 2000. (A cohort in this context refers to a group of people moving forward together in time.) All of these studies are still going, with the older studies now examining the lives of the participants in mid-life to old age. Data has been collected every few years from birth onwards. The studies are multidisciplinary, providing detailed information on physical and mental health, education, employment, family life, social participation, lifestyles and attitudes. This allows researchers to address questions about the interconnections between different life domains. The fact that the birth cohort studies track children's progress from birth, through the school years, and beyond, makes them a particularly exciting resource for education researchers. Figure 19.2 provides a summary of the birth cohort studies, their starting dates, and their initial sample sizes.

Next Steps

Next Steps, formerly known as the Longitudinal Study of Young People in England (LSYPE), follows the lives of around 16,000 people born in 1989–1990. The study began in 2004, when the cohort members were aged 13–14, and has collected information about their education and employment, economic circumstances, family life, physical and emotional health and wellbeing, social participation and attitudes. The Next Steps data has also been linked to National Pupil Database (NPD) records, which include the cohort members' individual scores at Key Stage 2, 3 and 4. Following the initial survey at age 13–14, the cohort members were visited every year until 2010, when they were age 19–20. The next survey takes place in 2015/16, when the cohort members are 25 years old.

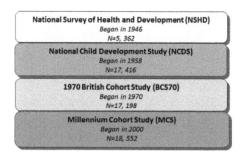

Figure 19.2   British birth cohort studies

Research examples

An enormous amount of work on education and social mobility has been carried out using the longitudinal datasets listed above. We highlight a few key examples here.

Douglas's 'The Home and the School' (Douglas, 1964) was a hugely influential early study of inequalities in education, carried out using data from the 1946 birth cohort. Douglas addressed the widening inequalities as children progressed through primary school, and highlighted the 'wastage of talent', particularly among working class children, evidenced by their low chances of gaining a grammar school place, and high chance of leaving school at 15.

More recently, Leon Feinstein's work on the 1970 birth cohort study highlighted inequalities in cognitive test scores that were apparent before the start of primary school (Feinstein, 2003).

Figure 19.3 shows children's cognitive test scores expressed in terms of where they came in the percentile ranking, from 22 months to ten years of age. Children from high SES (socio-economic status) backgrounds are compared to those from low SES backgrounds. The key finding is that poorer children who were doing well initially declined in the rankings, and were overtaken by richer children who had not scored so well at 22 months by the time they were ten. This finding has proved controversial, given the risk of measurement error in cognitive scores at a very early age, and of regression to the mean (Jerrim and Vignoles, 2012). Nevertheless, this paper is a useful illustration of the way longitudinal birth cohort data can be used to analyse trajectories of development over time, and the research helped to inform a policy focus on the need for investment in children's development in the early years (DfES, 2003; Field, 2010; Marmot et al., 2010).

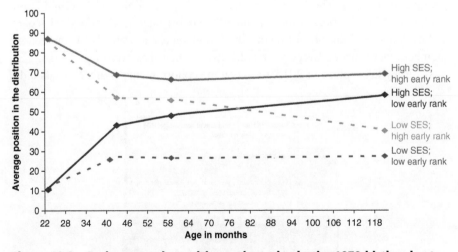

Figure 19.3   Early unequal cognitive trajectories in the 1970 birth cohort study

Unequal trajectories of attainment have persisted in the most recent birth cohort. Analysis of the children in the Millennium Cohort Study at age seven showed that parental social class continues to exert a strong influence on children's early test scores, and on their learning in the initial years of primary school, between the ages of five and seven (Sullivan et al., 2013). The authors analyse whether differences in working and middle class parenting styles and activities can explain the social class gap in children's learning. They conclude that, although parenting activities such as reading to children, are very important, these factors cannot 'explain away' the social class gap.

Analysis of Next Steps has assessed the educational attainments of pupils according to ethnic group (Strand, 2011). Strand finds that Pakistani, Bangladeshi, black Caribbean and black African pupils all received lower school test scores than whites at age 11. However, looking at progress between the ages of 11 and 14, the picture changed, such that Indian pupils had a statistically significant advantage over whites, and only black Caribbean pupils fared significantly worse than whites. This difference could not be explained entirely by differences in the social class backgrounds of pupils according to ethnic group.

Survey data can be enhanced by linking it to administrative data. For example, several studies have linked Next Steps to the National Pupil Database (NPD) (Meschi et al., 2014). The National Pupil Database contains information on all pupils in state schools in England, including test results and basic demographic characteristics (gender, ethnicity and free school meals).

One of the advantages of using the older birth cohort studies is that one can examine what happened to the cohort members in later years. A programme of research using the 1958 and 1970 birth cohort studies examined the impact of poor adult literacy and numeracy skills on people's lives (Bynner and Parsons, 2006). The consequences of poor basic skills included not just a higher risk of unemployment and poverty, but wider outcomes such as depression and reduced social participation. This work informed government policy on promoting adult basic skills.[2]

DATA COLLECTION

The design and conduct of surveys are extremely important in determining the quality of the survey. This section will briefly highlight a few of the most important design features: that is, sample design and frame, questionnaire design, and data collection approach. There is an extensive literature on survey design and implementation which readers should consult for further information and guidance (for example, Bryman, 2012; Converse and Presser, 1986; De Leeuw and Dillman, 2008; De Vaus, 2013; Groves et al., 2009; Lynn, 2009; Marsden and Wright, 2010; Payne, 2014 [1951]; Sudman and Bradburn, 1982).

Sample design and frame

In relation to sample design, a basic requirement for any survey is that a sampling frame is available. A sampling frame is a complete, or almost complete, list of all units of the population, for example, individuals, households and so on. The sample for the survey should be chosen from this list, using random probability methods. This allows statistical inference from the survey sample to the population of interest. In reality, often sampling frames do not have perfect coverage of the population. Under-coverage can occur where certain parts of the population are missing or excluded from the sampling frame, or conversely the sampling frame may include people who are not part of the population or may inadvertently include the sample people more than once. The difference between the population and the sampling frame is referred to as the coverage error of the survey. For most large-scale national surveys of the general population, robust sampling frames are available, but for surveys which focus on particular sub-populations, it can sometimes be more difficult to obtain a good sampling frame. In educational research, researchers are often interested in particular sub-population groups such as students or teachers. In general, relatively good sampling frames are usually available for these groups as educational establishments hold records of their staff and students. Sometimes it is necessary to negotiate access to these records with the establishments themselves, but not always. For example, the Department for Education maintains a National Pupil Database of all state-school students in England which can be used as a sampling frame for surveys of students and schools.

Most large-scale surveys use cluster sampling, where sampling units are grouped together in some way, often geographically, and all elements in these groups are sampled simultaneously, to facilitate more cost-effective data collection and/or stratified sampling, where the sampling frame is sorted into different groups representing different sub-populations and samples are drawn separately from each of these groups, to ensure representation of these sub-population groups in the sample.

Another key consideration in sample design is whether to sample all units or individuals in proportion to their prevalence in the population or whether to over-sample particular groups. It is relatively common for surveys to over-sample groups which are of particular interest but which make up only a relatively low proportion of the population, such as minority ethnic groups, in order to ensure that there is a sufficient sub-sample size to be able to carry out statistical analysis by ethnic group. Similarly, some surveys may oversample groups of particular interest to policymakers, such as disadvantaged or low-income groups or particular geographical areas. Design weights are used at the analysis stage to account for different probabilities of selection.

There are many textbooks on survey sampling including Groves et al. (2009) and Lohr (2010).

Questionnaire design

The content of the survey questionnaire is obviously vital. In general, the questionnaire content should be driven by research questions, which the survey aims to address. Clear research questions are essential to knowing what information the survey should collect. A key feature of the survey method is standardised measurement, which means asking the same questions in the same way to all respondents. This ensures that the same information is available for everyone in the same way and allows statistical comparisons to be made between different respondents and groups of respondents. In practice, surveys are often quite heavily routed so that different individuals get different questions depending on their circumstances and previous answers they have given.

Lots of different types of information is collected in surveys, including factual questions about relatively fixed attributes such as demographic characteristics, education levels, questions about current circumstances in key domains such as housing situation, work status and information about employment, income, family situation and health status and questions about behaviours, knowledge, attitudes and values. In longitudinal surveys it is also common to ask not just about current circumstances but also about life events and changes in circumstances since the last interview. Most longitudinal surveys collect full information about transitions over time in a respondent's housing, relationship and employment circumstances, often referred to as histories.

There are many different types of survey questions. As noted above, standardised measurement is a core component of any survey and for this reason most survey questions tend to be closed questions, where all respondents are given the same pre-specified list of response options. Occasionally open questions, where respondents' answers are recorded in their own words are used, though often these are coded later to categorical lists to allow statistical comparisons of answers given by different respondents.

Good questionnaire design is essential to getting accurate answers in surveys. In general it is good practice to use established sets of questions which have been thoroughly tested and validated, or to conduct through testing of any new questions before they are used to ensure they are measuring accurately what they are intended to measure. There is a large literature on how to test and evaluate survey questions, such as Presser et al. (2004). In particular, it is crucial that respondents can understand the survey questions, and are willing and able to answer them. In his classic book, Tourangeau et al. (2000) explores the psychological process that respondents go through when answering survey questions. The four stages are: comprehension of the question; retrieval of the required information from memory; judgement of the information retrieved; and finally deciding on a response. This theory of the response process has been very influential in questionnaire design, and has also led to the development of question-testing methodologies designed to elicit insight into this response process known as cognitive testing.

There is much established guidance on good questionnaire design, for example, Sudman and Bradburn, 1982; Converse and Presser, 1986, Payne 2014 [1951]. However, even with well-designed questionnaires, it is possible for survey answers to differ from the true value in the population. This is referred to as measurement error. This can occur for many reasons including difficulty recalling the required information accurately and misreporting, for example due to social desirability bias.

Data collection approach

The choice of data collection mode will be determined by the aims of the study and by practical constraints. In general, interviewer-administered survey modes, such as face-to-face or telephone interviewing lead to higher response rates than remote methods of data collection such as web or postal surveys (Hox and De Leeuw, 1994). However, face-to-face methods are also more expensive. The choice of mode also has an impact on measurement error and data quality. For some types of question, interviewer administration leads to better quality data as the interviewer can provide prompting and clarification for complex questions such as income. However, for other types of questions, particularly sensitive questions, self-administered modes lead to more honest answers and better data quality. Overall, factors associated with the choice of survey mode will include the topic and content of the survey, the length of the questionnaire, the survey population, the survey budget and also the amount of time available. There is an extensive literature on the development and implementation of different survey modes, for example Dillman et al. (2009), and on the growing use of web surveys, for example Callegaro et al. (2015).

Maximising response is important for surveys, as non-response can lead to bias in the survey estimates. In many countries there has been a downward trend in response rates to surveys over the last 30–40 years (De Leeuw and De Heer, 2002). The main sources or reasons for non-response in surveys are failure to make contact with the sampled units, that is, non-contact and failure to persuade sampled units to take part in the survey, that is, refusal. For longitudinal surveys, non-location is also a major source of non-response. In addition to mode, maximising response is also influenced by a number of other design features, such as the level of 'respondent burden' (how demanding the survey is for respondents), the level of respondent engagement (for example use of advance letters and leaflets), minimum call requirements, use of incentives and interviewer characteristics. However, as social surveys are voluntary, non-response is inevitable. Survey estimates can be adjusted for non-response using techniques such as weighting. There is an extensive literature on non-response in surveys, for example, Groves and Couper (1998), Groves et al. (2002).

It is important to value the contribution that participants make by responding to surveys. In the case of longitudinal studies, this contribution continues over many years. It goes without saying that without the study members, none of the science would be possible. Ethical requirements in carrying out surveys are essentially the same as for any other form of data collection. Survey members must give informed consent and be treated with respect. It is appropriate to share the findings of the study with participants where possible. For analysts carrying out secondary data analysis, the main ethical requirements concern data-security and not risking the identification of individuals.

DATA ANALYSIS

This topic is addressed in detail elsewhere in this volume. A range of different statistical analysis techniques can be used to analyse survey data. These range from simple to more sophisticated. The analyst should not underestimate the power of the simplest descriptive techniques. Basic descriptive findings telling us simple things about ourselves and our society can often generate the most interest – How many adults are illiterate?; How fat are our pre-school children? How many of us believe in god? Policymakers, the media and the general public alike are typically more interested in these kinds of findings than in the results of a complex statistical regression analysis. Spending sufficient time on descriptive analysis also means that you understand your data, and are less likely to make basic errors later on.

Statistical techniques can be classified as univariate, bivariate and multivariate. Univariate techniques are used for describing one variable, bivariate for the relationship between two variables and multivariate for the relationship between three or more variables.

More complex multivariate analysis techniques allow researchers to simultaneously control for multiple variables. For longitudinal surveys, specific analytical techniques are available such as event history analysis.

For all types of analysis, formal statistical tests, known as tests of statistical significance, are used to establish whether or not differences between groups or relationships between variables are statistically significant, meaning that they are very likely to be real differences rather than something which could have occurred by chance.

When analysing survey data it is often necessary to use design weights to account for the sample design of the survey and ensure that the survey estimates or statistics produced are valid for the population of reference and/or non-response weights to try to account for non-response which may bias the survey estimates or statistics.

There is an extensive range of textbooks aimed at providing guidance about statistical analysis of survey data (for example, Foster et al., 2014; Healey, 2014; Marsh and Elliott, 2008), and this topic is discussed in more detail in later chapters in this volume.

CONCLUSION

The potential to use survey data to address questions in education research is greater than ever. We have summarised a wide range of types of data available to education researchers, given examples of specific datasets, and provided illustrative examples of research studies which show some of the uses of different kinds of data. There is no single 'right' kind of data which is superior to the others, rather the design of the data must fit the research questions. We hope that this chapter will help researchers to choose the right tools for the job in hand.

Notes

1 www.data-archive.ac.uk/
2 The 'Skills for Life' programme.

WEBSITES

Information on datasets mentioned in this chapter

UK Data Archive www.data-archive.ac.uk/
UK data service www.ukdataservice.ac.uk/
Centre for Longitudinal Studies (home of 1958, 1970 and 2000 British birth cohorts, and Next Steps) www.cls.ioe.ac.uk/
NSHD www.nshd.mrc.ac.uk/
NatCen www.natcen.ac.uk/our-research/research/british-social-attitudes/
CLOSER (Cohort & Longitudinal Studies Enhancement Resources) www.closer.ac.uk/

FURTHER READINGS

De Vaus, David. 2013. *Surveys in Social Research*. London: Routledge.
Foster, Liam, Ian Diamond and Julie Jefferies. 2014. *Beginning Statistics: An introduction for social scientists*. London: Sage.
Gorard, Stephen. 2001. *Quantitative Methods in Educational Research: The role of numbers made easy*. London: Continuum.
Gorard, Stephen. 2008. *Quantitative Research in Education*. London: Sage.
Groves, Robert M., Floyd J. Fowler Jr, Mick P. Couper, James M. Lepkowski, Eleanor Singer and Roger Tourangeau. 2009. *Survey Methodology*. London: John Wiley & Sons.
Lynn, Peter. 2009. *Methodology of Longitudinal Surveys*. London: John Wiley & Sons.
Marsh, C. 1982. *The Survey Method: The Contribution of surveys to sociological explanation*. London: Allen and Unwin.
Marsh, Catherine and Jane Elliott. 2008. *Exploring Data: An introduction to data analysis for social scientists*. London: Polity.
Payne, Stanley Le Baron. 2014 [1951]. *The Art of Asking Questions: Studies in public opinion*, 3, Princeton, NJ: Princeton University Press.

REFERENCES

Blanden, Jo, Paul Gregg and Lindsey Macmillan. 2007. 'Accounting for intergenerational income persistence: noncognitive skills, ability and education'. *The Economic Journal*, 117(519): C43–C60.

Blanden, Jo, Alissa Goodman, Paul Gregg and Stephen Machin. 2004. 'Changes in intergenerational mobility in Britain'. *Generational Income Mobility in North America and Europe*: 122–146.

Bourdieu, Pierre and Jean Claude Passeron. [1977] 1990. *Reproduction in Education, Society and Culture*. London; Beverly Hills: Sage.

Bowles, Samuel and Herbert Gintis. 1976. *Schooling in Capitalist America: Educational reform and the contradictions of economic life*. New York: Basic Books.

Bryman, Alan. 2012. *Social Research Methods*. Oxford: Oxford University Press.

Bynner, John and Samantha Parsons. 2006. *New Light on Literacy and Numeracy*. London: National Research and Development Centre for Adult Literacy and Numeracy.

Callegaro, M., K. L. Manfreda and V. Vehovar. 2015. *Web Survey Methodology*. London: Sage.

Coleman, J., E. Campbell, C. Hobson, J. McPartland, A. Mood, F. Weinfield and R. York. 1966. *Equality of Educational Opportunity*. Washington, DC: US Government Printing Office.

Converse, Jean M. and Stanley Presser. 1986. *Survey Questions: Handcrafting the standardized questionnaire*. London: Sage.

De Leeuw. E. and W. De Heer (2002). Trends in household survey nonresponse: a longitudinal and international comparison. In R. M. Groves, D. A. Dillman, J. Eltinge and R. Little (Eds) *Survey Nonresponse* (pp. 41–54. New York: Wiley.

De Leeuw, Edith Desirée and Don A Dillman. 2008. *International Handbook of Survey Methodology*. London: Taylor & Francis.

De Vaus, David. 2013. *Surveys in Social Research*. London: Routledge.

DfES. 2003. 'Every child matters'. London: DfES.

Dillman, D. A., J. D. Smyth and L. M. Christian 2009. *Internet, Mail and Mixed-Mode Surveys: The Tailored Design Method*. London: Wiley.

Douglas, J. W. B. 1964. *The Home and the School: A study of ability and attainment in the primary school*. London: MacGibbon and Kee.

Feinstein, L. 2003. 'Inequality in the early cognitive development of British children in the 1970 cohort'. *Economica*, 70(1): 73–97.

Field, F. 2010. 'The foundation years: preventing poor children becoming poor adults', in *The Report of the Independent Review on Poverty and Life Chances*. London: HM Government.

Floud, J., A. H. Halsey and F. Martin. 1956. *Social Class and Educational Opportunity*. London: Heinemann.

Foster, Liam, Ian Diamond and Julie Jefferies. 2014. *Beginning Statistics: An introduction for social scientists*. London: Sage.

Glass, D. V. 1954. *Social Mobility in Britain*. London: Routledge and Kegan Paul.

Goldthorpe, J. and C. Mills. 2008. 'Trends in intergenerational class mobility in modern Britain: evidence from national surveys, 1972–2005'. *National Institute Economic Review*, 205: 83–100.

Goldthorpe, John H., C. Llewellyn and C. Payne. 1980. *Social Mobility and Class Structure in Modern Britain*. Oxford: Clarendon Press.

Gorard, Stephen. 2001. *Quantitative Methods in Educational Research: The role of numbers made easy*. London: A&C Black.

Gorard, Stephen. 2008. *Quantitative Research in Education*. London: Sage.

Gorard, Stephen and Chris Taylor. 2004. *Combining Methods in Educational and Social Research*. London: McGraw-Hill Education (UK).

Groves, Robert M., Floyd J. Fowler Jr, Mick P. Couper, James M. Lepkowski, Eleanor Singer and Roger Tourangeau. 2009. *Survey Methodology*. London: John Wiley & Sons.

Groves and Couper (1998). *Non-response in Household Interview Surveys*. Wiley: New York.

Groves, R. M, D. A. Dillman, J. Eltinge and R. Little (Eds) (2002) *Survey Nonresponse*. New York: Wiley.

Halsey, A., A. Heath and J. Ridge. 1980. *Origins and Destinations. Family, Class and Education in Modern Britain*. Oxford: Clarendon Press.

Healey, Joseph. 2014. *Statistics: A tool for social research*. London: Cengage Learning.

Heath, A. 2000. 'The political arithmetic tradition in the sociology of education'. *Oxford Review of Education*, 26(3–4): 313–331.

Hox, J.J. and De Leeuw, E.D. 1994. A Comparison of Nonresponse in mail, telephone, andface-to-face surveys. Applying multilevel modelling to meta-analysis. *Quality and Quantity,* 28(4): 329–344.

Jencks, C. 1972. *Inequality: A reassessment of the effect of family and schooling in America*. New York: Basic Books.

Jerrim, J. 2013. 'The reliability of trends over time in international education test scores: is the performance of England's secondary school pupils really in relative decline?' *Journal of Social Policy*, 42(2): 259–279.

Jerrim, J. and A. Vignoles. 2012. 'Social mobility, regression to the mean and the cognitive development of high ability children from disadvantaged homes'. *Journal of the Royal Statistical Society: Series A (Statistics in Society)* Online Preview.

Joshi, H., G. Makepeace and P. Dolton. 2007. 'More or less unequal? Evidence on the pay of men and women from the British Birth Cohort Studies'. *Gender, Work and Organization*, 14(1): 37–51.

Lohr, S. L. 2010. *Sampling: Design and analysis*. London: Brooks/Cole.

Lynn, Peter. 2009. *Methodology of Longitudinal Surveys*. London: John Wiley & Sons.

Marmot, M., J. Allen, P. Goldblatt, T. Boyce, D. McNeish, M. Grady and I. Geddes. 2010. 'Fair society, healthy lives: strategic review of health inequalities in England post 2010'. London: The Marmot Review.

Marsden, Peter V. and James D. Wright. 2010. *Handbook of Survey Research*. Bingley: Emerald Group Publishing.

Marsh, C. 1982. *The Survey Method: The Contribution of surveys to sociological explanation*. London: Allen and Unwin.

Marsh, Catherine and Jane Elliott. 2008. *Exploring Data: An introduction to data analysis for social scientists*. London: Polity.

Meschi, Elena, Anna Vignoles and Robert Cassen. 2014. 'Post-secondary school type and academic achievement'. *The Manchester School*, 82(2):183–201.

Nuttall, Desmond L., Harvey Goldstein, Robert Prosser and Jon Rasbash. 1989. 'Differential school effectiveness'. *International Journal of Educational Research*, 13(7):769–776.

Payne, Stanley Le Baron. [1951] 2014. *The Art of Asking Questions: Studies in public opinion*, 3. Princeton, NJ: Princeton University Press.

Pearson, Helen. 2016. *The Life Project: The extraordinary story of our ordinary lives*. London:: Penguin.

Presser, S., J. M. Rothger, M. P. Couper, J. T. Lessler, E. Martin, J. Martin and E. Singer. 2004. *Methods for Testing and Evaluating Survey Questionnaires*. London: Wiley.

Rutter, M. B., B. Maughan, P. Mortimore, J. Ouston and A. Smith. 1979. *Fifteen Thousand Hours: Secondary schools and their effects on children*. London: Open Books.

Strand, Steve. 2011. 'The limits of social class in explaining ethnic gaps in educational attainment'. *British Educational Research Journal*, 37(2): 197–229.

Sudman, Seymour and Norman M. Bradburn. 1982. 'Asking questions: a practical guide to questionnaire design'. San Francisco: Jossey-Bass Inc.

Sullivan, A. 2001. 'Cultural capital and educational attainment'. *Sociology*, 35(4): 893–912.

Sullivan, A. 2002. 'Bourdieu and education: how useful is Bourdieu's theory for researchers?' *Netherlands' Journal of Social Sciences*, 38(2): 144–166.

Sullivan, A., S. Ketende and H. Joshi. 2013. 'Social class and inequalities in early cognitive scores'. *Sociology*, 47(6): 1187–1206.

Tourangeau, R., L. J. Rips and K. Rasinski (2000). *The Psychology of Survey Response*. Cambridge: Cambridge University Press.

Zimdars, Anna, Alice Sullivan and Anthony Heath. 2012. 'Higher education: a limit to expansion? attitudes to university funding, fees and opportunities', in Alison Park, Elizabeth Clery, John Curtice, Miranda Phillips and David Utting (Eds) *British Social Attitudes* (Chapter 28). London: Sage.

20

'True' Experimental Designs

Carole J. Torgerson and David J. Torgerson

INTRODUCTION

In this chapter we will give an overview of the key elements of the design and conduct of 'true' experiments or randomised controlled trials (RCTs). This will include a discussion of both the main features of the basic RCT design and some of its variants and its main components.

There has been a recent resurgence in the use of RCTs to evaluate novel educational programmes and practices. This is to be welcomed as it is an uncomfortable truth (for some) that, in the presence of good teaching, changes to the curriculum or pedagogy may either have no effect, a small effect or, worst of all, a negative effect. It is, therefore, crucial that, before we spend scarce resources and make teachers change practice, any change proposed will be both effective and worthwhile (cost effective) in terms of resource expenditure.

There has been a reluctance to embrace experimental methods to evaluate educational approaches, strategies, curricular content or schooling structures. This reluctance may have been driven by misunderstanding of the RCT design, as some educational policymakers and researchers are concerned that it may be an unsuitable design to employ in order to evaluate complex educational changes.

However, we argue that the RCT can be used successfully to evaluate educational practices, as well as interventions in other areas of social life and public policy: its use is certainly not confined to health care research, specifically as the design of the double blind, placebo randomised controlled drug trial. Indeed, the more complex the intervention or setting in which the evaluation occurs, the greater the need is for the RCT to help disentangle the myriad of other influences

that might result in changes in educational achievement and be alternative explanations for any improvements observed. We hope that this chapter will address
some of these concerns.

Educational pedagogies and practices within countries and across the world
vary significantly. This variation is driven by a combination of things including:
resource availability (for example, larger class sizes in poorer countries); variations in language (for example, greater or less phonetic correspondence between
the spoken and written word); cultural traditions; and teacher preference. Some
rationales for the use of different teaching pedagogies and practices do not require
much evaluation. For instance, in a developing country, if the available teaching
resources mean that there is only a single teacher available to teach 80 children
in a school then, however much smaller classes are desirable, it will not be possible to resource them and evaluation in this context would not be a fruitful use of
financially constrained research funding. However, if funds became available to
employ a second teacher the question arises: should the resources be spent on a
second teacher or perhaps on two teaching assistants? Which intervention might
be more effective? Or, if we decide we will halve the class size by employing a
second teacher, how should this be done? Should we split the class by attainment
or have two classes of mixed attainment? Therefore the simple question of how
we should use a second teacher's salary opens a vista of potential different educational models. To find out which of these is most effective can best be explored
using experimental design, ideally the randomised controlled trial (RCT) design.
For example, Duflo and colleagues evaluated the halving of class size in Kenyan
primary schools by splitting class size by attainment and compared this intervention with mixed attainment classes using a RCT design (Duflo et al., 2008).

The RCT is the best design for demonstrating whether or not an innovative
educational intervention is effective (Torgerson and Torgerson, 2008). Most other
designs are susceptible to selection bias. Selection bias is when schools or students are selected into a curriculum group based on some characteristic that has
an effect on an educational outcome. For instance, if local or national government has decided to invest more resources in schools and each school is allocated
enough money to employ an extra teacher but each school can choose whether or
not to do so, this will lead to selection effects. Consequently, if a researcher wants
to see whether investment in new technology in a set of schools leads to better
results than in schools that choose to invest in additional teachers, simply comparing the outcomes from the two sets of schools may lead to biased results. This is
because the characteristics of the schools that choose to invest the money in new
technology rather than in additional teachers may be quite different. Whilst we
can statistically adjust for observable differences, such as school size, or socio-
economic context, it may be impossible or difficult to adjust for unmeasured or
immeasurable variables such as teacher motivation or quality. The only way to
be certain that any differences observed between schools that choose technology
over extra teaching staff is to *randomly* allocate the schools into two groups, with

one group spending the resource on technology and the other group spending the resource on extra teachers. Because the two groups have been formed by random allocation then, apart from any chance element potentially introducing bias, we know that the schools are equivalent in all measured (for example, school size) and unmeasured (for example, teacher motivation) characteristics. Consequently, if a difference in educational outcomes is observed after the intervention then this is attributable to the intervention.

Experimental research in the field of education has a long and distinguished history. The first randomised controlled trials (RCTs) among humans in the modern period were undertaken among United States (US) university students – 'freshmen' engineers – in the 1930s (Walters, 1931, 1932). School- or class-based randomisation and the principles of analysing such data were first described by Lindquist (1940). A significant number of large field trials, such as the Tennessee class size experiment (Nye et al., 1999) were undertaken in the US in the 1970s and 1980s. However, until comparatively recently, large policy or pragmatic trials were missing from the United Kingdom (UK) research literature. Over the last fifty or sixty years, educational psychologists have undertaken and published relatively large numbers of small trials manipulating the teaching of certain educational concepts. For example, there are quite a number (around 36) of RCTs and quasi-experiments (QEDs) evaluating the role of phonics teaching on literacy learning (Torgerson et al., 2006). However, these tended to be small and vary quite widely in their design quality. Nevertheless, in the last decade or so there has been a renaissance in the area of experimental research in education. In the US the Institute of Educational Sciences (IES) has supported a programme of experimental research with an emphasis on the RCT design. Similarly, in the United Kingdom (UK) the Educational Endowment Foundation (EEF) has, in the last five years, funded over one hundred evaluations which are primarily experimental in nature.

In this chapter we will discuss the key elements of a rigorously designed, conducted and reported RCT that could be used to inform educational policy and practice. For interested readers there are a number of textbooks on the design and conduct of RCTs in education (for example, Torgerson and Torgerson (2008) and a free online handbook has been published by the EEF on their website: https://educationendowmentfoundation.org.uk/uploads/pdf/Randomised_trials_in_education-revised250713.pdf).

DESIGN PROCESS

In the following we discuss the key processes and issues of trial design; but, as noted above, consultation with more detailed textbooks is advisable if you are planning to undertake a RCT. However, this chapter will discuss the key elements you need to consider and this will be informative with regard to whether your research question is amenable to a RCT design.

Systematic review

Although this chapter is not discussing review design and techniques it is important to state that, before a trial is planned, a systematic review of the literature is undertaken (Torgerson, 2003). This will, first, help prevent duplication in research and, second, aid the design of the proposed trial by addressing gaps and limitations in the existing literature. It is important that any review process is scientific, and adopts an explicit, replicable approach to identifying, quality appraising and synthesising the literature (Torgerson, 2003).

Research question

All research requires a clear, unambiguous research question (White, 2009). Furthermore, in the context of this chapter, the nature of research questions which can be addressed through the use of experimental design is that they aim to explore causal relationships. Put another way, they need to be efficacy or effectiveness questions. The RCT has many strengths but it is not appropriate for addressing correlational or descriptive questions. For instance, what is the proportion of children within a given age group being bullied and how does the bullying affect their psychological health? This question is best answered using a cross-sectional design which uses survey tools to explore children's perceptions. In contrast, if the question were 'What is the best method of reducing the incidence of bullying in schools?' as this is an effectiveness question, it can be tackled using an experimental design. Even when we have identified a question that can be addressed using a RCT design, we need to consider the merit of the different possible comparisons within the design. A 'no teaching' condition is very unlikely to be a helpful comparator for most educational questions. Rather, 'business as usual' or normal classroom teaching is likely to be the most useful comparison condition, in the absence of two or more clear novel interventions to be tested. Indeed, the most useful trials are so-called 'pragmatic' or 'field' trials. These trials possess a key characteristic in that they try to mimic 'real life' teaching conditions in every facet, with the exception that children, schools or teachers are randomly allocated to an intervention rather than being selected administratively or arbitrarily assigned. Such trials are distinct from the classic educational psychology trials that are typically undertaken under tightly controlled conditions with the intervention being delivered by a researcher. A pragmatic trial, in contrast, is set in a standard educational context with all the challenges, such as poor compliance, that this implies. Consequently, the observed effect size differences between intervention and control or comparison conditions are usually somewhat lower in 'real world' settings than in the rarefied laboratories of a university department. This need to develop trials that represent 'real life' rather than artificial conditions was first argued by Schwartz and Lellouch (1967) in health care trials in the 1960s.

Unit of allocation

One key issue to consider is what the unit of randomisation should be. In educational research we often, if not mostly, need to randomise in groups of individuals or 'clusters'. In contrast to health care research where patients are randomised as individuals, in education the natural unit of allocation is often a group. Therefore, classes, year groups, or whole schools might be randomised rather than individual students or pupils. The main reason for cluster randomisation is due to the potential for 'spill-over' or 'contamination' effects. Clearly most teaching takes the form of facilitating learning with groups of students. Therefore, a teacher cannot necessarily prevent 'control' students receiving a novel educational intervention if they are being taught in the same classroom as the intervention students. In addition to this potential for teacher level spill-over the possibility of student level contamination cannot be ignored. For example, if we were to randomise individual classes to a novel curriculum this may avoid the teacher level contamination but it would not prevent student level spill-over if there were strong friendship groups across classes, in which case the students in the intervention classes could communicate key elements of the novel curriculum to their peers in the control classes. If this were thought to be a real possibility we may decide to randomise at the level of the school year, as friendship groups are less likely to lead to cross-year spill-over effects. Or we could randomise at the level of school. Consequently, very early in the design process we need to decide the level of allocation.

Protocol

The first thing that needs to be developed is the trial protocol. Essentially a trial protocol is a road map of what is planned. The protocol should contain: the study design, and a description of the sample of schools/children to be recruited and randomised. It will also contain a description of the intervention and control or comparison conditions, the length of follow-up and the main outcome measures and statistical approach to data analysis. The protocol should be detailed as this will allow those who are working on the trial to know exactly what is to be done and when. Ideally it should follow methodological best practice, for example the CONSORT guidelines (www.consort-statement.org/) for the reporting of trials. The CONSORT statement, adopted by many academic journals in a variety of disciplines, including education, sets out the key items that need to be described in a trial report to enable the reader to assess first, whether it is a robust study, and second, how to replicate the study if required. Therefore, it is very useful to ensure that the RCT is planned in such a way as to conform to the reporting standards of CONSORT.

Registration

Once the protocol is completed it needs to be registered on a publicly available, searchable database: for example www.isrctn.com/. A detailed version of the protocol could also be published (for an example of a EEF protocol published on their website on online maths tutoring see: https://educationendowmentfoundation.org.uk/uploads/pdf/Online_Maths_Tutoring.pdf). The reasons for registration are as follows. First, it prevents duplication. When planning a proposed trial, other researchers can see if a similar study is already underway. This allows them to either potentially join the registered trial team or modify their design to address a different research question. Second, it reduces the problem of publication bias, sometimes known as the 'file drawer' problem (Torgerson, 2006). This is the tendency for researchers, and journals, not to prioritise for publication studies that have found negative or null results. Consequently, when people undertake a systematic review of RCTs, any snapshot of the literature tends to be biased towards the positive, as negative trials remain unpublished. This is a recognised problem and registration is one method of dealing with the issue. If a registered trial is unpublished then a reviewer can contact the authors for the results and, if these are not forthcoming, then an assumption of the trial having a negative finding can be used in the review. Finally, registration describes the key outcomes and statistical analysis, which prevents the primary outcome from changing to favour the intervention. For instance, if a study had measured 10 different outcomes and identified one of these as a primary outcome, which subsequently turned out not to be a statistically significantly different outcome then there could be a temptation by the researchers to reclassify one of the secondary outcomes, which *was* significantly different, as the new primary outcome. Prior registration allows other researchers to identify this practice and take it into account when evaluating the quality of the published trial.

Ethical approval

Before recruitment and randomisation of participants, RCTs, like most primary research (the exceptions might be the use of anonymised secondary data) require ethical oversight by an independent ethics committee. The ethics oversight is to ensure that the participants are not placed at any undue risk to their well-being. Furthermore, ethics committees can act as guardians of scientific quality as an inadequately planned RCT may be unethical as it can lead to a biased answer and place future students at risk of being offered a substandard educational intervention due to the mistaken belief it is actually effective.

Recruitment

Once ethical approval has been granted then schools and/or participants can be recruited. In the ideal world we would recruit a random sample of participants from the population within which we hope to implement the trial's results. Unfortunately, it is rarely possible to recruit such a sample, as both schools and students have the right to refuse participation. Furthermore, it might be difficult, logistically, to deliver the intervention across a wide geographical area. Consequently, we should try and recruit as representative a sample of participants as possible. If we intended that the intervention was to be aimed primarily among schools that are situated in areas of high deprivation we should endeavour to include such schools in our trial so we can be confident that the results will apply to all schools from deprived areas.

In terms of recruitment, we can classify the type of recruitment as 'trickle' or sequential recruitment or 'block' recruitment. In the former, which is most common in clinical trials, schools or students are recruited over a period of time and randomised shortly after recruitment. In block recruitment, which is more common in educational settings, we would recruit all, or most, of the schools in a short period of time and then randomise them all at once. In practice, however, it is often the case we combine the approaches. We might randomise 80–90 per cent of the schools at once and then randomise the remaining schools as they trickle into the study.

Pre-testing

Once recruitment has been achieved, and before randomisation, an optional step is to undertake pre-testing of recruited schools and students. The main rationale for pre-testing is that it improves statistical power. For example, if there is a correlation of 0.70 between the pre- and post-test then this will increase the power of the study to that of twice the recruited sample size. Pre-tests can take many forms. They can come from school records of past test performance – the key thing is for them to predict outcome. The pre-testing should occur *before* randomisation as this allows the tests to be unaffected by the allocation group. In addition, there may be some attrition by schools or students once the allocation is known and knowledge of their pre-test scores can allow some statistical adjustment (imputation) to take into account such loss of data. As a general rule, it is usually highly advantageous to have some pre-test in educational trials due to their very high predictive value. For some subjects, such as mathematics, the pre-test might have a correlation up to 0.9, which explains around 80 per cent of the variance in the post-test, which allows a massive reduction in the number of students needed, compared to having no pre-test; or conversely, it increases the power of the study for a given sample size. As noted above, this could be the use of existing test results from previous nationally-reported exams. Once we have collected the pre-test data then it is appropriate to randomise.

Randomisation

Randomisation is, in principle, simple, but in practice, can often go wrong. We could simply toss a coin and allow those schools/students that get heads to receive the intervention and those that get tails to receive the control condition.

However, in practice this should not happen. What a significant amount of methodological research has shown (Schulz et al., 1995; Kjaergaard et al., 2001; Hewitt et al., 2005) is that, when mechanical methods such as coin tossing or card shuffling are used, there is a temptation for some researchers to re-toss the coin or re-deal the deck of cards if the school or student does not get an intervention that either the school has flagged up as potentially benefitting from the intervention, or, if the researcher is keen for a particular trial result, they could be tempted to place schools/students who they think will do well with the intervention into that group. Because there is so much evidence that this is a significant problem across previously conducted RCTs it is recommended by key methodologists that the generation and assignment of the random allocation is undertaken by an independent third party. This is the most important aspect of randomisation, that is, it should be concealed from the person recruiting the school or student into the study. There are online facilities to undertake concealed allocation, which should be used for almost any trial.

Once an independent third party has been identified to undertake the randomisation, the next question is what kind of randomisation is to be used? The easiest form is simple randomisation, which is akin to tossing a coin. A computer can easily generate a simple randomisation list. We might take a list of schools or students and ask the computer to generate two random samples with half in the intervention and half in the control group. Such an approach will produce two groups of similar size and will, *on average*, produce two groups that are balanced on known and unknown characteristics that affect outcome. Note here the words in italics: *on average*. This means that, for some randomisations, the groups will not be balanced in key characteristics. If the trial is large, say 100+ individuals or schools, then we can use statistical methods (for example, regression analysis) to control for observed imbalances, such as school size, student age and so on (Rosenberger and Lachin, 2002). But if the sample size is smaller we can lose statistical power if we simply rely on adjustment. Therefore, we can use forms of restricted randomisation to ensure we do end up with balanced groups in observable variables (clearly we cannot do this with unobservable variables). One method is to use blocked randomisation. When we do this we split our sample of schools or students into two groups. If we were interested in balancing on school size we would split our sample into schools above and below the median school size. Then we might select blocks of four (that is, AABB, BBAA, ABAB, BABA, ABBA, BAAB) and randomly select two blocks of four allocations: one assigned to small schools and the other to large schools. In this way we can ensure that there are equal numbers of large and small schools in the intervention groups. Another approach that is used when there are small numbers of schools but there is a need to balance on several variables is 'minimisation' (Torgerson and Torgerson, 2007). This method is not strictly randomisation. What happens is that the first school is randomised, the second school goes into the control group and then the following units are allocated according to an algorithm that aims to 'minimise' any observed differences in values such as school size or past academic performance. More detail on how this can be done and other methods of ensuring balance can be found in detailed textbooks (Rosenberger and Lachin, 2002).

Compliance and intention to treat

Once we have randomised we need to put into place the intervention. At this stage we may find that the intervention is either refused or inadequately implemented. However, it is critical that schools/students who do not take part in the intervention as anticipated are retained in the trial for the final analysis. To avoid bias due to non-compliance we need to use 'intention to treat' as the primary analytic strategy. In this analysis, all the participants are retained in their randomised groups. This may seem counter-intuitive to those who question why, if a school or student did not receive an intervention, they would be analysed as if they *had* received it (and vice versa with the control condition)? This is because the principal analysis we are undertaking is to compare the 'offer' of the intervention and this analysis retains the randomisation which is the basis for the design warranting the causal inferences that we draw from the results (Shadish et al., 2002). It is often the case that some participants change their minds and refuse the offer of the intervention, but if we remove them from the analysis the corresponding students or schools will still be present in the control group which will introduce a potential source of bias. Those participants who refuse their allocated intervention are often systematically different from those who accept it. This difference might be in the form of prior attainment, socio-economic status or another variable which will affect outcome. Therefore, removing them from the analysis does not allow these characteristics to cancel out in the analysis; and, by allowing the expression of these variables on the outcome, a biased result will be produced. Nevertheless, if we wish to obtain an answer regarding the effect of the intervention on those who received it we can use a statistical method known as 'complier average causal effect' (CACE) analysis that enables us to retrieve an effect of fully compliant participants. This method, also known as the instrumental variable approach, hinges on two assumptions. First, the proportion of those in the control group who would have refused the intervention if they had been offered it is the same as the proportion in the treatment group who refused the intervention. This assumption must be true due the fact that randomisation on average produces equivalent groups (except for the play of chance). The second assumption, which may not be true, is that merely offering the intervention to the intervention participants has no effect on their outcomes. For instance, the process of offering one-to-one tuition in maths could have an effect on those who refuse the intervention as the offer may make the student work harder or find other forms of help. However, usually we can assume the mere offer of an intervention is ineffective: it is the actual use of the intervention that generates any effect (Hewitt et al., 2006). However, to generate such an estimate requires knowledge of the outcome scores of *all* randomised participants. Alternatives to CACE analysis commonly used include 'on treatment analysis' or 'per protocol' analysis, which are sometimes seen as being valid means of dealing with non-compliance in the analysis. Also it could be argued that their use would allow an assessment of whether the intervention has any likelihood of success (proof of concept). On treatment analysis means that, if a control student received the intervention either in error or due to spill-over effects, this student is included in the intervention group in the analysis. Similarly if an intervention student refuses the intervention then they are analysed as if they had been randomised to the control group. In a per protocol analysis these 'non compliers' are excluded from the analysis. Both these approaches are likely to produce biased treatment estimates. Even if we were tempted to use these methods in a proof of concept study, which could be used to signal further research we may be misled and waste valuable research resources. If we can measure non-compliance we can do a CACE analytical approach, which is a more robust method of assessing whether an intervention is likely to work or not.

Post-testing

Once we have followed up the participants for the required length of time we need to undertake a post-test in both randomised groups to compare them in order to assess whether or not the intervention has been effective. Ideally, this test should be supervised or implemented by a researcher/educator who is blinded or masked to the allocation to intervention and control groups. This is important because teacher assessments can be biased if the teachers have a conscious or unconscious preference for one or other of the interventions. Such preferences of the tester can bias the outcome measurement. For example, in the evaluation of the last UK Labour government's flagship numeracy policy Every Child Counts (Torgerson et al., 2013) the primary outcome was delivered by independent testers who did not know the group allocation of the children being tested: intervention or control. In contrast, a secondary outcome was delivered by the teachers themselves, who were fully aware of the allocated group. The secondary outcome showed a much larger effect size estimate than the primary, blinded, outcome measure (Ainsworth et al., 2014).

Primary outcome

At the protocol stage, and at trial registration, we should explicitly state the primary outcome. The rationale for this is that if we test on multiple outcomes then it is likely we will see a statistically significant difference in one or more outcomes purely by chance. Clearly there may be a rationale for having multiple outcomes so we can get an overall picture of the intervention. We may not be entirely focused on educational outcomes and may also wish to see an improvement in well-being outcomes, such as increase in happiness or reduction in anxiety or bullying. Nevertheless, our trial should state a primary outcome, which, if not statistically significant, means that the secondary outcomes should be of lesser importance.

Pre-test equivalence

Once we have finished our trial the first analysis is often to test that the randomisation 'has worked' by comparing pre-test variables. This is misleading unless we suspect some subversion of the allocation. If we have used random allocation then any baseline differences observed will have, by definition, occurred by chance. If we have significant attrition it is more useful to compare the baseline variables, by group, of the analysed population to assess whether the attrition has introduced bias. There is a view that if there is significant chance imbalance we should correct this in the analysis. However, we should use baseline variables in the analysis *only* if they strongly predict the outcome; if they do not then 'correcting' for them in the analysis could introduce bias in its own right as the variable correlates with randomisation and 'corrects' this out of the analysis. This is one of the problems of doing baseline testing: it may lead to adjustment for a chance imbalance that has little or no relationship with the main outcome, and leave – uncorrected – a 'non-significant' imbalance that is correlated with outcome, and which would, if corrected, have adjusted away the chance imbalance effects.

Outcome analysis

The simplest analysis is to compare the means or proportions at post-test. This is correct and will generally produce the same estimates as more complex methods. However, if we have a pre-test, which as noted earlier correlates strongly with outcome, this will add to the precision of our study (that is, reduce the uncertainty surrounding the estimator). Consequently, some form of regression analysis (for example, analysis of covariance) adjusting for pre-test score and other variables that might affect outcome such as age and gender would be necessary. Also if there is a chance imbalance in pre-test values then a regression analysis will correct for this and give a more valid treatment estimate than a simple post-test mean difference. Note, a common approach is to use change scores in an analysis when there are both pre- and post-test data. These generally give similar results to a regression approach using baseline as a covariate with post-test as the outcome *if* there is good balance on pre-test scores. If there is imbalance then change score analysis, due to the phenomenon of regression to the mean effects, will result in a biased estimate. Furthermore, it is more inefficient in terms of standard errors compared to a regression based approach.

Consequently, its use should be discouraged. Additionally, if we have undertaken randomisation of groups of students (for example, school or class randomisation) we need to take this into account in the analysis. If this is not undertaken we will obtain biased precision in that we would appear to see relatively little uncertainty when in reality uncertainty is present in the observed estimate.

Reporting uncertainty

For each analysis we have an estimate of the intervention's effect. Despite randomisation there could be several competing explanations for the observed effect. We hope that, with robust randomisation, intention to treat analysis, blinded follow-up and low attrition, the contribution of bias of generating an effect difference is minimal. The other contributor that can never be totally eliminated is that of chance. There are two statistical schools of thought on how to account for uncertainty: Bayesian and frequentist methods. It is beyond the scope of this chapter to go into detail about these methods, but Bayesian credibility intervals are probably often what people understand to be frequentist confidence intervals: that is, within the interval there is a probability that the 'true' difference lies. However, confidence intervals are not quite that and are more difficult to understand. A confidence interval is about replication. If any given trial were repeated many times then 95 per cent of them would produce intervals that contain the postulated effect size. Whilst there can be intense debate in the methodological literature as to the best approach in this respect, for trials with large sample sizes, both methods produce similar estimates of uncertainty (that is assuming the Bayesian interval uses a 'flat' or uninformative prior). For example, in a trial where there is a 1.47 point difference a 95 per cent confidence interval is 0.64 to 2.33 points, which is statistically significant. A Bayesian credibility interval on the same data yields 0.85 to 2.54, which is not too dissimilar to the confidence interval approach. Consequently, it probably does not matter too much which method is used as long as we account somehow for the imprecision of our treatment estimate. It is important that we are aware of sampling variation in our results. If we simply reported point treatment estimates of effect we would not know how confident we were of the size of the true intervention effect. A wide credibility or confidence interval, even if it is 'statistically' significant, still leads to a lot of uncertainty which we may decide to resolve by conducting a larger RCT.

Sample size calculation

Linked to the need to estimate precision of the intervention estimate from a completed trial is the need to ensure that we have a big enough sample size to enable us to show a hypothesised difference with a reasonable level of precision or confidence. The routine, or frequentist approach, is to identify a difference that would be educationally significant or cost-effective. This is the most difficult aspect of sample size calculation, and requires judgement by the researcher and some idea of the likely costs and benefits of implementing any given intervention. If the intervention is inexpensive and/or easy to implement then the difference between the groups that would make it cost effective might be very small, which would require a large sample size. In contrast, a very expensive intervention would require a large difference to be worthwhile, which would require a more modest sample size. It is worth noting that most novel educational interventions are likely to produce moderate or small effect sizes. This is because most will be compared with business as usual teaching as it would not make sense (or be ethical) to compare a teaching intervention against no teaching. Consequently, as students are actually receiving an effective intervention we are interested in looking for a smaller incremental or marginal gain. Therefore, we should plan to look for effect sizes (proportion of a standard deviation) in the area of 0.33 or more likely 0.20 or smaller. Once we have an idea of the hypothesised difference in effect then the method of calculating a sample size is relatively simple and can be done using a number of statistical packages. As noted previously, educational outcomes often have a strong relationship with pre-test measures – so a naïve sample size, not taking this into account will result in a sample size that is larger than necessary. Once we know the difference we are proposing to investigate then we need to know what we deem to be statistically significant (usually 5 per cent) and the power of the study (usually 80 per cent or 90 per cent). The latter is where, if we were to repeat the study on many occasions and the effect size we are looking for is the 'true' effect how often we would find a difference to be statistically significant. Thus, with 90 per cent power 9/10 trials would find a statistically significant difference between the groups assuming such a difference existed.

Often we want to undertake a pilot or feasibility trial before embarking on our main study. In this case, the sample size estimation becomes a little more challenging. In a pilot study we may only wish to look at 'process' measures, such as recruitment to the study or compliance with the intervention, so it becomes a little more difficult to decide on the relevant sample size. One approach, however, may be to use a sample size that is large enough to exclude the point estimate sought in the main trial. For instance, if we decide that, if we were to run the main trial we would want it to be large enough to identify a 0.30 effect size, such a trial would require about 356 participants (with 80 per cent power and 5 per cent significance). However, if we undertook a pilot trial of about 32 participants (that is, 9 per cent of the main trial size) this would enable us to calculate a one-sided 80% confidence interval that would exclude 0.30 of an effect size if the true difference was actually zero or less (Cocks and Torgerson, 2013). Other authors suggest the sample sizes for a pilot trial should not fall below 30 participants or for a cluster trial of eight clusters (that is, eight schools or classes) (Donner and Klar, 2000).

Randomisation ratios

In most RCTs participants are randomised in equal numbers to the two or more groups. When the total sample size is fixed then this is statistically the most efficient approach of obtaining the best power to show a difference between the groups. However, if the costs or logistics of delivering one of the interventions are different then it will be more efficient, both statistically and economically, to randomise using an unequal ratio favouring the cheaper group. For example, let us suppose we want to evaluate a mentoring programme for students, yet we only have sufficient mentoring resources for 64 students. If we use equal randomisation and recruit 128 students we would have 80 per cent power to show a half a standard deviation difference (assuming no pre-test). But let us assume we actually have 200 students available who could take part in the study. Using equal allocation we would 'waste' 72 students, but rather what we could do is to randomise 64 students into the intervention group and 136 into the control group. If we were to do this then the power of the study actually increases to 91 per cent. Therefore, whilst it is generally true that when the total sample size is fixed, power is maximised when equal allocation is used, but when resources are fixed and the sample size is not, then power is increased by using unequal allocation.

TRIAL DESIGNS

In the following we will discuss some of the different types of trial designs. The choice of design will be driven by a combination of factors including: cost; feasibility; and sources of bias. Perhaps the most important factor is minimisation of post-randomisation sources of bias. One of these sources of bias that can work in positive or negative ways is 'contamination' of the control group or spill-over effects into the control groups. This is a particular issue with educational trials. If, for example, we randomised schools to receive extra training in maths teaching and a senior teacher from each school attended the training we would welcome any 'contamination' or spill-over of the intervention to non-attending teachers. But in an evaluation where we want to assess a novel curriculum's effect on learning outcomes among students, then we do not want contamination of the control students. For example, if we wanted to see whether financial incentives among adult learners was effective at increasing class attendance we would not want to randomise individual students otherwise this may demoralise the non-incentivised students in the class (Brooks et al., 2008). Consequently we often need to use cluster randomisation.

Cluster randomised trials

As noted previously, a cluster, sometimes known as a group, randomised trial is when we do not randomise individuals but rather we randomise groups or clusters of participants. In educational research the common unit of allocation is the school, class, or school year group; however, it might be larger, such as school district. Sometimes time (for example, month) can be used as the unit of allocation. The randomisation of groups of individuals has some implications for the design and analysis of the trial. In terms of sample size the number of individuals in the trial needs to be larger than if we had randomised at the individual level. This is because the outcomes of the students tend to correlate within the group, whereas standard statistical methods assume the outcomes of individuals are independent from each other. Because of this correlation, which is known as the *intra cluster correlation coefficient (ICC)*, our sample size calculation needs to take this into account. However, this is relatively simple. First, we calculate the sample size as we would if there were no clustering and then we calculate an inflation factor or the *design effect*. This is estimated using a simple formula of: ((cluster size −1) × ICC) + 1. In educational trials the ICC is usually between 0.15 to 0.25. Therefore, let us calculate a sample size for a cluster trial that aims to find a 0.30 effect size difference. We know that if we randomised individual students this would require 356 participants. However, we propose to randomise by class. Assuming the class size is 30 and the ICC is 0.20, then we would need the following: ((30–1) × 0.20) +1 = *design effect* (6.8). Therefore we would need 356 × 6.8 = 2,421 or around 82 classes in our trial. In reality the study may be somewhat smaller, because if we had a pre- and post-test correlation of about 0.70 (which is common) then we would need around 40 classes in our study.

The next issue with respect to cluster trials is randomisation. First, it is important to identify the students and teachers *before* randomisation. This is to ensure that once the allocation is known students or teachers are not changed. For instance, if a school had the option of sending one of two teachers on the novel curriculum training course the knowledge of the allocation might affect the decision of which teacher to send, which could introduce a potential source of bias. Second, because we typically have fewer clusters available to randomise then some form of stratified or restricted randomisation is recommended to ensure that the schools or classes are balanced across the intervention groups.

Finally, for cluster trials the analysis is different from an individually randomised trial. Because the usual assumption of an individual's outcome being unrelated to any other individual no longer holds, then a different analytical approach is needed. The easiest, which was described back in 1940 by Lindquist, is to take the mean scores of each cluster and treat this as a single observation. For instance if we had 40 schools with 1,200 children we would calculate the average (mean) score of each school and then do a simple two sample t-test comparing the 20 intervention observations with the 20 control observations: thus the analytical sample size is 40 not 1,200. More complex methods have been developed to take individual characteristics into account, such as multi-level modelling or robust standard errors. However, it does not matter too much what method is used as long as it takes clustering into account.

Factorial trials

A factorial trial is where we randomise students or schools into two different interventions within the same trial. A factorial is an efficient design as it is possible to get two comparisons for the 'price of one' in terms of sample size. The simplest factorial is 2 × 2: this is where we have four groups with two different interventions. For instance, assume we wished to test whether a financial incentive and a new curriculum was effective either singly or in combination. We would then randomise to four groups: financial incentive alone; new curriculum alone; financial incentive and new curriculum; neither. In the analysis we would treat the groups as two separate trials. Consequently, if we wished to assess the impact of financial incentives we would combine the financial incentive alone group with the financial incentive plus new curriculum and compare the sum of these two groups with the sum of the remaining two groups (that is, no incentive plus new curriculum). The downside of a factorial design is that if there is an interaction this can remove the statistical advantages of performing such a design. If we have a qualitative interaction whereby the new curriculum works less well in the presence of financial incentives then the design will underestimate the effect of the new curriculum. Therefore, it is important to choose interventions that are unlikely to have a negative interaction.

Split plot design

A split-plot is a special form of a factorial design whereby we combine cluster randomisation with individual allocation. In a partial-split plot individuals are only randomised in one arm of the cluster allocation. For example, in a study of embedded grammar teaching (*Grammar for Writing*) we wanted to test whether there was also an impact of small group work (Torgerson et al., 2014). Pupils in schools that were randomised to teach literacy using a grammar approach were randomised to receive the grammar teaching in a whole class or to be taught the approach in small groups. Schools were initially recruited and asked to identify pupils who would be eligible for small group teaching or not. Those pupils in the intervention schools who were eligible were randomised to be taught in small groups or to be taught the intervention using a whole class approach. The analysis could then compare the effect of *Grammar for Writing* on class level outcomes between the two groups of schools. Comparing the two groups of schools, it was found that there was a 0.10 standard deviation difference in favour of *Grammar for Writing* schools. But this difference was not statistically significant (95 per cent CI -0.09 to 0.30). However, comparing the small group children with the class-taught children generated a larger effect size of 0.24, which was borderline statistically significant (95 per cent CI -0.01 to 1.56). Indeed, when the control cluster classes were compared with the intervention classes the effect size of 0.10 reduced to 0.06, suggesting even the modest, not statistically significant, effect was partly driven by the small group effect rather than the *Grammar for Writing* effect. If the split plot design had not been used, and instead all of the intervention children had received the teaching in small groups, then it would not have been possible to disentangle the effects of the novel curriculum from the delivery method. This design enabled the researchers to show that this particular version of embedded grammar teaching did not have a statistically significant effect on literacy outcomes, yet the small group teaching did (Torgerson et al., 2014).

REPORTING RCTS AND THE USE OF THE CONSORT STATEMENT

Most RCTs are inadequately reported in the sense that it is difficult to ascertain what exactly was done and by whom. This problem has been recognised across a number of different fields. In health care research, methodologists and journal editors proposed the CONSORT guidance for authors of RCTs to keep to when reporting their trials. The CONSORT statement has a 25 item checklist and a flow diagram for the reporting of randomised trials (www.consort-statement. org/). Following the statement allows the trials to have all the key elements of design reported to satisfy the readers as to whether a trial has been robustly undertaken or not. For example, the statement asks the authors to report: how the randomisation was done; whether intention treat was used; how many participants dropped out and from which group. This guidance with some modification has been adopted by many psychology and education journals, including the American Psychological Association journals.

CONCLUSIONS

It is important that RCTs are conducted robustly: a poor quality RCT could be more misleading than other forms of research as people often, naïvely, assume that all confounding must have been abolished in a RCT. In a well conducted trial this may often be true, but in a low quality study effect estimates may be biased. It might be an exaggeration to say that in education and the wider social policy world we are entering into a new age for randomised trials. For too long the use of trials in the field of health care research has dominated the experimental landscape. However, with recent initiatives across the world there has been a welcome increase in the number of randomised trials being designed and conducted. Randomised controlled trials (RCTs) are the best method of evaluating key questions of effectiveness in education and social policy. However, it is important that they are conducted rigorously so that their results are believable. A key element of a successful RCT is robust randomisation, which must be undertaken independently. Another key issue is that of sample size. Effective educational interventions will tend to produce relatively small effect sizes: differences between groups of a tenth of a standard deviation are not uncommon. But small differences, particularly if the intervention is inexpensive, are important. It is crucial to remember that most children/students will receive an effective educational intervention so we are only interested in relatively small increments. However, these small marginal effects will add up and a small effect spread over a national school population that might number millions will translate into many thousands of young people having improved educational outcomes and as a consequence favourably impact on their lives. Clearly this will also benefit society at large with a better educated population; economic productivity will increase and other social outcomes will improve.

It is sometimes argued that RCTs are unethical in that some students (or patients in health care research) will get the 'inferior' intervention. It is true that some will receive the inferior approach: but until we actually do the RCT we do not which is the effective intervention. It must be more ethical to test a novel intervention among a small group of participants, of which at least a proportion will get the superior intervention, compared with rolling it out to many thousands of children who may all get the inferior intervention. Some ethical and logistical objections may be addressed through the careful choice of design. A waiting list approach, for example, means that all eligible participants will eventually receive the new intervention, if it were demonstrated to be effective. Additionally, some schools or institutions may be reluctant to take part in the research if they think they might be allocated to a control group with 'no additional intervention'. Alternatives or complements to the waiting list approach might be to randomise schools to receive the intervention for different school years, or use a balanced design so that all schools receive an intervention but in different areas so that different interventions can be evaluated: two 'active' interventions with different characteristics to establish which is better. Consequently, with a little thought, many ethical and logistical difficulties can be addressed with the use of different types of RCTs.

REFERENCES

Ainsworth, H., Hewitt, C. E., Higgins, S., Wiggins, A., Torgerson, D. J. and Torgerson, C. J. (2014) Sources of bias in outcome assessment to randomised controlled trials: a case study. *Educational Research and Evaluation*, 21, 3–14.

Brooks, G., Burton, M., Coles, P., Miles, J., Torgerson, C. and Torgerson, D. (2008) Randomised controlled trial of incentives to improve attendance at adult literacy classes *Oxford Review of Education*, 34: 493–504.

Cocks, K. and Torgerson, D. J. (2013) Sample size calculations for pilot randomised trials: a confidence interval approach. *Journal of Clinical Epidemiology*, 66: 197–201.

Donner, A. and Klar, N. (2000) *Design and Analysis of Cluster Randomization Trials in Health Research*. London: Arnold.

Duflo, E., Dupas, P. and Kremer, M. (2008) Peer effects and impact of tracking: evidence from a randomized evaluation in Kenya. California Center for Population Research (CCPR-055–08).

Hewitt, C., Hahn, S., Torgerson, D. J., Watson, J. and Bland, J. M. (2005) Adequacy and reporting of allocation concealment: review of recent trials published in four general medical journals. *British Medical Journal*, 330: 1057–1058.

Hewitt, C. J., Torgerson, D. J. and Miles, J. N. V. (2006) Taking account of non-compliance in randomised trials. *Canadian Medical Association Journal*, 175: 347–348.

Kjaergaard, L. L., Villumsen, J. and Cluud, C. (2001) Reported methodologic quality and discrepancies between large and small randomized trials in meta-analyses. *Annals of Internal Medicine*, 135: 982–989.

Lindquist, E. F. (1940) *Statistical Analysis in Educational Research*. Boston: Houghton Mifflin.

Nye, B., Hedges, L. V. and Konstantopoulos, S. (1999) The long-term effects of small classes: a five year follow-up of the Tennessee class size experiment. *Educational Evaluation and Policy Analysis*, 21: 127–142.

Rosenberger, W. F. and Lachin, J. M. (2002) *Randomization in Clinical Trials: Theory and practice*. New York: Wiley & Sons.

Schulz, K. F., Chalmers, I., Hayes, R. J. and Altman, D. G. (1995) Empirical evidence of bias: dimensions of methodological quality associated with estimates of treatment effects in controlled trials. *Journal of the America Medical Association*, 273: 408–412.

Schwartz, D. and Lellouch, J. (1967) Explanatory and pragmatic attitudes in therapeutic trials. *Journal of Chronic Diseases*, 20: 637–648.

Shadish, W. R., Cook, T. D. and Campbell, D. T. (2002) *Experimental and Quasi-Experimental Designs for Generalized Causal Inference*. Boston: Houghton Mifflin Co.

Torgerson, C. J. (2003) *Systematic Reviews*. London: Continuum.

Torgerson, C. J. (2006) Publication bias: the Achilles' heel of systematic reviews. *British Journal of Educational Studies*, 54(1): 89–102.

Torgerson, C. J. and Torgerson, D. J. (2007) The use of minimization to form comparison groups in educational research. *Educational Studies*, 33: 333–337.

Torgerson, C. J., Brooks, G. and Hall, J. (2006) A systematic review of the research literature on the use of phonics in the teaching of reading and spelling. Department for Education and Skills Research Report RR711.

Torgerson, C., Wiggins, A., Torgerson, D., Ainsworth, A. and Hewitt, C. (2013) Every child counts: testing policy effectiveness using a randomised controlled trial, designed, conducted and reported to CONSORT standard. *Research in Mathematics Education*, 15: 141–153.

Torgerson, D. J. and Torgerson, C. J. (2008) *Designing Randomised Trials in Health, Education and The Social Sciences: An introduction*. Basingstoke: Palgrave Macmillan.

Torgerson, D., Torgerson, C., Mitchell, N., Buckley, H., Ainsworth, H., Heaps, C. and Jefferson, L. (2014) Grammar for Writing, Educational Endowment Foundation, February. Retrieved on 11 July 2016 from https://educationendowmentfoundation.org.uk/uploads/pdf/FINAL_EEF_Evaluation_Report_-_Grammar_for_Writing_-_February_2014.pdf

Walters, J. E. (1931) Seniors as Counsellors. *The Journal of Higher Education, 2*, 446–448.

Walters, J.E. (1932) Measuring effectiveness of personnel counseling. *Personnel Journal*, 11, 227–36.

White, P. (2009) Developing Research Questions, Basingstoke: Palgrave Macmillan.

21

Educational Action Research as Transformative Practice

Mary Brydon-Miller, Maricar Prudente
and Socorro Aguja

INTRODUCTION

Educational Action Research (EAR) provides a powerful framework for drawing upon the knowledge and experience of teachers, school leaders, students, and community members to address important educational, social, cultural, and political issues. Educational Action Research can be placed within the broader context of Action Research which has been defined as 'a participatory, democratic process concerned with developing practical knowing in the pursuit of worthwhile human purposes' (Reason and Bradbury, 2001, p. 1). Echoing this focus on participation, reflection, and action, Piggot-Irvine et al. have described action research as 'a collaborative transformative approach with joint focus on rigorous data collection, knowledge generation, reflection, and distinctive action/ change elements that pursue practical solutions' (2015, p. 4). Action research is represented in a wide range of disciplines including organizational development and management, nursing, geography, anthropology, public health, international development and, of course, education. But what brings the many traditions of Action Research together can perhaps best be thought of as a shared values stance which is grounded in 'a respect for people and for the knowledge and experience they bring to the research process, a belief in the ability of democratic processes to achieve positive social change, and a commitment to action' (Brydon-Miller et al., 2003, p. 15). This differs from other models of research design in its rejection of the notion of research as an expert-driven practice and instead views researchers as facilitators whose main role is to enable participants to take ownership of the research process from identifying key issues, to generating research questions and developing methods of collecting and analyzing data, to the final stages of disseminating and using the results of the research to create change.

Action Research is often described as an iterative, or cyclical, process in which the initial identification of an issue leads to planning of a possible strategy to address the concern, observation of the impact of the intervention, and finally reflection on the process and its outcomes which leads to the next action/reflection cycle. Ideally, action research projects go through a series of such iterations, although in some cases the presenting issue might be addressed in a single cycle. Oftentimes, publications describing action research processes focus on a single round of the research as a way to make the reflection process more explicit and to share the knowledge gained through the project to date with a broader audience.

Educational Action Research is a term used to describe a group of action research methodologies which involve working with educators in both formal and popular education sites to improve educational outcomes for students, address educational inequality, and create more critical and innovative educational practices. Classroom-based Action Research, Teacher-as-Researcher, and Practitioner Inquiry are specific approaches to Educational Action Research. In the context of Educational Action Research, the iterative process might entail identifying a question or problem in pedagogy, classroom management, curriculum development or any other aspect of educational practice, conducting initial investigations to develop a deeper understanding of the form and causes of the problem, creating strategies designed to address the problem based on the teacher's own experience as well as other sources of information, implementing and observing the results of these interventions, and then reflecting on the outcome and determining the next iteration of the research process. This process can be carried out by individual teachers in their own classrooms, by groups of teachers working in collaboration, or at a school, district, or community-wide level to address a common question or concern. Theory and practice are not seen as separate aspects of the research process, but are integrated with a focus on the importance of lived experience and shared knowledge as the basis for theory generation.

In this chapter we provide an overview of the history of Educational Action Research and discuss its distinct epistemological stance which distinguishes it from other educational research methodologies. After outlining some specific EAR methods, we present a set of quality criteria that can be used to evaluate EAR studies and pay particular attention to the ethical issues involved in conducting EAR. Throughout the chapter we draw upon examples of Educational Action Research projects being conducted in the Philippines. The Southeast Asian Region is a rich source of some of the most innovative and extensive EAR efforts currently being conducted anywhere in the world, and the Philippines has recently launched the Action Research Action Learning (ARAL) conferences as a way to highlight this work and to bring researchers from across the country and the region together. We hope that by using these studies as examples here we bring greater attention to this extraordinary contribution to the global community of educational researchers.

EDUCATIONAL ACTION RESEARCH: THE PHILIPPINE CONTEXT

In the Philippines, students in the Teacher Education Program and in the Masters' level of the Graduate Program (non-thesis track) conduct action research as a learning output in an integrating course, while in-service teachers in the basic education level are expected to conduct action research to examine impacts of new instructional programs or teaching/learning innovations. In 2012, recognizing the important role of School Division Superintendents (SDS) in instituting the needed reforms in basic education, the government's Department of Education (DepED) in collaboration with the Lasallian Institute for Development and Educational Research (LIDER) of De La Salle University (DLSU) and the Knowledge Channel Foundation Inc. conducted the SDS Leadership Program. This joint undertaking, funded by AusAID, was aimed at developing the superintendents into purposive change leaders who have a good grasp of the situation or context for the change process. It is hoped that the train-ing will empower them to initiate specific programs and projects that target the DepED's desired outcomes. The superintendents were also expected to install and institutionalize the changes they have initiated. A major realization of this leadership training program was that involvement of practitioners in research is important if changes and innovations in the education organization are desired. Hence, the School Division Superintendents initiated programs to intensify the conduct of action research among teachers, school principals, district supervisors and other school personnel. In 2015, to provide an avenue for the sharing of action research findings, LIDER took the lead in organizing the 1st National Congress on Action Research and dubbed it as ARAL – an acronym that stands for Action Research Action Learning and which is also the Filipino word for 'study'. The following year, ARAL2016 invited distinguished Action Researchers from Malaysia, Indonesia, and Myanmar to understand how action research is being done in these countries. This made ARAL2016 the 1st International Congress of Action Research in Education, initiating the formation of a network of action researchers in the ASEAN region.

When action research papers presented in ARAL2015 and ARAL2016 were reviewed and analyzed, changes in AR approaches were noted. A decrease in the number of individual teacher research and collaborative action research proj-ects was seen, while an increase in the number of school-wide action research studies was evident. These changing trends in AR approaches may be attributed to the increased participation of school heads/principals, who are addressing school-wide problems in their Action Research projects. Data also suggest that collaborative action research projects should be strengthened as it can help the DepED attain the goal of developing basic education teacher-researchers and at the same time enable university researchers to create and share new knowledge in the field. Further, the collaborative effort of universities to reach out to basic education teachers and extend a helping hand in the design and implementation of action research brings better chances of teacher promotion. DepED's criteria in assessing teachers for promotion hinge in large part on teacher education and meritorious accomplishment especially in research and development particularly on the conduct of action research. Hence collaborative action research can uplift teacher professionalization and teacher promotion for teacher quality and thereby improve the quality of education in the country.

Moreover, when AR papers submitted in ARAL2015 and ARAL2016 were categorized into AR types following the typology of Sagor (2005), it was observed that more than 50 percent of the papers were quasi-experimental, which involved evaluation of the impact of a previously implemented change such as a new curriculum or teaching method. While about 40 percent of the AR papers were of the descriptive type, which usually involved a study of a group (for example, a class of students) in order to analyze the probable causes for the issue under study. The remaining 10 percent of the AR papers were case studies that focused on an individual and involved either analysis of the probable cause of a behavior or evaluation of the impact of a previously implemented change. The types of AR presented in both ARAL2015 and ARAL2016 were observed to be similar.

During the First National Congress on Action Research in Education (ARAL2015) held on February 27–28, 2015 in the Philippines, a very interesting study was commended for its cultural significance. This action research was conducted by Loida Intong, a school district supervisor of Concepcion, Misamis Occidental. The Philippine government's Department of Education (DepEd) Indigenous Peoples Education Office (IPsEO) has identified six schools in Concepcion district with 90–100 percent IP (Indigenous People) learners, who all belong to the *Subanen* tribe. The *Subanen* tribe is one of the biggest non-Muslim indigenous cultural communities in Mindanao, the southern island of the Philippines. During her monitoring as District supervisor, Loida observed that Grade 1 pupils are not using the *Subanen* language, which is their mother tongue. In her discussions with teachers and parents, she found out that pupils of *Subanen* origin often experience discrimination at school; thus, they have chosen to adopt the language used by non-IP pupils. In an effort to ensure a more culturally-sensitive and learner-centered instruction, Supervisor Intong encouraged Grade 1 teachers in the district to develop instructional materials (IMs) integrating *Subanen* indigenous practices. This way, the *Subanen* pupils will take greater pride in their cultural heritage. The IMs incorporated *Subanen* greetings, songs, rhymes, and short stories in their classes. In developing these IMs, the teachers sought the help of *Subanen* tribal leaders, who willingly cooperated and provided the needed information. After a semester of using the IMs, Supervisor Intong observed classes and had focus group discussions with the teachers. It was found that pupils from the *Subanen* tribe began to display extrovert behaviors and were more participative in class discussions. The pupils were also observed to be more confident and exhibited pride in using their *Subanen* language. The study posited that the observed positive changes in pupils' behavior suggest that IP pupils' self-concept was enhanced because their indigenous cultural practices were given importance in school. This action research provided evidence that using indigenized learning materials can improve IP learner's performance. To date, elementary schools in the six districts where *Subanen* tribal communities reside, are now fully adopting IP-based instructional materials in cooperation with the Schools Superintendent, the parents, and the *Subanen* community leaders. Truly, this action research underscored the role of schools in promoting and preserving the cultural heritage of Indigenous People.

During ARAL2016, a descriptive action research study entitled *Enhancing the Level of Performance of Science III Students through Formative Assessment Classroom Techniques (FACTs)* was presented by a group of preservice teachers from Mariano Marcos State University-College of Teacher Education in Laoag City, Philippines. The study employed the three-step action research cycle outlined by Stringer (2008) to address the issue of enhancing the students' level of performance in Science III (Chemistry) through formative assessments. Stringer's three-steps include: (1) *Look*, (2) *Think*, and (3) *Act*, where *Look* involves gathering of information through careful observation; *Think* involves analyzing the information to assist the researcher in identifying significant features and elements of the issue at hand; and *Act* involves using the newly formulated information to design relevant solutions to the issue being investigated. Findings showed that the use of selected Formative Assessment Classroom Techniques (FACTs) enhanced the level of performance of the students in Science III.

In all forms of action research, and especially in Educational Action Research, the positionality of the researcher is an important issue that informs the research process. Action researchers often make the distinction between insider and outsider status in discussing the role of the researcher (Coghlan and Brannick, 2014). Many Educational Action Researchers are themselves teachers or school leaders conducting research within the context of their own schools and communities. This insider status affords the researcher a rich knowledge of the context which frames the issue, relationships which can support and enrich the research process, and most importantly, a deep commitment to the students, parents, and community within which the research takes place. This model sees teachers and other educational professionals as researchers in their own right and understands that EAR can serve as an ongoing process of deepening educational professional practice. At the same time university researchers also have an important role to play in providing research methods training, process facilitation, and an outsider perspective. This perspective is important since there are times when insider status can make it difficult to see beyond one's own experience and to imagine alternative ways to address problems, so in many instances it is helpful to bring together insider and outsider points of view through partnerships between school and university-based researchers.

Educational Action Research incorporates specific traditions including Teacher-as-Researcher, Classroom-based Action Research, and Practitioner Inquiry. Each of these traditions is grounded in the belief that educators themselves, as well as their students and community partners, must play a central role in guiding the development of classroom practice, curriculum development, and larger educational policy. In some instances EAR is focused on more technical questions regarding educational practice, while at the other end of the spectrum, it embraces the emancipatory potential of research and engages actively in efforts to challenge current trends toward increased standardization and exclusion, insisting instead that education be focused on increasing the ability of students to engage in critical thinking which challenges systems of oppression and marginalization. In our view, while research at both ends of this spectrum can be of value, the most important contribution of EAR lies in its ability to ask questions that challenge the status quo in significant ways in order to bring about changes that contribute to positive social change both within, and beyond, the educational system.

A BRIEF HISTORY OF EDUCATIONAL ACTION RESEARCH

Educational Action Research draws upon a rich history which includes the work of educational pioneers like John Dewey and Paulo Freire, whose writing, while separated by time and place, reflects the same belief in democracy and the transformative power of education. Both men translated these principles into specific theories of knowledge generation focused on the use of reflective practice, collaboration, and authentic problem solving as the basis for learning (Dewey, 1916, 1938; Freire, 1970/2000, 1998).

Other, more recent, contributors include Lawrence Stenhouse (1983) and John Elliot (2007), both from the UK, who helped to articulate the process of learning through reflection on practice that is at the heart of EAR. According to Elliot, it was Stenhouse who first made the link between 'teachers as researchers' and a specific theory of education, emphasizing the importance of teachers' own experience and insight. Citing her own training as one of Elliot's students, Bridget Somekh (2003) notes that respecting teachers' abilities to generate knowledge and to theorize about educational issues is essential in insuring that EAR continues to promote genuine forms of teaching and learning.

Wilfred Carr and Stephen Kemmis have also made important contributions by locating EAR in the context of critical theory and articulating the radical, political potential of EAR. Drawing upon the work of Jürgen Habermas, they define their notion of emancipatory action research as 'a form of research that seeks to create the kind of communicative space within which practitioners can participate in making decisions, taking action and collaboratively inquiring into their own practices, their understandings of these practices, and the conditions under which they practice' (Carr and Kemmis, 2009, p. 79). According to them, the most important aspect of EAR, which distinguishes it from other forms of research on education, is the explicit understanding that 'education is politics conducted by other means' (Carr and Kemmis, 2009, p. 74). This recognition of the political nature of all educational research challenges traditional positivist notions of objectivity and value neutrality and instead demands that educational researchers take responsibility for the ways in which research shapes educational policy and practice. This articulation of an explicit advocacy stance for the researchers themselves distinguishes this approach from conventional forms of both quantitative and qualitative research which understand their role as experts providing data to others – administrators, policymakers, and politicians, for example – to implement change.

In the United States, one long-standing EAR partnership was established in the public school system in Madison, Wisconsin in partnership with local university faculty members. Focusing on core principles which include treating teachers as knowledgeable professionals and giving participants control over research questions and methods, this program trained scores of teacher researchers and furthered the use of action research as a strategy for creating equitable classrooms (Caro-Bruce et al., 2007; Caro-Bruce et al., 2009; Zeichner, 2003).

Susan Noffke, another important contributor to the development of educational action research, described the ways in which EAR creates change at personal, professional, and political levels (Noffke, 1997, 2009). At the personal level, educators can come to understand their own motivations for teaching and experience transformations in how they identify and enact their own values through practice. They can also develop a greater sense of agency as they become more confident as active contributors to, rather than passive recipients of, knowledge regarding the theory and practice of education. At the professional level, EAR brings teachers, educational leaders, and university partners together to deepen their understanding of important issues regarding teaching and learning with a view to creating positive change in educational practice. And finally, at the political level, EAR sees the vital role of teachers and other educational professionals as active contributors to larger policy-related dialogues about educational reform.

The notion of Practitioner Inquiry as described by Marilyn Cochran-Smith and Susan Lytle (2009) provides another important acknowledgement of the central role that teachers themselves must play in the process of educational reform. But in order to do this, teachers must be empowered to take action. 'A core part of the knowledge and expertise necessary for transforming practice and enhancing students' learning resides in the questions, theories, and strategies generated collectively by practitioners themselves and in their joint interrogations of the knowledge, practices and theories of others' (Cochran-Smith and Lytle, 2009, p. 124).

Finally, while this chapter focuses on Educational Action Research within the context of more formal educational settings, there is also a rich and important contribution from the area of popular education. Action research has been described as the intersection of community-based research, popular education, and action for social justice (Brydon-Miller, 2001). Organizations like the Highlander Research and Education Center in the Southern United States, the Society for Participatory Research in India (PRIA) and many other initiatives around the world, have demonstrated the important role that popular education can have in giving communities the tools they need to address critical economic, environmental, and social issues (Brydon-Miller et al., 2009; Horton and Freire, 1990; Tandon, 2002; for another short history of Educational Action Research see also Noffke and Brennan, 2014).

EPISTEMOLOGICAL AND THEORETICAL FOUNDATIONS OF EDUCATIONAL ACTION RESEARCH

A careful consideration of the epistemology of EAR in contrast to other forms of educational research reveals a distinct understanding of knowledge generation not as an objective, value-neutral, expert-driven process but rather as an opportunity for collaboration and engagement that is clearly focused on creating more democratic, critical approaches to education. Action research 'emphasizes how knowledge is acquired in relationship, mutual intersubjectivity, and through action to create change' (Stoecker and Brydon-Miller, 2013, p. 22). This more engaged stance toward knowledge creation is in contrast to the positivist understanding that underlies many quantitative methodologies. That is not to say that quantitative research cannot be included in Educational Action Research studies, indeed many EAR projects rely upon quantitative data to support claims of positive change. The difference is in the insistence in EAR on democratic engagement and the articulation of a clear advocacy stance resulting from the research process. At the same time it is also distinct from the phenomenological and social constructionist approaches informing most qualitative research that, while reflecting the relational aspects of knowledge generation, often fail to include the idea that knowledge is created through taking action on the world. This focus on practical knowing, that is knowledge gained through actual experience and day-to-day interactions (Coghlan, 2011), informs all forms of Educational Action Research. As an illustration of how this epistemological framework informs the practice of EAR, in our opening example, it was the supervisor's and teachers' observations of the challenges facing indigenous students in their classrooms and their experience in using local knowledge to help children feel that their own culture was an important part of their shared learning, that led them to investigate how the incorporation of indigenized instructional materials might facilitate learning and contribute to the overall well-being of the children in their classrooms.

Educational action researchers draw upon a number of theoretical frameworks to inform their understanding of the process and findings of their research. As noted earlier, critical theory has been a key source for action researchers generally in challenging the dominant positivist perspective regarding research and knowledge generation. In particular the work of Jürgen Habermas with his notions of communicative space and communicative action (Habermas, 1984) helps to clarify the role of democratic processes and dialogue that are a foundation of action research. Critical pedagogy, centered on the work of Paulo Freire, but also including a range of scholars such as Sonia Nieto (2009), Antonia Darder (Darder et al., 2009), and Henry Giroux (2011), has also been an important influence in EAR. Feminist theory as well has had a profound influence, particularly the work of Patricia Maguire (1987; Brydon-Miller et al., 2004), who first articulated the need for greater integration of feminist theory and action research. Critical race theory (Dixson and Rousseau, 2006; Parker et al., 1999) and Post-Colonial Theory (Castle, 2001) also provide important lenses through which Educational Action Researchers can come to understand the issues facing students and communities more clearly.

EDUCATIONAL ACTION RESEARCH METHODOLOGIES

As noted above, EAR often draws upon both quantitative and qualitative methodologies to address specific research questions. The difference comes in who generates those questions, whose experience is understood as contributing valuable understandings of the issue, whose interpretations of the data gathered are privileged, and in the end, who owns the results of the research and how that knowledge is used to create positive social change.

In addition to traditional educational research methods, however, Educational Action Researchers have also developed or adapted a wide range of other more collaborative and creative methods designed to generate data that can be used to inform changes in educational practice and policy. Methods such as Lesson Planning, Photovoice and Digital Storytelling, Group Level Assessment, World Café, and Participatory Theatre are just some of the methods that have been used in the context of Educational Action Research projects (see Coghlan and Brydon-Miller, 2014, for brief descriptions and references).

One way in which action research projects are sometimes distinguished is by considering the scope or focus of the research question. Many Teacher-as-Researcher projects reflect a First-Person Action Research perspective in which the research question addresses some aspect of a single teacher's practice.

In Second-Person Action Research a group works together using more collaborative processes to address some issue of common concern. The intent in both of these cases might be to inform change within a single school or organization. Third-Person Action Research is intended to reach a wider audience, either through presentations or publication, to share the knowledge generated through the research process. At its best, EAR combines all three. As Coghlan notes, 'scholar-practitioners are not merely practitioners who do research; rather, they integrate scholarship into their practice and generate actionable knowledge' (Coghlan, 2013, p. 1).

QUALITY CRITERIA FOR EDUCATIONAL ACTION RESEARCH

The question of what constitutes high quality Educational Action Research merits serious consideration because the standard criteria by which educational research might be judged do not reflect the aims of EAR or are defined differently in the context of EAR. The Action Research journal, the primary journal for a broad range of action research articles, outlines seven specific criteria by which action research projects might be evaluated. These same criteria can be applied to the more specific field of Educational Action Research (see Stoecker and Brydon-Miller, 2013 for an expanded discussion of these criteria):

1 Articulation of objectives. It is essential in any form of research that the objectives for the study are clearly articulated. In Educational Action Research these objectives, translated into specific research questions, might be determined by a teacher who is interested in improving some aspect of her own practice, or they might be agreed upon by a group of teachers working on a collaborative project, or they might result from a broader more participatory discussion of issues facing schools or other community organizations. It is important that the objectives address some real issue or concern expressed by the participants themselves, rather than something imposed upon them by managers or organizational leaders. And it is also important that these objectives remain open to amendment throughout the process. As participants develop a deeper understanding of the issue, the objectives of the research should reflect these changes.
2 Partnership and participation. Even in First-Person Teacher-as-Researcher projects there is a participatory process involving teachers and students addressing some issue or question related to practice. In larger collaborations a group of teachers might work together, or might partner with university-based researchers to address some common concern. Articulating the nature of these partnerships, acknowledging how research questions are developed, how data are collected and analyzed, and how change is initiated and sustained as a result of the research process are important in determining the quality of Educational Action Research processes.
3 Actionability. Kurt Lewin, one of the pioneers of Action Research once said, 'Research that produces nothing but books will not suffice'. (Lewin, 1946, p. 35). Educational Action Research should be judged in part on how effective the process is in creating positive change. This is not to say that all EAR projects succeed in accomplishing their objectives – in fact important learning can come about through a critical examination of our failures – but the iterative nature of action research provides opportunities for us to apply the understanding gained through these failures to the next round of research.

4 Contribution to educational theory and practice. While actionability is vital to the EAR process, it is still important that the work of Educational Action Researchers make a substantial contribution to our understanding of the larger field of education. In EAR we tend to focus on the transferability of knowledge rather than on a more conventional notion of generalizability. In its formal sense, generalizability implies that the findings of a particular study can be replicated in another setting – a drug trial conducted in England will reach the same findings if the study is repeated in the Philippines. But no EAR setting is ever exactly like another. Each school, each classroom, each group of students is unique. Instead, EAR regards each setting as an opportunity to create local change while using the knowledge gained through these experiences to contribute to our broader knowledge of what constitute effective strategies to improve practice.

5 Methods and process. One of the ways in which this contribution to educational practice can be achieved is in a detailed and critical description of the interventions that have been developed and the methods used to assess their efficacy. By 'telling the story' of the research process, Educational Action Researchers are able to provide other researchers and practitioners with the kind of detailed narrative needed to understand, adapt, and apply the process in their own contexts.

6 Reflexivity. The basic process of EAR described earlier outlines the Plan, Act, Observe, Reflect cycle which is the basis of all forms of action research. In the context of EAR, this focus on the importance of reflexivity reinforces the notion of the teacher as researcher – someone who is able to frame an important question of practice, to design strategies to address this question, to observe the outcome of implementation, and then, most importantly, to critically evaluate the results and, based on this analysis, to initiate the next research cycle. Educational Action Researchers should articulate this process of reflection in their discussions of their research in order to allow others to follow their sense-making processes.

7 Significance. In the end, we must ask ourselves whether or not the research matters – matters to the children in our own classrooms, their parents, and community. And whether it provides useful knowledge to our fellow educators and others interested in improving the educational system.

Ethics of education action research

One of the other quality criteria outlined in Stoecker and Brydon-Miller (2013) relates to the question of ethics within an action research framework. Action research offers the opportunity for research to create tangible improvements in practice and to contribute to positive social change. But with this focus on creating positive change comes the possibility for causing harm. This may be especially true in the case of EAR in which those who will be affected by the change are students in our classrooms, their families, and communities.

As noted earlier, one characteristic shared by all forms of action research is a shared values stance which focuses on respect for people's knowledge, a commitment to democratic practice, and a belief in the possibility of creating positive social change (Brydon-Miller et al., 2003) – a possibility which implies an obligation to participate as active agents of this change. In the case of Educational Action Research this change most often takes place in complex, hierarchical systems that reflect (and perhaps even amplify) the challenges facing the larger community.

The importance of reflexivity discussed above is especially important in guiding educational action researchers – whether they are university-based researchers, teachers, school leaders, or others – in considering the values that inform their own practice. While most human subjects review processes focus on the principles of autonomy, beneficence and justice (all certainly laudatory), we would encourage researchers to consider the values that are most important to them and their research partners in guiding their actions. One strategy for articulating and operationalizing this set of values, at both a personal and a larger group level, is the Structured Ethical Reflection process (Brydon-Miller et al., 2015). This process invites researchers to identify a set of core ethical principles that they feel are most central in guiding their research practice, and to then consider how these principles are enacted at each stage of the research process. Participants in this process are encouraged to reflect upon how their own cultural experiences might inform these values. During a presentation at the Congress in the Philippines, for example, participants were asked to identify the values they felt were most central to their own understanding of EAR. One participant, Cyril Belvis, rose to offer the concept of *kakapa-kapa*, which he defines as an 'open-ness to the surprise our findings may reach, humility in front of our respondents, and playfulness towards serendipity' (personal communication). While on the one hand this value is clearly rooted in Filipino culture, it strikes us as also being a critical aspect of all good Educational Action Research.

EXEMPLARS OF EDUCATIONAL ACTION RESEARCH

Some exemplars of Educational Action Research were drawn from the works presented in ARAL2015 – The 1st National Action Research Congress held in the Philippines on February 27–28, 2015. As previously mentioned, Educational Action Research is grounded in the belief that educators themselves, as well as their students and community partners, must play a central role in guiding the development of classroom practice, curriculum development, and larger educational policy. Three specific traditions of Education Action Research are presented as follows:

Teacher-as-researcher

A Mathematics professor, Dr Maxima Acelajado examined the cognitive and non-cognitive gains resulting from employing the Flipped Classroom Approach on teaching selected topics in College Algebra. Two comparable intact freshman Algebra classes of the College of Education at De La Salle University-Manila, during the first term, SY2014–2015, participated in the study. The two classes were taught using the TCA (Traditional Classroom Approach) and the FCA (Flipped Classroom Approach), alternately. Pre-tests and post-tests in all topics under consideration were administered to determine the cognitive gains of the students in the TCA and FCA classes. To determine non-cognitive gains, a

Perceptions Inventory was administered to the students after their exposure to FCA. Cognitive gains such as the students' improved critical thinking ability when students were exposed to FCA were observed. Significant learning gains in every topic were also seen from the results of the t-test for dependent samples applied to the group's respective pre-test and post-test mean scores. To describe their learning experiences, students were asked to write in their journals. Examining students' journal writings revealed favorable responses from the students on the use of FCA. Non-cognitive gains were primarily on the improvement of attitudes toward mathematics. Dr Acelejado also reported that students in FCA classes seemed to be more motivated, confident, relaxed, responsible and active in their learning. A majority of the students indicated that they were happy to have control of their own learning. Using FCA enabled them to explore more mathematical concepts through various modes and resources outside the classroom at a time convenient for them. These findings provided evidence that using the FCA can lead to cognitive and non-cognitive gains, affirming the efficacy of the Flipped Classroom Approach in teaching Algebra. Moving to the next cycle of the research process, Dr Acelejado plans to employ FCA in her other classes in Mathematics to examine more ways of improving students' learning of Mathematics.

Classroom-based action research

Mr Danilo Rogayan, a Science teacher of Subic National High School in Zambales, Philippines developed an instructional technique to improve the laboratory report writing skills of second year high school students. Primarily, he utilized a Reflective Journal Writing Technique (RJWT) as a teaching strategy. Specifically, the instructional process, which he referred to as MENTOR, involves the following processes: (1) Motivate the students through reflective questioning; (2) Execute the lesson through concept formation; (3) Note students' participation in the discussion; (4) Team the students for reality check reflection; (5) Offer time for outputting; and (5) Run and monitor small group writing sessions. Summative tests prior to and after the RJWT-MENTOR teaching intervention were administered to measure effectiveness on students' laboratory report writing skills. Formative assessments such as written quizzes, journal entries, laboratory reports, and other written outputs were likewise employed and analyzed to determine changes in students' writing skills. Results showed that after the RJWT-MENTOR intervention, the class mean score in report writing skills improved significantly. Mr Rogayan shared that in employing this technique, regular checking of the entries in the journal is essential so that students will better understand their difficulties in writing based on the feedback provided by the teacher. He also expressed his plans to use varied and innovative motivational activities to encourage the students to actively participate in the microgroupings and in the writing sessions.

Practitioner inquiry

Jasmine Gaogao, a school principal, wanted to answer to the query: How can the *Gulayan sa Paaralan* (School's Vegetable Garden) Program in Maningcol Central School be revitalized? Principal Jasmine believes that addressing this inquiry will help the school in establishing sustainable means of providing a food source for the school's feeding program. This concern stemmed from the problem of poor nutrition among pupils in her school. In this action research, Principal Jasmine employed a community-based approach that involved a triad of stakeholders: 120 pupils, 45 parents, and 27 teachers as research participants. Focus group discussions (FGDs) among these three groups of stakeholders enabled Principal Jasmine to draw out ideas, issues, and problems that either promote or hinder involvement and cooperation for the school's feeding program. Analysis of FGD transcripts revealed that time constraints and communication gaps block the successful implementation of the *Gulayan sa Paaralan* program. Specifically, this action research provided evidence that the conduct of school–community based planning is necessary for the successful implementation of school programs. Reflecting on the participants' responses during the FGDs, Principal Jasmine initiated the *Lakas Ko, Kalusugan Mo* (My Strength, Your Health) Program to address the nutritional welfare of the pupils in her school. Principal Jasmine reported that the *Lakas Ko, Kalusugan Mo* is now a successful ongoing program that involves pupils, parents, and school teachers, actively working together to provide sustainable means for the school's feeding program.

Undoubtedly these three exemplars show that the most important contribution of Education Action Research lies in its ability to ask questions to draw upon local knowledge and practitioner experience to bring about changes in the educational system that contribute to positive social change both within, and beyond, the educational system. This research inspires us all to recommit ourselves to the notion of education as a basic human right and a source for positive social change and to reach out to one another to support this effort in our own communities and around the world. But doing so requires us to address some specific challenges to the continued development of EAR as a valid and vital contributor to our understanding of educational practices.

TACKLING THE CHALLENGES FACING EDUCATIONAL ACTION RESEARCH

One of our hopes in writing this chapter is to provide a clear and compelling case for Educational Action Research to other scholars and practitioners in the field. Too often, research methods courses still overlook EAR as an important contributor to our understanding of educational practice. Or, if it is included in teacher education programs, it is often seen by other scholars as a less rigorous form of research intended primarily to engage teachers in a kind of imposed self-improvement process. In this way there is the potential for what should be an open-ended, process-oriented approach to be co-opted in the interests of using teacher inquiry to advance externally defined objectives designed to advance political agendas around teaching and schooling. This can be countered by keeping teachers and students at the center of the research process.

If Educational Action Research is to reach its full potential as a source of critical, emancipatory understandings of the ways in which education can contribute to addressing issues of oppression and inequality, our approaches to teacher education must reflect the same kinds of respect for the knowledge our own students bring to our classrooms, and a willingness to challenge our institutions to create space and support for diverse student populations. And we must build strong international partnerships that celebrate cultural differences and create space for the voices of researchers, teachers, students, and community partners to enrich and deepen our understanding of the challenges and contributions of Educational Action Researchers around the world to the cause of creating rich educational opportunities for all.

REFERENCES

Brydon-Miller, M. (2001). Education, research, and action: Theory and methods of participatory research. In D. L. Tolman and M. Brydon-Miller (Eds) *From Subjects to Subjectivities: A handbook of interpretive and participatory methods* (pp. 76–89). New York: New York University Press.

Brydon-Miller, M., Davids, I., Jaitli, N., Lykes, M. B., Schensul, J., and Williams, S. (2009). Popular education and action research. In S. Noffke and B. Somekh (Eds) *The SAGE Handbook Of Educational Action Research* (pp. 495–507). Los Angeles: Sage.

Brydon-Miller, M., Greenwood, D., and Maguire, P. (2003). Why action research? *Action Research*, 1(1), 9–28.

Brydon-Miller, M., Maguire, P., and MacIntyre, A. (2004). *Traveling Companions: Feminism, teaching, and action research*. Westport, CT: Greenwood Press.

Brydon-Miller, M., Rector Aranda, A., and Stevens, D. (2015). Widening the circle: ethical reflection in action research. In H. Bradbury (Ed.) *The SAGE Handbook of Action Research*, 3rd edition (pp. 596–607). London: Sage.

Caro-Bruce, C., Flessner, R., Klehr, M., and Zeichner, K. (Eds) (2007). *Creating Equitable Classrooms through Action Research*. Thousand Oaks, CA: Corwin Press.

Caro-Bruce, C., Klehr, M., Zeichner, K., and Sierra-Piedrahita, A. M. (2009). A school district-based action research program in the United States. In S. Noffke and B. Somekh (Eds) *The SAGE Handbook of Educational Action Research* (pp. 104–117). Los Angeles: Sage.

Carr, W. and Kemmis, S. (2009). Educational action research: A critical approach. In S. Noffke and B. Somekh (Eds) *The SAGE Handbook of Educational Action Research* (pp. 74–84). Los Angeles: Sage.

Castle, G. (2001). *Postcolonial Discourses: An anthology*. Oxford: Blackwell.

Cochran-Smith, M. and Lytle, S. (2009). *Inquiry as Stance: Practitioner research for the next generation*. New York: Teachers College Press.

Coghlan, D. (2011). Action research: Exploring perspectives on a philosophy of practical knowledge. *Academy of Management Annals*, 5(1), 53–87.

Coghlan, D. (2013). Developing the scholar-practitioner. *DLSU Business Notes and Briefings*, 1(1), 1–6.

Coghlan, D. and Brannick, T. (2014). *Doing Action Research in Your Own Organization*, 4th edition. London: Sage.

Coghlan, D. and Brydon-Miller, M. (2014). *The SAGE Encyclopedia of Action Research*. London: Sage.

Darder, A., Baltodano, M. P., and Torres, R. D. (2009). *The Critical Pedagogy Reader*, 2nd edition. New York: Routledge.

Dewey, J. (1916). *Democracy and Education*. New York: Macmillan.

Dewey, J. (1938). *Logic: The theory of inquiry*. New York: Henry Holt.

Dixson, A. D. and Rousseau, C. K. (2006). *Critical Race Theory in Education: All God's children got a song*. New York: Routledge.

Elliot, J. (2007). *Reflecting Where the Action Is: The selected works of John Elliot*. London: Routledge.

Freire, P. (1998). *Teachers as Cultural Workers: Letters to those who dare teach*. Boulder, CO: Westview Press.

Freire, P. (2000). *Pedagogy of the Oppressed*. New York: Bloomsbury. (Original work published in 1970).

Giroux, H. A. (2011). *On Critical Pedagogy*. London: Bloomsbury Academic.

Habermas, J. (1984). *The Theory of Communicative Action (Volumes 1 and 2)*. Boston, MA: Beacon Press.

Horton, M. and Freire, P. (1990). *We Make the Road by Walking: Conversations on education and social change*. Philadelphia: Temple University Press.

Lewin, K. (1946). Action research and minority problems. *Journal of Social Issues*, 2(4), 34–46.

Maguire, P. (1987). *Doing Participatory Research: A feminist approach*. Amherst, MA: University of Massachusetts, Center for International Education.

Nieto, S. (2009). *Language, Culture, and Teaching: Critical perspectives*, 2nd edition. New York: Routledge.

Noffke, S. (1997). Professional, personal, and political dimensions of action research. In M. W. Apple (Ed.) *Review of Research in Education, 22* (pp. 305–343). New York: American Educational Research Association.

Noffke, S. (2009). Revisiting the professional, personal, and political dimensions of action research. In S. Noffke and B. Somekh (Eds) *The SAGE Handbook Of Educational Action Research* (pp. 6–23). Los Angeles: Sage.

Noffke, S. and Brennan, M. (2014). Educational action research. In D. Coghlan and M. Brydon-Miller (Eds) *The SAGE Encyclopedia of Action Research* (pp. 285–288). London: Sage.

Parker, L., Deyhle, D., and Villenas, S. (1999). *Race is … Race isn't: Critical race theory and qualitative studies in education*. Boulder, CO: Westview Press.

Piggot-Irvine, E., Rowe, W., and Ferkins, L. (2015). Conceptualizing indicator domains for evaluating action research. *Educational Action Research*. DOI:10.1080/09650792.2015.1042984.

Reason, P. and Bradbury, H. (2001). *Handbook of Action Research: Participative inquiry and practice*. London: Sage.

Sagor, R. (2005). *The Action Research Guidebook: A four-step process for educators and school teams*. Thousand Oaks, CA: Corwin Press.

Somekh, B. (2003). Theory and passion in action research. *Educational Action Research*, 11(2), 247–264.

Stenhouse, L. (1983). *Authority, Education, and Emancipation: A collection of papers by Lawrence Stenhouse*. London: Heinemann Educational Books.

Stoecker, R. and Brydon-Miller, M. (2013). Action research. In A. Trainor and E. Graue (Eds) *Reviewing Qualitative Research in the Social Sciences* (pp. 21–37). New York: Routledge.

Stringer, E. (2008). *Action Research in Education*. New Jersey: Pearson Education.

Tandon, R. (2002). *Participatory Research: Revisiting the roots*. Kelowna, Canada: Mosaic Books.

Zeichner, K. (2003). Teacher research as professional development for P-12 educators in the USA. *Educational Action Research*, 11(2), 301–326.

22

Systematic Review and Meta-Analysis

Sandy Oliver and Janice Tripney

An important way to make full use of high quality empirical studies by systemically combining findings from different studies to address a new set of research questions.

Many of us have ideas about the causes underlying problems, such as low academic achievement, or what works best to solve them, possibly favouring phonics-based instruction over whole language approaches to literacy. Under these circumstances it is all too easy to be convinced by confirmatory evidence we happen to come across, even if that evidence is not particularly reliable, and without looking for contradictory evidence. Worse, when looking for all the relevant studies, not just those reporting desirable outcomes, contradictory evidence may well be more difficult to find. Disappointing findings from a well-designed study (disappointing in that an exciting new programme did not live up to expectations) are less likely to be submitted or accepted for publication, especially in a high profile journal, than studies with positive findings. In addition, studies demonstrating a significant treatment effect are also more likely to be published in English, and more likely to be cited by others. This problem is known as publication bias (Egger and Smith, 1998). Because such haphazard approaches to publishing and reading studies poses a serious threat for advancing education research, reliable systematic reviews include extensive searches for primary studies, including unpublished evidence, and investigate whether their own findings may have been influenced by a bias towards publishing more positive results (Banks et al., 2012; Torgerson, 2006). In addition to the problem of readily available studies tending to offer positive findings, is the risk of encountering misleading findings from studies that have been poorly designed or poorly conducted, or limited findings from research taking a particular approach or conducted in a particular context.

Research methodologies for systematically identifying, appraising and synthesising existing research have been developed to overcome these challenges. An array of methods is now available for answering research questions, not with single studies, but with multiple studies. These multiple studies, if similar, can be aggregated to ascertain the consistency (or inconsistency) of their findings. Alternatively, studies addressing the same issue but in different ways or different contexts, can be configured to present a more comprehensive and detailed picture than is available from a single study alone. The following two sections consider first the principles underpinning analyses of multiple studies and then how these principles translate into practical steps for different review approaches. The subsequent three sections describe in more detail approaches to systematic reviewing for three different purposes: for testing associations and causal relationships, for generating theory and for exploring evidence within an existing theory or framework. Of these, more attention is paid to reviews of effects as these are more commonly advocated for informing decisions about education. Finally we consider the accepted standards in systematic reviewing and argue for adopting participatory approaches in order to take into account variations in context and values.

THE PRINCIPLES DRIVING ANALYSES OF MULTIPLE STUDIES

Reviewing systematically and synthesising existing literature is largely an applied science. A key purpose is to pool dispersed knowledge for the convenience of readers making policy, practice or personal decisions. For instance, when applied to policy decisions, research may be pooled systematically to advance understanding of problems being faced, to consider the viability of various options and to inform the implementation of collective endeavours (Lavis, 2009).

Systematic reviews address the problem that any single primary study, even if well-designed and executed, might be too small, poorly conducted, have spurious results, offer results from one particular perspective, or not share the same context as a reader considering a decision they face in their professional or personal life. The remedy is to accumulate evidence across many studies. This leads to a larger sample from which one might choose those studies that are better methodologically, and the opportunity to make use of an 'average' result, thereby reducing the influence of spurious studies. Alternatively, analysing more studies offers the opportunity to learn about how contextual factors, such as neighbourhood deprivation, may influence the implementation or effectiveness of a programme by comparing studies conducted in a range of contexts.

Such comprehensive summaries are required when clarifying and taking stock of what we know from science (Hunt, 1997), or when encouraging others to use available evidence in decisions that affect other people's lives. An example of the latter is the Sutton Trust-EEF Teaching and Learning *Toolkit*, which summarises educational research from the UK and around the world. This Toolkit, which prioritises systematic reviews of research and meta-analyses of experimental studies, is used by a growing number of teachers and schools to make best use of their resources to improve the attainment of pupils (Higgins et al., 2015).

Decision-makers cannot take their responsibility seriously if, when reading research reports or reviews, they cannot exercise any judgment over the information they allow to influence them. In this respect systematic reviews offer a number of advantages over traditional literature reviews. A key principle to reviewing research systematically is to do so transparently, so that readers can see how the literature has been framed, judged and summarised before conclusions have been drawn. An expectation that the methods will be explained and justified supports the definition of a systematic review as a review of research literature using systematic, explicit methods that are accountable to whoever paid for the review and whoever wants to use it (Gough et al., 2012). A term often used synonymously with *systematic review* is *research synthesis* (Cooper and Hedges, 1994). A dictionary definition of *synthesis* is 'the putting together of parts or elements so as to make up a complex whole; the combination of immaterial or abstract things, or of elements into an ideal or abstract whole' (OED Online, 2015). The term synthesis can be applied to the whole process or to the last stage alone in a systematic review.

Neither the definitions for systematic review and synthesis, nor the principle of transparency, are restricted to reviewing any particular type of study, although the practicalities of applying the principle may differ when inspecting studies of different designs or from different disciplines. Despite this, the term 'systematic review', for many people, brings to mind a particular type of review: a statistical meta-analysis, which pools the quantitative measures from similar studies (Glass et al., 1981; Hedges and Olkin, 1985). These types of reviews have been well developed methodologically to answer particular types of question with particular designs of studies, typically but not exclusively, controlled trials, that may or may not be randomised. They serve the purpose of testing well formulated hypotheses about the causes underlying problems, such as low academic achievement, or what works best to solve them. The latter estimate the impact of intervening in a particular way, and the degree of (un)certainty about the measure. Academics working in other methodological areas have sometimes equated this approach with all that systematic reviewing has to offer and therefore view it as irrelevant to their own work. However, as a set of statistical methods for combining effect estimates from individual studies, meta-analysis is only one of many diverse approaches to systematic reviewing that can be distinguished (Gough et al., 2012). Just as primary research benefits from a range of methodologies, so does systematic reviewing.

This chapter describes a spectrum of approaches to systematic reviewing that reaches from statistical meta-analysis to qualitative analysis such as thematic synthesis or meta-ethnography, with mixed methods syntheses in between. It recognises that people making decisions in the classroom, school office or local government may benefit from ready access to reviews that: clarify the nature and scale of a problem; explore the policy options in terms of the impact, feasibility or acceptability; or reveal challenges and offer solutions for implementing policy decisions (see Lavis, 2009 for a similar argument in health systems). Each of these steps in a policymaking process need radically different approaches to learning from the literature, differences that spring from the fundamentals of research methodology, as illustrated below.

For instance, a question asking 'What is the quantitative evidence for the impact of teaching thinking skills on pupils' attainment and attitudes in schools?' is well served by a statistical meta-analysis (Higgins et al., 2005). This meta-analysis identified all the similar studies addressing this question, aggregated their findings and reported an average, weighted by the size of each included study. This is analogous to hill walkers as they pass a turning point, each piling up an additional stone. The resulting cairn grows taller with successive walkers – and those behind, seeing a larger cairn, are more confident of the direction of travel.

A very different systematic review asked 'through what processes does the school environment (social and physical) influence student health outcomes?' (Jamal et al., 2013). This adopted a qualitative approach to reviewing. Configuring the findings of primary studies in this way is analogous to constructing a mosaic with pieces of broken tile to offer a meaningful picture of what the research is telling us.

Between these two extremes is the opportunity to take a mixed methods approach to systematic reviewing. This approach was used in a review that usefully collated the learning about young people's access to tobacco, where a synthesis of qualitative evidence of young people's views was presented alongside a statistical meta-analysis of survey data (Sutcliffe et al., 2011). *Aggregating* the survey data and *configuring* the qualitative data ensured the review benefited from both indicative and explanatory findings of the primary studies to offer a meaningful but imprecise picture of what the research is telling us. Combining the two generated additional learning, and identified gaps in our knowledge.

This spectrum of approaches is illustrated in Figure 22.1. On the left hand side are typical approaches to reviewing in order to generate theory to advance understanding or offer enlightenment for decisions (for example, meta-ethnography or thematic synthesis); on the right-hand side are typical approaches to reviewing in order to test theory with measures of association or causality (for example, statistical meta-analysis); and between the two are typical approaches for exploring options bearing in mind existing priorities, constraints or tentative theory (for example, framework synthesis, realist synthesis). The gradient in the shading implies that the boundaries between these different approaches are not clear cut. Although the different approaches share similar principles, because they are conducted for different purposes using different types of studies they differ in

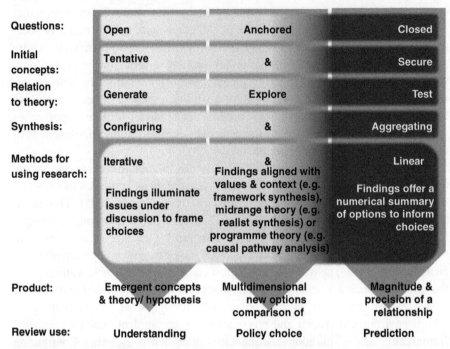

Figure 22.1 Spectrum of approaches to systematic reviewing research literatures

practical terms. The practical steps they share are described immediately below; how they differ in practice is described in each subsequent section addressing three different approaches to systematic reviewing.

THE PRACTICALITIES OF SYSTEMATIC REVIEWING

Conducting systematic reviews involves a number of key steps (Figure 22.2). To get started there is intellectual work to be done: exploring the problems being faced and the role of research in addressing it; developing a clear, important and answerable research question and the conceptual framework to shape the review; and deciding the work to be done, the scale and detail. Alongside the intellectual effort is organisational work of engaging people with a stake in the review or its findings, and building a team capable of completing the work. Of course, the intellectual and organisational tasks overlap as the aim is engage the stakeholders in the intellectual task of shaping the review in light of their understanding of the problems they face. The technical tasks involve identifying relevant studies, describing and synthesising them in terms of the conceptual framework and appraising the relevance and quality of the evidence to draw reliable conclusions.

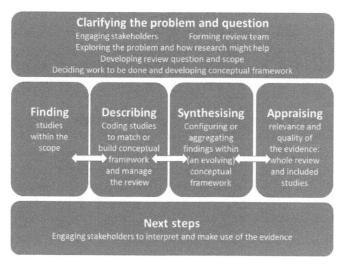

Figure 22.2 Key steps in conducting systematic reviews (Gough et al., forthcoming)

The final stage of considering the implications of the findings is better done in discussion with stakeholders who are well placed to make use of the findings. Precisely how each task is done, and in what order, varies depending on the type of question being asked. For instance, individual studies may be appraised when applying a quality threshold prior to synthesis (common when testing causal relationships) or during synthesis (when building theory). In contrast, appraisal following synthesis is applied to bodies of literature to assess the heterogeneity of studies and the confidence that can be placed in the findings (Guyatt et al 2008; Lewin et al 2015).

The following sections take systematic reviewing approaches from different positions on the spectrum (Figure 22.1) in turn and consider their core principles and the practical differences in how those principles are applied; namely differences in how evidence is identified, appraised and synthesised. In doing so, they also consider the role of conceptual frameworks in systematic reviews, and how they are constructed, whether these are employed as *hypotheses* to be tested, final products of a review, or ways of seeing problems and solutions that evolve during the review process.

SYSTEMATIC REVIEWS FOR TESTING HYPOTHESES

Reviews that collect empirical data to test hypotheses about associations or causal relationships can be thought of as using an 'aggregative' logic, in which they are adding up (aggregating) and averaging similar forms of data (Gough et al., 2012). The best known aggregative approaches are reviews of intervention effects based on causal analyses. Understanding causation is at the heart of the term 'impact evaluation'. A recent example of this type of review is a study which evaluated the impact of different truancy interventions on school attendance of chronic truant students (Maynard et al., 2013). An aggregative approach is also appropriate for systematic reviews assessing associative relationships between variables, such as the correlation between socioeconomic status (SES) and academic achievement (Sirin, 2005) or between amount of time spent on homework and academic achievement (Cooper et al., 2006).

For reviews that test hypotheses, rigour is enhanced by choosing in advance the type of studies to be included without being influenced by prior knowledge of research findings from relevant primary studies. In practice reviewers may be familiar with some of the relevant studies before they start, but they can still establish clear criteria for including or excluding studies for their review. To answer questions about the effects of interventions, establishing criteria for eligible studies means specifying the types of studies that are considered appropriate and valid for making causal inferences. Increasing the scope of an evidence-based approach to areas outside health care, such as to education, has renewed the importance of a long-standing discussion about which quantitative study designs are valid for causal inference, and which can provide only evidence of association. While randomised control trials (RCTs) will usually be the most internally valid method for assessing a causal relationship, it is increasingly being shown in practice that well-implemented quasi-experimental designs based on statistical methods are able to yield unbiased and comparable results (Cook et al., 2008; Hansen et al., 2011; Konnerup and Kongsted, 2012; Shadish et al., 2002).

Box 22.1 presents details of evaluation designs commonly included in an effectiveness review.

Choosing between these study designs is a decision for each review. Here, there are three main options:

- Exclude studies from which drawing causal inferences is less justified (for example, setting the bar at RCTs and rigorous quasi-experimental designs only). The consequent benefit of this approach is conclusions drawn from the findings of methodologically appropriate studies. Being too restrictive, however, may limit the ability to generalise, and another potential drawback is an empty or near empty review.
- Include all relevant studies in the review. Not limiting inclusion to particular study designs allows researchers to draw on a broader range of evidence, and provides more detailed information on the methodological weaknesses and inconsistencies of existing studies, and where there are research gaps. A clear drawback is that the findings from studies using different designs and methods of analysis may vary, and being too inclusive may increase the potential for including evidence that is misleading and so weaken the confidence that can be placed in the review findings. One solution is to separate evidence of correlations (or associations) from evidence of causality, with implications for policy drawn only from the latter. Another is to test whether the results differ depending on the study designs or methods (that is, sensitivity analysis or sub-group analysis) – more of this later.
- Include all relevant studies in the review while going no further than commenting on their design and methods. The emphasis here is on devolving responsibility for evaluating the implications for the review's overall conclusions to the reader.

Box 22.1   Examples of study designs included in reviews of effectiveness

- **Randomised controlled trial:** A study where the investigators allocate individuals (or other units such as classes or schools) at random – using centralised methods of randomisation, such as computer-generated allocation – to receive one of two or more interventions. One of these interventions is the standard of comparison, or control. The power of random assignment as a technique lies in accounting for all known and unknown extraneous variables by equating the groups at the start of an experiment.
- **Non-randomised controlled trial:** A study where the investigators allocate individuals (or other units) to receive one of two or more interventions using a method that is not random. One of these interventions is the standard of comparison, or control. Allocation may be pseudo-random or quasi-random (for example, by date of birth (odd or even dates), day of the week, medical record number, the date at which they are invited to participate in the study (odd or even dates), or allocating individuals alternately into the different study groups). These studies have a greater risk of bias than randomised trials because those enrolling study participants are able to predict the group to which the next enrolled person will be allocated, and can undermine studies by, for example, pressing invitations on individuals who have more to gain from the intervention being offered, or ignoring those who they think may not respond well.
- **Controlled before-and-after studies:** A study in which observations are made before and after the implementation of an intervention, both in a group that receives the intervention and in a control group that does not. Allocation to the different groups is not made by the investigators (for example, study comparing beneficiaries and non-beneficiaries of a training programme, where the trainees self-selected into the programme). These studies have a high risk of bias on account of unidentified baseline differences between the intervention and control groups that may affect changes in the outcome measure.
- **Interrupted time series:** A study – with or without a non-equivalent comparison group – that collects data at multiple time-points before and after an intervention (the 'interruption') in order to detect whether the intervention has had an 'effect' significantly greater than any underlying trend over time. A number of statistical techniques (for example, segmented regression analysis) can be used to analyse the data, depending on the number of data points available and other factors.

Without random assignment, groups being compared are less likely to be equivalent before the intervention. Designs that do not use randomised methods of allocating participants into intervention and control groups can be improved by using matching and/or statistical controls.

- **Comparisons with matched groups:** A non-randomised study in which individuals (or other units) receiving one of two or more interventions are compared after being matched on the measure of interest, such as attainment, time-invariant variables, such as relevant demographic characteristics (using observables, or propensity scores), and/or according to a cut-off on an ordinal or continuous variable (regression discontinuity design).
- **Accounting for differences between groups statistically:** A study in which individuals (or other units) are non-randomly allocated to receive one of two or more interventions, with statistical procedures (for example, multivariate or instrumental variables regression) used to control for differences between groups.

Identifying and describing studies for testing hypotheses

For reviews that intend to test a hypothesis or theory, the aim is to identify all or a representative sample of studies, similar to primary research where aggregating research seeks complete or statistically representative populations. With primary research, some populations are harder to reach: typically those that are rare, marginalised, stigmatised or not associated with mainstream structures (Marpsat and Razafindratsima, 2012). Similarly, for systematic reviews, some studies are harder to find because they are unfamiliar to some readers in their conceptualisation or language, report disappointing findings or are published in obscure places. The solution for reviews that are predominantly aggregative has been to seek all relevant research to minimise the threat to validity presented by a biased set of studies (Egger et al., 2001). This requires extensive, if not exhaustive, searches of bibliographic databases, specialist websites and library catalogues, journals, conference proceedings, dissertation abstracts and other sources, using electronic and hand-searching methods. Challenges specific to searching for literature in education, including a diverse literature, a lack of precise or agreed terminology, and a great variety and variability of bibliographic tools, have prompted a growing body of methodological research that can assist the social science reviewer when devising a comprehensive search strategy (Grayson and Gomersall, 2003; Mehdyzadeh, 2004; Papaionnou et al., 2010; Schucan Bird and Tripney, 2011). Detailed guidance for finding effectiveness studies in areas such as education is available from the Campbell Collaboration (Hammerstrøm et al., 2010). The principle of transparency requires matching clear descriptions of the studies to the inclusion criteria.

Appraising studies for testing hypotheses

Once studies have been assessed as meeting the inclusion criteria and clearly described, the next step is to identify potential biases affecting the reliability of the studies included in a review (internal validity) or limitations in the applicability of the studies to the research question or other settings (external validity). This process, called critical appraisal (or assessing risk of bias or quality assessment), determines how much weight is placed on the evidence of each study included in the final synthesis, and is essential because variations in the study design and conceptualisation of the problem and execution can affect the conclusions about the existing evidence (Gough, 2007). There are many published tools that are specifically designed for use in systematic reviews, each incorporating criteria relevant to design features of the particular studies being evaluated. Examples of well-known tools for assessing randomised controlled trials include the Cochrane Risk of Bias tool (Higgins et al., 2011) and the Jadad Scale (Jadad et al., 1996). These were used in recently published reviews investigating school-based education programmes for the prevention of child sexual abuse (Walsh et al., 2015) and interventions that can help reduce consumption of sugar-sweetened beverages in children (Avery et al., 2015) respectively. A large number of other appraisal tools are available, including those developed for quasi-experimental designs, though few have been rigorously developed or tested for validity and reliability.

Accuracy is maximised when the quality assessment is conducted by two or more reviewers working independently before comparing their judgements, and the results reported for each individual study. Subsequently there is a decision to be made about how the outcome of the critical appraisal exercise will be taken into consideration in the synthesis. Again, there are a number of options: set the quality threshold bar high a priori and include only studies judged to be of 'low risk of bias' in the synthesis; include all studies that were subject to quality appraisal and carry out sensitivity analyses and/or report results separately, according to risk of bias judgements; or include all studies in the synthesis and leave it to the reader to decide if the conclusions of the review are compromised.

Synthesising studies for testing hypotheses

Options for synthesising evidence for testing hypotheses include using statistical techniques to pool data from studies (meta-analysis), noting how many individual studies show a statistically significant result (vote-counting), and presenting the findings as a narrative and in summary tables. The preferred quantitative method for synthesising research results is meta-analysis, as developed in its current guise by Gene Glass and others. In the three decades or more since Glass' original meta-analytic work on psychotherapy (Smith and Glass, 1977) and class size (Glass and Smith, 1979), the concepts of meta-analysis have been developed and applied to a rapidly growing number of educational topics. A recent search of the ERIC database identified almost 3,000 articles published since 1980 that use or discuss meta-analysis. One such review is that by Cooper et al. (2006) who used meta-analysis to synthesise research conducted in the United States over the period 1987–2003 on the effects of homework on measures of student achievement. The remainder of this section provides an overview of meta-analysis. The aim is to briefly outline what it involves in practice, including some cautions and caveats to its use, rather than provide detailed explanations of procedures, which are elaborated elsewhere. Those wishing to apply meta-analytic procedures should consult the full overviews of meta-analysis that are available (for example, Borenstein et al., 2009; Cooper, 2016; Cooper et al., 2008; Durlak and Lipsey, 1991; Lipsey and Wilson, 2001).

The heart of meta-analysis is the effect size, a standardised, scale-free measure of the relative size of an 'effect', which is computed for each outcome of interest. Measures of the uncertainty and precision of the estimated effect size, its confidence intervals and standard error, are typically also calculated. There are many different types of effect sizes, but they fall into two main categories, those looking at the magnitude and direction of the difference between groups and those looking at measures of association between variables. Crucially, this is information that cannot be obtained solely by focusing on a particular p-value, since a p-value obtained in a research study is a function of both sample size and effect size (Sullivan and Feinn, 2012).

The type of metric used in a meta-analysis will depend on the type of outcome variable being measured. In the case of continuous dependent variables, like test scores, the usual approach is to calculate the standardised mean difference (SMD) using the reported means and standard deviations, though it can also be computed from other summary data, such as a t-test.. Cohen's term d is an example of this type of effect size index. For dichotomous outcomes like school attendance, it is usually the risk ratio (RR) or odds ratio (OR) that are calculated. Formulae that allow different effect size measures to be calculated are detailed in specialist texts on statistics (for example, Borenstein and Hedges, 2016; Cumming, 2012) including those for cluster-randomised designs (Hedges, 2007). To facilitate the computation of effect sizes there are also a number of web-based effect-size calculators, such as www.cem.org/effect-size-calculator, developed by the Centre for Evaluation and Monitoring at Durham University. Some websites also provide the means for transforming one metric into another (for example, SMDs into r). Finally, specialist software to conduct meta-analyses include Comprehensive Meta-Analysis (www.meta-analysis.com/), EPPI-Reviewer (http://eppi.ioe.ac.uk/cms/Default.aspx?alias=eppi.ioe.ac.uk/cms/er4), and the Cochrane Collaboration's Review Manager (http://tech.cochrane.org/revman).

When appropriate, the effect size measures are combined across studies and represented graphically in a forest plot to provide an overall measure of 'effect'. This involves taking a weighted average of the effect sizes across the different studies, and testing whether this estimate is significantly different from a null 'effect'. The weight is based on the standard error (specifically, the inverse of the squared standard error), and is employed so that studies with larger sample sizes are weighted more, as are those with greater precision (Lipsey and Wilson, 2001).

Although meta-analysis has many advantages over other methods of research synthesis, it is not always feasible or appropriate to conduct a meta-analysis. First, it is significantly more demanding than other research synthesis methods in terms of the reported outcome data required for analysis. The independence, data quality and adequacy of statistical reporting in primary studies is very variable. The validity and reliability of outcome measures may also be variable and not reported in any great detail. There are procedures for dealing with these problems, including imputing single values for missing estimates (for example, the mean), contacting the primary investigators to obtain additional data or clarification, and reporting the implications of data deficiencies. However, in some circumstances, the use of meta-analytics techniques may not be the best approach. Second, meta-analysis may be compromised by heterogeneity of its results. A common criticism of meta-analyses is that they often combine different kinds of studies in the same analysis. Individual studies that are brought together in a meta-analysis seeking answers to questions about the efficacy of education interventions, for example, will inevitably differ in at least some of their characteristics, with the potential for a mix of comparisons of different study designs, populations, interventions, settings and/or outcomes. In addition, the methods of calculating effects may not be the same across included studies. The challenge for the reviewer is deciding just how similar the studies need to be in order to pool in the same meta-analysis. If confidence intervals for the results of individual studies (generally depicted in the forest plot using horizontal lines) have poor overlap, this may indicate the presence of statistical heterogeneity. Statistical tests to assess whether the observed variability in study results (effect sizes) is larger than expected from sampling error alone are also available, such as the commonly used Q-test (Higgins and Thompson, 2002). Despite the existence of such tests, however, decisions concerning which studies should and should not be combined are inevitably subjective.

If (statistical) heterogeneity is identified it is important to carry out a number of checks, including checking the data are correct and that the most appropriate effect size measure was selected. It is also clearly of interest to determine the causes of heterogeneity, while bearing in mind that investigations of heterogeneity when there are very few studies are of questionable value. Ideally having specified a priori (that is, in the protocol of a review) what might cause the results of studies to differ, meta-analysis techniques can be used to examine potential variation in 'effects' due to characteristics of the study (for example, sample size), participants (for example, gender), intervention (for example, intensity), outcome measure (for example, choice of scale) or setting (for example, geographic area). Heterogeneity may be explored by conducting sub-group analyses using categorical models analogous to ANOVA (Lipsey and Wilson, 2001) or meta-regression, a more sophisticated tool for exploring heterogeneity involving a merging of meta-analytic and linear regression principles (Baker et al., 2009). Information on statistical methods for examining heterogeneity are available (for example, Deeks et al., 2001; Hedges and Pigott, 2004).

Despite the potential advantages of meta-analysis, the use and interpretation of effect sizes is not straightforward. For example, if studies included in a meta-analysis are based on a biased sample of all relevant studies, then the overall 'effect' computed by this meta-analysis will reflect this bias (Rothstein et al., 2005). Methods to assess the impact of missing studies on the results of the meta-analysis include visual tools such as funnel plots that plot effect size against standard error, and regression tests (Duval and Tweedie, 2000; Egger et al., 1997). A further challenge is that, once estimated, the reviewer must give some consideration to what the pooled estimate of 'effect' actually means, for the effect size itself is simply a number. Again, this is a subjective process. Cohen (1988) classified effect sizes as *small* ($d = 0.2$), *medium* ($d = 0.5$), and *large* ($d \geq 0.8$), and these benchmark categories have become part of the orthodoxy of effect size interpretation. However, although these designations can provide a general guide, they should be used with some caution, as they do not take into account other variables, such as the research context, costs and practicalities of implementing an intervention, and the value attached to any benefits associated with it (Durlak, 2009).

If used appropriately, meta-analysis provides a powerful set of tools for integrating the results of studies on the same topic. In some systematic reviews, however, insufficient data are available or studies are not sufficiently similar to allow a statistical approach to synthesis. This creates a challenge for the reviewer. As an alternative, some reviews use a vote-counting approach that focuses on the statistical significance of the primary studies to draw conclusions about the literature as a whole (Light and Smith, 1971). Despite the intuitive appeal of vote counting, it has serious failings as an inference procedure. It is limited in that it does not provide information about the size of the overall 'effect' or the consistency of 'effects' across studies. It also fails to take into consideration the dependence of statistical significance on sample size (Thompson, 2007). Given that most primary studies in education research are conducted with low statistical power, it can be very misleading to simply rely on statistical significance to gauge whether a relationship exists (Hedges and Olkin, 1980). The weaknesses of vote-counting were illustrated over 20 years ago by Hedges et al. (1994) who used meta-analysis to re-analyse data from a series of earlier reviews using this approach. Challenging Hanushek's widely cited conclusion that 'there is no strong or systematic relationship between school expenditures and student performance' (Hanushek, 1989: 47), Hedges concluded that the relationship between resource inputs and student outcomes was consistent and positive.

Systematic narrative methods of synthesis can also be used to synthesise quantitative studies when the studies included in a systematic review do not provide the necessary data for calculating effect sizes or are not sufficiently similar for a meta-analysis to be appropriate. By going beyond a simple summary of findings from individual studies (typically used in traditional, non-systematic narrative reviews), such reviews seek to generate new findings and recommendations (Snilstveit et al., 2012). Like the vote-counting method of aggregating studies, however, narrative reviewing cannot be conclusive regarding causality.

SYSTEMATIC REVIEWS FOR GENERATING THEORY

Although existing systematic reviews more often address questions about the effects of intervening in people's lives, a rational approach to making decisions starts with understanding the nature and scale of the problem, then frames and compares possible solutions, before testing the effects of likely solutions. Primary research offers a broad range of quantitative, qualitative and mixed methodologies for each of these tasks. Studies may involve convening interviews to hear people talk about their experiences and opinions, either individually or in groups – the mainstay of much qualitative research. Longitudinal qualitative research may involve extended interactions with a researcher embedded in a community in order to study it (ethnography) or detailed examination of one or more individual, event, institution, policy, or other 'case' over a sustained period of time (case study), often including quantitative as well as qualitative data. Such studies build theory from collecting and analysing rich sets of data.

Methods for drawing out the learning from multiple studies such as these were developed in the social sciences to develop theory rather than test it. Indeed, it was in the area of education that efforts were first made to extract concepts, metaphors and themes from different reports, then interpret and synthesize these into a 'line of argument'. This first example analysed school inspection reports to generate learning about school leadership (Noblit and Hare, 1988). This approach is the basis of meta-ethnography, which continues to inform our understanding of education. For instance, a meta-ethnography of English language learning synthesised 25 studies to emphasise the key roles played by four classroom teaching practices: instruction built around community; protracted language events for maximizing verbal activity; building on prior knowledge; and using multiple multimedia alongside text (Téllez and Waxman, 2006). More recently, a meta-ethnography of qualitative studies investigated through what processes the school environment (social and physical) influences young people's health (Jamal et al., 2013). From 19 studies they identified four overarching themes: aggressive behaviour and substance use as a source of status and bonding at schools where students feel educationally marginalised or unsafe; health-risk behaviours concentrated in unsupervised 'hotspots' at the school; positive relationships with teachers being critical in promoting student wellbeing and limiting risk behaviour; and unhappiness at school prompting students to 'escape' through unauthorized absence or through substance use.

Identifying studies for generating theory

When seeking data for examining processes or meanings (rather than testing hypotheses) the intention is not to seek representative samples of people (in primary studies) or studies (for reviews). Instead, generating new conceptual understanding relies on access to sufficient cases of people (for primary research) or studies (for reviews) whose characteristics or circumstances vary, within which to identify themes and explore patterns. Instead of an exhaustive search, more appropriate is a theoretical approach to searching to identify a sufficient and appropriate range of studies either through a rolling sampling of studies according to a framework that is developed inductively from the emerging literature (akin to theoretical sampling in primary research) (Strauss and Corbin, 1990). In practice, many reviews for generating theory start with a list of appropriate sources of studies and lists of key concepts translated into commonly used terms, just as is done for reviews testing causal relationships. However, authors may argue that, analogous to qualitative primary studies, a smaller choice of sources and terms may be appropriate and, having found a set of studies to analyse, they may focus more on the concepts therein, analysing themes until they reach saturation. In practice, reviewers of qualitative studies have not been able to rely on electronic searches of bibliographic databases as social science is frequently reported in sources that are not indexed electronically – books, chapters and informal publications ('grey' literature). Screening titles and abstracts in library catalogues, the contents pages of journals, and on websites, as well as asking authors of relevant papers if they know of more studies, can be very productive (Thomas and Harden, 2008).

Appraising studies for generating theory

Particularly helpful for generating theory are rich qualitative studies. Judging the quality of qualitative research remains contentious: whether to do it at all; to do so using clear criteria; to exclude poorer quality studies; or to qualify their findings in a synthesis. An assessment tool employed by the EPPI-Centre at UCL Institute of Education was built on the literature about the quality of qualitative research and subsequently developed over successive systematic reviews addressing young people's lives (Thomas and Harden, 2008; Rees et al., 2011). It is less a tool for applying explicit principles or standards by which a study may be judged, and more a tool for structuring a reviewer's judgement about quality (see Box 22.2). As such, the tool, together with its questions and guidance, supports reviewers preparing a narrative judgment about the quality of a study.

Two recent reviews have commented on the implications of using such a tool to exclude studies judged to be less methodologically appropriate based on their reports. In their meta-ethnography, Jamal et al. (2013) noted that some of the conceptually rich data could have been excluded from their synthesis because some methodological approaches (for example, interviews/focus groups) and certain academic disciplines (for example, anthropology) tend to report their methods less transparently. Rees et al. (2011) took this a step further by checking what themes would have been lost to our understanding of how young children view obesity, body size, shape and weight. In that review the themes evident in the six lowest quality studies were all supported by a number of other, higher quality studies. Excluding the lowest quality studies would not have modified the findings a great deal although, because of their focus, the findings relating specifically to girls, very overweight and very young children would have been weaker.

Box 22.2   Questions to assess the quality of a study about children's views

- Were steps taken to increase rigour in the sampling?
- Were steps taken to increase rigour in the data collected?
- Were steps taken to increase rigour in the analysis of the data?
- Were the findings of the study grounded in/supported by the data?
- Please rate the findings of the study in terms of their breadth and depth.
- To what extent does the study privilege the perspectives and experiences of children?
- Overall, what weight would you assign to this study in terms of the reliability/trustworthiness of its findings?
- What weight would you assign to this study in terms of the usefulness of its findings for this review?

Synthesising the findings of studies for generating theory

How studies have been synthesised is reported with increasing clarity. Meta-ethnography remains similar to the original work of Noblit and Hare (1988). The interpretations and explanations generated by the primary studies are treated as data, analogous to analysing interview transcripts. Jamal et al. (2013) described four steps. The first was reading and re-reading the studies to understand their findings, theories and concepts before constructing the reviewers' interpretation of each study. Second, the studies were grouped according to their main topics and the key concepts from individual studies within each health topic were synthesised within a list overarching themes (meta-themes) for each of the topics. The third step involved synthesising themes across topics, starting with a paper high in methodological quality and/or conceptual richness of findings, then comparing and contrasting the findings with a second study to synthesise their findings, before adding a third, and so on. The final step was interpreting the meta-themes to develop a 'line of argument' or theory about making changes in schools.

Other analytical methods developed for primary research also have their counterparts for analysing existing research rather than primary data. For instance, thematic analysis, widely used in primary research, is mirrored by thematic synthesis for drawing on multiple studies systematically by: coding the text 'line-by-line'; developing 'descriptive themes'; and generating 'analytical themes' which offer new interpretive constructs, explanations or hypotheses (Thomas and Harden, 2008). Thus, syntheses of qualitative studies with overlapping interests can provide more than a summary of each study; they can advance understanding as each study makes complementary contributions to building theory. A very practical application was a thematic synthesis of 15 studies seeking classroom-based interventions to improve the educational achievement of pupils identified as gifted and talented (Bailey et al., 2012). The findings supported the use of personalised learning and differentiation within the classroom; collaborative and group activities; and enrichment programmes for developing self-regulation and higher order thinking skills.

SYSTEMATIC REVIEWS FOR EXPLORING THEORY

Between these two extremes of syntheses that build theory from qualitative studies and syntheses that test theory with quantitative studies, are mixed methods syntheses that explore theories and assumptions. These reviews start with an existing framework or theory to direct the initial search for evidence and progress by amending the initial framework or theory in light of emerging evidence.

Identifying studies for exploring theory

Searching for studies to explore theory shares the principles of searching for studies to generate and test theory. It may start with a clear direction, as for testing theory, but because synthesis is framed in terms of prior assumptions, searching may take a new turn to explore details or fill gaps in the emerging body of knowledge, akin to purposive sampling in primary research (Miles and Huberman, 1994).

Appraising studies for exploring theory

Because reviews exploring theory or assumptions may draw on studies employing methods from different disciplines or methodologies (some of them even within the same study) the focus is on assessing how much confidence can be placed on particular findings. Depending on the conclusions to be drawn, assessment criteria might appropriately include the comparability of different groups within a study (for assessing causal relationships), or they might appropriately include effort to encourage respondents expressing their own opinions and reflections. Thus, assessing the quality of the evidence cannot be isolated from considering the findings.

Synthesising the findings of studies for exploring theory

Syntheses that explore theory neither pre-specify all key concepts (as is required for testing a hypothesis) nor rely wholly on 'open coding' which recognises themes from the included studies (as done when generating innovative theory). Instead, they structure evidence in an initial framework that is informed by prior assumptions, values and constraints, and is subsequently amended in light of new concepts emerging from the data. Such frameworks operate at different levels of detail, as described below.

Differing assumptions held by academics about conceptualisation, theory and empirical investigation have been explored systematically by meta-narrative reviews, initially to understand how novel ideas spread through public service organisations (Greenhalgh et al., 2005). Meta-narrative reviews may offer policymakers a way 'to understand and interpret a conflicting body of research and, therefore, to use it more effectively in their work' (Wong et al., 2014).

The implications of specific policies have been explored with framework synthesis, which applies framework analysis (Ritchie and Spencer, 1994) at the review level. This was the strategy to identify essential components and barriers to success for obesity prevention within the health promoting schools framework (Langford et al., 2015). In this study a framework approach facilitated analysis of intervention process data. Themes identified in advance focused on aspects of process (acceptability, fidelity) while others arose inductively from the data (family involvement, barriers/facilitators). Data from each study was summarised within a matrix comprising the final themes to identify their similarities and differences. Framework synthesis has the advantage of displaying the evidence clearly to readers throughout the research process, allowing the developing framework and emerging findings to be debated with people beyond the research team (Oliver et al., 2008).

Prior assumptions about the consequences of intervening in other people's lives may be developed further into causal pathways, thereby allowing evidence of feasibility, acceptability, effectiveness and costs to be displayed along that pathway. This has been advocated for reviews of international development (Waddington et al., 2012), where it has been called causal chain analysis (Snilstveit, 2012) and applied, for instance, to make sense of large literatures about interventions to enhance girls' education and gender equality in developing countries (Unterhalter et al., 2014). Causal chain analysis is also recommended for systematic reviews of health equity, where education also has an important influence (Welch et al., 2012). Even more detailed investigation of a causal chain involves identifying precise mechanisms (entities, processes or structures) that link interventions and outcomes in various contexts. This is the aim of realist synthesis, which is based on a realist philosophy of science and considers the interaction between context, mechanism and outcome (Wong et al., 2014).

STANDARDS, CONFIDENCE AND VALUES IN SYSTEMATIC REVIEWS

As methodologies for systematic reviewing have matured, so there has grown increasing consensus over what makes a good systematic review. Guidance is available for reporting systematic reviews. The Preferred Reporting Items for Systematic Reviews and Meta-Analyses (PRISMA) statement has focused primarily on randomised controlled trials (Moher et al., 2009) and has been extended to address issues of equity (Welch et al., 2012). Readers of such reviews can be guided by the AMSTAR tool to assess their methodological quality (Shea et al., 2007). Similar publication standards have been developed for meta-narrative reviews (Wong et al., 2013a) and realist reviews (Wong et al., 2013b). Reporting guidelines for meta-ethnography are in development (France et al., 2015).

Application of standards when conducting or appraising systematic reviews is complemented by judging the reliability of the evidence or the confidence that can be placed on the findings. This is necessary because the strength of evidence relies not only on how well a systematic review has been conducted, but also on the studies it finds. Methods are now available to assess what confidence to place in a body of literature, not just in the findings of individual studies. These are available when assessing the evidence about the effects of intervention (Guyatt et al., 2008), and when assessing qualitative evidence for making decisions about health and social intervention (Lewin et al., 2015).

As well as having confidence in how a systematic review and its included studies have been conducted, readers need confidence in the feasibility of applying an intervention to their local setting and the expectation of similar results as shown in a study (the external validity mentioned above). Where the findings of evaluations are fairly consistent across a range of settings they are assumed to be 'generalisable'. However, may studies fail to provide information about key contextual characteristics (Bonell et al., 2006; Ahmad et al., 2010); and where findings are not consistent, interpreting them for use in other contexts is a largely subjective exercise of taking into account characteristics of intervention providers; their host organisations; target populations; local culture, values, norms and resources; and the political environment (Wang et al., 2006).

Consideration of variations in context and values is not simply a task to be tagged on the end of the systematic review process. Rather, implicit or explicit values, assumptions and contexts influence the conduct of systematic reviews. They sensitise analysts to particular issues as they synthesise qualitative studies and influence which hypotheses and frameworks are chosen for testing or exploring theory. Qualitative researchers acknowledge their work as value laden and, being reflexive practitioners, take steps to make those values and their consequences explicit. However, conscious application of values can be a more inclusive process when hypotheses or frameworks are constructed in discussion with people who hold an interest in the funding, delivery or exposure to an intervention. For instance, construction of conceptual frameworks provides a way in for policymakers, teachers and pupils to influence the focus of a review (Rees and Oliver, 2012). This process of 'stakeholder involvement' was illustrated by reviews about supporting 'looked after' children to stay in school (Liabo et al., 2013), and conflict resolution, peer mediation and young people's relationships (Garcia et al., 2006). In each case young people chose the focus of the review and how the key concepts were interpreted for synthesising the relevant literature. A participatory approach such as this transforms systematic reviewing into an exercise in co-construction of learning from the existing literature, where methods are appropriately aligned with the question to be addressed, and chosen in light of the available literature, particularly whether it suits generating, exploring or testing theory.

Systematic review methods have developed in response to specific needs for evidence, largely in health but also for other public sectors and in the natural sciences. In our experience, whenever methods developed in one academic system or policy sector have been transferred to another, new challenges have been encountered and new methodological solutions developed, often solutions that can be usefully applied in the original area too. A recent challenge, in the form of particularly broad questions asked by policymakers, has emerged from the growing enthusiasm for systematic reviews to inform international development. A series of 'rigorous literature reviews' addressing education in developing countries purposely involved multidisciplinary teams to bring 'a wider range of disciplinary approaches, techniques, methodologies, questions and means of appraisal to focus on the themes and problems at the core of education research' (Department for

International Development, 2012). Such interests raise questions about how best to develop policy relevant questions to achieve systematic reviews that are both important and answerable, how to review literatures at different levels of granularity and how to navigate competing interests in the breadth and detail of any given literature. Just as individual systematic reviews are commonly shaped through dialogue between decision-makers asking the questions and review teams finding the answers, so too does overcoming methodological challenges depend upon dialogue between those preparing and those using systematic reviews.

ACKNOWLEDGEMENTS

This chapter is informed by research, scholarship and debate undertaken largely with colleagues at the EPPI-Centre, UCL Institute of Education. We are particularly grateful to Alison O'Mara-Eves, James Thomas and the anonymous peer reviewers for their comments on earlier versions of the text.

FURTHER READING

For a short, accessible and technically up-to-date book covering the full breadth of approaches to reviews from statistical meta-analysis to meta-ethnography, read: Gough, D., Oliver, S. and Thomas, J. (Second edition, forthcoming) *Introduction to Systematic Reviews*. London: Sage.

Further reading on the calculation and interpretation of effect sizes, complete with many worked examples from educational research, is available in an edited collection published by the National Foundation for Educational Research: Schagen, I. and Elliot, K. (Eds) (2004). *But What Does It Mean? The Use of Effect Sizes in Educational Research*. Slough: NFER.

The *Cochrane Handbook for Systematic Reviews of Interventions* is the official guide that describes in detail the process of preparing and maintaining Cochrane systematic reviews on the effects of health care interventions, and is a valuable reference for effectiveness reviews more generally (http://handbook.cochrane.org/).

The RAMESES project offers standards and training materials for conducting meta-narrative and realist reviews (www.ramesesproject.org/).

REFERENCES

Ahmad, N., Boutron, I., Dechartres, A., Durieux, P. and Ravaud, P. (2010) 'Applicability and generalisability of the results of systematic reviews to public health practice and policy: a systematic review', *Trials*, 11: 20 doi:10.1186/1745-6215-11-20.

Avery, A., Bostock, L. and McCullough, F. (2015) 'A systematic review investigating interventions that can help reduce consumption of sugar-sweetened beverages in children leading to changes in body fatness', *Journal of Human Nutrition and Dietetics*, 28(s1): 52–64.

Bailey, R., Pearce, G., Smith, C., Sutherland, M., Stack, N., Winstanley, C. and Dickenson, M. (2012) 'Improving the educational achievement of gifted and talented students: a systematic review', *Talent Development & Excellence*, 4(1): 33–48.

Baker, W. L., White, C. M., Cappelleri, J. C., Kluger, J., Coleman, C. I. and the HOPE Collaborative Group (2009) 'Understanding heterogeneity in meta-analysis: the role of meta-regression', *International Journal of Clinical Practice*, 63(10): 1426–1434.

Banks, G. C., Kepes, S. and Banks, K. P. (2012) 'publication bias: the antagonist of meta-analytic reviews and effective policymaking', *Education Evaluation and Policy Analysis*, 34(3): 259–277.

Bonell, C., Oakley, A., Hargreaves, J., Strange, V. and Rees, R. (2006) 'Assessment of generalisability in trials of health interventions: suggested framework and systematic review', *British Medical Journal*, 333: 346.

Borenstein, M. and Hedges, L. V. (2016) *Computing Effect Sizes for Meta-Analysis*. Chichester: Wiley-Blackwell.

Borenstein, M., Hedges, L. V., Higgins, J. P. T. and Rothstein, H. R. (2009) *Introduction to Meta-analysis*. Chichester: John Wiley & Sons.

Cohen, J. (1988) *Statistical Power Analysis for the Behavioral Sciences*, 2nd edition. Hillsdale, NJ: Erlbaum.

Cook, T., Shadish, W. and Wong, V. (2008) 'Three conditions under which experiments and observational studies produce comparable causal estimates: new findings from within-study comparisons', *Journal of Policy Analysis and Management*, 27(4): 724–750.

Cooper, H. M. (2016) *Research Synthesis and Meta-analysis: A step-by-step approach*, 5th edition. London: Sage.

Cooper, H. and Hedges, L. V. (1994) *The Handbook of Research Synthesis*. New York: Russell Sage Foundation.

Cooper, H., Hedges, L. V. and Valentine, J. C. (Eds) (2008) *The Handbook of Research Synthesis and Meta-analysis*. New York: Russell Sage Foundation.

Cooper, H., Robinson, J. C. and Patall, E. A. (2006) 'Does homework improve academic achievement? A synthesis of research, 1987–2003', *Review of Educational Research*, 76(1). doi: 10.3102/00346543076001001.

Cumming, G. (2012) *Understanding the New Statistics: Effect sizes, confidence intervals, and meta-analysis*. Hove: Routledge.

Deeks, J. J., Altman, D. A. and Bradburn, M. J. (2001) 'Statistical methods for examining heterogeneity and combining results from several studies in meta-analysis', in M. Egger, G. Davey Smith and D. G. Altman (Eds) *Systematic Reviews in Health Care: Meta-analysis in context*, 2nd edition (pp. 285–312). London: British Medical Journal Publishing Group.

Department for International Development (2012) DFID Research: Call for rigorous literature reviews in education. Retrieved from https://www.gov.uk/government/news/dfid-research-call-for-rigorous-literature-reviews-in-education (accessed 29 July, 2016).

Durlak, J. A. (2009) 'How to select, calculate, and interpret effect sizes', *Journal of Pediatric Psychology*, 34(9): 917–928.

Durlak, J. A. and Lipsey, M. W. (1991) 'A practitioner's guide to meta-analysis', *American Journal of Community Psychology*, 19: 291–332.

Duval, S. and Tweedie, R. (2000) 'Trim and fill: a simple funnel-plot-based-method of testing and adjusting for publication bias in meta-analysis', *Biometrics*, 56(2): 455–463.

Egger, M. and Davey Smith, G. (1998) 'Bias in location and selection of studies', *British Medical Journal*, 316: 61–66.

Egger, M., Dickersin, K. and Davey, S. G. (2001) 'Problems and limitations in conducting systematic reviews', in M. Egger, S. G. Davey and D. G. Altman (Eds) *Systematic Reviews in Health Care: Meta-analysis in context* (pp. 43–68). London: BMJ Books.

Egger, M., Davey Smith, G., Schneider, M. and Minder, C. (1997) 'Bias in meta-analysis detected by a simple, graphical test', *British Medical Journal*, 315(7109): 629–634.

France, E. F., Ring, N., Noyes, J,. Maxwell, M., Jepson, R., Duncan, E., Turley, R., Jones, D. and Unv, I. (2015) 'Protocol-developing meta-ethnography reporting guidelines (eMERGe)', *BMC Medical Research Methodology*, 15: 103. doi: 10.1186/s12874-015-0068-0.

Garcia, J., Sinclair, J., Dickson, K., Thomas, J., Brunton, J., Tidd, M. and the PSHE Review Group (2006) 'Conflict resolution, peer mediation and young people's relationships. Technical report', in ?? *Research Evidence in Education Library.* London: EPPI-Centre, Social Science Research Unit, Institute of Education, University of London. Retrieved from http://eppi.ioe.ac.uk/cms/Default.aspx?tabid=708 (accessed 14 September, 2016).

Glass, G. V. and Smith, M. L. (1979) 'Meta-analysis of research on class size and achievement', *Educational Evaluation and Policy Analysis*, 1(1): 2–16.

Glass, G. V., McGaw, B. and Smith, M. L. (1981) *Meta-analysis in Social Research.* London: Sage.

Gough, D. (2007) 'Weight of evidence: a framework for the appraisal of the quality and relevance of evidence', in J. Furlong and A. Oancea (Eds) *Applied and Practice-based Research. Special Edition of Research Papers in Education*, 22(2): 213–228.

Gough, D., Oliver, S. and Thomas, J. (2012) *Introduction to Systematic Reviews.* London: Sage.

Gough, D., Oliver, S. and Thomas, J. (Second edition, forthcoming) *Introduction to Systematic Reviews.* London: Sage.

Grayson, L. and Gomersall, A. (2003) *A Difficult Business: Finding the evidence for social science reviews.* ESRC UK Centre for Evidence Based Policy and Practice: Working Paper 19.

Greenhalgh, T., Robert, G., Macfarlane, F., Bate, P., Kyriakidou, O. and Peacock, R. (2005) 'Storylines of research in diffusion of innovation: a meta-narrative approach to systematic review', *Social Science and Medicine*, 61: 417–430.

Guyatt, G. H., Oxman, A. D., Vist, G., Kunz, R., Falck-Ytter, Y., Alonso-Coello, P. and Schünemann, H. J., for the GRADE Working Group (2008) 'Rating quality of evidence and strength of recommendations GRADE: an emerging consensus on rating quality of evidence and strength of recommendations', *British Medical Journal*, 336: 924–926.

Hammerstrøm, K., Wade, A. and Jørgensen, A. M. K. (2010) Searching for studies: a guide to information retrieval for Campbell Systematic Reviews, *Campbell Systematic Reviews*, Supplement 1. doi: 10.4073/csrs.2010.

Hansen, H., Klejntrup, N. and Andersen, O. (2011) *A Comparison of Model-Based and Design-Based Impact Evaluations of Interventions in Developing Countries.* FOI Working Paper 2011/16.

Hanushek, E. A. (1989) 'The impact of differential expenditures on school performance', *Educational Researcher*, 18(4): 45–65.

Hedges, L. V. (2007) 'Effect sizes in cluster-randomised designs', *Journal of Educational and Behavioural Statistics*, 32(4): 341–370.

Hedges, L., Laine, R. D. and Greenwald, R. (1994) 'Does money matter? A meta-analysis of studies of the effects of differential school inputs on student outcomes', *Educational Researcher*, 23(3): 5–14.

Hedges, L. V. and Olkin, I. (1980) 'Vote-counting methods in research synthesis', *Psychological Bulletin*, 88(2): 359–369.

Hedges, L. V. and Olkin, I. (1985) *Statistical Methods for Meta-analysis*. New York: Academic Press.

Hedges, L. V., and Pigott, T. (2004) The power of statistical tests for moderators in meta-analysis. *Psychological methods*, 9(4), 426–445.

Higgins, J. P. and Thompson, S. G. (2002) 'Quantifying heterogeneity in a meta-analysis', *Statistics in Medicine*, 21(11): 1539–1558.

Higgins, J. P. T., Altman, D. G. and Sterne, J. A. C. (eds) (2011) 'Assessing risk of bias in included studies', in J. P. T. Higgins and S. Green (eds) *Cochrane Handbook for Systematic Reviews of Interventions Version 5.1.0* (updated March 2011) (Chapter 8). The Cochrane Collaboration. Retrieved on 12 July 2016 from handbook.cochrane.org.

Higgins, S., Hall, E., Baumfield, V. and Moseley, D. (2005) 'A meta-analysis of the impact of the implementation of thinking skills approaches on pupils', in ??. *Research Evidence in Education Library*. London: EPPI-Centre, Social Science Research Unit, Institute of Education, University of London. Retrieved from http://eppi.ioe.ac.uk/cms/Default.aspx?tabid=339 (accessed 14 September, 2016).

Higgins, S., Katsipataki, M., Coleman, R., Henderson, P., Major, L. E. and Coe, R. (2015) *The Sutton Trust-Education Endowment Foundation Teaching and Learning Toolkit*. London: Education Endowment Foundation.

Hunt, M. (1997) *How Science Takes Stock: The story of meta-analysis*. New York: Russell Sage Foundation.

Jadad, A. R., Moore, R. A., Carroll, D., Jenkinson, C., Reynolds, D. J., Gavaghan, D. J. and McQuay, H. J. (1996) 'Assessing the quality of reports of randomized controlled trials: is blinding necessary?' *Controlled Clinical Trials*, 17: 1–12.

Jamal, F., Fletcher, A., Harden, A., Wells, H., Thomas, J. and Bonell, C. (2013) 'The school environment and student health: a systematic review and meta-ethnography of qualitative research', *BMC Public Health*, 13:798 doi:10.1186/1471-2458-13-798.

Konnerup, M. and Kongsted, H. (2012) 'Do Cochrane reviews provide a good model for social science? The role of observational studies in systematic reviews', *Evidence and Policy*, 8(1): 79–86.

Langford, R., Bonell, C., Jones, H. and Campbell, R. (2015) 'Obesity prevention and the Health promoting Schools framework: essential components and barriers to success', *International Journal of Behavioral Nutrition and Physical Activity*, 12: 15 doi:10.1186/s12966-015-0167-7.

Lavis, J. N. (2009). 'How can we support the use of systematic reviews in policymaking?' *PLoS Med*, 6(11): e1000141.

Lewin, S., Glenton, C., Munthe-Kaas, H., Carlsen, B., Colvin, C. J., Gülmezoglu, M., Noyes, J., Booth, A., Garside, R. and Rashidian, A. (2015) 'Using qualitative evidence in decision making for health and social interventions: an approach to assess confidence in findings from qualitative evidence syntheses (GRADE-CERQual)', *PLoS Med*, 12(10): e1001895. doi:10.1371/journal.pmed.1001895.

Liabo, K., Gray, K. and Mulcahy, D,. (2013) 'A systematic review of interventions to support looked-after children in school', *Child and Family Social Work*, 18 (3): 341–353.

Light, R. J. and Smith, P. V. (1971) 'Accumulating evidence and procedures for resolving contradictions among different research studies', *Harvard Educational Review*, 41: 429–471.

Lipsey, M. W. and Wilson, D. B. (2001) *Practical Meta-analysis* (Vol. 49). Thousand Oaks, CA: Sage.

Marpsat, M. and Razafindratsima, N. (2012) 'Survey methods for hard-to-reach populations: introduction to the special issue', *Methodological Innovations Online*, 5(2): 3–16.

Maynard, B. R., McCrea, K. T., Pigott, T. D. and Kelly, M. S. (2013) 'Indicated truancy interventions for chronic truant students. A Campbell systematic review', *Research on Social Work Practice*, 23(1): 5–21.

Mehdyzadeh, H. (2004) *Searching for the Evidence: An introduction to social science information retrieval.* Technical Paper No. 5. London: Department for Culture, Media and Sport.

Miles, M. and Huberman, A. (1994) *Qualitative Data Analysis.* London: Sage.

Moher, D., Liberati, A., Tetzlaff, J., Altman, D. G. and the PRISMA Group. (2009) '*P*referred *R*eporting *I*tems for *S*ystematic Reviews and *M*eta-*A*nalyses: The PRISMA Statement', PLoS Med, 6(6): e1000097. doi:10.1371/journal.pmed1000097.

Noblit, G. and Hare, R. D. (1988) *Meta-ethnography: Synthesizing qualitative studies.* Newbury Park, CA: Sage.

OED Online. March 2015. Oxford University Press. Retrieved on 1 May 2015 from www.oed.com/view/Entry/196574?redirectedFrom=synthesis.

Oliver, S. R., Rees, R. W., Clarke-Jones, L., Milne, R., Oakley, A. R., Gabbay, J., Stein, K., Buchanan, P. and Gyte, G. (2008) 'A multidimensional conceptual framework for analysing public involvement in health services research', *Health Expectations*, 11(1): 72–84.

Papaionnou, D., Sutton, A., Carroll, C., Booth, A. and Wong, R. (2010) 'Literature searching for social science systematic reviews: consideration of a range of search techniques', *Health Information and Libraries Journal*, 27(2): 114–122.

Rees, R. and Oliver, S. (2012) 'Stakeholder involvement', in D. Gough, S. Oliver and J. Thomas (Eds) *Introduction to Systematic Reviews* (pp. 17–34. London: Sage.

Rees, R., Oliver, K., Woodman, J. and Thomas, J. (2011) 'The views of young children in the UK about obesity, body size, shape and weight: a systematic review', *BMC Public Health*, 11: 188 doi:10.1186/1471-2458-11-188.

Ritchie, J. and Spencer, L. (1994) 'Qualitative data analysis for applied policy research', in A. Bryman and R. G. Burgess (Eds) *Analyzing Qualitative Data* (pp.173–194). London: Routledge.

Rothstein, H. R., Sutton, A. J. and Borenstein, M. (Eds) (2005) *Publication Bias in Meta-analysis: Prevention, assessment and adjustments.* London: Wiley.

Schagen, I. and Elliot, K. (Eds) (2004) *But What Does It Mean? The use of effect sizes in educational research.* Slough: NFER.

Schucan Bird, K. and Tripney, J. (2011) 'Systematic literature searching in policy relevant, inter-disciplinary reviews: an example from culture and sport', *Research Synthesis Methods*, 2(3): 163–173.

Shadish, W. R., Cook, T. D. and Campbell, D. T. (2002) *Experimental and Quasi-experimental Designs for Generalized Causal Inference.* Boston, MA: Houghton Mifflin.

Shea, B. J., Grimshaw, J. M., Wells, G. A., Boers, M., Andersson, N., Hamel, C., Porter, A. C., Tugwell, P., Moher, D. and Bouter, L. M. (2007) 'Development of AMSTAR: a measurement tool to assess the methodological quality of systematic reviews', *BMC Medical Research Methodology*, February 15, 7: 10. PMID: 17302989.

Sirin, S. R. (2005) 'Socioeconomic status and academic achievement: a meta-analytic review of research', *Review of Educational Research*, 75(3): 417–453.

Smith, M. L. and Glass, G. V. (1977) 'Meta-analysis of psychotherapy outcome studies', *American Psychologist*, 32, 752–760.

Snilstveit, B. (2012) 'Systematic reviews: from 'bare bones' reviews to policy relevance', *Journal of Development Effectiveness*, 4(3) 388–408.

Snilstveit, B., Oliver, S. and Vojtkova, M. (2012) 'Narrative approaches to systematic review and synthesis of evidence for international development policy and practice', *Journal of Development Effectiveness*, 4(3): 409–429.

Strauss, A. and Corbin, J. (1990) *Basics of Qualitative Research, Grounded Theory Procedures and Techniques*. London: Sage.

Sullivan, G. M. and Feinn, R. (2012) 'Using effect size – or why the *p* value is not enough', *Journal of Graduate Medical Education*, 4(3): 279–282.

Sutcliffe, K., Brunton, G., Twamley, K., Hinds, K., O'Mara-Eves, A. J. and Thomas, J. (2011) *Young People's Access to Tobacco: A mixed-method systematic review*. London: EPPI Centre, Social Science Research Unit, Institute of Education, University of London.

Téllez, K. and Waxman, H. (2006). 'A meta-synthesis of qualitative research on effective teaching practices for English language learners', in J. M. Norris and L. Ortega (Eds) *Synthesizing Research on Language Learning And Teaching* (pp. 245–277). Philadelphia: John Benjamins Publishing.

Thomas, J. and Harden, A. (2008) 'Methods for the thematic synthesis of qualitative research in systematic reviews', *BMC Medical Research Methodology*, 8: 45 doi:10.1186/1471-2288-8-45.

Thompson, B. (2007) 'Effect sizes, confidence intervals, and confidence intervals for effect sizes', *Psychology in the Schools*, 44: 423–432.

Torgerson, C. (2006) 'Publication bias: the Achilles' heel of systematic reviews?' *British Journal of Educational Studies*, 54(1): 89–102.

Unterhalter, E., North, A., Arnot, M., Lloyd, C., Moletsane, L., Murphy-Graham, E., Parkes, J. and Saito, M. (2014) *Interventions to enhance girls' education and gender equality. Education rigorous literature review.* Department for International Development.

Waddington, H., White, H., Snilstveit, B., Hombrados, J. G., Vojtkova, M., Davies, P., Bhavsar, A., Eyers, J., Koehlmoos, T.P., Petticrew, M., Valentine, J.C. and Tugwell, P. (2012) 'How to do a good systematic review of effects in international development: a tool kit', *Journal of Development Effectiveness*, 4(3): 359–387.

Walsh, K., Zwi, K., Woolfenden, S. and Shlonsky, A. (2015) 'School-based education programmes for the prevention of child sexual abuse: a systematic review', *Campbell Systematic Reviews*, 10. doi: 10.4073/csr.2015.10.

Wang, S., Moss, J. R. and Hiller, J. E. (2006) 'Applicability and transferability of interventions in evidence-based public health', *Health Promotion International*, 21(1): 76–83. doi: 10.1093/heapro/dai025.

Welch, V., Petticrew, M., Tugwell, P., Moher, D., O'Neill, J., Waters, E. et al. (2012) 'PRISMA-Equity 2012 extension: reporting guidelines for systematic reviews with a focus on health equity', *PLoS Med*, 9(10): e1001333. doi:10.1371/journal.pmed.1001333.

Wong, G., Greenhalgh, T., Westhorp, G. and Pawson, R. (2014) 'Development of methodological guidance, publication standards and training materials for realist and meta-narrative reviews: the RAMESES (Realist And Meta-narrative Evidence Syntheses – Evolving Standards) project', *Health Services and Delivery Research*, 2(30).

Wong, G., Greenhalgh, T., Westhorp, G., Buckingham, J. and Pawson, R. (2013a) 'RAMESES publication standards: meta-narrative reviews', *BMC Medicine*, 11: 20. doi:10.1186/1741-7015-11-20.

Wong, G., Greenhalgh, T., Westhorp, G., Buckingham, J. and Pawson, R. (2013b) 'RAMESES publication standards: realist reviews'. *BMC Medicine*, 11: 21. doi:10.1186/1741-7015-11-21.

23

Mixed Methods Approaches and their Application in Educational Research

Pamela Sammons and Susila Davis

INTRODUCTION

This chapter discusses the use of mixed methods (MM) approaches in educational research and provides a brief review of methodological literature on MM in social research. It explores the growing popularity of MM to study complex educational questions and issues in the design of MM investigations. The chapter also discusses the arguments made to support the use of mixed methods as well as some of the potential problems that may be encountered.

Some of the main defining features of MM studies are explored, building on, and elaborating, discussions by Tashakkori and Teddlie (2003, 2010a). The way MM research can be used to investigate complex social phenomena, reveal patterns and associations, provide findings that can support generalisations and develop and test theories and also provide rich descriptions and identify patterns that provide evidence to illuminate and extend understanding of educational topics is discussed. The chapter draws attention to the way both quantitative and qualitative data can be collected, analysed and integrated to link findings and to support new, synergistic understandings that go beyond the findings and interpretations that can be achieved from reliance on only one methodological perspective.

The chapter uses several studies as exemplars to highlight the potential of MM research in studying classroom practice to address broader research questions and illustrate the way both quantitative and qualitative data can be analysed and the results integrated. The chosen examples have a common educational focus on studying teachers' classroom practice and teacher effectiveness and all were conducted in England during the last 15 years.

Two are longitudinal research studies and one an evaluation with a longitudinal component. The first two examples examine the MM design of the Variations in Teachers' Lives Work and their Effects on Pupils (VITAE) research (Day et al., 2006, 2007, 2008a; Sammons et al., 2007) funded by the then Department for Children, Schools and Families (DCSF[1]) in England and the follow-up Effective Classroom Practice (ECP) study (Day et al., 2008b; Kington et al., 2011, 2014b) funded by the Economic and Social Research Council (ESRC)[2]. The third example studies the impact of 'Teach First'[3] teachers in schools because this also addresses the notion of effective classroom practice and shows how MM can support studies that are designed to evaluate educational initiatives, in this case the role of Teach First teachers in supporting school improvement. This study was commissioned as part of the Maximum Impact Programme funded for Teach First by the Goldman Sachs Foundation (Muijs et al., 2010; Muijs et al., 2012). Teach First is an alternative school based certification programme in England that was influenced by the earlier 'Teach for America' programme.

The VITAE research used national assessment data and contextualised value added approaches[4] (statistical methods based on multilevel models) to study teacher effectiveness, based on pupil outcome data (tests and national assessments). It also used questionnaires with teachers and students, and a series of in depth interviews with a sample of over 300 teachers. The research was longitudinal and studied teachers over more than three successive school years. The ECP study involved 81 teachers and adopted both quantitative and qualitative classroom observations conducted over two terms in one school year. It also employed teacher interviews and student surveys to gain information on classroom practice from different stakeholder perspectives. The Teach First evaluation also sought to triangulate its evidence base, employing questionnaire surveys, interviews with stakeholders, documents and performance data from students' test and examination results (again using value added multilevel statistical analyses[5]) to study the variation in teachers' classroom practice through observations and evaluate the impact of Teach First practitioners on their schools' performance.

This chapter seeks to develop a framework to aid the reader in understanding and evaluating the quality of MM designs and research results. It compares the kinds of research questions addressed by these three different studies. It also highlights the sequencing of the research, the ways different kinds of data were analysed and linked and the processes of integration and synthesis. In addition, the chapter notes some of the methodological challenges faced, the knowledge claims made and how the authors substantiated their findings and conclusions.

WHAT IS MIXED METHODS RESEARCH?

The use of methods from different research traditions is not a new phenomenon in social and educational research. It has a long history and has supported the advancement of many disciplines. However, the term 'mixed methods (MM)' research has only emerged in the last two decades and with this the notion of classifying different types of MM designs. As Guest (2013, p. 142) notes, 'Researchers in various disciplines were integrating qualitative and quantitative methods long before the field of mixed methods formally emerged and typologies were established'. Denzin (2010, p. 422) claims that the 'paradigm war' of the 1980s 'validated the use of mixed methods designs', rendering arguments denying the stronger inferences and diversity of findings offered by such designs as futile. Guest (2013) also highlights some interesting ways in which several classic early epidemiological and anthropological studies benefitted from the use of both quantitative and qualitative components to support groundbreaking and innovative investigations. For example, Guest points to John Snow's research into the nineteenth-century cholera epidemic in London, where the use of a variety of methods led to the eventual identification of a particular water pump as the source of the widespread infection. Snow talked to local residents about which water pumps they used regularly, produced a dot map of where each case of infection had taken place and made use of statistics correlating the quality of water and number of cholera cases to draw his final conclusions (Johnson, 2006). The roots of MM research are seen to go back more than half a century according to Hunter and Brewer (2003) although in this case the term 'multimethod' was used. Tashakkori and Teddlie (2003) sought to distinguish MM research from the more general term of multimethod to cover only those studies where both qualitative and quantitative components were intentionally incorporated at the research design stage and reserve 'multimethod' for studies using several techniques from within the same paradigm (either qualitative or quantitative).

MM research has been identified in different ways in the methodological literature (see Tashakkori and Teddlie, 2003, 2010a; Johnson, Onwuegbuzie and Turner, 2007). Teddlie and Sammons (2010) argue that MM research has emerged as an increasingly popular alternative to the traditional dichotomy evident between qualitative and quantitative research traditions in the social and behavioural sciences. Following the publication of the first and second *Handbooks of Mixed Methods Research* (Tashakkori and Teddlie, 2003, 2010a) and the inception of a special Journal of Mixed Methods Research, MM is becoming recognised as a third and alternative methodological approach of increasing popularity. Teddlie and Sammons (2010) argue that its growing popularity 'is largely due to its flexibility in simultaneously addressing multiple and diverse research questions through integrated QUAL and QUANT techniques' (Teddlie and Sammons, 2010, p. 116).

In their second Handbook devoted to the topic, while reflecting on the development of MM approaches, Tashakkori and Teddlie (2010a) argue that MM refers to:

> The broad inquiry logic that guides the selection of specific methods and that is informed by conceptual positions common to mixed methods practitioners (e.g., the rejection of

'either-or' choices at all levels of the research process). For us, this definition of methodology distinguishes the MMR approach to conducting research from that practiced in either the QUAN or QUAL approach. (Tashakkori and Teddlie, 2010a, p. 5)

These authors thus reject what they see as an arbitrary and often inappropriate opposition of qualitative and quantitative approaches as competing alternatives that researchers have to choose between, and the arguments that researchers must necessarily belong to only one or the other camp as suggested by, in their view, the sterile and false dichotomy evident in many discussions in the so called 'paradigm wars' debates and in many traditional methodological text books. The appeal of MM research is thus seen to lie in the ability to combine both 'numbers and a story' (Spalter-Roth, 2000) to generate new knowledge because 'the combination of both general numeric findings and specific cases exemplifying those findings generate a synergy that neither can alone' (Teddlie and Sammons, 2010, p. 116). Key to the definition is the notion of *integration* in terms of the way MM researchers choose to analyse, interpret and discuss their research in such a way that quantitative and qualitative components are seen to be purposively connected and findings 'mutually illuminating' (Bryman, 2007, p. 8).

Teddlie and Sammons (2010) suggest that such mutual illumination involves an inductive–deductive research cycle indicating a rejection of a linear approach to research and the creation of findings. They argue that MM research designs require creativity and flexibility in their construction and implementation. Although Tashakkori and Teddlie (2003) had distinguished a number of alternative ways of defining MM designs, some have suggested that the notion of typologies may not be that useful because 'the actual diversity in mixed methods studies is far greater than any typology can adequately encompass' (Maxwell and Loomis, 2003, p. 244). Nonetheless, it is generally recognised that a loose typology of MM research designs and analytic techniques can be helpful to distinguish between five main families of designs, while recognising that any individual MM study may well be unique in its particular way of conceptualising, analysing and integrating approaches, data and findings. Table 23.1 illustrates these five main 'families' of MM designs, their definition and the analytic approaches and techniques associated with each.

Creswell (2003) drew attention to the need to move beyond the traditional and often oppositional quantitative or qualitative divide in designing research and evaluating knowledge claims that are made. He argued that instead research approaches should be thought of as lying somewhere along a continuum, and that although much research may still be largely qualitative or largely quantitative the third main approach of MM (purposive integration where different features of a study might be at different places on such a continuum) had come of age by the start of the twenty-first century. Some go further to argue further that MM as a third methodological paradigm is particularly important for the investigation

Table 23.1   Typology of mixed methods research designs and analytic techniques

MMR Design 'Family'	Definition of Design 'Family'	Analytic Techniques Used with this Design 'Family'
Parallel Mixed Designs	Designs in which mixing occurs in an independent manner either simultaneously or with some time lapse; QUAL and QUAN *strands* are planned/implemented in order to answer related aspects of same questions	Parallel track analysis; Cross-over track analysis
Sequential Mixed Designs	Designs in which mixing occurs across chronological phases (QUAL, QUAN) of the study; questions or procedures of one *strand* emerge from or are dependent on the previous strand; *research questions* are built upon one another and may evolve as the study unfolds	Sequential QUAL→QUAN analysis; Sequential QUAN→QUAL analysis; Iterative sequential mixed analysis
Conversion Mixed Designs	Designs where mixing occurs when one type of data is transformed and then analysed both qualitatively and quantitatively	Quantitising narrative data; Qualitising numeric data (e.g. profile formation) Inherently mixed data analysis
Multilevel Mixed Designs	Designs where mixing occurs across multiple levels of analysis; Mixing occurs as QUAN and QUAL data from different levels are analysed and integrated to answer aspects of the same or related questions	Analyse data from each level separately; then integrate them vertically
Fully Integrated Mixed Designs	Family of MM designs in which mixing occurs in an interactive manner at all *stages* of the study; at each *stage*, one approach affects the formulation of the other	Combinations of all those above

Source: Adapted from Teddlie and Sammons (2010).

of complex social and behavioural phenomenon in the increasingly globalised and interconnected world of the twenty-first century. Creswell claims that the practice *of*:

> [R]esearch (such as writing a proposal) involves much more than philosophical assumptions. Philosophical ideas must be combined with broad approaches to research (strategies) and implemented with specific procedures (methods). Thus, a framework is needed that combines the elements of philosophical ideas, strategies, and methods into the three approaches to research. (Creswell, 2003, p. 4)

He goes on to propose three questions that should underpin the choice of research design:

1   What knowledge claims are being made by the researcher (including a theoretical perspective)?
2   What strategies of inquiry will inform the procedures?
3   What methods of data collection and analysis will be used?

These three questions are seen as helpful starting points in making an informed decision about whether a MM approach is deemed appropriate.

Creswell et al. (2011) provide an elaborated discussion of the role and nature of MM enquiry in a major review of the use of MM approaches in health related research. This defines MM in terms of five features as follows:

- focusing on research questions that call for real-life contextual understandings, multilevel perspectives, and cultural influences;
- employing rigorous quantitative research assessing magnitude and frequency of constructs and rigorous qualitative research exploring the meaning and understanding of constructs;
- utilising multiple methods (for example, intervention trials and in-depth interviews);
- intentionally integrating or combining these methods to draw on the strengths of each; and
- framing the investigation within philosophical and theoretical positions.

It is suggested that the three broad questions and this more elaborated set of five features outlined by Creswell (2003; Creswell et al., 2011) provide a basis for those designing educational research to examine the quality and appropriateness of a MM design to address its stated research purposes and questions.

Creswell (2003) compared four main knowledge positions or paradigms: post positivism, constructivism (often combined with interpretivism), advocacy/participatory and pragmatism. Many MM researchers adopt the philosophical position of pragmatism arguing for the primacy of the research aims and underlying research questions in driving the choice of research design (see Tashakkori and Teddlie, 1998, 2003 for a fuller discussion of pragmatism and the philosophical issues in relation to MM studies). A MM design thus should be adopted if the researchers judge that they will be better placed to achieve their purposes and address their research questions successfully through the application of methods from more than one tradition (qualitative or quantitative). Tashakkori and Teddlie (2003) refer to this primacy as the 'dictatorship' of the research questions in driving research designs and choice of methods. Heyvaert et al. (2013) explicitly adopt a pragmatist stance arguing:

> [T]his implies that one should apply the best suited combination of methods and modes of analysis to answer the posed research question(s): that can be a monomethod or an MM approach. Emphasizing processes of abduction, intersubjectivity, and transferability (Morgan, 2007), pragmatism offers the researcher alternatives to the dichotomous choice between (post)positivism and constructivism, driven by the question of utility. (Heyvaert et al., 2013, p. 303)

This is in strong contrast to those that see alternative positions as antagonistic and mutually exclusive with the integration of findings seen as incommensurate due to fundamental differences in underlying philosophical assumptions and world views.

Salomon (1991) meanwhile argues that the differences between chosen approaches go beyond the 'quantitative-qualitative' debate. For example, a more 'controlled study of how specific variables affect others' may take an 'analytic approach', while a study investigating the complexities of educational environments, or 'a whole dynamic ecology, the building blocks of which cannot be easily (or usefully) separated' (Salomon, 1991, p. 12) will require a more 'systemic approach'. Salomon, espousing the work of Lakatos (1978) in distinguishing between theoretical and empirical progress, argues that:

> [T]he strength of the analytic approach lies in its ability to lead to empirical progress by testing specific causal hypotheses but that the theories from which the hypotheses are derived ought to emanate from a more systemic approach, possibly better capable of suggesting rich descriptive theories. (Salomon, 1991, p. 15)

Denzin (2010, p. 421) charts a rich history of the so-called 'paradigm wars' and describes three distinct periods:

1 the postpositivist war against positivism (1970–1990);
2 the wars between competing postpositivist, constructivist, and critical theory paradigms (1990–2005); and
3 the current war between evidence-based methodologists and the mixed methods, interpretive, and critical theory schools (2005 to present).

Denzin (2010, p. 422) seemingly reinterprets Tashakkori and Teddlie's (2003, p. 24) 'third methodological movement' as a 'third moment' and sets it against a quite revolutionary stance at the time based in the 'critical interpretive social science tradition' which seeks to reject altogether the norms and assumptions of objectivity and focuses more on the 'subversion of dominant paradigms. Entrenched in what would be Denzin's (2010) first war, some recognition emerged that all paradigms (however defined), methods and modes of description, interpretation and articulation are partial or incomplete individually (Feyerabend, 1974; Merton, 1975; Eisner, 1986). Salomon (1991, p. 16) concludes with the idea that complementarity 'serves better, fuller, and more satisfying understanding', with each approach informing and guiding the other. The debated 'incommensurability' of paradigms fades when concepts are reframed (Onwuegbuzie and Leech, 2005). Salomon (1991, p. 16) for example argues that 'the analytic approach capitalizes on precision while the systematic approach capitalizes on authenticity'. More recently, Onwuegbuzie and Teddlie (2003) sub-divide research into methods which are 'exploratory' and 'confirmatory'.

Denzin (2010, p. 425) also calls for 'a moral and methodological community that honors and celebrates paradigm and methodological diversity'. Hall and Howard (2008, pp. 250–1) refer to a 'synergistic' approach, where the combination or mixing of methods results in a sum greater than those of their individual components. Although qualitative and quantitative findings may concur or support each other, there may be discrepancies revealed. However, qualitative descriptions that contradict quantitative effects may lead in new directions and provide more complete, holistic or intricate understandings of phenomena.

Heyvaert et al. (2013) draw attention to the need to develop appropriate general criteria and frameworks for the critical appraisal of MM studies, reflecting that this has become a recognised feature of good practice in evaluating the quality of quantitative and of qualitative research. They argue that developing such a recognised set of quality criteria is particularly important to enable MM studies to be properly evaluated and contribute to systematic reviews and best evidence syntheses. However, they note that, because any MM study should be more than just the sum of the individual qualitative and quantitative components, the application of qualitative and quantitative critical appraisal criteria to examine the separate components of a MM study is unlikely to be sufficient to establish the overall quality of an individual MM study. More is needed to address the *combination of methods* in the MM research and how this has shaped the overall findings. Heyvaert et al. (2013) make a comparison of different published critical appraisal frameworks for examining the quality of individual MM studies. They conclude that:

> The qualitative and quantitative strands of an MM study should not only be answering to strand-specific criteria; in addition, the strands should be appropriately mixed in order to answer the posed research questions, a rationale for the MMR approach should be provided, and the overall study should be coherent and insightful. (Heyvaert et al., 2013, p. 317)

Tashakkori and Teddlie (2003; Teddlie and Tashakkori, 2009) and Guest (2013) have discussed the merits and possible problems in seeking to develop typologies of MM designs. Tashakkori and Teddlie (2010a, p. 22) outline four main justifications for attempts to classify MM designs. Typologies:

- help to establish a 'common language' for the field;
- provide structure or 'blueprint' to the field;
- help to 'legitimise' the field; and
- are useful 'pedagogical tools' for students.

Leech and Onwuegbuzie (2009) present a framework involving three dimensions:

a) the level of mixing
b) time scale covered (distinguishing concurrent from sequential components), and
c) the primacy given to different approaches (are quantitative and qualitative components given equal status or is one dominant?).

The resulting typology outlines eight main types of MM design. Guest (2013) agrees that for novice researchers MM typologies may be useful in helping those unfamiliar with the conduct of MM enquiry in creating a workable design. This emphasises the didactic or pedagogical purposes of such classification, but he questions their value for experienced researchers and suggests they may be confusing or unworkable at least in some cases where the complexity and fluidity of some MM designs, especially those in larger projects, resists simple categorisation. In this chapter the position taken is to advise that for students and those new to the MM field typologies can be a very useful starting point to enhance their understanding of the different ways that MM designs can be conceived. However, they are best regarded as helpful illustrative tools, and should not be set in stone or applied slavishly. It is worthwhile for a researcher to see what can be learnt from such typologies and how far they may inform their own planning to achieve their particular research purposes. This can support methodological advancement (see above) but it is likely, and indeed one of the attractions and strengths of MM approaches that they are flexible and encourage creativity on the part of the researcher, that there may be differences in the particular ways they choose to combine methods in any individual study. Again, following the pragmatist position, it is argued that the design decisions should be guided by the research purposes and research questions the student or researcher wants to pursue. As Tashakkori and Teddlie concluded no one typology can be exhaustive and fit all cases.

Guest (2013) makes an alternative proposal. Rather than focusing attention on the design of a MM study as a whole, he suggests a move to consider what he terms the 'points of interface' between different datasets (qualitative and quantitative). He suggests this linguistic shift would help to identify more clearly the ways mixing occurs in any given study. The advantage claimed is that such a shift, 'would provide an alternative way to describe the inherent complexity and fluidity of many mixed methods studies' (Guest, 2013, p. 146). However, this does not eliminate the need to make explicit the actual MM design employed in any particular study as Guest (2013, p. 146) goes on to say: 'Note that the details of the design would not be lost; they would simply be presented in the methods section of the report or proposal, as they would with any study'. While there is much merit in making more explicit the points of mixing as Guest suggests, we remain convinced that thinking about the nature of any particular MM design as a whole and its main features (as advocated by the study of typologies) and documenting this in relation to other main categories of MM designs identified by typologies remains of value for the reasons noted above, though we agree that adding a stronger emphasis to identify the points and nature of mixing of data is also most helpful.

Likewise, we argue that providing a clear and sufficiently detailed description of any MM study and its methods is vital in judging the rigour of a study and the robustness of the knowledge claims that it makes. We agree with Guest (2013) that a diagram illustrating the various qualitative and quantitative research components and their application across the timescale of any investigation is likely to be helpful in understanding all MM studies and that it is vital in the case of complex, longitudinal MM studies where mixing occurs in more than one phase and in more than one way. Researchers should also seek to document clearly where, how, and why datasets are connected and mixed (the points of interface). This would help to highlight the way the various data collection, analysis, and interpretation stages of the research process are connected and, in particular, the way qualitative and quantitative data and findings are integrated. This is necessary to establish in what ways any MM attempts to achieve more than just being the 'sum' of its individual qualitative and quantitative components. Fetters and Freshwater (2015) provide further guidance on expectations from journal editors on publishing a methodologically mixed methods research article and what explanations and detail of the MM approach are deemed necessary. Their article also emphasises the value of diagrams to illustrate research designs and approaches to analysis.

Nine defining characteristics of MM research have been proposed by Tashakkori and Teddlie (2010a, 2010b). These defining characteristics provide a useful basis for informing, describing and evaluating MM designs.

- Methodological eclecticism;
- Paradigm pluralism;
- Emphasis on diversity at all levels of the research enterprise;
- Emphasis on continua rather than a set of dichotomies;
- Iterative, cyclical approach to research;
- Focus on the research question (or research problem) in determining the methods used within any given study;
- Set of basic 'signature' research designs and analytical processes;
- Tendency toward balance and compromise that is implicit within the 'third methodological community'; and
- Reliance on visual representations (for example, figures, diagrams) and a common notational system.

Tashakkori and Teddlie (2010b) argue that these help to distinguish MM from mono or multimethod approaches and suggest that four of these characteristics are particularly relevant to the notion of putting the 'human' back in 'human' research methodology that they view as especially relevant to social and behavioural research. They suggest that the researcher shares concerns that link with the notion of humans as essentially 'everyday problem solvers' while using research knowledge and expertise in ways everyday problem solvers do not, and they use some educational examples to illustrate this idea. The four distinguishing characteristics they highlight in this connection are the strong focus on the research question in determining the methods used in any given study, the emphasis on adopting diversity in methods, methodological eclecticism, and an iterative, cyclical approach to the research and analysis.

EXEMPLARS OF MM RESEARCH IN EDUCATION: A FOCUS ON TEACHERS' CLASSROOM PRACTICE

Sammons (2010) and Teddlie and Sammons (2010) have drawn attention to the potential of MM approaches in educational effectiveness and improvement research. They suggest that MM designs can prove helpful in removing the historic over reliance on statistical analysis of student outcome data evident in many studies of school effectiveness that reveal the limitation of a narrow focus on measured outcomes, and the opposing tendency for school improvement research to be limited to small-scale, typically qualitative case studies of stakeholder perceptions and processes without reference to outcomes or ways of making generalisations. They argue that the focus on both 'numbers and a story' (Spalter-Roth, 2000) enables the combination of general statistical findings and thick descriptions of particular cases,

> has the potential to generate new insights and increase understanding of educational effectiveness research (EER) topics that neither can achieve alone … that allows MM research to add 'extra value' to research studies seeking to better describe, predict, and understand social phenomena, such as the variation in and contributors to differences in educational effectiveness. (Sammons, 2010, p. 699)

Thus the use of MM approaches can help in both theory generation and theory testing in education, using a combination of inductive and deductive cycles where there is a 'to and fro' between analyses and findings across qualitative and quantitative components. This can enhance understanding of school and classroom processes. The combination of rigorous quantitative models, high quality case study and other qualitative approaches has the potential to further advance the educational effectiveness field and support closer links with that of school improvement. It can generate knowledge and evidence of more practical relevance and accessibility to practitioners as well as contribute to theoretical model building, testing and understanding. Such research can also provide another way to study linkages across levels (school and classroom for example) in qualitative ways to add depth to the statistical models.

Here MM research studies are illustrated using three examples of studies of teachers' classroom practice. It is argued that the flexibility allowed by MM designs is particularly suited to the study of such a complex educational topic.

Example 1: Variations in Teachers' Work Lives and their Effects on Pupils (VITAE)

The VITAE research (Day et al.; 2006, 2007) was commissioned by the Department for Education and Skills (DfES) and conducted between 2001 and 2005. It involved a nationally representative sample of 300 primary (Key Stage 1 and 2)[6] and secondary (Key Stage 3 English and mathematics) teachers working in 100 schools across seven local authorities (LAs)[7] in England. Schools were selected to be representative of those in England in terms of levels of social disadvantage and attainment. The research sought to describe and analyse influences on teachers' professional and personal lives, their identities and effectiveness (both perceived and measured by student outcomes), and explore their interconnections. It also investigated connections between the school contexts in which they worked and these features. VITAE was included as an Associate Project of the Teaching and Learning Research Programme (TLRP). The study involved a team of researchers and a longitudinal MM design was chosen (Day et al., 2006; Sammons et al., 2007) to reflect the complexity of the overarching research purposes and key questions that were all addressed by the both qualitative and quantitative components.

1   Does teacher effectiveness vary from one year to another and in terms of different pupil outcomes and do teachers necessarily become more effective over time?
2   What are the roles of biography and identity?
3   How do school and/or department leadership influence teachers' practice and their effectiveness?
4   What particular kinds of influence does continuing professional development (CPD) have on teachers' effectiveness?
5   Are teachers equally effective for different pupil groups or is there differential effectiveness relating (for example) to gender or socio-economic status?
6   Do the factors which influence effectiveness vary for teachers working in different school contexts, or for different kinds of outcomes?
7   Do factors influencing teachers' effectiveness vary across different sectors (primary and secondary) and different age groups (Key Stage 1, 2 and 3)?

Day et al. note that although government funded, the VITAE study:

> [W]as not intended to serve a policy research agenda, nor did it attempt to evaluate any interventions; nevertheless, it was certainly conducted in the context of the high government priority of raising standards in teaching and student attainment. The project specification included a focus on measurable student attainment but not to the exclusion of a wide-ranging investigation aimed at a more holistic, nuanced understanding of teachers' work and lives. (Day et al., 2008a, p. 330)

The complex purposes and research questions led the researchers to use MM to investigate (a) a range of direct and indirect contributory influences on teachers' perceived effectiveness; (b) how the teachers managed these influences in various personal, professional, and policy contexts; and (c) whether there were associations between (a) and (b) and the measurable progress and attainment of the students under study rather than only 'seeking simplistic cause-and-effect relationships' by a narrower quantitative focus just on effectiveness as measured by statistical analyses of student outcomes.

The study design thus sought to link mainly quantitative research on teacher (and school) effectiveness on the one hand, and mainly qualitative research on teachers' work and lives on the other and integrate these different perspectives in order to better address the central research questions. In a methodological paper Day et al. (2008a, p. 331) sought to demonstrate how conceptual and methodological integration 'led to synergistic understandings that enabled the discovery and delineation of key findings that were both more enlightening and more robust than would have been the case if one method or another had dominated'. They used examples of two key findings to illustrate how the MM design and points of interface in the analysis of datasets had enabled such synergy that went beyond the individual quantitative or qualitative findings of the research.

In addition to presenting details about the sample diagrammatically linked to the various data collection methods over the course of the longitudinal research that involved data collection across three full school years for sample of over 300 teachers, the authors provided more detailed tables indicating the methods used and the processes of data analysis (both qualitative and quantitative) and the way these were mixed across the course of the study (Sammons et al., 2007; Day et al., 2008a). They provide an explicit account of how they sought to use case studies of the large teacher sample, to support data analysis and integration arguing that:

> [T]he construction of teacher case studies, the prime focus of the study, used three main sources of data: interviews, teacher and student questionnaires, and annual student assessment data. Case studies were developed for all 300 teachers, a process that involved qualitizing quantitative evidence, quantitizing qualitative evidence, and integrating the two (followed by a consequent synergistic interpretation). This interactive combination of data collection, ongoing analysis, tentative hypothesis generation, and testing and interpretation of results (see Day et al., 2006, for an account of this process) provides greater mapping, analysis, interpretation, and holistic understandings of the research area than would be gained by relying on a single paradigm or approach. (Day et al., 2008a, pp. 333–4)

The authors also draw attention to the role of the mixed methods team and the focus on dialogue of both team members and data through regular meetings where the research process, data collection methods, initial analyses and emerging results were regularly discussed as part of an iterative cyclical process. These involved the development of productive research relationships and understandings within the team, that included members with qualitative and quantitative, expertise, and experience. The role of 'regular project workshops that focused on building shared understandings of data analyses, interpretations, and emergent themes' was highlighted and this promoted 'the building of genuine good will and mutual support' (Day et al., 2008a, p. 339). This was seen as a key factor in the processes of conceptual and methodological integration and synergy. The authors also state 'we would emphasize, especially, the need to sustain productive dialogue (in which the different data "talk" to each other) throughout the project' (Day et al., 2008a, p. 341).

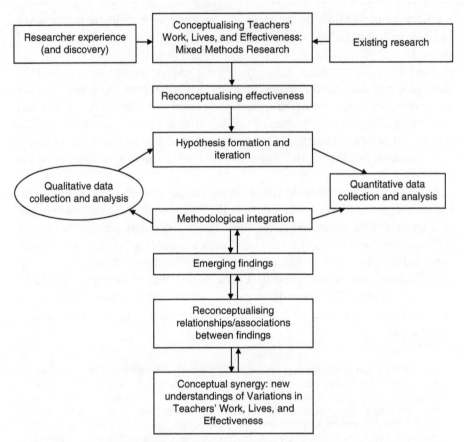

Figure 23.1   A tentative model of synergy in mixed methods research

Source: Adapted from Day et al. (2008a, p. 340).

The authors proposed a tentative model of how the research moved from conceptual and methodological integration to synergy (reproduced in Figure 23.1).

Example 2: Effective Classroom Practice (ECP)

The ECP project (Day et al., 2008b; Kington et al., 2011, 2014a) was separate from but built on the earlier VITAE research described in Example 1. It involved a number of the same team members (Day, Sammons, Kington) but was funded by a research council, not the government. It was initiated because it was recognised that lack of funding for a classroom observation component was a significant limitation of the original VITAE study. The ECP research sought to address this through a strong focus on observation. It had three broad aims:

1   To describe, analyse, and explain the variation in primary and secondary school teachers' classroom behaviours and practice, focusing on English and mathematics teaching;

2 To explore typical and more effective classroom practice of teachers in Years 2, 6, and 9, across different school contexts, professional life phases, and ages in relation to professional, situated, and/or personal factors, which are perceived to affect observed practice over time; and,

3 To draw out implications from the findings of (1) and (2) above for policymakers concerned with raising standards for schools and for teacher development.

The researchers make it clear that, 'the research was not trying to identify whether particular teachers were effective, rather to explore the practices, strategies, and methods used in classrooms by effective practitioners' (where effectiveness indicators had already been developed to aid sampling) (Kington et al., 2014a, p. 31). They chose to use a purposive sample of teachers identified from previous research who either worked in schools in England that had been identified as significantly more effective in value added statistical analyses of national pupil performance data or had been identified as typical or more effective in analyses of pupil performance data in their own classes from the earlier VITAE research. The study was conducted between 2006 and 2008.

The researchers made an explicit case for using a MM design through linked concurrent quantitative and qualitative strands involving description, the study of patterns and associations and the deliberate integration of findings from different sources of data.

In an article on the research methodology published in the *Journal of Mixed Methods Research* the study's authors claimed: 'The strength of the study was in its mixed methods design with the actual observation of classroom practice the principal part of the research design' (Kington et al., 2011, p. 10). These observations, conducted on two separate occasions in two different school terms involved the use of two quantitative systematic observation instruments: the International System of Teacher Observation and Feedback (ISTOF) and the Quality of Teaching (QoT) schedules. Interestingly, the ISTOF schedule was developed by the Methodology of Research on Educational Effectiveness group using a MM process based on a review of literature on teacher effectiveness and the collection of qualitative data in the form of expert opinion from researchers across more than 19 countries (Teddlie et al., 2006). The QoT instrument was based on a collaborative project between the Dutch and English inspectorate and also involved expert opinion (van de Grift et al., 2004; van de Grift, 2007). It has now been employed in published comparative quantitative studies of the variation in teachers' classroom practice across at least six countries in Europe (van de Grift et al., 2014).

In addition to these two quantitative schedules, the ECP study laid equal emphasis on the collection of qualitative observation data using, 'rich descriptive field notes to describe the lesson, which included detail on the structure, organization, and flow of the lesson; nature of lesson activities; interaction; classroom climate; and comments on the teacher's persona' (Kington et al., 2011, p. 10).

Teachers were also interviewed about their lives and work and their classroom practice to provide further detailed qualitative evidence. Both pre and post observation semi-structured interviews were conducted for each of the two observation lessons. Further quantitative data was obtained from teacher and pupil surveys.

The study also used repertory grids a technique developed through personal construct theory. These involved individual interviews with teachers to try and tap their personal constructs about teaching and effective classroom practice. Each teacher's personal constructs were written down and this provided additional rich qualitative evidence on teachers' perspectives, in addition to that obtained from the more traditional semi-structured interviews (see Kington et al., 2014b).

The authors use a discussion of the analysis of the repertory grid data to describe the analytic approach with involved both qualitative and quantitative elements and which enabled the development of a new quantitative instrument, a group grid that was based on the analysis of the original qualitative personal construct data. The constructs contained in the individual grids (more than 600 were identified across the teacher sample) were then categorised into 'themes' as part of the qualitative analysis process. They explained that,

> The categorization process was done by the researchers involved in the actual construct elicitation interviews with participants. At the end of the categorization process, some 18 themes had been identified and these were expressed as bipolar constructs by eliciting the opposite poles to the themes. A new standard repertory grid (or group grid) was then designed using the original elements and the new bipolar construct themes. Ratings from the original grids were then inserted into the new standard grid, where there was a 'match' between a construct used in the original grid and the new standard grid. (Kington et al., 2011, p. 14)

18 themes emerged from the categorisation of teachers' personal constructs. These were then included in a group grid that could be used to establish the relative importance attached to different constructs across larger samples of teachers.

The ECP research addressed five main questions. The authors argued that to address these complex questions adequately required a variety of sources of evidence and this again is linked with the rationale for using MM. These five questions that drove the research design are reported in Table 23.2 which shows how the various multiple data sources were linked with each question.

Kington et al. (2011) use a diagram (Figure 23.2) to provide a visual representation of the ECP design and this illustrates various points of qualitative and quantitative linkage over the course of the research. They note also that there were some elements that worked sequentially within each of the phases of data collection in which the findings from one method were elaborated and expanded through another method (for example, factors identified via teacher questionnaire explored in pre- and post-observation interviews). The design also allowed for data collected by one method to feed into more than one

Table 23.2   Range of different methods in Effective Classroom Practice study linked to research questions

Key Research Questions	Main Data Collection Methods
1. What are the factors that influence typical and more effective teachers' classroom practices in primary and secondary schools?	Teacher questionnaire Pre-observation interview Classroom observation Post-observation interview Pupil survey Pupil focus group interview Existing VITAE datasets
2. What are the relationships between typical and more effective teachers' perceived effectiveness and their classroom practice and organisation?	Pre-observation interview Classroom observation Post-observation interview School leader interview Existing VITAE datasets
3. What are the similarities and differences in the factors that influence classroom practice in different school phases and subjects?	Teacher questionnaire Pre-observation interview Classroom observation Post-observation interview School leader interview Pupil survey Pupil focus group interview Existing VITAE datasets
4. What are the implications of this for key stakeholders who are involved in raising standards in schools?	Pre-observation interview Post-observation interview School leader interview
5. What are the relationships between observed classroom practice and school context in different school and teacher career phases?	Teacher questionnaire Pre-observation interview Classroom observation Post-observation interview School leader interview Pupil survey Pupil focus group interview Existing VITAE datasets

Source: Adapted from Kington et al. (2011, p. 111).

subsequent research instrument, examining the focus of the study from different perspectives (for example, first round of teacher interviews fed into later interviews with school leaders and the pupil questionnaire. In view of this level of mixing the authors make the claim that the ECP approximates to a 'fully mixed, concurrent, multiphase, equal status, triangulation design' (Kington et al., 2011, p. 107).

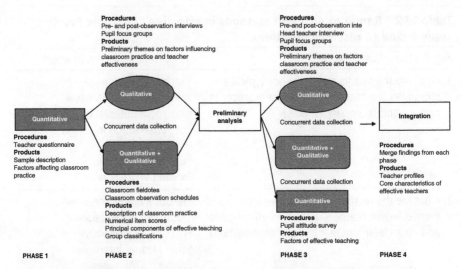

Figure 23.2   Illustration of fully mixed, concurrent, multiphase, equal status design of Effective Classroom Practice project

Source: Adapted from Kington et al. (2011, p. 108).

Kington et al. (2014a, p. 33) provide a further discussion of the ECP's MM approach with a focus on design decisions. They claim that 'the demands of this project led to the development of an integrated, holistic approach involving the combination of a range of research techniques, including those traditionally associated with both "quantitative" and "qualitative" paradigms'.

In the authors' view this enabled the ECP study to provide 'further insight and understanding of the factors that influence effectiveness and the relationships between (a) observed practice; (b) teacher, head teacher, and pupil perceptions; and (c) the analytical lenses of teachers' professional life phase and teachers' identity' (Kington et al., 2014a, p. 33). In line with the earlier VITAE study the researchers again chose to create individual teacher case studies as their prime focus for the point of interface where the mixing of the various qualitative and quantitative data took place. However, they also sought to provide an integration of the qualitative and quantitative approaches in relation to all stages of the research from the conceptualisation of research questions, data collection, data analysis, and data interpretation as the following quote illustrates.

> To avoid qualitative (stories) and quantitative (statistical) elements of the research being designed and conducted separately ... the process of integration began at the point of developing the research questions and continued through sampling, data collection, analysis, and reporting. The more detailed and holistic combination of approaches also allowed data, investigator, and methods triangulation (Denzin, 1978) and provided greater mapping, analysis, interpretation, and comprehension of the research area. (Kington et al., 2014a, p. 33)

Example 3: Evaluation of Teach First

The evaluation of Teach First (Muijs et al., 2010; Muijs et al., 2012) sought to investigate the link between pedagogy and student outcomes as part of an evaluation of the impact of Teach First an alternative teacher certification programme.

The authors sought to conduct a 'theory based' evaluation adopting the theoretical framework of the Dynamic Model of Educational Effectiveness, DMEE (Creemers and Kyriakides, 2008) to inform its approach. They reported their two underlying purposes (evaluation and theory testing) as follows:

> The key aim of this study was to explore the extent to which Teach First teachers were effective classroom practitioners and could have a positive impact on student learning, and what factors could support them in being effective. On a theoretical level, we were interested in whether this study could provide any additional support to the DMEE. (Muijs et al., 2012, p. 35)

Five linked research questions were described:

1 To what extent are Teach First teachers effective classroom practitioners, as perceived by school staff, external observers and colleagues?
2 Do Teach First teachers employ pedagogical approaches which are considered to be effective?
3 Is there any evidence that can support a positive impact on learning?
4 What factors can help or hinder them becoming effective practitioners?
5 Does this evaluation provide support for the DMEE?

In contrast to many MM investigations the authors made a particular emphasis on the value of adopting a theory driven approach to their investigation, with a strong link to the notion of 'a theory of action'. They argue that:

> A theory-driven evaluation approach assumes that we can use evaluation methodologies to illuminate theoretical models, linking evaluation of specific programmes to theories of change and action.... A key element of theory-driven evaluation is that the evaluation goals and mechanisms are not driven exclusively by stakeholders and evaluation commissioners, but also relate to the theoretical underpinnings that may explain intended outcomes and mechanisms by which they are to be achieved. (Muijs et al., 2012, p. 32)

Their rational for adopting a MM design was linked to the need to collect a range of measures that linked with the Dynamic Model that underpinned the theory of change and action. These authors were of the opinion that tapping the variables of interest necessitated both qualitative and quantitative techniques. 'A mixed methods approach was used in this study, as the different variables in our view require different data collection strategies. This design aimed to provide breadth and depth, while ensuring the collection of rigorous and replicable data' (Muijs et al., 2012, p. 33).

The Teach First evaluation involved using secondary data analysis from the English National Pupil Database plus quantitative classroom observations. These were analysed to identify the impact on teaching quality and student achievement. In addition, 'qualitative data from case studies and interviews were used to develop deeper understanding of processes and facilitators and barriers to success' (Muijs et al., 2012, p. 33).

The MM evaluation team of researchers combined members with qualitative and quantitative expertise and the case study element of the evaluation was itself MM in approach. In total a sample of 16 schools and 47 Teach First (TF) teachers were studied. The schools varied in location but were all in areas of high social disadvantage, reflecting the aims and placement of TF teachers. For the classroom observations the ISTOF instrument (Teddlie et al., 2006) was adopted (in line with the ECP study noted in example 2) chosen because it had been internationally validated to measure effective classroom practices. In addition a range of semi-structured interviews with TF teachers, their line managers and school head teachers were conducted.

The authors argued that there were many points of interface in their design that enabled the integration of the different sources. They described the iterative process of analysis and the way this allowed earlier analyses results to inform later data collection stages. In addition they described how qualitative data were quantitised as a further round of analysis after initial qualitative analysis had taken place.

> Qualitative data collection and data analysis were closely integrated.... This strategy allowed the team to check out hypotheses as they emerged from data analysis and refine data collection strategies as the study progressed. In addition to qualitative analysis, interview data were also analysed using content analytic methods. Content analysis is a summarising, quantitative analysis of messages that relies on the scientific method (including attention to objectivity-inter-subjectivity, a priori design, reliability, validity, generalizability, replicability, and hypothesis testing) and is not limited as to the types of variables that may be measured or the context in which the messages are created or presented ... A coding scheme was developed and results quantified. (Muijs et al., 2012, p. 37)

The Teach First evaluation acknowledged a major weakness in its reliance on secondary analysis of pupil attainment because it was only possible to link students' results to schools not to individual teachers. This meant that they could only test the quantitative hypothesis that the number of TF teachers in a school might be related to value added measures of effectiveness in terms of student outcomes. This hypothesis was informed by the qualitative data analysis which had suggested that the numbers of TF teachers in a school could influence the school culture in terms of the notion of a critical mass as the following quote articulates. Again this provides an explicit illustration of the 'point of interface between the quantitative and qualitative data and its uses.

In a second phase of the analyses, we explored whether the number of Teach First teachers who had worked in each of the Teach First schools affected the impact of their school. The hypothesis here is that a larger number of Teach First teachers might have a greater impact as a result of a greater impact on school culture, or through the facilitating effect of a critical mass of Teach First teachers as indicated in some of the qualitative data. (Muijs et al., 2012, p. 39)

Quantitative data on correlations between the number of TF teachers in the school were explored over time to test whether the critical mass hypothesis was supported by the data. In addition the qualitative data found that the critical mass of TF teachers in schools was borne out in terms of the analysis of barriers and facilitators of success.

The content analysis of interviews from line managers and head teachers was used to study the characteristics these stakeholders associated with TF teachers, and these qualitative themes were then quantitised to identify their relative prevalence and importance. Interviews with TF teachers themselves explored their perceptions of their own teaching approaches. It was revealed that they saw elements of constructivist and direct instruction teaching approaches, although a stronger emphasis on the latter. This finding was further tested from the quantitative observation data in terms of the ISTOF systematic observation rating scale.

Diagrams were used by these authors to illustrate the Dynamic Model link to their evaluation and to illustrate their quantitative analyses but, in contrast to the first two examples, they did not use a diagram to illustrate their research design. Nor did they seek to label their chosen design in terms of one of the five main design families discussed by Tashakkori and Teddlie (2003). In our view the TF study can be viewed as most closely aligned to the family of a Parallel Mixed Design. In addition, though not explicitly mentioned, the authors' position again suggests a pragmatist philosophical position where the research design is, at least in part, driven by the research aims and research questions, including the wish to test the utility of the Dynamic Model for evaluation purposes.

OVERVIEW

This chapter has provided an introduction to the rationale for, and conduct of, MM research. It has discussed the rise of MM studies as a third methodological approach that is distinctive from either qualitative or quantitative approaches that have been more commonly used in past social research. In addition, it has examined the way MM designs may be classified and evaluated. Three examples of different MM studies that have sought to study teachers' classroom practice have been chosen to illustrate the variety in the way MM designs can be developed and linked using an educational focus. These examples indicate the way research purposes and research questions typically drive the choice of a MM approach, either explicitly or implicitly linking with a pragmatist philosophical position.

In addition these examples have been used to illustrate the importance attached to the inductive–deductive 'to and fro' of the research process linking qualitative and quantitative components so that they are mutually informative. The notion of the 'point of interface' as propounded by Guest (2013) has been introduced and instances to illustrate this identified in the three chosen examples. The value of typologies to document and examine different MM designs and the role of diagrams to illustrate such designs and the ways qualitative and quantitative components of a study (samples, methods, analysis phases) are combined has been highlighted.

Approaching the end of this chapter, we offer an 'alphabetical' set of linked questions which can help readers to critically appraise, interrogate and so better understand published MM research studies. We suggest these may also be useful to those who are interested in the potential of MM research but have not yet used such designs as a basis to support their decision-making in designing a new MM investigation.

The MM 'alphabet': questions to support the critical appraisal of MM studies

Petticrew and Roberts (2006) remind us that the criteria which are deemed to constitute 'methodological perfection' are likely to change over time, and that the goal of critical appraisal is to:

> [Assess] the degree to which a study is affected by bias and whether the degree of bias is large enough to render the study unusable. It is not simply a matter of 'sorting the wheat from the chaff', but an assessment of whether the research is 'fit for purpose'. (Petticrew and Roberts, 2006, p. 131)

In relation to how environments of research and discovery evolve over time, we would therefore like to conclude this chapter by drawing a parallel between social science and the physical sciences or as Northcutt and McCoy (2004, p. 1) phrase, the 'ethereal world of subatomic particles':

> The qualitative researcher finds that the nature of both elements and relationships depends on complex interactions between the phenomenon that the system represents and the purpose and methods of interpretation brought to the phenomenon by the researcher ... [which] creates a fascinating paradox.... There are no universals or principles or grand *met-anarrative*. On the other hand, seemingly disparate phenomena are often discovered to be fundamentally similar when analyzed from a systems point of view ...'. (Northcutt and McCoy, 2004, p. 1)

There is an often mistaken belief that the definitions and criteria of measurement in the natural sciences rarely change; fleeting classifications and

Figure 23.3 Critical analysis: an A to Z for appraising MM studies

A. What was the overall purpose of this study (aims/objectives)?

B. What are the quantitative research questions?

C. What are the qualitative research questions?

D. How are the quantitative and qualitative questions linked?

E. What is the sample for the quantitative component of the study? How was it selected?

F. What is the sample for the qualitative component of the study? How was it selected?

G. What is the overall sampling frame and how are the qualitative and quantitative samples linked/related?

H. What are the quantitative data collection instruments/sources?

I. What are the qualitative data collection instruments/sources?

J. What are the joint quantitative/qualitative data collection instruments/sources (if any)?

K. What kinds of quantitative analyses strategies are used and how have they addressed the quantitative research questions?

L. What are the qualitative analyses strategies are used and how have they addressed the qualitative research questions?

M. What are the 'points of interface' linking the qualitative and quantitative data analyses?

N. What is the priority accorded to the qualitative and quantitative components of the study?

O. How were concerns about the quality of the quantitative data addressed (e.g. reliability, validity, generalisability)?

P. How were concerns about the quality of the qualitative data addressed (e.g. trustworthiness of findings)?

Q. What attempts were made to link or integrate the qualitative and quantitative components of the study?

R. How far do the quantitative and qualitative findings align? What efforts were made to reconcile/explain any differences in the findings of the qualitative and quantitative components of the study?

S. Are there any examples of any quantitising of qualitative data?

T. Are there any examples of any qualitising of quantitative data?

U. How rigorous is the description of the research design and methods?

V. Have the authors used a diagram to illustrate the MM design and the way different components are linked?

W. Do the researchers make an explicit case for adopting a MM design?

X. What is the philosophical position underpinning the research and how does it link with the research aims and purposes?

Y. Do the researchers make new knowledge claims that are based on the integration and synthesis of qualitative and quantitative data and findings?

Z. Is there evidence that the MM design has produced findings/ added new knowledge that is more than the 'sum' of the quantitative or qualitative parts?

Source: Adapted from Teddlie and Tashakkori (2009, pp. 37–8).

meanings are reserved specially for the social sciences. One need only study the evolution of something seemingly 'basic' such as the definition of the 'metre' as a unit of length to see that definitions change over time in *all* sciences, albeit within different mechanisms and resulting in different outcomes. Woolgar (1988, pp. 18–19) argues that the 'organisation and conception of science has, at a general level, itself varied over time. In other words, the way in which science might be defined has itself varied in response to the organisational and social factors which bear upon its boundedness'. Niaz (2008) in his review of MM research programmes in education suggests that MM:

> [P]rovides a rationale for hypotheses/theories/guiding assumptions/presuppositions to compete and provide alternatives. This facilitates the reconstruction of historical episodes in physical science and cognitive psychology based on Galilean idealisations. The historical reconstruction helps to juxtapose empirical evidence in the context of arguments and counter-arguments of the different competing groups of researchers. (Niaz, 2008, p. 298)

Analogous to MM is the basis for chemical synthesis, which necessitates the breaking of existing bonds and formation of new ones (Encyclopaedia Britannica, 2015):

> For many compounds, it is possible to establish alternative synthetic routes ... [K]nowledge of the reaction mechanism and the function of the chemical structure (or behaviour of the functional groups) helps to accurately determine the most-favoured pathway that leads to the desired reaction product.

Moving beyond even Lakatos' (1978) 'revolutions of science' and criteria for 'subsumption' (Walker, 2010, p. 438), MM may constitute a partial 'bridge' between ideas around the history and philosophy of science that still prevail today: Kuhn's 'scientific revolutions' and Popper's principle of 'falsification'. Teddlie and Tashakkori (2009) explain that making inferences in MM research 'is both an art and science' and:

> [I]nvolves elements of creativity, intuition, and meaning making as well as the ability to compartmentalize components or aspects of a phenomenon, understand each, and then reconstruct them for a full understanding. (Teddlie and Tashakkori, 2009, p. 289)

Nowhere else is the contribution of MM approaches and techniques seen more clearly than in the area of educational effectiveness and improvement (Muijs, 2012):

> Working within a pragmatic paradigm that essentially rejects paradigmatic fundamentalism, and interested in both quantifiable impacts and the complex processes related to them, mixed methods were seen as providing a route towards integrating these two

interests.... Improvement researchers also frequently employed similar mixed methods designs, where, again, schools were selected on the basis of performance trajectories (have they improved significantly), which is then followed by case study work to ascertain what factors were related to this improvement trajectory. (Muijs, 2012, p. 59)

Notwithstanding Latour's (1993) declaration that 'we have never been modern', in an age where physicists, in an attempt to understand the Big Bang, are investigating and publically articulating new approaches to fuse the seemingly irreconcilable General Theory of Relativity and Quantum Theory (SciTechDaily, 2015), perhaps social scientists are at least getting closer to 'being open to new discoveries in *both* QUAL and QUAN research' (Teddlie and Tashakkori, 2009, p. 291). MM research continues to face the challenges of integrating and reconciling different paradigms, realities and epistemologies (amongst other factors) and also of creating appropriate integration and synthesis of findings with a MM lens to deepen understanding and create new knowledge that goes beyond what may be established using either a quantitative or qualitative perspective alone. This is certainly an exciting position of discovery, particularly for researchers of complex educational and social science topics, where before them lie a range of research problems to understand and explain, using the opportunities made available by the pursuit of rigorous and creative MM research.

Notes

1 UK Department for Education known by different names under successive governments: 'Department for Education and Skills (DfES)' – 2001–2007; 'Department for Children, Schools and Families (DCSF)' – 2007–2010; 'Department for Education (DfE)' – 2010 to present.

2 Economic and Social Research Council, one of seven research councils (and a public body) that funds and supports peer-reviewed research in the UK.

3 A charity launched in 2002 to train and provide 'excellent' teachers in secondary schools within low-income communities in England and Wales. One of the main aims of the programme is to develop inspirational leaders in order to reduce educational inequalities. It is an alternative certification programme that built on the earlier Teach for America model.

4 A statistical measure of pupil progress from one stage of education to a later stage (e.g. across one or more school years) that takes into account pupils' prior attainment as well as controlling external factors such as social deprivation.

5 A measure of pupil progress from one stage of education to a later stage (e.g. across one or more school years). Attainment is measured based on pupils' prior attainment. [See also Note 4.]

6 A stage of pupils' education at different points during their school life in the UK. Each key stage marks expected levels of knowledge at various ages. Key Stage 1: ages 5–7, years 1 and 2; Key Stage 2: ages 7–11, years 3, 4, 5 and 6; Key Stage 3: ages 11–14, years 7, 8 and 9; Key Stage 4: ages 14–16, years 10 and 11.

7 An administrative body that governs a particular geographical area in the UK

REFERENCES

Bryman, A. (2007) The research question in social research: what is its role?. *International Journal of Social Research Methodology Theory and Practice*, 10(1): 5–20.

Creemers, B. P. M. and Kyriakides, L. (2008) *The Dynamics of Educational Effectiveness*. London: Routledge.

Creswell, J. W. (2003) *Research Design: Qualitative, quantitative and mixed methods approaches*. Thousand Oaks, CA: Sage.

Creswell, J. W., Klassen, A., Plano Clark, V. L. and Clegg Smith, C. (2011) *Best Practices for Mixed Methods Research in the Health Sciences*. Bethesda, MD: Office of Behavioral and Social Sciences Research, National Institutes of Health. Retrieved on 10 December, 2015 from http://obssr.od.nih.gov/scientific_areas/methodology/mixed_methods_research/index.aspx

Day, C., Sammons, P. and Gu, Q. (2008a) Combining qualitative and quantitative methodologies in research on teachers' lives, work, and effectiveness: from integration to synergy. *Educational Researcher*, 37(6): 330–342.

Day, C., Sammons, P., Stobart, G., Kingston, A. and Gu, Qing (2007) *Teachers Matter*. Milton Keynes: Open University Press.

Day, C., Stobart, G., Sammons, P., Kington, A., Gu, Q., Smees, R. and Mujtaba, T. (2006) Variations in teachers' work, lives and their effects on pupils: VITAE Report (DfES Research Rep. No. 743). London: Department for Education and Skills.

Day C., Sammons P., Kington A., Regan, E., Ko J., Brown E., Gunraj, J. and Robertson D. (2008b) *Effective classroom practice (ECP): A mixed-method study of influences and outcomes*. End of Award Report submitted to the Economic and Social Research Council, School of Education, The University of Nottingham, Reference No. RES-000-23-1564.

Denzin, N. K. (1978) *The Research Act: A theoretical introduction to sociological methods*. New York: Praeger.

Denzin, N. K. (2010) Moments, mixed methods, and paradigm dialogs. *Qualitative Inquiry*, 16(6): 419–427.

Eisner, E. (1986) The primacy of experience and the politics of method. *Educational Researcher*, 17(5): 15–20.

Encyclopaedia Britannica (2015) *Chemical Synthesis*. Retrieved on 10 December, 2015 from www.britannica.com/science/chemical-synthesis.

Fetters, M. and Freshwater, D. (2015) Publishing a methodological mixed methods research article. *Journal of Mixed Methods Research*, 9(3): 203–213.

Feyerabend, P. (1974) How to be a good empiricist: a plea for tolerance in matters epistemological. In P. H. Niddick (Ed.) *The Philosophy of Science* (pp. 12–39). Oxford: Oxford University Press.

Guest, G. (2013) Describing mixed methods research: an alternative to typologies. *Journal of Mixed Methods Research*, 7(2): 141–151.

Hall, B. and Howard, H. (2008) A synergistic approach conducting mixed methods research with typological and systemic design considerations. *Journal of Mixed Methods Research*, 2(3): 248–269.

Heyvaert, M., Hannes, K., Maes, B. and Onghena, P. (2013) Critical appraisal of mixed methods studies. *Journal of Mixed Methods Research*, 7(4): 302–327.

Hunter, A. and Brewer, J. (2003) Multimethod research in sociology. In A. Tashakkori and C. Teddlie (Eds) *Handbook of Mixed Methods in Social and Behavioural Research* (pp. 577–594). Thousand Oaks, CA: Sage.

Johnson, R. B. Onwuegbuzie, A. and Turner, L. (2007) Towards a definition of mixed methods research. *Journal of Mixed Methods Research*, 1(2): 112–133.

Johnson, S. (2006) *The Ghost Map*. London: Penguin Group.

Kington, A., Reed, N. and Sammons, P. (2014b) Teachers' constructs of effective classroom practice: variations across a career. *Research Papers in Education*, 29(5): 534–556.

Kington, A., Sammons, P., Day, C. and Regan, E. (2011) Stories and statistics: describing a mixed method study of effective classroom practice. *Journal of Mixed Methods Research*, 5(2): 103–125.

Kington, A., Sammons, P., Regan, E., Brown, E. and Ko, J. with Buckler, S. (2014a) *Effective Classroom Practice*. Maidenhead: McGraw Hill Open University Press.

Lakatos, I. (1978) *The Methodology of Scientific Research Programs*. Cambridge: Cambridge University Press.

Latour, B. (1993) *We Have Never Been Modern*. Cambridge, MA: Harvard University Press.

Leech, N. and Onwuegbuzie, A. (2009) A typology of mixed methods research designs. *Quality & Quantity*, 43(2): 265–275.

Maxwell, J. A. and Loomis, D. M. (2003) Mixed methods design: an alternative approach. In A. Tashakkori and C. Teddlie (Eds) *Handbook of Mixed Methods in Social and Behavioral Research* (pp. 241–272). Thousand Oaks, CA: Sage.

Merton, R. K. (1975) Structural analysis in sociology. In P. Blau (Ed.) *Approaches to the Study of Social Structure* (pp. 112–138). New York: The Free Press.

Morgan, D. L. (2007) Paradigms lost and pragmatism regained: methodological implications of combining qualitative and quantitative methods. *Journal of Mixed Methods Research*, 1(1): 48–76.

Muijs, D. (2012) Methodological change in educational effectiveness research. In C. Chapman, P. Armstrong, A. Harris, D. Muijs, D. Reynolds and P. Sammons (Eds) *School Effectiveness and Improvement Research, Policy and Practice: Challenging the orthodoxy?* (pp. 58–66). Oxford: Routledge.

Muijs, D., Chapman, C. and Armstrong, P. (2012) Teach first: pedagogy and outcomes. The impact of an alternative certification programme. *Journal for Educational Research*, 4(2): 29–64.

Muijs, D., Chapman, C., Collins, A. and Armstrong, P. (2010) *Maximum Impact Evaluation. The impact of Teach First teachers in schools: An evaluation funded by the Maximum Impact Programme for Teach First Final Report*, University of Southampton and University of Manchester.

Niaz, M. (2008) A rationale for mixed methods (integrative) research programmes in education. *Journal of Philosophy of Education*, 42(2): 287–305.

Northcutt, N. and McCoy, D. (2004) *Interactive Qualitative Analysis: A systems method for qualitative research*. Thousand Oaks, CA: Sage.

Onwuegbuzie, A. J. and Leech, N. L. (2005) Taking the 'Q' out of research: teaching research methodology courses without the divide between quantitative and qualitative paradigms. *Quality & Quantity*, 39(3): 267–296.

Onwuegbuzie, A. J. and Teddlie, C. (2003) A framework for analyzing data in mixed methods research. In A. Tashakkori and C. Teddlie (Eds) *Handbook of Mixed Methods in Social and Behavioral Research* (pp. 351–383). Thousand Oaks, CA: Sage.

Petticrew, M. and Roberts, H. (2006) *Systematic Reviews in the Social Sciences*. Oxford: Blackwell Publishing.

Salomon, G. (1991) Transcending the qualitative–quantitative debate: the analytic and systemic approaches to educational research. *Educational Researcher*, 20(6): 10–18.

Sammons, P. (2010) The contribution of mixed methods to recent research on educational effectiveness. In A. Tashakkori and C. Teddlie (Eds) *SAGE Handbook of Mixed Methods in Social and Behavioural Research*, 2nd edition (pp. 697–723). Thousand Oaks, CA: Sage.

Sammons, P., Day, C., Kington, A., Gu, Q., Stobart, G. and Smees, R. (2007) Exploring variations in teachers' work, lives and their effects on pupils: key findings and implications from a longitudinal mixed methods study. *British Educational Research Journal*, 33(5): 681–701.

SciTechDaily (2015) *Physicists Take a New Approach to Unify Quantum Theory and Theory of Relativity*. Retrieved on 10 December, 2015 from http://scitechdaily.com/physicists-take-new-approach-unify-quantum-theory-theory-relativity/.

Spalter-Roth, R. (2000) Gender issues in the use of integrated approaches. In M. Bamberger (Ed.) *Integrating Quantitative and Qualitative Research in Development Projects* (pp. 47–53). Washington, DC: The World Bank.

Tashakkori, A. and Teddlie, C. (1998) *Mixed Methodology: Combining qualitative and quantitative approaches*. Thousand Oaks, CA: Sage.

Tashakkori, A. and Teddlie, C. (Eds) (2003) *Handbook of Mixed Methods in Social and Behavioural Research*. Thousand Oaks, CA: Sage.

Tashakkori, A. and Teddlie, C. (Eds) (2010a) *Handbook of Mixed Methods in Social and Behavioural Research*. Thousand Oaks, CA: Sage.

Tashakkori, A. and Teddlie, C. (2010b) Putting the human back in 'human research methodology': the researcher in mixed methods research. *Journal of Mixed Methods Research*, 4(4): 271–277.

Teddlie, C. and Sammons, P. (2010) Applications of mixed methods to the field of educational effectiveness research. In B. P. M. Creemers, L. Kyriakides and P. Sammons (Eds) *Methodological Advances in Educational Effectiveness Research* (pp. 115–152). London: Routledge Taylor & Francis.

Teddlie, C. and Tashakkori, A. (2009) *Foundations of Mixed Methods Research: Integrating quantitative and qualitative approaches in the social and behavioural sciences*. Thousand Oaks, CA: Sage.

Teddlie, C., Creemers, B., Kyriakides, L., Muijs, D. and Yu, F. (2006) The international system for teacher observation and feedback: evolution of an international study of teacher effectiveness constructs. *Educational Research and Evaluation*, 12: 561–582.

van de Grift, W. (2007) Quality of teaching in four European countries: a review of the literature and application of an assessment instrument. *Educational Research*, 49(2): 127–152.

van de Grift, W., Helms-Lorenz, M. and Maulana, R. (2014) Teaching skills of student teachers: calibration of an evaluation instrument and its value in predicting student academic engagement. *Studies in Educational Evaluation*, 43: 150–159.

van de Grift, W., Matthews, P., Tabak, L. and de Rijcke, F. (2004) *Comparative Research into the Inspection of Teaching in England and the Netherlands* (HMI 2251). London: Ofsted.

Walker, T. (2010) The perils of paradigm mentalities: revisiting Kuhn, Lakatos, and Popper. *Perspectives on Politics*, 8(2): 433–451.

Woolgar, S. (1988) *Science: The very idea*. Chichester: Ellis Horwood.

24

Using Secondary Data Analysis

Pamela E. Davis-Kean and Justin Jager

One of the advances in educational research in the last century has been the collection of large-scale educational studies for understanding the various issues of schooling as children enter the primary grades and matriculate from secondary school. These data collections were premised on the idea that we needed to understand how children are learning and interacting with the educational context across time. Many countries, including the US and UK have invested a considerable amount of money in trying to understand and describe the experiences of children in schools and how they achieve both academically as well as socio-emotionally in the schooling context. International datasets such as the PISA and TIMMS have also been develop in order to track differences in achievement across multiple countries in order to compare and contrast the learning and training experiences across different education policies, funding, ideology, and pedagogy of different nations. Thus, a robust set of data is available to data scientists who are interested in answering important questions in education that is both important within countries but also across countries as well.

Some of the important questions that are often asked involve how groups differ across important demographic groups such as socio-economic status, race/ethnicity, and country of origin. The availability of these datasets has allowed researchers and educators to detail the gap in trajectories of achievement within countries (Fryer and Levitt, 2004; Lee and Burkam, 2002) as well as across countries (Mullis et al., 2009). These achievement gaps have important education policy implications and many changes have been made to how schools and countries address disparities in education based on the findings from these various datasets. For example, the emphasis on math and science education across developed countries was in part due the international comparisons done in the Trends in International Mathematics and Science Study-TIMMS (http://timssandpirls. bc.edu/) study. Policymakers and educators could see how students across the world ranked on maths achievement tests that were created to be comparable across countries. Even though many of these datasets are available for examining the issues of education within and between countries with the statistical power to find small differences between groups, the majority of the research in education in all countries is still generated from smaller community and classroom studies. In this chapter, we discuss the advantages of using existing datasets to study a range of important educational questions, the challenges, hurdles and limitations associate with using these datasets, and how to obtain theses datasets for use by the research community. We will also discuss and give examples of how important questions in the field of education can be rigorously answered by using these datasets and thus provides an important addition to the methods used in educational research and science.

WHY USE SECONDARY DATA TO ANSWER EDUCATION QUESTIONS?

It is often difficult to define a specific question that pertains to education due to the breadth of this field of study. Education researchers are not only interested in the context of schooling, such as the classroom or the school, but are often also interested in the individual learning of the student in these contexts. One cannot study learning unless you understand how that student learns and this is often informed by the home environment and parenting that the student receives (Davis-Kean and Sexton, 2009). However, when it comes to contexts, education researchers must extend their focus beyond the family because the educational climate within a school is predicated on the policies in various states and countries regarding the allocation of funding for education and the policies surrounding how to meet the criteria for proficiency and achievement. In the United States, for example, schools are decentralized and emphasize local control of schools and so policies related to schooling are decided at district levels within cities, counties and states (Bray, 1999). The state is the primary funder of education and sets the policies within the state regarding education. Other countries like Canada and the United Kingdom have a more centralized system, where the policies are decided at the federal level (Cole and Hill, 2013). Thus, how to understand an individual characteristic like achievement can be quite complex and the data needed to account for various factors that influence achievement demands access to complex data that represents the breadth of how individuals are educated. Luckily, for education scientists around the world there are datasets available that can be used to look at multiple levels influencing the education of an individual as well as education systems in general.

PRIMARY VERSUS SECONDARY DATASETS

For some researchers, the idea of using secondary datasets to answer their questions will be a novel idea. Many researchers from education and associated areas (for example, psychology) are trained to collect new data to answer their questions. This is to ensure that they have appropriately tested the theories or models that they have proposed and to use the best measurements of the constructs in these models. This type of data collection is considered *primary* data collection because the data is collected by the person who designed the data collection and the measures for the study. There are many advantages to this type of data collection including having control over the design and measurement of the study, being able to make changes to protocols when events may warrant changes (for example, a measure proves to be too difficult for age of children sampled, translations are needed for certain populations), having the only access to the data for publications, and being able to secure relationships with schools, teachers, parents, and students for future data collection. Basically, the researcher is in full control of the content and rigor of the data being collected through primary data collection. There are also disadvantages to this approach.

For quantitative researchers, primary data collection is often disadvantaged by the amount of time it takes to collect the appropriate sample for studying a phenomenon. In order to ascertain the sample size needed to statistically power the types of studies done in education and educational psychology, hundreds of schools and thousands of children are often needed. The recruitment of a sample can take months and then scheduling the interviews and testing can take additional time. These studies are vulnerable to small samples, large amounts of missing data, non-representation of the population, and lack of diversity across race and socio-economic status (SES)/class (Davis-Kean and Jager, 2012). The precision that is gained by using strong measurement may be lost in the lack of generalizability of the research to the general populations. Since the goal of most educational research is to be able to generalize findings to the population of focus, losing the ability to generalize is a large cost of the primary data collection. Many of the issues, however, can be solved by using secondary sources of data.

Unlike primary data, secondary data are data designed and collected by another researcher or research organization. For educational researchers these are often collected for the sake of tracking educational trends within or across countries. In the US the National Center for Educational Statistics (NCES, https://nces.ed.gov/) is one of the largest repositories of datasets collected for the purpose of monitoring and providing data for research on educational changes. In the UK, the Data.Gov.UK archive is an excellent resource for data including multiple datasets from the Department for Education (https://data.gov.uk/publisher/department-for-education) complete with a map of where the data was collected (see Table 24.2 for additional resources). These datasets generally offer data about students, teachers, and schools and are representative of the population in their respective country. They are also generally large enough (statistically powered) that subgroups of the population (gender, race, SES/class, geographical area) can be adequately studied. Many (if not most) are longitudinal so that changes (or growth) in achievement can be monitored and various influences that predict these changes can be examined. These are all excellent reasons to use these datasets but perhaps the most important for the educational scientist or student is the ability to access this data without waiting the years required to collect this extensive amount of data across schooling. Many educational research questions can be answered using these datasets with a scientific rigor that cannot be matched in the primary datasets. Even though these datasets are able to overcome many of the issues of primary data, there are still limitations to them that should be acknowledged.

Perhaps the primary limitation for secondary data is the lack of control that a researcher has in the questions or assessments that are administered. Thus, the educational scientist may have questions that cannot be answered with the dataset of interest. More common is that there is some measurement of a construct of interest but the full measure is not available because it had to be shortened in order to be added to a large survey and thus maybe less reliable and valid than the original measure.

A similar issue relates to change in measurement across time. This is a problem for both primary and secondary datasets in trying to ascertain growth or change in various outcomes of interest to educational researchers. Achievement measures are generally standardized and well validated and can be used with some precision across the years of schooling and into adulthood. Measures of socio-emotional change, however, are not generally standardized and it is often not obvious how they might change and grow across time (Davis-Kean et al., 2008). Thus, when using secondary datasets, you have to carefully read the manuals to understand what has been measured when and how often they are measured across time if understanding change or growth in an educational outcome is a goal of the study. Using these datasets, however, are not without controversy as demonstrated in an interesting debate by Feinstein et al. (2015) over the issue of historical ways that class and cognitive ability have been examined in older datasets like the British Cohort Studies and newer cohorts such as the Millennium Cohort Study in the UK and whether or not analyses on these more historic datasets provide useful information on current education policy or even ways that education should be considered with more current issues such as differences in immigration status. Thus, another important concept to consider with secondary data analyses is whether you want to look at historical changes or are trying to examine current educational issue in order to allow for intervention. These questions are dictated by the question and intent of the researcher and there are secondary forms of data including administrative data available to help in answering the questions but historically and contemporaneously.

As noted above, the fact that most secondary data are longitudinal in design is certainly a strength; however, a longitudinal design can also be weakness if the data from a decade ago is no longer a valid way to examine educational trends.

The policies regarding education change almost yearly and certainly as frequently as the politicians change at state and federal levels. Hence, depending on the age of the secondary dataset, it may not be capturing the contemporaneous issues that are happening with curriculum, teaching, and schools. Primary data collection is more versatile regarding major historical changes in education policy though the change would need to be quite formidable to see short term changes in education.

Another advantage in many of the secondary datasets, especially those that have been archived in data repositories, is the strong documentation of the measures and study, in general. The codebooks are generally well detailed and though it is often a challenge to understand the complexity of the dataset, the documentation allows for the easy extraction of the data. There are still issues with data being incorrectly labelled or coded but much less than occurs in primary datasets that are used by a small set of researchers that manage the data.

Finally, any researcher using the larger scale population education datasets will need statistical sophistication in understanding the complex weighting of these samples in order for them to represent the population of interest. Although this knowledge is relatively easily achieved; however, there are many programs that may not teach these skills because they are oriented to smaller scale data collection. In the next section we review some of the important concepts that are needed to understand how to use weights when using population studies to examine educational questions (Davis-Kean et al., 2015).

Whilst both primary and secondary datasets have their advantages, there are strong reasons for considering the use of secondary data analyses to answer educational questions. The ability of national datasets to represent the population of interest is perhaps the strongest reason for considering the use of secondary datasets. Since interventions are often the focus of educational research it is essential that we understand who is struggling to be proficient or achieve in the various schooling contexts in the country of interest. This demands large scale education data so that all groups in a society can be examined. No single researcher can accomplish this on their own and so the availability of this data for analyses makes it possible to answer questions on the achievement gap, socio-economic differences in education, curriculum differences, teacher effects on achievement, and many other questions related to the policies within a school. Adding secondary data analyses as a statistical method in educational research will increase the rigor and generalizability of our findings, which is a very important tool to add to the statistical toolbox (Davis-Kean and Jager, 2012).

OVERCOMING KEY ANALYTICAL HURDLES TO THE USE OF SECONDARY DATA

In this section we highlight and describe three analytical hurdles associated with the use of large-scale, educational data and provide readers with the necessary information to meet these challenges. While the first two hurdles revolve around the incorporation of sample weights into one's analysis, the third hurdle entails adjusting for the effects of a complex sampling design. For purposes of illustration, we use the National Center For Education Statistics' Early Childhood Longitudinal Study, Kindergarten Class of 1998–1999 (ECLS-K), which is a national, longitudinal study of US students that spans from Kindergarten to 8th grade (Tourangeau et al., 2009). We use the ECLS-K to illustrate the three analytical hurdles associated with large-scale, educational data because not only does the ECLS-K provide clear and straightforward examples of the problems associated with each hurdle, it also provides examples of the prototypical solutions to each hurdle. However, we wish to stress that although the ECLS-K is particularly well-suited to illustrate the analytical hurdles as well as the hurdles' solutions, the hurdles we describe here are by no means unique to the ECLS-K or even to US data more generally. Instead, these analytical hurdles hold for most large-scale, educational datasets, including those from the UK.

Hurdle 1: Apply sample weights to avoid estimate bias

Because oversampling of one or more subpopulations is common with large-scale educational data, educational researchers often must apply a sample weight if they want their findings to generalize to the target population (that is, the population that the study purports to represent). For example, as part of ECLS-K, Asian students were purposely oversampled at Kindergarten to help insure a sufficient number were included in the sample. Because Asian children were purposely oversampled at Kindergarten, within the ECSL-K the Spring Kindergarten (Spring-K) percentage of Asian students is inflated relative to the target population (Figure 24.1, Table 24.1). Specifically, although the percentage of Asian Kindergarten students among the target population is around 3 percent (the ECLS-K administrators based this percentage on the fact that Asian children comprised around 3 percent of population of 5-year-olds within the United States at the time of data collection), the percentage of Asian kindergarten students among the Spring-K sample was around 7 percent, or around 2.3 times larger than among the target population.

Sample weights correct for the estimate bias introduced by purposeful non-random sampling. Generally, sample weights average out to 1.0, with subpopulations that are underrepresented in the sample relative to the target population (students other than Asian students in the ECLS-K) have sample weights larger than 1.0 while the opposite holds for subpopulations overrepresented in the sample relative to the target population (Asian students in the ECSK-K). Moreover, the more underrepresented in the sample a subpopulation is, the larger its sample weight (the farther it is from 1.0), and more the more overrepresented in the sample a subpopulation is, the smaller its sample weight (the closer it is to zero). When no sample weights are applied it is as if a sample weight of 1.0 is uniformly

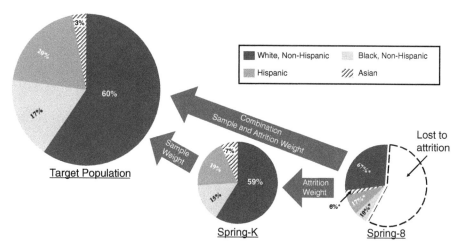

Figure 24.1 Target population and samples, and the distinct functions of sample, attrition, and combination weights

*Represents percentage among those retained at Spring-8th. Spring-K – Spring Kindergarten Sample; Spring-8 = Spring 8th grade sample

applied to all subpopulations. This, in effect, assumes all subpopulations are accurately represented within the sample, leading to biased estimates when this assumption does not hold. Typically, the appropriate set of sample weights and its corresponding variable name is clearly identified within a dataset's documentation file(s). For example, according to the ECSL-K user's manual (Tourangeau et al., 2009), we should apply the following sample weight for the Spring-K data: C2CW0. After applying this weight (Table 24.1) the Spring-K percentage Asian Students (3 percent) matches that of the Target Population percentage (3 percent).

Hurdle 2: Harmonize weights and missing data strategy to maximize power and minimize bias

Many large-scale educational datasets utilize a longitudinal design. When working with large-scale longitudinal data, attrition is common. The problem that attrition poses is that it is typically differential or non-random (that is, certain types of study participants, such as those from lower socio-economic backgrounds, are more likely to drop out of the study). As a result of differential attrition, the demographic composition of a study's sample changes across waves, which complicates comparisons of estimates across multiple waves. For example, within the ECLS-K a disproportionate amount of Black Non-Hispanic students were lost to attrition across the Spring-K and the Spring of 8th Grade (Spring-8; Figure 24.1, Table 24.1). More specifically, whereas Black students comprised 15 percent of the Spring-K sample, they only comprised 10 percent

Table 24.1   Race/ethnic composition and weighted percentages at kindergarten and 8th grade, by target population and samples

	No weight applied				Spring-K sample weight applied				Spring-8 combination weight applied			
	White, non-Hispanic	Black, non-Hispanic	Hispanic	Asian	White, non-Hispanic	Black, non-Hispanic	Hispanic	Asian	White, non-Hispanic	Black, non-Hispanic	Hispanic	Asian
Target Population	60%	17%	20%	3%	–	–	–	–	–	–	–	–
Spring-K	59%	16%	19%	7%	60%	17%	20%	3%	–	–	–	–
Spring-8	67%	10%	17%	6%	–	–	–	–	60%	17%	20%	3%

of the Spring-8 sample. To be clear, the problem that differential attrition across race poses is that differences in achievement across time could in part be a function of differences in the racial composition of the sample across time. Here we discuss and compare and contrast two general approaches to adjusting for the effects of attrition: (1) the use of weights and (2) the use of missing data techniques such as Full Information Likelihood (FIML) and multiple imputation (MI).

Generally, there are two categories or types of weights that can be used to adjust for attrition. The first type is aptly named an 'attrition weight'. In contrast to sample weights, which adjust for sampling bias, attrition weights correct for bias introduced by attrition. Thus, the objective of attrition weights (Figure 1) is to render subsequent waves of data (here the ECLS-K Spring-8 sample) comparable to the initial wave of data (here the ECLS-K Spring-K sample). Combination weights (also called longitudinal weights) are the second type of weight that can be used to adjust for attrition. The reason these sorts of weights are referred to as 'combination' weights is because they adjust for *both* sampling bias and attrition bias. Returning to our example involving the ECLS-K, the objective of combination weights is to render the Spring-8 sample comparable to the target population (Figure 1). As is often the case with large-scale longitudinal data, ECLS-K does not provide attrition weights but does provide combination weights. According to the ECSL-K user's manual, given the combination of waves of data we are using here (that is, Spring-K through Spring-8), we should apply the following combination weight: C2_7FC0. After applying the weight (Table 24.1) the Spring-8 percentages of Asian Students (3 percent) and Black students (10 percent) match those of the Target Population.

Instead of using weights to adjust for attrition, researchers can take advantage of more advanced missing data approaches, such as FIML and MI. Because an introduction to FIML and MI is beyond the scope of this chapter, we direct readers who are interested in a primer on these techniques to please see either Enders (2013) or Graham (2009). We do wish to note here that both techniques are available in most statistical software packages (for example, SAS, Stata, SPSS, and Mplus) and therefore accessible to the general researcher. Moreover, of the two techniques, FIML is simpler to implement (that is, in some cases FIML is the default option and in most other cases applying FIML is as simple as adding a single line of syntax or checking a box in a drop-down menu). We also believe that, of the two techniques, FIML is less prone to 'user error'. Consequently, while both FIML and MI are effective and proven strategies to adjust for attrition, for researchers who are unfamiliar with both techniques FIML might prove easier to both use and use correctly.

Typically, data administrators instruct users of their data to use combination weights when carrying out longitudinal analyses because they assume that users of their data will fail to adjust for attrition some other way, such as through the use of FIML or MI. However, counter to what data administrators often recommend, we recommend avoiding the use of both attrition and combination weights and instead using FIML or MI. Put another way, consumers of large-scale secondary educational data should use sample weights (when available) to adjust for the effects of sampling bias and use FIML or MI to adjust for the effects of attrition. We make this recommendation because relative to FIML and MI, attrition weights (including combination weights) have two key disadvantages. First, unlike FIML and MI, attrition weights often sharply reduce one's analytical sample and, thereby, statistical power. This is because typically only those with data at every wave are assigned an attrition weight and only those with an attrition weight are included in the analyses. Within the ECLS-K example, where the Spring-K unweighted $N = 19,967$ and the unweighted N for those who reported data at every wave through Spring-8 = 8,503, one's analytical N would be 8,503 with attrition weights (or combination weights that incorporate attrition weights) but 19,967 with FIML or MI. Second, there is reason to believe that FIML and MI, provided a large set of auxiliary variables (that is, non-model variables related to missingness) are incorporated, are more effective in adjusting for attrition bias than are attrition weights.

Hurdle 3: Adjust for complex sampling design to avoid Type I errors

Most large-scale datasets utilize complex sample designs. Avoiding the particulars of complex sampling, here we highlight that complex sampling entails a multi-staged or clustered sampling design (for example, schools are randomly sampled and then all students within the selected schools are sampled). For example, the ECLS-K utilized a multi-staged sampling design that consisted of three stages: (1) US counties were randomly sampled, (2) then within sampled counties, schools were randomly sampled, and (3) then within sampled schools, kindergarteners were randomly sampled. Because a multi-staged or clustered sampling design reduces variance (for example, 100 students from the same school are likely more similar to one another demographically then are 100 students from 100 different schools), it also reduces standard errors and thereby inflates the chance for Type I errors (Davis-Kean and Jager, 2012). For more information on complex sample designs please see Bornstein et al. (2013) or Levy and Lemeshow (2013). To adjust for these design effects a 'primary sampling unit' variable (for example, schools) and potentially a 'stratification' variable are incorporated into one's analyses. Most statistical packages (for example, SAS, Stata, SPSS, and Mplus) are capable of adjusting for a complex sampling design and typically the appropriate primary sampling unit and, if necessary, stratification variables are clearly identified within a dataset's documentation file(s). For example, according to the ECSL-K user's manual, given the combination of waves of data we are using here (that is, Spring-K through Spring-8), we should apply a specific PSU variable (that is, C27FCPSU) and a specific stratum variable (that is, C27FCSTR).

HOW TO FIND SECONDARY DATA

When searching for a secondary dataset, chances are you will not be able to find one that is perfectly suited to address your research question; after all, the designers of a given secondary dataset likely did not have your particular research question in mind when developing and designing their dataset. Consequently, when searching for a secondary dataset, your goal is to identify the dataset that is *best* equipped to address your research question. With that goal in mind, a data archive is likely the best place to start your search. Table 24.2 lists three major data archives – Interuniversity Consortium for Political and Social Research (ICPSR); The Murray Research Archive (MRA), and the Consortium of European Social Science Data Archives (CESSDA) – as well their websites. Though based at US universities, both ICPSR and MRA contain archival data from a host of different nations and both are accessible to those from outside the US (although for ICPSR one needs to be affiliated with an ICPSR membership institution). Finally, CESSDA houses archives from 13 European nations and while the archives are generally available to all, the steps required for access do vary somewhat by nation. Also listed in Table 24.2 is an international selection of secondary datasets that have wide applicability for education-focused research. For each dataset listed in Table 24.2 we also indicate whether it is a public or private use dataset as well as its nationality. It is important to keep in mind that 'private' datasets are still typically accessible to the average researcher provided he or she follows a given dataset's protocol for gaining access, which usually entails providing a brief description of how you plan to use the data as well as a description of a data security plan. For each of the private datasets listed in Table 24.2, the particulars of the dataset's protocol for gaining access can be found on its website. It is also important to keep in mind that these datasets were not all necessarily developed by educational researchers or with the primary aim of tracking and understanding educational outcomes. Nonetheless, all of the datasets listed in Table 24.2 do have rich educational data. Chances are, between the datasets available within the data archives and the specific datasets listed in Table 24.2, you will be able to find an existing dataset adequately equipped to address your research question.

EXAMPLES OF RESEARCH USING SECONDARY DATA

So far in this chapter we have discussed the advantages and disadvantages of using secondary data for answering questions in educational science. We have also detailed the additional statistical steps that are needed to in order to adequately generalize to the population with using representative datasets. In this section we will give comprehensive examples of how using secondary datasets can lead to answering important questions in education that are rigorous and replicated.

Table 24.2   Resources for secondary educational data

Resource	Public/Private	Nationality	Website
Data Archives			
Murray Research Archives (MRA)	Both	Many	www.murray.harvard.edu
Inter-University Consortium for Political and Social Research (ICPSR)	Both	Many	www.icpsr.umich.edu/icpsrweb/ICPSR
Data.Gov.UK	Public	UK	https://data.gov.uk/publisher/department-for-education
UK Data Service	Public	UK	www.ukdataservice.ac.uk/
UK Data Archive	Public	UK	www.data-archive.ac.uk/
Consortium of European Social Science Data Archives (CESSDA)	Both	Many	www.cessda.net
Secondary datasets			
The National Longitudinal Study of Adolescent Health (Add Health)	Both	US	www.cpc.unc.edu/projects/addhealth
Monitoring the Future (MTF)	Both	US	www.monitoringthefuture.org/
Early Childhood Longtitudinal Study-Birth Cohort (ECLS-B)	Public	US	www.nces.ed.gov/ecls/birth.asp
Early Childhood Longitudinal Study-Kindergarten Classt of 1998-1999 (ECLS-K)	Public	US	www.nces.ed.gov/ecls/kindergarten.asp
Early Childhood Longitudinal Study-Kindergarten Class of 2010-2011 (ECLS-K:2011)	Public	US	www.nces.ed.gov/ecls/kindergarten2011.asp
National Child Development Study (NCDS)	Both	UK	www.cls.ioe.ac.uk/
British Cohort Study (BCS)	Both	UK	www.cls.ioe.ac.uk/
Millennium Cohort Study (MCS)	Both	UK	www.cls.ioe.ac.uk/

Example 1: Achievement gap

Defining the Question

For many years there has been a clear achievement gap between race groups in the US. Many researchers have examined this across different cohorts and tried to explain the effect by taking into account demographic, school and classroom, parenting, and individual difference but even though accounting for these factors reduced the differences in the groups, the gap was not eliminated. One of the issues with this large body of research was that the gap was always examined as a between race gap that perpetuated the idea that anyone of a particular race would, on average, score more poorly than those of another race group. In 2014, Davis-Kean and Jager asked the question in a different way. They were concerned that there might be race groups where lower performers were more represented and when examining the average differences were masking the fact that there were also high achievers in this population. Indeed, they posited that high achievers may have similar trajectories of achievement no matter what the race of a student, but what differed was the proportion of high achievers in each race. If the proportion of low achievers was substantial then examining the average trajectory or average achievement of a given race would miss that there were high achievers within that race group in and, in turn, misrepresent the achievement levels of that race group. Thus, the goal was to represent the achievement profiles within race groups and to examine how they changed across schooling.

Locating the appropriate dataset

In order to answer these questions, the researchers needed to obtain a dataset that adequately sampled multiple race groups so that the research could be representative of those populations, had at least three time points of achievement data available in order to describe trajectories, and collected a large enough sample so that the race groups could be compared, and was representative of schooling in the US. In this case, the dataset with the most recent information available on schooling with adequate sample and available data and time points was the Early Childhood Longitudinal Survey-Kindergarten cohort (ECLS-K).

This survey collected data on approximately 20,000 children across the United States as the entered Kindergarten in 1998. These children were followed through 8th grade when the study was ended. The dataset contains information from students, parents, teachers, schools and administrative data across all waves of data collection. It sampled public, private, and parochial schools and represents students in these schooling contexts. The weighting and sampling used for this dataset is detailed in the previous section and was implemented in this study.

Answering the Question

In order to answer the questions of the study, Davis-Kean and Jager (2014) used a Latent Class Analysis to obtain profiles of achievement trajectories within groups. They found that each race group had a representation of high, average, and low achievers and that socio-economic status was related to many of the differences (but not all) that were found in these groups. They were able to show that each race group had different proportions of achievers in these high, average, and low trajectories but that high achievers did not look the same in each of the race groups. There was still an achievement gap present between race groups even for the highest achievers. There were also able to show the various trajectories of achievement across time for these groups that differed within and between groups. Thus, new information was available to the literature on the achievement gap. Namely, that not only are there differences between race groups but significant differences within groups that are related to the socio-economic status within those race group. Davis-Kean and Jager (2012) were also able to show that some children with low scores at Kindergarten were able to 'catch-up' in achievement across the first six years of schooling and did not look different from those on the high performing trajectory by 5th grade.

Example 2: Fractions and algebra

Defining the Question

For many years, educators and researchers discussed the important link between learning fractions early in elementary school and performance in algebra in junior high and high school. However, when researchers looked in the literature to find the study that showed this relation, they were unable to find a single study that showed this relation. A group of researchers (Siegler et al., 2012) decided to see if there was indeed a relation between early fraction ability and later performance in algebra above that of other early math skills such as addition, subtraction, multiplication and division. They wanted to generalize to the population and since they were looking at issues of prediction from about 4th grade to 8th and 9th grade, needed a longitudinal dataset that had tested these concepts at those time points. They also had a secondary goal to test the rigor of the finding by replicating this finding across multiple datasets (Duncan, 2015).

Locating the Appropriate Dataset

In order to answer the questions they sought out datasets that had information on students starting at 8–9 years of age and again at 12–13 years of age. These datasets also needed to contain and have available the items that were used to test the various groups of math topics (addition, subtraction, multiplication, division, fractions, and algebra) so that they could be correctly coded to test the primary question of the study – do fractions matter for later algebra ability above that of other basic math skills. The research team was able to locate two studies, one in the US called the *Panel Study of Income Dynamics-Child Development Supplement* (PSID-CDS) and one in the UK called the *British Cohort Studies* (BCS) that met all the requirements. The ability to use the UK dataset made another question available to be answered: how universal is the relation between fractions and algebra given different education systems. These datasets represented the population of each of the countries, could be generalized to those populations, and allowed for the ability to replicate findings in two different countries.

The Panel Study of Dynamics – Child Development Supplement

The Panel Study of Income Dynamics began in 1968 by drawing a nationally representative sample of over 18,000 individuals living in 5,000 families in the United States. Information on these individuals and their descendants has been collected continuously (annually through 1993, biennially since then). The information includes data on employment, income, wealth, expenditures, health, marriage, childbearing, child development, philanthropy, education, and numerous other topics.

In 1997, all PSID families who had children between birth and 12 years of age were recruited to participate in the Child Development Supplement of the PSID (Hofferth et al., 1998). The CDS includes up to two children selected randomly from each PSID family that agreed to participate (CDS-I). The CDS-I collected data on 2,394 families (88 percent of eligible families) and their 3,563 children. The families who remained active in the PSID were reassessed in 2002 and 2003 (CDS-II). The CDS-II collected data on the 2091 families (91 percent of those in the CD-I) and their 2,907 children. Data and documentation are available at http://psidonline.isr.umich.edu/.

The British Cohort Studies

British Cohort Study (BCS). The 1970 British Cohort Study is a longitudinal study that follows into adulthood all individuals born in Great Britain during a single week in April, 1970 (1). Data collection sweeps for BCS have taken place when the cohort members were aged 5, 10, 16, 26, 30, 34, and most recently 38 years (2). The birth sample of 17,196 infants was approximately 97 percent of the target birth population. The responding sample at age 10 was 14,350 (83 percent) and at age 16 was 11,206 (65 percent). Data and documentation are available at http://www.cls.ioe.ac.uk/.

Answering the Question

Siegler et al. (2012) answered the questions of the study by examining multiple regressions of both datasets which took into account multiple alternative explanations for their findings. One of the limitations of the studies was that in order to compare two studies Siegler et al. had to reduce the variables that could be examined to a smaller set that both datasets had in common. Even with this reduction in variables, the major math variables were consistent across both datasets as were a robust set of socio-demographic indicators. The findings were consistent across both datasets that fractions were indeed a significant predictor of later math skills even after taking into account the basic math skills. There was also an unexpected finding. Division independent of fractions was also a predictor of later math skills and this was true in both the US and UK datasets. Thus, a replicated finding that there are two fundamental math skills needed in early elementary school in order to achieve in later algebra and advance math skills: fractions and division. These findings have important implications for teaching mathematics in both countries and, importantly, were shown to generalize to the populations of both the US and the UK. Also of note, is that these findings were consistent even though both countries have different educational systems and training.

These examples show how secondary data analyses can be a powerful methodological tool for answering questions in educational research. Even though there are limitations to the depth of measurement in some of the studies, the breadth and generalizability of the research surpasses that of the community based educational studies. As was shown in the examples, important research questions can be answered and even validated and replicated across multiple datasets which allows for a rigorous test of models and hypothesis.

SUMMARY

The use of secondary datasets to study human behavior is fairly commonplace in the social sciences (for example, economics, sociology, and political science). These disciplines are interested in generalizing to the populations they are studying as well as accounting for potential differences and biases related to issues such as race and socio-economic differences. Even though there are multiple representative educational datasets available to be used by educational researchers, many researchers are not aware of them or do not know how to appropriately weight them to represent the population of interest. In this chapter we have provided guidance on how to use these datasets to answer educational questions and to increase the rigor of educational studies.

We have chosen to focus on national, population studies because these datasets represent the countries in which they are drawn. There are, however, many datasets that have been collected by researchers that are not representative but may also be useful for examining topics of interest to the broader educational community. Many of these can be found in data archives and we have provided information on how to obtain these in Table 24.2. These datasets will be limited in their generalizability to the population but may be rich in variables that look at issues of curriculum or classroom activities. The important point is that there is wealth of data available that has been collected across time and in many countries that can be useful in answering many educational questions of importance to educational researchers.

In this chapter we also highlight some of the limitations to using this data. These limitations include limited constructs being measured, reduced scale information, dominance of self-report methods, and retrospective measures. Even with these limitations, a secondary data analysis provides a powerful tool for the educational researcher in answering important questions for the education sciences.

The possibility to generalize to the population and to increase the rigor of the science by replicating across similar datasets creates advantages for the research literature as well as educational policymakers. Thus, secondary data analyses for educational researchers and scientist provides an important methodological tool to consider in answering important educational questions in the future.

REFERENCES

Bornstein, M. H., Jager J., and Putnick, D. L. (2013). Sampling in developmental science: shortcomings and solutions. *Developmental Review*, 33(4), 357–370.

Bray, M. (1999). Control of education: issues and tensions in centralization and decentralization, in R. F. Arnove, and C. A. Torres (Eds) *Comparative Education: The dialectic of the global and the local*. Lanham, MD: Rowman & Littlefield.

Cole, M., and Hill, D. (2013). *Schooling and Equality: Fact, concept and policy*. London: Routledge.

Davis-Kean, P. E., and Jager, J. (2012). The use of large-scale data sets for the study of developmental science. In B. Laursen, N. Card, and T. D. Little (Eds) *Handbook of Developmental Research Methods* (pp. 148–162). New York: Guilford Press.

Davis-Kean, P. E., and Jager, J. (2014). Trajectories of achievement within race/ethnicity: 'catching up' in achievement across time. *The Journal of Educational Research*, 107(3), 197–208.

Davis-Kean, P. E., and Sexton, H. R. (2009). Race differences in parental influences on child achievement: multiple pathways to success. *Merrill-Palmer Quarterly (1982–)*, 285–318.

Davis-Kean, P. E., Jager, J., and Maslowsky, J. (2015). Answering developmental questions using secondary data. *Child Development Perspectives*, 9, 256–261. doi: 10.1111/cdep.12151.

Davis-Kean, P. E., Huesmann, L. R., Jager, J., Collins, W. A., Bates, J. E., and Lansford, J. E. (2008). Changes in the relation of self-efficacy beliefs and behaviors across development. *Child Development*, 79, 1257–1269. doi: 10.1111/j.1467-8624.2008.01187.x.

Duncan, G. J. (2015). Toward an empirically robust science of human development. *Research in Human Development*, 12(3–4), 255–260.

Enders, C. K. (2013). Dealing with missing data in developmental research. *Child Development Perspectives*, 7(1), 27–31.

Feinstein, L., Jerrim, J., Vignoles, A., Goldstein, H., French, R., Washbrook, E., … and Lupton, R. (2015). Comment and debate: social class differences in early cognitive development. *Longitudinal and Life Course Studies*, 6(3), 331–376.

Fryer, R. G., and Levitt, S. D. (2004). Understanding the black-white test score gap in the first two years of school. *Review of Economics and Statistics*, 86, 447–464.

Graham, J. W. (2009). Missing data analysis: making it work in the real world. *Annual Review of Psychology*, 60, 549–576.

Hofferth, S., Davis-Kean, P.E., Davis, J., and Finkelstein, J. (1998). The child development supplement to the Panel Study of Income Dynamics: 1997 user guide, retrieved on July 12, 2016 from https://psidonline.isr.umich.edu/cds/cdsi_usergd.pdf. The University of Michigan, Survey Research Center Institute for Social Research, Ann Arbor, MI.

Lee, V. E., and Burkam, D. T. (2002). *Inequality at the Starting Gate: Social background differences in achievement as children begin school*. Washington, DC: Economic Policy Institute.

Levy, P. S., and Lemeshow, S. (2013). *Sampling of Populations: Methods and applications*, 4th edition. Hoboken, NJ: Wiley & Sons.

Mullis, I. V. S., Martin, M. O., Robitaille, D. F., and Foy, P. (2009). *TIMSS advanced 2008 international report: Findings from IEA's study of achievement in advanced mathematics and physics in the final year of secondary school*. Chestnut Hill, MA: TIMSS & PIRLS International Study Center, Boston College. Retrieved on July 12, 2016 from http://timssandpirls.bc.edu/timss_ advanced/ir.html.

Siegler, R. S., Duncan, G. J., Davis-Kean, P. E., Duckworth, K., Claessens, A., Engel, M., …, and Chen, M. (2012). Early predictors of high school mathematics achievement. *Psychological Science*, 23(7), 691–697.

Tourangeau, K., Nord, C., Lê, T., Sorongon, A. G., and Najarian, M. (2009). *Early Childhood Longitudinal Study, Kindergarten Class of 1998–99 (ECLS-K), Combined User's Manual for the ECLS-K Eighth-Grade and K–8 Full Sample Data Files and Electronic Codebooks* (NCES 2009–004). National Center for Education Statistics, Institute of Education Sciences, US Department of Education. Washington, DC.

25

Researching in Digital Environments

Rebecca Eynon

The variety and availability of networked devices such as tablets, mobile phones, and laptops, and the proliferation of online environments such as social networking sites, and computer gaming worlds are reconfiguring learning and education. As Haythornthwaite suggests, new technologies are 'rewriting communication networks, creating new spaces and relationships, restructuring knowledge networks, challenging identities, and changing the location, evaluation, and accessibility of information resources and people' (Haythornthwaite, 2015, p. 292). Given this context, it is important to conceptualise and research the digital aspects of learning and education. Indeed, the proliferation of the digital into all aspects of education and social life means that investigating the role of new technologies becomes a concern for all those engaged in education research.

It is important to define what we mean by a digital environment. Crook offers three ways to conceptualise this term: as an environment characterised by access to and interaction with digital objects (for example, images, music, documents); as a bounded virtual world, characterised by feelings of presence and immersion; and as an augmented, intelligent environment characterised by the ubiquity of networked devices (Crook, 2013, p. 31). These three conceptualisations helpfully offer researchers a range of different ways to begin thinking about how to research such environments for the purposes of learning and education.

The starting point for this chapter is that the majority of current understandings of education research remain highly relevant to research in the digital realm. A focus on the digital is best considered as a topic that cuts across all epistemological positions, theoretical frameworks, research approaches and analytical techniques. Given this large scope, it is not possible to cover all the perspectives and methods that are available to researchers interested in examining some aspect of the digital realm in education. Indeed, there are now whole handbooks dedicated to digital social science research (for example, Fielding et al., 2016), and learning and technology research in particular (Haythornthwaite et al., 2016; Price et al., 2013). Here the focus will primarily be on the new opportunities and challenges that researching digital environments offers researchers, while at the same time stressing the importance of existing understandings and research frameworks from education and the social sciences.

The first section below examines some key substantive and practical considerations when carrying out research in digital environments in education. In the second section, the focus moves to some specific, and relatively novel, techniques through the exploration of three core concepts often of interest to education researchers – interaction, content and experience. The third section addresses the importance of being aware of and reflective about the ethical choices that are made when planning, executing and writing up the research in this fast-moving field, whilst the concluding section focuses on the future of research in this area and the kinds of research skills that will likely be required.

RESEARCHING DIGITAL ENVIRONMENTS: (DIS)CONTINUITIES WITH OTHER TOPICS OF EDUCATIONAL RESEARCH

Why study digital environments?

The digital is embedded within learning and education in multiple forms. For example, technology can be used in various ways to support learning (for example, using a word processor to support writing, a search engine to help extend knowledge of a particular topic, email for additional support, watching educational videos, gaining feedback from peers, participating in a forum, participating in a online game or joining a Massive Open Online Course). The form and organisation of educational institutions have also altered as the use of digital technologies become an accepted part of daily life (Cornford and Pollock, 2003 Robins and Webster, 2002). Furthermore, working with technology potentially enables people to augment their achievements, with implications at both the individual and societal level (Crook, 2013; Pea, 1998). Indeed, there are few aspects of learning and education that technology has not influenced to some degree, making it is important to research the digital components of all these practices.

A focus on the digital aspects of learning and education can also offer methodological opportunities. As an increasing number of activities involve using technology, more 'digital traces' are created. These may include, for example, email trails, forum discussions, and hyperlinks between different sites. Researchers can collect and analyse such data, potentially making parts of the learning process

(McDougall and Jones, 2006) and wider behaviours and processes relevant to education more visible than was possible previously.

For example, interest has burgeoned in recent years around the development and uptake of the Massive Open Online Course (MOOC). MOOCs offer an opportunity to observe and analyse various patterns of online behaviour, such as watching a video clip, logging on to a virtual learning environment, participating in a forum or completing a quiz (for example, Breslow et al., 2013). Others have collected data from Social Networking Sites, such as Facebook, to obtain insight into the talk around learning that takes place outside the classroom, examined the interactions in online games and related these patterns to a variety of learning outcomes, or studied academic interactions in an online research environment to explore interdisciplinary practices. It has always been possible to document classroom discussions and other forms of interaction to some degree. However, the comprehensive nature of the data that it is possible to collect in these online contexts, over the entire time period of interest from the start to finish, is relatively unique. Such data may give education researchers an opportunity to explore some of the processes relevant to learning and education that are often to a large extent hidden from view.

The promise of such data to transform our understanding of learning and education is perhaps a little overstated based on current evidence, yet there is certainly a great deal of potential here. Indeed, the rise of learning analytics and educational data mining are two subfields of education research (discussed in chapter 46) that demonstrate the current focus on this area. It is important to note that, while often used primarily to uncover learning processes, such data is not limited to learning. The digital traces that are left behind when people interact with technology can also allow us to explore wider questions relevant to education, such as the power structures and communication networks both within and across educational institutions.

A second opportunity is to capitalise on the rise of mobile-networked devices, and use them as a research tool. For example, smartphones offer a range of digital trace data from information about physical interactions with the device, geolocated information and physical movement (Raento et al., 2009; Lathia, 2012). Yet these devices offer more possibilities. Alongside this kind of data that can in a sense be 'found' as a product of a person using the device, such technologies are particularly useful for capturing data that is essentially 'made' (Jensen, 2011). With technical support, researchers can create apps that can be designed to collect all kinds of affective and experiential data from participants as educational events take place. If well-designed, these apps can make it easier for participants to record their experiences in real time and can generate data that can be very insightful for certain kinds of education research (Raento et al., 2009).

Third, a focus on the digital can lead to the use of technology to develop more creative approaches to traditional social science methods. For example, encouraging people to create photos, videos or recordings to better communicate their experiences, or presenting people with the data collected about them online and asking them to reflect on these activities. Furthermore, with the increasing focus on linking datasets it may become increasingly possible to follow learners across a range of platforms, supporting researchers taking a Learning Lives, Networked Learning and/or Learning Ecologies perspective (Barron, 2004; Erstad and Green 2016; Jones, 2015.

Studying digital environments also has some practical advantages. Attention to the digital may enable researchers to focus on education systems or initiatives that are geographically dispersed, or difficult to access. The use of digital methods can be more cost effective, saving researchers' time and resources. Some digital environments, such as games and online courses, can be places where it is easier to have more control over random assignment to different groups or where certain experiments can be carried out that would be difficult and costly to arrange in traditional school settings. However, all of these benefits offer some challenges too. These include the skill sets required by researchers, ethical considerations, and the low entry to some field sites in the digital realm leading to poorly conducted and thought-through work that causes problems for the future of study in this area.

Nevertheless, given the relative newness of this area of study, and the possibilities to develop novel approaches to methods as technologies develop, researchers also have an opportunity to reflect and write about existing and new methodological and analytic techniques for studying education.

Conceptualising the digital

As is highlighted throughout this handbook, the research questions asked, the methods used and the analytical approach taken in any study depend on the researchers' epistemological and ontological frameworks. Regardless of the perspective taken, there is a strong set of philosophical and theoretical foundations from which education researchers can draw. However, while these conceptual resources remain an important source for those interested in studying digital environments, there have been, quite correctly, some critiques of this area of study for not properly conceptualising the digital or technological aspects of the research.

Indeed, there are multiple ways of conceptualising and theorising technology that are well explored in wider social science perspectives of technology but are often overlooked by Education researchers (see Oliver, 2013, 2016 and Selwyn, 2013). In essence the majority of research on digital environments in education tends to view technology as an instrumental tool, where research questions are essentially about efficiency and effectiveness of technology for a particular learning experience. A smaller, but important, body of work conceptualises technology more in terms of practices or culture, where questions of meaning, experience and value are the focus (Hamilton et al., 2004; Oliver, 2016, drawing on Peters, 2006). Regardless of the view taken the need for a strong, explicit theoretical basis for undertaking this work cannot be over emphasised. Furthermore, there is a need to look beyond theories of learning, which tend to dominate this area towards a wider conceptualisation of education, understood within cultural, economic and political terms (Selwyn, 2010, 2013).

Delineating research boundaries

In the early days of research about digital environments, many researchers made a clear demarcation between the 'offline' or 'real' settings and the 'online' or 'virtual' space. The associated research projects followed a similar pattern, where the primary effort was on what happened online (for example, in an online distance learning course or a learning experience in an online game) with limited focus or consideration of 'real' life. As the field matured, there has been a shift towards a more careful debate about the distinction between on and offline (Lee et al., 2008) and a more nuanced recognition of the links between the two, where technology is seen 'not as discrete entities, but as constituents of layered social and technological networks' (Jensen, 2011, p. 46).

For example, researchers may design a study that looks both at activity on an online forum, site or world, alongside observation or interviews in people's homes, workplace or learning environment. Such an approach can enable researchers to consider both the digital and face-to-face practices as part of the same study, which is perhaps closer to many educators and learners 'blended' experience. Previous studies have, for example, investigated the use of social networking sites as part of the learning experience for campus based higher education students (Stirling, 2015) or teenagers' uses of technology outside school (Leander and McKim, 2003).

Of course, the precise focus varies from study to study, and depends on the way a digital environment is conceptualised as outlined in the introduction (Crook, 2013). Yet the way that the digital environment is conceptualised has implications for the way the study is framed or bounded. In reality, defining the boundaries of learning or educational practice has never been straightforward but consideration of digital environments has made it somewhat more complex (Erstad et al., 2016). Indeed, the issue of bounding field sites has captured the attention of anthropologists and Internet researchers alike. Thus, researchers interested in digital environments in education can turn to a rich body of literature about this issue (for example, Burrell, 2009; Hine, 2015).

'Traditional' versus 'digital' methods

The 'digital' can be an object of study or a tool to research with, and is often both in studies of digital environments. For example, when examining a digital environment education researchers could select from a range or combination of methods: 'traditional' well established techniques in social science research, such as face-to-face interviews; methods with a digital component (for example, a survey delivered online); methods carried out entirely in the digital realm (for example, a visualisation of all the digital trace data available in a Massive Open Online Course or a link analysis of all the connections between universities in the UK). Some of these techniques are very similar to the methods that researchers are already familiar with but others require a new or additional set of skills. This could be learning how to interview people at a distance via email or Skype, or learning how to collect Twitter data to examine the lifecycle of an educational debate. Indeed, there is a growing literature around the use of digital techniques in social science research (Lee et al., 2008; Price at al., 2013).

Categorising digital methods

Given the plethora of possibilities, there is no ready way of neatly categorising the different methods that can be used. One solution is to group these into the following four areas that reflect different kinds of research skills and ethical considerations:

- gathering data directly from individuals (for example, online surveys and interviews, photo-elicitation, diary studies and think aloud via digital means);
- observing small and medium group interactions (for example, observations of interactions in forums and virtual environments, non-automated content analysis);
- analysis of large scale digital trace data (for example, social network analysis, analysis of click-stream data, use of location-aware devices; visualisation);
- performing secondary analysis of existing datasets (for example, educational data mining, merging of large-scale datasets and re-use).

Such approaches can be used in isolation or in combination. Of course, this does not cover every aspect of research in education, but it does provide some kind of insight into the possibilities for using digital methods for researchers working in this area (Eynon et al., 2016).

As noted above, methods need to be understood within the wider theoretical and epistemological frame (Jensen, 2011). Different kinds of research designs, for example, participatory methods such as action research versus more experimental approaches, will have embedded within them different relationships and assumptions about the role of the researcher and the researched which will also inform the way methods are utilised. In the next section, some of these methods are explored in more detail.

DIGITAL METHODS: INVESTIGATING INTERACTION, CONTENT AND EXPERIENCE

As noted above, a digital environment can take numerous forms, and the precise choice of methods remains based on the appropriateness and feasibility of that method to enable the researcher to construct or collect data that best addresses the aims of the research. The focus in this section is on specific analytical and methodological techniques that are appropriate for capturing three core aspects of learning and education in digital environments: interaction, content and experience.

Analysis of interactions

Many education researchers are interested in some form of interaction, whether this is between institutions, policymakers and educators, teachers and students, between humans and digital objects, or peer-to-peer conversations. The study of interactions allows researchers to explore aspects of education such as the formation and enactment of government educational policy, power relationships between stakeholders, the impact of academic research on practice, and the process of learning at an individual and/or group level. The possibilities are multiple and significant. Interestingly, all of these forms of interaction have some kind of digital component. This could be, for example, policymakers seeking consultations on the creation of a new policy, or the links to research in a policy report, or online interactions in a forum to support student learning.

While 'interaction' is not a straightforward and agreed upon term, particularly in digital environments (Kiousis, 2002 cited in Jensen, 2011, p. 46), all forms of digital traces that may represent interaction can be analysed. One particular technique is Social Network Analysis (SNA). Indeed, the socially networked structure of daily life has been the focus of some forms of sociological research for a significant period of time (Wellman and Rainie, 2012). Network analysis is a method of investigating how actors, including those in educational contexts, interact (Easley and Kleinberg, 2010). SNA helps model the spatially and temporally influenced social relationships between individuals, groups or communities. It is a way of understanding the overall structure of the interaction. Often used for interactions between individuals (for example, by those interested in computer supported collaborative learning and networked learning) it can also be used to examine interactions with and between various kinds of political, cultural, education and economic institutions that make up society as a whole (Jensen, 2011).

Through visualisation and numerical analysis, it is possible to use this technique to inform researchers about the actors who are likely to be important in the network, in terms of who is interacting with whom. It is possible to see the power of different participants, how cohesive the group is, the kinds of influence different actors have (Haythornthwaite, 2002; Jimoyiannis and Angelina, 2012; De Laat et al., 2007), and the extent to which specific subgroups or communities are forming within the network as a whole (De Laat et al., 2007; Gillani et al., 2014; Haythornthwaite and De Laat, 2010; Haythornthwaite, 2015).

There are a range of techniques that can be used to collect the data necessary to conduct SNA. For a very useful general overview, see Hogan (2016), and for one specific to learning see (Haythornthwaite, 2008). For example, researchers can understand social networks by asking people specific questions to recall their network via the completion of a sociometric survey (for example, Quardokus, and Henderson, 2015). However, more automated approaches that do not require self-report can be used. This data is sometimes made freely available to academics or it can be accessed directly from some sites (see for example, Lampe, 2013). Indeed, as a technique, SNA has appeared to increase in popularity and use with the rise of 'big data' (Boyd and Crawford, 2012).

In the field of education, SNA has been used for a variety of purposes. Carolan (2013) suggests three big areas of focus: social capital, diffusion and peer influence. For example, SNA has been used to explore interactions amongst students (and teachers) in MOOCs (Gillani and Eynon, 2014 – see Box 25.1); online forums (Palonen and Hakkarainen, 2000; Cho et al., 2007; Haythornthwaite and De Laat, 2010); blogs (Jimoyiannis and Angelina, 2012); and Facebook (Garcia et al., 2015). Yet, it is also used for other kinds of topics: to examine how Twitter is (or is not) being used by Higher Education Institutions to reinforce status in global rankings (Shields,, 2016); to investigate publishing relationships between academics at different institutions (Kuzhabekova et al., 2015); or university industry co-operations (Pinheiro et al., 2015).

When carrying out SNA it is important to reflect on the choices being made in the creation of the model, as this will have important implications for the network structure and conclusions drawn. These include the level of the analysis (for example, individual actors or the complete network); how relationships between different actors are defined; and how time is conceptualised and addressed (for example, is the network structure at the end of the course, or how it develops over time that is of most interest) (Haythornthwaite, 2015; Lampe, 2013). There is no one right approach, but visualisation techniques and qualitative observation can help to inform the decisions taken (Eynon et al., 2016).

Box 25.1   The use of SNA to explore interactions in a MOOC

Taking one Massive Open Online Course of over 87,000 students, Gillani and Eynon used Social Network Analysis (SNA), alongside demographic data and course outcome measures to examine who was participating in the discussion forums, the kinds of interactions that were happening and if using the forums was related to course outcomes. From the analysis they found that forum participants tended to be young adults from the Western world, and that the groups that form on the forums could be characterised as crowds – rather than communities – of learners. The use of SNA showed how some students engaged in rich discussions around topics of shared significance but overall the study found that forum use was largely inconsistent and non-cohesive. By linking the forum data to learning outcomes, they found that those that engaged explicitly in the discussion forums were often higher-performing than those that did not, although the vast majority of forum participants received 'failing' marks. In this study, the authors show the value of SNA in understanding some aspects of the learning experience, but also stress the value of a more mixed method approach and the challenges of how to measure learning outcomes in these kinds of settings (Gillani and Eynon, 2014).

Network analysis is a powerful tool, but it is important to remember that the data that such networks are built from is, like all forms of data, a partial representation of the practice of interest. For example, when data is scraped from a forum or other online context it is typically taken from one platform and only represents those who are active on that particular site. Participants who read but do not post or post on other sites are not represented (Lampe, 2013).

Another challenge is that the visualisation of networks or associated statistical network measures provide limited information about why these interactions might be meaningful on an individual or group level. Often researchers also want to know the content of the interactions or the wider context to help explain the relationships that have been identified. Indeed, SNA is often used alongside other methods, either linking these networks to outcomes of interest, such as interactions in a forum and performance on a test (Garcia et al., 2015; Vaquero and Cebrian, 2013) or linking measurements of social capital based on student data and later drop out (Eckles et al., 2012); or interviewing key members of the network and/or analysing the content (for example, De Laat et al., 2007). It is to the issue of how to analyse content that we now turn.

Analysis of content

An important aspect of educational research is what is said or what is created, by individual learners, groups, or organisations. Education researchers may often be interested in the discourse around particular topics, or digital artefacts that are created by learners and other groups.

Researchers interested in dialogue can capture and analyse data about the content of any naturally occurring interactions that are made online and these can then be analysed through relatively traditional techniques such as content, discourse analysis or conversational analysis (Giles et al., 2015). Indeed, such approaches have often been used to better understand learner interactions that take place online (for example, Stahl, et al., 2006; De Weaver et al., 2006) in informal and formal settings (Guzzetti and Foley, 2014), informed by a range of learning theories that highlight the importance of dialogue in varied ways such as the work of Pask, Papert and Vygotsky (Ravenscroft, 2001). As reflected in the debates common to those working within the field of Computer Supported Collaborative Learning (CSCL) such a focus can take a number of theoretical positions and analytical approaches.

Despite the diversity, there are a number of decisions that have to be made when thematically coding such data in some way. These range from how to operationalise the concepts of interest, the sampling strategy, the unit of dialogue (for example, the word, the sentence or the entire response), and how to ensure reliability and enhance validity (Schrire, 2006) and the focus of the analysis, that is, at the individual or group level (Stahl, 2005). Depending on the analytical approach taken, there may be existing frameworks that can be drawn upon such as the Community of Inquiry Model (Garrison et al., 2000) and Bloom's Taxonomy (Bloom and Krathwohl, 1956).

Such thematic analysis can vary in complexity and can operate at a number of different levels and measure different components of the activity at one time. For example, van Aalst coded students' use of knowledge forum according to knowledge, sharing, construction and creation discourses reflecting different theoretical orientations to learning (van Aalst, 2009). Schrire proposes a scheme that incorporates interaction, cognition and content (Schrire, 2006). Gillani and colleagues coded MOOC forum data on five dimensions: knowledge construction (Gunawardena et al., 1997); communicative intent (Clark et al., 2007; Erkens and Janssen, 2008); the topic of the post; the level of emotion; and relevance of the post to the ongoing discussion (Gillani et al., 2014). The precise decisions and focus will vary from project to project and depend on the original theoretical foundations.

As the scale of online learning increases, in some contexts thematic analysis of data by hand becomes challenging. In such settings, one option is to sample the data to make the process of conducting content analysis more feasible within the limited time frame and resources of most research (for example, De Laat and Lally, 2004). Another increasingly popular method is to opt for more automated data coding approaches drawing on fields of text mining, natural language processing and computational linguistics. For example, Wen and colleagues used sentiment analysis to determine affect while learning in MOOC forums to assist with understanding drop out (Wen et al., 2014). Sentiment analysis has also been used to explore perceptions of MOOCs on Twitter (Shen and Kuo, 2015), and emotions of students learning fractions while using an adaptive online learning tool in a classroom environment (Grawemeyer et al., 2015). A final approach to coding large-scale data includes crowdsourcing the data, for example using Mechanical Turk to categorise speech acts in MOOC forums (Arguello and Shaffer, 2015).

However the data is analysed, it is again important here to reflect on what this data represents. A number of researchers have pointed out the differences in spoken and text communication that need to be considered when using such data to understand learning. For example, the permanence of text may lead to changes in what is discussed, typing involves drafts and revisions not necessarily made visible on the site where data is collected, the software utilised will necessarily shape the interaction, the sense of audience may differ, and the commitment by participants to a continuing dialogue may be different (Giles et al., 2015). Drawing on the work of Claude Shannon and Yuri Lotman, Hamilton and colleagues usefully point out that

an educational conversation is a noisy thinking device because it struggles not only with the content of the communication but also the distribution and redistribution of knowing. Each utterance is both a performance and the product of an earlier performance. Performance and product condense in an educational conversation, and combined provide new opportunities for students to participate in knowing and acquire knowledge. (Hamilton et al., 2004: 850)

It is important to explore or consider the mediated and complex nature of these digital interactions as part of the process of interpretation (Thomas, 2002).

As noted above, a focus on learning processes has perhaps been the most popular kind of study using thematic analysis of content from online contexts. Yet such approaches can be used more broadly. Studies focused on aspects of digital environments that have used various forms of discourse analysis include analysis of the rise of the MOOC (Selwyn et al., 2015); the formation of teacher identity (Irwin and Hramiak, 2010); and the implementation of technology in schools (Sasseville, 2004). While the methods varied in each case (in some cases gathering texts into a corpus manually), the potential to scrape data about a wide range of educational topics and to analyse these has considerable potential value. It is important to stress that the analysis of content can go beyond text into other forms (see Box 25.2).

A second, related, area of focus when investigating content are digital artefacts that are intentionally produced either as part of a research project where students (or other stakeholders) are invited to create artefacts as part of the research process (Lally, 2015), or as part of enhancing the learning process (Bereiter, 2005) that can then be researched.

Indeed, as an example of the former of these two areas, participatory design is an important strand of work in research into the design of digital environments (Druin, 2009); the creation of artefacts for research has a broader history in education research which can be utilised to tackle issues of power and representation in the research process (Ruddock, 2002). Once it was only researchers who captured or created visual images (through photos, film or drawings), but now participants are involved in creating these artefacts in ways that provide them

---

Box 25.2 Analysing Video Data

Analysing content of interactions beyond text can take a number of multimodal forms. For example, in a classroom or in a virtual world like Second Life, it is possible for researchers to record not only what is said, but also the gestures and body language and the wider social setting of the interaction. Using practical examples and providing details of a range of tools and frameworks from which researchers can draw, Derry and colleagues provide a very thorough and useful overview of the issues that education researchers need to consider when using video in their research. Derry and colleagues note a range of factors that make the use of video in research feasible in a wide range of learning settings both formal and informal: technical advance, increase in accessibility and affordability, and the increasing scope for researchers to engage in interdisciplinary work. They draw attention to four issues in analysing video data when examining issues about learning: how to focus the analysis with such a wealth of data, the choice of analytical framework, the technological tools to aid the analysis, and the ethical considerations of sharing and re-using the data collected (Derry et al., 2010).

(it is hoped) with a stronger voice and say in how their experiences are represented in research (Buckingham, 2009).

With the rise of constructivist/knowledge building theories of learning, educators from an array of backgrounds are looking to technology to create content to support learning (for example, Hoban et al., 2015). For example, virtual worlds such Second Life offer one way for students to learn through the creation of objects (Hew and Cheung, 2010). In a review of the 'digital turn' in New Literacy Studies, Mills highlighted a wide range of studies where such artefacts had been produced including fan-fiction sites, videos, photography, and digital art (Mills, 2010). Indeed, in media education and new or digital literacy research these creative works have been a primary focus of attention for researchers both within, outside, or cutting across formal educational contexts and informal settings for some time (for example, Buckingham, 2007; Kress, 2003).

Again, it is important to be clear about what content of this kind represents. Crook suggests that artefacts are essentially a representation of understanding for the individual and for relevant others (Crook, 2013). Relatedly, Buckingham cautions researchers not to naively assume that these artefacts are more 'truthful' than any other kind of research, arguing that they are not a direct window on experience, and require proper analysis in order to explore their complexity and multiple meanings. This remains important regardless of whether such artefacts are seen from more of a research or learning angle. Numerous factors will influence what is created. These include the technology used, the participants' understanding of the research, and the understandings of the affordances of the technology that the participant has (Buckingham, 2009). Thus, experience needs to be understood as part of this process. It is this issue which is the focus of the next section.

Analysis of experience

How people experience and understand their own and others' educational experiences is a core aspect of research in digital environments. Perhaps due to the increase in the availability of digital trace data there has been a return to some extent of behaviourist approaches to learning (Skinner, 1954) and at times a premium placed on data that represents action or behaviour over other kinds of foci. This is a mistake; as it risks neglecting the wealth of existing research in this area, the partial representation such datasets offer, and the potential benefits of combining such data with insights from other approaches. Indeed, there is significant value of mixed method approaches to research in digital environments, in order to connect online behaviours and interactions with the content of these interactions, to the ways that people experience them, regardless of the topic being explored (Wesler et al., 2008).

Experiential processes can be captured in a variety of ways. They include online versions of traditional social science approaches (that is, surveys and interviews, for example, Couper, 2000; James and Busher, 2009) where people are asked about their past and current experience, diary studies, and various forms of cognitive task analysis – essentially any technique where people are prompted to reflect on their behaviour and experience.

One technique that is increasingly used as portable devices have become more readily available is photo-elicitation. Photo-elicitation enables participants to take photos of their experiences over a set period of time, either when they feel a particular event is pertinent to the research topic or in response to an automated request at certain time intervals. Typically these photos are then discussed with the participant during an interview. Such techniques provide researchers with insights into experiences or practices not easily accessed by other means, such as how the digital environment of interest relates to wider experiences of learning and education. At the same time such an approach gives participants control over what photos are taken and how their experiences are framed. Video diaries are another technique that can offer similar advantages, often offering more information and greater depth of experience (Groundwater-Smith et al., 2015). Such techniques can be used in three main ways: as a way for participants to communicate particular perspectives; to provide a way for participants to observe and record their own behaviours and practices; to facilitate meta-cognition (Schuck and Kearney, 2006). The design of such studies can take a variety of forms. For example, as part of a yearlong study into the use of project-based learning approaches, Smith explored the use of reflective videos as a way into capturing understanding the learning that happened as part of the entire process (Smith, 2016).

A second set of approaches are those that encourage participants to reflect on practices and behaviours made automatically visible by technology. For example, critical event recall can be used effectively when asking students to reflect on their experience and roles of participating in online discussion (De Laat and Lally, 2004). In this study, the summary of the content analysis of the forums was used as the prompt plus the full transcripts as stimulus for the discussion with the learner (De Laat and Lally, 2004).

Experience sampling using mobile devices can also be an interesting way of getting experiential data from people engaged in particular tasks over time (Raento et al., 2009); such as asking reflections on lessons by teachers over a two-week period using PDAs (Malmberg et al., 2014). Such techniques can be powerful, as reflection happens at the time of the behaviour. In a similar fashion, other ways of encouraging talk could include Wizard of Oz Studies, traditionally used in HCI studies for the development and usability testing of new technologies, to encourage people to reflect upon and discuss their learning goals, experiences and actions while using technology through via 'think aloud' approaches (Eynon and Davies, 2010).

When using such techniques, there are some practical considerations, such as who has access to – and the skills to use – technical devices to take photos, or make video recordings, or respond immediately to a text. Of importance also are issues of ownership of the images and privacy (particularly taking photos of others who have not consented to be part of the research), and how to deal with self-reports (such as video diaries) being very much structured by norms and expectations of how the participants feel they should act on camera (Groundwater-Smith et al., 2015).

Analysis can also be quite challenging due to the amount (Groundwater-Smith et al., 2015) and nature of multimodal data that is typically created from such techniques. There is significant guidance from multimodal and visual research that those in digital environments can draw upon (for useful overviews see Jewitt, 2008; Pink, 2009).

ETHICAL CONSIDERATIONS FOR CURRENT AND FUTURE RESEARCH

There are well-established ethical guidelines in the field of Education (see Chapter 4). These include the guidelines on ethics from British and American Educational Research Associations (BERA and AERA) and the Australian Association for Research in Education (AARE). These echo the principles set out in the Belmont Report. For example, BERA sets out five core ethical principles: minimising harm, respecting autonomy of participants, protecting privacy, offering reciprocity and treating people equitably (Hammersley and Traianou, 2012, pp. 2–3).

However, while there has been some recognition by professional associations in the field of education about the need to examine the ethical implications for research using technology to gather data (for example, a useful bibliography provided by BERA); professional associations and governing councils' guidelines for ethics have been slow to recognise the need for full consideration of this issue (Kanuka and Anderson, 2007). Indeed, to date there have been limited professional resources for researchers in the field of education and technology to guide their ethical choices (Moore and Ellsworth, 2014).

The use of digital methods offers researchers new ways of carrying out explorations in learning and education, yet alongside these opportunities come some new ethical challenges. With new technical innovations that make possible the capture of a wider array of learner data, the rise of big data, the open data movement, the everyday integration of technology such as smartphones into a wide range of learning contexts, and the increasingly blurred boundaries between researcher, educator, and learner, it is important that researchers are aware of, and reflective about, the ethical implications of their work.

It is not possible to go into depth here. However, there are a number of key issues that researchers working in this area need to be aware of, including:

- the need to be sensitive to the context of the environments where the research is carried out, and adjust ethical decisions accordingly throughout the project;

- the relevance of the human subjects model versus a more humanities-based model to guide ethical decision-making (that is, should researchers view publically available data as text – or does it represent human interaction or dialogue that requires permission) (Bassett and O'Riordan, 2002);
- the concept of privacy in public. In other words is every interaction online truly public data (even if it is publically traceable)? For example, when talking in a public park, people anticipate privacy if having a one to one conversation – is it reasonable to expect the same online? (Nissenbaum, 1998);
- the ethics of using other people's content, and issues of copyright (Buckingham, 2009);
- the use of direct quotes in academic work from public online sources that are instantly traceable online – compromising anonymity (Markham, 2012);
- issues of working with younger age groups (Groundwater-Smith et al., 2015), and related issues of establishing consent at a distance (Eynon et al., 2008);
- who is and is not represented in research projects involving digital environments (Eynon et al., 2009; Lee et al., 2008).

Given that few review boards will have sufficient expertise in this evolving area, there is a significant responsibility on the individual researcher to make considered ethical choices. (For further guidance, see Eynon et al., 2016 and the guidelines provided by the Association of Internet Research, Markham and Buchanan, 2013).

CONCLUSION: FUTURE RESEARCH IN DIGITAL ENVIRONMENTS

There is a great deal of potential in researching the digital aspects of learning and education, and using digital methods to do so. Yet is important to note that such techniques draw heavily on existing understandings of educational research. Despite the wealth of data many of these techniques generate, they do not and cannot replace existing approaches to educational research. Importantly, for any method and analytical technique to be useful, they need to be grounded within a strong epistemological and theoretical framing.

As the specific tools and technology available to researchers and educators are constantly changing, then a key aspect for education researchers working in this area is not to get too captivated by the technology, and instead remain focused on developing theoretical as well as practical understanding, raising questions and encouraging reflection. New skills will constantly be required (particularly some comfort or awareness with computational techniques), and the ability to work in multi-disciplinary teams will become increasingly valuable. Most important is the need to encourage an ongoing conversation about the opportunities and challenges of digital research so that it becomes more of a mainstream part of educational researchers 'toolkit' and less of a specialist or niche area of work.

REFERENCES

Arguello, J. and Shaffer, K. (2015). Predicting Speech Acts in MOOC Forum Posts. In Proceedings of the 9th international conference on web and social media.

Bassett, E. and O'Riordan, K. (2002). Ethics of Internet research: contesting the human subjects research model. *Ethics and Information Technology*, 4(3), 233–247.

Barron, B. (2004). Learning ecologies for technological fluency: Gender and experience differences. *Journal of Educational Computing Research*, 31(1), 1–36.

Bereiter, C. (2005). *Education and Mind in the Knowledge Age*. London: Routledge.

Bloom, B. and David, R. (1956). *Taxonomy of educational objectives: The classification of educational goals, by a committee of college and university examiners*. Handbook 1: Cognitive domain. New York: Longmans.

Boyd, D. and Crawford, K. (2012). Critical questions for big data: Provocations for a cultural, technological, and scholarly phenomenon. *Information, Communication & Society*, 15(5), 662–679.

Breslow, L., Pritchard, D., DeBoer, J., Stump, G., Ho, A. and Seaton, D. (2013). Studying learning in the worldwide classroom: research into edX's first MOOC. *Research & Practice in Assessment*, 8, 13–25.

Buckingham, D. (2007). Digital media literacies: rethinking media education in the age of the Internet. *Research in Comparative and International Education*, 2(1), 43–55.

Buckingham, D. (2009). 'Creative' visual methods in media research: possibilities, problems and proposals. *Media, Culture & Society*, 31(4), 633–652.

Burrell, J. (2009). The field site as a network: a strategy for locating ethnographic research. *Field Methods*, 21, 181–99.

Carolan, B. V. (2013). *Social Network Analysis and Education: Theory, methods and applications*. London: Sage.

Cho, H., Gay, G., Davidson, B. and Ingraffea, A. (2007). Social networks, communication styles, and learning performance in a CSCL community. *Computers & Education*, 49(2), 309–329.

Clark, D., Sampson, V., Weinberger, A. and Erkens, G. (2007). Analytic Frameworks for Assessing Dialogic Argumentation in Online Learning Environments. *Educational Psychology Review*, 19(3), 343–374.

Cornford, J. and Pollock, N. (2003). *Putting the University Online: Information, Technology and Organizational Change*. London: Routledge

Couper, M. P. (2000). Review: Web surveys: A review of issues and approaches. *The Public Opinion Quarterly*, 64(4), 464–494.

Crook, C. (2013). The field of digital technology research. In S. Price, C. Jewitt and B. Brown (Eds) *The SAGE Handbook of Digital Technology Research* (pp 26–40). London: Sage.

De Laat, M. F. and Lally, V. (2004). It's not so easy: researching the complexity of emergent participant roles and awareness in asynchronous networked learning discussions. *Journal of Computer Assisted Learning*, 20(3), 165–171.

De Laat, M., Lally, V. Lipponen, L. and Simons R-J (2007). Investigating patterns of interaction in networked learning and computer-supported collaborative learning: a role for Social Network Analysis. *International Journal of Computer-Supported Collaborative Learning*, 2(1), 87–103.

Derry, S. J., Pea, R.D., Barron, B., Engle, R. A., Erickson, F., Goldman, R. and Hall, R. (2010). *Conducting Video Research in the Learning Sciences: Guidance on selection, analysis, technology, and ethics*. London: Routledge

De Weaver, T., Schellens, M., Valcke, H. and Van Keer (2006). Content analysis schemes to analyze transcripts of online asynchronous discussion groups: A review. *Computers & Education*, 46 (1), 6–28.

Druin, A. (2009). *Mobile Technology for Children: Designing for interaction and learning*. Burlington, MA: Morgan Kaufmann.

Easley, D. and Kleinberg, J., (2010). *Networks, crowds, and markets: Reasoning about a highly connected world*. Cambridge: Cambridge University Press.

Eckles, J. and Stradley, E. (2012). A social network analysis of student retention using archival data. *Social Psychology of Education*, 15(2), 165–180.

Erstad, O. and Sefton-Green, J. (2016). *Learning Identities, Education and Community: Young Lives in the Cosmopolitan City*. Cambridge: Cambridge University Press.

Erstad, O., Kumpulainen, K., Mäkitalo, Å., Schrøder, K.C., Pruulmann-Vengerfeldt, P. and Jóhannsdóttir, T. (eds)., (2016). *Learning Across Contexts in the Knowledge Society*. London: Springer.

Erkens, G. and Janssen, J. (2008). Automatic coding of dialogue acts in collaboration protocols. *International Journal of Computer-Supported Collaborative Learning*, 3(4), 447–470.

Eynon, R. and Davies, C. (2010). A companion for learning in everyday life. In Y. Wilks (Ed.) *Close Engagements with Artificial Companions. Key social, psychological, ethical and design issues* (pp. 211–222). Amsterdam: John Benjamins.

Eynon, R., Schroeder, R. and Fry, J. (2009). New techniques in online research: challenges for research ethics. *21st Century Sociology*, 4(2), 187–199.

Eynon, R., Fry, J. and Schroeder, R. (2008). The Ethics of Internet Research. In, N. Fielding, R. Lee and B. Grant (Eds.) *The SAGE Handbook of Online Research Methods* (pp. 47–72) London: Sage.

Eynon R., Schroeder, R. and Fry, J. (2016). The Ethics of Learning and Technology Research. In, C. Haythornthwaite, R. Andrews, J. Fransman and E. Meyers (Eds). *The SAGE Handbook of E-learning Research*, 2e (pp. 221–232). London: Sage.

Eynon, R., Hjoth, I., Yasseri, T., and Gillani, N. (2016). Understanding Communication Patterns in MOOCs: Combining Data Mining and qualitative methods. In, S. ElAtia, D. Ipperciel, and O. Zaïane (Eds.), *Data Mining and Learning Analytics: Applications in Educational Research*. Wiley.

Fielding, N., Lee, R. and Blank, G. (2016). *Handbook of Online Research Methods* (2nd edition). London: Sage.

Garcia, E., Elbeltagi, I. and Dungay, K. (2015). Student use of Facebook for informal learning and peer support. *International Journal of Information and Learning Technology*, 32(5), 286–299.

Garrison, D., Anderson, T. and Archer, W. (2000) Critical inquiry in a text-based environment: Computer conferencing in higher education. *The Internet and Higher Education*, 2, 87–105.

Giles, D., Stommel, W., Paulus, T., Lester, J. and Reed, D. (2015). Microanalysis of online data: the methodological development of 'digital CA'. *Discourse, Context & Media*, 7, 45–51.

Gillani, N. and Eynon, R. (2014). Communication patterns in massively open online courses. *The Internet and Higher Education*, 23, 18–26.

Gillani, N., Yasseri, T., Eynon, R. and Hjorth, I. (2014). Structural limitations of learning in a crowd – communication vulnerability and information diffusion in MOOCs. *Scientific Reports*, 4.

Grawemeyer, B., Holmes, W., Gutiérrez-Santos, S., Hansen, A., Loibl, K. and Mavrikis, M. (2015). Light-bulb moment? Towards adaptive presentation of feedback based on students' affective state. Proceedings of the 20th International Conference on Intelligent User Interfaces, 400–404. ACM.

Groundwater-Smith, S., Dockett, S. and Bottrell, D. (2015). Innovative methods. In D. Bottrell, S. Dockett and S. Groundwater-Smith (Eds) *Participatory Research with Children and Young People* (pp. 101–139). London: Sage.

Gunawardena, C. N., Lowe, C. A. and Anderson, T. (1997). Analysis of a global online debate and the development of an interaction analysis model for examining social construction of knowledge in computer conferencing. *Journal of Educational Computing Research*, 17(4), 397–431.

Guzzetti, B. J. and Foley, L. M. (2014). Literacy agents online. E-discussion forums for advancing adults' literacy practices. *Journal of Adolescent and Adult Literacy*, 57(6), 472–482.

Hamilton, D., Dahlgren, E., Hult, A., Roos, B. and Soderstrom, T. (2004). When performance is the product: problems in the analysis of online distance education. *British Educational Research Journal*, 30(6), 841–854.

Hammersley, M. and Traianou, A. (2012). *Ethics in qualitative research: Controversies and contexts*. London: Sage.

Haythornthwaite, C. (2002). Building social networks via computer networks: creating and sustaining distributed learning communities. In K. A. Renninger and W. Shumar (Eds) *Building Virtual Communities: Learning and change in cyberspace* (pp. 159–190). Cambridge: Cambridge University Press.

Haythornthwaite, C. (2008) Learning relations and networks in web-based communities. *International Journal of Web Based Communities*, 4(2), 140–158.

Haythornthwaite, C. (2015). Rethinking learning spaces: networks, structures, and possibilities for learning in the twenty-first century. *Communication Research and Practice*, 1(4), 292–306.

Haythornthwaite, C. and De Laat, M. (2010). Social networks and learning networks: using social network perspectives to understand social learning, 7th International Conference on Networked Learning. Aalborg, Denmark.

Haythornthwaite, C., Andrews, R., Fransman, J. and Meyers, E. M. (2016). *The SAGE Handbook of e-Learning Research*, 2nd edition. London: Sage.

Hew, K. F. and Cheung, W. S. (2010). Use of three-dimensional (3-D) immersive virtual worlds in K-12 and higher education settings: a review of the research. *British Journal of Educational Technology*, 41(1), 33–55.

Hine, C. (2015). *Ethnography for the internet: embedded, embodied and everyday*. Bloomsbury Publishing.

Hoban, G., Nielsen, W. and Shepherd, A. (2015) (Eds) *Student-generated Digital Media in Science Education: Learning, explaining and communicating content*. London: Routledge.

Hogan, B. (2016). Online Social Networks: Concepts for data collection and analysis. In, N. Fielding, R. Lee and B. Grant (Eds.) *The SAGE Handbook of Online Research Methods* (pp. 92–108) London: Sage.

Irwin, B. and Hramiak, A. (2010). A discourse analysis of trainee teacher identity in online discussion. *Technology, Pedagogy and Education*, 19(3), 361–377.

James, N. and Busher, H. (2009). *Online interviewing*. London: Sage.

Jensen, K. B. (2011). New media, old methods – internet methodologies and the online/offline divide. In M. Consalvo and C. Ess (Eds) *The Handbook of Internet Studies* (pp. 43–59). London: John Wiley & Sons.

Jewitt, C. (2008). *Technology, Literacy and Learning: A multimodal approach*. Abingdon: Routledge.

Jimoyiannis, A. and Angelina, S. (2012). Towards an analysis framework for investigating students' engagement and learning in educational blogs. *Journal of Computer Assisted Learning*, 28(3), 222–234.

Jones, C. (2015). *Networked learning: an educational paradigm for the age of digital networks*. New York: Springer.

Kanuka, H. and Anderson, T. (2007). Ethical issues in qualitative e-learning research. *International Journal of Qualitative Methods*, 6(2), 20–39.

Kuzhabekova, A., Hendel, D. and Chapman, D. (2015). Mapping global research on international higher education. *Research in Higher Education*, 56(8), 861–882.

Kress, G. (2003). *Literacy in the New Media Age*. London: Routledge.

Lally, V. (2015). Alongside virtual youth using the internet: creating and researching learning interactions. In D. Wyse, L. Hayward and J. Pandya (Eds). *The SAGE Handbook of Curriculum, Pedagogy and Assessment* (pp. 278–293) London: Sage.

Lampe, C. (2013). Behavioural trace data for analyzing online communities. In S. Price, C. Jewitt and B. Brown (Eds) *The SAGE Handbook of Digital Technology Research* (pp. 236–250). London: Sage.

Lathia, N. (2012, June). Using idle moments to record your health via mobile applications. In Proceedings of the 1st ACM workshop on mobile systems for computational social science (pp. 22–27). ACM.

Leander, K. and McKim, K. (2003). Tracing the everyday 'sittings' of adolescents on the Internet: a strategic adaptation of ethnography across online and offline spaces. *Education, Communication & Information*, 3(2), 211–240.

Lee, R. M., Fielding, N. and Blank, G. (2008). The Internet as a Research Medium. In N. Fielding, R. Lee and B. Grant (Eds) *The SAGE Handbook of Online Research Methods* (pp. 3–20). London: Sage.

Malmberg, L. E., Hagger, H. and Webster, S. (2014). Teachers' situation-specific mastery experiences: teacher, student group and lesson effects. *European Journal of Psychology of Education*, 29(3), 429–451.

Markham, A. (2012). Fabrication as ethical practice: qualitative inquiry in ambiguous internet contexts. *Information, Communication, and Society*, 5(3), 334–353.

Markham, A. and Buchanan, E. (2013). Ethical decision-making and Internet research 2.0: recommendations from the AoIR ethics working committee. Association of the Internet Research Ethics Working Committee.

McDougall, A. and Jones, A. (2006). Theory and history, questions and methodology: current and future issues in research into ICT in education. *Technology, Pedagogy and Education*, 15(3), 353–360.

Mills, K. A. (2010). A review of the 'digital turn' in the new literacy studies. *Review of Educational Research*, 80(2), 246–271.

Moore, S. L. and Ellsworth, J. B. (2014). Ethics of educational technology. In, J. Spector, M. Merrill, J. Elen, and M. Bishop (Eds.) *Handbook of Research on Educational Communications and Technology* (pp. 113–127). New York: Springer

Nissenbaum, H. (1998). Protecting privacy in an information age: the problem of privacy in public. *Law and Philosophy*, 17, 559–596.

Oliver, M. (2013). Learning technology: theorising the tools we study. *British Journal of Educational Technology*, 44(1), 31–43.

Oliver, M. (2016). What is technology? In N. Rushby and D. Surry (Eds) *The Wiley Handbook of Learning Technology* (pp. 35–57). London: John Wiley & Sons.

Palonen, T. and Hakkarainen, K. (2000). Patterns of interaction in computer-supported learning: a social network analysis. In B. Fishman and S. O'Conner-Divelbiss (Eds) *Fourth International Conference of the Learning Sciences* (pp. 334–339). Mahwah, NJ: Erlbaum.

Pea, R.D. (1993). Practices of distributed intelligence and designs for education. In, G. Salamon (Ed.) *Distributed Cognitions: Psychological and Educational Considerations* (pp. 47–88). Cambridge: Cambridge University Press.

Peters, M. A. (2006). Towards philosophy of technology in education: mapping the field. In J. Weiss, J. Nolan, J. Hunsinger and P. Trifonas (Eds) *The International Handbook of Virtual Learning Environments* (pp. 95–116). The Netherlands: Springer.

Pinheiro, M. L., Lucas, C. and Pinho, J. C. (2015). Social Network Analysis as a new methodological tool to understand university–industry cooperation. *International Journal of Innovation Management*, 19(1).

Pink, S. (2009). *Visual interventions: Applied visual anthropology* (Vol. 4). Berghahn Books.

Price, S., Jewitt, C. and Brown, B. (Eds) (2013). *The SAGE Handbook of Digital Technology Research*. London: Sage.

Quardokus, K. and Henderson, C. (2015). Promoting instructional change: using social network analysis to understand the informal structure of academic departments. *Higher Education*, 70(3), 315–335.

Raento, M., Oulasvirta, A. and Eagle, N. (2009). Smartphones an emerging tool for social scientists. *Sociological Methods & Research*, 37(3), 426–454.

Ravenscroft, A. (2001). Designing e-learning interactions in the 21st century: Revisiting and rethinking the role of theory. *European Journal of Education*, 36(2), 133–156.

Robins, K. and Webster, F. (2002). *The Virtual University? Knowledge, markets, and management*. Oxford: Oxford University Press

Ruddock, J. (2002). The transformative potential of consulting young people about teaching, learning and schooling. *Scottish Educational Review*, 34(2), 123–137.

Sasseville, B. (2004). Integrating information and communication technology in the classroom: a comparative discourse analysis. *Canadian Journal of Learning and Technology*, 30, 5–28.

Schrire, S. (2006). Knowledge building in asynchronous discussion groups: going beyond quantitative analysis. *Computers and Education*, 46(1), 49–70.

Schuck, S. and Kearney, M. (2006). Capturing learning through student-generated digital video. *Australian Educational Computing*, 21(1), 15–20.

Selwyn, N. (2010). Looking beyond learning: notes towards the critical study of educational technology. *Journal of Computer Assisted Learning*, 26(1), 65–73.

Selwyn, N. (2013). *Distrusting Educational Technology: Critical questions for changing times*. London: Routledge.

Selwyn, N., Bulfin, S., & Pangrazio, L. (2015). Massive open online change? Exploring the discursive construction of the 'MOOC' in newspapers. *Higher Education Quarterly*, 69(2), 175–192.

Shen, C. W. and Kuo, C-J. (2015). Learning in massive open online courses: evidence from social media mining. *Computers in Human Behaviour*, 51(B), 568–577.

Shields, R. (2016). Following the leader? Network models of 'world-class' universities on Twitter. *Higher Education*, 71(2), 253–268.

Skinner, B. F. (1954). The Science of Learning and the Art of Teaching. *Harvard Educational Review*, 24, 86–97.

Smith, S. (2016). (Re)counting meaningful learning experiences: using student-created reflective videos to make invisible learning visible during PjBL experiences. *Interdisciplinary Journal of Problem-Based Learning*, 10(1).

Stahl, G. (2005). Group cognition in computer-assisted collaborative learning. *Journal of Computer Assisted Learning*, 21(2), 79–90.

Stahl, G., Koschmann, T. and Suthers, D. (2006). Computer-supported collaborative learning: An historical perspective. In R. K. Sawyer (Ed.) *Cambridge handbook of the learning sciences* (pp. 409–426). Cambridge: Cambridge University Press.

Stirling, E., (2016). Technology, time and transition in higher education–two different realities of everyday Facebook use in the first year of university in the UK. *Learning, Media and Technology*, 41(1), 100–118.

Thomas, M. J. W. (2002). Learning within incoherent structures: the space of online discussion forums. *Journal of Computer Assisted Learning*, 18(3), 351–366.

Vaquero, L. and Cebrian, M. (2013). The rich club phenomenon in the classroom. *Scientific Reports*, 3, 1174.

van Aalst, J. (2009). Distinguishing knowledge-sharing, knowledge-construction, and knowledge-creation discourses. *International Journal of Computer-Supported Collaborative Learning*, 4(3), 259–287.

Wellman, B. and Rainie, L. (2012). *Networked: The New Social Operating System*. Cambridge: The MIT Press.

Wen, M., Yang, D. and Rose, C. (2014). Sentiment Analysis in MOOC Discussion Forums: What does it tell us? In Proceedings of Educational Data Mining. July 2014.

Wesler, H. T., Smith, M., Fisher, D. and Gleave, E. (2008). Distilling digital traces: computational social science approaches to studying the Internet. In N. Fielding, R. Lee and B. Grant (Eds) *The SAGE Handbook of Online Research Methods* (pp. 116–140). London: Sage.